www.wadsworth.com

wadsworth.com is the World Wide Web site for Wadsworth and is your direct source to dozens of online resources.

At *wadsworth.com* you can find out about supplements, demonstration software, and student resources. You can also send email to many of our authors and preview new publications and exciting new technologies.

wadsworth.com
Changing the way the world learns®

LEARNING

BEHAVIOR AND COGNITION

Third Edition

David A. Lieberman

University of Stirling
Scotland

Wadsworth
Thomson Learning

Australia • Canada • Denmark • Japan • Mexico • New Zealand • Philippines
Puerto Rico • Singapore • South Africa • Spain • United Kingdom • United States

Executive Editor: *Vicki Knight*
Acquisitions Editor: *Marianne Taflinger*
Editorial Assistant: *Suzanne Wood*
Marketing Manager: *Jenna Opp*
Project Editor: *John Walker*
Print Buyer: *Stacey Weinberger*
Permissions Editor: *Bob Kauser*

Production Service: *Robin Gold /*
  Forbes Mill Press
Copy Editor: *Robin Gold*
Cover Designer: *Laurie Anderson*
Compositor: *Wolf Creek Press*
Cover and Text Printer/Binder:
  R.R. Donnelley & Sons, Crawfordsville

**Library of Congress
Cataloging-in-Publication Data**

Lieberman, David A.
  Learning : behavior and cognition / David A. Lieberman. —3rd ed.
    p. cm.
  Includes bibliographical references.
  ISBN 0-534-33925-5
  1. Learning, Psychology of. 2. Paired-association learning.
3. Conditioned response. I. Title.
BF319.5.P34L54 1999
153.1'526—dc21   99-36080

For more information, contact
Wadsworth/Thomson Learning
10 Davis Drive
Belmont, CA 94002-3098
USA
www.wadsworth.com

International Headquarters
Thomson Learning
290 Harbor Drive, 2nd Floor
Stamford, CT 06902-7477
USA

UK/Europe/Middle East
Thomson Learning
Berkshire House
168-173 High Holborn
London WC1V 7AA
United Kingdom

Asia
Thomson Learning
60 Albert Street #15-01
Albert Complex
Singapore 189969

Canada
Nelson/Thomson Learning
1120 Birchmount Road
Scarborough, Ontario M1K 5G4
Canada

 This book is printed on acid-free recycled paper.

To Myra and Mark,
with love

CONTENTS

PART III

OPERANT CONDITIONING

CHAPTER FIVE

REINFORCEMENT   193

CHAPTER SIX

APPLICATIONS OF REINFORCEMENT   253

CHAPTER TEN

THE ROLE OF THE REINFORCER   417

CHAPTER ELEVEN

LEARNING IN AN EVOLUTIONARY CONTEXT   467

PREFACE

I love studying and teaching learning. The topic is profoundly important—learning affects almost everything we do—and it is exciting when researchers are able to penetrate the complex surface of human behavior to provide glimpses of the elegant processes underneath. The development of the scientific method during the last few hundred years seems to me one of the greatest achievements in human history, and I find it exhilarating when clever experimenters are able to use the sharp blade of logic and reason to discover the processes that determine our behavior.

In writing this text, I have tried to communicate the challenge and excitement of learning researchers' voyages of discovery. The purpose of this preface is to explain the assumptions that guided my efforts. Briefly, my goal was that the text be *stimulating, clear, practical,* and *cognitive*.

Intellectual Stimulation

One of my fundamental goals was to present ideas in a way that would be intellectually rigorous and stimulating. All textbook authors face the difficult problem of how to balance the need for broad coverage against the dangers of superficiality—of losing students in a forest of facts. My own bias is toward depth rather than breadth: I think students gain more from a deep understanding of fundamental ideas than from a superficial familiarity with a much larger set of facts. In writing this text, I have tried to explore the most important issues in associative learning in depth, rather than to provide shallower coverage of all topics.

One example of this approach is the treatment of experimental design. If students are to be helped to think critically, it is vital that they understand the logic of experiments rather than just memorize their conclusions. To encourage this understanding, Chapter 1 provides an introduction to the experimental method: the advantages and disadvantages of experiments, why learning researchers sometimes study animals, and so on. Subsequent chapters build on this foundation by analyzing selected experiments and issues in depth while providing briefer summaries of other studies. Where this selective approach has meant that coverage of some issues has had to be curtailed, I have provided references that the interested reader can consult for more information.

I have taken a similar approach to presenting theories, concentrating on presenting a small number in depth rather than providing more superficial coverage of them all. In the case of classical conditioning, for example, I have focused on the theory I consider the most important: the Rescorla-Wagner model. Through extensive analysis of this model, I have tried to convey a feeling for how theories can be used to explain known phenomena and to generate novel and sometimes counterintuitive predictions. This material is not easy, but I've found that students feel that the model's remarkable achievements makes the effort to understand it worthwhile.

Clarity

No matter how stimulating ideas may be in principle, they will not have this effect in practice unless readers understand them. I have tried very hard, therefore, to present ideas clearly and simply; I hope reading the text will feel more like participating in a conversation than listening to a formal lecture.

Practical Applications

A third goal in writing this text was to show how learning principles can be practically applied in everyday life. Students sometimes find courses on learning boring because of an understandable disinclination to believe that experiments on rats can shed any light on human behavior. It is not enough for teachers and textbooks to assert that laboratory research is relevant: This relevance has to be demonstrated.

I have done this by interweaving material on laboratory research and practical applications throughout the text. The chapters on classical conditioning, for example, discuss the effects of conditioning on human emotions such as fear and sexual arousal, and on our reactions to drugs such as heroin. I have also discussed how conditioning principles have been used to treat problems such as phobias and alcoholism.

A similar approach is taken in the chapters on reinforcement. Chapter 5 discusses the basic principles of reinforcement and illustrates each principle with a practical application. Because of the importance of reinforcement, issues arising from its use are also examined in more depth in a separate chapter.

Chapter 6 demonstrates the power of reinforcement when it is used properly, but it also discusses potential problems—for example, that reward might undermine interest in enjoyable activities. The chapter concludes with a discussion of two alternative strategies for encouraging desirable behavior, modeling and self-control.

Chapter 7, on punishment, continues the emphasis on the relationship between laboratory research and practical applications. The chapter begins with an exploration of the principles of punishment established in the laboratory and then turns to studies of the applied use of punishment with children, examining punishments such as time out and response cost, and also the use of reinforcement as an alternative to punishment.

A Cognitive Approach

I was an undergraduate at Columbia College, which was then one of the centers for the Skinnerian or behaviorist approach to learning. Nate Schoenfeld, one of the great teachers in this tradition, was my first professor, and I found his approach so exciting that I even sat in on lectures he gave in other courses.

I still value the Skinnerian emphasis on analytical rigor and on the practical application of learning principles. Over time, however, I became convinced that psychologists not only must discover the empirical principles of learning—for example, are rewards more effective when they are immediate?—but also must understand the processes that produce these effects. One of the central themes of this text has thus been understanding the cognitive processes that underlie learning.

In developing this theme, I have focused on the conflict between associative and cognitive theories of learning. This conflict has fundamentally shaped current views of learning, and I have devoted considerable space to tracing the evolution of these theories, and their gradual convergence under the pressure of accumulating evidence. Chapter 8, for example, describes the conflict between S–R and cognitive theories of reinforcement, and considers the possibility that both were right, as learning involves the development of both relatively simple associations and more complex expectations. Chapter 9 then traces the role of memory and attention in producing this learning, and Chapter 10 includes an extensive analysis of how we use the information we have learned in deciding how to respond.

Chapter 12 returns to the conflict between associative and cognitive views of learning in the context of concept learning. We discuss the evidence for concept learning in both animals and humans and look at current theories of how these concepts are formed. I conclude the chapter by introducing one of the most remarkable developments in psychology in recent years, neural network models. These models provide a new synthesis of associative and cognitive approaches. Learning is still seen as involving cognitive processes of considerable complexity, but these are in turn explained in terms of simple associative processes at a neural level. Although these models are still very new, there is provocative evidence that they might be able to account for instances of learning ranging from classical conditioning in slugs to language learning in humans, and the chapter considers the potentially revolutionary implications of these models for our understanding of the human mind.

Key Changes to the Third Edition

All the key figures in the history of research on learning—Pavlov, Thorndike, Hull, Tolman and Skinner—regarded research on animals as a means to an end, that end being understanding human behavior. For a variety of reasons, however, learning in animals and humans has often been studied in different courses—courses on Learning, for example, often concentrate on learning in animals, while human learning is studied in courses such as Behavior Modification and Cognition.

In the first two editions of this text, I tried to incorporate material on learning in humans as well as animals, and perhaps the key feature of the third edition is the continuation of that effort to bring the two areas together. In part, that has been achieved by increased coverage of applications of conditioning principles—for example, Lovaas' work with autistic children, the controversy over whether reinforcement undermines intrinsic motivation, and greatly expanded coverage of the effects of punishment in children. In addition, I have substantially increased coverage of areas of human learning that are directly relevant to associative learning—examples include new sections on causal learning, concept learning (with detailed analysis of prototype, exemplar, and rule-based theories), and theories of human decision making (including economic models and the work of Tversky and Kahneman on heuristics). I see this material not as expansion of the scope of the learning course but rather a return to integrating evidence from animal and human research, recognizing both similarities and differences.

There have also been a number of other changes, including new sections on determinism, choice behavior, and complex learning in animals (including cognitive maps, timing and counting). Existing sections have also been revised to allow coverage of new material such as Ralph Miller's work on the role of performance in classical conditioning and LeDoux's demonstration of two neural pathways in fear conditioning.

Finally, there have been two changes in the overall organization of the text. Chapter 2 in the second edition provided an extended introduction to classical and operant conditioning, but one result was that similar material was often discussed in two or more places; I have returned to the simpler format used in the first edition, with a brief introduction to these forms of learning at the end of Chapter 1. I have also extensively reorganized Part IV, on theories of learning, to allow a smoother flow of ideas. This section now begins with the question of what is learned during conditioning (Chapter 8) and then examines the role of memory and attention in producing this learning (Chapter 9). Chapter 10 focuses on the role of the reinforcer in triggering these processes, and also in determining performance. Chapter 11 then discusses the evolution of learning, suggesting that although there are differences in learning in different situations and species, there is also an underlying continuity, as the different processes appear to be based on a small number of basic building blocks.

Finally, Chapter 12 discusses concept learning, a more sophisticated form of learning but one that nevertheless blends the associative and cognitive processes encountered in earlier chapters. The discussion concludes with an examination of the potential of neural network models to provide an integrated framework for understanding all learning, from classical conditioning to concept learning and language.

Aids to Studying

To help readers to absorb the sometimes challenging material in each chapter, an extensive Summary is provided at the end of each chapter. In addition, each chapter contains a Glossary section that provides more formal definitions of the main terms introduced in the chapter and a series of Review Questions. If students can answer these questions, they can be confident that they have understood the main themes of the chapter.

Acknowledgments

I hope that this text is both challenging and interesting, and that it provides a sense of the importance and excitement of research on learning. If the text achieves any of these aims, credit will be due to many individuals. One is Ralph Haber, who warmly encouraged me when I first contemplated what to me was the awesome prospect of writing a text. Another is my first editor, Ken King, who strongly believed in what I was trying to do and supported me even in cases such as the Rescorla-Wagner model, where my approach differed substantially from that of existing texts.

I am also grateful to many friends and colleagues who have read and commented on the manuscript at various stages of its preparation. For the first edition,

Tony Dickinson of Cambridge University
Vin LoLordo of Dalhousie University
Glyn Thomas of Birmingham University

were all kind enough to read the entire manuscript. I also received helpful comments from

Pete Badia of Bowling Green State University
David L. Brodigan of Carleton College
John Capaldi of Purdue University
Alexis C. Collier of Ohio State University
Robert L. Greene of Case Western Reserve University
Nancy K. Innis of the University of Western Ontario
Donald F. Kendrick of Middle Tennessee State University
Steve Maier of the University of Colorado
Mary Jane Rains of the University of Wisconsin, Stout
Mark Rilling of Michigan State University

In preparing the second edition, I was helped by comments from

Pamela Jackson-Smith of the University of Utah
Michael E. Rashotte of Florida State University
Gene D. Steinhauer of California State University at Hayward

who read the first edition and offered suggestions for how it could be improved. Once my draft was complete, the following individuals read the entire revision and provided valuable comments:

Michael S. Fanselow of the University of California at Los Angeles
Sandra J. Kelley of the University of South Carolina at Columbia

In addition, two colleagues were kind enough to comment on the section dealing with evolution:

Bill McGrew of the University of Stirling
Cliff Henty of the University of Stirling

For the third edition, I received helpful suggestions on areas for improvement from

Harvard Armus, University of Toledo
Stephen Buggie, University of New Mexico, Gallup
Robert Madigan, University of Alaska, Anchorage
Louis Manza, Lebanon Valley College
Steven Meier, University of Idaho
Joseph Snyder, Concordia University, Loyola Campus
Elizabeth Street, Central Washington University
David Washburn, Georgia State University, Language Research Center

I believe the text benefited substantially from the comments of all of these reviewers, and I am grateful for their efforts. I did not always follow their advice, however, and, accordingly, they should not be held responsible for any errors or omissions that remain.

In a slightly different context, I am again grateful to Mike Rashotte of Florida State University, who was kind enough to allow me to incorporate some of the exam questions he used in his course in the Instructor's Manual. And I am grateful to Robin Gold, of Forbes Mill Press, who acted as copy editor and supervised the production of this edition. Despite literal storms and power failures, she managed to improve my grammar and get this book out on time (or so she has assured me . . .). She did a wonderful job, and I am grateful for her efforts.

Finally, I would like to thank two other women. Marianne Taflinger became my editor when production of the text was transferred from Wadsworth to Brooks/Cole; she has strongly supported my efforts and I am very grateful for her help. And I would also like to express my appreciation to my wife Myra. Writing a text can be a ferociously time-consuming activity that absorbs the energies of its author for unconscionably long periods; Myra accepted the resulting burdens without complaint, and I am deeply grateful for her warmth, good humor, and love.

David A. Lieberman

LEARNING

Behavior and Cognition

PART I

INTRODUCTION

CHAPTER ONE

Some Basic Assumptions

In the old television series *Dragnet*, police sergeant Joe Friday was forever being confronted by incoherent witnesses to a crime. He would stoically endure their babbling until, his patience finally exhausted, he would interrupt, "We want the facts, Ma'am, just the facts." Psychologists too want the facts, but, with experience, they acquire a certain wary respect for the problems involved in determining facts.

What is a fact? Of course everyone knows what a fact is; a fact is . . . , well . . . it's a *fact*, something that everyone knows to be true. Or is it? Was it a fact that the earth was flat because everyone before Columbus believed it to be so? Or that the earth was the center of the universe before Galileo single-handedly moved it into orbit around the sun? And if we cannot be sure of the truth in cases as obvious as these ("Can't you feel that the earth is still? Can't you see that the sun is moving?"), how much more difficult must it be when the truth is more obscure, and when experts can't even agree among themselves? If one scientist claims that the moon is composed of blue cheese, and a colleague tartly replies, "So's your mother," how are we to decide which of their scientific views is correct?

In older sciences, such as physics and chemistry, disputes over scientific facts are less obvious: Over the years, basic concepts such as the atom and gravity have become firmly established; only after considerable training to learn dispute-free "facts" are new initiates to the profession gradually introduced to the ambiguities and uncertainties of current research. In psychology, which is a relatively new science, these disputes cannot be obscured so easily: The dividing line between "old established facts" and "new controversial hypotheses" is less clear, and there is not a comforting bedrock of certainty and accomplishment to support a student when he or she feels overwhelmed by conflicting claims. Consider such a relatively simple problem as the use of corporal punishment: Is corporal punishment an effective and ultimately humane way to eliminate a

3

person's harmful behavior, or is it a barbaric relic of our primitive past? There is evidence to support both views, and it can be more than a little frustrating to try to analyze the polemics of each side, and more than a little tempting to give up in disgust, crying "a plague on both your houses."

In their attempts to resolve such disagreements—to decide what is a fact and what is not—psychologists have relied on several assumptions. These assumptions are now so widely accepted that psychologists rarely question them, but this does not necessarily mean that they are correct. It is perhaps worth emphasizing in advance that the assumptions we will be examining in this chapter really are assumptions, slowly developed over several centuries within a particular cultural and scientific tradition, and indeed not universally accepted even among psychologists. There are good grounds for you to approach these assumptions with a healthy skepticism and to form your own views of their validity. The better you understand these assumptions, however, the better you will understand why research on learning has followed the paths that we will be tracing in subsequent chapters.

One purpose of this chapter, then, is to examine the methodological assumptions that have guided psychological research: why psychologists rely on experiments to understand learning, and the logic that guides them in designing these experiments. Before considering how to do research, however, we will begin by focusing on an even more fundamental issue: Why study learning in the first place?

1.1 IS BEHAVIOR LAWFUL?

The most fundamental assumption underlying research into the laws of learning is that there *are* laws of learning-if people's behavior was simply capricious or random, there would be little point in trying to discover the laws governing it. To clarify the issue, let us begin by defining more precisely what we mean by a law. Within science, a law is essentially a statement of the form "If A, then B." That is, if some condition A exists, we predict that event B will occur. The statement "The sun rises every morning," for example, predicts that if it is morning, then the sun will rise. Similarly, Einstein's famous equation $E = mc^2$ says that if m has a value of 1 and c has a value of 2, then the value of E will be 4 (the real value of c is much greater). The assertion that behavior is lawful, therefore, is essentially a claim that behavior is in principle predictable: Whenever a certain set of conditions arises, the same behavior will always follow.

Determinism versus Free Will

Most of us believe that at least some aspects of behavior are predictable. However much we might dislike some powerful bully, for example, we don't usually walk over to him and punch him in the nose, because we know very well that his reaction will not be random but intensely and unpleasantly predictable. Opinion varies, however, as to the extent of this predictability or lawfulness.

Determinism. At one extreme, some believe that *all* behavior is predictable. According to the doctrine of **determinism,** people's behavior is entirely determined by their heredity and environment (as used here, the word "environment" refers to past experiences as well as present environment). Your decision to go to college, for example, will have been influenced by factors such as the educational background of your parents, the grades you received at school, the economic advantages of a degree, and so forth. According to determinism, these factors made it inevitable that you would eventually choose to go to college, whether or not you were consciously aware of their influence.

Dramatic advances in physics and chemistry have accustomed us to the idea that nature is inherently orderly, even though our ignorance sometimes makes it appear capricious. But is the behavior of a living organism just as lawful, just as determined, as the orbit of a rocket or the ticking of a clock? Are we really just helpless pawns in the grasp of environmental and genetic forces beyond our control?

Free will. Within Western civilization, strict determinism of this kind has generally been rejected. Humans, according to most Western religions, are fundamentally free: We all have the power to determine our actions; this **free will** makes each of us responsible for our behavior and provides the basis for our concepts of morality and responsibility. Aside from formal religious teachings, however, a deep strain within all of us resents the notion that we are only insignificant links within a causal chain, like billiard balls hurtling blindly through space, propelled by forces we cannot resist. Our resentment of being controlled was eloquently expressed by the novelist Dostoevsky:

> *Out of sheer ingratitude man will play you a dirty trick, just to prove that men are still men and not the keys of a piano. . . . And even if you could prove that a man is only a piano key, he would still do something out of sheer perversity—he would create destruction and chaos—just to gain his point. . . . And if all this could in turn be analyzed and prevented by predicting that it would occur, then man would deliberately go mad to prove his point.*
> (Quoted in Skinner, 1955, p. 49)

Given our resentment of being controlled, why do many research psychologists nevertheless believe in determinism? The reasons are complex, and in the following sections we will consider some of them. As you read this material, some of the arguments might strike you as more philosophical than psychological, and you might wonder why a textbook on learning should be devoting so much attention to this issue. The answer is that a belief in determinism plays an important role in guiding psychological research. If you carry out a study to find a lawful relationship and it fails, you are much more likely to persist if you are convinced that there really are laws. As a result, many of the most crucial discoveries about learning have been made by psychologists with a stubborn, even fanatical belief that behavior is lawful. (See, for example, the discussions of Pavlov and B. F. Skinner in Chapters 2 and 5.) In the sections that follow, we will consider some arguments that have led to this belief.

Examples of Lawful Behavior

One reason for believing that behavior is lawful is simply empirical: evidence that in some situations our environment does seem to control our behavior strongly. There are many examples, but we will start by looking at three: obedience, child abuse, and aggression.

Obedience. One of the most striking examples of how strongly our environment can influence us, to the point of engaging in behavior we strongly oppose, comes from Stanley Milgram's research on obedience (Milgram, 1963, 1974). Milgram was horrified by the behavior of German soldiers during World War II who participated in the murder of millions of Jews and other groups in concentration camps. Though some of those involved may have been evil, many seemed to be ordinary soldiers obeying orders, no matter how vile those orders were.

To understand the conditions that could have produced such obedience, Milgram designed an experiment that he hoped would allow him to study obedience in the laboratory. He recruited ordinary people from the New Haven area through newspaper ads, and told them that they would be participating in a study on the effects of peer-delivered punishment on learning. They were asked to give their partners an electric shock whenever they made an error on a memory problem. The intensity of the shock was controlled by a series of 30 switches, ranging from 15 to 450 volts, and the experimenter instructed subjects to increase the intensity of the shock after every error by the partner, who was in an adjoining room. Unknown to the subject, the partner was actually a confederate of the experimenter and never received the shocks.

Milgram had hoped to use the highest shock intensity his subjects were willing to administer as a measure of their obedience to authority—in this case, a scientist in a white lab coat. The astonishing result, which Milgram had not anticipated, was that there were essentially no limits to his subjects' obedience. Sixty-five percent continued to administer shocks even when their partners pounded on the wall and refused to answer any questions and when the switch on the shock control panel was labeled 450 volts . . . Danger: Severe Shock. His subjects became extremely upset as the experiment continued, some laughing hysterically and pleading with the experimenter to let them stop, but almost all continued to administer shocks when ordered to do so. One observer reported,

> I observed a mature and initially poised businessman enter the laboratory smiling and confident. Within 20 minutes he was reduced to a twitching, stuttering wreck, who was rapidly approaching the point of nervous collapse. He constantly pulled on his earlobe, and twisted his hands. At one point he pushed his fist into his forehead and muttered: "Oh, God, let's stop it." And yet he continued to respond to every word of the experimenter, and obeyed to the end.
> (Milgram, 1963, p. 377)

It has been argued that the extraordinary behavior of the participants in Milgram's study was atypical, a product of the experiment's artificial conditions (Baumrind, 1964). The behavior of German soldiers during World War II argues against this view—obedience to authority, even when it means injuring others, is not a phenomenon confined to the laboratory. Another poignant example comes from the Vietnam War in the 1960s. In one of the most notorious incidents of that war, a group of American soldiers entered a small Vietnam village, My Lai, in search of enemy soldiers. When the American soldiers failed to find the enemy, they obeyed the orders of their officers and slaughtered everyone in the village, killing hundreds of defenseless women and children. Although the terrible conditions of war undoubtedly play a major role in producing such behavior, Milgram's research suggests that obedience is not confined to such situations. We are more sensitive to social control—to the opinions of our parents, our friends, even our neighbors—than we sometimes realize. (See also Cialdini, 1993.)

Child abuse. A further example of how powerfully our environment can determine our behavior comes from studies of children who are physically or sexually abused. Approximately two thirds of children who are abused develop serious symptoms, ranging from anxiety and bed-wetting to depression and self-destructive behavior (Kendall-Tackett, Williams, & Finkelhor, 1993). One of the saddest of these after-effects is that many of these children have a greatly increased likelihood of themselves becoming abusers when they become parents. Kaufman and Zigler (1987) reviewed the many studies in this area and concluded that "approximately one-third of all individuals who were physically abused, sexually abused, or extremely neglected will subject their offspring to one of these forms of maltreatment" (p. 190). Conversely, most adults who abuse children were themselves abused as children. In one typical study, Kasper and Alford (1988) studied 125 men who had sexually abused children and found that approximately 85% were themselves abused. The experience of abuse can profoundly influence a child's present and future behavior.

Aggression. Aggression provides an example of how heredity, and our environment, can influence our behavior. It is well known that children who have aggressive parents are themselves more likely to be aggressive, as indexed by such measures as delinquency, criminality and antisocial personality. The fact that aggression often runs in families, however, does not tell us whether the cause is genetic (the children have inherited a predisposition to behave aggressively) or environmental (the children become aggressive as a result of being targets of aggression). One way to separate these effects is to compare the behavior of identical twins who are reared together with those who are adopted and thus grow up in different families. (To the extent that behavior is genetically determined, the behavior of identical twins should be similar even if reared in different environments.) In a recent review of the literature in this area, Miles and Carey (1997) concluded that as much as 50% of aggressive behavior in adults can be accounted for by heredity. Put another way, if an adult is aggressive, there is roughly a 50/50 chance that he or she inherited this trait.

The Feeling of Freedom

The examples we have considered so far involve strong social pressures—orders from powerful authorities; sustained and intense parental abuse. Perhaps these situations are atypical, and in the more normal conditions of everyday life we have much greater freedom to decide how we will behave. In these more normal settings we do not experience any sense of compulsion or constraint. We can do what we want, go where we want, say what we want. How can our behavior be determined if we constantly feel so free?

The answer proposed by determinists is that although we may *feel* free in such situations, our behavior is being controlled just as surely as in Milgram's experiments. The difference is simply that in everyday life we are less aware of the forces that are affecting us.

Advertising. A classic example of how we can be influenced without realizing it is advertising. Most of us believe that we are not taken in by advertisements—we are not seduced by their glitz and instead base our decisions solely on evidence. Some research, however, suggests that we are all more susceptible to advertising than we realize. In one study on this point, Smith and Engel (1968) showed 120 adults a picture of an automobile. For half the subjects, the photograph showed only the car, whereas for the other subjects a sexy redhead, dressed in black lace panties and a sleeveless sweater, was standing in front of it. After examining the picture, participants were asked to evaluate the car on several dimensions. Those who saw the car with the attractive female next to it rated the car as significantly more appealing and better designed. They also estimated it to be more expensive (by an average of $340), faster (by 7 mph), and less safe. When a subset of the subjects were later asked if their ratings had been influenced by the presence of the model, however, 22 of the 23 subjects interviewed denied it. One respondent claimed, "I don't let anything but the thing itself influence my judgments. The other is just propaganda." Another commented, "I never let myself be blinded by advertising; the car itself is what counts." Thus although the model's presence clearly altered the participants' ratings of the car, virtually no one believed that he had been affected.

Sexual attraction. Another illustration of how the environment can influence us without our realizing it comes from research on sexual attraction. Why is it that we are sexually attracted to some individuals but not others? Psychologists are still in the early stages of trying to understand attraction, but some interesting evidence has begun to emerge. One study, by Dutton and Aron (1974), was carried out in an unusual setting for a psychology experiment, a deep river gorge in British Columbia. There were two ways of crossing the river: a narrow, wobbly footbridge located some 230 feet above rapids, or a much more substantial wooden bridge only 10 feet above a small rivulet. Males were approached as they crossed either bridge by an attractive female who asked if they would answer some questions for a research project she was conducting. When the interview was over, she gave the males her telephone number in case they later had any questions.

The real purpose of the study was to measure sexual attraction—would the males later phone to ask for a date? Many did, but the study's striking finding was that the proportion asking for a date depended on where the interview took place: Half the men interviewed after crossing the rickety bridge later phoned for a date, compared with only 12% of those interviewed after crossing the solid bridge.

On the surface this result might seem bizarre—why should the location of the interview determine whether males think a female is attractive? Dutton and Aron, however, had predicted precisely this result on the basis of a theory of emotion previously proposed by Schachter and Singer (1962). We will not review the theory in detail, but in essence it proposes that all emotions are characterized by similar states of physiological arousal—increased heart rate, rapid breathing, and so on. Schacter and Singer argued that we therefore need to rely on environmental cues to help us identify what emotion we are experiencing. According to this theory, males would have experienced strong arousal when crossing the high bridge; when they encountered the attractive interviewer, they would have unconsciously thought "Aha, it must be her beauty that is making me feel so excited." And believing that they were attracted to her, they would have been more likely to ask her for a date.

An alternative explanation might already have occurred to you, though, namely that the differences could have been the result of differences in the men who used the two bridges. Perhaps the higher bridge attracted men who were more adventurous and thus would also have been less timid about asking for a date. To control for this possibility, Dutton and Aron ran a second experiment.

Both groups now consisted of men who crossed the high bridge, with one group interviewed while they were on the bridge and the other at least 10 minutes after they had crossed, so that any arousal had time to dissipate. If the earlier results had been an artifact of differences in adventurousness, the two groups should now be equally likely to phone for a date, since both consisted of men who chose the high bridge. If the results had been caused by arousal, however, then the group interviewed while still on the bridge should again have been more likely to phone, and this is what the authors found.

The most likely explanation for Dutton and Aron's findings seems to be that the males who crossed the high bridge misinterpreted their arousal, attributing it to sexual attraction rather than the more prosaic experience of crossing a rickety bridge. When they later decided to ask for a date, they almost certainly believed this to be a free choice, but they were being influenced by factors of which they were entirely unaware.

Further evidence for the role of unconscious factors in attraction, this time pointing to the importance of heredity, comes from a study by Singh (1993). It has often been noted that standards of beauty can vary considerably across times and cultures. At one time, for example, Western cultures put special value on white skin, whereas now people will pay large sums for holidays in the sun or tanning treatments. Similarly, ideals of female size have changed considerably over time, with thin shapes being preferred at some times and more voluptuous shapes at other times. This variation might suggest that ideals of physical beauty are entirely cultural, but Singh speculated that some aspects of beauty might be genetically determined. To find out, he looked at variations in the American ideal of female beauty from 1920 to 1990, using the measurements of Miss America winners and Playboy Playmates of the Month as an indicator of what shapes were considered most desirable.

He found variation in some measurements such as weight, but he also found remarkable consistency in one, the ratio of waist size to hip size. In Playmates, for example, the waist/hip ratio varied only from .68 to .71, and in Miss America winners from .69 and .72. To assess the desirability of this shape further, he also obtained measurements for fashion models. Overall, they were far thinner than, say, Playmates, but their waist/hip ratios proved to be virtually identical, varying only between .68 and .69. It appears as if American males are most strongly attracted to a very specific shape, even though the preferred weight has varied substantially over this period.

Singh suggested that males are attracted so strongly to this shape because it is a strong predictor of female fertility. The size of a woman's waist and hips is controlled by the female hormone estrogen, which stimulates the deposit of fat at the hips while inhibiting deposits at the abdomen. The more estrogen a women has, therefore, the lower her waist/hip ratio will be. Singh argued that estrogen levels are also strongly correlated with fertility: In one study of married women, for example, women with lower waist/hip ratios were found to have less difficulty in becoming pregnant. Males attracted to this shape would thus be somewhat more likely to mate successfully and to leave offspring sharing their genes. Over many generations, the result would be an increase in the proportion of the population attracted to this shape.

If Singh is right, evolution might have led men to unconsciously prefer females with a particular shape. (For information on what factors make males attractive to females, see Singh, 1995.) Thus in one of the situations where we might assume that we are most free, choosing a partner, environmental and genetic factors might be influencing our choices without our awareness. Feeling free does not necessarily mean that we are free.

Neural Determinism

Further evidence for the determinist view comes from our rapidly growing understanding of the brain's role in determining behavior. We will discuss the mechanisms involved in more detail in Chapter 2, but in essence the brain consists of a vast network of interconnected cells called neurons, and the transmission of electrical signals through these cells determines our behavior. When we see a friend, for example, the light falling on receptors located at the back of the eye produces electrical signals, and these are then transmitted by means of a series of neurons to the cortex and then ultimately to the muscles that cause us to raise our hand in greeting or to move our lips to say hello. If physicists are correct, and the behavior of all particles in the universe is lawful, then the transmission of these electrical impulses through our brain must also be lawful. (Indeed, neurophysiologists already have a good understanding of the chemical processes that govern the propagation of electrical signals through neurons, and how the arrival of a signal at a neuron's terminal leads to the release of chemicals, which then activate the next neuron in the chain.) If our brains control our behavior, and if the brain's operations are lawful, it follows that our behavior must also be lawful.

This argument is important enough that we will sketch it out in a little more detail, focusing on the brain's role in three fundamental activities: movement, emotion, and thought.

Movement. Our movements are entirely controlled by the transmission of electrical impulses though our neurons. When we move an arm, for example, this movement is caused by the contraction of muscles within the arm, and these contractions are in turn controlled by neurons. There are neurons connected to every muscle in the body, and the arrival of electrical impulses at the terminals of these neurons trigger the release of chemicals that in turn initiate muscular contractions. If these neural connections are damaged—for example, if the spine is damaged in an automobile accident so that neural messages can no longer be transmitted from the brain to certain muscles—then we lose the ability to control these muscles. Similarly, the tremors seen in Parkinson's disease are due to degeneration of the basal ganglia, one of the regions of the brain controlling movement, and it is possible to treat Parkinson's by administering L-DOPA, a drug that restores the functioning of the affected neurons. Evidence of this kind makes it clear that movement is entirely controlled by the nervous system.

Emotion. In a similar way, our emotions are controlled by what regions of our brains are active. One early experiment demonstrating the brain's role in emotions was reported by Olds and Milner (1954), who found that delivering a tiny electrical current to certain areas of a rat's brain seemed to produce pleasurable sensations in the rat, as the rat would press a lever as often as 2,000 times per hour to turn on this current. A neurosurgeon, Heath (1963), reported similar effects in humans. One of his patients suffered from narcolepsy, a debilitating condition in which sufferers will suddenly and uncontrollably fall into a deep sleep, even in the middle of a conversation. In an effort to help this patient to stay awake, and thereby retain his job, Heath and his colleagues implanted small electrodes into several areas of the patient's brain. They provided the patient with a control panel that he could use to initiate stimulation of these areas. He described one of the buttons on this panel as his "happy button," saying it gave him a drunk feeling, while another stimulated sexual arousal.

Drugs such as alcohol, heroin, and Ecstasy work in a similar way; by altering chemical activity in the brain, they change the emotions we experience. In both animals and humans, it is possible to produce emotions ranging from rage to euphoria by altering neural activity.

Thought. Increasing evidence suggests that thinking also depends on neural activity in different regions of the cortex. Early evidence for the brain's role in thought came from studies of epilepsy reported by a Canadian neurosurgeon, Wilder Penfield.

Epileptic seizures are triggered by abnormal activity in one small region of the brain, and in severe cases it is important to identify the precise region involved so that it can be removed surgically. One way of doing this is to remove part of the skull and use electrodes to stimulate various parts of the brain while the patient is conscious; the patient can then report when they are experiencing the sensations that normally precede their seizures, so that the surgeon can remove the region producing these feelings. (This technique might sound gruesome, but the scalp is anesthetized first, and because there are no pain receptors in the brain, the patient suffers no discomfort.) Penfield discovered that stimulation of some areas would give rise to specific thoughts or images. Depending on the area stimulated, patients reported hearing someone calling their name, waiting at a station for a train, or hearing music. If the stimulation was stopped, the sensation would cease, but it would return if the same spot was stimulated again (for example, Penfield, 1958). Activity in particular cortical areas thus seemed to control what thoughts a patient experienced.

More recent evidence for the brain's role in determining thinking has come from the development of brain scans, procedures that allow doctors and psychologists to observe ongoing activity in different areas in the brain. These scans have revealed very precise correlations between activity in different areas and what thoughts participants are experiencing at the time. If you are working on a mathematics problem, for example, one area of your brain will become more active, but if you then begin to imagine a musical passage, activity will switch to another area. We can now actually watch activity moving from region to region as a person thinks!

Some of the most dramatic evidence for the correlation between brain activity and thought has come from studies of stroke victims. Strokes are caused by blood clots cutting off the flow of blood to particular regions within the brain, resulting in the death of the cells in that area. Depending on how large an area is starved of blood, the damaged area can be quite small, and in some instances the resulting impairment of the person's cognitive functioning can be extraordinarily specific. In one case reported by Caramazza and Hillis (1991), a female stroke patient developed problems with just one class of words, verbs. She could still use verbs in sentences, and she could understand them if she read them, but she was unable to write them down. If she heard a sentence containing the verb "crack," for example ("Don't crack the nuts in here"), and was then asked to write it, she could write down all the words except for "crack." If she heard a sentence in which "crack" was used as a noun, however ("There's a crack in the mirror"), she could write the word normally! In this remarkable case the damage seemed to be specific not only to one class of words, verbs, but also to the ability to reproduce this class in writing. (In other studies, brain-damaged patients have had difficulties with even narrower word categories, such as fruit or vegetables—see Damasio, 1990.)

In summary, it appears as if every aspect of our behavior—movement, emotion and thought—depends on the transmission of electrical impulses within neurons. If this neural activity is lawful, the behavior that it controls must also be lawful.

Evaluation

It seems clear that our heredity and environment do influence a wide range of our behaviors, including how we react to advertisements, who we find attractive, and whether we are aggressive. The fact that our behavior is influenced, however, does not necessarily mean that it is totally determined. Even when under the most intense environmental pressure, it is possible that we still retain some freedom to choose, however circumscribed. Consider again the effects of sexual abuse on children. We have seen that roughly one third of children who are abused go on to become abusers as adults. By the same token, however, this means that two thirds of these children do not. Proponents of free will can thus argue that even under the most terrible pressures, each of us retains some capacity to choose our own path.

Determinists can counterargue that behavior is the product of multiple influences acting together, and that if individuals vary in their response to a situation, this simply reflects differences in their other experiences. Researchers have already identified several factors that influence whether abused children become abusive parents, including whether they remember their abusive experiences, whether they have a supportive spouse, and how much stress they are under (Belsky, 1993). In this light, the fact that abused children respond differently can be seen not as evidence against determinism but as still more evidence in its favor, as reactions to abuse depend on the individual's subsequent environment. The fact that individuals respond differently, in other words, does not necessarily mean that their behavior is not lawful. Consider how individuals vary in the symptoms they develop when they catch a cold—some are particularly likely to have sore throats, others runny noses, still others ear aches. The fact that the same virus produces different symptoms does not mean that the processes involved are not lawful, but simply that the effects depend on many factors.

In the end, it is unlikely that the debate between determinism and free will will ever be resolved conclusively. Not even the most optimistic determinist believes that we will ever be able to predict every aspect of a person's behavior—we would have to know every law and record every moment of the person's life to be able to calculate the cumulative impact of all these experiences. If we can never fully predict behavior, however, then it will always be possible for believers in free will to argue that this lack of predictability reflects an essential inner freedom, while determinists claim that it reflects only limitations in our current state of knowledge.

It is thus doubtful whether we will ever know whether behavior is completely lawful. The evidence we have reviewed, however, suggests that environment and heredity do powerfully influence our behavior, whether or not they fully control it.

1.2 How Should We Discover Any Laws?

If behavior is lawful, at least to some degree, how should we go about discovering these laws? We will start by examining two alternatives: consulting authorities and observing the workings of our own minds.

Authority

Historically, the most common answer to the problem of obtaining knowledge has been to consult an authority. Over the centuries, reliance on authorities has been a constant feature of human society, and defiance of such authorities has often been at the risk of life and limb. In ancient Greece, the heresies of Socrates led to his being poisoned with hemlock. Fifteen centuries later, Galileo's challenge of the teachings of Socrates and Aristotle (which, ironically, had become dogma) almost led to his being burned at the stake. The stifling effects of medieval orthodoxy were humorously but accurately satirized in a story by Francis Bacon, written in 1605:

> In the year of our Lord 1432, there arose a grievous quarrel among the brethren over the number of teeth in the mouth of a horse. For 13 days the disputation raged without ceasing. All the ancient books and chronicles were fetched out, and wonderful and ponderous erudition, such as was never before heard of in the region, was made manifest. At the beginning of the fourteenth day, a youthful friar of goodly bearing asked his learned superiors for permission to add a word, and straight-away, to the wonderment of the disputants, whose deep wisdom he sore vexed, he beseeched them to unbend in a manner coarse and unheard-of, and to look in the open mouth of a horse and find answer to their questionings. At this, their dignity being grievously hurt, they waxed exceedingly wroth; and, joining in a mighty uproar, they flew upon him and smote him hip and thigh, and cast him out forthwith. For, said they, surely Satan hath tempted this bold neophyte to declare unholy and unheard-of ways of finding truth contrary to all the teachings of the fathers. After many days more of grievous strife the dove of peace sat on the assembly, and they as one man, declaring the problem to be an everlasting mystery because of a grievous dearth of historical and theological evidence thereof, so ordered the same writ down.
>
> (Quoted in Munn, 1961, p. 4)

Lest you think this attack on authority to be unfounded or unduly harsh, consider the advice of the respected seventeenth-century German physician John Loselius, on the proper treatment of gout:

> Shave with a razor the hair off both legs, and at the same time cut the nails off hands and feet. This should be in the spring when the sap is flowing, and the day before the new moon. Make a hole right into the heartwood of a poplar or oak tree and insert the hair and nails. Stop it tight with a plug made of a branch of the tree, and the transplantation is perfect. Cut off close to the tree that part of the plug that sticks out, and the next day plaster the place well with cow dung. If the patient does not in the next three months feel the malum again, he can credit it to the tree.
>
> (Quoted in Roueche, 1954)

In our more skeptical era, the power of authority is no longer as absolute as it once was. Yet such authoritarian nonsense is not the exclusive province of the past. Twentieth-century medicine and science have had more than their share of absurdities, including such nightmares as prefrontal lobotomies, a widely accepted treatment for certain mental disorders involving the surgical removal of a substantial section of the brain, thereby curing patients by reducing them, in some cases, to vegetables. It should be clear that authority, whether religious, medical, or scientific, is not the last word. Indeed, even authors of textbooks have been known to err!

Introspection

An alternative means of gaining knowledge has been **introspection,** a person's examination of his or her own thoughts or feelings. We are all introspective on occasion, and literature abounds with references to people "searching their souls" or "plumbing the depths of their hearts" in an attempt to understand themselves. The first systematic application of this technique, however, was the work of a German psychologist of the late nineteenth century, Wilhelm Wundt (1832–1920). The essence of Wundt's technique was extremely simple: Subjects were exposed to a stimulus and then asked to report the sensations aroused by it. In actual practice, however, this technique required long and arduous hours of training. It was important, for example, that a subject report not simply what he or she saw (such as a chair), but the exact sensations the object elicited, the quality and intensity of such sensations, how they changed over time, and so on.

This precise analysis of sensations is not easy. A naive observer exposed to a brightly lighted piece of coal and a dimly lighted paper, for example, will invariably report that the coal appears darker, even though physically it might actually be reflecting far more light. Observers in such cases are not reporting what they actually see but what they expected to see. Wundt's subjects underwent extended training to overcome this and similar errors. Once the observers were properly trained, Wundt hoped to use their reports to analyze the complex patterns of human thought into their constituent elements and then discover the laws by which these elements are combined to produce the richness and variety of mental life.

Though the rigorous demands of Wundt's technique now seem somewhat daunting, the underlying logic has great intuitive appeal. If we want to understand the processes of learning, what better way is there than by studying these processes at work within our own minds? In the end, we must all rely on the judgment of our senses—it is a brave person who strides forward when his or her eyes tell of an abyss ahead. In the same way that our peripheral senses provide us with our most reliable information about the external world, introspection would seem to be the best guide to the world of the mind.

The unconscious. Yet, despite its obvious attractions, introspection gradually fell into progressively greater disrepute, until eventually it almost disappeared from psychology. One reason for this collapse was that even as Wundt was painstakingly beginning to train his subjects, a Viennese physician named Sigmund Freud was developing his revolutionary theories—theories that, in an offhand way, were ultimately to destroy the rationale for introspection. Freud exposed for the first time the Byzantine world of the unconscious, its primitive swirl of emotions hidden from consciousness behind powerful defensive barriers. This metaphor of hidden, subterranean forces had devastating implications for introspection, attacking its very foundation: a faith in the accessibility of all thought to conscious analysis. Unless every aspect of human thought and emotion could be observed and analyzed, introspection could at best provide only an incomplete and fragmented picture of the causal mechanisms of behavior. And Freud's theories suggested that consciousness was but the visible tip of the iceberg, with vast areas of the mind forever hidden in the murky depths of the subconscious.

Freud's theories suggested for the first time that there might be severe limits to the power of conscious analysis, but it seems likely that these limits would have become apparent in any case. Consider, for example, what happens when you try to prove a geometry theorem. You may struggle for minutes or even hours, doggedly searching for a solution, when suddenly the correct answer occurs to you. What happened exactly? How did you suddenly pass from a state of complete and utter confusion to one of confidence in the right answer? Clearly some important mental processes intervened between these two states, but, introspectively, all is a blank, your mind an empty vacuum from which the correct solution emerged as if by spontaneous generation. To take an even more homely example, how is it that we are able to control and coordinate our bodily movements? Try, for example, to introspect as you repeatedly flex your thumb. Concentrate intensely and try to feel every sensation. You might be able to feel your thumb's movement, but can you feel the command that initiates that movement? What is making your thumb move? What is the link between your eyes scanning this page and the actual flexing of your thumb in that far-off extremity? Our inability to trace the processes involved even in such simple acts as thumb flexing suggests serious limits to the usefulness of introspection in analyzing complex thought and learning.

The problem of confirming reports. Considerations such as these suggest that introspection can at best play only a limited role in helping us understand behavior. It would seem, however, that we should at least be able to use introspection in analyzing that fraction of our experience that is accessible to consciousness. Again, however, critics have raised serious objections to the use of introspection even in this limited domain. The problem, fundamentally, is one of confirmability: How are we to confirm the accuracy of an introspective report when it is based on private events that are inaccessible to any outside observer? If a person says she or he is feeling angry, for example, how do we know whether the person is really feeling anger or fear, or perhaps some subtle combination of the two?

It might seem churlish to question the honesty of such a report (isn't a person the best judge of her or his own feelings?), but studies of perception in other situations suggest a need for greater caution. Just as our visual senses are not flawless—the moon is *not* larger at the horizon, and desert oases glimpsed from afar have a dismaying tendency to recede as we approach—so, too, introspection can yield data that are not necessarily accurate.

The problem of evaluating observers' reports is not, of course, unique to introspection. A person who says he feels hungry is really no different from a scientist who reports seeing a rat or, for that matter, a flying saucer. Each of these statements is simply a report of subjective experience; the fact that the stimulus for one example originated outside the body rather than inside it does not give the former report any greater validity. Whatever the original stimulus for these reports, we are faced with the problem of evaluating their accuracy—that is, evaluating how closely the original events and the verbal reports correspond.

Reports of external events can be confirmed by establishing either their reliability (for example, by comparing the reports with those of other observers in the same situation) or their consistency with other data (for example, radar reports in the case of flying saucers). In the case of introspective reports, however, confirmation is not so easy. To start with, how are we to estimate the reliability of an introspective observer when no other observer can detect the private events on which the report is based? One sensible solution adopted by introspectionists was to expose several observers to the same external stimulus; if they independently reported the same reactions, this would support the view that they were reporting their experiences accurately.

This approach worked well in some situations, but it proved less successful in others. One of its most spectacular failures arose in a controversy over "imageless thought." Some psychologists believed that the meaning of any word was simply the image that it produced—the meaning of the word "chair," for example, would be the image that comes to mind when you think about this word. This approach seems plausible when we consider concrete nouns like chair, but what of more abstract words such as "truth" or "meaning"—do these words also produce images? One influential introspectionist, Oswald Kulpe, reported that when he and his colleagues introspected they could not detect any trace of an image while thinking of such words. Another leading introspectionist, however, insisted that even the most abstract words produced images if you introspected carefully enough. In the case of *meaning,* for example, he reported seeing "the blue-gray tip of a kind of scoop which has a bit of yellow about it (probably a part of the handle) and which is digging into a dark mass of what appears to be plastic material" (Titchener, 1915, p. 519). This image had its origins, he suggested, in injunctions from his youth to "dig out the meaning" of Latin and Greek phrases. Each side insisted that the other was wrong, and there was no way to resolve their disagreement.

Evaluation.   The realization that much of the mind's functioning is unconscious, coupled with the difficulty of reliably observing even those areas that ostensibly are conscious, led eventually to the virtual abandonment of introspection as a scientific technique. Do not conclude that introspection is totally without value. It is still a fertile, if informal, technique for generating hypotheses about the causes of behavior, and it can sometimes provide confirmable information that can be highly valuable. (See, for example, Lieberman, 1979.) For the most part, however, psychologists have abandoned introspection as a systematic technique for acquiring knowledge.

In thus rejecting introspection, we must admit that we seem to be turning our backs on much of the richness and fascination of the mental world—indeed, of the entire world, for what else does any of us directly know or experience besides the workings of our own minds? It is perhaps worth emphasizing, therefore, that this rejection was not prompted by petulance, or by a Calvinistic desire to make psychology seem cold or dreary. Psychology originated as a branch of philosophy, and for centuries it was concerned exclusively with the contents and processes of the mind. These genuinely fascinating problems were finally put aside only when psychologists became convinced that direct study of the mind was futile so long as observers could not reach agreement on even its most elementary properties. In domains where agreement is obtainable, introspection can still serve as a useful tool; but for the substantial areas of mental functioning that are unconscious, it can play little role.

1.3 BEHAVIORAL AND COGNITIVE APPROACHES

The growing evidence for the limitations of introspection as a tool for studying the mind led to the emergence of a new approach within psychology called **behaviorism.** Behaviorists such as John B. Watson argued that since it is not possible to study the mind accurately, psychologists should instead focus on people's visible or overt behavior instead. Rather than studying subjective feelings such as hunger, we should study people's objectively observable behavior such as eating or travelling to a restaurant. An objective observation, in this sense, is simply one on which all observers can agree. "John is eating a hamburger," for example, is an objective report, because it is at least potentially confirmable by independent observers, whereas "John feels hungry" is not. Note that an objective report is not necessarily more valid than a subjective report: Subjective reports can be quite true (John really does feel hungry), and, conversely, objective reports can be quite false (even though all observers agree that the sun looks larger when it is just above the horizon than when it is at its zenith, this is in fact an illusion). By focusing on behavior that could be described objectively, however, behaviorists hoped that psychologists would at least be able to agree on their data, thus allowing theories to be evaluated by solid evidence rather than by the eloquence or prestige of opposing theorists.

Skinner's Radical Behaviorism

Although all behaviorists agree on the importance of objective observations of behavior, they disagree concerning what attention, if any, should be paid to mental states. One influential approach was developed by B. F. Skinner (for example, Skinner, 1953). Like Watson before him, Skinner believed that the goal of psychology should be practical, helping with problems such as the best ways of rearing children, coping with phobias, and making education more enjoyable as well as more effective. All these problems involve changing behavior, and the only way to change anyone's behavior is to change his or her environment. If you want to convince someone to vote for a particular political party, for example, you could try to do so by talking to him about the party's merits, but your words would then represent a change in the person's environment, and you would be hoping that this would lead to a consequent change in his voting behavior. If you want to change people's behavior, therefore, you must understand what environmental conditions lead to what behaviors.

To provide a concrete focus for understanding Skinner's approach, suppose that a friend tells you that she has decided to vote for candidate X for president. Why has she reached this decision? One obvious possibility is simply that she likes this candidate. Skinner did not doubt the existence of feelings such as liking, but he argued that psychologists should explain behavior not in terms of feelings but rather in terms of the environmental conditions that give rise to these feelings—in this case, perhaps a speech that your friend heard the candidate make. For Skinner, the cause of your friend's decision is not her liking of the candidate but the experiences that produced this feeling of liking.

Skinner attempts to explain behavior in terms of the environment, rather than thoughts or feelings, for two reasons. One, as we have already seen, is that it is difficult to observe other people's thoughts and feelings. If we attribute someone's behavior to his or her feelings, it is difficult to determine whether this explanation is correct. Moreover, Skinner argued that once we attribute someone's behavior to a mental state, we tend to be satisfied with this explanation, and we do not go on to try to identify the environmental conditions that generated this state. If someone eats because he or she is hungry, we need to ask *why* that person is hungry. If they vote for a candidate because they like him, we need to understand *why* they like him. Unless we understand the environmental conditions that shape behavior, we cannot hope to change behavior.

Consider the hypothetical sequence represented in Figure 1.1, in which an environmental condition gives rise to a mental state, which in turn produces behavior. To change this behavior, we must understand the environmental conditions that produce it, and Skinner argued that we should study the relationship between environmental conditions and behavior directly. He argued that studying the mental processes in this chain would not only be of limited value but could even be harmful. It would be of little value because the limitations of

FIGURE 1.1   Two behavioral perspectives. Behaviorists agree that introspection is of limited value in understanding the mind, but they disagree about whether other techniques should be used instead. Cognitive psychologists advocate using other techniques to study the mind indirectly; Skinner recommended ignoring the mind and focusing on the direct relationship between environmental conditions and behavior.

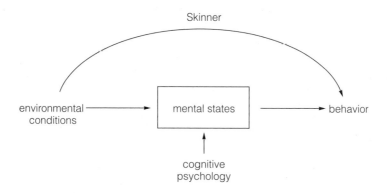

introspection mean that we can say very little about these mental processes; it is potentially harmful because any effort we put into speculating about them is effort that could be invested more profitably in investigating the effects of different environments. It is not easy to ignore the mind—since our private worlds are largely dominated by our own thoughts and feelings, we are inevitably fascinated by the possible thoughts and feelings of others—but Skinner argued that we must resist the siren call of the mind if we are to maximize psychology's ability to change behavior.

Cognitive Approaches

A rather different approach to the role of the mind in psychology emerged from cognitive psychology. (*Cognition* refers to the processes involved in thinking; cognitive psychologists try to understand these processes.) Cognitive psychologists are also behaviorists, in that they believe that most of the operations of the brain are unconscious, and thus that introspection can provide little information about these processes. If you ask someone her telephone number, for example, she will probably respond immediately, but if you ask her how she managed to retrieve this fact from the many hundreds of thousands of other facts stored in her memory, she will probably just stare at you. The reason is that the processes involved in storing and then retrieving information from memory are almost entirely unconscious, so that we have no idea how we do it. Similarly with other cognitive processes, introspection allows us to glimpse only the conscious tip of the mental iceberg; most of the brain's operations are hidden from view. (If you are not yet convinced, try closing your eyes and wiggling one of your thumbs. Can you feel any of the processes that occur in the interval between your decision to move your thumb and its movement? In fact, hundreds of different muscles are involved, including muscles in your back and legs, because you need to maintain your balance while engaging in this movement, but introspection provides us with no hint of this intricate and coordinated sequence of movements.)

Cognitive psychologists thus agree with other behaviorists that our ability to observe the mind's activities is seriously limited. However, they argue that this need not prevent us from studying cognitive processes. Physicists, for example, cannot directly observe the existence of atoms, but this has not stopped them from developing theories about the properties of atoms and other invisible particles, and these theories have led to discoveries that have transformed our world. (In addition to nuclear power, an understanding of atomic particles has also provided the foundation for the development of televisions, computers, and so on.) Similarly, cognitive psychologists believe that theories of how the mind works would deepen our understanding, which in turn would inevitably increase our ability to help people with problems.

In essence, the disagreement between Skinner's approach and that of cognitive psychologists concerns the desirability of theories about the mind. Both sides agree that introspection is of limited value in understanding the mind and, thus, that the primary data of psychology must be objective observations of behavior. They disagree, however, about whether there is a useful role for theories about the mind. Skinnerians argue that because behavior is ultimately determined by environmental conditions, our effort should go into studying the effect of these conditions on behavior. Cognitive psychologists argue that because cognitive processes form a critical part of the causal chain that controls behavior, a deeper understanding of these processes will inevitably lead to practical applications.

The Approach of This Text

The approach taken here can be seen as a blend of the Skinnerian and cognitive approaches. We think Skinner was right to emphasize the importance of environmental conditions in determining behavior. His emphasis on the practical application of learning principles played a crucial role in encouraging applied research, and we will be devoting considerable attention to the applications that resulted.

We think that Skinner was also right in recognizing the potential hazards in speculating about the mind—it is all too easy to attribute behavior to invisible mental states, without any evidence that these states really exist. However, we also agree with cognitive psychologists that these dangers can be avoided if theories are stated in such a way that they lead to testable predictions, and that under these circumstances they can substantially enrich our understanding of behavior. Suppose, for example, that a theorist proposed that reading involves a sequence of 32 cognitive processes. If there was no way to test the truth of this claim, the theory would be useless. On the other hand, if the theory led to testable predictions, and these were confirmed, then our understanding of the nature of these processing steps might allow us to identify the stage at which reading is impaired for different individuals, and thereby help us to develop treatments tailored to their individual problems.

For a cognitive approach of this kind to be useful, its claims must be testable. Suppose that we gave a rat a pellet of food every time it scratched its back, and as a result it begins to scratch its back at a very high rate. Would we be justified in claiming that it is scratching because it knows that this action will produce food? The answer is that it depends on whether this explanation is testable. If we make this claim purely on the basis of intuition—"If I were in that situation, I would know that food depended on scratching, and so I'm sure the rat does too"—this would not be a scientifically acceptable explanation, because there would be no way to determine whether it is true. In science, the fact that an explanation sounds plausible is *not* a valid argument for accepting it; as we shall see, many seemingly obvious explanations of behavior have proved to be totally and utterly wrong. (See Sections 4.4, 5.4 and 8.2 for some examples.) It is not enough, therefore, that an explanation sound good; it must lead to testable predictions if it is to have scientific value.

We will discuss the issues involved in deciding whether animals form expectations at greater length in Chapter 8, where we will encounter evidence that animal behavior probably is guided by expectations in some situations, but that in others their behavior appears more blind than calculating. Our purpose in raising the issue now, before its exploration in Chapter 8, is that in our discussions of learning before that chapter we will sometimes speculate about what subjects in experiments might be thinking—for example, whether a rat is responding to obtain food, or whether it remembers obtaining food on some past occasion. It is important to remember that these kinds of references to mental states must not be taken as self-evident facts, but only as speculations or hypotheses. These explanations might be correct, but, equally, they might be wrong, so they must be treated cautiously unless appropriate evidence is available to support them.

1.4 THE EXPERIMENTAL METHOD

The new concern with behavior was accompanied by an increasing emphasis on experimentation. Instead of passively observing behavior in the hope of noticing what antecedent conditions might have caused it, the essence of the experimental approach is to manipulate those conditions actively. The aspect

FIGURE 1.2   Four independent variables (IVs) simultaneously influencing a dependent variable (DV).

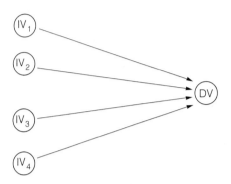

of the environment that we manipulate is called the **independent variable,** and the behavior we observe is called the **dependent variable.** Briefly, then, the experimental method consists simply of manipulating some independent variable and observing its effect on some dependent variable. A consistent relationship between them—for example, environmental variable A is always followed by behavior B—is called a **law.**

If experimentation were really so simple, discovering the laws of behavior should be easy: All we would have to do would be to manipulate our independent variables, observe their effects, and combine the resultant laws into a comprehensive account of behavior. The problem is that *we must manipulate only one independent variable at a time.* If several independent variables changed simultaneously (see Figure 1.2), then it would be impossible to say which one was responsible for the resulting behavior. And, as we shall see, it is extraordinarily difficult to ensure that only one independent variable changes at a time.

A Hypothetical Experiment

To illustrate the kinds of problems that can arise, consider the following example. Suppose that a psychologist reported a new and highly effective treatment for severe depression. The fundamental cause of depression, she argued, was a lack of self-confidence. Therefore, what psychologists need is a way of bolstering people's self-confidence. To this end, she arranged for her patients to participate in weekend expeditions in which they engaged in demanding physical sports—mountaineering, canoeing, sailing, and so on—and learned that they could overcome difficult problems. At the end of one year's treatment, she reported, 93% of the participants in her program were substantially or fully recovered.

On the basis of this evidence, would you conclude that the new therapy was effective? According to the logic of the experimental method, you would first need to satisfy yourself that no other variable that could have accounted for the observed improvement had been present. In the following section, we will consider several alternative explanations, but before proceeding to that section you might find it fun to see how many of these explanations you can think of by yourself. Assume that you had conclusive evidence that patients who received the treatment improved; what other evidence would you want before you would recommend this expensive treatment to a friend who is severely depressed?

The Search for Alternative Explanations

Time. One independent variable that could account for the improvement observed in this study is the building of self-confidence, but another variable is simply the passage of time. Depression is rarely a permanent condition, and the patients might have improved just as much had they simply been left alone for one year.

In situations in which more than one independent variable is present, the simplest way to determine the effects of one of these variables is physically to eliminate the others. If you found that an injection of penicillin and Aureomycin was effective in treating flu, for example, then, to evaluate the contribution of penicillin on its own, you could remove Aureomycin from the injection. This elimination strategy, however, cannot be applied to our depression example because there is no way of "eliminating" time: Patients cannot be given confidence-boosting experiences without time also passing.

In cases in which an unwanted variable cannot be eliminated physically, its effects can instead be neutralized through the use of an appropriate control group. To eliminate time as a factor, we could arrange for a control group that receives only the passage of time (that is, is left untreated for a year). In effect, both treatment and control groups would receive the time variable, but only the experimental group would receive the treatment in which we are primarily interested:

> *experimental group:*   time + confidence building
> *control group:*   time

If at the end of the year the experimental group showed substantially more improvement, this difference could not be explained by the passage of time, since both groups received equal exposure to this variable. This design, in other words, controls for the effect of time by arranging for it to affect both groups equally: If the groups still differ, some factor other than time must be at work.

Subject expectations. Suppose, then, that we ran our proposed experiment and found that the experimental group still improved substantially more: Could we now conclude that confidence building is an effective treatment for depression?

Again, the answer is no, because other independent variables are present in the experimental group that could account for the improvement. One such variable is subject expectations. When subjects are asked to participate in a treatment program, they typically assume that the treatment is likely to be effective; otherwise, the experimenter would not waste time investigating it. Such expectations of improvement may themselves be sufficient to produce improvement. In the field of medicine, for example, studies of cold medicines have repeatedly shown that most of the popular remedies have no direct effect; it is the fact that patients expect to improve that underlies any improvement, with placebos (pills that have no active ingredients) being just as effective as commercial products that do have active ingredients.

Another example of the importance of subject expectations comes from studies of hypnosis, in which hypnotized subjects can often perform quite remarkable feats such as lying rigid between two chairs while supporting a great weight, or withstanding intense pain. Most, if not all, of these feats have been found to be due to subjects' expectations: When subjects believe that they can do something, this belief allows them to perform feats that normally would be beyond their ability. When nonhypnotized subjects are told that they really can perform these feats, their performances match those of hypnotized subjects (Barber, 1976).

In our depression experiment, then, subjects might have improved simply because they expected to, rather than because of any real increase in self-confidence engendered by sailing, climbing, and so on. To control for this possibility, we could redesign the study so that all subjects would expect to improve equally, whether or not they received the experimental treatment. We might rerun the experimental group but compare it with a control group that also receives a highly plausible treatment (for example, weekly injections of vitamins, explained on the basis that vitamin deficiency plays a crucial role in depression). If the only factor in this experiment is expectation of improvement, both groups should improve equally. Suppose that we again found substantially greater improvement in the experimental group; could we now conclude that confidence building is an effective therapy for depression?

Experimenter expectations.   You might not be altogether surprised to hear that the answer is again no. Although our experimental and control groups are matched in terms of subject expectations, they might still differ in terms of experimenter expectations. That is, the experimenter who ran the study might have believed in the importance of self-confidence and, thus, expected the experimental group to improve more.

At this point you could be forgiven if you were beginning to feel exasperated. We seem to be nitpicking. Even if an experimenter did expect one group to do better than another, could this really have determined the outcome of the experiment? Surprisingly, the answer is yes. In an experiment by Rosenthal (1966), for example, subjects were shown pictures of faces and asked to rate whether the pictures appeared to be of successful people. (The rating scale ranged from −10 for faces of people thought to be very unsuccessful to +10 for faces of people looking very successful.) Each group of about a dozen subjects was read standard instructions and then shown slides of the different faces. The study used different experimenters for the different groups, and these experimenters were led to expect different outcomes. One group of experimenters was told that they were being given a special set of subjects who would probably produce positive scores, whereas a second group of experimenters was led to expect negative scores. In fact, subjects were assigned to the experimenters at random. Under these circumstances, could experimenter expectations make any difference? The results were that they did: Experimenters expecting positive results obtained significantly higher scores than did those expecting negative results. Thus, despite the fact that all subjects saw the same faces and were read the same instructions, their ratings of the faces were strongly influenced by what their experimenters expected.

How could an experimenter's expectations affect a subject's evaluation of a picture? We know very little about the underlying processes, but some evidence suggests that subtle cues from the experimenter are involved. One of the classic examples of such cues is the case of Clever Hans. (See Pfungst, 1965.) Hans was a horse that lived on a farm in Germany at the turn of the century. Hans wasn't an ordinary horse, though: He was the only horse in Germany that could add! When asked the sum of two plus two, for example, Hans would slowly begin to tap the ground, one, two, three, four . . . and then stop. Nor was this simply a trick he had memorized, because he could add virtually any numbers, and it didn't even matter who asked the question. Moreover, addition wasn't his only skill: He was equally proficient at subtraction and, incredibly, multiplication and division. An obvious explanation for his prowess was some sort of signal from his master, but when a blue-ribbon panel of experts convened to investigate Hans's extraordinary powers, they found that Hans performed equally well in his master's absence.

The explanation for Hans's apparent genius was eventually discovered in a brilliant series of experiments by Oscar Pfungst, a German psychologist. Pfungst found that Hans's accuracy was considerably reduced if the person who asked the question didn't know the correct answer. Furthermore, the further away the questioner stood, the less accurate was Hans's answer. Finally, putting blinders around Hans's eyes totally destroyed his performance. Clearly, Hans could answer questions only if he could see someone who knew the correct answer. But what possible visual cues could the questioner have been providing? The answer, Pfungst discovered, was that questioners tilted their heads slightly forward as they finished their questions, and this was Hans's cue to begin tapping. As the tapping approached the correct answer, the observers tended to straighten up in anticipation, and this slight tensing was Hans's cue to stop. Hans was extraordinarily sensitive to such cues, responding to the raising of eyebrows or even the dilation of nostrils, and Pfungst was eventually able to control Hans's tapping completely by producing these cues deliberately. Hans truly was an extraordinary horse, but his genius lay more in his powers of observation than in any arithmetic ability.

And now, at long last . . .   Let us now return to our depression experiment. Suppose that we redesigned our experiment yet again to ensure that the experimenter who ran the study expected both groups to improve equally, and we again found substantially greater improvement in the experimental group. Now, at long last, would we have proved that building self-confidence is an effective treatment for depression? Yet again, the answer is no. Why not? What other variable could possibly have been present? It is not easy to identify other variables, but the fact that we can't identify alternative explanations doesn't prove that there aren't any. The blue-ribbon panel was unable to find any plausible explanation for Hans's dazzling performance, but that didn't prove that it was the result of a genuine mastery of arithmetic. In a similar vein, for centuries naturalists were unable to explain the mysterious ability of bats to navigate in total darkness, but that didn't prove that it was the result of some occult power. (The discovery of radar in the 1930s eventually led to the solution.) An experiment, in other words, can never prove that a particular explanation is correct because it is always possible that some alternative explanation will eventually be found.

The Nature of Scientific Progress

We started with a seemingly simple experiment, but the more we analyzed it, the more alternative explanations for its outcome we identified. This is always the case. The goal of the experimental method is to change only one independent variable at a time, but this ideal can never be fully realized. We can control for the effects of particular variables, such as time and subject expectations, but there are always changes that we cannot control—fluctuations in humidity, the occurrence of sunspots, the death of an earthworm in China. The fact that we cannot control for all possible variables has some important implications for the nature of scientific progress.

The slowness of scientific progress.   One implication concerns the slowness and confusion with which science sometimes progresses. A popular image of science has the scientist in an antiseptic white lab coat, progressing inexorably through rigorous analyses. In practice, scientific progress is often much more confused and halting. As we have seen, it is impossible to control for all possible variables; we can only control for those variables that seem most important. Our notions of what variables are important, however, are often wrong. For example, one of the most dangerous things a woman in Victorian England could do was enter a maternity hospital; many thousands of women died every year after giving birth. When Joseph Lister suggested that doctors could prevent these deaths if they washed their hands with soap, his proposal was greeted with incredulity: How could washing hands with boiled-down animal fat prevent a woman from dying? Now, with our greater understanding of the existence and nature of germs, his suggestion makes sense, but at the time it seemed utterly preposterous. Similarly, in the case of Clever Hans, few would have believed beforehand that a horse could be so sensitive to minute changes in people's postures.

There is thus a built-in Catch-22 to scientific progress: To discover scientific laws, you must control all important variables; unfortunately, you can only identify what variables are important if you already know the laws. This problem is not insurmountable. We just have to plug away, identifying important variables as best we can in experiments that may initially lack important controls. This bootstrapping process means that progress will initially be slow and frustrating as we struggle to identify the important variables.

The need for humility. A second implication of the difficulty of controlling all variables is the need for some caution, and even humility, in interpreting experimental evidence. However certain we might be that a particular explanation is correct, it is always possible that it will eventually be superceded by a better explanation. The astronomer Ptolemy, for example, believed that the earth was the center of the universe, with the sun and stars revolving around it. Using a model based on this assumption, he was able to predict the movements of the planets through the sky with remarkable success. His model was sufficiently accurate to allow sailors to use it to navigate the seas for more than 1400 years, even though we now know that his theory was totally wrong. Similarly, Newton's theory of gravity has been one of the cornerstones of modern physics, but this did not prevent Einstein from developing a theory of relativity that fundamentally recast some of Newton's most basic assumptions about the nature of time, space, and gravity. In interpreting scientific evidence, then, we need to recognize that even the best scientific explanations can be wrong—or, at any rate, incomplete.

The artificiality of experiments. A third implication of our analysis concerns the inherent artificiality of experiments. To isolate the effects of one variable, you need to hold others constant, but the more you control the environment, the less like real life it becomes. The underlying strategy is summarized in Figure 1.3: You start with a complex environment and, by *analysis*, try to break this complex environment into simpler ones so you can study the effects of constituent elements (A, B, C, and so on) one at a time. Then, once you have determined the effects of each variable on its own, you use the method of *synthesis* to begin recombining them, studying what happens when two or more variables act together (AB, ABC, and so on). The scientific method thus proceeds by first analyzing complex environments into simpler ones, then gradually returning to the more complex environment that was the original focus of interest.

FIGURE 1.3   Using the experimental method, the experimenter analyzes a complex environment to isolate
variables and then synthesizes the variables in progressively more complex combinations.

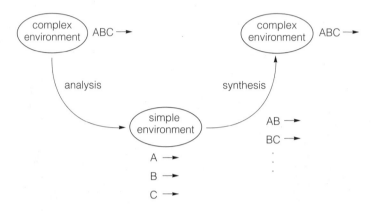

In psychology, most research is still analytical, with the result that it is very easy to feel depressed by its artificiality. "It's all so meaningless," you might say. "What does the behavior of a student in an artificial laboratory setting have to do with real life?" The answer lies in the assumptions we have been tracing in this chapter. If behavior is lawful, and if the best way of discovering these laws is through well-controlled experiments, then eventually the principles discovered in these artificial settings will help us understand behavior in the more complex conditions of the real world.

In other sciences, this faith in the experimental method has paid off handsomely. In genetics, for example, Gregor Mendel discovered the principles of genetics by studying how the color of pea flowers determined the colors of their progeny. In one sense, his experiments were highly artificial: Peas and humans would seem to have little in common. By studying the transmission of traits in this simple setting, however, geneticists have been able to identify genetic principles that also apply to the vastly more complex genetic system of humans, an advance that has already made possible test-tube babies, as well as significant progress toward the cloning of humans from single cells. In less than 100 years, we have moved from the investigation of the garden pea to an understanding of some of the most profound mysteries of human life.

1.5 THE USE OF ANIMALS

Having decided to study the laws of learning, and to do so through careful experimentation, we now come to the question of what species to study. If our goal is to understand human behavior, the answer might seem obvious: We should study humans. Given the blinding clarity of this logic, why have psychologists often studied animals instead?

The Advantages of Using Animals

Control of the environment.   The reasons that psychologists study animals are complex, but all are rooted in the problems of experimental control discussed in the last section. We said then that one of the crucial problems in psychological research is to manipulate only one independent variable at a time while holding all others constant. In practice, this requires extensive control over the subject's environment. For both moral and practical reasons, such control is easier to attain with animal subjects than with human subjects.

For example, one problem of considerable importance in human behavior concerns the effects of a child's early environment on her or his development. Freudians have long argued that the first years of life are crucial in determining personality. More recently, educators have suggested that early sensory and social deprivation is an important factor in the poor school performance of some children (particularly from underprivileged homes) and have urged governments to invest in compensatory childcare programs for young children. How are we to determine whether the role of early experience is really so crucial and, if so, which aspects are most important? To determine the importance of early sensory experience, for example, should we run controlled experiments in which half the children are reared normally while the other half are permanently confined to a barren environment, devoid of all stimuli? Similarly, to determine the importance of a mother's role in a child's normal development, should we compare children reared with their mothers and children taken away from their mothers and reared in isolation? Such experiments would hardly be humane or practical. The questions involved are significant, with serious implications for the future structure of our schools and even our families, but the experiments necessary to answer such questions are clearly unacceptable.

Using animals as subjects, however, psychologists have conducted experiments to answer precisely these questions, with often fascinating results. Harry Harlow, for example, reported a series of experiments in which infant rhesus monkeys were reared in varying degrees of social isolation. When taken away from their mothers immediately after birth and reared in total isolation, these infants became highly neurotic, spending much of their time huddled in corners, rocking back and forth and sucking their thumbs. Furthermore, this pattern of disturbed behavior persisted into adulthood, and most were unable to function normally in a group, or even to mate.

These early studies supported the critical role of early experience in social development, and in later experiments Harlow and others isolated some important variables. The presence of the mother, for example, is not necessarily critical; infants taken away from their mothers but reared with other infants show significantly less disturbance (Harlow & Harlow, 1965). Another finding, with poignant social implications for certain humans, is that male rhesus monkeys, which normally play an insignificant role in child rearing, can, if necessary, replace the mother with no apparent ill effects to either child or father (Mitchell & Brandt, 1972).

A similar line of experiments has examined the role of early sensory experience in the development of rats. Some rats were reared in "enriched" environments that included other rats and a variety of toys, platforms, colors, and sounds; other rats were reared in "deprived" environments that lacked these stimuli. Animals reared in the enriched environments developed larger brains (Rosenzweig, 1984), with considerably more complex interconnections among their neurons (Turner & Greenough, 1985). These results suggest that early stimulation plays a critical role in the brain's development and thus in our capacity for learning in later life.

Simpler systems.   One advantage of using animals as subjects, then, is that we can more easily control their environments and thus determine which variables are important. A related advantage is studying simpler systems. To isolate the effects of a single variable, one strategy is to control the environment so that few variables will be present; an alternative strategy is to study a simpler system, in which fewer variables exert an influence. Suppose, for example, that you wanted to understand the principles of electronics. You would obviously find it easier to understand these principles if you began by studying a transistor radio rather than a giant computer: The simpler the system, the easier it is to understand its operations. Thus, scientists were able to isolate the fundamental principles of genetics by first studying two lower life forms—the fruit fly and the pea—that offer simpler systems. If, instead, they had first tried to understand these principles in a more complex system-for example, the inheritance of human intelligence, which is almost certainly influenced by many thousands of genes—it is unlikely that they would yet have learned much at all about the principles of genetic transmission.

The simpler the system, the easier it is to determine its fundamental principles. Determining the principles of behavior in animals, however, can help us to understand human behavior only if these principles are similar. Is this assumption justified? Do the principles of learning in rats or even monkeys have any relevance for human behavior?

Are Animal and Human Behavior Similar?

Throughout history, the notion that animals and humans are similar would have been met with indignation and disbelief, but in 1859 Charles Darwin published a book that for the first time challenged the complacent view of human beings that they are the unique culmination of creation. Darwin dared to suggest that human beings are not unique, that they are only one of many species of animals on Earth, all shaped by the same environmental forces and evolved from the same common ancestors. It follows that, if humans and other animals are so closely related, important similarities must exist between them.

Biologically, the proof was not long in coming; indeed, much of it had already been assembled. Despite the incredible diversity of animal species (there are now thought to be more than three million species, ranging in size from virtually invisible microorganisms to the mammoth blue whale, whose tongue alone weighs more than an elephant), the underlying biological principles are surprisingly similar. Our understanding of human neurophysiology, for example, is built largely on the pioneering work of Hodgkin and Huxley on the giant squid. Similarly, our understanding of human vision is based on Hartline and Ratliff's investigations of the eye of the horseshoe crab, a primitive species almost unchanged from primordial times. And when we begin to examine species more closely related to humans, the similarities become even greater. The basic principles of digestion, vision, respiration, locomotion, and so forth are, for all practical purposes, identical across the various mammalian species. Indeed, it is precisely because of this fundamental equivalence that modern medicine has been able to develop so quickly. The drugs and surgical techniques on which our lives now depend were generally pioneered not with people, but with mice, monkeys, and the famous guinea pig—that much put-upon rodent whose name has become synonymous with the concept of experimentation.

Tool use. For post-Darwin scientists, animals and people were clearly similar, at least in regard to physical construction. Behaviorally, on the other hand, this similarity was less obvious. Even if humans had once been a simple ape, so the argument went, they had long since begun a unique evolutionary path that left them the only animal capable of using tools, of transmitting culture, and of symbolic communication. More recently, however, evidence has accumulated that human beings are not unique even in these areas. Chimpanzees, for example, use twigs to reach into termite nests and gather the tiny insects to eat. Nor is this use of tools fortuitous: If an appropriate twig is not available, the chimp will modify one until it is of the correct size and shape (Goodall-van Lawick, 1968).

It might be argued that only higher primates such as chimpanzees have the capacity to use tools, but even this no longer appears to be true. On the Galapagos Islands, where Darwin did much of his research, there is a finch that faces a problem similar to that of the chimpanzee. The finch likes to eat insects that live under the bark of trees; although it can drill a hole through the bark, its beak is not long enough to catch its prey. The finch solves this problem by searching for a cactus spine and then, holding it in its beak, poking the spine around the hole. When the surprised insect emerges, the finch drops the spine and quickly eats the insect. And, like the chimpanzee, the finch is selective in its approach, rejecting spines that are not the right size for the hole it wishes to attack (Millikan & Bowman, 1967). As these and other instances of tool use and even culture were reported (Miyadi, 1964; Wrangham, McGrew, de Waal & Heltne, 1994), it became increasingly clear that humans are not unique even in these abilities, although we still seemed to be the only animals with a sophisticated language and the intellectual capacities that language implies.

Problem solving. Chimpanzees have also demonstrated impressive abilities in thinking and problem solving. In one experiment by Premack and Woodruff (1978), a chimpanzee named Sarah was shown videotapes of humans struggling to solve a problem. In one of those situations, illustrated in Figure 1.4, a man is trying to escape from a locked cage. After the videotape was over, Sarah was shown a set of pictures suggesting possible solutions—for example, a picture of a key and of an irrelevant object such as an electric plug—and asked to choose one; the experimenter remained outside the room, so as not to influence her choice. The result was that Sarah chose the correct solution every time. In a second experiment, the choices were made more difficult; for example, a phonograph was not working, and Sarah was shown pictures of a plug attached to a wall, an unattached plug, and an attached plug that had been cut. Again, Sarah's performance was essentially perfect; she chose the correct solution for 11 out of 12 problems.

To solve these problems, Sarah had to understand the nature of the problem confronting the person, the correct solution, and the fact that she was being asked to provide a solution. (After all, the pictures could have been presented simply to determine which one she liked best.) The solutions had never been taught deliberately to Sarah; she could have learned them only by observing routine activities in the laboratory. Sarah's performance under these conditions suggests a remarkably high level of intelligence.

Language. Perhaps the final step in the evolution of our species' self-image stemming from Darwin may have begun in 1969 with the publication in the journal *Science* of an article by Allan Gardner and Beatrice Gardner. The article reported their efforts over the preceding two years to teach a baby chimpanzee named Washoe to use sign language. The results were dramatic. Washoe quickly learned a great many signs and used them reliably in a wide variety of situations. The sign for *dog*, for example, was elicited by a wide variety of dogs, both alive and in pictures, and even by the barking of a dog that could not be seen.

Although there has been some controversy over whether Washoe's use of signs was really comparable to that of humans (see, for example, Terrace, 1985), subsequent research has largely confirmed the Gardners' claims. Some of the most impressive evidence has come studies of another species of chimpanzee, the bonobo, and in particular from a young male named Kanzi.

FIGURE 1.4   The pictures on the left are taken from four videotaped enactments of problems: trying to escape from a locked cage, shivering after struggling with a malfunctioning heater, attempting to wash a floor with no water emerging from the hose, and trying to play a phonograph. After seeing each of these 30-second videotapes, the chimpanzee was offered a choice between two of the four pictures shown on the right: a key, a lit torch, a hose connected to a faucet, and a plug connected to a wall socket. (Premack & Woodruff, 1978)

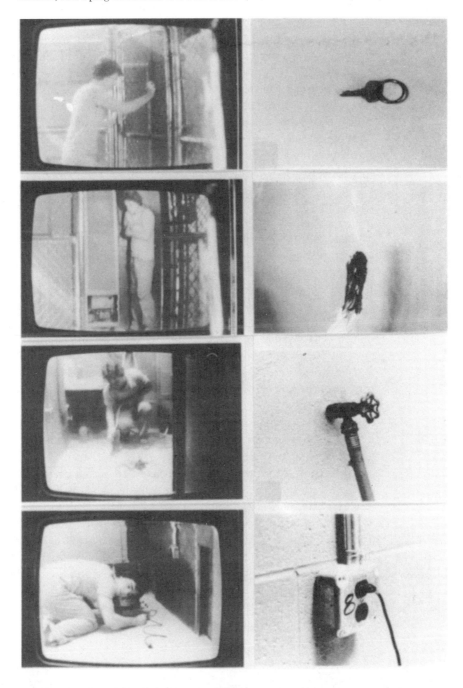

We shall discuss Kanzi's achievements in more detail in Chapter 12, but we can anticipate our discussion there by saying that Kanzi was reared among humans and that when he was five years old his caretakers accidentally discovered that he had learned the meaning of a number of English words simply by listening to the conversations going on around him. If given an instruction such as "Take the potato outside and get the apple," for example, he could respond accurately even though he had never been exposed to this particular combination of words before. A series of tests revealed his comprehension of spoken English to be equivalent to that of a 2½ year-old child (Rumbaugh & Savage-Rumbaugh, 1994)!

Only a small number of chimpanzees have been given language training, and it is difficult to predict how much further they and others will progress as training methods improve. It is already clear, however, that the gap between chimpanzees and humans in language is far smaller than virtually anyone believed possible a few decades ago.

Almost before psychologists could absorb the evidence for language in chimpanzees, even more startling evidence was reported for sophisticated language skills in parrots. Pet owners have long been aware of parrots' skill in learning to repeat what is said to them ("Polly want a cracker?"), but everyone assumed that the parrots were simply blindly repeating what they heard, without comprehension. Pepperberg (1993), however, has trained a parrot named Alex to master more than 40 English words, and Alex can not only understand these words when spoken by others but also use them himself to answer questions or make requests. When shown an object he has never seen before, for example, Alex can verbally describe its shape and color; he can say how many objects have been placed in front of him (up to 6) and whether or not two objects have the same appearance.

This research is quite recent, and needs to be replicated with other parrots, but it raises the intriguing possibility that language skills may be present in many more species than previously thought possible. When we hear animals in a zoo making what sound to us like meaningless noises, might the problem sometimes lie in our lack of understanding rather than in theirs? (See also Cheney, Seyfarth, & Silk, 1995.)

If learning in animals and humans is more similar than we have traditionally assumed, this does not mean that it is identical, and that all or even most research into learning should be done with animals. Every species is unique, and it would be foolish to expect to gain a complete understanding of people from the study of pigeons or white rats. Because humans and other species have shared millions of years of evolution in common, however, it would be surprising if they were not similar in important respects, and the available evidence supports this assumption.

It may be as well to pause at this point to note that the language we have been using is potentially misleading. We have referred to animals and humans as if they were entirely separate categories, but in fact the human species, *homo sapiens*, is just one of many species within the animal kingdom. Humans, in other words, *are* animals.

Rather than discussing humans and animals, we should have distinguished between humans and nonhuman animals. This more accurate terminology is a bit cumbersome, and we have chosen to use the simpler and more conventional term, *animals*, but it should be clear by this point that humans and animals are not separated by an unbridgeable chasm; humans are, in fact, a species of animal, albeit one with some rather remarkable characteristics.

Ethical Issues

We have seen that the use of animal subjects in experiments can have significant advantages. Because of the possibility of more stringent control over the environment, we can analyze phenomena in animals that, for moral or practical reasons, might otherwise be inaccessible. Insofar as the learning processes in animals are simpler, this can actually be an advantage, because we can more easily analyze these processes. On the other hand, the similarity of animal and human behavior means that we must take seriously the ethical issues raised by the use of animals in experiments. If animals are similar to us in intelligence, and presumably also in feelings, how can we justify confining them in cages and, in some cases, subjecting them to painful stimuli such as electric shock?

One view is that such research cannot be justified, because animals are living creatures with just as much right to life and freedom as humans have. This position is attractive in its strong value for all life, but few people hold it in its pure form. Suppose, for example, that you had a child who contracted rabies, and that the only way to obtain a vaccine to save the child's life required killing a mouse. Would you do it? Very few people faced with this dilemma would not choose to save the child, implicitly valuing a child's life more than that of a mouse.

Rightly or wrongly, then, most people do value human welfare more than that of animals, but this does not imply that animal life is worthless. Thus, the problem remains of deciding whether the benefits of particular experiments with animals outweigh the cost to the animals. To assess this, we need some method of quantifying both the benefits and the costs; in practice, though, this is difficult if not impossible. Suppose, for example, that we wanted to assess the cost to the subjects of an experiment on the effects of punishment. How could we decide how much pain a rat would experience if it were given an electric shock? What if we substituted a fish or a cockroach as the experimental subject? Do they also feel pain? If so, is it more or less than that experienced by the rat?

If it is difficult to find any objective way of assessing the costs of animal research, it can be equally difficult to assess its benefits. In our hypothetical rabies example, we assumed that killing the mouse would save the life of the child, but the benefits of experiments are rarely this predictable. Experiments that seem minor at the time they are performed can eventually have momentous theoretical and practical benefits. In a study by Comroe and Dripps (1977), for example, physicians were asked to rate the ten most important advances in cardiovascular and pulmonary medicine and surgery that had benefited their patients. A total of 663 studies were found to have been crucial in leading to these breakthroughs; 42% of them involved experiments that, at the time they were reported, seemed totally unrelated to the later clinical application. When doing basic research, it is difficult to predict what benefits might eventually be derived from enhanced understanding of a fundamental mechanism.

In deciding whether a planned experiment is justifiable, then, it is difficult to assess either the costs to the animals used or the long-term benefits to humans. There are no simple guidelines; all we can say here is that an assessment of the benefits to be gained depends heavily on the validity of the assumptions discussed in this chapter. If behavior is lawful, if experimental research is the best way to discover these laws, and if animal and human behavior is similar in important respects, then research on animals might play an important role in increasing our understanding of human behavior.

1.6 An Overview of Associative Learning

Summarizing our discussion until this point, we have suggested that research on learning has been based on several assumptions: that behavior is lawful, that the best way to discover these laws is through controlled experiments, and that studies of learning in animals can shed light on how learning occurs in humans. Before proceeding to examine the research that has resulted from these assumptions, though, we need to address one final question, namely what this book is about. You might think that the answer is already obvious—its title, after all, is *Learning*—but a problem arises from the fact that learning is such a vast topic. It affects almost everything we do, from making friends to riding a bicycle to learning organic chemistry. As a result, it is impossible to cover every aspect of learning in a single course, and it has become customary to study different aspects in different courses: Courses on developmental psychology deal with one aspect, courses on educational psychology with another, courses on memory and cognition a third, and so on.

Within this division, courses on learning generally concentrate on a particular form of learning called *associative learning*. To explain what associative learning is, we will begin by examining what we mean by the broader term learning.

Learning

Some stimuli always elicit the same reaction. If you accidentally touch a hot pan, for example, it will make you pull your hand back every time; if a sudden gust of wind hits you in the eye, it will make you blink every time. In cases like this, in which a stimulus always elicits the same response, we call the stimulus-response relationship a **reflex.**

$$Reflex: \quad S \rightarrow R$$

Habituation. Our definition of a reflex requires that the stimulus always elicits the same response, but under some conditions the strength of a reflexive response can change with experience. Suppose, for example, that you were quietly studying in your room one day when you suddenly heard a deafening noise—a particularly hideous burglar alarm in the building next door to you had just gone off. This sudden, intense noise would almost certainly make you jump, a reaction that is known as the startle reflex. The first time it happened, your reaction would be very intense, but if it happened again five minutes later, you would probably react less strongly; a third repetition would produce even less of a reaction, and so on. This decrease in the strength of a reflex when the stimulus is repeated a number of times is called **habituation;** it is a common characteristic of reflexes, especially when the stimulus is repeated within a relatively short period of time.

One experiment illustrating habituation was reported by Davis (1974). He placed rats in a cage that was mounted on springs, so that if they made a sudden movement he could measure the magnitude of this movement by measuring the movement of the floor. He then presented a loud tone to the rats a number of times. As shown in Figure 1.5, he found that the tone initially produced a strong startle response, but that the magnitude of this response decreased over successive presentations.

Why did the rats' reactions to the tone habituate when it was presented repeatedly? One possibility is sensory fatigue—frequent presentations of the tone could have impaired the capacity of the sensory system to react. A closely related possibility is motor fatigue—as the rats responded to the tone on successive trials, they could have become progressively more tired and thus physically less able to respond. Although sensory and motor fatigue undoubtedly can occur, habituation is rarely caused by such fatigue. If, at the conclusion of his experiment, Davis had presented a test trial in which he had increased the intensity of the tone, he would almost certainly have observed an increase in the vigor of the startle response back to its original level. If so, the rats' sensory and motor systems would clearly have been capable of producing a response, and the weakened responding on earlier trials could not have been caused by fatigue.

FIGURE 1.5   Magnitude of the startle response of rats to successive presentations of a tone. (Adapted from Davis, 1974)

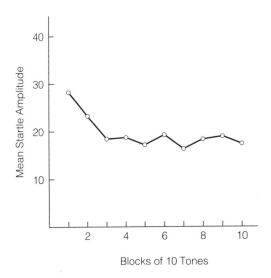

Defining learning. Habituation, then, is not caused by fatigue in either the senses or the muscles; by elimination, it seems to involve some sort of change in the nervous system that links them. Specifically, habituation seems to involve learning that a potentially dangerous stimulus is not, in fact, followed by any harmful experience, and thus that we can safely ignore the stimulus.

Changes in behavior of this kind illustrate what we mean by learning. It is difficult to define learning precisely, but one simple definition would be a change in behavior as a result of experience. As sometimes happens with simple definitions, however, this one quickly runs into difficulties.

One problem, as we have already seen in our discussion of habituation, is that there are some changes caused by experience that are really not what we mean by learning. If your behavior changed because you had not eaten for several hours, for example, or because you had been paralyzed in an accident, these would not be what we mean by learning. What we really mean are experiences that result in the storage of information in your brain, information that alters your capacity to respond, whether or not you actually use it. If you were taught to ride a bicycle, for example, this would be an example of learning whether or not you later choose to use this skill.

To capture the meaning of learning more precisely, we will redefine **learning** as a change in our *capacity* for behavior, as a result of particular *kinds* of experience. This definition is regrettably more cumbersome, but it comes closer to what we really mean when we talk about learning.

Associative Learning

In the case of habituation, learning occurs as a result of the presentation of a single stimulus. (However, see Whitlow & Wagner, 1984.) A more elaborate form of learning occurs when two events occur together and we learn about the relationship between them. If we use the symbol E_1 to represent one event and E_2 to represent the second event, then in **associative learning** we learn about the association or relationship between the two events:

$$E_1 \rightarrow E_2$$

The two events could potentially be anything: a drop in air pressure warning of a storm to come; a television theme tune announcing *Star Trek*; a tone of voice signaling annoyance. Learning psychologists, however, have been particularly interested in instances of associative learning where the second event is biologically important—food, say, or bodily injury—and survival might depend on being able to predict this event. Suppose, for example, that a lion always visited a watering hole at 4:00 in the afternoon; if antelopes that also used this water could learn this stimulus-stimulus relationship (4:00 P.M. → lion), this would allow them to avoid the area at this time and thereby prolong their lives. Or consider a related situation from the lion's point of view: Suppose that whenever it stalked an antelope while remaining downwind of it, it was more likely to succeed. If it could learn this response-stimulus relationship (downwind stalking → succulent antelope), then it too would have a longer career.

Classical and Operant Conditioning

In those cases where an important event is reliably preceded by a stimulus, the stimulus often comes to elicit the same behavior as the event it predicts. If a light is repeatedly followed by a puff of air to the eye, for example, we eventually begin to blink as soon as the light is presented, without waiting for the puff. This is an example of **classical** or **Pavlovian conditioning.** Classical conditioning allows us to prepare for forthcoming events; in our eyeblink example, if we blink before the puff arrives, the lid closure can prevent particles being blown into the eye.

When an important event follows a response rather than a stimulus, the result is often a change in the response's probability, and this is called **instrumental** or **operant conditioning.** If your parents gave you a sports car every time you received an A for a course, for example, the amount of time you spent studying would be very likely to increase. This example illustrates one of the two subtypes of operant conditioning, reinforcement and punishment, which differ in whether the change in responding is an increase or a decrease. In **reinforcement,** the consequence that follows a response is desirable and the effect is to strengthen it—the use of a reward to increase studying, for example. In **punishment,** on the other hand, the consequence is undesirable and the effect is to weaken the response. Children who burn their hands when touching a hot pan quickly learn not to repeat this behavior.

As summarized in Figure 1.6, the essential distinction between classical and operant conditioning lies in whether an important event follows a stimulus (for example, light → air puff) or a response (for example, touching pan → burn). In real life, distinguishing between these forms of learning can be surprisingly difficult, but we will defer further consideration of their relationship until we have a better understanding of each on its own. (See Chapter 10.)

These two forms of conditioning are the focus of this text. As we shall see, both play a major role in shaping our lives. This might not be obvious for classical conditioning because classical conditioning often occurs without our awareness. (See Chapter 4.) Also, the best-known conditioned responses are salivation and blinking, neither of which would probably make a "top 10" list of critical skills. However, classical conditioning also affects far more important aspects of our behavior, including emotions such as fear and sexual arousal, what foods we like, and the effects of drugs such as heroin and alcohol. Learning psychologists have been able to use an understanding of the processes involved to develop therapies for problems such as phobias, alcoholism, and bedwetting. We will look at what behaviors can be conditioned in Chapter 2 and at practical applications in Chapter 3.

The importance of reinforcement and punishment is probably more obvious, but even here we tend to underestimate their significance. As in the case of classical conditioning, this is partly because we are not always aware of their effects. Attention from others, for example, can be very reinforcing, and when parents and teachers pay attention to a child who is misbehaving they sometimes inadvertently reinforce the behavior they are trying to eliminate. Also, reinforcement and punishment sometimes appear ineffective because they are not used optimally. Improved understanding of the principles involved has allowed psychologists to develop techniques for reducing children's misbehavior, for teaching convicts to master a year's worth of school in only a month, and for helping autistic children to lead normal lives. We will look at the principles of reinforcement in Chapter 5 and at how they can be applied in Chapter 6.

Is Associative Learning Simple or Complex?

In trying to understand classical and operant conditioning, psychologists have tended to adopt one of two very different perspectives. One is to assume that conditioning is basically a simple, automatic process. If a light is followed by a puff of air to your eye, for example, the assumption is that this strengthens a connection

FIGURE 1.6   Varieties of associative learning. Associative learning involves the detection of relationships between events (E), where the events concerned can be responses (R) or stimuli (S), and the stimuli can be positive (S^{POS}) or negative (S^{NEG}).

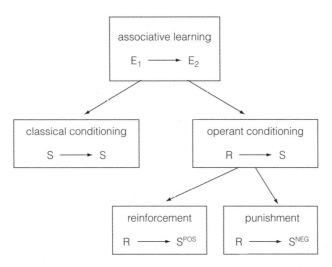

in your brain between representations of these events, so that the next time you see the light it automatically elicits a blink. Such a simple, automatic process would be adaptive because it would allow you to respond very rapidly, without needing to think.

There is, however, an alternative way of viewing associative learning, which is as a sophisticated process for detecting causal relationships. According to this view, the world is an extraordinarily complex place in which we are constantly being bombarded by sights, sounds, and other experiences. Associative learning is the process by which we identify the causal or predictive relationships that are embedded within this flux of events, even when the related events are separated by hours or even days. To use a phrase suggested by one of the proponents of this view (Dickinson, 1980), only if we can understand the "causal texture" of the world around us do we have any chance of influencing events. Associative learning provides the knowledge of the world on which we base our decision making.

So, which view is correct—is associative learning a simple, automatic process or a much more sophisticated one for detecting relationships? This issue has preoccupied learning researchers for more than a century, and it is a major theme in this text, one to which we will return repeatedly in different contexts. Whichever view you currently think is correct, you might be surprised by some of the evidence you will encounter.

1.7 SUMMARY

The focus of this text is associative learning—the learning that occurs when two events are paired together. In subsequent chapters, we will be looking at the principles of associative learning, how these principles can be applied practically (for example, how rewards and punishments can be used more effectively), and theories about the nature of the underlying processes. In this first chapter, we began by examining the assumptions that underlie the research we will be discussing.

The first assumption we considered is that behavior is lawful. According to determinism, our behavior is entirely determined by our heredity and environment. There is little doubt that these factors do strongly affect our behavior, sometimes without our awareness, and we considered examples ranging from the effects of advertising to sexual attraction to child abuse. A second argument for determinism is based on the role of the brain in controlling behavior. The brain controls movement, and growing evidence indicates that it also controls thought and emotion. If neural activity in the brain controls behavior, and if this neural activity is lawful, then the behavior that these neurons control must also be lawful.

There is now substantial evidence that environment and heredity do exert a powerful influence on our behavior. Less clear is whether behavior is totally determined by these factors, or whether, even under the most intense pressures, we retain some freedom to choose our own paths.

Assuming that behavior is lawful at least in part, the next question is inevitably how to go about discovering these laws. One attractive option is introspection—carefully observing our own mental processes to discover the laws governing our thoughts. Introspection was the main tool of psychologists in the nineteenth century, but it quickly fell into disfavor as introspectionists discovered that much of the mind's functioning is unconscious and thus hidden from introspection. Moreover, even where mental processes appeared to be accessible, subjects' introspective accounts often proved unreliable. At best, therefore, introspection could provide only a limited account of why people behave the way they do.

In reaction to the difficulties involved in observing the mind, a new approach called behaviorism emerged. Behaviorists believed that psychologists should focus on observable behaviors rather than thoughts and feelings; only by studying behaviors that could be observed could psychology hope to advance. One form of behaviorism, advocated by Skinner, advocated studying the relationship between environmental conditions and behavior, with little regard to any thoughts or feelings that might intervene. Another, that of cognitive psychology, argued that these intervening processes were an important part of the causal chain producing behavior, and thus should also be a legitimate focus of investigation. Rather than accepting subjects' introspective reports about the nature of these processes, however, cognitive psychologists developed theories about these processes and then evaluated the theories by seeing how well they predicted behavior. The approach taken in this text is a blend of the two approaches, though leaning more toward the cognitive perspective.

To understand the relationship between environmental conditions and behavior, psychologists run experiments in which they manipulate some aspect of the environment (the independent variable) to assess its effect on some aspect of behavior (the dependent variable). A systematic relationship between the independent and dependent variables would then define a law.

In outline, the experimental method is almost trivially simple: To discover the laws of behavior, all we have to do is manipulate some aspect of the environment and observe its effects on behavior. In practice, it is difficult, if not impossible, to manipulate only one independent variable at a time. One approach is to control the environment physically to at least minimize the number of variables present; when this is not possible, the experimenter can assess the effects of extraneous variables through comparison with control groups.

Because scientists cannot control all possible variables, they try to control only those that seem most important. There is thus a built-in Catch-22 to scientific progress: To discover scientific laws, we need to control all important variables, but we can only identify the important variables if we already know the scientific laws! This problem can be overcome gradually through trial and error, but the result is that scientific progress can be frustratingly slow.

A further implication of the impossibility of controlling all variables is the need for caution and humility in interpreting experimental evidence: However convincing an explanation might seem, it is always possible that an alternative explanation will eventually be discovered. Finally, the need to control the environment as fully as possible means that experiments are inevitably artificial: The more stringently we control the experimental environment, the less it will resemble the natural environment. Progress in other sciences, however, suggests that once we have analyzed the effects of individual variables in artificial environments, we can then synthesize their combined effects in progressively more complex and realistic settings.

The importance of controlling the experimental environment is the main reason for the use of animals in psychological experiments—it is much easier to control the environment of animals. Also, because animals are simpler than humans, it is easier to isolate the effects of single variables on their behavior. These advantages, however, are only meaningful if the principles of learning in animals and humans are similar. The precise relationship between learning in animals and humans remains an open question, but research in recent decades has made it clear that animals have a sophisticated capacity for thinking, learning, and language. This does not mean that learning can only be studied in animals; nor does it mean that the principles of learning in animals are identical to those in humans. Insofar as these principles are similar, though, studies of learning in animals could help us to understand learning in humans.

The evidence for similarities in animal and human learning also sharpens the ethical dilemma of using animals in research: If animals resemble us in intelligence and perhaps in feelings, do we have the right to force them to participate in experiments? There is no easy way to balance the benefits of animal research against the costs to the animals, but our calculation of the benefits will depend critically on the validity of the assumptions reviewed in this chapter: If behavior is lawful, and if the best way to discover these laws is through controlled experimentation, then it is likely that animal experiments will ultimately lead to important practical applications. The evidence in subsequent chapters will help you to form your own views of the validity of these assumptions.

We concluded our introduction to associative learning by examining what we mean by learning. Some stimuli always elicit the same response—this fixed relationship is called a reflex—but sometimes the response to a stimulus changes as a result of experience. The first time you hear a loud noise, for example, it might make you jump, but if the noise is repeated your startle response might habituate. If this decrement was the result of sensory or motor fatigue, we would not consider it learning; only changes caused by certain kinds of experiences (in principle, those that result in the storage of new information in the brain) would qualify as learning. We defined learning more formally as a change in the capacity for behavior as a result of certain kinds of experience.

In subsequent chapters we will be focusing on associative learning, in which we learn about the relationship between two events that occur together. In particular, we will concentrate on two forms of associative learning, classical and operant conditioning. In classical conditioning, a stimulus reliably precedes an important event such as food, and the typical result is that the stimulus begins to elicit some of the same behaviors as the food. In operant conditioning, the important event follows a response, and the result is a change in the response's probability. One form of operant conditioning is reinforcement, in which a response is strengthened by the consequence that follows it; another is punishment, in which the response is weakened. As we shall see, all these forms of conditioning play a fundamental role in shaping our behavior.

To account for associative learning, learning psychologists have considered two very different theories. One is that associative learning is a simple, even primitive form of learning in which contiguous events are automatically associated. A very different view is that associative learning is a sophisticated process for detecting relationships between events that may be widely separated in time. So, is associative learning simple or complex? One of our goals in subsequent chapters will be to try to answer this question.

Glossary

Determinism The belief that all behavior is caused by either environmental or genetic factors.

Free will The belief that people have the power to determine their own actions, regardless of any external pressures.

Introspection A person's examination of his or her own thoughts or feelings.

Behaviorism The view that the basic datum of psychology should be visible behavior, rather than mental states. (See Chapter 8 for a fuller definition.)

Independent variable The aspect of the environment that an experimenter manipulates during an experiment.

Dependent variable The observable behavior that occurs as a result of manipulation of the independent variable during an experiment.

Law A consistent relationship between the independent and dependent variables in which the occurrence of some condition A always leads to outcome B.

Reflex A stimulus-response relationship in which a stimulus reliably elicits the same response innately, without prior experience.

Habituation A decrease in the strength of a reflex as a result of repeated presentations of the stimulus by itself.

Learning A term devised to embarrass learning psychologists, who tie themselves into knots trying to define it. We have defined it as a change in our capacity for behavior as the result of particular kinds of experience.

Associative learning Learning about the association or relationship between two events that occur together.

Classical or **Pavlovian conditioning** An increase in responding to a stimulus because of pairings of that stimulus with an important event. (See Chapter 2 for a fuller definition.)

Operant or **instrumental conditioning** These terms refer to a change in the probability of a response as a result of its being followed by an important event. The terms *instrumental conditioning* and *operant conditioning* both refer to learning in which a response is modified by its consequence, but, because of the way in which these terms emerged historically, some psychologists use them to refer to slightly different situations for studying learning. In this usage, the term instrumental conditioning is used to describe situations in which only a single response can be made on a trial (for example, a rat that runs through a maze a single time and is then removed), while the term operant conditioning is used to describe situations in which subjects are free to respond continuously (for example, a rat that is left in a cage and allowed to press a lever repeatedly). Because the principles of learning in these two situations are basically identical, many learning psychologists now treat the terms as equivalent, and we will follow this usage here. Further discussion of the definition of operant conditioning can be found in Chapter 5.

Reinforcement A subtype of operant conditioning in which the probability of a response increases because it is followed by an important event. (See Chapter 5 for a fuller definition.)

Punishment A subtype of operant conditioning in which the probability of a response decreases because it is followed by an aversive event. (See Chapter 7 for a fuller definition.)

Review Questions

1. Is behavior governed by laws? What are the arguments for and against this view?

2. What developments undermined the use of introspection in psychology?

3. In what ways do the views of Skinner and of cognitive psychologists differ? In what respects are they the same?

4. How do experiments control for unwanted variables?

5. What are the strengths and weaknesses of the experimental method?

6. Why do psychologists believe that the results of experiments carried out in highly artificial laboratory settings can tell us anything about behavior in the real world?

7. What are the arguments for and against the use of animals in psychological research?

8. What evidence suggests that animals might be more similar to humans in learning and intelligence than traditionally assumed?

9. Why is learning difficult to define?

10. What are the two main theoretical views concerning the nature of associative learning?

CLASSICAL CONDITIONING

CHAPTER TWO

FOUNDATIONS OF CLASSICAL CONDITIONING

A dog stands motionless in the middle of a room, immobilized by a leather harness. The room is very quiet, all outside sound blocked by one-foot-thick concrete walls. A bell rings, and the dog turns toward the bell but otherwise shows little reaction. Five seconds later, the dog is presented food powder through a long rubber tube. The silence returns. Ten minutes pass; the bell sounds again and, as before, is followed by food. Ten more minutes pass. Again the bell sounds, but this time the dog begins to move restlessly in its harness, saliva dripping from its mouth. As the trials continue, the dog becomes increasingly excited at the sound of the bell, with more and more saliva flowing into a tube that has been surgically implanted in the dog's mouth. The saliva flows through the tube into an adjoining room where technicians record the number of drops.

When word of this experiment reached other scientists, the news was greeted with tremendous excitement. Within a few years, the experimenter, Ivan Petrovich Pavlov, was known to virtually every psychologist in the world. Within a few decades, his research had become perhaps the best known in the history of science, ranking with the legendary fall of an apple onto Isaac Newton's head.

Why all the excitement? What was so interesting about the fact that a dog could be trained to salivate? The answers to these questions have their roots deep in the history of Western intellectual thought, and we will need to explore that history briefly to understand the reaction to Pavlov's experiments.

2.1 THE ASSOCIATIVE TRADITION

The Reflex

Early explanations of human behavior were generally religious in character. Human behavior was seen as unpredictable, determined by fate or the whim of the gods. The advent of Christianity produced significant changes in these beliefs, but behavior was still seen as fundamentally unpredictable. Individuals were believed to have free will because they had souls. For almost 1700 years there were few significant departures from this theme, until the publication in 1650 of *The Passions of the Soul* by René Descartes. Descartes was a brilliant mathematician (Cartesian geometry was named after him), but he was also an outstanding philosopher, of such eminence that he was invited to Sweden to serve as the personal tutor to Queen Christina, then one of Europe's most powerful monarchs. He wanted to decline the queen's invitation politely, but she dispatched a warship to collect him, and he apparently then found the honor too great to refuse. Conditions, however, proved less than ideal: Classes were held at five o'clock in the morning, in the unheated library of the castle. It was apparently an unusually rigorous winter even by Swedish standards, and Descartes died of pneumonia, at the age of 54, before the winter ended (Boring, 1950).

Aside from its somber implications for those contemplating careers in philosophy, Descartes's life is important to us because he was the first major figure in Western civilization to offer a detailed, mechanistic explanation for human behavior. According to Descartes, our senses and muscles are connected by a complex network of nerves, and the flow of "animal spirits" through these nerves makes possible the instinctive reactions necessary for survival. If a person were to step into a fire accidentally, for example, the nerves in the foot would be stimulated and would transmit this excitation to the brain. The brain would then release animal spirits into the nerve, which would flow back to the calf muscle and cause it to swell, resulting in the foot's withdrawal from the flame. (See Figure 2.1.) This simple mechanism—a receptor activating a muscle through a direct, innate connection—Descartes called a *reflex*, and he proposed that these reflexes underlie all automatic, involuntary reactions.

Voluntary behavior, however, was an entirely different matter. Descartes was a dualist, believing that the body and the mind exist in two entirely separate spheres. He believed that the body is physical and can be understood in terms of simple physical mechanisms, whereas the operations of the mind are controlled by the soul, a spiritual force that is independent of the physical universe. How then, you might ask, is the mind ever able to influence the body's operations, as, for example, in voluntary movements such as turning a page? The answer, according to Descartes, was that the soul was localized in an area of the brain known as the pineal gland,[1] and this gland was also a reservoir containing animal spirits, the physical fluid that produced the contractions of the

---

[1] Descartes's choice of this seemingly minor organ for such a lofty role was by no means arbitrary. He knew that most of our sensory organs come in pairs—two eyes, two ears, and so on—and yet we perceive only one unified image. It was obvious, therefore, that all of our senses must converge on one center, where their disparate impressions can be blended together. And since the pineal gland, by virtue of its location in the exact midline of the brain, was the only organ not duplicated in the left and right hemispheres, Descartes concluded not unreasonably that it must be the seat of the soul.

FIGURE 2.1   Descartes's illustration of the reflex arc.

muscles. By tipping the pineal gland in the desired direction, the soul was able to decant these fluids into the appropriate nerve, where they would flow to the appropriate muscle and initiate whatever movement was desired.

Mental Associations

Descartes's analysis showed how seemingly complex movements of the body could be explained by the same simple mechanisms that governed machines, but he was not prepared to allow a similar determinism in the operation of the mind. This audacious step was first taken some 40 years later by an English physician named John Locke, secretary to the Earl of Shaftesbury. As was the custom of those times, Locke met weekly with educated friends to discuss current issues in areas such as science and theology. At one of these meetings, the disagreements became particularly intense, and it puzzled Locke that intelligent men could hold such different opinions regarding the same basic facts. He resolved to prepare a brief paper for the next meeting analyzing how each of us forms our ideas of the world and why our ideas are so different. Twenty years later, he finally completed this analysis, and it was published as a lengthy book, *An Essay Concerning Human Understanding*. The ideas in this essay were elaborated by later philosophers such as David Hartley and James Mill; together, these ideas form the doctrine that has become known as British Associationism.

The British Associationists.   According to the Associationists, thought is simply a succession of ideas through our minds, so that the basic unit of all thought is the idea. Descartes had believed many of our ideas to be innate, but Locke argued that our minds at birth are a tabula rasa, or blank slate. Any ideas we may have, he said, could only be acquired through experience. Locke suggested that any sensations that occur together will become associated so that if one of these sensations later recurs it will automatically elicit the second sensation. A stone, for example, produces a variety of visual and tactile sensations, which become associated through repeated pairings. It is this compound sensation (associated sensations) that forms our idea of a stone.

Ideas, in other words, are nothing more than sensations that have become associated together. This process of association also explains the sequence in which ideas occur to us.

> Our ideas spring up, or exist, in the order in which the sensations existed, of which they are the copies. This is the general law of the "Association of Ideas." . . . Of the successive order of our ideas, many remarkable instances might be adduced. Of these none seems better adapted to the learner than the repetition of any passage, or words; the Lord's Prayer, for example, committed to memory. In learning the passage, we repeat it; that is, we pronounce the words, in successive order, from the beginning to the end. The order of the sensations is successive. When we proceed to repeat the passage, the ideas of the words also arise in succession, the preceding always suggesting the succeeding, and no other. Our suggests father, father suggests which, which suggests art; and so on, to the end. How remarkably this is the case, anyone may convince himself, by trying to repeat backwards even a passage with which he is as familiar as the Lord's Prayer.
> (James Mill, Analysis of the Phenomena of the Human Mind, 1829)

The laws of association.   The concept of association can thus explain not only the existence of ideas but also the order in which they occur. The fundamental principle underlying the formation of associations was **contiguity,** which stipulates that associations are formed between events that occur together. In the Lord's Prayer, the word *our* is followed by *father,* and as a result an association is formed between them. The word *which* also follows soon after, but the longer delay between *our* and *which* means that *our* is associated more strongly with *father* than with *which,* so that *our* is more likely to make us think of *father.*

A second principle of association was *frequency:* The more often two words occurred together, the more strongly they would be associated. The Lord's Prayer again provides an example: The more often we hear it, the more strongly we associate the words, and thus the better we recall it.

A third principle determining the strength of an association was said to be the *intensity* of the feelings that accompanied the association.

> [*The ideas*] *which naturally at first make the deepest and most lasting impression are those which are accompanied with pleasure or pain. . . . A man receives a sensible injury from another, thinks on the man and that action over and over, and by ruminating on them strongly or much in his mind, so cements those two ideas together that he makes them almost one; never thinks on the man, but the pain and displeasure he suffered comes into his mind with it, so that he scarce distinguishes them, but has as much an aversion for the one as the other.*
> (John Locke, *An Essay Concerning Human Understanding,* 1690)

Thus, by the nineteenth century, the historical groundwork was in place for a theory of human behavior based on the fundamental notion of the association. Descartes had shown how the movements of the body could be explained through simple associations, or connections, between senses and muscles, and the British Associationists had extended his analysis to the mind, showing how thought could also be explained in terms of associations between ideas, and how ideas could in turn be analyzed into associations among sensations. The key to understanding human behavior, therefore, seemed to lie in an understanding of how associations come to be formed.

Cortical Associations

This belief in the importance of associations was further reinforced as physiologists began to understand how the brain works. In discussing this knowledge, we will temporarily abandon our historical approach and present an overview of our current understanding of the brain's operations, rather than the picture as it existed in Pavlov's time. This updated review will allow us to introduce information that will be useful in later chapters, but will not greatly distort the situation that existed in Pavlov's era, when scientists already knew the broad outlines if not all the details.

The neural basis of behavior. Consider again Descartes's example of a man pulling his foot out of the fire. How is this movement actually produced? Descartes was right that there is a sense in the foot that will detect heat, and that it is connected through a nerve to the muscles that will withdraw the foot, but the properties of this nerve are somewhat different from those he imagined. Far from being hollow tubes that carry animal spirits, nerves are composed of cells called **neurons** that are specialized to carry electrical signals. Figure 2.2 shows a schematic representation of a typical neuron. The neuron consists of a set of branching tendrils, called **dendrites,** that receive information from other neurons; a *cell body*; a long section called an **axon;** and, at the end of the axon,

FIGURE 2.2   Schematic representation of a typical neuron.

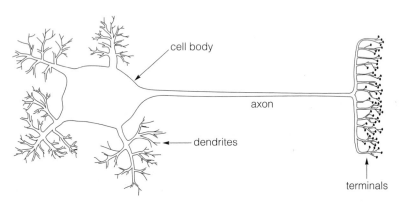

a set of *terminals* that make contact with the dendrites of other neurons. A neuron can be thought of as a battery that produces electrical energy, together with a wire that carries this energy somewhere else. The cell body is, in effect, the battery that produces an electrical signal; this signal is then conveyed along the axon, which is the wire, until it reaches another neuron. As shown in Figure 2.3, there is a very small space called the **synaptic cleft** between the terminals of one neuron and the dendrites of another. When the electrical signal arrives at the terminals of the first neuron, it causes the release of chemicals called **neurotransmitters** that are stored in the terminals. These neurotransmitters move across the synaptic cleft to the second neuron, where their arrival stimulates that neuron to produce an electrical signal, and so on.

In our fire example, the fire would stimulate a sensory receptor in the skin, inducing electrical activity in a very long *sensory neuron* that would carry an electrical signal from the foot to the spinal cord. The signal would then be transmitted through an *interneuron* in the cord to a *motor neuron*, which would then convey the signal to a muscle in the calf. The arrival of the impulse would trigger electrical activity in the muscle, causing it to contract, thereby pulling the foot out of the fire. This account is oversimplified in that postural reflexes actually involve the integrated activity of many muscles: Raising a leg requires compensatory adjustments elsewhere to ensure that the body does not fall over! Nevertheless, there really are simple reflexes of the type we have described in which only three neurons—a sensory neuron, an interneuron, and a motor neuron—combine to produce a reflexive response. Indeed, there are even simpler reflexes involving only a direct connection between a sensory and a motor neuron. Thus, although the details of how neurons carry messages differ from those proposed by Descartes—the mechanism is electrical rather than hydraulic—in its broad outlines the system is surprisingly similar to the one he portrayed.

FIGURE 2.3   Illustration of the synaptic cleft between the axon terminal of one neuron and the dendrites of a second neuron. The axon terminal contains neurotransmitters stored in structures called vesicles. When an electrical impulse arrives at the terminal, it causes the release of these neurotransmitters, which then move across the synaptic cleft and induce electrical activity in the second neuron.

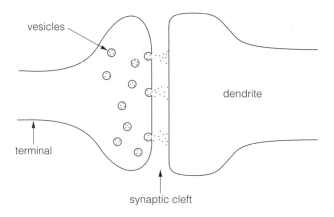

What, then, of voluntary behavior? Suppose, for example, that a doctor asked you to raise your foot during an examination. How would you do it? Voluntary movements of this kind involve the brain, which is a massive collection of neurons—approximately 10 *billion* neurons—organized into complex subsystems. Different sections of the brain are specialized to carry out different functions: One system deals with vision, another controls eating, a third is responsible for language, and so on. Higher cognitive functions such as thought and language are largely concentrated in the outer layer of the brain called the **cerebral cortex.** If the cortex is damaged or anesthetized, we generally lose conscious awareness. Conversely, electrical stimulation of the cortex can produce conscious experiences. A Canadian neurosurgeon, Wilder Penfield, exposed the cortex of epileptic patients in the course of operations to treat their conditions. He found that if he stimulated certain areas of the cortex with very small electrical currents, his patients would report experiences such as hearing someone call their name or standing on a railway platform waiting for a train (for example, Penfield, 1958).

Returning to our foot-raising example, the doctor's words would trigger receptors in your ear, which would transform them into a series of electrical impulses that would then be conveyed to the auditory area of the brain. This region, as most others, consists of an almost unimaginably dense web of interconnected neurons; a single neuron within the cortex may receive inputs from as many as 50,000 other neurons. Eventually, a set of signals would be conveyed to the motor cortex, and from there to the spinal cord and then to the leg muscles.

Thus, in contrast to reflexes, which can involve just a single connection between a sensory and a motor neuron, more complex activities such as language and voluntary movement can involve the transmission of electrical signals within a network of many millions of neurons.

The neural basis of learning. The picture of the brain we have painted so far might seem to suggest that our reactions to a situation should always be the same because the sensory input the situation produces would always be routed through the same neurons to the same muscles. The reason that this does not happen is that the connections between neurons in the brain are not fixed: The strength of these connections can be altered by experience. Our understanding of how neural connections are altered is still developing, but one mechanism appears to be a change in the number of neurotransmitters produced by a neuron when it is stimulated repeatedly. Under certain conditions, repeated stimulation will result in an increase in the number of neurotransmitters a neuron releases, thereby increasing the likelihood that its electrical activity will be transmitted to the next neuron in the chain (Kandel, 1991). Thus, although learning in the brain is almost certainly a very complex activity, if for no other reason than the vast number of neurons involved, at a cellular level learning is now thought to depend on simple changes in the strength of the connections between individual neurons. The strength of these connections determines how electrical impulses are routed through the brain, thereby determining our behavior.

We can now return to our historical argument. By the end of the nineteenth century, introspective and physiological evidence both suggested that much if not all of the mind's operations might be explicable through simple associations, so that if we could understand how associations are formed, we might have the key to understanding the mind. Philosophers' attempts to identify the principles of association, however, had become bogged down. Different philosophers had suggested different principles, but because these principles were derived from introspection, there was no obvious way to decide which of the alternatives was correct. If only there were an objective method for studying the formation of associations. . . .

2.2 PAVLOV'S CONDITIONED REFLEXES

Ivan Petrovich Pavlov was born in a small village in Russia in 1849. His early years were spent preparing for the priesthood at the local church school. His plans eventually changed, and in 1870 he walked hundreds of miles across Russia to enroll in St. Petersburg University as a student of physiology. His particular interest was in the physiology of digestion, and he developed ingenious surgical procedures for the measurement of salivary and gastric secretions in dogs.

Saliva is secreted by special glands within the cheek and then carried by ducts to the cheek's inner surface. By surgically redirecting one of these ducts, Pavlov was able to divert the saliva to the external surface of the cheek, where it could be collected through a connecting tube and then analyzed. Using this surgical preparation, known as a *fistula*, Pavlov found that salivation was an automatic, reflexive response that was elicited whenever food came into contact with the mucous membranes of the mouth.

After his dogs had been tested for several sessions, Pavlov noticed a strange phenomenon: The dogs began to salivate not only when food was placed in their mouths but also at other times. Many scientists would either have ignored this salivation, considering it irrelevant, or sought actively to prevent it because its occurrence would contaminate their measures of the pure reflex to food. Pavlov, however, was fascinated. If salivation is a reflexive response, lawfully elicited only by very specific stimuli such as the presence of food in the mouth, why should it suddenly begin to occur in the absence of these stimuli?

An Associative Analysis

In analyzing this "psychic" secretion, which at first appeared to have no cause, Pavlov noticed a pattern to when it occurred. For example, the dogs were particularly likely to salivate when they saw the experimenter enter the room, or when they heard his footsteps approaching. Was it possible that the dogs had come to associate these stimuli with the delivery of food, and this was why they were salivating? Or, in Pavlov's terminology, that in addition to the innate or *unconditioned reflexes* with which every animal was born, they were able to form new, *conditioned reflexes?*

Stating his hypothesis in physiological terms, Pavlov began by assuming that the presentation of any stimulus would produce activity in a set of neurons in the brain that effectively represented that stimulus (a "center"). When food was presented in a dog's mouth, for example, this would activate the food center in the brain, and activity in the food center would then be transmitted through an innate connection to the salivary glands, causing salivation (Figure 2.4). If a stimulus such as a tone preceded the food, this stimulus would activate its own cortical center. So far, this analysis conformed closely to physiologists' understanding of the brain's functioning at the time, but Pavlov now introduced a critical new assumption. If two centers of the brain were active at the same time, he suggested, the connection between these centers would be strengthened. In our example, the fact that activity in the tone center was closely followed by activity in the food center would mean that the connection between these centers would be strengthened. The next time the tone was presented, therefore, activity in the tone center would be transmitted to the food center, and from there to the salivary glands.

FIGURE 2.4   Pavlov's view of the connections involved in classical conditioning. If the sight of
Pavlov preceded food, the visual representation of Pavlov in the dog's brain would be
connected to the food center (the broken line). Excitement in the food center would
then be transmitted via an innate pathway (solid line) to the dog's salivary glands.

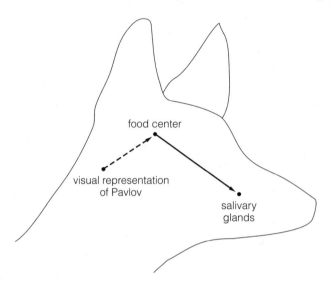

food center

visual representation
of Pavlov

salivary
glands

If this analysis was correct, Pavlov saw that it could have far-reaching implications. As we saw in the preceding section, behavior depends on the routing of
electrical impulses through the brain, and this routing depends on the strength
of the connections between individual neurons. If we could understand how the
strength of neural connections is altered, we would understand the crucial mechanism underlying the brain's operations. Because of the brain's complexity, however, it is normally extremely difficult to study the formation of new connections.
Suppose, for example, that we wanted to study the neural changes that occur as
a child memorizes a poem in school. How would we observe changes in connections between individual neurons in the child's brain? And even if we had a
technique for doing so, how would we know which of the brain's 10,000,000,000
neurons to monitor? If Pavlov's hypothesis was correct, however, he could monitor the formation of new connections simply by measuring a dog's salivation:
The stronger the connection between the tone and food centers, the more electrical impulses would be transmitted to the food center and from there to the
salivary glands, resulting in greater salivation. The amount of salivation, therefore, provides a simple index of the strength of this connection. To determine
the laws governing the formation of neural connections, therefore, all Pavlov
needed to do was to manipulate possible variables and observe their effects on
the amount of salivation. If, as he believed, all education and training "are really

nothing more than the results of an establishment of new nervous connections" (Pavlov, 1927, p. 26), then studying how dogs learn to salivate might lead to an understanding of the mechanism underlying all learning.

Conditioning

Excited by this possibility, Pavlov abandoned his research on digestion, even though it had already made him world famous and was soon to earn him the Nobel prize. Instead, he set out to study how new associations were formed by deliberately pairing stimuli with the presentation of food and observing how the conditions of pairing influenced the development of salivation.

Controlling the conditions. Pavlov recognized from the outset that the task was not going to be an easy one: The brain was an enormously complex organ, sensitive to countless stimuli from the outside world, so that the effects in which he was interested might easily be lost in the flood of stimuli constantly washing over his subjects.

> *Unless we are careful to take special precautions the success of the whole investigation may be jeopardized, and we should get hopelessly lost as soon as we began to seek for cause and effect among so many and various influences, so intertwined and entangled as to form a veritable chaos. It was evident that the experimental conditions had to be simplified, and that this simplification must consist in eliminating as far as possible any stimuli outside our control which might fall upon the animal.*
> (Pavlov, 1927, p. 20)

To achieve this, Pavlov conducted his initial studies in an isolated room, where no one but the experimenter was allowed to enter. This precaution, however, proved inadequate, as even the slightest movement of the experimenter, such as a blink, was enough to distract the dogs. Pavlov tried placing the experimenter outside the room, but this did not solve the problem, as the dogs continued to be affected by stimuli such as the footsteps of passersby and even a cloud that temporarily reduced the amount of light coming in the window. Finally, Pavlov was driven to designing a completely new laboratory which, with the aid of a "keen and public-spirited Moscow businessman," he had built in St. Petersburg.

The laboratory looked like a fort, with walls more than a foot thick, encircled by a trench filled with straw to reduce vibrations. The actual test rooms were widely dispersed through the building to minimize distracting noises. Figure 2.5 illustrates a typical test room. The dogs were strapped into loose-fitting harnesses to reduce movement, and any salivation was carried off through a tube to an experimenter in an adjacent, soundproof room. With the aid of a variety of electrically operated signal devices, Pavlov was now able to control almost completely

FIGURE 2.5   Apparatus used in Pavlov's study of salivary conditioning in dogs. Saliva flowed through a tube connected to the dog's cheek and traveled to another room where it could be recorded. (After Yerkes & Morgulis, 1909)

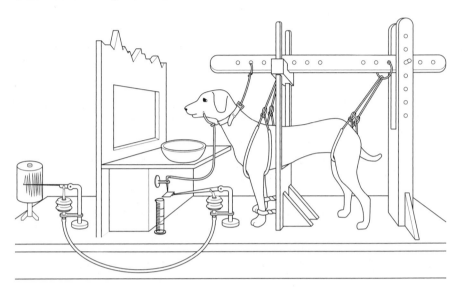

any external stimuli that reached his subjects, and thus was ready to make a systematic study of how associations are formed.

A typical experiment. We can illustrate the quality of the results Pavlov now obtained with an experiment by one of his students. Anrep (1920) first presented his dogs with a tone by itself and found that it had no effect on salivation. He then paired the tone with food: The tone was sounded for five seconds; then, two seconds later, food was presented. Each of these tone-food pairings was called a **trial,** and Anrep presented a trial every few minutes. (The actual time between trials varied between 5 and 35 minutes.) On an average of once every ten trials, the tone was presented by itself for 30 seconds so the experimenter could measure the amount of salivation elicited solely by the tone.

The results for two subjects are shown in Figure 2.6, where we can see that the magnitude of salivation on the test trials gradually increased from 0 drops to a maximum level, or *asymptote*, of about 60 drops after 30 pairings. One striking feature of these results is the smoothness and regularity of the learning curves. It normally requires averaging the results of many subjects to eliminate random variations and produce curves of this smoothness, but because of the extraordinary control Pavlov achieved over the environment, he and his colleagues were able to produce beautifully clear and uniform data even in single

FIGURE 2.6   Salivary conditioning in dogs. (Data from Anrep, 1920)

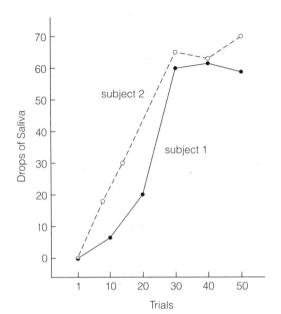

subjects. Even more dramatic evidence of the underlying lawfulness of behavior in this situation is the similarity of the learning curves of the two subjects: Even though the subjects were tested separately, their behavior was virtually identical on trial after trial.

Pavlov called the salivation elicited by the food an **unconditioned response (UR),** because no training was necessary to establish it, whereas the salivation to the tone was a **conditioned response (CR)**—that is, a response whose occurrence depended on particular conditions of training. Similarly, the food was an **unconditioned stimulus (US)** for salivation—that is, a stimulus that elicits a response without training. Finally, the tone was called a **conditioned stimulus (CS)**—a stimulus that, through training, elicits a response.[2] (See Figure 2.7.) The entire procedure, in which the pairing of a CS with a US results in an increase in responding to the CS, has come to be known as Pavlovian or **classical conditioning.**

---

[2] Pavlov actually used the term *conditional response* because the occurrence of the response was conditional on previous pairings of the CS and the US. The term was mistranslated as *conditioned response*. Some authors are now returning to Pavlov's original terminology, referring to conditional and unconditional stimuli and responses.

FIGURE 2.7   A typical classical conditioning procedure.

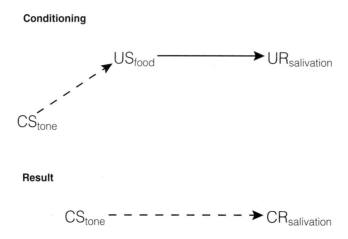

Conditioning

$US_{food} \longrightarrow UR_{salivation}$

CS_{tone}

Result

$CS_{tone} - - - - - - - - \rightarrow CR_{salivation}$

Extinction

Pavlov saw conditioning not simply as a useful tool for studying the formation of associations but as a process of fundamental importance in its own right. As we have seen, animals are born with a variety of innate reflexes that allow them to respond quickly to important events—for example, blinking when a gust of air brings the danger of particles being blown into the eye, or lifting a foot when it touches a burning surface. Unlearned reflexes such as these are important in allowing animals to cope with situations that always require the same response. Some features of the environment, however, vary in what response is appropriate, and Pavlov saw classical conditioning as a vital mechanism that allowed animals to adjust their behavior to new circumstances. Grizzly bears, for example, feed on salmon, but rivers contain salmon only during the brief migration season of that fish. If a bear visits a river one day and finds it teeming with salmon, the bear will clearly have a better chance of survival if it can learn that the river is a good source of food and therefore return the next day.

Once the salmon migration is over, however, a river that was once full of fish might become empty. What happens to an established association when the CS no longer reliably signals the US? The answer is shown in Figure 2.8, which presents the results of an experiment in which a previously conditioned stimulus was presented a number of times without the US. The result was that the conditioned response gradually disappeared, a phenomenon referred to by Pavlov as **extinction.** Although answering one question, however, this result raised another—namely, *why* did the response disappear? If a neural connection had been established in the brain between the CS and the US, could

FIGURE 2.8   Extinction of a conditioned response when the conditioned stimulus is presented by itself. (Data from Pavlov, 1927)

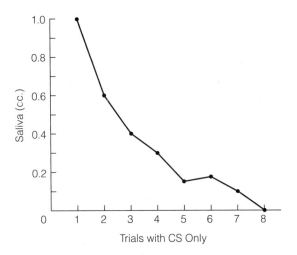

this connection have been obliterated simply by presenting the CS by itself a few times?

To Pavlov, this was implausible. There was no physiological evidence that neural connections suddenly disintegrated in this way, and observations of the dogs' behavior also suggested that the connections formed during conditioning were still present after extinction. If, for example, an interval of time was allowed to elapse after extinction had been completed, and if the CS was then presented again, the previously extinguished response would suddenly reappear. Figure 2.9 shows that after a series of extinction trials in which salivation was progressively reduced to zero, the CS was reintroduced after a lapse of two hours and again elicited a significant amount of salivation. This **spontaneous recovery** of the response was only temporary; with further presentations of the CS, the recovered response would again be rapidly extinguished. The recovery clearly demonstrated, however, that a connection still existed between the CS and the response.

The concept of inhibition.   If the CS were still associated with salivation, why had the dog stopped salivating during the earlier extinction trials? The answer, according to Pavlov, was not that the old, excitatory connection had been destroyed, but that the CS had also acquired the capacity to inhibit responding. In an elaboration of Pavlov's ideas proposed by Konorski (1948), pairing of the CS and US was assumed to establish an excitatory connection between the corresponding brain centers, so that activation of the CS center would be transmitted

FIGURE 2.9   Spontaneous recovery of an extinguished response. (Data from Pavlov, 1927)

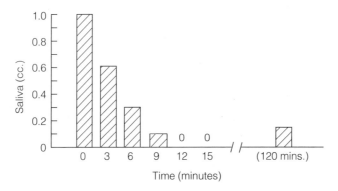

to the US center. If the CS were then presented on its own, a new, inhibitory connection would be established between the centers so that activity in the CS center would now tend to block or inhibit activity in the US center as well as to excite it.

During Pavlov's time, no direct evidence was available for the existence of inhibitory connections in the brain, but physiological research since his time has confirmed their existence. As we saw earlier, when an electrical impulse arrives at a neuron's terminal, it causes the release of chemical neurotransmitters that flow across the synaptic cleft to the next neuron in the chain. In excitatory connections, the neurotransmitters produce changes in the cell membrane of the second neuron which eventually cause it to initiate an electrical signal. Different neurons, however, produce different neurotransmitters, and some have the effect of blocking changes in the cell membrane. Thus if two neurons converge on the same target neuron, and one releases excitatory neurotransmitters while the other releases inhibitory ones, their effects might cancel each other, resulting in no change in the target neuron's electrical activity.

During conditioning, Pavlov suggested, an excitatory connection is established between the CS and US (Figure 2.10a). During extinction, a parallel inhibitory connection is developed (Figure 2.10b—the length of the line is being used to represent the strength of the association). As the inhibitory connection becomes stronger, it is increasingly effective in preventing the response until eventually, when the excitatory and inhibitory tendencies are equally balanced, the conditioned response is no longer elicited (Figure 2.10c).

Conditioned inhibition. Direct evidence for the existence of inhibition came from the phenomenon of **conditioned inhibition**—the tendency of a stimulus to block, or inhibit, responding as a result of previous training. The training procedure used by Pavlov was to alternate between trials in which the CS+ (positive

FIGURE 2.10   Pavlov's view of the development of inhibitory connections during extinction: (a) By the end of conditioning, an excitatory connection has been formed between the CS and US (solid line). (b) Presentation of the CS by itself produces a new, inhibitory connection (broken line). (c) With repeated presentations of the CS by itself, the inhibitory connection becomes stronger (represented by a longer broken line).

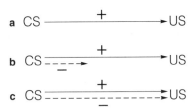

stimulus) was paired with food and trials in which the CS+ and the CS– (inhibitory stimulus) were presented together without food. The CS– signaled that food would not be forthcoming and acquired the capacity to inhibit salivation. Suppose, for example, that we conditioned salivation to a metronome, but that on certain trials we presented a whistle simultaneously with the metronome and did not present food.

metronome → *food*

whistle + metronome → ____

After a series of such trials, subjects would respond vigorously when the metronome was presented by itself, but not when the metronome was presented in conjunction with the whistle. The reason, according to Pavlov, was that pairing the metronome with food had resulted in the establishment of an excitatory connection between the corresponding neural centers, whereas pairing the whistle with no food had resulted in an inhibitory connection between the whistle and food. When the metronome was presented by itself, it excited the food center and thus elicited salivation, but when the whistle was also presented, it inhibited the food center, with the net result that no response was elicited.

The fact that subjects learned not to respond when the whistle accompanied the metronome, however, does not necessarily mean that the whistle was actively inhibiting responding. Another possibility is that the compound stimulus created by presenting the whistle and the metronome together was perceived as a unique stimulus or configuration, rather than as two separate elements. (See also Pearce, 1994). When we see a friend's face, for example, we do not see it as a collection of eyes, ears, and so forth but, rather, as a single configuration. Similarly, when the whistle (A) and the metronome (B) were presented together, Pavlov's subjects might have perceived them as an integrated configuration (C), rather than as separate elements (A + B). If so, the reason that subjects did not respond when A and B were presented together might not have been that A was inhibiting responding to B; it could simply have been that the configural stimulus C had never been followed by food and hence was neutral.

To be sure that the CS– in the conditioned inhibition paradigm is actively inhibiting responding, therefore, further evidence is required. One test was developed by Pavlov himself and is called a **summation test.** In a summation test, an inhibitory stimulus is tested by combining it with a new CS+. In the experiment by Pavlov that we have been describing, at the end of the conditioned inhibition phase he presented the whistle (CS–) together with a tactile stimulus that he had previously paired with food.

whistle + tactile stimulus → *?*

As shown in Table 2.1, when the tactile stimulus was presented by itself it elicited copious salivation, but when it was combined with the whistle, salivation declined drastically. Note that a configural explanation cannot easily account for this decline: If the whistle was simply neutral, we would not expect it to reduce responding so dramatically.

A summation test on its own, however, is not conclusive—it is still possible to account for these results without assuming that the stimulus is actively inhibiting responding. (For details, see Rescorla, 1969). For this reason, a **retardation test** is sometimes also used in which a stimulus suspected of being inhibitory is repeatedly paired with a US. The idea is that if a stimulus is inhibitory, it should require more conditioning trials than usual to convert it into a strong excitatory stimulus. (Conditioning is compared with a control group that receives the same number of conditioning trials, but without the earlier inhibitory training.) Although neither the summation test nor retardation test is definitive on its own, together they can provide compelling evidence that a stimulus is inhibiting responding (Williams, Overmier, & LoLordo, 1992; Cole, Barnet, & Miller, 1997).

Returning to the phenomenon of extinction, most learning psychologists now agree that extinction does not involve the destruction of the excitatory association formed during conditioning but rather the formation of a new, inhibitory association. (See Delamater, 1996, for a review.) As extinction trials continue, the inhibitory connection becomes progressively stronger until, eventually, it equals the excitatory tendency in strength and responding ceases.[3]

---

[3] Although, as we have noted, most learning psychologists now accept Pavlov's explanation of extinction in terms of the development of an inhibitory association, one continuing problem for this analysis concerns spontaneous recovery. If responding ceases during extinction because the excitatory and

TABLE 2.1   A Test for Conditioned Inhibition (Data from Pavlov, 1927, p.77)

Time	Stimulus Presented for One Minute	Drops of Saliva During One Minute
3:08 P.M.	Tactile	3
3:16 P.M.	Tactile	8
3:25 P.M.	Tactile + whistle	<1
3:30 P.M.	Tactile	11

Other Phenomena

Pavlov and his colleagues built up an extraordinarily detailed picture of the basic processes of conditioning. Indeed, there was a time in the 1950s when it could still be argued plausibly that every single major fact about conditioning had been anticipated by Pavlov some 50 years earlier. We cannot convey the richness of Pavlov's work in the space available, but we shall summarize briefly a few of the other phenomena he discovered.

Second-order conditioning. Having conditioned a response to a CS, Pavlov found that he could then use that CS to condition the response to yet another stimulus. In one demonstration, a dog was first given conditioning trials in which a metronome was paired with food. Then, once the metronome elicited salivation reliably, food presentations were discontinued and a black square was paired with the metronome:

1. *metronome* → *food*
2. *black square* → *metronome*

After several trials, the black square also began to elicit salivation, even though it had never been followed by food. Pavlov called this phenomenon **second-order conditioning** and considered it to be the outcome of a double associative

---

inhibitory connections are equally strong, why should the passage of time cause the extinguished response to reappear? Pavlov suggested that inhibitory associations are more fragile than excitatory ones, and more recently Bouton (1993) has proposed that inhibitory associations remain in memory but become harder to retrieve. It is not obvious, however, why excitatory and inhibitory associations should differ in either fragility or retrievability, and none of the explanations of spontaneous recovery so far proposed seem able to encompass all the available evidence (for example, Delamater, 1996; Brooks & Bouton, 1993; Rescorla, 1997a). Though spontaneous recovery is on the surface a trivially simple phenomenon, it has stubbornly resisted theorists' efforts to explain it.

chain, from the square to the metronome, and then from the metronome to food. (See Rescorla, 1980a, for an alternative interpretation.)

Counterconditioning. In addition to extinction, Pavlov discovered another way to eliminate a conditioned response, which was to pair the CS that elicited it with a US that elicited a different response. If the new response is incompatible with the old one, so that only one of them can occur at a time, then the more strongly the new response is conditioned the less likely it is that the old response will occur again. This technique has come to be known as **counterconditioning.** Pavlov provided a particularly dramatic demonstration of its power by showing that it could be used to suppress even unconditioned responses. In one experiment, he used an electric shock that normally elicited violent escape reactions and repeatedly followed it with presentations of food. Provided that the intensity of the shock employed was not too severe, he found that the dogs' normal defensive reactions were eventually suppressed almost entirely. Rather than jumping or showing any signs of discomfort on being shocked, a dog's only visible reaction was "turning its head to where it usually received the food and smacking its lips, at the same time producing a profuse secretion of saliva" (Pavlov, 1927, p. 30).

Generalization. Pavlov found that conditioning resulted in salivation not only to the CS presented during training but also to other stimuli that were similar to it. In one experiment, he conditioned salivation to a tone of 1000 Hz.[4] After conditioning, the dogs salivated not only to the 1000-Hz tone but also to tones of 1100 Hz, 1200 Hz, and so on, with the greatest increase in salivation occurring to the tones most similar to the training stimulus (that is, 900 Hz and 1100 Hz). This phenomenon was called **generalization,** and to Pavlov it had clear adaptive advantages. In nature, we rarely if ever encounter exactly the same stimulus twice; even a human face is never viewed from exactly the same angle or in exactly the same light. It is crucial, therefore, that a response is not restricted to the precise stimulus encountered on conditioning trials but generalizes to similar stimuli.

Discrimination. In some situations, however, it might be very important *not* to respond in the same way to similar stimuli. The appropriate response to a mushroom, for example, might not be at all appropriate to a toadstool. To test whether his dogs could learn to distinguish, or discriminate, between similar stimuli, Pavlov tried pairing a tone with food many hundreds of times, in the hope that salivation would increasingly come under the control of the

---

[4] The pitch of a tone is determined by the frequency with which its basic sound pattern is repeated each second. Frequency is measured in units called hertz (Hz), where one Hz equals one cycle per second.

FIGURE 2.11   Idealized representation of discrimination learning. On half the trials, a tone was followed by food (CS+); on the remaining trials, another tone was not followed by food (CS–).

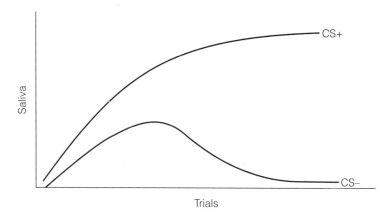

precise tone that was being presented. Simple repetition of this kind, however, did not sharpen control significantly. Pavlov found that it was far more effective to use *discrimination training* in which conditioning trials with a positive stimulus (CS+) were alternated with presentations of a negative stimulus (CS–).

$$CS+ \rightarrow food$$

$$CS- \rightarrow \underline{\quad\quad}$$

In a typical experiment, a 1000-Hz tone would be presented, followed by food, on half the trials; on the remaining trials, a 900-Hz tone would be presented without food. The typical results of such an experiment are shown in Figure 2.11. At first, the subjects responded to both stimuli, as responding conditioned to CS+ generalized to CS–. As training continued, responding was increasingly restricted to CS+. The subjects had learned to discriminate, or respond differentially to, the two stimuli.

As with many other terms in learning, the term **discrimination** can be used in several different ways, although the core meaning is similar in each case. In perhaps the most common usage, we say that someone discriminates between two stimuli if he or she responds differently to them. However, the term is also sometimes used to refer to the procedure that produces this outcome (repeated presentations of two stimuli, only one of which is followed by the US), or to the process in the brain assumed to generate this behavior. These different meanings are potentially confusing, but in most cases the intended meaning is clear from the context.

2.3 The Need for Control Groups

When they learned of Pavlov's research, Western psychologists also wanted to study classical conditioning. Did classical conditioning occur in humans? If so, was it confined to relatively minor responses such as salivation, or could it affect far more important aspects of our behavior?

Conditioning Fear in Little Albert

One of the first attempts to extend classical conditioning to other responses was reported by John B. Watson, the founder of behaviorism. Watson believed that psychologists should be concerned with overt behavior rather than the hidden processes of the mind, and he argued for a greater concern with practical applications. Thus, in 1920, together with Rosalie Raynor, Watson set out to discover whether fear could be classically conditioned in humans in the same way as salivation in dogs.

Their subject was a nine-month-old infant; his name was given in their published paper as Albert B., though he was later to be immortalized as Little Albert. Albert was normally a "stolid and unemotional" infant who almost never cried. As the first step in their experiment, Watson and Raynor presented Albert with a white rat and found that it elicited no signs of fear; Albert's only discernible reaction was an attempt to play with the animal. They then began conditioning trials in which every presentation of the white rat was followed by a loud noise that had previously been found to elicit strong fear. Almost immediately, Albert began to show signs of distress on presentation of the rat, and these signs increased over succeeding trials. When they presented the rat on the eighth trial, they recorded Albert's behavior as follows:

> The instant the rat was shown the baby began to cry. Almost instantly he turned sharply to the left, fell over on left side, raised himself on all fours and began to crawl away so rapidly that he was caught with difficulty before reaching the edge of the table.
> (Watson & Raynor, 1920, p. 5)

This fear reaction also generalized to similar stimuli that, before conditioning, had been neutral (for example, a rabbit and a fur coat). Albert's fear reaction showed no signs of fading with time and was still present on a test trial given almost a month later. The experiment had to be terminated at this point because Albert's mother ceased working at the hospital where they had been testing him.

The results they obtained were very convincing: After only seven conditioning trials, Albert's reaction to the rat was converted from one of mild curiosity to one of apparent terror. But could the change in Albert's behavior really be attributed to classical conditioning? The answer depends on exactly what we mean by conditioning. The essential element in Pavlov's procedure seems to be that a stimulus acquires the capacity to elicit a response as a result of pairings with a second stimulus that already elicited it. Putting this same idea slightly more technically, we defined classical conditioning earlier in the chapter as an increase in the probability of a response to a CS as a result of pairings of that CS with a US. The loud noise used in Watson and Raynor's experiment certainly seemed to function as an unconditioned stimulus for fear; why, therefore, should we doubt whether Albert's fear of the rat was the result of conditioning?

Alternative Explanations

The problem is that, although the observed fear response might have been the result of pairings of the CS and US, the response could also be explained in other ways.

Sensitization. One possible explanation is that Albert's fear increased simply because of the repeated presentations of the rat. This might seem very un-likely: If the rat did not elicit fear initially, why should continuing to present it repeatedly by itself endow it with the capacity to do so? The first point to note is that this explanation is possible even if it doesn't seem very likely. As we saw in Chapter 1, explanations that initially seemed wildly implausible some-times turn out to be correct. In this case, moreover, there is evidence that such effects really do occur. In Chapter 1 we discussed an experiment by Davis (1974) in which rats received repeated presentations of a tone. Initially, each tone presentation caused a startle response, but with repetitions this startle re-sponse diminished in magnitude (habituation). In a second experiment, how-ever, Davis exposed his rats to exactly the same sequence of tones, but this time with an 80-db. noise present throughout the experiment. Under these conditions the startle response to the tone became *stronger* over trials. Such an increase in the strength of a reflexive response when a stimulus is repeated is called **sensitization.**

Why should the presence of a loud background noise reverse the effects of repeating a tone? For our current purposes, the explanation doesn't really mat-ter—the crucial point is that sensitization can occur—but Groves and Thomp-son (1970) have proposed an explanation in terms of arousal. When we are asleep, our arousal level is low, and any stimulation will produce only a muted response. When we are awake, we respond to stimuli more strongly, and the greater our arousal, the more vigorously we tend to respond. When a loud noise was added in Davis' experiment, its continuous presence caused a steady in-crease in the rats' level of arousal, and this in turn amplified their response to the tone. Returning to the Watson and Raynor experiment, if the rat did elicit a small amount of fear initially, it is entirely possible that it was simply the re-peated presentations of the rat that increased Albert's fear (perhaps because the

FIGURE 2.12   Change in the level of fear displayed by two groups, one receiving
pairings of the CS with a US, and the other receiving the CS by itself.

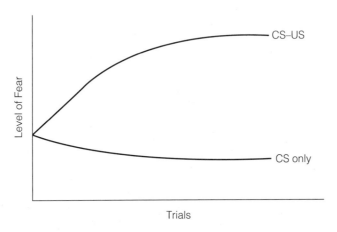

experimental situation was itself inducing increasing levels of arousal), not the
pairings of the rat with the loud noise.

Pseudoconditioning. Psychology experiments must now adhere to a number
of ethical standards, and adherence is generally monitored by an ethics com-
mittee at the institution where the research is carried out. By modern standards, it is doubtful whether an experiment such as Watson and Raynor's could
now be carried out, because of the distress that Albert suffered. To allow us to
explore further the methodological issues involved in assessing classical conditioning, however, let us suppose that we had available a procedure for measuring fear that did not actually produce fear! Armed with this procedure, suppose
that we repeated the Watson and Raynor experiment but controlled for sensitization effects by using two groups of subjects: an experimental group that received pairings of the rat (CS) with the noise (US), and a control group that
only received the CS. If Albert's fear was due solely to repeated presentations
of the CS, the CS-only control group should show just as must fear as the conditioning group.

In all likelihood, the results of this experiment would resemble those shown
in Figure 2.12: Rather than increasing over trials, fear levels in the control
group would decrease. (When a stimulus is repeated, the response it elicits is
generally much more likely to habituate than to become sensitized.) If we obtained this result, could we conclude that the increase in response in our experimental group was due to conditioning? The answer is still no: The increase
might have been caused not by pairings of the CS with the US, but rather by
presentations of the US by itself. In this case, repeated exposure to the loud

noise might have made Albert more and more upset, so that almost any new stimulus might have produced fear.

Experimental evidence that presenting a US by itself really can affect responding to other stimuli comes from an experiment on eyelid conditioning by Kimble, Mann, and Dufort (1955). The experimental group received 60 pairings of a light with a puff of air to the eye. A control group received the identical treatment for the first 20 trials, but on trials 21–40 they received only the US. Finally, on trials 41–60 they again received paired presentations.

Trials	Experimental Group	Control Group
1–20	CS–US	CS–US
21–40	CS–US	US
41–60	CS–US	CS–US

How much improvement in responding to the CS should we expect during trials 21–40? The experimental group received 20 pairings of the CS and US during this period, whereas the control group received only the US. If pairing is important, only the experimental group should have improved; if presentation of a US by itself can increase responding to a CS, then responding in the two groups should have been similar. As shown in Figure 2.13, the improvement in the two groups was not merely similar but almost identical. Thus, although the results of the experimental group on their own would have seemed impressive evidence for conditioning, the inclusion of the control group showed that this improvement was due solely to presentation of the US.

An increase in responding to a CS because of presentation of a US by itself is known as **pseudoconditioning** and is perhaps not as mysterious as it seems initially: It is not really surprising that subjects given repeated blasts of air to the eye should become jumpy enough that they blinked whenever any sudden stimulus was presented. (For another possible explanation of pseudoconditioning, see Wickens & Wickens, 1942.) Although pseudoconditioning is not usually as powerful as Kimble and associates found it to be, it is certainly possible that Albert's increased fear of the rat was caused solely by repeated experiences of the loud noise, not by its pairings with the rat.

Interaction effects. Suppose that with our newfound wisdom we again redesign our experiment, this time including a second control group that receives only the US by itself. (To assess conditioning in this group, we would introduce the CS by itself on a single test trial at the end of training.) Figure 2.14 shows the hypothetical results: Presentation of the US by itself increased fear on CS test trials, but not nearly as much as paired presentations of the CS and US. Now, at last, can we conclude that we have demonstrated conditioning?

FIGURE 2.13   Eyeblink conditioning. The experimental group received 60 pairings of a light with an air puff; the control group received CS–US pairings on trials 1–20 and 41–60 but only the air puff during the intervening interval. (Adapted from Kimble, Mann, & Dufort, 1955)

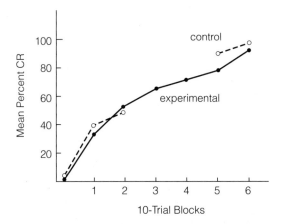

FIGURE 2.14   Level of fear displayed by three groups—one given CS–US pairings, one given the CS by itself, and the third given the US by itself for the same number of trials followed by a single trial of the CS by itself.

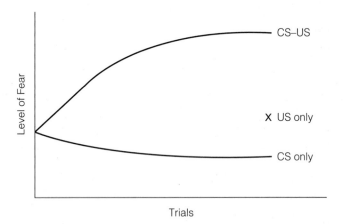

The answer, frustratingly, is no. Although we have controlled for the separate effects of the CS by itself and the US by itself, we have not controlled for the possibility that, when presented concurrently, their combined effect might be greater than the sum of their individual effects. A nonadditive effect of this kind, when two variables are presented together, is known as an **interaction effect.** To clarify this concept, consider the following situation: Imagine yourself studying

FIGURE 2.15   The unpaired control procedure for classical conditioning. The CS and US are presented at widely separated time intervals.

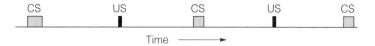

for an exam in a dingy hotel room. A dripping faucet in an adjacent room might bother you, but you might still be able to study; a flashing neon light outside your window might bother you, but again you might be able to ignore it. If both were going on simultaneously, however, their combined effects might drive you up the wall, in a way that you could not predict by considering the effects of each factor in isolation. In the same way, the combined effects of CS and US presentations might be much greater than the sum of their effects measured separately.

It is not enough, then, to control for the effects of the CS and US separately; we also need to control for any interaction between them. One simple procedure for doing this is to use an **unpaired control**—a control group in which the CS and the US are presented at widely separated times (Figure 2.15). Subjects in an unpaired control receive the same number of CS and US presentations as experimental subjects who receive normal conditioning trials, but these presentations are arranged so that the CS and US never occur together. If pairing of a CS and US produces an association, then the experimental group should respond more; if responding is due simply to the combined effects of receiving the CS and US separately, then responding in the two groups will be equal.

The analysis we have been pursuing might seem tedious or unimportant: What do the details of the control procedure matter, you may ask; what we want to know are the facts! As we saw in Chapter 1, however, it can be very difficult to determine what a fact is, because the facts for one generation have a nasty habit of becoming the laughable superstitions of the next generation. Indeed, as we shall see, more recent research has shown that the unpaired control also has important limitations as a control for assessing conditioning. For the moment, though, let us stop beating this not-quite-dead horse and accept that this control provides us with at least a rough tool for assessing conditioning. Can we now say whether fear can be classically conditioned?

2.4 WHAT BEHAVIORS CAN BE CONDITIONED?

With an acceptable procedure for assessing conditioning, we can now try to answer the question of what responses can be classically conditioned. To provide some structure for our discussion, we will begin by examining simpler responses, and only then turn to more complex responses such as emotions.

We can divide behavior into two broad classes, based on the subsystem of the nervous system involved in controlling the response. Two semi-independent systems are involved in transmitting impulses from the central nervous system to other parts of the body. The *skeletal nervous system* controls striped muscles, so called because their alternating bands of dark and light fibers give them a striated, or striped, appearance when examined under a microscope. Most of the muscles we think of when we hear the word muscle—biceps, triceps, deltoids, and so on—are in fact striped muscles, whose function is to adjust the position of the body in space. The *autonomic nervous system,* on the other hand, controls the smooth muscles and glands, both of which are involved in regulation of the internal environment. Smooth muscles, as you might imagine, have a uniform or smooth appearance under the microscope; they are responsible for movements within the body. Rhythmic contractions of the smooth muscles lining the gullet, for example, are responsible for the movement of food from the mouth to the stomach (contractions known as peristalsis); glands secrete chemical substances such as adrenaline and saliva.

The skeletal nervous system is thus responsible for coping with the external environment through bodily movement, whereas the autonomic nervous system regulates the internal milieu. The bodily movements controlled by the skeletal nervous system are called **skeletal responses;** the glandular and smooth muscle activities controlled by the autonomic nervous system are called **autonomic responses.** We will begin our exploration of what responses can be conditioned with autonomic responses; we will then look at skeletal responses and, finally, at more complex responses such as motives and emotions.

Autonomic Conditioning

We have already encountered evidence that at least one response controlled by the autonomic nervous system can be conditioned: salivation. For many years, however, it was unclear whether all autonomic responses, or only a limited subset of responses, could be conditioned. Soviet investigators reported successful conditioning of a wide range of autonomic responses—for example, urine formation in the kidney and insulin release by the pancreas. (See Bykov, 1957.) Psychologists in the West initially had difficulty evaluating these claims because only brief summaries were available in translation and few Western psychologists had the surgical skills required to study autonomic responses. Research over recent decades, however, has strongly confirmed the earlier Soviet reports. We cannot cover all this research, but we will illustrate it with a few examples.

Arousal. When we encounter new or stressful situations, our bodies prepare for action through a complex set of responses known collectively as arousal. The adrenal gland secretes the hormone adrenaline, heart rate increases, blood pressure changes, and so on. One component of arousal is perspiration, and we can measure this component by passing a very small electrical current through the skin and measuring the current that is transmitted. The skin's conductivity defines the **galvanic skin response,** or **GSR,** which is thus just a measure of perspiration: The more we perspire, the more readily our skin conducts an electric current. By measuring perspiration, therefore, the GSR gives us a simple index of a person's arousal. (The GSR is also sometimes referred to as the *skin conductance response*, or *SCR*).

Because it measures arousal, the GSR has been of considerable interest to psychologists. It can be used to assess concentration—the harder subjects concentrate, the more aroused they might become—and also the presence of emotions. The GSR is used as the main component of polygraph, or lie detector, tests: When people are lying, they tend to become aroused, so that by measuring the GSR we can obtain indirect evidence about whether someone is lying. (It is important to emphasize, however, that polygraph tests are very far from infallible. The fact that someone becomes aroused when asked an incriminating question does not necessarily mean that the person is lying; the person might just be embarrassed or frightened.)

The important point in the present context is that arousal, as measured by the GSR, is readily conditioned. If a person receives a mild electric shock, for example, arousal occurs; if this shock is preceded by a tone, the tone will also acquire the capacity to elicit the GSR. Champion and Jones (1961) have shown that this increase is genuinely due to classical conditioning: If the tone and shock are presented separately, in an unpaired control group, the GSR to the tone does not increase.

Insulin and blood sugar levels. A central concept in understanding the activities of the autonomic nervous system is **homeostasis,** or the activities of the body that are directed to maintaining a stable internal environment. For example, we need to maintain the body's temperature at a constant level to survive; deviations in any direction, either up or down, can have lethal consequences. In a similar way, we act to maintain constant levels of water, energy, and so on. There is now evidence that many of the autonomic activities that regulate our internal environment can be conditioned.

One example involves the amount of glucose (a form of sugar) circulating in the blood. Siegel (1972) gave rats a number of injections of insulin, a hormone that decreases the level of glucose in the blood. Pavlov had hypothesized that the cues associated with the injection of a drug would act as conditioned stimuli, with the systemic effects of the drug then becoming conditioned to these cues. To test this hypothesis, Siegel gave his subjects a test injection of saline, a neutral fluid that normally has no effect. The saline injection did indeed elicit a strong conditioned response, but it was an *increase* in blood glucose rather than the decrease produced by the insulin. Appropriate controls showed that this result was due to the pairing of the injection with insulin.

Why was the conditioned response the opposite of the unconditioned response in this case, when in every other example of classical conditioning we have encountered the two responses were the same? Siegel (1978) has suggested that the answer could lie in the body's efforts to maintain a stable internal environment. When insulin is injected, it produces a fall in blood glucose below the optimal level; when the body senses this fall, it reacts by increasing glucose levels. It was this *compensatory response* that was conditioned, a system that might have evolved because by taking compensatory action in advance of a disturbance, the body can minimize the harmful effects of the disturbance.

An alternative explanation has been proposed by Eikelboom and Stewart (1982), who argue that the conditioned and unconditioned responses to insulin *are* the same; they appear to differ only because the unconditioned response has been incorrectly identified. Suppose, for example, that you accidentally cut your hand; would the bleeding that followed be an unconditioned response? They argue that it would not: Bleeding is a direct physical reaction to an opening in the skin, whereas an unconditioned response is a reflexive reaction that is mediated by the central nervous system. Similarly in the case of insulin, they suggest that insulin normally acts directly on the cells of the body to cause the removal of glucose from the blood, without any involvement of the central nervous system. However, when glucose levels then fall, this drop is detected by receptors in the brain, which then trigger an increase in blood glucose to compensate. The drop in glucose levels, in other words, is an unconditioned stimulus that produces an increase in glucose levels as an unconditioned response, and this increase is then conditioned to the stimulus of the injection. (See Ramsay & Woods, 1997, for a recent elaboration of this hypothesis.) If this argument is accepted, the conditioned and unconditioned responses to insulin are both increases in blood glucose, with the common purpose of opposing the damaging effects of a shift from optimum levels.

Note that the issue here is not whether an increase in glucose levels can be conditioned—all sides agree that it can; the only issue is whether the unconditioned response is better understood as the initial decrease in glucose that follows an insulin injection, or the subsequent increase. The question of whether conditioned and unconditioned responses are the same has potentially important theoretical implications, as we shall see in Chapter 4, but for our current purposes the important point is that glucose levels can be conditioned.

Pain sensitivity. Siegel (1975) also investigated whether the effects of morphine can be conditioned. Morphine is one of the most effective painkillers, or analgesic drugs, that we have. (*Algesia* is derived from the Greek word meaning pain, and *an* means not; an analgesic drug is thus one that reduces pain.) With repeated administration, however, morphine loses its potency, a phenomenon known as *tolerance*. The reason for this loss of potency, Siegel suggested, could be classical conditioning. As far as a person in pain is concerned, any reduction in pain is highly desirable, but from the body's point of view, the morphine is interfering with the pain system which protects us by ensuring that we *do* react to harmful experiences by feeling pain. Thus, when an injection of morphine reduces pain (*analgesia*), the body responds with an increased sensitivity to pain, or *hyperalgesia*, so as to return sensitivity to its appropriate, homeostatic level. Siegel hypothesized that this compensatory, hyperalgesic reaction would be conditioned to the cues of being injected. Every time the morphine was administered, the conditioned hyperalgesic response would become stronger, and this would explain why the morphine loses its effectiveness: The analgesic effect of the morphine is being opposed by the conditioned hyperalgesic response.

To test this hypothesis, Siegel (1975) gave rats a series of morphine injections. If a compensatory reaction had been conditioned to the cues of being injected, then a test injection of saline should now cause an increase in the rats' sensitivity to pain, rather than decreasing it as morphine does. To measure pain sensitivity, Siegel used an ingeniously simple technique in which he placed the rats on a moderately hot metal plate and recorded the time until the rats licked their paws; the greater their pain sensitivity, the sooner they would lick their paws. Rats who had previously received morphine, he found, were more sensitive to pain following a saline test injection, and appropriate controls established that this was the result of conditioning.

Siegel found that this compensatory reaction was conditioned not only to the injection but also to the room in which the injection was given: Pain sensitivity was greater in the room where morphine had been administered than in other rooms. This effect, moreover, can be very powerful. Tiffany, Maude-Griffin, and Drobes (1991) repeatedly injected rats with morphine in a distinctive environment. When they later tested pain sensitivity in that environment following an injection of morphine, they found that rats previously injected in that environment required six times as much morphine as control rats did to produce a set level of analgesia.

Siegel has suggested that the conditioning of compensatory reactions to environmental cues could also explain drug overdoses. Heroin, for example, will elicit compensatory reactions, and these responses become conditioned to the environment in which the heroin is injected. If an addict then takes heroin in a new setting, the conditioned compensatory reaction will be weaker and the effects of the heroin correspondingly magnified. In support of this hypothesis, Siegel (1984) interviewed survivors of heroin overdoses and found that 70 percent of the overdoses occurred when heroin was injected in an unfamiliar setting. Further evidence comes from a study by Siegel, Hinson, Krank, and McCully (1982) in which rats received daily injections of heroin to develop their tolerance and were then given a greatly increased dose in the test phase. Of the rats that were given the overdose in their same training environment, 32 percent died. If the overdose was administered in a different environment, however, 64% of the subjects succumbed. When drugs are administered repeatedly, conditioned compensatory reactions seem to play a vital role in determining how they affect us.

Taste-aversion learning. Many of the autonomic responses to illness can also be classically conditioned. When we become ill after eating spoiled food, for example, the nausea that we experience may become conditioned to the taste of the food. In one of the first demonstrations of **taste-aversion learning,** Garcia and Koelling (1966) began by offering rats a choice between two water bottles, one of which contained normal water and the other a water solution with a distinctive flavor. Once they had established that the rats had no preference between the two, they ran a conditioning phase in which the rats were allowed to drink the flavored water for 20 minutes and then exposed to X rays that would make them ill. After the rats had recovered, Garcia and Koelling again offered them a choice between the two solutions. They found that while the rats were still willing to drink the normal water, consumption of the flavored water was substantially reduced. It appeared that the aversive properties of illness had been conditioned to the taste that preceded it, so that the rats were no longer willing to drink it. (See Section 3.3 for a fuller account of this study and its implications.)

In the Garcia and Koelling study, no direct measure of the conditioned response was available; the experimenters could only infer that the flavor made the rats feel ill from the fact that they refused to drink it. In some subsequent studies, however, this assumption has been confirmed more directly. In a dramatic study by Gustavson, Garcia, Hankins, and Rusiniak (1974), for example, coyotes were made ill after eating meat; the next time they were offered this meat, they all avoided it and some actually vomited. Studies of taste-aversion learning in humans also suggest that the tastes paired with illness become repugnant. In a survey by Logue, Ophir, and Strauss (1981), for example, 65% of the college students interviewed reported at least one aversion to a food that had been acquired through association with illness, and of this subgroup 83% reported that the food tasted aversive. Interestingly, many reported disliking this taste even though they knew that their illness had actually been caused by something else, such as the flu. Such results suggest that classical conditioning may not be a conscious or rational process: Even if we are confident that a CS will no longer be followed by a US—that eating a certain food will not make us ill, or that new techniques mean that going to a dentist will not be painful—the CS might still elicit emotions that were conditioned to it in a previous incident. (See Section 4.6 for further discussion of this possibility.)

Taste-aversion learning might play an important role in determining what foods we eat. One practical illustration concerns the use of chemotherapy as a treatment for cancer. Many patients who receive chemotherapy lose a substantial amount of weight. It was generally assumed that this weight loss reflected some direct effect on metabolic processes, but Bernstein (1978) suggested that at least part of this weight loss might be due to classical conditioning. Perhaps, she suggested, the foods eaten before each treatment become aversive through conditioning. As treatment continues, and more and more foods are followed by illness, patients' normal diet may increasingly elicit feelings of nausea, leading to the observed reduction in the amount eaten.

To test this hypothesis, Bernstein (1978) gave a group of cancer patients a distinctively flavored ice cream to eat one hour before undergoing chemotherapy. As predicted, they developed an aversion to this flavor. These results suggest that at least some of the weight loss caused by chemotherapy could be due to taste-aversion learning. (See also Jacobsen et al., 1993.) If so, it may prove possible to reduce this harmful effect in the future by applying conditioning principles—for example, having patients eat a special diet before treatment sessions, so that conditioning will occur to this food rather than to the normal diet.

Allergies. Classical conditioning might also be involved in allergies. Hay fever, for example, is an allergic reaction to pollens and grasses. The immune system reacts to these foreign substances by producing *antibodies* to destroy them; in allergic individuals, the body reacts too strongly and produces antibodies in quantities that actually damage tissues. This then causes symptoms such as sneezing and itchy eyes. Research on animals has shown that some of these allergic reactions can be classically conditioned. In one study guinea pigs were repeatedly sprayed with a substance that produced asthmatic attacks. The spraying apparatus produced a hissing sound, and eventually presentation of the hissing sound on its own was sufficient to produce an asthmatic attack (Justesen, Braun, Garrison, & Pendelton, 1970).

Conditioning of this kind might help to explain "psychosomatic" reactions in which individuals become ill in the absence of any apparent physical cause. In one striking case, a patient with an allergy to roses became ill when shown an artificial rose; in another, a patient who was allergic to goldfish suffered an asthmatic attack when shown a picture of a goldfish. (See Gauci, Husband, & King, 1992.) Such reactions are normally dismissed as psychosomatic, but they could be the result of classical conditioning. In the case of the rose, for example, the patient would typically have seen a rose before inhaling the allergens that triggered an allergic reaction; the conditioning of this reaction to the visual cues would then explain the allergic response to the sight of the artificial rose.

In summary, research on the conditioning of autonomic responses has burgeoned in recent years, largely because of the pioneering work of Siegel and also of Ader and Cohen (1985). In addition to the responses we have discussed, other autonomic responses that have been conditioned include the production of killer cells by the immune system, changes in body temperature, and reactions to amphetamines. The autonomic system controls a bewildering array of responses, and it is beginning to look as if a high proportion, perhaps all, can be classically conditioned.

Skeletal Conditioning

Conditioning is pervasive and powerful, insofar as autonomic responses are concerned. The list of skeletal responses that can be conditioned is not quite as impressive—in part because conditioning requires the existence of an unconditioned stimulus capable of eliciting the desired behavior, and the number of skeletal behaviors that can be elicited in this way is relatively small. Nevertheless, a significant number of skeletal responses can be conditioned—the eyeblink, the patellar or knee-jerk reflex, aggression, and so on—and in at least some of these cases the association formed is remarkably strong.

Autoshaping. A particularly interesting example was discovered almost by accident in the course of research into the effects of rewards. To study the effects of a reward on animal learning, it is typically necessary first to train the animal to perform some desired response, and this is done by shaping—first rewarding a response vaguely similar to the target behavior, then reinforcing a somewhat closer approximation, and so on. In research involving pigeons, for example, the birds typically are trained in a test cage that has a circular plastic disk, or key, mounted on one of its walls. To train the birds to peck the key, the experimenter first gives the birds food whenever they face the wall containing the key, then for moving their heads slightly toward the key, and so on.

 This process can be laborious and time-consuming, and there was thus considerable interest when Brown and Jenkins (1968) announced the discovery of an automatic procedure for shaping key-pecking, which they called **autoshaping.** All the experimenter had to do was place the bird in a box and then collect it half an hour later; automatic programming equipment did the rest. Roughly once a minute, the key was illuminated for eight seconds, at the end of which the bird was given access to food for four seconds. Within two sessions, all 36 birds tested were pecking the key when it was illuminated.

 At first, autoshaping was seen largely as a convenient practical tool, but it eventually struck people that something very strange was going on. There was no need for the birds to peck; they received food at the end of every trial regardless of their behavior. Nevertheless, the birds all soon responded vigorously on every trial. Did the birds just like pecking lighted keys, or was it conceivable that the pecking behavior elicited by the food was being conditioned to the preceding key light? Evidence for the conditioning interpretation was actually present in the original study, because Brown and Jenkins had included a condition in which the key light followed the food rather than preceding it. Only 2 out of 12 birds exposed to this condition began to peck the key. In other words, pigeons do not simply peck lighted keys; the response develops only when the key light and food are paired. (See also Jenkins & Moore, 1973.)

Sign tracking. Brown and Jenkins specifically measured pecking at the key as the conditioned response, but subsequent research has made it clear that birds and other animals will engage in a variety of behaviors to bring themselves into contact with stimuli predicting food. If the bird is at the opposite end of the box when the light comes on, for example, it will come to the key to peck. Rats will also approach and contact a bar whose illumination is paired with food (Peterson, Ackil, Frommer, & Hearst, 1972). Pavlov (1941) also observed such behavior in his experiments: When a dog was removed from its harness after conditioning trials in which a light was paired with food, it would go over to the light and lick it!

In the natural environment, behavior of this kind would generally be adaptive, because the stimulus that most reliably precedes the ingestion of food generally is the food, or, more accurately, aspects of the food such as its appearance or odor. There is thus adaptive value to an animal's tracking and making contact with any stimulus that reliably precedes the ingestion of food. For this reason, Hearst and Jenkins (1974) have suggested **sign tracking** as a generic term to cover autoshaping and similar situations in which animals approach and contact a stimulus that signals a US. Under the artificial conditions of the laboratory, sign tracking can produce seemingly useless behaviors such as a pigeon pecking a plastic key, but in real life it is more likely to result in the pigeon's approaching and pecking grain lying on the ground, or a lion tracking the sounds made by an antelope moving through the bush. These behaviors are crucial to survival, and classical conditioning plays an important role in guiding animals to the stimuli that predict food.

Conditioned Motivation

The skeletal and autonomic responses we have examined so far have all involved relatively discrete, easily specified responses such as salivation, blinking, and perspiration. In some cases, however, the conditioned response appears to be a more complex state, which, when aroused, has the capacity to motivate any of a wide range of responses.

Hunger. To illustrate the distinction between a specific response and a motivational state, consider the following experiment by Weingarten (1983). Seven hungry rats were exposed to repeated pairings of a 4.5-minute tone with the presentation of food. Then, in a test phase, the rats were given continuous access to food so that they were sated. Nevertheless, when the tone was again presented, they immediately began to eat, consuming approximately 20 percent of their normal daily ration within a short period. A CS that had been paired with food, in other words, seemed to acquire the capacity to elicit hunger, so that the rats would eat whenever the CS was presented.

You might have experienced a comparable phenomenon in passing a bakery, where the smell of freshly baked bread suddenly made you feel hungry. The conditioned response in this case does not seem to be a single, well-defined response, but rather a broader motivational state that could lead to any of a number of behaviors directed toward satisfying it, such as buying the bread or hurrying home to eat a snack. (See also Zamble, 1967.)

Growing evidence indicates that classical conditioning plays a pervasive role in regulating every aspect of eating, from triggering hunger through guiding our choice of food to ending our meal. The first evidence for this role came from Pavlov, who suggested that we learn what foods are edible partly through conditioning. Puppies reared on milk did not salivate when shown solid food for the first time, suggesting that they did not recognize it as food. Only after the visual appearance of the food was paired several times with ingestion did the sight of the food begin to elicit salivation.

Conditioning might also influence our preferences between different foods. We tend to assume that our food preferences are innate, and up to a point this is so—infants, for example, have an innate preference for sweet tastes over bitter ones. The components of foods that are good for us, however, do not always have distinctive tastes. We all need the vitamin thiamin, for example (thiamin deficiency causes a deadly condition called beriberi), but foods containing thiamin do not have a distinctive taste. How, then, do we manage to regulate our diet in a way that ensures sufficient quantities?

Zahorik (1977) has summarized extensive research on the regulation of thiamin intake in rats, evidence that points to an important role of classical conditioning. If rats are fed a diet lacking in thiamin, they become ill, and as a result they develop an aversion to the foods they eat during this period. This leads the rats to switch to other foods, and if they recover while eating these foods they develop a positive preference for them. In other words, food tastes paired with illness become aversive, whereas tastes paired with recovery from illness become preferred, a conditioning process that allows rats to home in on the foods they need to survive.

In a similar fashion, rats develop a preference for foods that are high in calories. In an experiment by Capaldi, Campbell, Sheffer, and Bradford (1987), rats were given a flavored liquid and then, 30 minutes later, a meal. The greater the caloric value of the meal, the more the rats preferred that flavor in a later choice test. (See also Lucas & Timberlake, 1992.) Finally, conditioning can also induce satiety: If a stimulus that has been associated with high-calorie meals is presented to rats while they are eating, they will reduce how much they eat. It thus appears that conditioning influences not only when we feel hungry but what foods we choose to satisfy this hunger and when we stop eating them. (For reviews, see Rozin & Zellner, 1985; Capaldi, 1996.)

Fear. Another motivational state that can strongly influence our behavior is fear. Before we can decide whether fear is conditionable, however, we need a way to measure it. In the case of human subjects, we could simply ask them how frightened they are, but people are not always aware of their fear, and even when they are they may not want to admit it. Thus, although introspective reports can provide some information, psychologists want a more objective method of measuring fear. One early solution for measuring fear in animals was to count feces: The more frightened a rat is, the more it will urinate and defecate. Feces counts, however, not only are unpleasant for the experimenter but also have severe technical limitations. Although feces counts give a good indication of a rat's initial fear level, there are distinct physiological limits to how long a rat will defecate. Thus, there are limits to the usefulness of this method for assessing long-term fear.

A far more satisfactory solution on all counts was devised by Estes and Skinner (1941) and is known as the **conditioned emotional response (CER)** procedure. It is based on the simple observation that frightened animals in a cage tend to freeze. By observing how long an animal remains immobile in the presence of a stimulus, therefore, we can gain a rough idea of how frightening that stimulus is. Estes and Skinner developed an ingeniously simple technique for measuring freezing automatically, without the experimenter having to be present. (As we shall see again in Chapter 6, Skinner was concerned throughout his career with finding the most efficient ways to run experiments.) The first step in their procedure was to train rats to press a bar to obtain food. At first, the rats received a pellet of food for every press, but the proportion of responses that produced food was gradually reduced, until eventually the rats would press the bar steadily, without pausing, for long periods. At this point, the experimenters could present the stimulus they wanted to test. If the stimulus elicited fear, the rats would freeze, with the obvious result that their responding on the bar would be reduced. By counting the number of bar-presses made in the presence of a test stimulus, therefore, we obtain a simple and objective measure of the rats' fear.

In practice, a more useful index of fear is obtained by calculating a statistic known as a **suppression ratio.** If a tone is presented for three minutes, for example, we count the number of bar-presses that occur not only during the tone (B) but also during the preceding three minutes (A). The suppression ratio is then defined as

$$suppression\ ratio = \frac{B}{A + B}$$

Suppose, for example, that a rat responded 50 times during the period before the tone was presented. If the tone was not frightening, the rat would continue to respond at roughly the same rate in its presence, so that it would also respond 50 times during period B. The suppression ratio would thus be:

$$\frac{B}{A + B} = \frac{50}{50 + 50} = 0.50$$

If, on the other hand, the tone elicited fear, the rat would freeze for as long as the tone was on, yielding a suppression ratio of:

$$\frac{B}{A + B} = \frac{0}{50 + 0} = 0$$

We thus have a somewhat unusual measure in which a lower score represents greater fear, with 0 representing the maximum measurable fear and 0.50 representing no fear.

Using the CER as a measure, many experiments have demonstrated that fear does become conditioned to stimuli that precede aversive events. To cite just one example, Annau and Kamin (1961) trained rats to press a bar to earn food, and then occasionally presented a three-minute noise followed by an electric shock. Different groups received shock intensities varying from 0.28 to 2.91 milliamps; Figure 2.16 shows the suppression ratios for the different groups on successive conditioning trials.

The first time the noise was presented, on day 1, it produced no fear in any of the groups (a suppression ratio of 0.50). In the group that received a very mild shock (0.28 volts), this remained the case on subsequent days: Presentation of the noise had no effect on bar pressing, and the suppression ratio remained at 0.50. For subjects receiving a 0.49 milliamps, responding was reduced by the noise, leading to a sharp fall in the suppression ratio. As training continued, however, the noise began to have less effect, and the suppression ratio began to increase. A noise paired with a mild shock, in other words, did induce fear at first, but with continued exposure subjects seemed to adapt to the shock and find it less frightening. Finally, when more severe shocks were used, a single conditioning trial was sufficient to suppress responding almost totally (the suppression ratio on trial 2 was close to 0), and it remained suppressed on subsequent trials. These results suggest that more intense shocks produce stronger conditioning of fear, and this fear is more likely to endure.

Sexual arousal. The conditioning of sexual behavior was first reported in a study of Japanese quail by Farris (1967). Courtship in these birds normally involves a ritualized display by the male in which it circles the female while holding its body horizontal and strutting on its toes; eventually, the male begins to puff out its feathers and emit hoarse, vibrating calls. To see if this ritual could be conditioned, Farris placed male quail in a cage, sounded a buzzer for 10 seconds, and then opened a door, giving the male access to a receptive female. Within 15–20 pairings, all the males began to strut around the cage when the buzzer sounded, and within a few more trials they were puffing out their feathers

FIGURE 2.16   Acquisition of a conditioned emotional response (CER) over 10 days. Different groups received electrical shocks ranging in intensity from 0.28 milliamps to 2.91 milliamps. (Annau & Kamin, 1961)

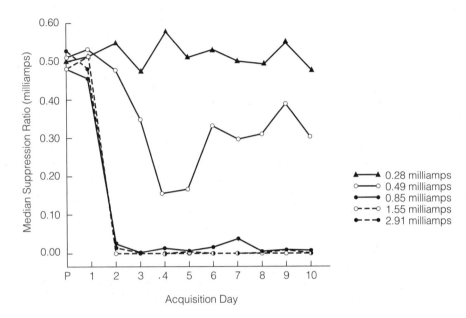

and vibrating vigorously! Subjects in an unpaired control, on the other hand, showed no reaction to the buzzer.

Farris's results suggest that stimuli associated with sexual intercourse (or even with the appearance of a member of the opposite sex) can come to elicit sexual arousal. Although we tend to think of sexual attraction as innately determined, learning seems to play an important role for many species. Studies of rats, for example, have shown that experienced male rats come to prefer the odor of receptive females to that of nonreceptive females (Carr, Loeb, & Dissinger, 1965), and it seems plausible to think that this could be the result of a conditioning process in which the receptive female's odor is paired with intercourse. This conditioning interpretation is supported by a later study in which male rats were exposed to a distinctive odor followed by access to a receptive female; subsequent presentations of this odor increased secretion of testosterone, a hormone that plays a critical role in male sexual behavior (Graham & Desjardins, 1980). Such evidence suggests that classical conditioning plays a significant role in many species in focusing males' sexual behavior on appropriate stimuli (Domjan, 1992).

Evidence that classical conditioning also plays an important role in human sexual behavior comes from a study by Rachman and Hodgson (1968). The subjects were seven male volunteers, and the unconditioned stimuli used to produce sexual arousal were 40 slides of nude women. Each slide was preceded by a CS, a picture of knee-length, black, fur-lined boots. The picture of the boots was projected for 30 seconds, followed by 10 seconds of one of the nude slides. To assess sexual arousal, penile erection was measured by means of a rubber tube whose stretching could be monitored by an automatic recording system.

Initially, none of the subjects showed any sign of arousal to the boots. After only 30 pairings, however, strong arousal had been conditioned in five of the seven subjects, with an erection occurring every time the boots were presented. This response, moreover, generalized to similar stimuli: Three of the subjects also became aroused to brown fur boots, two to high-heeled black shoes, but none to low-heeled black shoes or sandals. At the conclusion of the experiment, sexual arousal to the boots was extinguished by repeatedly presenting the boots by themselves.

This experiment might arouse mixed feelings (it is almost sinister in some respects, hilarious in others), but its implications are potentially important. If sexual arousal is conditioned to the stimuli present when we become aroused, this conditioned arousal could influence what stimuli we then find exciting, and thus channel our sexual behavior. For example, conditioning of this kind could play an important role in the development of abnormal behaviors such as fetishes. In one case reported by McGuire, Carlisle, and Young (1965), a 17-year-old male saw through a window a girl dressed only in her underwear. Thereafter, he often masturbated while recalling this image and eventually developed a strong sexual obsession with female underwear, which he bought or stole. Whether all fetishes develop in this way, it appears that classical conditioning can play a significant role in channeling sexual behavior.

2.5 A Universal Process?

Pavlov proposed that if two brain centers are active at the same time, the link between them will be strengthened. If so, this should occur not only when a CS is paired with a US, but also when *any* stimuli occur together and thus their cortical centers are active at the same time. If a tone is closely followed by a light, for example, these stimuli should become associated in exactly the same way as a tone and food.

Sensory Preconditioning

Support for this prediction has come from research on **sensory preconditioning**. Demonstrations of this phenomenon involve three phases. In the first, two neutral stimuli—for example, a tone and a light—are presented together. In the second, one of these stimuli is paired with a US. Finally, the stimulus not

FIGURE 2.17   Sensory preconditioning: (a) illustrates the procedures used to produce sensory preconditioning; (b) presents one interpretation of the associations that are formed as a result.

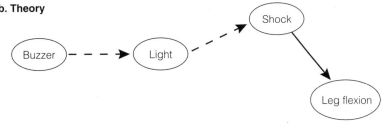

a. Procedure

Sensory preconditioning: Buzzer ⟶ Light

Conditioning: US_{shock} ⟶ $UR_{leg\ flexion}$

CS_{light}

b. Theory

Buzzer ⤏ Light ⤏ Shock ⟶ Leg flexion

paired with the US is presented to see if it too will now elicit a conditioned response. In one of the first demonstrations of this phenomenon, Brogden (1939)
gave dogs preliminary training in which a buzzer was paired with a light. Then,
in the conditioning phase, he paired the light with a mild shock to the paw,
which elicited leg flexion (Figure 2.17a). When he then presented the buzzer, it
too elicited flexion.

The most plausible explanation of this phenomenon is that when the buzzer
was paired with the light during the preconditioning phase, an association was
formed between them. During conditioning, a second association was formed
between the light and the shock (Figure 2.17b). When the buzzer was presented
during testing, excitation was transmitted from the representation of the buzzer
to the light, and from there to the shock. Or, in terms of expectations, the dogs
had learned that the buzzer was followed by light and then that the light was
followed by shock; when they heard the buzzer during the test phase, they expected the shock to follow and therefore flexed their legs.

Sensory preconditioning can take place when two events are presented simultaneously, as well as when one precedes the other. In an experiment by
Rescorla (1980b), for example, rats were allowed to drink water flavored with
two distinctive tastes, and one of these tastes was then paired with illness. A

test phase revealed that the rats had developed an aversion to both tastes, and a control group established that this occurred only if the tastes were presented together in the first phase. Results such as these support the view that associative learning is a general process in which any stimuli that occur together can become associated.

Contextual Conditioning

Further evidence that brain centers active at the same time become associated has come from research on the role of contextual cues in conditioning. In a typical conditioning experiment in which a light is paired with food, the light is not the only stimulus present when food is presented. For example, the experiment takes place in a particular setting—perhaps a room in a laboratory, or a cage—and the visual appearance and odors of the setting provide contextual cues that are present throughout the experiment.

If associations are formed whenever stimuli occur together, we might expect the US to become associated with these contextual cues as well as with the CS, and this prediction has been confirmed in several experiments. One example we have already encountered comes from Siegel's (1975) research on morphine conditioning. He found that compensatory responses to morphine could be conditioned not only to the CS of injection but also to the room in which the injection was given, as rats returned to that room showed an increased sensitivity to pain.

The term **contextual conditioning** is used to describe conditioning to environmental cues that are present throughout an experiment. In Siegel's experiment, the context was simply associated with the US, but contextual cues can also influence the association formed between the CS and the US. We can illustrate this more complex role of contextual cues with an experiment by Bouton and Bolles (1979). In the first phase of this study, rats were given fear conditioning trials in which a tone was paired with shock. Then, to extinguish this fear, subjects were repeatedly presented with the tone on its own. For some subjects, these extinction trials took place in the same box used during the conditioning phase, but for others the tone was presented in a second box with a very different appearance. Finally, all subjects were returned to the first box for a CER test to see if the tone still elicited any fear:

Conditioning	Extinction	CER test
Tone → shock	Tone → __	Tone → ?

The results for the first group, given conditioning and extinction trials in the same apparatus, were as you might expect: The extinguished tone produced no signs of fear. The results for the group given extinction trials in a different apparatus, however, were drastically different: Not only did the tone elicit strong fear, but the level of fear was exactly the same as in a control group given conditioning but not extinction. In other words, the extinction trials in the second box might just as well never have taken place, as the tone elicited the same amount of fear in box 1 as it had at the end of conditioning.

What appears to have happened is that during conditioning subjects learned that the tone signaled shock. When the tone was presented on it own in a second box, they did not learn simply that the tone no longer signaled shock, but rather that *the tone did not signal shock in box 2*. When returned to box 1, therefore, the rats assumed that the tone still signaled shock in this apparatus just as it had previously, and so became frightened. The implication is that when a CS is paired with a US, subjects might learn not simply that they are related but that they are related in a particular environment. In the Bouton and Bolles study, the rats appear to have learned that whether a tone signals shock depends on what box they are in at the time.

Often a signal has one meaning in one context but quite a different meaning in another. If you see a group of adolescents shouting "kill them," for example, this can have a very different meaning if said at a high school football game than in an alley late at night. Contextual cues help us to interpret the meaning of such signals, and they seem to play the same role in classical conditioning. (For more extensive reviews of the diverse roles played by contextual cues in conditioning, see Balsam & Tomie, 1985; Bouton, 1994; Swartzentruber, 1995.)

Multiple Associations

The evidence for sensory preconditioning and contextual conditioning supports the view that any stimuli that are contiguous will become associated. If so, the number of associations formed during conditioning trials might be much greater than our analysis until this point has implied. Suppose, for example, that rats in a taste aversion experiment were allowed to drink a water solution containing two distinctive tastes and were then made ill. Each of these tastes would probably become associated with the US, but the evidence we have reviewed in this section suggests that a number of other associations would probably also be formed. To start with, the two tastes would be likely to become associated with each other. Also, the contextual cues might become associated with the US. And, though we have not presented evidence on this point, there is good reason to suppose that these contextual cues would also become associated with the tastes (for example, Rescorla, Grau, & Durlach, 1985). In other words, the situation during conditioning would not be the simple one represented in Figure 2.18a, but rather something closer to that represented in Figure 2.18b, with associations being formed between all the stimuli present.

We shall see in later sections that this picture is not quite right: Contiguous stimuli are not always associated. (See Chapters 4 and 9.) Nevertheless, the true picture in conditioning experiments seems to be closer to the multiple-association

FIGURE 2.18   Associations formed during classical conditioning. (a) The CS–US association.
(b) Other associations that can also be formed.

a.

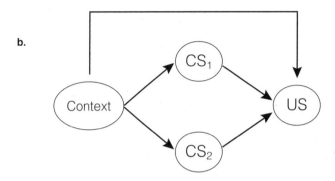

b.

analysis presented in *b* than to the single-association view presented in *a*. As Pavlov and the British Associationists suggested, the brain does have a strong tendency to associate whatever events occur together.

2.6 SUMMARY

The first attempt to explain human behavior through lawful principles was by Descartes, who attributed involuntary movements of the body to simple connections—which he called reflexes—between sensory receptors and muscles. The British Associationists extended Descartes's argument by proposing that thinking was also controlled by simple principles. Ideas were formed through associations between sensations, and thought was guided by associations between ideas that had previously occurred together. The idea that associations were critical in regulating behavior received further support when physiological research revealed that activity in the brain is determined by the transmission of electrical signals between cells called neurons, and thus that the strength of the connections between neurons is ultimately the crucial factor determining all behavior and thought. If we could understand the processes involved in the formation of associations, therefore, we might have the key to understanding human behavior.

This belief explained much of the excitement over Pavlov's discovery of the conditioned reflex. Pavlov found that if a tone (the CS) was paired with food (the US), dogs would eventually salivate to the tone just as they had to the food. To explain this result, Pavlov suggested that the CS and US each triggered activity within some region of the dog's brain, and that when two centers within the brain become active within a short period of time, the connection between these centers is strengthened. By studying how salivation was conditioned under highly controlled conditions, Pavlov hoped that it would be possible to discover the laws governing the formation of all associations.

One of the characteristics of classical conditioning discovered by Pavlov was extinction: If a CS was presented by itself after conditioning, the conditioned response would gradually weaken, or extinguish. The excitatory connection between the CS and US was clearly still present, however, because responding to the CS spontaneously recovered with the passing of time. To explain the disappearance of responding during extinction, Pavlov postulated the formation of a new, inhibitory association that counterbalanced the excitatory connection. Support for this inhibitory process comes from the phenomenon of conditioned inhibition, in which a CS– occasionally accompanies the CS+, and the US is not presented on these compound trials. As a result, the inhibitory CS– acquires the capacity to block, or inhibit, responding. This inhibitory potential can be measured using a summation test, in which the CS– is presented with a new CS+ that has been paired with the same US, or a retardation test, in which the CS– is itself paired with that US until conditioning occurs.

Pavlov discovered another way to eliminate a conditioned response, which was to condition a new response to the CS that was incompatible with the old response; this procedure is called counterconditioning. If a mild shock is paired with food, for example, it will eventually cease to elicit any signs of fear, and instead the dog will simply salivate.

Pavlov also found that the response conditioned to one CS could be transferred to a second CS by pairing the two stimuli. Such second-order conditioning might play an important role in establishing emotional or evaluative responses to stimuli; this might be why candidates' speeches in political advertisements are accompanied by patriotic music.

Yet another characteristic of conditioning discovered by Pavlov was generalization, in which the response conditioned to a CS would spread, or generalize, to similar stimuli. Generalization can be reduced, however, if subjects are given discrimination training in which a CS+ and a CS– are alternated, with only the CS+ followed by the US. At first, subjects tend to respond to both stimuli, but with continued training only the CS+ will elicit the response.

When psychologists in the West learned of Pavlov's research on salivation, they wanted to explore what other aspects of behavior could be conditioned, but it gradually became apparent that there were serious methodological problems in assessing conditioning. To determine whether a response is conditionable, it is not enough to pair a CS with a US and then see if the CS elicits the response. Any change could reflect sensitization (caused by presentation of the CS by itself), pseudoconditioning (caused by presentation of the US by itself), or an interaction between them. One way to control for these effects is to use an unpaired control group, in which the CS and US are presented separately.

Using this control, psychologists found that conditioning affects a wide range of skeletal and autonomic responses. Among the autonomic responses that can be conditioned are arousal (in the form of the GSR), blood sugar levels, sensitivity to pain, aversions to food, and activation of the body's immune system. The range of skeletal responses that can be classically conditioned is smaller, but one that has proven of particular importance for research purposes is key-pecking in pigeons, which can be autoshaped by pairing illumination of a key with the presentation of food.

In addition to these specific responses, conditioning can elicit more general motivational states. If a tone is paired with food, for example, the tone might come to elicit not only salivation but also hunger, which then can motivate a wide range of behaviors directed toward obtaining food. Among the motives that can be conditioned in this way are hunger, fear, and sexual arousal.

Far from being confined to salivation, then, conditioning is a remarkably general phenomenon, affecting responses ranging from blinking and salivation to our most powerful emotions. In the words of Hilgard and Bower (1981, p. 58), "It would seem that almost anything that moves, squirts or wriggles could be conditioned." If we only knew the principles involved—that is, what factors determine the strength of conditioning—then we might be able to use conditioning to significantly alter human behavior. In Chapter 3 we will examine what we now know about these principles, and consider how successful psychologists have been in their attempts to apply them.

The fact that conditioning occurs with so many different CS's and US's supports Pavlov's hypothesis that any brain centers that are active at the same time will become associated. Further evidence for this view comes from the phenomenon of sensory preconditioning, in which two neutral stimuli are presented together and then one of them is paired with a US. The typical result is that both stimuli acquire the capacity to elicit the conditioned response, an outcome that suggests that the stimuli became associated when they were presented together in the first phase. Additional support for this view comes from contextual conditioning, in which responding is conditioned not only to the CS but also to the apparatus or place in which conditioning occurs. Although we shall later find that we need to modify this hypothesis, it appears that the brain has a strong tendency to associate any stimuli that occur together.

Glossary

Contiguity A fundamental principle believed to underlie the formation of associations. This principle stipulates that events that occur together become associated.

Neuron A cell in the body specialized to produce and transmit electrical impulses.

Dendrites Fibers that branch out from the cell body of a neuron to make contact with other neurons.

Axon The elongated section of a neuron that transmits an electrical impulse generated in the cell body to other neurons or muscles.

Synaptic cleft The very small space that separates the axon terminals of one neuron from the dendrites of a second neuron. Neurotransmitters flow across this gap to transmit signals from the first neuron to the second one.

Neurotransmitters Chemicals that are stored within the terminals of a neuron. When an electrical signal arrives at the terminal, it causes the release of neurotransmitters, which then move across the synaptic gap to stimulate another neuron.

Cerebral cortex The outer section of the vertebrate brain. It is the center of higher functions such as thought and language.

Trial In a learning experiment, a discrete opportunity for a subject to learn. In classical conditioning, a single pairing of a CS and a US is called a trial.

Conditioned response (CR) The response to a conditioned stimulus caused by pairings of the CS with a US.

Unconditioned response (UR) The response elicited by an unconditioned stimulus.

Conditioned stimulus (CS) A stimulus that, through pairing with an unconditioned stimulus, elicits a response.

Unconditioned stimulus (US) A stimulus that elicits a response without training.

Classical conditioning An increase in the probability of a response to a conditioned stimulus (CS) as a result of pairings of that stimulus with an unconditioned stimulus (US). Older definitions of conditioning required that the response to the CS be the same as the response to the US, but it is now clear that these responses sometimes differ.

Rescorla (1988) has proposed defining classical conditioning more broadly as the learning of relationships among events. We prefer the term associative learning for the broader case, with classical conditioning restricted to instances of associative learning in which both events are stimuli and the second stimulus elicits an unconditioned response (or, in the case of second-order conditioning, the second stimulus elicits a conditioned response).

Extinction The weakening of a conditioned response when a CS is presented by itself.

Spontaneous recovery An increase in the strength of an extinguished response after a period of time following the last extinction trial.

Conditioned inhibition A tendency for a stimulus to inhibit, or block, the response normally elicited by a CS. A variety of different procedures can be used to establish a stimulus as a conditioned inhibitor, but generally the conditioned inhibitor signals that a US that normally would have occurred is not going to be presented. As a result, the conditioned inhibitor acquires the capacity to block the conditioned response normally elicited by the CS. One way of measuring the inhibitory properties of a stimulus is with a **summation test,** in which the stimulus is presented together with a CS+ to see if it will reduce responding. A second measure is a **retardation test,** in which the stimulus is paired with a US to see if conditioning will be slower.

Second-order conditioning Learning that takes place as a result of pairing a stimulus with a previously conditioned stimulus.

Counterconditioning A technique for eliminating a conditioned response that involves pairing a CS with another US to condition a new response. If the new response is incompatible with the old response, so that only one response can occur at a time, then the new response can replace the old one.

Generalization Responding to a test stimulus as a result of training with another stimulus. The response is said to have generalized from the training to the test stimulus.

Discrimination Differential responding to two stimuli. In classical conditioning, this can be achieved by discrimination training, in which one stimulus (CS+) is followed by a US but the second stimulus (CS−) is not. As with many other terms in learning, the term *discrimination* can refer to the training procedure (alternating presentations of the CS+ and the CS−, with only the CS+ followed by the US) or to the result of this procedure (greater responding to CS+ than to CS−). The context in which the terms are used generally makes it clear which definition is intended.

Sensitization An increase in the strength of a reflex due to repeated presentations of the stimulus by itself.

Pseudoconditioning An increase in responding to a CS as a result of presentations of the US by itself.

Interaction effect An effect that can result when two variables are presented. Whenever the effect of two variables acting at the same time is different from the arithmetic sum of the effects of the two variables measured separately, an interaction effect is said to have occurred.

Unpaired control A control group in which the CS and the US are presented at widely separated times. An unpaired control is sometimes referred to as an explicitly unpaired control.

Skeletal responses Bodily movements controlled by the skeletal nervous system.

Autonomic responses Glandular and smooth muscle activities controlled by the autonomic nervous system.

Galvanic skin response (GSR) A measure of arousal in which electrodes are placed on the skin, and an electrical current is passed between them. The greater a person's arousal, the more they perspire and thus the stronger the current that will be conducted. Also known as the skin conductance response (SCR).

Homeostasis The attempts by the body to maintain a stable internal environment.

Taste-aversion learning A form of classical conditioning in which a subject develops an aversion for the taste or odor of a food because of that food's association with illness.

Autoshaping A procedure in which pigeons are trained to peck a key through pairings of illumination of that key with food.

Sign tracking The behavior of approaching and contacting a stimulus that has preceded an unconditioned stimulus such as food.

Conditioned emotional response (CER) A procedure for measuring fear based on the observation that frightened animals generally freeze. The stimulus to be tested is presented while subjects are responding to obtain a reward such as food. The reduction in their rate of responding to obtain food can be used as an indirect measure of their freezing, and thus of their fear.

Suppression ratio A statistical index used to measure the reduction in responding during a CER test. The index is $B/(A + B)$, where B is the number of responses during the test stimulus and A is the number of responses during an equivalent period immediately before the test stimulus.

Sensory preconditioning Learning resulting from a procedure in which two neutral stimuli are presented together and then one of them is paired with an unconditioned stimulus. The typical result is that responding is conditioned not only to the conditioned stimulus but also to the stimulus paired with it during the preconditioning phase.

Contextual conditioning Conditioning to the environmental cues that are present when unconditioned stimuli are presented.

Review Questions

1. Why did Pavlov's research attract so much attention?

2. What were the laws of association according to the British Associationists?

3. Pavlov believed that learning is "nothing more than the results of an establishment of new nervous connections." Is this consistent with what we know about how the brain works?

4. Why did Pavlov attribute extinction to an inhibitory process? What evidence supports his interpretation?

5. What is the difference between second-order conditioning and sensory preconditioning?

6. What is an unpaired control group? Why is it necessary?

7. What skeletal and autonomic behaviors can be classically conditioned? Why is the CR sometimes different from the UR?

8. What is the difference between an overt response and a motivational state? What evidence suggests that motivational states can be classically conditioned?

9. What role might classical conditioning play in determining food preferences, sexual arousal and psychosomatic illnesses in humans?

10. Describe the CER procedure and the use of suppression ratios to measure fear.

11. Pavlov believed that associations would be formed whenever two cortical centers were active at the same time. What evidence supports this view?

CHAPTER THREE

PRINCIPLES AND APPLICATIONS

The research reviewed in the previous chapter makes it clear that classical conditioning is not confined to relatively innocuous behaviors such as salivation; classical conditioning affects some of the most important aspects of our behavior, including the foods we eat, the functioning of our immune systems, and emotions such as fear and sexual arousal. If we understood the principles of conditioning, therefore, it might allow us not only to understand our behavior better but also, potentially, to use these principles to change our behavior. In the case of fear, for example, could we use conditioning to reduce our fear in situations where it incapacitates us (for example, in job interviews or dating)? Conversely, could we learn to increase our fear in situations where this might be desirable—for example, could a smoker who wanted to quit make smoking aversive by pairing the sensations of smoking with a painful consequence? In this chapter we will try to answer these questions. We will begin by reviewing laboratory research on what factors determine the strength of conditioning, and we will then look at some attempts to apply these principles to problems such as phobias and alcoholism.

3.1 THE LAWS OF ASSOCIATION

The British Associationists, sitting in their armchairs several centuries ago, identified a number of laws of association, of which the most important were contiguity, frequency, and intensity. We will begin our survey of the principles of conditioning by considering the extent to which these laws have been supported by experimental research.

Contiguity

The most important principle of association was thought to be *contiguity*. The very concept of an association—a bond between two events that occur

FIGURE 3.1   Paradigms for four varieties of classical conditioning. The bars on the time line indicate periods during which a stimulus is presented. In simultaneous conditioning, for example, the US occurs at the same time and for the same duration as the CS.

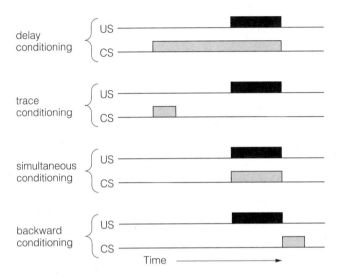

together—implicitly assumes that contiguity is necessary, and considerable effort has been devoted to exploring the role of contiguity in classical conditioning.

The CS–US sequence. As with most other aspects of conditioning, it was Pavlov who first investigated the role of contiguity in establishing a strong conditioned response. He experimented with four different temporal arrangements between the CS and the US. (See Figure 3.1.) In **delay conditioning,** once the CS came on, it remained on until the US was presented. In **trace conditioning,** the CS was terminated before the US began. As the British Associationists would have predicted, Pavlov found that conditioning was much stronger in the delay conditioning paradigm, where the CS and US were on at the same time.

The results obtained with the other two paradigms investigated by Pavlov, however, were not what the Associationists would have predicted. In **simultaneous conditioning,** the CS and the US came on at the same time. If contiguity is critical, as the Associationists believed, then conditioning should have been maximal, but in fact Pavlov found virtually no conditioning. Similarly, the CS and US were contiguous in **backward conditioning,** in which the US was presented before the CS, but again conditioning was poor.

These results seem contrary not only to the predictions of the Associationists but also to the evidence presented in Section 2.5 that any stimuli that are contiguous will be associated. In the sensory preconditioning experiment by Rescorla (1980b), for example, rats that drank a solution containing two distinctive tastes were later found to have associated them strongly. Why should simultaneous associations be formed easily in sensory preconditioning but only with great difficulty in simultaneous conditioning?

One possible explanation is distraction. In simultaneous conditioning, a CS and a US are presented at the same time. Because the US is invariably a much more powerful stimulus, attention to it may divert attention from the less salient CS and therefore reduce conditioning. (This is also known as *overshadowing*.) In sensory preconditioning, on the other hand, the two stimuli are both neutral, and subjects are probably more likely to attend equally to both. (See Rescorla, 1981, for an alternative interpretation.)

Another possibility, proposed by Matzel, Held, and Miller (1988), is that simultaneous and backward conditioning *do* produce strong CS–US associations; the problem is not that subjects don't learn about their relationship but rather that this knowledge is not translated into performance. In effect, the argument is that subjects know that the CS and US occur together, but that precisely because they occur together there is no point in making a conditioned response—there is not enough time to make a conditioned response before the US occurs, and so no reason to respond. In other words, as a contiguity analysis would suggest, simultaneous pairings of a CS with a US do result in the formation of a strong association between them; the problem is simply that this association does not lead to a response. (For further discussion of the issues involved in whether associations are translated into responses, see Section 4.5.)

It now appears that any arrangement in which a CS and a US are contiguous—whether the CS precedes the US, occurs simultaneously, or follows—can result in the formation of an association. Simultaneous and backward conditioning are much less likely to produce conditioned responses than is delay conditioning, but at least in part this seems to be caused by problems in performance rather than by a failure to form an association. In a sense, the British Associationists and Pavlov were both right. If the issue is whether associations are formed between contiguous stimuli, the evidence favors the Associationists: Simultaneous and backward conditioning can both produce strong associations. If the issue is how best to produce conditioned responses, however, then Pavlov's findings still provide the best guide: To obtain strong conditioning, the CS should precede the US and remain on until the US occurs.

The CS–US interval. Western psychologists conducted a series of experiments to determine systematically how the strength of conditioning changed as the interval between the CS and US increased. In a typical study, Moeller (1954) looked at the effects of the CS–US interval on GSR conditioning. He used a trace conditioning paradigm in which a 100-millisecond burst of white noise was followed after a delay by a weak electric shock, with the interval between the onset of the CS and the onset of the US (the interstimulus interval, or ISI) set at either 250, 450, 1000, or 2500 milliseconds (ms). Moeller's results are

FIGURE 3.2   GSR conditioning as a function of the CS–US interval during training.
(Adapted from Moeller, 1954)

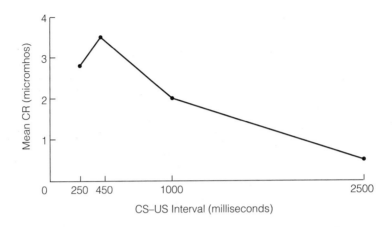

illustrated in Figure 3.2, which shows that the strength of the conditioned response was greatest in the group with a 450-ms gap, and that little or no conditioning occurred at delays of 1000 and 2500 ms. Also, as Pavlov's experiments on simultaneous conditioning had suggested, Moeller found that conditioning became weaker as the CS–US interval became very short, and thus the onset of the CS and US came closer to being simultaneous. In other studies, the decrement at short delays has been even more pronounced (McAllister, 1953).

Whatever the reasons for the difficulty of simultaneous conditioning, the optimal interval for GSR conditioning is roughly one-half second (about 500 ms), with trace conditioning becoming impossible at around two seconds (2000 ms). (For further discussion, see Rescorla, 1982; Hawkins & Kandel, 1984.) Both the optimum interval and the maximum interval that will sustain conditioning vary somewhat for different responses, but as a general rule the shorter the interval between the CS and the US, the better the conditioning. (See Cooper, 1991, for a discussion of the exceptions.)

Testa (1975) has reported evidence that conditioning is also influenced by spatial contiguity. He exposed rats to a light followed by a blast of air and found that fear conditioning was strongest if both stimuli came from the same area of the box. This result makes good sense if we think of conditioning as a mechanism that has evolved to help us detect causes and react to them appropriately. If we suddenly experience pain, for example, it is vital that we accurately identify the source of that pain so that we can avoid it in the future. One good clue to an event's cause is temporal contiguity: If the pain is in your foot, it is much more likely to have been caused by something you just stepped on than something you encountered an hour ago. Similarly, cause and effect are usually contiguous in space: Your foot pain is more likely to have been caused by something you stepped on, such as a snake, than by something overhead, such as a circling eagle. By making the likely cause of pain frightening, conditioning maximizes the chances that we will avoid the pain in the future.

Frequency

A second variable that the British Associationists thought determined the strength of an association between two events was the frequency of their pairing. Pavlov's research on salivary conditioning strongly supported this view (see Figure 2.6) and so has subsequent research. In general, the strength of the conditioned response seems to increase most during the early trials of conditioning, with the rate of increase gradually declining as training continues, until performance eventually reaches a stable plateau, or **asymptote.**

Intensity

The third major principle proposed by the British Associationists was that the strength of any association depends on the vividness or intensity of the stimuli involved; associations involving emotional or traumatic events, for example, will be remembered better. Again, controlled research on conditioning strongly supports this principle. Annau and Kamin (1961), for example, found that the amount of fear conditioned to a tone depends on the intensity of the shock used (see Figure 2.16). There is also evidence that the intensity of the CS is of some importance, although this effect appears weaker. (See Grice, 1968.)

On the whole, then, the speculations of the British Associationists have been strongly confirmed by research under controlled conditions. Associative learning really does depend on contiguity, frequency, and intensity.

3.2 CONTINGENCY

Until 1966, all the available evidence converged on a coherent and satisfying picture of conditioning in which the foundation stone was contiguity: If two events are contiguous, then an association will be formed between them. The strength of this association might be modulated by other factors such as the intensity of the stimuli involved. Fundamentally, though, conditioning appeared to be a simple process in which associations were automatically formed between contiguous events. In 1966, however, two landmark papers were published in *Psychonomic Science,* ironically a relatively obscure journal with a reputation for publishing competent but minor studies. These two papers posed a fundamental

FIGURE 3.3   Three CS–US contingencies: (a) The CS and the US are presented at random intervals. (b) The CS immediately precedes the US and is thus a perfect predictor of its occurrence. (c) The US tends to follow the CS but does not always do so.

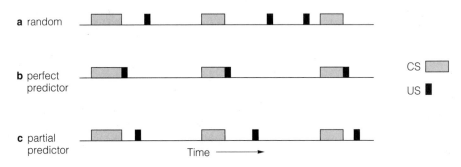

challenge to traditional views of the role of contiguity and unleashed an intellectual ferment—revolution would not be too strong a word—that continues to this day.

The Concept of Contingency

The first of these papers was the work of Robert Rescorla, then a graduate student at the University of Pennsylvania. In his paper, Rescorla suggested that contiguity between two events was not sufficient for conditioning; something more was needed. Specifically, Rescorla suggested that a CS must not only be contiguous with a US but must also be an accurate predictor of the occurrence of the US. Suppose, for example, that we expose rats to a sequence of tones and shocks delivered according to one of the three arrangements diagrammed in Figure 3.3. In all three cases the shocks are delivered at randomly chosen intervals, but the conditions differ in the timing of the tones. In **a,** the tones also are delivered at random, so the occurrence of a tone is of no value to the rat in predicting when the next shock is likely to occur; in **b,** a tone is presented just before each shock, so the tone is a highly accurate predictor; in **c,** an intermediate condition, shock is more likely when a tone has been presented but also occurs at other times.

A CS, then, can vary widely in its ability to predict a US, and it would be convenient if we had some mathematical measure of its predictive value. Indeed, several such measures are available, but we will focus on one measure termed a **contingency.** A contingency is a statistic derived from two probabilities: the probability that a US will occur in the presence of a CS—symbolized by $p(US \mid CS)$—and the probability that it will occur in the absence of the CS—$p(US \mid no\ CS)$. By combining these two probabilities with the appropriate formula, it is possible to calculate a contingency coefficient that measures the extent to which the CS and US occur together.[1]

In situation **a,** for example, suppose that the probability of a shock during a one-minute tone is 0.10, and that its probability in the absence of the tone is also 0.10:

$$p(shock \mid tone) \quad = 0.10$$
$$p(shock \mid no\ tone) = 0.10$$

Because the likelihood of a shock is the same regardless of whether the tone is presented, the tone is of no predictive value, and the contingency in this case is zero.

In **b,** on the other hand, the shock always occurs when the tone is presented and never occurs when it is absent:

$$p(shock \mid tone) \quad = 1.0$$
$$p(shock \mid no\ tone) = 0$$

The tone is a perfect predictor of the shock's occurrence, and the calculated contingency is 1.0.

Let us turn finally to situation **c.** We have seen that a shock is more likely during the tone than in its absence, but we have also seen that the tone is not a perfect predictor. Let us assume the following probabilities:

$$p(shock \mid tone) \quad = 0.60$$
$$p(shock \mid no\ tone) = 0.20$$

Given these probabilities, the contingency would be 0.41.

A contingency, in other words, gives us a simple mathematical summary of the degree of relationship between two events. If two events occur at random with respect to one another, there is no contingency. But the greater the linkage between their occurrences, the greater their contingency, to a maximum

---

[1] In the examples that follow, we have calculated the contingency between the tone and shock by using a nonparametric statistic called the *phi coefficient*. (See Siegel & Castellan, 1988.) To see how this works, imagine a simplified situation in which a session is divided into one-minute intervals, and that each of these intervals contains a CS, a US, both, or neither. We will use A to represent the number of intervals in which the CS and the US both occur; B the number of intervals in which only the CS occurs; C the number of intervals in which only the US occurs; and D the number of intervals in which neither occur. Under these conditions, the phi coefficient can be calculated as follows:

$$phi = \frac{\mid AD - BC \mid}{\sqrt{(A + B)\ (C + D)\ (A + C)\ (B + D)}}$$

This equation is presented only as background information; you will not need it to understand the examples that follow.

value of 1.0 when the two events always occur together. The greater the contingency between two events, the more useful one is as a predictor of the other.

You can check how well you understand all this by considering the following hypothetical situation: Suppose that you are a farmer who has just moved to a new county, and you need to be able to predict the probability of rain to decide whether to plant your corn. A salesperson for a weather forecasting company approaches you and tells you that the company has developed a new forecasting system that is far more accurate than any existing method. As proof, the salesperson shows you evidence that last year the company predicted rain on 100 days and it actually rained on 95 of those days. Should you buy the new forecasting service?

The answer, from the point of view of contingency, is no—or, at least, not necessarily. To determine the value of the company's predictions, you need to know not only the probability of rain when it was forecast, but also the probability when it was *not* forecast. Suppose, for example, that you had just moved to an area where it always rains on 95 days out of 100. Knowing the company's predictions would clearly be of very little aid in deciding whether rain was imminent. To evaluate the accuracy of any forecast or prediction, in other words, you need to consider not only how often the predicted event occurs when it is predicted but also how often it occurs when it is not predicted. If these probabilities are similar, then the prediction will not help you very much.

Contingency and Conditioning

A subject in a classical conditioning experiment faces a problem similar to that of the farmer who wants to predict rain. Consider, for example, a rat that suddenly becomes ill. If this illness were caused by food it had eaten earlier, it would obviously be advantageous for the rat to avoid that food in the future. In searching for a cue that could predict illness, however, the rat (like the farmer) might be seriously misled if it relied solely on contiguity. If the rat became ill after eating lima beans, for example, this would not necessarily mean that the lima beans had made the rat ill; if the rat became ill on days when it didn't eat lima beans as well as on days when it did, there would be no point to its avoiding lima beans in the future. In seeking to identify the true cause of an event, in other words, animals and humans would do better if they considered the contingency between two events as well as their contiguity.

Figure 3.3b illustrates a typical conditioning experiment. The CS and US are contiguous in time, and because they always occur together, there is also a perfect contingency between them. This contingency had largely been ignored by previous psychologists, who instead focused their experimental efforts on the role of contiguity. The assumption that an association will be formed between contiguous events was, after all, at the heart of the Associationist tradition, so it was only natural to assume that conditioning, too, would depend solely on

FIGURE 3.4   The procedure used by Rescorla (1968). Note that a tone is indicated by a shaded bar and a shock is indicated by a solid bar. A solid bar inside a shaded bar indicates that the tone and the shock occurred simultaneously. In the random group, the tone and the shock were presented at random. In the contingency group, shock was presented only during the CS. As indicated by the broken lines, both groups received the same number of shocks in the presence of the CS.

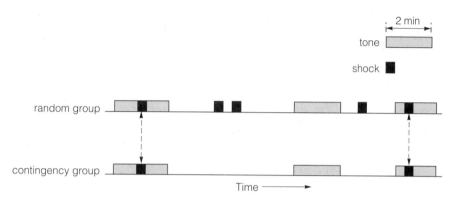

the contiguity of the CS and US. Rescorla, however, wondered whether animals might also take into account the degree of contingency between the two stimuli. What would happen, he asked, if a tone and shock were presented contiguously, as in most fear-conditioning experiments, but the shock was also presented in the absence of the tone, thereby eliminating their contingency?

Positive contingencies. Although Rescorla's initial work on contingency was published in 1966, we will look first at the results an experiment he reported in 1968. Figure 3.4 illustrates the design of this experiment. In the random group, rats received a series of tones and shocks delivered totally at random. Subjects in the contingency group received tones whenever their counterparts in the random group did, and they also received some—but not all—of the shocks delivered to subjects in the random group. Specifically, they received the shocks given to the random group while the tone was present but not when the tone was absent. Both groups thus received the same number of tones and the same number of pairings of the tone with the shock.

How should conditioning in the two groups compare? If conditioning depends simply on contiguity, then conditioning should be equal, since both had the same number of tone-shock pairings. If contingency also matters, however, then we should expect very different levels of conditioning in the two groups. In the contingency group, there is a strong contingency between the tone and shock; in the random group, there is no contingency. Insofar as contingency is important, therefore, conditioning should be substantially weaker in the random group, despite their receiving exactly the same number of pairings of tone

FIGURE 3.5   Fear conditioning as a function of tone-shock contingency. The probability of shock in the presence of the tone was 0.4 in all groups, but the probability of shock in the absence of the tone varied from zero to 0.4. Note that a suppression ratio of zero indicates strong fear; a suppression ratio of 0.5 indicates no fear. (Based on data from Rescorla, 1968)

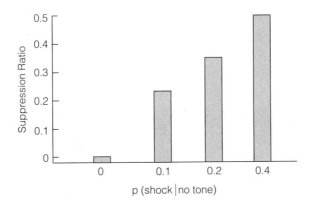

with shock. In accordance with this prediction, Rescorla found powerful conditioning in the contingency group: The rats totally stopped responding when the tone was presented in a CER test. But he found no conditioning whatsoever in the random group. In a second experiment, he varied the degree of contingency between the tone and shock by varying the probability of the shock in the tone's absence. He set the probability of shock in the presence of the tone at 0.40; he set the probability of shock in the absence of the tone at either 0, 0.10, 0.20, or 0.40. The more similar the probability of shock in the presence and absence of the tone, the weaker the contingency between them, and, as Figure 3.5 shows, the poorer the conditioning.

Negative contingencies. Conditioning, then, depends on the degree of contingency between the CS and the US: The more likely the US is in the presence of the CS compared with its absence, the greater will be the conditioning. What would happen, though, if there were a *negative* contingency between the two stimuli—if, for example, a shock occurred in the absence of the tone but not in its presence? You might be able to anticipate the answer: The CS now signals a reduced likelihood of shock and, therefore, will reduce or inhibit fear. Evidence for this conclusion comes from Rescorla's original report (1966), in which he compared groups exposed to either a positive, a negative, or a zero contingency between tone and shock.

Subjects in the zero-contingency, or random, group received 24 shocks and 24 tones, spaced randomly over a one-hour session. Subjects in the positive contingency group received the identical treatment, except that they received only those shocks that were programmed to occur within 30 seconds of the tone's

FIGURE 3.6   Rates of performing avoidance response before, during, and after the presentation of a five-second CS. During preceding conditioning trials, there was either a positive, a negative, or a zero (random) contingency between the CS and the shock. (Adapted from Rescorla, 1966)

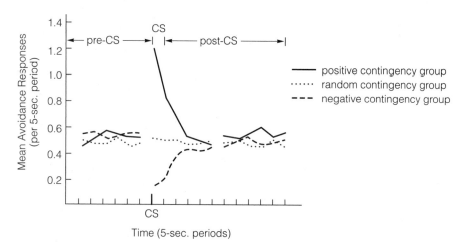

onset. Finally, the negative contingency group received the same 24 tones but only the shocks that were not scheduled to occur within 30 seconds of a tone. Thus, in the positive contingency group, a shock was more likely when a tone had been presented, whereas in the negative contingency group it was less likely.

To measure conditioned fear, Rescorla presented the tone while his subjects were responding on a Sidman avoidance task in which they had to jump over a barrier to prevent the delivery of electric shocks. The shocks were programmed to occur every 10 seconds, but whenever the subject jumped over the barrier, all shocks scheduled for the following 30 seconds were canceled. Subjects trained on this task quickly learn to jump over the barrier to avoid the shock, and their rate of jumping provides a sensitive index of their fear: The greater their fear, the more frequently they jump over the barrier (Rescorla & LoLordo, 1965).

Rates of performing the avoidance response before and during the presentation of a tone are shown in Figure 3.6. In the positive contingency group, responding doubled when the tone was presented, suggesting that substantial fear conditioning had taken place. In the random group, the tone had no effect, whereas in the negative contingency group the tone actually reduced responding. Just as a positive contingency between a CS and a US produces excitatory conditioning, a negative contingency produces inhibitory conditioning. Combining these results, it appears as if a CS must predict some change in the likelihood of the US for conditioning to occur. If the CS predicts an increase in the likelihood of the US, then we find excitatory conditioning; if the CS predicts a reduced likelihood, then we find inhibitory conditioning.

That conditioning depends on the contingency between the CS and US is really just a fancy way of saying that conditioning depends on the extent to which the CS predicts the US. In one sense, this is hardly surprising. If a tone and shock occur at random, for example, so that the tone signals no increase in the likelihood of the shock, it is not surprising that the tone elicits no fear. When viewed from the traditional perspective of contiguity, however, these results are deeply disturbing. If an association is formed when a CS and US occur contiguously, why was no conditioning found in Rescorla's random group? The tone and shock were paired repeatedly, and we know that such pairings can produce very powerful fear conditioning. How could occasional presentations of the shock by itself have prevented fear being conditioned to this tone?

Attempts to answer this question have opened up a veritable Pandora's box, since the apparent simplicity of conditioning has been found to conceal an elaborate and intricate network of cognitive subprocesses. Because of the complexity of the processes involved, we will postpone answering this question until we can explore these processes more systematically (Chapters 4 and 9). Before leaving Rescorla's experiments, however, we will consider one other implication of his results, concerning the appropriate control group for conditioning.

The random control. In Chapter 2, we suggested that to control for interaction effects we needed a group in which subjects received both CS and US, but unpaired. Specifically, we discussed the use of the unpaired control in which the CS and US are never presented together. Given Rescorla's results, however, we can now see that an unpaired group actually represents a negative contingency between the CS and US: The US never occurs in the presence of the CS, but it does occur in its absence. The CS in the unpaired group will not be neutral but will actually inhibit responding. If we want a control group in which no conditioning of any kind occurs, therefore, the unpaired group is clearly not appropriate. Rescorla (1967) suggested that we use a **random control**—a group for which the CS and US are presented completely at random rather than deliberately separated. The occasional pairings of the CS and US in this group might result in some conditioning, especially early in training (Kremer, 1971). However, if we present enough trials, the CS eventually becomes neutral, in the sense that it neither elicits nor inhibits the conditioned response (Keller, Ayres, & Mahoney, 1977).

It might seem that we have at long last found the ideal control group, but you might not be surprised to learn that the random control also has its problems. Seligman (1969) has argued that subjects exposed to a random contingency between tone and shock *do* learn: They learn that there is no correlation between the two events, and this knowledge can then affect their behavior in a variety of ways. Mackintosh (1973), for example, has shown that rats exposed to random presentations of a tone and shock have a difficult time learning to associate these events if they are later paired. It is as if the pretreatment phase teaches the rats that the two events are unrelated; as a result, they find it difficult to reverse this belief.

If what we are looking for is a control group in which no learning will occur, there probably is no such beast. As long as an organism is alive, learning of some kind about the environment is probably going to take place. We can control for the effects of contingency by using a random control, and we can control for the effects of contiguity by using an unpaired control. But no single procedure will simultaneously control for all possible alternative explanations.

Over the years, then, we have seen a substantial shift in the control groups used in conditioning experiments. As we have seen, it is not possible to control for all possible variables, just those that seem most plausible. As our understanding of a phenomenon increases, however, our knowledge of which variables affect it, and thus need to be controlled, will also increase. In the case of conditioning, the discovery of pseudoconditioning and the importance of contingency both led to major changes in control group methodology. Scientific progress thus involves a peculiar paradox: To determine which variables are important, we need to be able to control for the effects of other potentially important variables, but to do so we must know what variables are important—which is precisely what we are trying to establish in the first place! Fortunately for the sake of researchers as well as students, the paradox is not absolute and can be overcome by painstaking effort. The task is not nearly so simple as it might at first appear, though (Williams, Overmier, & LoLordo, 1992).

3.3 PREPAREDNESS

The second seminal paper of 1966 was by Garcia and Koelling, and they also challenged the assumption that any two events that were contiguous would be associated. In particular, these researchers challenged the idea that it did not matter what stimulus was chosen as a CS. Pavlov had claimed, "Any natural phenomenon chosen at will may be converted into a conditioned stimulus . . . any visual stimulus, any desired sound, any odor, and the stimulation of any part of the skin" (1928, p. 86). Subsequent research almost universally supported Pavlov's position—that is, until the publication of Garcia and Koelling's paper.

Taste-Aversion Learning

Garcia and Koelling's experiment had its origins in naturalistic observations of animal behavior—in particular, of a phenomenon in rats called bait-shyness. Rats, it turns out, resist human efforts to exterminate them. When left poisoned bait, they tend to take only the smallest taste at first; then, if they survive, they never touch that food again. Classical conditioning provides a possible explanation for the rats' avoidance of the bait: Ingestion of the poisoned bait produces nausea, and this reaction becomes conditioned to the gustatory and olfactory cues that precede the nausea. On future occasions, the rats avoid the bait because its odor or taste makes them ill. As we saw in Chapter 2, this phenomenon is known as taste-aversion learning.

As plausible as this explanation is, it cannot account for one aspect of the rats' behavior. Although the poisoned rats later avoided the bait, they showed no reluctance to return to the place where they had been poisoned and consume other foods there. If associations form between any contiguous events, then we should expect place cues to be associated with illness as readily as taste and odor cues, but this did not appear to be happening. Was it possible that the rats associated nausea with taste and odor, but for some reason were unable to form similar associations involving visual cues?

To test this hypothesis under controlled laboratory conditions, Garcia and Koelling allowed rats to taste distinctly flavored water from a drinking tube that was wired so that every lick produced not only water but a brief noise and light flash. Following exposure to this taste-noise-light compound, they received a dose of radiation sufficient to induce gastrointestinal disturbance and nausea. Then, on a test trial, the rats were exposed to each of the compound stimuli separately, to determine which ones had become aversive. A lick produced either the flavored water or plain water plus the noise-light compound. Drinking was found to be severely depressed by the presence of the flavor but was unaffected by the light and noise (Figure 3.7a). An aversion thus seemed to be readily conditionable to gustatory cues, as suggested by naturalistic observations, but not at all to stimuli from the external environment. An alternative explanation, however, was possible: Perhaps the noise and light used were simply too faint to be detected, so conditioning would not have been possible no matter what unconditioned stimulus had been employed. To test this hypothesis, Garcia and Koelling repeated their experiment with the same compound CS, but with electric shock as the US instead of X rays. The results for the suppression test are shown in Figure 3.7b, which illustrates that the audiovisual stimulus produced suppression of drinking and the taste stimulus had no effect. We thus face this strange situation in which nausea cannot be conditioned to a noise, nor fear to a taste, even though each of these conditioned stimuli is easily associated with the other US.

Subsequent research has established that it is possible to associate taste with shock and noise with illness, but it is much more difficult, requiring many more trials (for example, Best, Best, & Henggeler, 1977). Seligman (1970) has coined the term **preparedness** to refer to the fact that we seem prepared to associate some CS–US combinations more readily than others. To the traditional principles determining the strength of conditioning—contiguity, frequency, and intensity—we can thus add two more: contingency and preparedness.

FIGURE 3.7   Water intake before (pre) and after (post) conditioning: (a) when X rays were used as the US; (b) when shock was used as the US. The open bars represent intake of the flavored water; the solid bars represent intake of plain water when licking produced a noise and light. (Based on Garcia & Koelling, 1966)

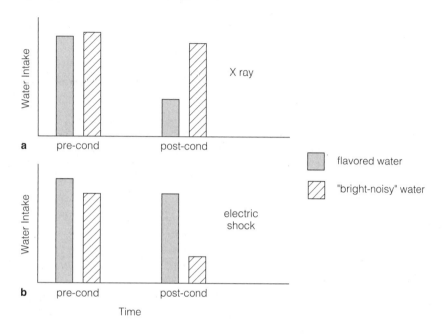

Implications of Taste-Aversion Learning

Garcia and Koelling's experiment has proved to be one of the most influential studies on learning ever published. In part, this is because their study provided the first clear evidence for the existence of taste-aversion learning, a process that plays a major role in determining food preferences. (See Chapter 2.) In addition to its practical significance, taste-aversion learning proved to have important implications for how psychologists view learning, and, indeed, for our understanding of scientific discovery. Before we complete our discussion of Garcia and Koelling's work, therefore, we will look briefly at these implications.

The role of contiguity in associative learning. According to the traditional view, all that matters in conditioning is contiguity: If two events are contiguous, then they will be associated. The evidence for preparedness, however, clearly shows that this is not the case. In the taste-aversion experiment, for example, noise was just as contiguous with illness as taste was, but this contiguity did not result in learning. Contiguity, therefore, is not sufficient for learning to take place. Other evidence, moreover, has shown that contiguity is not even necessary. In the Garcia and Koelling experiment, there was a delay of at least 20 minutes between the presentation of the taste and the animals' becoming ill; in a subsequent, memorable experiment by Etscorn and Stephens (1973), conditioning occurred despite a delay of 24 hours. Clearly, conditioning is not due simply to the linking of events that happen to occur contiguously: Some other process or processes must be involved. Garcia and Koelling's experiment thus contributed to a major theoretical shift in the way we view conditioning—from a simple process to one of considerable sophistication and complexity. We will examine this shift in greater detail in subsequent chapters.

The role of paradigms in science. Garcia and Koelling's paper was published in *Psychonomic Science* not because they submitted it there first, but because the paper had been vehemently rejected by every major psychology journal to which they had sent it (Garcia, 1981). In part, these rejections might have reflected some genuine weaknesses in their paper, including ambiguities in the description of their procedure. (If you read accounts of their work in different texts, you will find significant differences in the descriptions of their procedure; the reason is simply that their own description was not clear, and different authors have interpreted it differently.) The fundamental reason for the paper's rejection, however, was that the reviewers simply did not believe their results. Reviewers felt that it just wasn't possible that a taste could be associated with illness and yet not be associated with an electric shock. Everyone knew (or, rather, believed) that the laws of conditioning were uniform for all responses.

This attitude might sound extraordinarily unscientific. In a fascinating and influential analysis of science entitled *The Structure of Scientific Revolutions*, however, Thomas Kuhn (1970) argues that the ignoring of evidence in this way is actually a common feature of science and in many ways is even healthy. Scientific research, he suggests, is guided by **paradigms**—sets of shared assumptions about the nature of the world and about what constitutes important and worthwhile problems. It is not possible to study everything; scientists have limited resources and must concentrate on problems that seem likely to yield productive answers. Our paradigms—fundamental, almost unconscious assumptions about what is important—guide these decisions.

If reported evidence contradicts a fundamental premise, the normal scientific reaction is to reject or discount the evidence. Skeptical scientists would claim, "The experiment could not have been properly carried out." In the overwhelming majority of cases, this rejection is probably justified. For example, if a physicist claimed that he could fly through the air unaided, by sheer willpower, other physicists would almost certainly be right to ignore the claim rather than spend time, money, and effort exploring this new phenomenon. Paradigms thus play a positive role by directing our attention to problems that are likely to be important. Faith in their ultimate correctness helps give scientists the courage to persevere in the face of failure. Recall, for example, Pavlov's building of a new laboratory when his early experiments were inconclusive. Sometimes, though, paradigms blind us to new evidence simply because this evidence contradicts older findings that have hardened into dogma.

The uniformity of associative learning. From Pavlov's time, nearly all learning theorists have shared a fundamental assumption that the basic mechanisms of learning are the same across situations and species. When Pavlov began his research, he anticipated that some stimuli would be associated more easily with food than other stimuli would, and in his early experiments he distinguished between "natural" stimuli, such as the sight and smell of food, and "artificial" stimuli, such as a light or buzzer. He eventually dropped this distinction, however, when it became clear that the results of his experiments with "natural" and "artificial" stimuli were indistinguishable. It did not matter what stimuli he used; the principles governing the formation of an association were always the same.

Garcia and Koelling's results clearly contradict this assumption: It *does* matter what CS is paired with what US; some CS–US combinations are learned much more easily than others. We will consider some implications of this finding in the next section, and again at greater length in Chapter 11; at this point, we simply note that associative learning is not the entirely general process that Pavlov and others imagined, capable of associating any events that happen to occur together. We seem to be innately predisposed to learn the relationships between some events more readily than others.

The Adaptive Value of Conditioning

Why is it that some associations are easier to learn than others? In trying to answer this question, it might be helpful to begin by standing back a bit and addressing the broader question of why classical conditioning occurs at all.

The value of conditioning. In discussing Pavlov's research, we referred repeatedly to his view that the process of conditioning has evolved because it helps animals to survive in their natural environments. One way of thinking about conditioning is as a means of identifying stimuli that cause or predict important events: If an animal knows where food is available, for example, or which of the other animals in its vicinity is likely to attack it, then it can use this information to guide appropriate action. Culler (1938) expressed this view with some eloquence:

> [Without a signal] the animal would still be forced to wait in every case for the stimulus to arrive before beginning to meet it. The veil of the future would hang

just before his eyes. Nature began long ago to push back the veil. Foresight proved to possess high survival-value, and conditioning is the means by which foresight is achieved.
    (Culler, 1938, p. 136)

Salivary conditioning provides one example of the advantages of foresight: If a dog knows when food is coming, it can begin to salivate beforehand, and this will allow it to consume the food more quickly—not a small advantage when predators or other hungry dogs are around. Similarly, if a rat learns to freeze whenever it sees a predator, this freezing may enhance its chances of escaping detection and thus surviving.

In these examples, we can only speculate about the functional value of the conditioned response, but in some cases we have direct evidence. One example concerns the conditioning of sexual arousal. In an experiment by Zamble, Hadad, Mitchell, and Cutmore (1985), male rats were given access to a sexually receptive female. In one group, the female's appearance was preceded by a signal; in the other group, it was not. When the female's appearance was signaled, males initiated copulation more quickly and reached the point of ejaculation sooner. However unromantic such behavior might seem, a male that approaches a female faster is likely to have an advantage over competing suitors, and a male that finishes more quickly will have spent less time in a position where it is highly vulnerable to attack. The conditioning of sexual arousal will give this male a significant advantage in reproducing, thus ensuring that its genes—including those responsible for the conditioning of sexual arousal—will be passed on to succeeding generations (Hollis, Pharr, Dumas, Britton, & Field, 1997).

Another example comes from Hollis (1984), who studied the conditioning of aggression in a species of fish called the blue gourami. The males of this species establish territories, and then attack other males who intrude. Hollis gave her males conditioning trials in which the appearance of another male was reliably preceded by a light, and found that the aggressive behavior that was initially directed toward the intruder began to occur as soon as the light was presented. This could be seen as wasted effort—why engage in aggressive displays when no other male is around?—but Hollis found that if she now preceded test presentations of the intruder by the CS, the resident male was much more likely to win the ensuing fight. We do not yet know how the conditioning of aggression helped the resident to triumph: Perhaps hormones were released that ensured it was fully ready for battle, or perhaps the fact that it was already engaged in an aggressive display by the time its rival appeared helped to frighten that rival away. Whatever the mechanism, as the quotation from Culler would suggest, a forewarned fish proved to be a forearmed one.

The value of preparedness. Returning now to the question of why some associations are learned more easily than others, this analysis suggests that it is likely to be because these associations are of greater value in the animal's natural environment. Consider, for example, a rat that became ill after eating rancid meat. If the only learning system it possessed was an all-purpose mechanism that associated all contiguous events, then it would have developed an aversion to all the stimuli present when it became ill. Insofar as this included the taste of the rancid meat, the aversion would have helped it to survive, but it would have been equally likely to develop an aversion to a bird that happened to be singing just when it became ill. If it thereafter ran for cover whenever it heard a singing bird, it would have been more likely to die of exhaustion than to prosper. The pressures of natural selection would thus favor rats that associated illness with preceding tastes, which were likely to have genuine predictive value, rather than potentially irrelevant lights or sounds.

This analysis is very speculative: We don't *know* that rats rely more on gustatory than visual cues to identify food, however plausible this seems. However, this analysis does lead to an interesting prediction: The cue that an animal will associate most readily with illness should be whatever cue it relies on to identify food in its natural environment, no matter what that cue is. Rats forage for food at night; they are thus likely to rely on taste and odor, rather than visual appearance, to identify their food. For rats, therefore, it makes sense to associate taste cues with illness more readily than visual cues. Birds, on the other hand, rely on visual cues to identify their food; according to an adaptive analysis, therefore, birds should be more likely to associate visual cues with illness. In accordance with this prediction, Wilcoxon, Dragoin, and Kral (1971) found that when quail were made ill following the ingestion of blue, sour water, they developed a stronger aversion to the color than to the taste. Thus, although the analysis presented in this section is speculative, there is some reason to think it might be right.

3.4 BLOCKING

The 1960s were a difficult time for the principle of contiguity. First, Rescorla showed that temporal contiguity between a CS and a US is not sufficient to ensure conditioning; the CS must also be a good predictor of the US. Then Garcia and Koelling showed that even valid predictors are not always conditioned. In 1969, a third event undermined still further the traditional view of contiguity, and suggested an alternative analysis to replace it. This event was the publication of a paper by Leo Kamin.

The Phenomenon of Blocking

Kamin (1969) gave rats fear-conditioning trials in which two stimuli, a noise (N) and a light (L), were paired with an electric shock. The noise and the light came on together, remained on for three minutes, and were immediately followed by the shock. To assess conditioning to the light, Kamin used a CER test in which the light was presented while the rats pressed a bar to obtain food. The suppression ratio for the light was 0.05, indicating substantial fear conditioning. (Recall that a suppression ratio of 0.50 indicates no fear and zero indicates maximal fear.)

Kamin was interested primarily in a second group, though. The subjects in this second group received identical pairings of the noise-light compound with shock, but these compound trials were preceded by trials in which the noise by itself was paired with shock.

	Pretraining	*Conditioning*
blocking group:	N → shock	NL → shock
control group:		NL → shock

For subjects in the blocking group, therefore, the noise already elicited fear when the compound trials began. What effect should we expect this to have on conditioning to the light?

According to a contiguity analysis, we should expect strong conditioning to the light in both groups, because, in both, the light was repeatedly and contiguously paired with the shock. The results for the two groups, however, were very different. The suppression ratio in the control group was 0.05; the ratio for subjects given preliminary conditioning to the noise was 0.45, a statistic only barely distinguishable from the 0.50 level representing no fear. In other words, prior conditioning to the noise had blocked conditioning to the light. Kamin thus called this phenomenon, in which prior conditioning to one element of a compound prevents conditioning to the other element, **blocking.**

Kamin's Memory-Scan Hypothesis

Why should previous conditioning to one element of a compound block conditioning to the other? Kamin's explanation is intriguing. When an important event such as shock occurs, he said, animals search their memories to identify cues that could help to predict the event in the future. Imagine, for example, that a rat foraging for food in a forest is suddenly attacked by an owl. If the rat survives the attack, it will search its memory to identify cues that preceded the attack and thus help it avoid such an event in the future. If the rat had seen the owl in a tree just before the attack, for example, then the next time it saw an owl it would dive for cover.

Kamin first assumed, then, that unconditioned stimuli trigger memory searches for predictive cues. He further assumed that such searches require effort. In taste-aversion conditioning, for example, we have seen that animals may develop an aversion to foods consumed up to 24 hours earlier, indicating that any memory search must cover events spread over at least this time period. Such a search would require considerable time and effort, and Kamin speculated that, to save energy, subjects would scan their memories only if the US were unexpected or surprising. If the US were expected, then by definition some cue predicting its occurrence must already have been available, so that no further search would be needed.

To see how this analysis can account for blocking, consider first the control group that received only the compound trials. The first shock would have been unexpected and would have triggered a memory search for the cause. The rats would remember the preceding noise and light, and thus both cues would be associated with the shock.

Similarly in the blocking group, when the shock was presented in the preliminary phase, it would initially have been surprising and would have triggered a memory search in which the rats remembered the preceding noise and associated it with the shock. As this association was strengthened over trials, the rats would have learned to expect the shock. When the shock again followed the noise on the compound trials, therefore, the rats would not have been surprised; they would not have searched their memories for a cause, and thus would not have associated the preceding light with the shock.

At an empirical level, the phenomenon of blocking demonstrates that contiguous pairing of a CS with a US does not always result in conditioning. In particular, conditioning to a CS depends on the other stimuli present at the time. If another CS is present that has already been associated with the US, conditioning might not occur. According to Kamin, this is because conditioning involves an active search through memory for causes, and only an unexpected US will trigger this search.

May the Better Predictor Win

We will consider the validity of Kamin's explanation in later chapters, but there can be no question about the reality of blocking as an empirical phenomenon. Blocking thus adds to the growing evidence that contiguity is neither necessary nor sufficient for conditioning. The evidence that contiguity is not necessary is that taste and illness can be associated even with intervals between them of 24 hours. Conversely, contiguous pairings of a CS with a US do not always result in conditioning, so contiguity is shown to be insufficient for conditioning. Rescorla showed that the CS must also be a good predictor of the US: If a US is as likely to occur in the absence of a CS as in its presence, little or no conditioning occurs. Garcia and Koelling showed that conditioning also depends on the particular CS–US combination involved. Finally, blocking shows that conditioning is reduced or eliminated if another stimulus that already predicts the US is present.

This evidence does not mean that contiguity between a CS and a US is unimportant. As we have seen, the strength of a conditioned response depends critically on the CS–US interval, and we shall see in Chapter 4 that some of the evidence that seems most damaging to a contiguity account can be explained by a more sophisticated version of this approach. (See also Janssen, Farley, & Hearst, 1995.) Clearly, though, the strength of conditioning depends on more than simply whether a CS and a US occur together.

The fact that conditioning does not occur to any stimulus that happens to precede a US is fortunate, because the consequences otherwise could be quite catastrophic. Consider again the rat attacked by an owl. Developing a fear of owls would undoubtedly help the rat survive, but what if it also became frightened of other stimuli present at the time, such as trees, grass, and other animals? If it ran for cover every time it saw a blade of grass, it would die of exhaustion.

It is crucial, then, that unconditioned stimuli not be associated with every stimulus that precedes them, and the conditioning system has evolved to ensure that this does not happen. Instead, conditioning seems to concentrate on stimuli that are good predictors of a US—either because, in the evolutionary history of the species, these stimuli have been more likely to be its cause (Garcia & Koelling, 1966) or because they are currently the best available predictors of its occurrence (Rescorla, 1966, and Kamin, 1969; see also Wagner, 1969). Conditioning, in other words, is a beautifully adaptive system that targets the cues most likely to be the true causes or predictors of important events. How this is achieved is one of the most important issues currently debated by learning theorists, and one to which we will return in Chapter 4.

3.5 APPLICATIONS OF CONDITIONING

Throughout this chapter, we have traced psychologists' efforts to unravel the mysteries of associative learning through experimental analysis of both animal and human behavior. By studying conditioning in the controlled environment of the laboratory, where extraneous stimuli could be rigorously excluded, Pavlov and his successors hoped to be able to tease apart the complex processes involved in the formation of associations. The problem of manipulating only one variable at a time proved more difficult than was perhaps anticipated. Over the years, though, scientists have made considerable progress, as evidenced by Pavlov's brilliant dissection of the excitatory and inhibitory processes underlying extinction, and by Rescorla's more recent demonstration of the role of contingency in conditioning. Having isolated some of the principles of association under the artificial conditions of the laboratory, can we now combine or synthesize them to predict behavior in more complex and volatile environments? Can we, in other words, apply these principles to help people living not in the highly simplified, one-stimulus-at-a-time conditions of a concrete laboratory in St. Petersburg, but amid the complexity and chaos of the real world?

Systematic Desensitization

The first speculations about the possibility of applying classical conditioning principles to practical problems appeared in the study by Watson and Raynor (1920), discussed in Chapter 2, in which they conditioned "little Albert" to fear a rat by pairing the rat with presentations of a loud noise. At the end of their published report, they suggested that fear conditioning in children of the kind that they had demonstrated might explain many of the phobias and anxieties found in adults. They also offered several suggestions about how it might be possible to eliminate such fears—suggestions that eventually formed the basis for most of the current therapies for phobias.

Peter and the rabbit. One of Watson and Raynor's suggestions for eliminating fear was to associate the feared stimulus with a pleasurable experience, such as eating or sexual stimulation. The pleasant feelings elicited by these events would be incompatible with fear, they reasoned, so that if these reactions could be conditioned, then fear might be suppressed. This is, of course, the counterconditioning procedure originally described by Pavlov. The first human application of this counterconditioning strategy was in an experiment by Mary Cover Jones (1924). One of her subjects, a boy named Peter, was terrified of rabbits, and, following Watson and Raynor's suggestion, she resolved to introduce the rabbit while Peter was engaged in the pleasurable activity of eating. Obviously, she didn't want to introduce the rabbit too suddenly; if she had simply dropped the rabbit on Peter's lap while he was eating, it is unlikely that his fear would have diminished. So she introduced the rabbit only very gradually over a period of days, first keeping it at a distance and then moving it progressively closer to the boy's chair. The result was nothing short of spectacular, as Peter not only lost all fear of the rabbit but actively began to seek out opportunities to play with it.

Wolpe's procedure. By 1924, then, both conditioning and elimination of fear had been demonstrated successfully with humans, but for reasons that are still obscure, there was little further research into this area for almost 30 years. The next significant development was not until the mid 1950s, when Joseph Wolpe (1958) reported a therapy he had developed called **systematic desensitization.** Wolpe's technique was similar to that of Jones, except that his counterconditioning procedure used relaxation rather than eating as the response. In addition, instead of actually presenting the fear stimuli, he asked his patients to imagine the stimuli. A therapist using Wolpe's technique would ask patients to describe situations that frightened them and then would arrange these stimuli in a hierarchy based on their aversiveness. A patient who had a fear of snakes, for example, might find the idea of looking at a toy snake to be only somewhat threatening. Other stimuli involving snakes would then be arranged in ascending order according to their fearfulness, until the most frightening situation was reached—perhaps picking up a live snake. The therapist would train the patient in special techniques to encourage deep relaxation. (See Wolpe & Lazarus, 1966.) Typically, a patient would start with the lowest stimulus in the hierarchy and alternately visualize that frightening scene and then relax. Only when the patient reported complete relaxation while imagining that scene would the therapist ask the patient to visualize the next scene, and so on.

Wolpe reported remarkable success with this technique in eliminating phobias, and subsequent studies have largely confirmed his claims. In a study by Paul (1969), for example, students who had severe anxieties about public speaking were treated with either systematic desensitization or insight-oriented psychotherapy (which focuses on identifying the cause of the phobia). When examined two years later, 85% of those given desensitization showed significant improvement relative to pretreatment levels, compared with 50% in a psychotherapy group and only 22% in an untreated control group. The effectiveness of systematic desensitization varies depending on the phobia being treated, but it is one of the most effective treatments currently available for phobias involving specific objects such as snakes or blood, or activities such as flying (Borden, 1992; Thyer & Birsinger, 1994).

A Freudian slip. Despite this impressive evidence, Wolpe's claims were initially met with considerable skepticism, largely because of his theoretical rationale. Wolpe believed that phobias and other neuroses were really learned behaviors, and he thought it should be possible to modify these behaviors by using the same conditioning principles that had generated them in the first place. Most practicing therapists, however, subscribed to a very different interpretation of neurosis, one originally developed by Sigmund Freud. Freud saw neuroses as only external manifestations of much more fundamental conflicts within the mind. The mind, Freud believed, is composed of three fundamental forces—the id, the ego, and the superego—and the goals of these forces are often in opposition. The intense conflicts that result from such opposition are very painful and are therefore suppressed in the unconscious; but they sometimes become too powerful to be contained in this way and erupt in partially disguised, symbolic forms such as dreams or phobias. The important point in this interpretation is that phobias are only symptoms of underlying disturbances, much as yellow skin is only a symptom of jaundice rather than the disease itself. To treat only the external behavior, Freudians argued, was useless, since the underlying malaise would still be present, and eliminating one symptom would only result in its replacement by another—an effect referred to as **symptom substitution.** Snakes, for example, were seen by Freud as a sexual symbol, and fear of snakes was thus a disguised, external manifestation of anxiety about sex. Freudians believed that even if systematic desensitization succeeded in eliminating a fear of snakes, the underlying fear of sex would still be present and would inevitably emerge in some other form, such as a facial tic.

The Freudian and conditioning analyses lead to different predictions on two key points. The first concerns the origin of phobias. As we have seen, Wolpe assumed that phobias develop through a traumatic experience with the phobic stimulus, whereas Freud believed that phobias were only indirect expressions of other problems. One simple way to separate these accounts is to interview phobics to determine whether their fears were precipitated by a traumatic experience. The results turn out to depend partly on the phobia being examined, but in the case of specific phobias—those involving clearly definable stimuli such as blood, dogs, injections, and so on—the evidence generally supports the conditioning interpretation (Davey, 1992). Kleinknecht (1994), for example, interviewed University students with phobias involving blood, injury, and injections. Of those who could remember when their fears first appeared, 73% reported that a traumatic incident had caused it.

Even in those cases where patients could not directly recall a traumatic incident, it is possible that such an incident occurred but was later forgotten or repressed. One of the students in Kleinknecht's study, for example, had no memory of how her injection phobia had started, but interviews with her family revealed that when she was five a physician giving her an injection had had great difficulty in inserting the needle; her family had had to help hold her still, and she had suffered considerable pain and distress. Classical conditioning is probably not the cause of all phobias, but it does seem to play a role in a substantial proportion. (See also Kuch, Cox, Evans, & Shulman, 1994.)

The second area in which conditioning and Freudian accounts yield different predictions concerns symptom substitution. We have seen that Freud believed that eliminating one symptom would result in its replacement by another, but the evidence to date has not borne out this prediction. Paul, for example, reexamined his patients two years after the conclusion of treatment and found no recurrence of the old symptoms or emergence of new ones. Indeed, in some cases the elimination of phobias has been found to lead to a general improvement in other areas of functioning such as marital relationships. As predicted by a conditioning analysis, therefore, most phobias appear to have their origins in traumatic experiences, and elimination of phobias does not normally result in their replacement by other symptoms.

Is it really conditioning? Even if phobias are generally caused by classical conditioning, it does not necessarily follow that the success of systematic desensitization in treating them also depends on classical conditioning. For one thing, the stimuli employed during desensitization are very different from those commonly used in the laboratory. The CS, for example, is often an *imaginary* event rather than an event experienced directly. In treating a snake phobia, for example, the client might be asked to imagine a snake while relaxing—is it likely that whatever process of association is involved is the same as that in salivary conditioning? Recent research suggests that the answer may be *yes*. We will discuss this evidence in more detail in Section 9.6, but it suggests that emotions can be conditioned to stimuli that we are thinking about in the same way as to stimuli that are physically present. If so, pairing an image of a snake with relaxation could result in classical conditioning.

A further objection raised against a conditioning interpretation was that the success of the treatment might not have been the result of pairing of the feared stimulus with relaxation. As we saw in our discussion of control groups in Section 2.3, we can only conclude that a change in behavior is caused by conditioning if it is the result of pairing of the CS and the US; if the change is due to the presentation of only one of these stimuli, then it is not conditioning. The success of systematic desensitization could have been caused by only one of the treatment components. For example, success could have been simply the result of training subjects how to relax—this could have led to a general reduction in anxiety levels, so that subjects were less likely to become frightened in all situations.

To establish whether the effectiveness of systematic desensitization truly depends on pairing of the CS and US, Davison (1968) ran a further study incorporating several control groups. The subjects were college students with an intense fear of snakes, and Davison began by measuring their fear. He gave each subject a 13-step test involving progressively greater contact with snakes, ranging from simply approaching a jar containing a snake to actually picking up the snake bare-handed and holding it for 30 seconds; the number of steps a subject could complete provided an objective measure of their fear levels. Davison then gave students in the desensitization group standard training in which he asked them to imagine progressively more aversive scenes involving snakes while simultaneously engaging in deep relaxation exercises. He guided students in a second group through an identical relaxation procedure, except that the images they were asked to create concerned childhood events rather than snakes. Since childhood disturbances are widely thought to underlie phobias, subjects in this group should have expected to improve just as much as subjects in the first group, the only difference between them being whether relaxation was conditioned to snakes or to childhood memories. The experimenter asked students in a third group to imagine snakes but did not train the students in relaxation techniques. Students in a fourth group received no treatment. In effect, the first group received pairing of the CS (snakes) and the US (relaxation), whereas the second group received the US only, the third received the CS only, and the fourth received no treatment. When the students were later retested on the 13-step fear inventory, the desensitization subjects were the only ones to show any significant improvement; they improved by an average of five steps.

Subsequent studies have suggested that pairing exposure to a stimulus with relaxation is not always necessary—simply allowing patients to experience a feared situation without harmful consequences following (that is, extinction) can be sufficient (for example, Ost, Stridh, & Wolf, 1998). When the phobia is strong, however, relaxation does seem to enhance treatment (Morrow, 1986). Another factor that increases treatment effectiveness is exposing patients to the stimulus they fear directly—for example, having them sit in the same room as a snake—rather than having them imagine this stimulus (Larkin & Edens, 1994). Treatment where the feared object is physically present is called *in vivo* exposure, and its success is probably because the therapeutic situation is more similar to real life, so that any reduction in fear is more likely to generalize.

Aversion Therapy

A second major application of conditioning principles has been **aversion therapy,** in which the goal is not to eliminate fear but rather to harness it to produce avoidance of a harmful situation. This principle is by no means new, with some of the most imaginative—and gruesome—applications stemming from ancient times. Pliny the Elder, for example, recommended a treatment for alcoholism that consisted of covertly putting the putrid body of a dead spider in the bottom of the alcoholic's tankard. When the drinker would innocently tip the contents into his mouth, the resulting revulsion and nausea supposedly would deter him from ever drinking again. A somewhat more modern example (technically, at any rate) involved the treatment of a 14-year-old boy who wanted to give up smoking (Raymond, 1964). The boy was given injections of apomorphine, a drug that produces intense nausea, and each injection was timed so that it would take effect while the boy was in the middle of smoking.

> On the first occasion he was given an injection of apomorphine 1/20g, and after seven minutes he was told to start smoking. At eleven minutes he became nauseated and vomited copiously. Four days later he came for the second treatment, and said that he still had the craving for cigarettes, but had not in fact smoked since the previous session because he felt nauseated when he tried to light one. . . . Two months later he left school and started working. He said he had "got a bit down" at work and wanted to "keep in with the others," so he had accepted a proffered cigarette. He immediately felt faint and hot, and was unable to smoke. It is now a year since his treatment, and his parents confirm that he no longer smokes.
> (Raymond, 1964, p. 290)

Although Raymond's results were highly impressive, early attempts to apply his procedures to problems such as smoking and alcoholism were less successful. In retrospect, the main problem in these early studies was probably the unconditioned stimulus used. Raymond used apomorphine; because this is a dangerous drug that requires medical supervision, many of the early follow-up studies used electric shock instead. As we saw in our discussion of preparedness, however, stimuli such as the taste of alcohol or the odor of cigarette smoke are difficult to associate with shock, and this could account for the higher failure rate in these studies (Lamon, Wilson, & Leaf, 1977). Once research on taste-aversion learning in rats made this problem clear, researchers switched to USs that would be easier to associate. For alcoholism, nausea-inducing drugs such as lithium and emetine were used; for smoking, smoking itself was used as the aversive stimulus! In a study by Tiffany, Martin, and Baker (1986), for example, smokers were asked to smoke very rapidly, inhaling deeply every 6 seconds, and to continue smoking either for 3 minutes or until they felt unable to continue. Such rapid smoking induces strong feelings of nausea, and the experimenters hoped that this nausea would become conditioned to the taste and smell of cigarette smoke. When they measured cigarette smoking six months after treatment, they found that 59% of their patients no longer smoked, compared with only 35% in control groups.

A further problem in the early studies was that even where treatment was effective initially, patients often relapsed after treatment was discontinued. One reason was probably discrimination learning. For example, patients rapidly learn that whereas drinking alcohol in the clinical setting is followed by illness, drinking in their neighborhood bar or with friends has no such consequences. Rather than learning not to drink, patients simply learn not to drink in the presence of the experimenter. More recent studies have therefore incorporated other forms of training to help patients cope with temptation once treatment has ceased.

One approach has been to provide counseling during treatment to teach strategies for coping with the urge to smoke or drink when it arises. In the Tiffany, Martin, and Baker study of smoking described earlier, for example, the experimental group received counseling as well as aversion therapy, while control groups received one of the components at full strength but only a diluted version of the other—for example, full counseling but a less stressful version of aversion therapy in which they smoked at a slower rate. The treatment involving full versions of the two components was substantially more effective in reducing smoking than treatment where one of the components was reduced.

Another approach has been to provide posttreatment "booster" sessions to help maintain the aversion established during treatment. In one study using this approach, Boland, Mellor, and Revusky (1978) paired alcohol with lithium during treatment and arranged additional conditioning trials after patients had been discharged. When they assessed their patients six months after discharge, they found that 50% of the chronic alcoholics in the treatment group were still abstinent, compared with only 12% of the controls.

The use of multicomponent treatments in which aversion therapy has been combined with other approaches has contributed to an improvement in the long-term effectiveness of aversion therapy (Hall, Rugg, Tunstall, & Jones, 1984; O'Farrell et al., 1996). In a review, Elkins (1991) reported that approximately

FIGURE 3.8   Behavior therapy versus psychotherapy. Behavior therapy focuses on the role of the environment in controlling behavior, whereas psychotherapy focuses on the role of the mind.

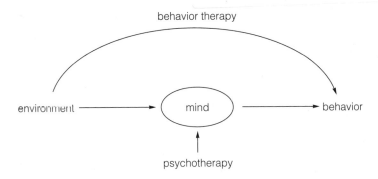

60% of alcoholics treated with aversion therapy were still abstinent one year after treatment, an impressive result for a problem that is notoriously difficult to treat. However, this does not mean that aversion therapy is always appropriate. The need for hospitalization means that aversion therapy for alcoholism is expensive, and its unpleasant nature leads to higher drop-out rates during treatment. Where milder forms of treatment are possible, therefore, they are preferred. For patients suffering from chronic alcoholism, however, aversion therapy appears to be an effective alternative.

Behavior Therapy versus Psychotherapy

Behavior therapy. Both systematic desensitization and aversion therapy are examples of **behavior therapy,** which emphasizes the environmental determinants of behavior rather than the patient's mental state. On the assumption that our current and past environment determines how we think and feel and that these mental states then determine how we behave (Figure 3.8), traditional psychodynamic therapies emphasize changing patients' minds; they generally involve a therapist talking to patients, trying to give patients greater insight into their problems. Behavior therapies, on the other hand, focus on an overt problem behavior and try to modify the behavior by altering the patient's environment.

We can further illustrate the difference between these approaches by considering their divergent attitudes toward *enuresis*, or bed-wetting. Freudians view enuresis as a symptom of an underlying psychological conflict, and they attempt to treat it through extensive therapy sessions in which the child is helped to recognize the underlying conflict and come to terms with it. Behavior therapists, on the other hand, view bed-wetting simply as an undesirable response, and they search for learning principles that might help to change the behavior.

The most effective treatment for enuresis, developed by Mowrer and Mowrer (1938), consists simply of a moisture detector wired to the child's bed in such a way that a buzzer will sound whenever the bed is wet. The rationale for this treatment is classical conditioning. The buzzer acts as an unconditioned stimulus to wake the child when he or she wets, and this waking response is hypothesized to become conditioned to the full-bladder cues that precede it. In the future, then, the child will wake up before he or she urinates. (For a discussion of alternative interpretations, see Doleys, 1977.)

This treatment has proved very effective, with average success rates of between 60 and 80% across studies (Doleys, 1977; Houts, Berman, & Abramson, 1994). No symptom substitution occurred, and observations of the children following treatment suggested that they were "happier, less anxious, and more grown-up . . . with dramatic positive changes in self-image" (Baker, 1969, p. 49). Because relatively few controlled studies have been carried out on the effectiveness of psychotherapy for enuresis, it is difficult to make precise comparisons, but a recent review by Houts, Berman, and Abramson (1994) concluded that that percentage of patients who stopped bed wetting after completion of treatment was almost twice as great for patients trained with the urine alarm as for those given psychotherapy or drugs.

Cognitive-behavioral therapy. The success of conditioning-based treatments for enuresis and phobias, and, less clearly, for alcoholism, suggests that behavioral treatments can be highly effective—sometimes far more so than psychodynamic therapies. This success, however, does not necessarily mean that behavior analysis is superior in all respects. In our discussion of the origins of phobias, for example, we noted that many phobias can plausibly be attributed to traumatic experiences with the feared object, but in some cases subjects cannot recall such experiences. In at least some of these cases—and especially those that emerged in adulthood, and thus where forgetting of the cause seems less likely—the Freudian interpretation of phobias as a symbolic expression of some other problem may be worth considering more seriously. (For an interesting defense of Freud's overall contribution to psychology, see Westen, 1998.)

An interesting example comes from a case reported by Lazarus (1971) in which a patient came for treatment because of a phobia about bridges. Probing further, Lazarus discovered that the patient had never had any unpleasant experiences involving bridges, and that his phobia had appeared suddenly, soon after he had been offered a promotion at work—a job that he could reach only by crossing a bridge. The patient had deep fears about his ability to handle the work required by this promotion, and Lazarus eventually concluded that the fear of bridges had emerged as a more socially acceptable excuse for avoiding the promotion. Lazarus used desensitization to treat the patient's fears related to the promotion, and the patient's fear of bridges soon disappeared.

Lazarus's approach combines elements from behavioral and psychodynamic approaches: The therapist concentrated on the patient's concealed fears, rather than accepting the behavioral symptom at face value, but once the underlying source of the patient's anxiety was identified, Lazarus used conditioning principles to help the patient overcome the anxiety.

This case illustrates how therapists can use elements from both behavioral and psychodynamic approaches, focusing on patients' thoughts and feelings as well as their overt behaviors. This synthesis lies at the heart of **cognitive-behavioral therapy,** which has become the dominant approach in clinical psychology in recent decades (Craighead, 1990). Cognitive-behavioral therapists focus on people's thoughts (cognitions) as well as on their overt behaviors. For example, we sometimes think about events in overly black-and-white terms ("I must be the best in everything"; "A low mark on this quiz will ruin my life"), and a cognitive-behavior therapist would try to help clients who were thinking in this way to change their counterproductive thoughts as well as to develop new skills and habits. A full exposition of this approach is beyond the scope of this text; for our purposes, the important point is that treatments based on classical conditioning have proven helpful both on their own and in conjunction with other techniques.

3.6 SUMMARY

Until 1966, almost 70 years of research on conditioning had supported an attractively simple model: An association is formed whenever two stimuli are contiguous, with the strength of the association depending on their temporal and spatial contiguity, their intensity, and the frequency of their pairing. The weakness of simultaneous and backward conditioning seemed to pose problems for this analysis, as conditioning was substantially poorer than the temporal contiguity of the CS and US in these paradigms would have predicted, but the low levels of responding in these paradigms now seem attributable to problems in performance rather than learning.

In the period between 1966 and 1969, however, three papers were published that fundamentally challenged this view. The first paper, by Rescorla (1966), showed that conditioning depended not only on the time separating the CS and US but also on their contingency—the extent to which two events occur together over time, as measured by the probability of a US in the presence of a CS and in its absence. If the probability of the US is greater in the presence of the CS than in its absence, then the CS signals that the US is more likely, and excitatory conditioning occurs; if the probability of the US is lower following the CS, then the CS signals that the US is less likely, and inhibitory conditioning occurs; if the probability of the US is the same in the presence of the CS as in its absence, then little or no conditioning occurs. Identical pairings of a CS and a US can thus increase, decrease, or have no effect on conditioning, depending on how often the US occurs in the absence of the CS.

The second seminal paper of 1966 was by Garcia and Koelling. They exposed rats to a compound stimulus composed of a taste, a noise, and a light, followed with a dose of radiation sufficient to induce illness. The rats developed a strong aversion to the taste but not to the light or the noise. When the researchers changed the unconditioned stimulus from radiation to an electric shock, they obtained the opposite result: The rats avoided the light and noise but not the taste. The fact that a CS and US are contiguous, then, does not guarantee conditioning, because rats are selectively prepared to associate some CS–US combinations more readily than others. The reason for the evolution of this selective mechanism is almost certainly its adaptive value. You are much more likely to survive if you avoid what you had eaten before you became ill; avoiding what you had seen or heard has less bearing on survival.

The third critical paper was published three years later by Leo Kamin (1969). Using rats as subjects, Kamin found that if fear had been previously conditioned to one element of a compound, this would block conditioning to the other element. Thus, if an experimenter paired a noise-light compound with electric shock, no fear would be conditioned to the light if the noise had previously been paired with the shock. The reason, Kamin suggested, was that unexpected unconditioned stimuli trigger a search through memory for cues that predict their occurrence. If a US is expected, however, then by definition an adequate predictor must already be present, so no further search is necessary. In the blocking experiment, previous conditioning to the noise established it as a reliable predictor of the shock, so no memory search was initiated on the compound trials and thus no association formed between the light and shock.

Each of these findings has important implications, ranging from the appropriate control group for conditioning to how paradigms guide scientists' evaluation of evidence. But the most important implication concerns the roles of contiguity in learning. The traditional view—that an association would be formed whenever two stimuli were contiguous—clearly needs to be modified. Tone and shock were contiguous in Rescorla's experiment, but little conditioning occurred if the US also occurred in the absence of the CS. Light and illness were contiguous in Garcia and Koelling's experiment, but conditioning occurred almost exclusively to the taste. And light was contiguous with shock in Kamin's experiment, but little or no conditioning was found if the accompanying noise had previously been paired with shock. Contiguity does not ensure conditioning.

The common thread uniting these experiments is that conditioning does not occur equally to whatever stimuli happen to precede a US; conditioning is much stronger to those stimuli that are good predictors of the US. In the case of preparedness, the knowledge that tastes are better predictors of illness than noise seems to be innate. In contingency learning and blocking, however, we learn the best predictors through experience.

From the time that Pavlov's work on dogs became known, psychologists were intrigued by its possible implications for human behavior. Watson and Raynor (1920) showed that fear could be conditioned in young children, and they speculated that many adult fears might be acquired in this way. If fears were acquired through conditioning, they suggested, then it should also be possible to eliminate them through conditioning. One technique they advocated was counterconditioning, which eventually became the basis of systematic desensitization, a therapy in which phobics are asked to imagine progressively more frightening scenes while relaxing. This has proved to be one of the most effective therapies for treating phobias.

Another important application of conditioning principles is aversion therapy, in which undesirable habits are eliminated through pairing with painful stimuli. To treat alcoholism, for example, the drinking of alcohol is paired with a chemical agent that induces nausea. Aversion therapy has been found to be highly effective in the initial treatment of both alcoholism and cigarette smoking, but patients sometimes return to drinking or smoking after treatment is discontinued. Research is now increasingly directed toward finding techniques for preventing relapses or treating them once they occur.

Systematic desensitization and aversion therapy are both examples of behavior therapy, in which therapists try to change clients' environments to change their behaviors, rather than trying to change their mental state. Some forms of behavior therapy have proven highly effective, but so too have treatments based on more cognitive approaches in which therapists aim to give clients' greater insight into their problems and help them to change their ways of thinking about these problems. Although historically these approaches emerged as opposing interpretations, it is possible to combine elements of both, and cognitive-behavioral therapies have become increasingly common in recent decades.

Glossary

Delay conditioning A technique in which a CS is presented and then continues until a US is presented. Some definitions further restrict this term, confining it to situations in which there is also a long interval between CS onset and US onset.

Trace conditioning A technique that involves presenting the CS and terminating it before presenting the US.

Simultaneous conditioning A technique that involves presenting the CS and US at the same time.

Backward conditioning A technique that involves presenting the US before presenting the CS.

Asymptote In mathematics, a stable value that a curve on a graph approaches but never quite reaches. As used in learning, it generally describes the level of performance at which improvement ceases, so that further training would produce no additional improvement.

Contingency A measure of the extent to which two events occur together, or covary, over time. A contingency coefficient is a mathematical statistic determined by two probabilities—the probability that a US will occur in the presence of a CS, and the probability that it will occur in the absence of the CS.

Random control A control group in which the CS and US are presented completely at random rather than deliberately separated. A random control is also known as a truly random control, to distinguish it from the unpaired control group in which the CS and US are always kept separate.

Preparedness The tendency to associate some CS–US combinations more readily than others. Other terms for this phenomenon include *relevance* and *selective association*.

Paradigm A set of shared assumptions about the nature of the world and about what constitutes important and worthwhile problems.

Blocking A phenomenon in which prior conditioning to one element of a compound reduces conditioning to other elements.

Systematic desensitization A therapy for phobias based on counterconditioning. Patients visualize fear-evoking stimuli while relaxing, to associate the stimuli with relaxation instead of fear.

Symptom substitution The replacement of one problem behavior (believed to be symptomatic of an underlying malaise) by another behavior that is equally undesirable.

Aversion therapy A procedure for eliminating an unwanted behavior by conditioning fear to stimuli associated with that behavior.

Behavior therapy A form of therapy that focuses on environmental determinants of behavior rather than on the patient's mental state.

Cognitive-behavioral therapy An extension of behavior therapy that emphasizes changing people's irrational or maladaptive thoughts about their problems (their cognitions) as well as their overt behaviors. This approach differs from behavior therapy in giving greater weight to people's thoughts; it differs from more traditional forms of psychotherapy in emphasizing current thoughts and behaviors rather than unconscious feelings developed in childhood.

Review Questions

1. Why did simultaneous and backward conditioning seem to pose problems for the principle of contiguity? How can these apparent anomalies be explained?

2. How did Rescorla disentangle the roles of contiguity and contingency in conditioning?

3. What is the purpose of the random and unpaired control groups? What are the arguments for and against using the random control as the control group for classical conditioning?

4. How did Garcia and Koelling show that the conditioning of a stronger aversion to a taste than to a light was not simply the result of greater salience of the taste as a conditioned stimulus?

5. What is Kuhn's concept of a paradigm? Do you think the advantages of scientific paradigms outweigh their disadvantages?

6. How might classical conditioning contribute to an animal's survival? Why might it be better not to associate a US with all the stimuli that are contiguous with it?

7. How did Kamin account for blocking?

8. Is contiguity necessary or sufficient for conditioning? Explain.

9. How could the Pavlovian concepts of generalization and counterconditioning be used to account for the success of systematic desensitization?

10. Is the success of systematic desensitization really the result of classical conditioning? Explain.

11. What are the differences between behavior therapy and psychodynamic therapy? What arguments support each approach?

CHAPTER FOUR

THEORIES OF CONDITIONING

The phenomenon of classical conditioning is basically very simple: If a CS and a US are repeatedly presented together, the CS will eventually begin to elicit the same response as the US does by itself. Pavlov proposed an equally simple theory to account for this evidence, namely that whenever two centers in the brain are active simultaneously, the connection between them will be strengthened. In essence, all that matters is contiguity: If a CS and a US occur together, they will be associated.

This account is delightfully simple, and for more than 50 years it was used to explain virtually all the known facts about conditioning. The discovery of contingency, preparedness, and blocking in the 1960s, however, posed a fundamental challenge. In the case of contingency, for example, Rescorla showed that conditioning would not occur if a US was equally likely to occur in the absence of a CS as in its presence. The fact that a CS and US occur together, in other words, does not guarantee conditioning, and thus conditioning must involve more than simply linking whatever centers in the brain are active simultaneously.

In this chapter we will consider what this "more" might be and examine current theories about what really happens when a CS and a US occur together. We will see that although Pavlov was not totally wrong, conditioning involves a much more intricate system of subprocesses than a simple contiguity account suggests.

4.1 THE RESCORLA-WAGNER MODEL

Rescorla's research revealed that animals are remarkably sensitive to the probability of the US both in the presence of the CS and in its absence. The obvious way to account for this sensitivity is to assume that animals are somehow capable of computing probabilities. If rats sometimes receive shocks in the presence of a tone and sometimes in its absence, for example, they might count how many shocks occur while the tone is present and also assess how much time has elapsed. Using this data, they could determine the average probability of the shock in the presence of the tone and, in a similar fashion, compute the shock's probability in the tone's absence. Finally, they could compare the two probabilities to determine whether they should be frightened when they hear the tone because it signals an increase in the likelihood of shock.

It is possible that animals do carry out the complex processes implicit in this account—measuring time, counting event frequencies, and computing probabilities. In 1972, however, two psychologists published a theory that offered a much simpler account. Robert Rescorla and Allan Wagner, from Yale University, offered an account for almost every major aspect of conditioning—the occurrence of conditioning itself, extinction, blocking, the effects of contingency, and so on. And they achieved all this using only a single, simple equation!

The Rescorla-Wagner model has proved to be one of the most remarkable and influential models in psychology, and we therefore will begin our exploration of theories of conditioning by examining it in some detail. Before we begin, it might be worth noting that some sections of the exposition are difficult and might require careful rereading. This might seem to contradict the previous claim that the model is simple, but once you understand the model, it really is simple. The catch is that it is stated in mathematical form, so you will have to master unfamiliar symbols and concepts before the model begins to make sense. Mastering this new terminology is not easy, but the potential reward is an insight into how a few simple assumptions can explain what seems to be a bewildering array of unrelated facts.

The Importance of Surprise

The foundation of the Rescorla-Wagner model was Kamin's work on blocking. As we saw in Chapter 3, Kamin found that when a noise-light compound was followed by shock, no fear was conditioned to the light if the noise had previously been presented by itself with the shock. From the perspective of contiguity, this result was bewildering: Why, when the light was paired with a powerful electric shock, was fear not conditioned to it? Kamin explained the results in this way: For conditioning to occur, the unconditioned stimulus must be unexpected, or surprising. If a US is surprising, subjects search their memory for possible causes; if the US is expected, though, then an adequate predictor of its occurrence must already be available—hence no memory search occurs, and no learning takes place.

For Kamin, then, the key to learning lay in the concept of surprise. In other words, learning depends to some extent on the discrepancy between what happens to us and what we expected to happen. If we expect a shock to occur, we do not learn; but if the same shock occurs unexpectedly, then it upsets us far more, and we search for an explanation. Thus, the same event can have very different effects, depending on our initial expectations.

A Mathematical Model

Rescorla and Wagner took this fundamental insight of Kamin's and modified it in several important respects. Where Kamin had assumed that surprise determines *whether* conditioning occurs, Rescorla and Wagner extended this assumption and said that surprise would also determine *how much* conditioning occurs. If a rat was very surprised when a shock followed a tone, for example, then the amount of fear conditioned on this trial would be greater than if the shock was largely expected. The more unexpected the US, the stronger the conditioning.

The learning curve. To enable researchers to predict the precise amount of conditioning, Rescorla and Wagner stated their model in mathematical form. They began by substituting the language of association for Kamin's cognitive terminology. When a CS and a US are paired, they said, an association would be formed between them, and they used the symbol V to represent the strength of this association. They assumed that if the CS–US pairings were repeated, the strength of the association would increase in roughly the manner shown in Figure 4.1a. One important point to note about this learning curve is that the increase in associative strength is not constant over trials. On the first trial, V increases by a substantial amount. Over successive trials, the increase in V on each trial gets progressively smaller, until eventually V approaches a stable value.

Rescorla used the symbol ΔV to represent the change in associative strength on each trial (Δ, or delta, is the mathematical symbol for change). The change in associative strength produced by the first trial was ΔV_1, the change on trial 2 was ΔV_2 and so on. As we saw in Chapter 3, a stable value that a curve approaches but never quite reaches is called an *asymptote*, and we will use the symbol V_{max} to represent the asymptotic value of V (Figure 4.1b).

Quantifying surprise. We can summarize the model to this point by saying that associative strength increases over trials until it reaches a stable maximum value; in mathematical symbols, V increases by ΔV on each trial until it approaches V_{max}. To predict the strength of association, then, we need a formula to predict ΔV. A number of formulas were possible; in choosing one, Rescorla and Wagner were guided by their assumption that the amount of conditioning depends on the amount of surprise. To quantify surprise, they focused on the relationship between V and V_{max}. At the beginning of conditioning, when V is much less than V_{max}, the subject will not expect the US and hence will be surprised when it occurs. As V increases over trials and approaches V_{max}, the occurrence of the US will be progressively less surprising. The difference between V and V_{max}, therefore, provides us with a useful index of surprise: The smaller the difference between V and V_{max}, the less surprising the occurrence of the US will be.

Figure 4.2 illustrates this point by focusing on two trials, one early on in conditioning and the other later. Early in conditioning (point 1), there will be

FIGURE 4.1   How associative strength (V) increases over conditioning trials (n) according to the Rescorla-Wagner model: (a) a typical learning curve; (b) the same curve, showing the change in associative strength on each trial (ΔV) and the asymptotic value of associative strength (V_{max}).

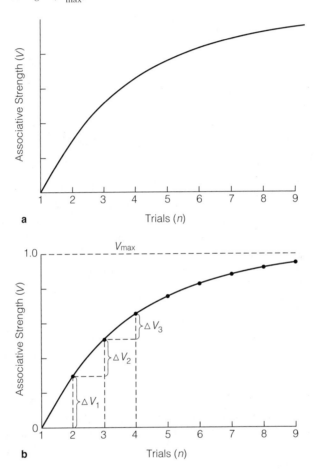

a large difference between V and V_{max}, and substantial conditioning will occur. As conditioning proceeds, however (point 2), the difference between V and V_{max} will decrease, and the US will be less surprising. The notion that the amount of conditioning depends on the amount of surprise, therefore, can potentially be translated into mathematical form by saying that the amount of conditioning on any trial n (ΔV_n) will depend on the difference between V and V_{max}:

$$\Delta V_n \approx V_{max} - V_n$$

FIGURE 4.2   The relationship between V and V$_{max}$ early and late in conditioning. Early in conditioning (point 1), the difference between V and V$_{max}$ is great. Later (point 2), the difference is much less.

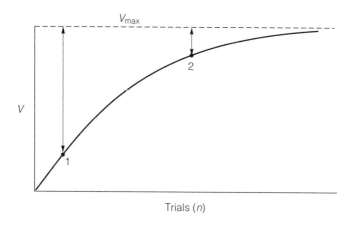

where

V_n = the strength of the association at the beginning of trial n
ΔV_n = the change in the strength of the association produced by trial n

Parameters. In our presentation of the model to this point, we have talked as if the learning curve shown in Figure 4.1 is the one found in all conditioning curves, but this is not quite right. The overall shape of the curve—increasing over trials, but at a declining rate—is indeed uniform, or at least roughly so, but the asymptotic level of conditioning and the rate at which this asymptote is reached vary across experiments. In the Annau and Kamin (1961) experiment on fear conditioning, for example, intense shock produced much higher asymptotic levels of fear than milder shocks did (see Figure 2.16).

Figure 4.3 illustrates the difference between the asymptote and the rate of conditioning, portraying a range of possible learning curves. In Figure 4.3a, the curves differ in asymptotic levels of conditioning but reach this level after the same number of trials; in Figure 4.3b, the curves reach the same asymptote but vary in the rate at which they get there.

If the growth in associative strength differs in different experiments, how can we use a single equation to predict these different outcomes? In mathematical formulas this is achieved through the use of constants called **parameters.** Suppose, for example, that we linked two variables, X and Y, by the equation

$$Y = c\, X$$

FIGURE 4.3   Variations in the asymptote (broken line) and rate of conditioning: (a) two learning curves that change at the same rate but approach different asymptotes; (b) two curves that approach the same asymptote but at different rates.

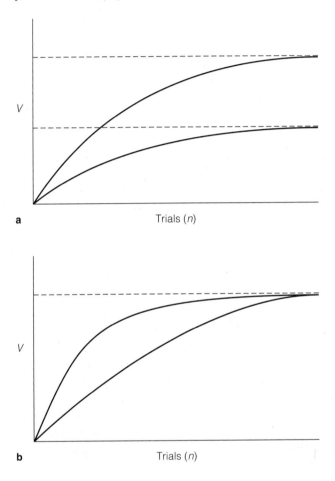

where c is a constant. If the value of the parameter c was set at 2 (Y = 2X), then the value of Y would increase twice as fast as the value of X; if the value of c was set at 3 (Y = 3X), Y would increase three times as fast. By varying the value of the parameter c, then, we can use the same basic equation to predict a range of different results.

    To enable theorists to predict variations in the rate and asymptotic value of conditioning, Rescorla and Wagner used two parameters. To predict the asymptotic level of conditioning, they used V_{max}, and to take into account different speeds of conditioning they introduced the parameter c.[1] The complete statement of the equation was thus:

$$\Delta V_n = c\,(V_{max} - V_n)$$

The greater the value of the parameter c in this equation, the greater the change in associative strength; this in turn means that conditioning will reach its asymptotic value faster, as associative strength will increase more rapidly on the early trials.

4.2 THE RESCORLA-WAGNER MODEL: DERIVING PREDICTIONS

We now have an equation with which we can predict the precise change in associative strength on any trial. To test the model, therefore, it might seem that all we need to do is present a series of CS–US trials, calculate the predicted value of V for each trial, and see if these predictions are correct. This simple summary, however, hides several serious practical difficulties.

One problem is that V represents the strength of a theoretical association. We can see a dog salivate, but we cannot directly observe the association assumed to produce this behavior. If the strength of association was 14, for example, how many drops of saliva should we expect to see? Before we can test the model's predictions, we need rules relating associative strength to overt behavior.

Parameter Estimation

A second problem is that we need to know the values of c and V_{max} before we can predict V. V_{max}, for example, refers to the maximum strength of the association, but if we cannot observe an association, then we have no rational basis for deciding its maximum strength. If we paired a tone with 5 grams of food, for example, would the maximum strength of association be 1 unit or 5 or 77?

---

[1] The value of the parameter V_{max} was assumed to be determined solely by the US used, whereas the value of c was determined by both the CS and the US. In fact, Rescorla and Wagner used two different constants, α and β, to represent the effects of the CS and US, rather than the single parameter c, and they also used the symbol λ to represent asymptotic conditioning rather than V_{max}. We have altered the symbols to make the exposition of the model easier to follow. Should you read the model in the original, you will find the equation stated as

$$\Delta V_n = \alpha\beta(\lambda - V_n)$$

The value of c in our version of the equation must lie between 0 and 1.

One solution is to try out a variety of values, chosen at random, and see which one leads to the most accurate prediction of behavior. If we found that setting V_{max} at 7 when the US is 5 grams resulted in highly accurate predictions, we could then use this value in further applications involving this US. Again, though, this solution is far more difficult in practice than it sounds. Suppose, for example, that after choosing a set of parameter values and selecting a rule for converting V into drops of saliva we found that our prediction was wrong. How could we locate the source of the error? It might have been in just one of the parameters or in all of them; it might not have been in the parameters at all but in the rule for translating V into behavior. In a complex model with many assumptions, it can be frustratingly difficult to identify the source of any error and thus to correct it.

Given these difficulties, you might not be altogether surprised to learn that in the entire history of learning theory there has been only one sustained effort to develop a comprehensive mathematical model of the kind we have been discussing (Hull, 1943) and that after more than a decade of effort the researchers involved largely abandoned the effort. This failure convinced many conditioning theorists that mathematical models were more trouble than they were worth, and for almost 20 years there was little further interest. (For a notable exception, see Estes, 1959.) Rescorla and Wagner's work has rekindled interest, however, by showing that it is not necessary to know the exact values of a model's parameters to test it. Instead of estimating the real values of the parameters c and V_{max}, they derived predictions using totally arbitrary values.

The use of arbitrary values might seem pointless, but although this strategy precludes *quantitative* predictions, it turns out that the model can still make some very interesting *qualitative* predictions. That is, although the exact points on the learning curve depend on the values of c and V_{max} used in the equation, no matter which values are chosen, the equation always predicts a learning curve of the same general shape. Thus although we cannot predict the exact number of drops of saliva, we can still make qualitative predictions about whether salivation will increase or decrease, and, as we shall see, even simple statements of this kind can sometimes lead to surprising and interesting predictions.

To see how this can happen, we will first consider how the model accounts for relatively straightforward phenomena such as conditioning and extinction. Then, once the basic operations of the model are a bit clearer, we will turn to some of its more striking predictions. To begin, though, let us take a look at how the model accounts for the basic shape of the learning curve during conditioning.

Conditioning

Suppose that we repeatedly paired a tone with food, as in the hypothetical experiment whose results are illustrated by the learning curve presented in Figure 4.1. To see what sort of results the model might predict in this situation, let

TABLE 4.1   Using the Rescorla-Wagner Model to Predict Conditioning

Trial	V_n	$\Delta V_n = c\,(V_{max} - V_n)$
1	0.00	$\Delta V_1 = 0.30\,(1 - 0.00) = 0.30$
2	0.30	$\Delta V_2 = 0.30\,(1 - 0.30) = 0.21$
3	0.51	$\Delta V_3 = 0.30\,(1 - 0.51) = 0.15$
4	0.66	$\Delta V_4 = 0.30\,(1 - 0.66) = 0.10$

us arbitrarily assume that the value of V_{max} appropriate to the amount of food we are using is 1.0, and the value of c is 0.30. How much learning should we then expect?

As shown in Table 4.1, associative strength at the beginning of trial 1 is assumed to be zero, so the amount of conditioning on that first trial would be:

$$\Delta V_1 = c\,(V_{max} - V_1) = 0.30(1.0 - 0) = 0.30$$

At the beginning of trial 2, the strength of the association would thus be 0.30, and the change in associative strength produced by that trial would be:

$$\Delta V_2 = c\,(V_{max} - V_2) = 0.30(1.0 - 0.30) = 0.21$$

The predicted values for V on the next two trials are shown in the table. As you can see, they correspond exactly to the values plotted in Figure 4.1.

Our success in predicting these hypothetical data is perhaps not too surprising (especially when you consider that the calculations were done first and the graph simply plots these calculations), but it does indicate the capacity of the model to generate learning curves of the shape found in most conditioning experiments. The predicted shape of the curve is the same, moreover, regardless of what values of c and V_{max} are used. These parameters alter the height of the asymptote and the speed with which it is reached, but in all cases the basic shape of the curve remains the same. (You might find it useful to verify this for yourself by working through some calculations using other values. You can use any value for V_{max}, but the value of c must lie between 0 and 1.0.)

Extinction

What about other aspects of conditioning? For example, can the model explain decreases in responding as well as increases? Yes, and it does so using exactly the same equation used to predict conditioning. The key to understanding how one equation can predict diametrically opposite results lies in V_{max}. We have said that V_{max} is the strength of the association that would be produced if a CS

FIGURE 4.4   An example of extinction as predicted by the Rescorla-Wagner model.

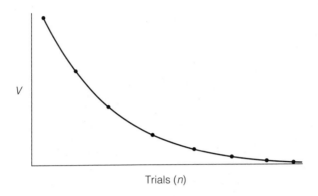

Trials (*n*)

and US were paired repeatedly. In extinction, we know that the level of conditioning reached after extended training is zero. The value of V_{max} on any trial in which a US is not presented, therefore, must also be zero.

To see the implications of this, suppose that after the third conditioning trial in our previous example we began to present the CS by itself. On the first extinction trial, V would have an initial value of 0.66 (see Table 4.1), but as a result of nonreinforcement on that trial, its associative strength would be changed by:

$$\Delta V_1 = c\,(V_{max} - V_1) = 0.30\,(0 - 0.66) = -0.198$$

The strength of the association, in other words, would be decreased by approximately 0.20, and its new strength would be:

$$V_2 = 0.66 - 0.20 = 0.46$$

A second extinction trial would decrease its strength by a further −0.14, and so on, until eventually V would approach its asymptotic value of zero. (See Figure 4.4.) Using only a single equation, therefore, the model can predict extinction as well as conditioning.

Blocking

We can also use the model to explain blocking. Before doing so, however, we need to consider how conditioning is affected if two stimuli instead of just one are present on a trial.

Compound trials. We said earlier that conditioning on any trial depends on how surprising the US is, which in turn depends on how much the subject expected the US to occur. Rescorla and Wagner assumed that if two condi-tioned stimuli, a and b, were presented together, the subject would take both stimuli into account in estimating the likelihood of the US. Specifically, they proposed that the association or expectation at the beginning of a trial would be the sum of the strengths of each of the stimuli present:

$$V_{ab} = V_a + V_b$$

Suppose, for example, that a and b had been paired separately with food and had associative strengths of 0.30 and 0.50, respectively. If the two stimuli were presented together, subjects would assume that food must really be likely. The associative strength of the compound would be:

$$V_{ab} = V_a + V_b = 0.30 + 0.50 = 0.80$$

In calculating unexpectedness, we need to take into account all the stimuli present. Thus, the amount of conditioning on a compound trial in which a and b occur together[2] would be

$$\Delta V_a = \Delta V_b = c \left(V_{max} - V_{ab} \right)$$

where

$$V_{ab} = V_a + V_b$$

Kamin's blocking experiment. We can now explain the results of Kamin's blocking experiment. Recall that a noise was paired with shock for a number of trials, and then a noise-light compound was paired with shock. During the noise trials, the associative strength of the noise would have increased until it essen-tially reached asymptote. If we assume that V_{max} for the shock was 1.0, then by the end of conditioning,

$$V_{noise} = 1.0$$

---

[2] In this example, and in all examples that follow, we have assumed that a and b are equally salient stimuli and that the values of c are the same for both. (Recall that c is determined by the CS as well as the US.) If a and b are not equally salient, a different value of c will be needed for each, and the amount learned on a compound trial will be:

$$\Delta V_a = c_a (V_{max} - V_{ab})$$
$$\Delta V_b = c_b (V_{max} - V_{ab})$$

FIGURE 4.5   The direction of learning as determined by the relationship between V and V_{max}. When V is less than V_{max} (point 1), associative strength increases. When V is greater than V_{max} (point 2), associative strength decreases. When V equals V_{max} (point 3), associative strength does not change.

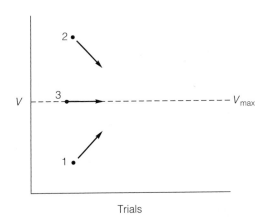

If the noise were presented with the light, then their combined associative strength would be:

$$V_{nl} = V_{noise} + V_{light} = 1.0 + 0 = 1.0$$

The amount of conditioning to the light on this trial would therefore be

$$\Delta V_{light} = c\,(V_{max} - V_{nl}) = 0.3(1.0 - 1.0) = 0.3(0) = 0$$

In other words, no conditioning would occur, which is exactly the result Kamin found.

This derivation illustrates again the fundamental principle that the amount of conditioning depends not simply on the US (in the model, the effect of the US is mediated by V_{max}), but also on what the subject expects (V). Suppose, for example, that a rat received a 10-volt electric shock. If the rat had not been expecting shock, this would cause a large increase in its fear; if it had expected precisely this shock, its fear would not change from the original expectation; and if it had been expecting a 20-volt shock, its fear would actually decrease. The same shock, in other words, could lead to either an increase, a decrease, or no change in fear, depending on the rat's initial expectation.

Restated in the associative terminology of the model, whether conditioning will increase or decrease when a US is presented depends on the relationship between V and V_{max}:

1. If V is less than V_{max}, as it normally is during conditioning, then ($V_{max} -$ V) is positive, and associative strength increases (point 1 in Figure 4.5).

2. If V equals V_{max}—for example, if conditioning has reached asymptote— then the quantity ($V_{max} - V$) will equal zero, and there will be no change in associative strength (point 2 in the figure).

3. If V is greater than V_{max}, then the quantity ($V_{max} - V$) will be negative, and associative strength will be reduced (point 3). One way in which this can happen is if the US presented on a trial is weaker than the US used on previous trials. Suppose, for example, that after fear conditioning has approached asymptote ($V = V_{max}$), the intensity of the shock is reduced. The value of V_{max} for the new US will be lower than for the previous US, with the result that the quantity ($V_{max} - V$) will be negative, and associative strength will be reduced.

Exactly the same US, therefore, can produce either an increase in conditioning, no change, or a decrease, depending on the strength of the association at the beginning of the trial.

4.3 EVALUATING THE RESCORLA-WAGNER MODEL

The Rescorla-Wagner model, then, is able to account for such basic conditioning phenomena as the occurrence of conditioning itself, extinction, and blocking, and it can do so using only a single basic equation. The model is in many respects an extraordinary achievement, but the real test of any model lies not so much in its ability to describe known phenomena as in the ability to predict new ones. To assess the model's success in this crucial respect, we will focus on one of its strangest and most counterintuitive predictions: In some circumstances, pairing a CS with a US will result not in conditioning but in extinction.

New Predictions: Overexpectation

Suppose that we were to expose rats to a series of conditioning trials in which a tone and a light were separately paired with an intense shock:

$$tone \rightarrow shock$$

$$light \rightarrow shock$$

Then suppose that the tone and light were presented together on the next conditioning trial:

$$tone + light \rightarrow shock$$

What effect should this have on fear of the tone? Because the tone is again being followed by an unpleasant shock, you might expect a further increase in fear, but, according to the Rescorla-Wagner model, the situation is not necessarily that simple. As we've already seen, the amount of conditioning in any situation depends not simply on the US but also on the associative strength at the beginning of the trial. Suppose, for example, that only a few trials were given before the compound trial, so fear levels to the two stimuli were only moderate:

$$V_a = V_b = 0.20$$

On the compound trial, V_{ab} would be 0.40, so that the change in associative strength on that trial would be

$$\Delta V_a = \Delta V_b = c\,(V_{max} - V_{ab}) = 0.3(1.0 - 0.4) = 0.18$$

In accordance with common sense, in other words, the model predicts an increase in fear conditioning on this trial.

Now suppose that extensive conditioning to the tone and light took place before the first compound trial, with this result

$$V_a = V_b = 0.9$$

In this case, the associative strength of the compound would be 1.8, so that on the compound trial:

$$\Delta V_a = \Delta V_b = c\,(V_{max} - V_{ab}) = 0.3(1.0 - 1.8) = -0.24$$

Even though the compound is still being followed by a powerful electric shock, the model now predicts a decrease in fear levels!

This prediction was tested in an experiment by Rescorla (1970). In the first phase, rats were given extensive pairings of both a tone and a light with shock, so that fear conditioning to each would be essentially at asymptotic levels. An experimental group was then given 12 compound trials in which the tone and the light were presented together and followed by the same shock as in training; a control group received no further training. Finally, fear conditioning to the two stimuli was assessed by presenting them separately in a CER (conditioned emotional response) test. (See Chapter 3 for a discussion of the CER test.)

Figure 4.6 shows the results of this experiment. Let us look first at the results for the light: Note that responding was suppressed much more in the control group (suppression ratio of 0.03) than in the experimental group (suppression ratio of 0.17). The initial pairing of the light with shock, in other words, had resulted in strong fear conditioning, but the additional pairings in the experimental

FIGURE 4.6   Fear elicited by a light and a tone following simple conditioning or after additional conditioning trials in which the tone and light were presented jointly, followed by shock. (Based on data from Rescorla, 1970)

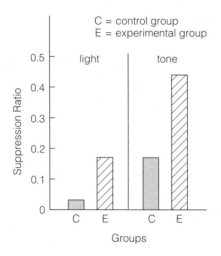

group actually reduced that fear. The effect on the tone was, if anything, even more dramatic, with the extra compound trials resulting in an even greater decrease in fear. Indeed, the tone no longer appeared to elicit any fear at all; the observed suppression ratio of 0.44 was virtually indistinguishable from the neutral point of 0.50. Extra pairings of the tone and light with shock not only did not increase fear, as common sense might predict, but actually reduced or even eliminated it! It is a bizarre result, but precisely what the model predicts.[3]

Implications for Contingency

In some circumstances, then, pairing a stimulus with shock can actually reduce fear of that stimulus. This finding provides us with the key to understanding another fundamental property of conditioning: the effects of contingency. In Chapter 3, we saw that if a CS and a US are presented noncontingently—that is, if the US occurs as often in the absence of the CS as in its presence—then no conditioning occurs. Why, though, does presenting the US by itself interfere with conditioning? According to the principle of contiguity, any event paired with a US should become associated with it, so that when the noncontingent

---

[3] The result is not nearly so strange when viewed from the perspective of the model, because the associative strength of the compound at the beginning of the extra-pairings phase was far greater than V_{max}. If the net fear level is greater than that justified by the shock that actually occurs, it is quite reasonable that subjects will react by reducing their level of fear.

group receives the CS and US together, conditioning should occur. How can presenting the US by itself interfere with the formation of this association?

The key to answering this question, according to Rescorla and Wagner, lies in recognizing that the US is not presented by itself. No stimulus ever occurs in a vacuum; there are always other stimuli present. For a rat in a fear-conditioning experiment, a given stimulus (a) might not be present during shock, but a variety of other cues will be present—visual cues from the walls, tactile cues from the floor, and so on. Some of these background cues (b) will be present uniformly throughout the session; they will be present when a is paired with the shock and also when shock occurs in the absence of a. A more realistic depiction of the actual course of events, then, is this:

$$ab \rightarrow US \ldots \ldots b \rightarrow US \ldots \ldots ab \rightarrow US \ldots \ldots b \rightarrow US$$

Given a sequence of such trials, how much conditioning should we expect to occur with a and b? Intuitively, it is very difficult to say. This is one case in which a mathematical model has an advantage over a more intuitive formulation such as that of Kamin. Figure 4.7 shows the model's prediction.

Initially, conditioning occurs to both a and b, because both are paired with the shock. Eventually, though, conditioning reaches a point where, although V_a and V_b individually are less than V_{max}, their combined strength on a compound trial will exceed V_{max}. In such situations, as we have just seen, the shock will actually reduce the fear associated with a and b. When b by itself is paired with the shock on the next trial, V_b will still be less than V_{max}, so $(V_{max} - V_b)$ will be positive and the associative strength of b will again increase. Over a series of such trials, the model predicts that the strength of b will alternately increase and then decrease, depending on whether a is also present, but that the net effect will be a long-term increase. Because a occurs only on compound trials, however, and because the combined associative strength of a and b on such trials always exceeds V_{max}, the model predicts that a will continue to lose associative strength.

Thus, the model predicts that when shock is presented noncontingently, fear will be strongly conditioned to the background cues but not to the CS. These predictions have been confirmed. Odling-Smee (1975) reported that noncontingent shock results in much greater fear of the apparatus than does contingent shock; as we saw in Chapter 4, Rescorla (1966) reported no fear of the nominal CS. Once confirmed, of course, this prediction makes good sense. The apparatus is a strong predictor of shock because the rat receives shocks only when it is inside the apparatus. Therefore, the apparatus comes to elicit strong fear. The probability of shock when the CS appears, however, is no greater than in its absence, so the rat is quite right not to become more frightened when it is presented.

The seemingly mysterious effects of presenting a US noncontingently, then, can be accounted for if we consider each US presentation as a conditioning

FIGURE 4.7   Changes in associative strength predicted by the Rescorla-Wagner model when a CS and a US are presented noncontingently. It is predicted that the CS will not develop associative strength, but that strong background stimuli such as the test apparatus will develop associative strength.

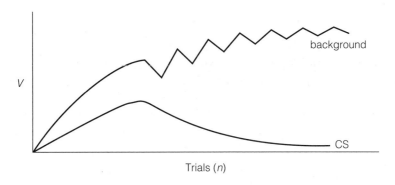

trial in which the US becomes associated with whatever stimuli are present at the time. Conditioning, in other words, *can* be explained in terms of contiguity, provided that we realize the following:

1. The strength of conditioning depends not just on the characteristics of the US but also on whether it was expected.

2. Conditioning occurs not just to the nominal CS but also to background cues that are present.

With these assumptions, we can use the model to explain the effects of noncontingent pairings simply in terms of the associations that form between contiguous stimuli. The end result is impressively sophisticated: Subjects behave as if they are calculating complex probabilities. The actual mechanism, however, might be surprisingly simple, with contingency effects emerging from a series of conditioning trials in which a US is simply associated with the stimuli present at the time.

The Model's Limitations

We have examined in some detail one prediction of the model; other predictions have also been tested and many have been confirmed (for example, Blough, 1975). In some important respects, however, the model's predictions have proved incorrect. We will consider three examples here.

Configural learning.   According to the model, the associative strength of a compound is the sum of the strengths of its components. Suppose, for example, that two stimuli, a and b, were independently paired with a US so that each had an associative strength of 0.5. If the two were presented together, their combined associative strength would then be:

$$V_{ab} = V_a + V_b = 0.5 + 0.5 = 1.0$$

In other words, when two conditioned stimuli are presented together, the model predicts greater responding to the compound than to either of the elements on its own. As plausible as this prediction seems, there are some situations in which the response to a compound is substantially *less* than to its components.

In one experiment demonstrating this point, Bellingham, Gillette-Bellingham, and Kehoe (1985) gave rats discrimination training that involved mixing conditioning trials. Trials in which a tone and a light were paired separately with water alternated with compound trials in which the tone and light were presented together without water:

tone → *water*

light → *water*

tone + *light* → ____

The rats learned to respond at a high rate to the tone and the light by themselves, responding on 90% of trials. When the tone and light were presented together, the model's "additive sum" rule predicts that responding should be even stronger, but in fact it was substantially less, as subjects responded on only 30% of compound trials. (See Figure 4.8.) The associative strength of the compound in this situation was clearly not the sum of its components.

The rats behaved as if they understood that the tone and light on their own signaled food but that, when presented together, they did not. In effect, they were responding to the compound as a unique stimulus or configuration, c, rather than as simply a + b. This phenomenon, in which subjects respond to a compound stimulus in a dramatically different way than they would respond to its elements presented separately, is known as **configural learning.** Pearce (1994) has summarized extensive evidence, much of it from his own laboratory, that configural learning plays a central role in conditioning, with responding often conditioned to a unified configuration of all the elements present rather than separately to each element. We cannot review all this evidence here, but clearly the model's "additive sum" rule is not always right. (For further discussion of configural learning, see Section 9.4.)

Attention. A second instance in which the predictions of the model have proved incorrect involves preexposure to a stimulus before it is paired with a

FIGURE 4.8   Configural learning. Responses to a tone (T+), a light (L+), and a tone-light compound (TL–). The tone and light were followed by water when they were presented on their own but not when they were presented together. (Adapted from Bellingham, Gillette-Bellingham, & Kehoe, 1985)

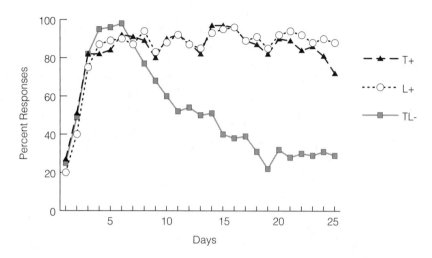

US. In an experiment by Lubow and Moore (1959), a group of sheep and goats were repeatedly shown a flashing light. The animals then received conditioning trials in which the same light was paired with shock. A control group received the identical conditioning trials but without preexposure to the light.

How should preexposure to the light affect subsequent conditioning? According to the Rescorla-Wagner model, when a light is presented by itself during preexposure, no conditioning will occur because no US is presented. In mathematical terms, V_{max} is always zero when no US is presented. If the light is initially neutral ($V = 0$), then

$$\Delta V = c\,(V_{max} - V) = c\,(0 - 0) = 0$$

At the beginning of conditioning in Lubow and Moore's experiment, therefore, the light should have had no associative strength in either group, and learning in the two groups should have proceeded identically. Contrary to this prediction, Lubow and Moore found that conditioning was significantly slower in the group preexposed to the light, a phenomenon they termed **latent inhibition** because they believed that the CS becomes inhibitory during the preexposure phase. Subsequent evidence, though, has made it clear that the CS is neither excitatory nor inhibitory; it is simply difficult to condition. (See Reiss & Wagner, 1972.) To prevent confusion, therefore, many researchers now prefer to use the term **CS preexposure effect** rather than latent inhibition.

Whatever it is called, the most likely explanation for this phenomenon is that when a stimulus is repeatedly presented by itself, we learn to ignore it. Kaye and Pearce (1987) have reported direct evidence that rats really do reduce attention to a stimulus when it is presented repeatedly. The researchers placed their subjects in a test cage containing a light, and occasionally turned on the light. They then simply recorded the percentage of occasions on which the rats turned toward the light when it was presented. At first, the rats oriented to the light about half the time, but over a number of sessions this gradually fell to approximately 15%. When the light was then paired with food, conditioning was significantly slower than in a control group that had never seen the light before. (See also Section 9.5.)

Latent inhibition, then, is a simple phenomenon in which presenting a stimulus by itself reduces its subsequent conditionability, and it can be explained equally simply by reduced attention to the stimulus. As simple as this account is, however, the Rescorla-Wagner model cannot accommodate it, because the model does not include any mechanism for changing the amount of attention paid to a stimulus.

On the surface, modifying the model to allow it to handle changes in attention should not be too difficult. Indeed, several theories have been proposed to this end, but although each has had some impressive successes, none as yet appears able to account for all the available evidence. (For some alternatives, see Mackintosh, 1975; Pearce & Hall, 1980; Wagner, 1981). Schmajuk, Lam, and Gray (1996) have recently proposed a new theory that incorporates the Rescorla-Wagner model and that they argue can integrate existing evidence more successfully, but there has not yet been sufficient time to evaluate its ability to predict new phenomena. Thus although a solution might not be too far off, the Rescorla-Wagner model in its current form cannot account for changes in attention. (See also Chapter 9.)

Occasion setting. A third difficulty for the model emerged with the discovery of a phenomenon known as **occasion setting.** In one experiment illustrating this phenomenon, Rescorla (1985a) trained pigeons that a five-second key light was followed by food on trials when the light was preceded by a noise, but not when it was presented on its own:

$$noise \rightarrow light \rightarrow food$$

$$light \rightarrow \underline{\quad\quad}$$

The noise, in other words, "set the occasion" for when the light would be followed by food, and the birds learned to behave appropriately, pecking the lighted key at a much higher rate on trials in which it had been preceded by the noise.

FIGURE 4.9   Possible explanations for occasion setting: (a) The occasion setter becomes associated directly with the US. (b) The occasion setter enables or facilitates the transmission of excitation between the CS and US.

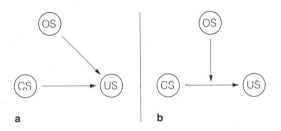

a   b

In itself, this result poses few problems for an associative analysis. Because the noise and the light were both present on reinforced trials, both stimuli would have become associated with the food. On trials in which the noise and light were present together, therefore, the total activation reaching the food center would have been greater than on light-only trials, leading to a stronger tendency to peck. To test this explanation, Rescorla presented the noise on its own 144 times, so that any association between the noise and food would be completely extinguished, and thus the noise should no longer enhance responding to the light. When the noise was again presented with the light during a test phase, however, the birds responded almost three times as often as when the key light was presented by itself. Indeed, the results from a control condition showed that the extinction trials had not produced any decrease whatsoever in the effectiveness of the noise as an occasion setter (OS). The strength of the association between the OS and food was clearly not a very important factor in the capacity of the OS to increase responding.

But if an OS does not increase responding because of its association with food, then why does an OS increase responding? Holland (1985) has proposed that occasion setters are not directly associated with a US (Figure 4.9a), but rather modulate or facilitate the association between the CS and US (Figure 4.9b). According to this analysis, when the noise was presented in Rescorla's experiment, it facilitated the transmission of a signal between the light and food centers; in the absence of such facilitation, the light was less effective in activating the food center.

If this analysis is correct, then classical conditioning is not based simply on the formation of associations between active centers. (See also Swartzentruber, 1995.) Rather than learning a linear association between two centers, the birds apparently learned a three-term, hierarchical relationship in which a higher-order center (the OS) modulated the association between two lower centers. Schmajuk, Lamoureux, and Holland (1998) have recently proposed an explanation for this phenomenon in terms of neural networks, a topic that we will consider in detail in Chapter 12. Their explanation is still based on the formation of associations, and indeed it still uses a variant of the Rescorla-Wagner to describe the formation of these associations, but it supposes a longer sequence of associations than the original model. Occasion setting thus provides simultaneously a serious challenge to the Rescorla-Wagner model—it cannot be explained in terms of the single associations between CS and US centers assumed by the model—and further evidence of the model's potential power when suitably modified.

Evaluation

Using only a single equation (in essence, a simple comparison of V and V_{max}), the Rescorla-Wagner model can explain an astonishing range of facts about conditioning, including why conditioning, extinction, and blocking occur; why presentation of a US by itself interferes with conditioning; and so on. In addition, this model makes a variety of counterintuitive predictions—for example, that a conditioning trial can reduce associative strength—and many of these predictions have been supported. As researchers have continued to test the model's predictions, however, evidence has accumulated that there are also many phenomena that the model cannot explain. (For a thorough exploration of the model's weaknesses, see Miller, Barnet & Grahame, 1995.)

One problem is that the model focuses on the formation of a CS–US association, and gives little consideration to events occurring before and after this association is formed. Before a CS can activate a center in the cortex, for example, extensive processing occurs in the brain to identify what that stimulus is. As part of this processing, we might attend to only some of the stimuli impinging on our senses (causing latent inhibition), and we might then perceive the elements we do notice as a unitary configuration rather than as a set of separate elements (leading to configural learning). Once a CS center is activated, moreover, the evidence concerning occasion setting suggests that conditioning involves more than just the association of this center with other centers that are active; at a minimum, the brain can form more complex, hierarchical associations involving several centers. And, as we shall see in Section 4.5, even after a CS–US association has been formed, still other processes can come into play when the CS is next presented. (These determine whether the CS–US association that has been formed leads to the activation of a response.) Conditioning, in other words, involves far more than just associating a CS center with a US center, so that even if the Rescorla-Wagner model were entirely accurate in its description of this stage in conditioning, the model would still need to be modified to account for processes occurring both before and after this moment.

Does this mean that the Rescorla-Wagner model should be rejected as just another failed theory? No, for two reasons. First, as already suggested, it might turn out that the model is not so much wrong as incomplete. Thus although it might require modification and extension, the equation at the heart of the model seems to capture a fundamental component of the conditioning process, and this equation might be retained in future models of conditioning. (For examples of some current models that incorporate the equation, see Van Hamme &Wasserman, 1994, and Schmajuk, Lam, & Gray, 1996).

Furthermore, even if the model is ultimately found to be wrong, it has provided a remarkable demonstration of how a few simple assumptions can explain a wide range of seemingly complex phenomena, and in this way contributed to a rebirth of interest in the power of psychological models. The Rescorla-Wagner model has also been successfully applied in other areas of psychology, such as perception, concept learning and social psychology, leading Siegel and Allan (1996) to conclude that "there have been few models in experimental psychology as influential as the Rescorla-Wagner model." Predicting the future is not easy, but it seems likely that the Rescorla-Wagner model will prove to be a major landmark in the development of our understanding of learning.

4.4 WHAT IS LEARNED DURING CONDITIONING?

The Rescorla-Wagner model provides us with a powerful tool for predicting the strength of the association formed on any trial, but the model is silent about the nature of this association. When a tone is paired with food, for example, what exactly is it that the dog associates? Pavlov's view, as we have seen, was that simultaneous activity in the tone and food centers of the brain results in the formation of a new associative pathway between them, so that when the tone is presented, the excitation it produces is transmitted to the food center, and from there to the salivary glands. An alternative analysis, first proposed by Clark Hull (1943), is that when the tone is followed by salivation, an association forms between the tone and salivary centers so the tone will elicit salivation directly.

S–S or S–R Associations?

Pavlov's formulation is sometimes referred to as an **S–S theory,** because it assumes that an association is formed between two stimuli, the CS and the US. (See Figure 4.10a.) Hull's view, on the other hand, is known as an **S–R theory,** because it postulates a direct link between the conditioned stimulus and the response. (See Figure 4.10b.) One way to test which theory is right is to alter the value of the US after conditioning has occurred. Suppose, for example, that after pairing a tone with food we could induce an aversion to that food, so that the dog no longer would eat it. According to Pavlov, presenting the tone leads to excitation of the food center, which is then transmitted to the salivary center. If the link between the food and salivary center is broken, the tone should

FIGURE 4.10   Two versions of what a subject learns during conditioning: (a) The S–S theory holds that an association is formed between the CS and US centers in the brain; excitation is then transmitted from the US center to the UR center through an innate link. (b) The S–R theory holds that an association is formed directly between the CS and the UR. (c) If the link between the US and the UR centers were broken, S–S theory predicts that the CS would no longer elicit a response, whereas S–R theory predicts that it would.

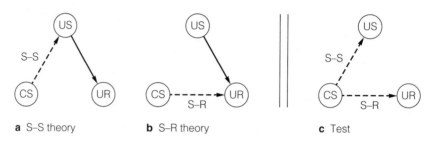

a S–S theory   b S–R theory   c Test

no longer elicit salivation. (See Figure 4.10c.) According to S–R theory, on the other hand, conditioning results in a direct association between the tone and salivation. *Postconditioning devaluation* of the food cannot alter this association, and thus the tone should continue to elicit salivation.

Holland and Straub (1979) tested these predictions in an experiment on rats. During the conditioning phase, a 10-second noise was followed by the delivery of food pellets. The experimenters measured conditioning by the rats' general activity (such as movement around the cage) during the noise. After conditioning was established (the rats' activity doubled when the noise came on), subsequent trials made food unattractive by pairing it with the highly aversive experience of rotation at high speed. The rats were allowed to eat freely from a large dish of pellets for five minutes and were then placed in a cage mounted on a phonograph turntable inclined at 45 degrees and rotated at 120 revolutions per minute for 10 minutes. Finally, the noise was presented again one day later to see if it would still elicit activity.

If the rats had associated the noise with food (S–S theory), then devaluing the food should prevent the noise from eliciting activity. S–R theory, in contrast, predicted that the noise-activity association would still be intact and conditioned activity would be unaffected. In fact, Holland and Straub found a significant decrease in activity to the noise. This reduced activity, moreover, could not be attributed simply to the fact that the rats had been ill because conditioned activity was unaffected in control subjects whose illness was not associated with food. It was the devaluation of the US that weakened the conditioned response.

Signal or Substitute?

That a change in US value affects the conditioned response strongly implies that a representation of the US must form part of the causal chain linking the

CS and the response. There are very different views, however, about the nature of this CS–US link. According to one of the earliest cognitive theorists of associative learning, Edward Tolman (1932), the link was in the form of an expectation: If a tone is followed by food, a dog will form an expectation that future tones will also be followed by food. Tolman was not very specific about how this expectation would then be translated into a conditioned response, but the general notion was that the dog would take whatever action was appropriate to prepare for the expected food. Thus, a dog would salivate when it expected food because such anticipatory salivation would help it to digest the food more quickly and efficiently (see Hollis, 1982); a rabbit would blink when it expected a puff of air to its eye because this blink would protect the eye.

Stimulus substitution. Pavlov's interpretation was very different. As we have seen, he believed that the CS and the US centers became linked so that activation of the CS center would lead to activation of the US center. The CS would therefore elicit exactly the same behaviors as the US did; in effect, it was as if the CS had *become* the US—hence the term **stimulus substitution.** For Tolman, the CS became a signal that food was coming (imagine the dog thinking, "Oh boy, I'm about to get food"); for Pavlov, it effectively became a substitute for that food, in that it elicited the same responses (imagine the dog thinking, "Oh boy, what lovely food this is"). Note, though, that both of these interpretations are *theoretical* statements about what might be going on in the dog's brain; we have no ways of knowing what the dog was actually thinking in either case.

At first, Pavlov's substitution theory might seem silly. A dog may not be a brilliant scholar, but surely it has enough sense to be able to distinguish a tone or a light from food! On closer examination, however, this claim is perhaps not as outrageous as it sounds. First, the assumption that a dog knows that a light is not food begs the important question of how it knows. We tend to think that identifying food is trivially simple; everyone knows, for example, that apples are edible but pebbles are not. Babies, however, do not know this and will often try to ingest objects that are emphatically not edible.

In many species, the young must actively learn to identify food, either by observing their parents or through their own experience. Birds, for example, have quite different pecking movements for eating food and drinking water, but when a newly hatched chick is presented with a drop of water for the first time, it initially attempts to eat it rather than drink it. After only one or two pecks, however, it abruptly changes to the more appropriate drinking response (Hunt & Smith, 1967). What appears to happen is that the presence of water in the chick's beak triggers an innate recognition response. The chick associates this response with the visual cues that preceded ingestion, so that the sight of water will thereafter trigger appropriate drinking behavior.

For the dogs in Pavlov's experiments, therefore, the experience of a light followed by food could have triggered an innate mechanism identifying the light as food, so that it would then elicit salivation and all the other responses appropriate to food. But if the dog really believed the light was food, you may ask yourself, why doesn't the dog try to eat the light? The answer is, the dog does! Pavlov found that when a dog is released from its harness after pairings of a light bulb with food, it eagerly runs over to the light bulb and licks it. The dogs didn't actually chew or swallow the bulb, but this might have been because the bulb's hardness inhibited the dog's swallowing reflexes.

In some studies in which the physical characteristics of the CS have been more appropriate, evidence has been reported that animals *will* try to ingest the CS. One example we have already encountered is autoshaping, in which a pigeon exposed to pairing of a circular key light with food will begin to peck the key. The existence of this phenomenon is very difficult to explain in terms of expectations: If the key light is simply a signal that food is imminent, why does the pigeon bother to peck it? If the lighted key has been identified as food, on the other hand, this pecking at the key becomes more understandable: The bird is trying to eat it.

Powerful support for this interpretation comes from a classic experiment by Jenkins and Moore (1973), who paired a lighted key with food in one group and with water in another. As we have already noted, a bird's responses to food and water are different. When given food, a pigeon pecks with its beak open; when given water, its beak is almost closed, and the pigeon uses its tongue to pump the water into its mouth. Also, a pigeon pecks water with its eyes open, but it pecks food with its eyes closed. (Food pecking is much more forceful, and the pigeon might close its eyes to protect them from ricocheting pebbles.) According to the substitution hypothesis, therefore, pigeons exposed to light-food pairings should try to eat the key with an open beak and closed eyes, whereas those exposed to light-water pairings should peck with a closed beak and open eyes. As Figure 4.11 shows, this was exactly what happened. The pigeons seemed to be trying to eat the key paired with food and to drink the key paired with water.

Further evidence of the power of the mechanism involved, and of its apparent irrationality, comes from another study by Jenkins (reported in Hearst & Jenkins, 1974), in which the key light was located along one wall of a six-foot-long box and the food source along another (Figure 4.12). The key light was occasionally presented for five seconds, followed by the raising of a grain magazine so that the grain was accessible for four seconds. Because of the layout of the box, if the pigeons approached the key and pecked it when the light came on, they could not return to the food dispenser in time to obtain all the available food. Nevertheless, Jenkins found that his birds would run over to the light as soon as it came on, peck it, and then quickly hurry back to the food magazine. Because of the length of the box, they missed most or all of the food on the trials in which they pecked. Despite this, they continued to peck the key in session after session. (See also Williams & Williams, 1969.) Pecking the key seemed more important to the birds than eating.

FIGURE 4.11   Typical responses of key-pecking during autoshaping trials. The photographs on the left show trials in which water was the US. The photographs on the right show trials in which food was the US. (Jenkins & Moore, 1973; photographs courtesy of Bruce Moore)

FIGURE 4.12   Top view of the apparatus used by Jenkins to study autoshaping in pigeons. (Adapted from Domjan & Burkhard, 1986)

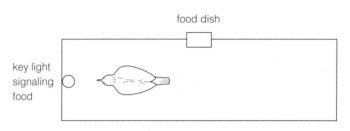

Expectations. Pavlov's substitution theory thus needs to be taken seriously: In many situations, animals do behave as if a CS paired with food really is food, and they will persist in trying to eat the CS even if it costs them real food. On the other hand, evidence also supports Tolman's view that a CS acts as a signal that the US is coming. One source of support comes from observations of dogs' behavior during salivary conditioning experiments. They do not just salivate; they will also turn toward the food tray and, if released from the harness, approach the tray (Zener, 1937). Their behavior strongly suggests that they expect to find food there, and similar results have been obtained in other experiments. In Jenkins' long-box experiment, for example, the pigeons usually approached the key light when it was illuminated, but in some cases they moved toward the food dispenser instead.

Other evidence suggests that animals not only know that a US is about to be presented but know exactly what that US is going to be. In an experiment by Colwill and Motzkin (1994), for example, rats were given conditioning trials in a chamber containing a food magazine on one wall; within the magazine were dispensers for delivering food pellets and liquid sucrose. CS_1, was presented on some trials and followed by access to sucrose; on the remaining trials, a second conditioned stimulus, CS_2, was presented, followed by access to food pellets:

$$CS_1 \rightarrow sucrose$$

$$CS_2 \rightarrow food\ pellets$$

After a few trials, the rats began to approach the food magazine when either CS was presented, indicating that they knew that food would be delivered there. However, the experimenters wanted to know more precisely what the rats were expecting. When CS_1 was presented, for example, did the rats have only a general expectation that food would be presented, or did they know that it would be sucrose?

To find out, the experimenters arranged a postconditioning devaluation phase in which they allowed the rats to drink sucrose for a period of up to 20 minutes, and then gave them an injection of lithium chloride to induce illness. As expected, this conditioned a strong aversion to the sucrose, so that the rats would no longer drink it when it was made available. The experimenters then returned the subjects to the test chamber and again presented CS_1 and CS_2. If the rats knew that CS_1 signaled the availability of sucrose, then they should not approach the magazine when this stimulus was presented, but they should still approach when CS_2 was presented. The results confirmed this prediction, as the devaluation of sucrose had its greatest effect on the response to CS_1. Comparable results were obtained when the food pellets were devalued—this resulted in fewer approaches to the magazine when CS_2 was presented. In this experiment, the rats behaved as if they knew whether the CS would be followed by food pellets or sucrose; in an experiment by Capaldi, Hovancik, and Friedman (1976), they seemed to know whether a CS would be followed by one food pellet or five. When a CS is paired with food, therefore, rats seem to learn exactly what that food is going to be. However, it is important to note that the claim here is not that rats are *consciously* expecting food, but rather that they are behaving *as if* they have such an expectation. We have no way of knowing a rat's conscious thoughts, and it is possible that any knowledge about future events is held in some unconscious form. When we use the term **expectation** in subsequent sections, therefore, all we mean is that subjects have acquired some sort of knowledge about what US is imminent, not necessarily that this knowledge is conscious. (For a more detailed analysis of how expectations might be defined, see Dickinson, 1989.)

A Two-Level Hypothesis

We now have what seems a distinctly confusing situation in which animals sometimes behave as if a CS paired with food actually is food, and try to eat it, but at other times behave as if the CS is simply a signal that food is coming and initiate appropriate action to obtain it. (See also Jenkins, Barrera, Ireland, & Woodside, 1978; Timberlake, Wahl, & King, 1982.) One way to resolve this conflict is to assume that both views are correct, and that the reason why the outcome varies is that classical conditioning actually involves two distinct learning systems—an *associative* system in which the CS elicits responses automatically, and a *cognitive* system in which expectations guide responding. Perhaps the first learning system to evolve was a relatively primitive one in which the CS was simply associated with the US and thus elicited the same responses. In the course of time, a more sophisticated system developed that involved active anticipation of the US; this allowed subjects to flexibly select from a range of preparatory responses, taking into account other information available at the time. Insofar as both systems still coexist in vertebrates, this would explain why animals sometimes act as if the CS is a signal for food and at other times as if it actually is food.

The idea that the brain contains two distinct learning systems has been proposed by a number of theorists over the years (for example, Konorski, 1967; Razran, 1971; Squire, 1992). Each theorist has attributed somewhat different properties to the two systems, but a common theme has been that one system is essentially simple and automatic, whereas the other involves some sort of expectation about the properties of the forthcoming US. We will call the assumption of two systems, one associative and the other more cognitive, the **two-level hypothesis.**

The brain's evolution. Indirect evidence for two learning systems comes from what is known about the evolution of the vertebrate brain. Studies of fossil records and of the brains of living species suggest that the vertebrate brain has changed enormously in the course of evolution. These changes, however, have consisted not so much in the disappearance of old structures—most of the primitive structures of an alligator or rat brain can still be easily recognized, almost unchanged, in that of a human—as in the elaboration of new structures. In particular, there has been a massive increase in the outer covering of the brain known as the *neocortex*.[4] The proportion of the brain devoted to neocortex in humans is 150 times greater, relative to body weight, than in the tree-shrew-like mammals from which we are thought to have descended. The functions of this vastly expanded neocortex include cognitive processes such as thinking and language. The neocortex is also the center of awareness. (If the neocortex is damaged or anesthetized, a person loses consciousness.)

In the course of evolution, the anatomy of the central core of the brain has remained unchanged to a remarkable extent, with emerging cognitive functions concentrated in a massively expanded outer region. Insofar as the older core has retained its old functions as well as structure, a relatively primitive associative system might still be present in vertebrates along with a more advanced cognitive one. Epstein (1994) has recently proposed a similar hypothesis to account for human emotions, suggesting that a largely preconscious system evolved first, and that this system remained when a more rational and analytical system emerged. In his words,

> It is inconceivable that, with the advent of language and the capacity for analytical thought, the hard-won gains of millions of years of evolution were summarily abandoned. It can more reasonably be assumed that the same principles . . . that apply to nonhuman animal cognitions apply as well to human cognitions, wherein

---

[4] The outer covering of the brain is called the *cortex*. Some form of cortex is present in most vertebrates, but it is expanded considerably in mammals, and the larger, newer section of the cortex is called the *neocortex*. In humans, most of the cortex consists of neocortex.

they influence and are in turn influenced by a newly acquired verbal-analytical rational system. (p. 714)

Two routes to fear. More direct evidence for the existence of two learning systems has come from recent research on the physiological mechanisms underlying fear conditioning. On the basis of this research, LeDoux (1994) has proposed that the area of the brain primarily responsible for the conditioning of fear is a structure called the *amygdala*. When the amygdala is surgically removed, for example, rats do not learn to fear a tone that signals shock. LeDoux found two different pathways leading from the senses to the amygdala: a direct path that can trigger a fear response very quickly, and an indirect path that goes first to the cortex and only then to the amygdala. He suggested that the direct path allows a rapid, automatic response to signals of possible danger, whereas the cortical path, although slower, allows subjects to evaluate the signal more carefully and decide whether fear is really appropriate.

LeDoux's research was carried out with rats, but a recent study by Bechara, Tranel, Damasio, Adolphs, Rockland, and Damasio (1995) suggests that similar systems exist in humans. Bechara and colleagues exposed their subjects to a series of colored slides, presented in random order. When the color blue appeared, it was followed by a loud blast of a horn. They used subjects' GSR to assess fear conditioning, and at the end of the conditioning trials they also asked subjects which color had been followed by the horn.

One of their subjects had a hereditary condition that causes damage to the amygdala. This subject showed no increase in GSR to the blue slide, indicating no fear. When later asked which of the colors had been followed by the horn, however, the subject correctly identified the color as blue. We thus have a rather unusual situation where even though the subject knew that blue would be followed by an unpleasant noise, blue did not elicit fear. The cortical system still produced an expectation of the aversive stimulus, but the amygdala was not translating this expectation into fear.

The same procedure was used with a second patient who had suffered accidental damage to the hippocampus, an area of the brain that is known to play an important role in certain kinds of memory. This patient showed normal conditioning, with a significantly stronger GSR to blue than to any of the other colors. When asked which color was followed by noise, however, the subject was unable to say. Together with the results for the first subject, these findings suggest that fear conditioning and conscious knowledge of the relationship between the CS and the US can occur independently, with damage to the brain eliminating one system but leaving the other unaffected. (See also Knowlton, Mangels, & Squire, 1996.)

There is suggestive evidence, then, for the existence of two distinct systems in conditioning: a relatively primitive system based on associations, and a cognitive system based on expectations. The existence of separate systems could help explain situations where we feel frightened but cannot say why. In one clinical example, a woman who had been raped had no conscious memory of the incident, but she became extremely upset when returned to the scene of the crime (Christianson & Nilsson, 1989). In situations like these, unconscious associations can elicit fear even though we have no conscious awareness of why we feel anxious.

Despite its intuitive appeal, as a scientific theory the two-level hypothesis suffers from regrettable vagueness. What are the exact properties of the associative and cognitive systems that are being proposed? And if there really are two systems, what is the relationship between them? We can illustrate the problem with an experiment on rats by Timberlake, Wahl, and King (1982). The researchers occasionally gave the rats food pellets, and before each delivery they rolled a metal ball across the floor of the cage. If the time interval between the ball's appearance and the delivery of food was short, then when the rats saw the ball they ran over to the pellet dispenser and waited, acting as if they knew that food was coming. If the time interval was long, on the other hand, the rats picked up the rolling ball and chewed it, acting as if it was food. Our two-process account can explain both behaviors, but it gives us no basis for predicting in advance which system will control responding, or how the output of the two systems might combine to jointly determine behavior. Thus, although a two-level account offers us a plausible framework for understanding conditioning, at present it is more of a promissory note for the future ("Here is the framework—details to be filled in later") than a fully worked-out theory. The portrait is attractive, but we will need more evidence before we can decide if it provides a good likeness.

4.5 The Determinants of Performance

Suppose that we give a dog conditioning trials in which a tone is followed by food, and that these pairings lead to the formation of a strong tone–food association. If we now present the tone by itself, can we predict how the dog will respond?

Choosing the Conditioned Response

The CR and the UR. This question might seem a bit strange, because all the research we have considered to this point suggests that the answer is so obvious as to be trivial: The response to a CS is always the same as the response to the US, so that in this case the dog will salivate. We did encounter evidence in Chapter 2 that conditioned responses to drugs sometimes differ from the unconditioned responses—insulin, for example, produces an decrease in blood sugar, whereas the conditioned response is an increase. We noted, however, that this divergence might be the result of a misunderstanding of the unconditioned response; if we properly identify the unconditioned response as the response mediated by the nervous system, the conditioned and unconditioned responses are the same.

Insofar as autonomic conditioned responses are concerned, then, the assumption that the conditioned response is the same as the unconditioned response appears to be valid. If we turn to skeletal conditioned responses, however, the picture becomes more complicated. In some cases, the conditioned skeletal response is the same as the unconditioned response—the eyeblink is a classic example—but in other cases these responses differ considerably. One early example was reported by Zener (1937), who trained dogs in a salivary conditioning experiment in which a bell was paired with food. The dogs responded to the food by licking and chewing it. The bell, however, elicited none of these responses, and the dogs instead engaged in behaviors such as orienting to the food tray, panting rapidly, and yawning.

Another example concerns electric shock. If a rat is placed in a cage and given shock through the floor, its unconditioned response to the shock is to jump and prance about the cage in an effort to escape it. If the shock is preceded by a tone, however, the rat's conditioned response to the tone is to freeze (Fanselow, 1989).

Still a third example comes from an experiment by Holland (1977) in which rats were exposed to pairings of a tone with food. Holland found that his subjects began to jerk their heads when the tone was presented, even though neither the tone nor the food elicited this response before they were paired. At least insofar as skeletal responses are concerned, therefore, there are many situations in which the CR and UR are not the same. (See also Wasserman, 1973; Timberlake & Grant, 1975.)

This evidence poses problems for both the associative and cognitive theories of learning that we have been considering. According to an associative account, a CS activates first the CS center and then the US center. The response to the CS, therefore, should be exactly the same as the response normally elicited by the US. A cognitive or expectancy analysis is rather vaguer—it essentially says that subjects should take "appropriate" action when expecting a US, but provides little guidance about what that preparatory action should be. (Why, for example, did Holland's rats begin to jerk their heads when they were expecting food?) An expectancy analysis thus offers us little guidance about what response to expect; stimulus-substitution theory offers us clear guidance, but the guidance is wrong. What now?

A behavior-system analysis. Fortunately, a number of theorists have converged on very similar explanations for why conditioned responses sometimes differ from unconditioned responses (for example, Jenkins, Barrera, Ireland, & Woodside, 1978; Timberlake, 1984). In effect, this explanation emphasizes the role of motivation in determining the conditioned response. We saw in Chapter 2 that when a CS is paired with a US, one result is the conditioning of a motivational state. If food is used as a US, for example, the CS paired with it will come to elicit hunger. Hunger will then elicit behaviors appropriate to obtaining food as well as consuming it. If you were a lion and saw an antelope in the distance, for example, you would not immediately begin to make chewing movements: You would need to stalk and kill the antelope before trying to eat it. Similarly in a classical conditioning situation, the CS will elicit behaviors directed toward *obtaining* the US as well as *consuming* it.

To see how this assumption can help us explain the form of conditioned responses, we will begin by outlining a more formal version developed by Timberlake (1984), which he called a behavior-system approach. The first assumption is that behavior is organized within relatively independent systems, with each system determining the initiation and sequencing of the behaviors that it controls. A rat, for example, must perform many activities to survive—finding food and water, avoiding predators, obtaining a mate—and each of these activities is controlled by a different **behavior system.**

Suppose, for example, that a rat is hungry. This hunger will activate the rat's feeding system, which will in turn activate alternative subsystems for obtaining food. Figure 4.13 presents a highly simplified outline of a possible feeding system, involving only three subsystems; the actual feeding system is thought to be considerably more complex. (The account presented here is not Timberlake's, but a synthesis of systems proposed by Timberlake & Lucas, 1989, and Davey, 1989.) The example assumes that the rat can choose among three main strategies for obtaining food: chasing a live prey, foraging alone for foods such as wheat grains, or foraging together with other rats. (Rats are nocturnal animals that live in colonies and often search for food together.) Which of these subsystems is activated will depend on the stimuli present at the time. If a small moving object is visible, this might activate the predatory system; a small object resembling a wheat grain might activate the foraging system; the presence of other rats might activate social foraging. Whichever system is activated, it will prime a further set of possible responses, such as chasing and biting; again, which of these primed responses occurs will depend on the stimuli that are present.

The stimuli that guide these responses resemble Pavlovian unconditioned stimuli in some respects, in that they innately elicit certain responses. Whether an animal responds to one of these stimuli, however, depends on the animal's motivational state. If a lion has just eaten, for example, then even the most succulent-looking antelope will not elicit stalking behavior. Stimuli that have the potential to release responses, rather than reliably eliciting them in every case, are referred to as *releasing stimuli* or *releasers*. (In the lion example, the antelope is a releaser for stalking behavior.)

In summary, behavior-system analyses assume that behavior is organized into a number of motivational systems. When one of these motivational systems is activated, it primes a set of potential responses. If a releasing stimulus is

FIGURE 4.13   A possible behavior system for feeding in rats. Hunger is assumed to prime a set of possible food-obtaining responses; a primed response will occur if its natural releasing stimulus is present.

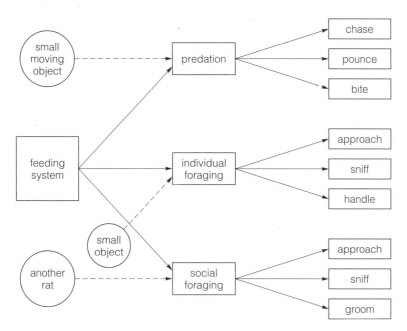

present, it will then trigger one of these primed responses. The end result is that behavior in any situation is jointly determined by an animal's motivational state and the releasing stimuli that are present.

Implications for conditioning.   How does all this help us to understand the conditioned response? If a CS is paired with a US, we have seen that one result will be the conditioning of a motivational state. If a rat is exposed to pairings of a tone with food, for example, then the tone will come to elicit hunger. What the rat does when it is hungry, however, will depend on the stimuli that are present. In particular, behavior-system theorists have suggested that the response will depend on *whether the CS resembles a releaser for feeding behavior.* If the CS is a small moving object, for example, then it might resemble the releaser for predatory behavior, and the rat might chase the CS. On the other hand, if the CS is very small and stationary, it might look like the sort of grains that elicit foraging behavior, and the rat might approach and sniff it.

This analysis can also help us understand why rats' unconditioned response to shock is escape but the conditioned response is freezing. A rat's defensive system includes several responses; one of the main determinants of which response will occur is how far away a potential predator is. (See

Fanselow, 1989.) If a predator is distant, a rat will freeze to avoid detection; if the predator is close and attacks the rat, the rat will struggle to escape. For the rat, shock in an experiment is probably the equivalent of being attacked by a predator, and the shock thus elicits attempts to escape. However, if the shock is preceded by a warning signal, and if this signal is similar to the properties of a predator seen at a distance, then the rat will respond by freezing. (Because of the importance of detecting predators, and their potential concealment, it seems a reasonable guess that in this case almost any stimulus is accepted as a sign of a possible predator.)

One problem with this account is that we do not know enough about the releasers that control an animal's behavior to be able to predict whether a CS such as light or a tone will resemble one of these releasers, and thus it is difficult to predict in advance what conditioned response will occur. This problem is by no means insoluble—all we need is more research to identify releasers and measure their similarity to conditioned stimuli—but it does mean that although the behavior-system approach provides a useful framework for thinking about conditioning, it has not yet led to many testable predictions. In the few cases where prediction has been possible, however, the results so far have been encouraging. (See also Timberlake, 1994; Silva & Timberlake, 1997.)

Learning without Performance

We started this section by asking how a dog would respond to a tone associated with food. We have taken it for granted that the tone would elicit a response—the only issue has been what this response would be. However, Ralph Miller and his colleagues at the State University of New York at Binghamton have argued that the existence of a CS–US association, even a strong one, does not necessarily mean that the CS will elicit a conditioned response. To see how this could be so, it might be helpful to step back for a moment and consider the distinction between *learning* and *performance*. Essentially, learning is about what we *know*, whereas performance is about what we *do*. You may have learned that it is important to study to get good grades, but when the time comes to study, you might be swayed by other factors such as a wonderful party that you have heard a friend is giving. Learning, in other words, is not always translated into performance.

Classical conditioning might at first seem a much simpler situation in which a CS will elicit a response automatically, but Miller and his colleagues have argued that here too subjects may consider a number of factors before deciding whether to respond (for example, Miller & Matzel, 1989). We will not give the details of this theory here, but we can illustrate the general approach with research on simultaneous conditioning. As we saw in section 3.1, simultaneous conditioning is a procedure in which a CS and US are presented simultaneously. The principle of contiguity suggests that conditioning should be

FIGURE 4.14   Procedure for the Matzel, Held, and Miller (1988) experiment. During the sensory preconditioning phase, a click was paired with a tone; during the subsequent simultaneous conditioning phase, the tone was presented at the same time as a shock.

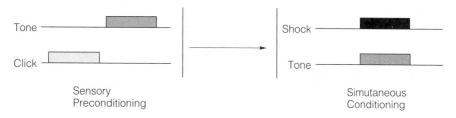

particularly strong with this procedure because the CS and US are presented
without any gap between them, but in fact this procedure normally results in
little or no conditioning.

The failure of conditioning with this procedure has generally been taken to
mean that an association is not formed when a CS and US occur simultaneously, but Matzel, Held, and Miller (1988) suggested another interpretation.
Suppose, they said, that an association *is* formed, but that this association is not
translated into performance. In most conditioning experiments the CS precedes the US; the CS thus provides information about when the US will occur,
and subjects use this information to decide when to respond (Miller & Barnet,
1993). The purpose of this response is to prepare for the forthcoming US, but if
the CS and US occur simultaneously then there is no time to prepare, and
hence no purpose in responding to the CS.

According to Matzel et al.'s analysis, simultaneous conditioning produces a
strong association between the CS and the US, but the experimental situation
does not provide subjects with a motive to respond. To reveal this latent or hidden association, they devised an ingenious procedure involving sensory preconditioning (Section 2.5). During the first phase of their experiment, Matzel and
colleagues presented rats with a click followed by a tone. Then, in the conditioning phase, they presented the tone simultaneously with shock (Figure 4.14).
Finally, they presented the click and the tone separately in a modified CER test
to see whether the two stimuli elicited fear. The results were that the click produced fear but that the tone did not.

The fact that the tone did not produce fear is not surprising: The tone and
the shock were presented at the same time on conditioning trials, and simultaneous conditioning is rarely successful. Why, though, did the click produce fear,
given that it was never paired with shock? The answer, according to Matzel and
his colleagues, is that when the click was presented, subjects knew from the sensory preconditioning phase that it would be followed by the tone, and they knew
from the simultaneous conditioning phase that the tone would be accompanied

by shock. When the click was presented, therefore, the rats expected shock to follow and they thus became frightened.

A control group established that this result was obtained only if the tone and shock were presented together during the conditioning phase—if they were presented separately, the click did not elicit fear on test trials. Clearly, therefore, simultaneous presentations of the tone and shock did produce learning, even though this was not revealed when the tone was presented. This supports Miller's claim that the absence of a response following conditioning does not necessarily mean that there was no learning. In the case of simultaneous conditioning, subjects do seem to learn about the relationship between the CS and the US, but they do not respond when the CS is presented because there is insufficient time to prepare for the US.

More broadly, this evidence provides further support for the view that when a CS is presented, it does not elicit a response automatically. Instead, it initiates what might be called a decision process in which subjects consider several factors before deciding whether to respond. (For further details, see Miller & Matzel, 1989; Miller & Barnet, 1993.) One such factor appears to be whether there is time to prepare; another factor is whether the CS resembles stimuli that release innate behaviors designed to obtain food or avoid dangerous situations.

Once again, then, conditioning appears to be a more complicated process than Pavlov imagined. We saw earlier that animals do not just associate brain centers during conditioning; they can also form detailed expectations about when and where the US will be presented. And, once this information has been acquired, there appears to be a separate, decision-making phase in which subjects use this information to decide whether to respond, and, if so, how.

4.6 CONDITIONING IN HUMANS

Most of the evidence on conditioning that we have considered has come from experiments on animals, but we have seen that the same principles often apply in humans. In fear conditioning and taste-aversion learning, for example, conditioning in animals and humans occurs in about the same number of trials, varies with the contiguity and contingency of the stimuli, and so on. The human capacity for language, however, makes it possible for us to ask questions about conditioning in humans that we cannot ask in animals—for example, whether conditioning can occur without awareness. In this section we will examine two of these more specialized aspects of conditioning.

Conditioning without Awareness

One reason for the initial interest in conditioning—and one reason the word *conditioning* has acquired ominous overtones, suggesting brainwashing and the world of George Orwell's 1984—is that it seems a wholly automatic process, occurring without our awareness and even against our wishes. Pavlov rings a bell and the dog salivates; a dictator—or advertiser—says the critical word and the conditioned masses respond with instant fear or rapture. But is this image realistic? Can conditioning really occur without our awareness?

Eyeblink conditioning. The two-level hypothesis says that conditioning involves two distinct learning systems: A relatively primitive system based on associations and a more cognitive system that involves anticipation of the forthcoming US and its properties. It seems plausible that processing in the associative system would be automatic, whereas processing in the cognitive system would be more likely to involve conscious awareness of the relationship between the CS and the US. (See also Öhman, 1988.) If so, then we should expect conditioning in humans normally to be accompanied by awareness; if the influence of the cognitive system could be eliminated, however, then conditioning should be controlled exclusively by the associative system and hence occur without awareness.

Evidence for this hypothesis has come from a series of experiments by Kenneth Spence (1966). Spence noted that extinction of eyeblink responses in animals is a very slow process, often requiring more than 500 trials, but that the conditioned response in humans disappears after only one or two extinction trials. Spence believed that the slow extinction in animals was due to the response's being controlled by a more primitive associative system. In humans, the cognitive system plays a more dominant role: As soon as subjects realize that the CS is no longer being followed by the US, they immediately stop blinking. The fact that extinction is rapid, however, does not necessarily mean that the slow associative system is no longer present. Spence believed that this slower system remains active in humans, but that its output is being overridden by the dominant cognitive system. If the cognitive system could be eliminated, he argued, then extinction in humans would follow the same gradual time course observed in animals.

To test this hypothesis, Spence needed some way to eliminate the cognitive system. One solution would have been to remove the cortex surgically. Perhaps anticipating the difficulties that he would have faced in recruiting subjects, Spence devised an ingenious alternative. Rather than eliminating the cognitive system physically, he eliminated it functionally, by giving his subjects a demanding distraction task. If the task were sufficiently difficult, Spence reasoned, the processing capacity of the cognitive system would be fully absorbed, and any conditioning would be under the control of the associative system.

Spence, Homzie, and Rutledge (1964) used two groups of college students as subjects and gave both groups trials in which a tone was followed after half a second by an air puff. The experimental group was told that the purpose of the study was to examine the effects of distraction on problem solving. When a warning

FIGURE 4.15   Extinction of a conditioned eyeblink response. The experimental subjects were given a
distraction task to prevent awareness of the change in contingency; control subjects were
not. On the x-axis, C indicates responding at the end of the conditioning phase. (Spence,
Homzie, & Rutledge, 1964)

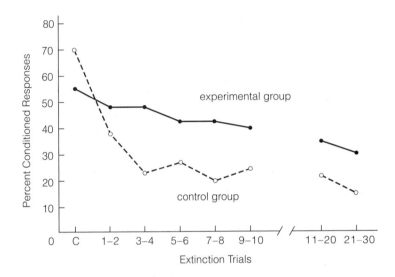

light came on, the subjects were supposed to push a button indicating which one
of two lights they believed would be illuminated two seconds later. To distract
them, it was further explained, irrelevant tones and air puffs would be presented
during the two-second decision period. A control group received the same pairings of tone and air puff, but without the concurrent problem-solving task.

After 50 pairings of the tone and air puff, extinction was begun. Instead of
omitting the air puff, however, the experimenters lengthened the CS–US interval from 0.5 to 2.5 seconds. Previous research had shown that conditioned
blinking would extinguish at this interval; by continuing to present the air puff,
the experimenters hoped to draw the subjects' attention away from the change
in CS–US contingency. The two-level hypothesis predicts that, with the cognitive system eliminated, blinking should extinguish gradually. As Figure 4.15
shows, this is what the experimenters found. Responding in the control group
extinguished very quickly, dropping from around 70% to 25% in only three trials. Conditioned responding in the experimental group, however, declined
much more gradually, and after 10 trials had fallen by only 14%. Postexperi-
ment interviews confirmed that subjects in the experimental group had not noticed the change in the CS–US interval during extinction, whereas almost all
of the control subjects had noticed the change. As predicted by the two-level

hypothesis, therefore, extinction was rapid when subjects were aware of the change in contingency but slow when they were not.

GSR conditioning. Spence prevented subjects from becoming aware of the relationship between a CS and a US by distracting their attention from this relationship. An alternative, potentially even more powerful, solution is to prevent them from detecting the CS in the first place! In one experiment using this approach, Öhman and Soares (1998) gave subjects GSR conditioning trials in which a picture of an animal (a snake or a spider) was paired with a mild electric shock. They used a discriminative conditioning procedure in which one picture, CS+, was followed by shock, while the other was not:

$$CS+ \rightarrow shock$$

$$CS- \rightarrow \underline{\qquad}$$

To prevent subjects from being aware of which CS had been presented, each picture was presented for only 30 milliseconds (0.03 seconds), immediately followed by a masking stimulus—in this case, a meaningless jumble of dark and light shapes. (Research has shown that masking stimuli interrupt the processing of brief stimuli that precede them, so that these earlier stimuli are effectively erased before subjects become consciously aware of them.)

Despite the use of this mask, conditioning occurred, and CS+ elicited substantially higher GSRs than CS–. To test whether the mask had really blocked awareness of the CS, the experimenters used an additional group in which there was a four second gap between the presentations of the CS and US, and subjects were asked to report during the gap whether the picture had been of a snake or a spider. The percentage of correct responses was almost exactly at chance (50.5%), confirming that subjects had no idea what stimulus had been presented. And yet, despite subjects having no awareness of the CS, presentation of the stimulus elicited a strong GSR.

These results, together with those of Spence, support the view that conditioning can occur without subjects' awareness. (See Shanks & St. John, 1994, for a more skeptical view.) The results also fit nicely with our earlier discussion of the two-level hypothesis. There we reviewed the Bechara et al. experiment in which brain-damaged subjects were given conditioning trials in which the color blue was followed by a blast of a horn. One subject showed GSR conditioning despite having no awareness of the relationship between the two stimuli, while another subject was aware of the relationship but developed no fear. These results suggest that learning can occur in parallel in two separate systems: A relatively primitive system in which associations are formed without conscious awareness and a more sophisticated cognitive system that produces conscious expectations. Because these systems normally are in operation at the same time, we usually become aware of the relationship between the CS and US during conditioning. If the cognitive system is distracted or damaged, however, then conditioning can still proceed in the associative system without our awareness. (See also Ince, Brucker, & Alba, 1978.)

Advertising. Conditioning without awareness can play an important role in our daily lives. Certainly, much advertising is based on what seems to be a conditioning process. By pairing a product with highly positive stimuli, advertisers hope that our feelings about the positive stimuli will be transferred, without our awareness, to the target. A picture of an automobile, for example, is accompanied by an attractive female, and a commercial for a political candidate is set against a scenic background and accompanied by patriotic or other stirring music. At least some evidence indicates, moreover, that such juxtapositions do result in the conditioning of emotional reactions to the target stimulus. In a study by Janis, Kaye, and Kirschner (1965), subjects who read a persuasive message while eating were significantly more likely to accept the positions advocated than were subjects who read the identical articles while not eating. Gorn (1982) found that attractive music played during a commercial significantly increased preference for the product. And, as we discussed in Chapter 1, Smith and Engel (1968) found that the presence of an attractive woman standing next to an automobile powerfully influenced subjects' evaluation of that car. In both these studies, the authors interviewed their subjects at the completion of the experiments and found that almost all subjects denied that their rating of the product had been affected by the attractive stimulus that accompanied it. (For additional evidence, see Cacioppo, Marshall-Goodell, Tassinary, & Petty, 1992, and De Houwer, Baeyens, & Eelen, 1994.)

Under some circumstances, then, conditioning does seem to be automatic, and our behavior can be influenced without our realizing it. The popular image of involuntary brainwashing, however, is almost certainly exaggerated. In most cases subjects are aware of what is happening during conditioning, and even in the case of advertising, where we sometimes seem unaware of how our emotions are being manipulated, there is evidence that the effects of this conditioning are neither as powerful nor as long-lasting as more reasoned presentations of logical arguments (Petty & Cacioppo, 1986). Human behavior seems to be based on a complex amalgam of reason and emotion, and we need to take both aspects into account in predicting how people will behave.

Causal Learning

In previous sections we have traced a gradual shift in psychologists' understanding of classical conditioning. At first, they saw conditioning as a basically simple process in which associations were formed between whatever centers were active at the time. There was some uncertainty whether a connection went directly from the CS center to the response, or indirectly through a US center, but, either way, activation of the CS center led directly and automatically to a response.

Several discoveries over the years have led to profound changes in this view. Research on contingency and blocking suggested that conditioning did not occur indiscriminately to whatever stimuli happened to precede a US but instead became focused on the stimulus that was the best predictor. Research on expectations further suggested that conditioning is not simply a matter of connecting CS and US centers. In salivary conditioning, for example, dogs learn when and where food is coming, and they will orient to the place where food is to appear. Finally, research on sensory preconditioning demonstrated that the system for detecting relationships between events is not confined to pairings involving a US. If a light is followed by a noise, for example, then rats will learn about this relationship in the same way that they learn that a light is followed by food.

Together, these findings suggest that conditioning involves far more than just the formation of associations; it appears to be a sophisticated system for detecting relationships between events, allowing us to anticipate when events are going to occur and take preparatory action. (See also Rescorla, 1988.)

Causal learning and conditioning. If this recent perspective is correct, and classical conditioning has at its core a system for detecting relationships between events, it raises the question of whether the same system might be involved in other situations where we detect relationships between events. In our daily lives, we are constantly making judgments on issues such as how our behavior affects others' liking for us, what foods are causing our allergies, whether a medicine is really helping us, and so on. Could the processes involved in classical conditioning also play a role in these other instances of causal judgment or **causal learning?**

If the processes involved in conditioning and causal learning were similar, we should expect the principles and properties of the two forms of learning to also be similar. To a perhaps surprising degree, this does appear to be the case. For example, we have seen that conditioning depends on factors such as the contiguity and contingency between two events, and the same is true in causal learning. (See Allan, 1993; Young, 1995.) Similarly, phenomena such as blocking and inhibitory conditioning have been demonstrated in human causal learning (for example, Dickinson, Shanks and Evenden, 1984). Perhaps the most striking evidence for the similarity of classical conditioning in animals and causal learning in humans, though, has come from an experiment by one of the early researchers in this area, Edward Wasserman.

Sickening strawberries. Wasserman (1990) asked participants in his study to imagine that they were doctors treating a patient with an allergy; their task was

FIGURE 4.16   Judgments of causality by college students and pigeons. Both groups were given training in which AC and BC compounds were sometimes followed by an outcome, and the probability of the outcome following the compounds varied in different conditions. The x-axis shows the degree to which AC was a better predictor of the outcome than BC. The y-axis shows (a) college students' ratings of whether A, B and C caused the outcome, and (b) pigeons' pecks at equivalent stimuli. (Adapted from Wasserman, 1990)

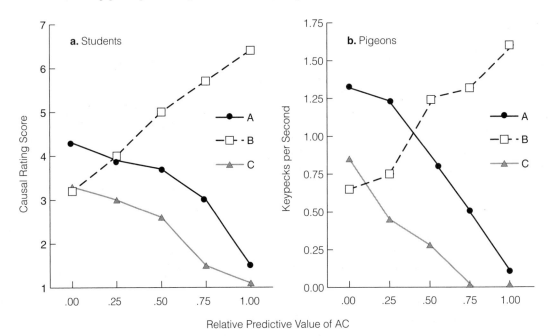

to discover which of the foods he ate were producing his allergic reaction. They were told what foods he ate each night, and whether he became ill after each meal. It turned out the patient had an extraordinarily boring diet: Dinner each night consisted of either shrimp and strawberries or shrimp and peanuts. The main variable in the experiment was the probability of becoming ill after eating these two meals. The average probability of becoming ill after eating a meal was always .50, but the distribution of illness following the two kinds of meals was varied: In one group, the probability of becoming ill was the same after both meals, in another it was somewhat higher after eating the meal containing strawberries, in a third it was higher still, and so on. After viewing the contents of each meal and the outcome, subjects were asked to rate the degree of causal relationship between eating each food and becoming ill.

Figure 4.16a shows subjects' causal ratings for the three foods as a function of the different outcomes. In one respect, the results are predictable. As the probability of becoming ill after the strawberry meal increased, subjects rated the strawberries (A) as a more likely cause of illness, and the peanuts (B) as a less likely cause. Somewhat less predictably, the rating of shrimp (C) also changed between conditions, even though the average probability of becoming ill after eating a shrimp meal was .50 in all groups. (We will not derive the prediction here, but this result follows directly from the Rescorla-Wagner model.) The most striking aspect of Wasserman's results, however, was the similarity of the data to data he had previously obtained in an autoshaping experiment with pigeons (Figure 4.16b). Though the exact details of the two procedures inevitably differed (the stimuli in the pigeon experiment were colors rather than food names, the outcome to be predicted was grain rather than an allergy, and so on), the conditioned responses for the pigeons exhibit a quite extraordinary parallel with the rating judgments of the humans. When similar conditions were arranged, the two species appeared to be evaluating the causal relationships involved almost identically.

It is important to emphasize that we are not claiming that the processes involved are identical: The conditioning of an eyeblink and a doctor's decision about whether a patient is suffering from pneumonia are unlikely to involve exactly the same processes. Nevertheless, the processes involved might be similar in important respects. We tend to think of human decision making as a highly rational and sophisticated process, and conditioning as a very primitive one, but they might not differ as dramatically as this summary suggests. We have already seen that classical conditioning is a much more complex process than it appears; conversely, in Chapter 10 we will find that human decision making is often much less sophisticated, than we realize. The gulf between these two classes of behavior might thus be narrower than it seems; if so, it is possible that the processes that have evolved over many hundreds of thousands of years to help animals detect causal relationships also play a role in human judgments. Cheng (1997) has recently proposed an impressive theory of causal learning in humans, and in the conclusion to her paper she notes that many of the phenomena that she has tried to explain in humans are also present in animals. Perhaps, she speculates, her theory will prove equally applicable in both domains. It will be difficult to evaluate this possibility until we have a deeper understanding of the processes involved in each, but it is possible that both are based on a sophisticated system that has evolved to allow animals to detect relationships between important events.

4.7 SUMMARY

Pavlov believed that an association would be formed whenever a CS is paired with a US. Research on blocking and contingency, however, showed that contiguity is not enough: Conditioning will not occur unless the CS is a good predictor of the US (contingency), and indeed a better predictor than the other stimuli present (blocking). This means that conditioning becomes focused on stimuli that are good predictors of the US, which makes conditioning a highly adaptive process, but it also poses a challenge for learning theorists: How do animals identify the best predictor?

A surprising answer was provided in 1972 by Rescorla and Wagner, who proposed that the amount of conditioning on any trial is determined not simply by the US but by the subject's expectation that the US will occur. According to this model, the change in associative strength (ΔV) on any trial is determined by the relationship between the strength at the beginning of the trial (V) and the asymptotic strength that could be supported by the US (V_{max}):

$$\Delta V = c\,(V_{max} - V)$$

When two or more stimuli are present on a trial, the associative strength of the compound is the sum of the strengths of the elements:

$$V_{ab} = V_a + V_b$$

To derive quantitative predictions from the model, it is necessary to assign values to the parameters c and V_{max}. Rescorla and Wagner showed that even if the true values of these parameters are not known, so that arbitrary values have to be assigned, the model can still make qualitative predictions about whether associative strength will increase or decrease. These qualitative predictions proved surprisingly powerful, and the model can account for phenomena as diverse as conditioning, extinction, and blocking using only a single equation.

The key to these predictions lies in the relationship between V and V_{max}: When V is less than V_{max}, ($V_{max} - V$) is a positive number and associative strength is predicted to increase; when V is greater than V_{max}, ($V_{max} - V$) is negative and associative strength is reduced; when V equals V_{max}, then associative strength remains unchanged. According to the model, therefore, the same US can increase, decrease, or have no effect on conditioning, depending on whether current associative strength is above or below V_{max}.

One prediction that follows from this analysis is that if the combined associative strength of two conditioned stimuli is greater than V_{max}, then a conditioning trial in which they are presented together should reduce conditioning. Researchers have confirmed this prediction, and this also allows the model to explain why conditioning does not occur when a CS and a US are presented noncontingently. At first, the US is associated with all the stimuli that are present, including the CS and background cues. Eventually, though, a point is reached where the combined strength of the CS and the background cues is greater than V_{max}, leading to a reduction in associative strength on these CS trials. Associative strength continues to increase on background trials, however, because the associative strength of the background on its own remains less than V_{max}. The result is that conditioning is eventually concentrated on the background cues, with the associative strength of the CS returning to zero.

By considering the associative strength at the beginning of a trial, then, the Rescorla-Wagner model can account for both blocking and contingency, the phenomena that seemed to pose the most serious challenge to the principle of contiguity. The end result of conditioning is impressively sophisticated, with responding concentrated on the stimuli that are the best predictors of the US, rather than just on those that happen to precede it, but the underlying mechanism might simply be the strengthening of associations between contiguous stimuli.

As impressive as the model's achievements have been, the Rescorla-Wagner model cannot account for all aspects of conditioning. Configural learning, latent inhibition, and occasion setting are examples of phenomena that the model cannot explain in its present form. The model thus will have to be modified if it is to continue to be used. This, of course, is ultimately the fate of all theories; what makes the Rescorla-Wagner model distinctive is its remarkable success in accounting for so many aspects of conditioning using so few assumptions. In the words of Williams (1996), "Its graceful account of the selective nature of the conditioning mechanism captures what is most striking about the process of Pavlovian conditioning" (p. 115), and the model is likely to prove to be one of the major landmarks in the development of our understanding of learning.

If classical conditioning involves the formation of associations, can we say anything more about the nature of these associations? According to Pavlov, associations are formed between the CS and US centers in the brain (S–S associations). An alternative possibility is that the CS becomes directly connected with the unconditioned response during conditioning (an S–R association). One way to distinguish between these alternatives is to pair a US such as food with an aversive stimulus, so that the food will no longer elicit its customary response. If an S–S connection was formed during conditioning, then the CS should no longer elicit a response if the US is devalued, and this prediction has been confirmed.

Different theories were proposed concerning the nature of this S–S association. According to Pavlov, a simple connection allowed activity in the CS center to be transmitted to the US center and from there to the response. A CS would therefore elicit the same response as the US, so that, in effect, the CS becomes the US. As this analysis predicts, animals sometimes respond to a CS in exactly the same way as they do to the US: Dogs have been observed to lick a light bulb paired with food, pigeons have tried to drink an illuminated key paired with water, and so on. In some of these same experiments, however, animals also behaved as if they knew the US was coming—for example, orienting toward the area where food was to be delivered. It was thus not clear whether the CS served as a signal that the US was coming or became a substitute for it.

One way to account for this conflicting evidence is to assume that both views are correct. In the course of evolution, two distinct learning systems might have evolved—a relatively primitive one based on associations, and a more sophisticated system based on expectations. Research on the effects of brain damage has supported the existence of two separate systems: If a CS is paired with an aversive noise, some subjects develop fear but don't know why; others know that the noise is about to occur but have no fear.

Once an association or expectation has been formed, how do these forms of learning lead to a response? Pavlov's theory was very simple: Once activation spread from a CS center to a US center, this led through an innate connection to activation of the UR. According to this analysis, the conditioned response should be the same as the unconditioned response, and for autonomic responses this appears to be so. Conditioned skeletal responses, however, sometimes differ considerably from the unconditioned responses.

To account for these differences, behavior-system theories propose that conditioned stimuli arouse motivational states that in turn prime innately organized response systems directed at obtaining or avoiding the US, whichever is appropriate. Which of these responses actually occurred would depend on the releasing stimuli present at the time—if a lion was hungry, for example, the sight of an antelope would release the lion's hunting behavior. In the context of conditioning, the conditioned response elicited by a CS would depend in part on how closely the CS resembles the natural releasing stimuli for that species. If a rat receives conditioning trials in which a metal ball is rolled across its cage just before it receives food, for example, the rat might chase the ball because this small moving object resembles the releasing stimuli for its hunting behavior.

In the concluding section of the chapter, we considered several issues concerning classical conditioning in humans. One such issue is whether conditioning can occur without our awareness, and the answer seems to be yes. Normally we are aware of the relationship between the CS and US, but if our attention is distracted from this relationship, or if the stimuli used are ones that we cannot consciously detect, then conditioning can occur without our knowledge.

Classical conditioning is now seen much more as a process for detecting relationships between stimuli than as a simple system for forming associations. In line with this emerging perspective, we considered whether the processes involved in detecting CS–US relationships might also be involved in detecting other causal relationships—for example, in trying to trace the causes of allergies. There appear to be impressive similarities between classical conditioning and causal learning—manipulating the contingency between two events, for example, has similar effects on both. This might be another instance in which learning in animals and humans is more similar than we normally assume.

On the surface, classical conditioning is almost the simplest learning system that could be imagined—all we do is pair a CS with a US—but after nearly 100 years of research, we are still not entirely sure what animals or humans learn in this situation, nor how this learning is translated into performance. Pairing one event with another is indeed simple, but the processes we use in detecting such relationships, and then in deciding how to respond, are not.

Glossary

V The strength of the association that is formed when a CS and a US are paired.

Parameters Constant factors used in mathematical formulas. The value of a parameter is a fixed quantity, not a variable. By varying the values of parameters, researchers can use the same basic equation to predict a range of experimental results.

Configural learning Learning to respond to a compound stimulus in a manner sharply different than to its components—for example, responding much more to the compound than to its elements presented separately. Subjects behave as if they have learned to perceive the compound as a unique stimulus, or configuration, that is more than the sum of its components.

Latent inhibition Presentations of a stimulus by itself that retard subsequent conditioning to that stimulus. Also known as the **CS preexposure effect.**

Occasion setting A classical conditioning procedure in which a CS is followed by a US only when a third stimulus, the occasion setter, precedes the CS. The third stimulus signals, or "sets the occasion," when the CS will be reinforced.

S–S theory The term applied to Pavlov's view of conditioning, which assumed that an association is formed between two stimuli, the CS and the US.

S–R theory A view of conditioning that, in contrast to Pavlov's view, assumes there is a direct link between the conditioned stimulus and the response.

Stimulus substitution Pavlov's interpretation of the process that occurs during conditioning. He believed that activation of the CS center of the brain would be transferred to the US center and would therefore elicit the same behaviors as the US. In his view, the CS essentially becomes the US.

Expectation A belief in the present that some event will occur in the future. In everyday usage, expectations are normally assumed to be conscious, but in learning theory the term is typically used when subjects behave *as if* they knew that some event was coming, without assuming that this expectation exists in conscious form.

Two-level hypothesis A proposal that two different learning systems can be involved when we learn about the relationship between two events: A relatively primitive system that forms an association between the events, and a cognitive system that forms an expectation.

Behavior system A regulatory system that links motivational states with innate stimulus–response units. The assumption is that a motivational state primes a set of possible responses; whether one is then triggered depends on whether a natural releasing stimulus is present.

Causal learning Learning that one event is the cause of another.

Review Questions

1. What is the equation used by Rescorla and Wagner to predict learning? What does each symbol represent?

2. How is Kamin's concept of surprise incorporated within the Rescorla-Wagner model?

3. What effect does the choice of the parameters c and V_{max} have on the shape of the learning curve? How are the values of these parameters related to the CS and US used on a trial?

4. Why didn't Rescorla and Wagner try to determine the real values of the parameters c and V_{max}? What approach did they use instead, and what are the implications of this approach for deriving predictions from the model?

5. How can the same equation be used to predict both conditioning and extinction?

6. How does the model account for blocking?

7. There are two crucial tests of any theoretical model: Can it account for known phenomena, and can it accurately predict new ones? What is an example of the Rescorla-Wagner model's new predictions?

8. The Rescorla-Wagner model shows how a few simple assumptions can be used to account for seemingly complex behavior. How does the model's explanation of contingency illustrate this?

9. How do configural learning, latent inhibition and occasion setting show the Rescorla-Wagner model's limitations?

10. To test your understanding of the model, you might like to try to figure out for yourself how the model could be used to account for conditioned inhibition.

11. Does classical conditioning involve the learning of S–S or S–R associations?

12. What was Pavlov's stimulus-substitution hypothesis? What is the evidence for this hypothesis?

13. What is the difference between signal and substitution accounts of conditioning? What evidence supports each account?

14. What is the two-level hypothesis? How does it account for the conflicting evidence on whether a CS functions as a signal or a substitute for the US? And how does physiological research on fear conditioning support the claim of two different learning systems?

15. What is the distinction between learning and performance? How is research on simultaneous conditioning relevant to this distinction?

16. What evidence suggests that the CR is not always the same as the UR? How would Timberlake's behavior-system analysis account for the cases in which these responses differ?

17. What evidence suggests that conditioning can occur without awareness?

18. What is the relationship between classical conditioning in animals and causal learning in humans?

OPERANT CONDITIONING

REINFORCEMENT

One of the most obvious ways to encourage a behavior is to reward it. Parents praise children's good behavior; companies pay salespeople bonuses for high output; universities promote productive researchers. There is nothing new or profound about the idea of using rewards to encourage behavior—the principle was probably known and used long before the discovery of fire.

If the principle of reward is so obvious, though, why is behavior often so hard to change? Why do parents find it so difficult to get their teenage children to clean their rooms? Or, to take a more immediately relevant example, why do students often find it so difficult to make themselves study? There are, after all, very powerful rewards for studying: in the short term, good course grades; in the longer term, a better job. Yet students often leave studying until the last minute, and sometimes don't get around to it even then. Similarly, smoking and overeating can take years off our lives, and people are often desperate to give up these habits; yet the habits persist. Why is behavior in these situations apparently so irrational, when rewards as potent as a good job and longer life have little effect? Clearly, the principle of reward cannot be quite as simple as it sounds.

To understand why rewards seem to control behavior in some situations but not others, we will examine experimental research into the principles that determine the effectiveness of rewards. Then, in Chapter 6, we will examine some of the attempts that have been made to apply the principles discovered in the laboratory in real life, and what these attempts have revealed about both the strengths and weaknesses of rewards as a tool for altering behavior. We will begin, though, with the first experimental study of rewards, by Edward Lee Thorndike.

5.1 THORNDIKE'S LAW OF EFFECT

Thorndike's research, like Pavlov's, had its roots in the philosophy of Associationism, but its most immediate antecedent was the publication of Charles Darwin's

Origin of Species. Darwin's theory of evolution had proposed that man was but one animal species among many, and this claim triggered a surge of interest in the intelligence and reasoning powers of animals. If Darwin was right, if we are closely related to other animal species, then the traditional view that animals are dumb brutes becomes far less attractive. After all, if our close relatives were dumb, what might that imply about us?

Are Animals Intelligent?

To lay the basis for a more realistic judgment, a contemporary of Darwin named George Romanes collected observations of animal behavior from reliable observers around the world. When published, the material in Romanes's *Animal Intelligence* seemed to strongly support Darwin's thesis, as anecdote after anecdote revealed impressive powers of reasoning. The following account of the behavior of captive monkeys in Paraguay—drawn, as it happens, from one of Darwin's own books—is representative:

> *Rengger, a most careful observer, states that . . . after cutting themselves only once with any sharp tool, they would not touch it again, or would handle it with the greatest caution. Lumps of sugar were often given them wrapped up in paper; and Rengger sometimes put a live wasp in the paper, so that in hastily unfolding it they got stung; after this had once happened, they always first held the packet to their ears to detect any movement within.*
> (Romanes, 1882)

These observations, and others like them, provided persuasive evidence that animals possessed intelligence and reasoning power of an impressively high order. But were these observations trustworthy? Thorndike thought not. In the first place, he doubted the accuracy of some of the anecdotal material:

> *One has to deal not merely with ignorant or inaccurate testimony, but also with prejudiced testimony. Human folk are . . . eager to find intelligence in animals. They like to. And when the animal observed is a pet belonging to them or their friends, or when the story is one that has been told as a story to entertain, further complications are introduced. Nor is this all. Besides commonly mis-stating what facts they report, they report only such facts as show the animal at his best. Dogs get lost hundreds of times, and no one ever notices it or sends an account of it to a scientific magazine. But let one find his way from Brooklyn to Yonkers and the fact immediately becomes a circulating anecdote. Thousands of cats on thousands of occasions sit helplessly yowling, and no one takes thought of it or writes to his friend, the professor; but let one cat claw at the knob of a door supposedly as a signal to be let out, and straightaway this cat becomes the representative of the cat-mind in all the books.*
> (Thorndike, 1898, p. 4)

FIGURE 5.1   Thorndike's puzzle box. (Thorndike, 1911)

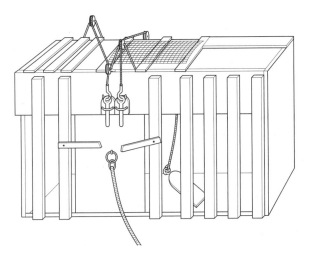

The Law of Effect

Anecdotal observations, then, might not be accurate, and, even when they are, they might not be representative. The animal's success could have been the result of chance, rather than any powers of rational analysis. "To remedy these defects," Thorndike (1898) argued, "experiment must be substituted for observation and the collection of anecdotes. Thus . . . you can repeat the conditions at will, so as to see whether or not the animal's behavior is due to mere coincidence." Thorndike, therefore, began to study learning in animals systematically, using an apparatus that he called a *puzzle box*. Basically, it was little more than a wooden crate with a door that could be opened by a special mechanism, such as a latch or rope (Figure 5.1). Thorndike placed a dish containing food outside the box but visible through its slats, then put the animal to be tested inside and observed its reactions.

When a hungry cat was placed in the box, Thorndike found that it would initially scramble around the box, frantically clawing and biting at the sides of the apparatus to escape and reach the food. After approximately 5 to 10 minutes of struggling, the cat would eventually stumble on the correct response and, finding the door open, would rush out and eat the food. According to Romanes's anecdotes, this success should have led to the immediate repetition of the successful response on the following trial. Instead, Thorndike found that the animal generally repeated the frantic struggling observed on the first trial. When the cat finally did repeat the correct response, however, the **latency** of this response— the time from being put in the box to performing the response—was generally shorter than it had been on the first trial, shorter still on the third trial, and so on. Figure 5.2 presents representative records of the performance of two cats.

FIGURE 5.2   Changes in the latency of escape from the puzzle box over trials for two of Thorndike's cats. (Thorndike, 1911)

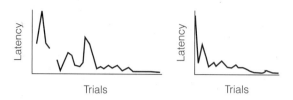

Progress in both cases was gradual and marked by occasional reversals, but on average the time to escape became progressively shorter as training continued.

What was the explanation for the improvement in the cats' performance? The gradual nature of the improvement convinced Thorndike that the cats had not formed a rational understanding of the situation. Rather, he argued, the food reward was gradually stamping in an association between the box cues and the escape response:

> The cat does not look over the situation, much less think it over, and then decide what to do. It bursts out at once into the activities which instinct and experience have settled on as suitable reactions to the situation "confinement when hungry with food outside." It does not ever in the course of its successes realize that such an act brings food and therefore decide to do it and thenceforth to do it immediately from decision instead of impulse. The one impulse, out of many accidental ones, which leads to pleasure, becomes strengthened and stamped in thereby, and more and more firmly associated with the sense-impression of that box's interior. .Accordingly it is sooner and sooner fulfilled.
> (Thorndike, 1898, p. 45)

Thorndike repeated this experiment with other responses and also with other species, including chicks, dogs, and monkeys. The basic pattern of the results was almost always the same: a gradual improvement over many trials. This uniform pattern suggested that the gradual strengthening effect of rewards was not confined to a single situation or species, but represented a general law of behavior, which Thorndike formalized as the **Law of Effect:**

> Of several responses made to the same situation, those which are accompanied or closely followed by satisfaction to the animal will, other things being equal, be more firmly connected with the situation, so that, when it recurs, they will be more likely to recur. . . . The greater the satisfaction . . . the greater the strengthening . . . of the bond.
> (Thorndike, 1911, p. 24)

Some Controversial Issues

When Thorndike's findings were published, they aroused considerable interest. He had moved the question of how animals learn from the realm of speculation to the experimental laboratory, where the processes involved could be carefully studied. Once in the lab, moreover, he was able to observe systematic patterns in his subjects' behavior and codify these observations in the Law of Effect, one of the first laws of behavior in the history of psychology. Thorndike's statement of this law, however, aroused considerable controversy.

I can't get no satisfaction. One source of controversy was Thorndike's use of the term *satisfaction*, which refers to a subjective or mental state. Since we can't see into the mind of a cat, how can we know whether it is experiencing satisfaction? This difficulty in assessing satisfaction makes the Law of Effect potentially circular: A response will increase if it is followed by a satisfying outcome, but the only way we know whether the outcome is satisfying is if the response increases!

In fact, Thorndike was aware of this problem, and he proposed an independent and objective test for determining whether a consequence was satisfying:

> By a satisfying state of affairs is meant one which the animal does nothing to avoid, often doing such things as attain and preserve it.
> (Thorndike, 1911, p. 245)

In other words, if a cat repeatedly tries to obtain food in one situation—for example, by jumping up onto a table where food is kept—then by definition this food must be satisfying, and the Law of Effect now allows us to predict that the food will also be an effective reward for other behaviors, such as escaping from the puzzle box. Meehl (1950) later labeled this property of rewards *transituationality*.

Thorndike's objective definition of satisfaction saves the Law of Effect from circularity, but the term still bothered learning theorists because of its subjective connotation that a reward is emotionally satisfying. An experiment by Sheffield, Wulff, and Backer (1951) illustrates the dangers. To study what events are rewarding, they used an apparatus called a straight-alley maze, which consists of a start box and a goal box connected by a long alley. (See Figure 5.3.) To find out if a stimulus is rewarding, the stimulus is placed in the goal box and the subject in the start box, and the experimenter records how long it takes for the subject to run to the goal box. If the stimulus is rewarding, it should strengthen the response of running, and the speed of running down the alley should thus increase over trials.

The experimenters used male rats as subjects and a receptive female in the goal box as the reward. The normal copulatory pattern in rats consists of a series of 8 to 12 intromissions and withdrawals by the male until it finally ejaculates.

When the male reached the goal box, the experimenters allowed it two intromissions, and then abruptly removed it from the goal box before it could ejaculate. It is not obvious that this sequence would be particularly satisfying for the male, but it proved to be a very powerful reward, as the males' speed of running down the alley increased over trials by a factor of eight!

Such evidence makes it at least questionable whether all events that strengthen behavior are emotionally satisfying, and it has led learning theorists to prefer the more objective term *reinforcer* to *reward*. A **reinforcer** can be defined as an event that increases the probability of a response when presented after it. Similarly, we can define **reinforcement** as an increase in the probability of a response caused by the presentation of a reinforcer following that response.

Association or expectation?   A second controversy arose over Thorndike's assumption that learning is an associative process. In the case of the puzzle box, for example, Thorndike proposed that food stamped in an association between the stimulus of the box and the response of escaping, so that the box stimuli would thereafter elicit the correct response automatically. We have seen that he had good grounds for this interpretation—the erratic nature of cats' improvement over trials did not support the view that the cats had any deep understanding of what they were doing or why. Other psychologists, however, believed that animals are far more intelligent than Thorndike's analysis implied. An Austrian psychologist, Kohler, said that the apparent stupidity of cats in Thorndike's puzzle box was a reflection not so much on the cats' intelligence as on Thorndike's! Specifically, Kohler argued that Thorndike's tasks were difficult because the causal relationships were concealed. The physical relationship between the release mechanism and the door was not visible to the animals in most cases, so that they could not directly perceive the relationship. If the relationship was made visible, Kohler suggested, animals would behave far more intelligently.

In one test of this prediction, Kohler (1927) provided a chimpanzee with a stick in her cage and then placed a bunch of bananas outside the cage just beyond her reach:

> She grasps at it, vainly of course, and then begins the characteristic complaint of the chimpanzee: she thrusts both lips—especially the lower—forward, for a couple of inches, gazes imploringly at the observer, utters whimpering sounds, and finally flings herself on the ground on her back—a gesture most eloquent of despair. . . . Thus, between lamentations and entreaties, some time passes, until—about seven minutes after the fruit has been exhibited to her—she suddenly casts a look at the stick, ceases her moaning, seizes the stick, stretches it out of the cage, and succeeds, though somewhat clumsily, in drawing the bananas within arm's length. . . . The test is repeated after an hour's interval; on this second occasion,

the animal has recourse to the stick much sooner, and uses it with more skill; and,
at a third repetition, the stick is used immediately, as on all subsequent occasions.
(Kohler, 1927, pp. 32–33)

This abrupt change in behavior, Kohler concluded, revealed a sudden *insight* into the problem.

We thus have two very different interpretations of animal learning: that it is a gradual process based on associations, or a cognitive process involving the perception of relationships. Determining which of these accounts is correct proved very difficult, and we will defer detailed consideration of this issue until Chapters 8 and 12. We can foreshadow that discussion, however, by saying that we will encounter evidence supporting both views. As with classical conditioning, there is reason to think that reinforcement involves two separate learning systems, an associative system in which the association between a stimulus and a response is strengthened gradually, and a cognitive system in which we learn about the relationship between our behavior and its consequences. The result is that in some situations stimuli elicit responses automatically, whereas in others we consider the possible consequences of our behavior before deciding whether to respond.

Reinforcement versus conditioning. As psychologists learned of Pavlov's research as well as Thorndike's, one issue that arose concerned the relationship between the two forms of learning. The procedures used by Pavlov and Thorndike clearly differed. Pavlov arranged a contingency between two stimuli: food, for example, was presented following a tone. Thorndike, on the other hand, arranged a contingency between a response and a stimulus: Food was presented following a correct response. If we represent the consequence by the symbol S*, then we can represent the two forms of learning as follows:

$$Classical\ conditioning: \quad S \rightarrow S^*$$
$$Reinforcement: \quad\quad\quad R \rightarrow S^*$$

Carrying this point a bit further, in classical conditioning food follows a CS: Whether a dog salivates has no effect on whether food is presented. In reinforcement, on the other hand, presentation of food depends crucially on the subject's response: No response, no food.

In procedural terms, then, classical conditioning and reinforcement clearly differ. This does not necessarily mean that the learning processes involved are also different: A single learning process could be involved in detecting relationships between events, whether the first event is a stimulus or a response. Thus although the procedures used in classical conditioning and reinforcement are different, the underlying mechanism could be the same.

Again, the issues here are too complex for us to try to resolve here, and we will postpone examination of this question until Chapter 10. In the meantime, it is important that you understand the distinction between the two procedures. In both reinforcement and classical conditioning, a response is strengthened because of the presentation of an event such as food: In reinforcement, food is delivered following a response, whereas in classical conditioning the food is delivered following a stimulus.

5.2 BASIC PROCEDURES

Thorndike devised the puzzle box to study reinforcement, but most subsequent research has been carried out using two other pieces of equipment: the maze and the Skinner box.

The Maze

At almost the same time as Thorndike was carrying out his research, W. S. Small at Clark University was using a maze to study learning in rats. The history of mazes goes back at least as far as the ancient Egyptians, and outdoor mazes became extremely popular in the eighteenth century. Outdoor mazes were constructed using tall hedges, and the game was to find one's way through the intricate network of connecting passages. Small reasoned that such mazes would provide an ideal apparatus for studying learning in rats, because many rats lived in complex underground burrows and thus should be equipped to solve such problems.

Small (1901) based his maze on a famous garden maze built at Hampton Court Palace in England; Figure 5.3a shows its layout. Small placed the rats at the entrance, observed how long it took them to find their way to the central section that contained food, and recorded how many errors (entries into blind alleys) they made in the process.

As research with mazes continued, it became clear that this problem was too complex for the learning processes involved to be easily analyzed, and researchers began to design progressively simpler mazes. One of the most popular mazes proved to be the *T-maze* shown in Figure 5.3b, in which the rat only had to learn a single turn. The subject was placed in the start box and allowed to run down a straight alley to a choice point, where it could turn either right or left. Both choices led to goal boxes, but only one contained food. Learning was measured by how many trials were needed for the rat to learn to choose the correct alley consistently.

Even the T-maze, however, proved undesirably complex for some purposes, and many experiments were carried out using the *straight-alley* maze (Figure 5.3c) referred to earlier. All the rats had to do in this apparatus was run from the start

FIGURE 5.3   Three mazes for studying learning.

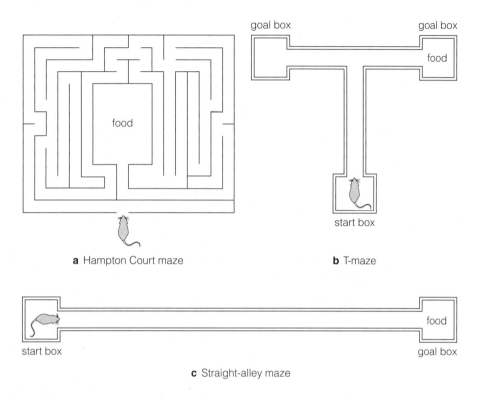

a Hampton Court maze   **b** T-maze

c Straight-alley maze

box to the goal box, and learning was measured by the change in the animal's speed of running down the alley.

Skinner's Contributions

The culminating step in the trend toward simpler procedures to study reinforcement was taken by B. F. Skinner, who, along with Pavlov and Thorndike, has been one of the most influential figures in the study of associative learning.

The Skinner box. To study the effects of reinforcement in rats, Skinner modified Thorndike's puzzle box. Instead of having subjects leave the box to obtain food located outside it, Skinner placed a supply of food pellets in a magazine mounted on the outside of the box, and designed a mechanical system to deliver pellets to a tray located within the box. (See Figure 5.4.) A horizontal bar or lever was located near the food tray, and every time the rat pressed the bar down, it automatically received a pellet of food. To keep the stimulus environment as constant as possible during training, Skinner placed the cage inside a

FIGURE 5.4   A Skinner box, or operant chamber, for rats. When the rat presses the bar, a food pellet is delivered to a tray located below the bar. A light mounted above the bar illuminates the chamber. This illustration is drawn from a computer program called Sniffy, The Virtual Rat; the program simulates a rat's behavior and can be used to demonstrate both classical and operant conditioning.

ventilated, soundproof chamber. (Note the similarity to Pavlov's fort.) This apparatus is popularly known as a *Skinner box*, though Skinner himself did not like the term. In journal articles, the apparatus is more commonly described as an *operant chamber*.

To ensure that the rat would eat the food pellet as soon as it was presented (and thus that the reinforcer would follow the bar press with as little delay as possible), Skinner began each experiment by giving his subjects *magazine training*, which consisted of presenting the food at periodic intervals. Because eating repeatedly followed the sound of the food delivery, the rats soon learned to approach the food magazine as soon as they heard the sound. Skinner could then ensure that the rat received food almost immediately whenever it pressed the bar.

The cumulative recorder. Another of Skinner's innovations was a device for automatically producing graphs of an animal's behavior. The device, called a

FIGURE 5.5   A cumulative recorder. Rotation of the drum moves the paper to the left; a motor pulls the
pen one step toward the top of the paper every time the subject makes a response.

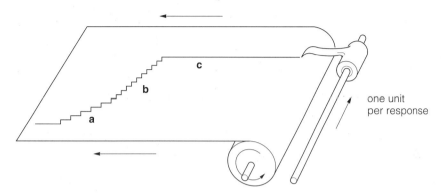

one unit
per response

cumulative recorder, consists of a rotating drum with a pen resting above it;
the rotation of the drum moves a strip of paper under the pen, and the pen is
moved one step along the drum every time the subject makes a response (Figure 5.5). If no response is made, the pen remains in the same position while the
paper is moved beneath it, the result being a horizontal line. If the rat presses
the bar, the pen moves one step vertically; the more often the animal responds,
the higher the pen rises up the paper. The height of the pen at any point thus
provides a measure of the total, or cumulative, responses emitted since the beginning of the session. Because the total number of responses emitted can never
fall, a cumulative record can only rise or remain constant, and the angle at
which the curve rises reflects the rate of the subject's responding.

The cumulative record in Figure 5.5 illustrates these points. At the beginning of the session, the subject responded at a steady rate of 10 responses per
minute; this is shown as an ascending, stepped line (segment **a**). After 10 minutes, the subject's rate of responding doubled, and the stepped line rises more
steeply (segment **b**). Finally, after 20 minutes, the subject stopped responding.
Because the cumulative number of responses since the beginning of the session
remains at 300 responses, the response curve is now horizontal (segment **c**). In
other words, the steepness of the line in a cumulative record indicates the rate
of response: The faster a subject responds, the more steeply the line rises.

The operant. In sum, the Skinner box offers significant advantages for studying learning. There is no need to place animals in the maze and then remove
them after each trial; instead, the experimenter simply places the animal in the
box and leaves it there. The animal can then respond repeatedly without further intervention by the experimenter, because delivery of the food and recording of the response all occur automatically. As a result, a single experimenter

can study learning in a number of Skinner boxes simultaneously, and in many learning laboratories animals are being studied in 4 to 8 boxes at the same time.

Skinner called responses such as bar-pressing operants because they operate on the environment to change it. An **operant** can be defined as a response that produces a particular change in the environment, but the term is more commonly used to refer to a class of responses rather than to a single response. When a rat is trained to press a bar, for example, it can do so by biting the bar, by pressing the bar with its left paw, and so on. All these variants are normally treated as members of a single operant class because they all have the same effect on the environment—in this case, moving the bar. The term *operant level* refers to the initial rate at which an operant is performed before reinforcement is made contingent on it. Finally, the training procedure—in the case of a rat, allowing it to press a bar repeatedly during a session to obtain food—is referred to as a *free-operant* procedure because subjects are free to respond when and as often as they like. The free-operant procedure can be contrasted to the *discrete-trial* procedure used in a maze or in Thorndike's original puzzle box, in which only one response can occur per trial.

5.3 THE REINFORCER

Having reviewed techniques for studying reinforcement, we can now begin to examine the principles that determine whether reinforcement is effective. One of the most important steps in using reinforcement effectively is to identify potential reinforcers (as in the old recipe for elephant stew, the first step of which was to "catch an elephant"), and much early research on reinforcement was concentrated on this task.

Primary Reinforcers

One obvious set of candidates were stimuli that are needed for survival, such as food and water. It makes sense that such stimuli would become reinforcing in the course of evolution because an animal that repeats a response that has led to food is likely to have a better chance of obtaining food in the future. Thus, a gene that established food as a reinforcer would be likely to be transmitted to future generations. It therefore came as no surprise when early research demonstrated that stimuli such as food, water, and sex were all reinforcing.

In the early 1950s, however, evidence began to accumulate that not all reinforcers were necessary for survival, at least not in the simple physical sense that food is. In an experiment by Butler (1954), for example, monkeys were placed in an enclosed cage with two wooden panels, one painted yellow and the other blue. If a monkey pushed open the blue door, it was allowed to look out into the experimental room beyond for a period of 30 seconds. If it pushed against the yellow door, an opaque screen immediately came down, terminating the trial. Not only did the monkeys quickly solve this problem, learning to push only the blue door, regardless of the side on which it was presented, but they proved remarkably persistent in performing the response. In one experiment in which there was a trial once a minute—that is, a 30-second opportunity to look out into the room, followed by a 30-second blank interval—one subject responded on every single trial for nine hours without a break. A second subject responded for 11 hours, and a third for an extraordinary 19 consecutive hours. Visual access to the surrounding room was clearly not necessary for the monkeys' survival in any direct sense, but it proved a remarkably potent reinforcer. As Butler commented, "That monkeys would work as long and as persistently for food is highly unlikely."

Visual stimulation now appears to be only one example of a large set of events that Kish (1966) has referred to as *sensory reinforcers*. These are stimuli whose physical effects seem largely confined to the receptors and nerves involved in their detection and have no effect on general metabolism. Intuitively, their most important characteristic seems to be that they provide variety in our perceptual environment. Rats, for example, prefer to explore complex mazes with many turns rather than to explore simple ones (Montgomery, 1954); humans confined in a dark room will push a button that turns on a panel of flashing lights, with the rate of button-pushing increasing as the pattern of lights becomes less predictable (Jones, Wilkinson, & Braden, 1961).

The reinforcers we have discussed to this point—food, water, and sensory stimulation—are effective essentially from birth. This point is most obvious in the case of food and water, but it is true in the case of sensory reinforcers as well. Siqueland and DeLucia (1969) found that sensory stimulation was reinforcing for infants as young as three weeks, who would increase their rate of sucking on a rubber nipple if this resulted in presentation of photographic slides. Reinforcers that require no special training to be effective are called **primary reinforcers.**

The Premack principle. The evidence that sensory stimulation can be reinforcing suggests that reinforcers are not all physically necessary for survival. Is there any other characteristic, then, that is shared by reinforcers such as hamburgers, sex, and flashing lights? Perhaps the most useful integrating principle is one suggested by David Premack (1965, 1971). Premack argued that different experiences all have different values for us, and that these values can be inferred by observing the amount of time in which we engage in these activities when they are freely available. The common characteristic of reinforcers, said Premack, is that they are all high-probability activities. Is it possible, then, that *any* high-probability activity will reinforce any response that has a lower probability?

Suppose for example, that a group of children were given free access to a number of foods and were found to prefer potatoes to spinach, but to strongly prefer ice cream to both of them. If high-probability responses reinforce lower-probability responses, then—as all parents know—we should be able to use access to ice cream to reinforce eating spinach. However, we should also be able to use access to potatoes to reinforce eating spinach, albeit less effectively, because eating potatoes is also a higher-probability response. Premack (1965) tested predictions like these in a series of experiments involving rats and children, and on the whole the results were positive. The suggestion that more probable responses will reinforce less probable responses thus became known as the **Premack principle.** One prediction, however, was not supported. In our example, the Premack principle says that access to potatoes will not reinforce eating ice cream, because eating potatoes is a less probable response. This prediction seems obvious—what child would eat more ice cream to gain access to potatoes? The answer, however, turns out to be that they all will, provided that they genuinely like potatoes, and that eating ice cream is the only way they can obtain them. (For supporting evidence, see Eisenberger, Karpman, & Trattner, 1967; Allison, 1989.)

The response deprivation hypothesis.   To explain this finding, Timberlake and Allison (1974) suggested a modification to the Premack principle. When we are given a free choice among various activities, they noted, we have a preferred way of distributing our time among these activities. According to Timberlake and Allison's **response deprivation hypothesis,** if we are not allowed to perform a response at the level we prefer—if we are, in effect, deprived of the response—then access to this activity will be reinforcing. In our potato example, if you are unable to eat potatoes at your preferred level, then you will perform other responses to obtain potatoes, even if those other responses are themselves more valued, such as eating ice cream.[1]

The response deprivation hypothesis retains Premack's emphasis on activities as reinforcers. What determines the reinforcement value of an activity, however, is not whether it is more probable than the response to be reinforced, but rather whether the current level of the activity is below its optimum level. The further an activity is below its preferred level, the more reinforcing it will be; conversely, the more you prefer an activity, the more reinforcing it will be when you are deprived of it. In this respect, the response deprivation hypothesis points to the same conclusion as the Premack principle: If you want to find a good reinforcer, look for activities that people like to engage in when they have a free choice.

---

[1] However, you will not increase your consumption of ice cream sufficiently to obtain all the potatoes you would normally eat if this would require you to eat too much ice cream. According to Timberlake and Allison, we have a preferred or optimum way of allocating our time among competing activities— what they call a *bliss* point—and if we have to increase the time we spend on one activity to gain access to another, we will compromise on a level of performance that keeps both activities as close as possible to the behavioral bliss point.

Although the Premack principle has had to be modified, it has contributed significantly to liberating psychologists from an overly narrow view of what events are reinforcing. Earlier theorists tended to sort events into rigidly defined categories, but Premack's work has suggested a much more fluid and relativistic interpretation: What is reinforcing varies from moment to moment and from individual to individual. Whatever someone voluntarily spends his or her time doing—whether it is pulling weeds, skydiving, or sitting by the fireside knitting—that is what is likely to be reinforcing for that person.

A childish application. A particularly delightful application of this principle has been reported by Homme, deBaca, Devine, Steinhorst, and Rickert (1963). The subjects were unruly three-year-olds who repeatedly ignored their nursery school teacher's instructions and, instead, raced around the room screaming and pushing furniture. This kind of behavior can be wearing on even the most patient adults, but it is particularly hard to bear for those responsible for the children's safety. One common reaction of parents in such situations is to lose their tempers and punish the children to get them to do as they are told. Instead, Homme and his co-workers set out to reinforce good behavior through a judicious application of the Premack principle. They reinforced the children's behavior whenever the children sat and played quietly for a specified period of time, with the reinforcer being several minutes of uninterrupted running and screaming! Within only a few days, the children were obeying the teacher's instructions almost perfectly, so that "an observer, new on the scene, almost certainly would have assumed extensive aversive control was being used" (Homme et al., 1963). Later on, new and even better reinforcers were developed through continued observation of the children's behavior, including such decidedly unusual rewards as allowing the children to throw a plastic cup across the room, to kick a wastepaper basket, and, best of all, to push the teacher around the room in a swivel chair on rolling wheels!

The moral to this story is that it is a mistake to think of reinforcers in terms of a restricted list of "approved" stimuli. There is no magic list of reinforcers; the best way to determine what will be reinforcing for someone is to observe that person's behavior.

Secondary Reinforcers

In contrast to primary reinforcers, which are effective from birth, some of the most powerful reinforcers affecting our behavior are **secondary** or **conditioned reinforcers,** which have acquired their reinforcing properties through experience. Money, for example, is not at first a very effective reinforcer; showering an infant with dollar bills is unlikely to have any discernible impact on the infant's behavior. As we grow older, though, money becomes increasingly important; in some cases, it becomes an obsession. How, then, do secondary reinforcers, such as money or the word good, acquire their reinforcing properties?

One of the first attempts to answer this question was by John B. Wolfe (1936), who examined whether the powerful effects of money in real life could be reproduced in the animal laboratory. Using six chimpanzees as subjects, Wolfe first trained them to place a token into a vending machine to obtain grapes. Once they had mastered this task, they were given a heavy lever to operate to obtain further tokens; Wolfe found that they would work as hard to operate the lever when the reward was tokens as when it was the grapes themselves. Furthermore, their behavior bore some striking similarities to that of humans with regard to money. In one experiment in which the chimpanzees were tested in pairs, Wolfe found that the dominant member of the pair sometimes would push aside its subordinate to gain access to the lever. If the subordinate had already amassed a pile of tokens, then the dominant one might simply take them away. In one of the pairs, however, the subordinate, Bula, developed an effective counterstrategy. She would turn toward her partner, Bimba, extend her hand palm up, and begin to whine. This apparent begging was invariably successful: As soon as Bula began to whine, Bimba would quickly hand her one of the tokens and would continue doing so until she stopped whining . . .

The reinforcing properties of the tokens in this study were not innate. Wolfe used tokens of different colors, and he found that if tokens of a particular color were no longer exchanged for grapes, the chimpanzees would quickly lose interest in them. Wolfe considered several explanations of why the tokens became reinforcing, one of which was that the reinforcing properties of the food had become classically conditioned to the tokens because of their temporal contiguity. If this explanation was correct, then the strength of a secondary reinforcer should depend on the same associative principles that determine conditioning: contiguity, frequency, intensity, and so on.

Although the suggestion that secondary reinforcement is based on classical conditioning is still debated, research has confirmed that their principles are very similar. (For reviews, see Fantino, 1977; Williams, 1994a.) To establish the word *good* as a secondary reinforcer, for example, it should be paired with a primary reinforcer (such as candy) as closely and as often as possible. And, as in classical conditioning, it is important not to present a secondary reinforcer too often by itself. If you repeatedly say "good" to a child without any other reinforcing consequences following, the reinforcing properties of the word will extinguish (for example, Warren & Cairns, 1972).

Social Reinforcers

A third possible category of reinforcers (one not usually treated separately) is **social reinforcers**—stimuli whose reinforcing properties derive uniquely from the behavior of other members of the same species. In practice, the meaning of this term is clearer than its definition and includes such things as praise, affection, and even just attention.

One reason for treating social reinforcers separately is that they are a blend of both primary and secondary reinforcers. Poulson (1983) found that an adult's smile could reinforce behavior in infants as young as three months, suggesting that smiling is innately reinforcing. But considerable evidence also indicates that the power of social reinforcers can be altered by pairing them with other reinforcers. The reinforcing properties of the word *good*, for example, can be increased by following it with candy (Warren & Cairns, 1972). Thus, although social reinforcement might have an innate basis, experience also plays an important role.

Our second reason for treating social reinforcers separately is to emphasize their importance. Social reinforcers such as praise and attention are probably the reinforcers we encounter most often in our daily lives, and they play an important—and often underestimated—role in controlling our behavior.

We can illustrate the power of social reinforcers with a study by Allen, Hart, Buell, Harris, and Wolf (1964). The subject was a four-year-old girl, Ann, who had just started nursery school. From the time of her arrival, she spent most of her time interacting with adults rather than playing with other children, and as time went on she developed a variety of behavioral problems. She complained frequently about skin abrasions that no one else could see; she spoke in a low voice that was very difficult to hear; and she spent increasing amounts of time standing by herself, pulling at her lower lip and fingering her cheek.

One possible analysis of Ann's behavior might have been that she was an insecure and unhappy child, and thus needed as much comfort and reassurance as possible to help her adjust to her new surroundings. The authors' analysis, however, was quite different. They noticed that a common feature of all Ann's problem behaviors was that they elicited adult attention. If she stood by herself, for example, a teacher was soon likely to come over to ask what was wrong. If adult attention was reinforcing, the teachers might have been encouraging the very behaviors they were trying to eliminate. The authors' advice to the teachers, therefore, was to change the reinforcement contingencies by paying attention to Ann whenever she played with others but ignoring her when she stood alone. When Ann did talk or play with other children, a teacher would come over to Ann, smile, and talk to her about what she was doing.

The result was a dramatic transformation in Ann's behavior. After just a single day, the proportion of her time spent in social play increased from 10% to 60%, and this higher level was maintained over subsequent weeks. The frequency of reinforcement was then gradually reduced and eventually faded out altogether, but Ann's social play remained at a high level. (As her skills in playing with other children increased, this play probably produced its own source of reinforcement.)

Social reinforcers can be very powerful: Even a small shift in adult attention—not money, not candy, but just attention—was sufficient to substantially alter Ann's behavior. Also, as often happens, the crucial role of social reinforcement in directing Ann's behavior was not at first appreciated. Actions such as paying attention to someone are such a common part of our lives that we take them for granted, but, as we shall see again in other applications, social reinforcement can play a very powerful role in controlling behavior.

5.4 DELAY OF REINFORCEMENT

Having identified a set of potential reinforcers, we now turn to the question of what determines whether they will be effective in strengthening behavior. One likely factor is the delay between the response and the reinforcer. The British Associationists believed that the contiguity between two events was the most important factor determining whether they would be associated; as we have seen, this belief was strongly confirmed in research on classical conditioning, in which delays of even one or two seconds were generally sufficient to impair learning or prevent it altogether. It thus seemed highly likely to early learning researchers that contiguity would prove equally critical in reinforcement. Their attempts to confirm this hypothesis in the laboratory, however, quickly ran into difficulties.

Does Delay Matter?

The early studies. In a study by Wolfe (1934), the experimenter tested rats in a T-maze with food always available in the goal box on one side. (This is known as a *spatial discrimination*, because the subject has to learn to go to a particular location in space.) Wolfe modified the apparatus by inserting delay boxes between the choice point and the goal boxes. By varying how long subjects were held in the delay box before the door to the goal box was opened, Wolfe could control precisely the delay between the rat's making a correct choice response and receiving food. Up to a point, his results confirmed the importance of contiguity: Lengthening the delay from 0 to 60 seconds in different groups led to a similar increase in the number of trials required for solution. Increasing the delay beyond 60 seconds, however, had little effect, and Wolfe found some evidence of learning even when food was delayed for 20 minutes.

If delays of even a few seconds normally prevented learning in classical conditioning, how did learning take place for Wolfe's rats when the correct response and food were separated by 20 minutes? Hull (1943) suggested that the answer might lie in secondary reinforcement. As soon as the rat was released from the delay box on the correct side, it received food; thus, the stimuli associated with this box—its color, odor, and so on—were contiguous with food. As a result, these stimuli could have become secondary reinforcers, and the next time the rat made the correct response and entered the delay box it would have received immediate reinforcement. According to Hull, then, the rat developed a preference for the correct side not because it realized that this response led to food, but because it produced immediate secondary reinforcement.

This explanation is highly counterintuitive. Would a rat really develop a preference for the correct side of a maze simply because the delay box on that side was reinforcing? To find out, Perkins (1947) repeated Wolfe's experiment but randomly interchanged the delay boxes between trials, so that both delay boxes were on the correct side on half the trials and thus both would become secondary reinforcers. Therefore, secondary reinforcers would follow incorrect as well as correct responses, which would mean that secondary reinforcement could not contribute to a preference for the correct side. According to Hull's analysis, the rats in this condition should no longer have had any reason to prefer the correct side. In accordance with this prediction, Perkins found that learning in this group was significantly slower than in a control group for which the delay boxes were not interchanged. However, although learning was slower, some learning did occur nevertheless, despite the fact that reinforcement following a correct response was delayed for 45 seconds. In a second experiment, Perkins varied the delay of reinforcement for groups with interchanged delay boxes and found that learning would occur with delays of as long as 2 minutes.

In one respect these results support Hull's analysis: When secondary reinforcement was eliminated, the maximum delay at which learning was possible was reduced from 20 minutes to 2 minutes. The fact that learning occurred with a delay of as long as 2 minutes, however, was still puzzling. If events must be contiguous to be associated, how could a response be associated with food that was presented 2 minutes later?

Spence's hypothesis. A possible answer was provided by one of Hull's colleagues, Kenneth Spence (1947), who suggested that although Perkins had eliminated one source of secondary reinforcement, a second source still remained. When a rat turned right or left at the choice point, the muscular contractions involved would have stimulated receptors in the muscles called *proprioceptors*. When muscles contract, these proprioceptors generate electrical signals that are then transmitted to the brain. If you move your thumb, for example, you can feel its movement even with your eyes closed; this sensation is made possible by *proprioceptive stimuli* from the muscle. In contrast, stimuli originating outside the body are called *exteroceptive stimuli*.

Neuroanatomical studies had established the existence of proprioceptors, but to this base of empirical evidence Spence added a crucial theoretical assumption. Whenever a muscle contracts, he said, a trace of the proprioceptive stimulus produced lingers on in the nervous system even after the movement is completed, with the intensity of this trace decaying gradually over time (Figure 5.6). If a flashbulb goes off while you are sitting in a dark room, for example, you will experience a bright afterimage that then fades. Spence hypothesized that a similar decaying trace would persist after physical movements. In

FIGURE 5.6   Hypothetical curve of how the intensity of a proprioceptive trace decays over time.

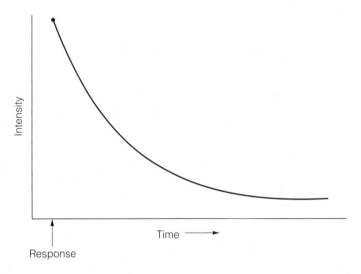

Perkins's experiment, a rat's turn to the correct side would have produced a distinctive proprioceptive stimulus, and if a trace was still present when food arrived this stimulus would have acquired reinforcing properties. The next time the rat made the correct response, the proprioceptive stimuli produced would have provided immediate secondary reinforcement. In effect, the rat was now reinforcing itself for correct turns!

Spence's hypothesis also explained why learning was better in Wolfe's study than in Perkins's. As we saw earlier, the laws governing the establishment of a secondary reinforcer are essentially identical to those of classical conditioning. One of these principles, first established by Pavlov, is that conditioning depends not only on the time between the onset of a CS and a US, but on whether the CS remains present throughout the interval. Delay conditioning, in which the CS remains present until the US arrives, is substantially more effective than trace conditioning, in which the CS terminates beforehand. In Wolfe's experiment, the delay box was present throughout the delay interval; in Perkins's experiment, only a trace of the proprioceptive stimulus would have remained. According to a conditioning analysis, therefore, the delay box should become a stronger secondary reinforcer than the proprioceptive trace. Thus, learning in Wolfe's experiment should have been stronger than in Perkins's, as it was.

By assuming that proprioceptive stimuli could function as secondary reinforcers, Spence was able to provide a comprehensive—and rather neat—account for all the available experimental evidence. Moreover, although some details of his analysis were untestable (there was no direct evidence that movements gave rise to slowly decaying traces, much less that these traces then functioned as secondary reinforcers), the theory as a whole did lead to a testable prediction. For learning to occur, Spence said, some form of immediate reinforcement is required. If proprioceptive as well as exteroceptive secondary reinforcement could be eliminated, Spence predicted, then even a brief delay in the presentation of food should seriously impair learning.

But how could proprioceptive secondary reinforcement be eliminated? As long as a response produces a proprioceptive stimulus, it is impossible to prevent a trace of this stimulus from being paired with food, and thus from functioning as a secondary reinforcer for future responses.

Grice's test. A solution to this conundrum was soon provided in a brilliant experiment by one of Spence's students, G. Robert Grice (1948). Recognizing the impossibility of preventing secondary reinforcement of the correct response, Grice instead devised an ingenious procedure to control for its effects. In Chapter 1, we saw that the occurrence of some extraneous variables such as the passing of time cannot be physically prevented, but their role can nevertheless be disentangled through the use of an appropriate control group for comparison. In a similar fashion, Grice now set out to control for the effects of secondary reinforcement by comparing two responses. One, R_1, was followed by a secondary reinforcer (S^r), and then, after a delay, by food. The second response, R_2, produced the same secondary reinforcer but not the food:

$$R_1 \rightarrow S^r \xrightarrow{\hspace{5cm}} food$$
$$R_2 \rightarrow S^r$$

Because the secondary reinforcer followed R_2 as well as R_1, it would strengthen both responses equally. Any difference in the strength of the two responses, therefore, could only be caused by the food acting across the delay interval to strengthen R_1 directly.

The apparatus Grice used is shown, in overhead view, in Figure 5.7. At the entrance to the maze, the rats could enter either a black or a white alley. Whichever alley they chose, they then entered a delay box painted gray, and, after confinement for a set period, were released into the goal box. The positions of the black and white alleys were alternated randomly over trials: On half the trials, white was on the left; on the other half, white was on the right. Food was always available in the goal box following the white alley. Thus, in contrast to the spatial discrimination used by Wolfe and Perkins, in which food was contingent on the choice of a particular side, this was a *visual discrimination* in which reinforcement was contingent on the choice of a particular color, regardless of its location.

Because food was available equally often on both sides of the apparatus, turns to both left and right were followed by food. Proprioceptive stimuli from

FIGURE 5.7   Overhead view of the visual discrimination maze used by Grice. The section containing the choice alleys could be moved so that the black alley was either to the rat's left or to its right. (Adapted from Grice, 1948)

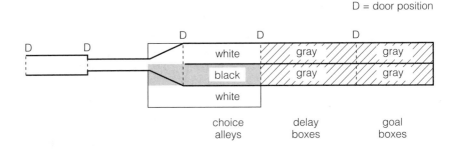

both of these responses were thus paired with food; whether the rat made a correct or incorrect response on any trial, it would receive immediate proprioceptive secondary reinforcement. Similarly, because both delay boxes were followed by food, both would become secondary reinforcers. Thus, whether the rat chose the black alley or the white alley on any trial, it would receive the same amount of exteroceptive and proprioceptive secondary reinforcement. The only way it could learn the correct response would be by directly associating this response with the delayed food.

As Spence had predicted, even short delays of reinforcement now profoundly disrupted learning. Figure 5.8 shows the percentage of correct responses over trials for groups trained with different delays. The group with no delay learned the correct response quite rapidly, requiring an average of only 20 trials to reach a criterion of 90% correct. A group for whom reinforcement was delayed for half a second, however, required five times as many trials to reach the same criterion. Delays of 1 and 2 seconds impaired learning even more severely, and at 10 seconds learning proved virtually impossible: Three of the five subjects in this group showed no preference for the correct response even after 1440 trials! Just as Spence had predicted, when all sources of immediate reinforcement were effectively eliminated, then even small delays of reinforcement had catastrophic effects on learning.[2]

When learning is studied in a Skinner box rather than in a maze, learning is also seriously impaired when reinforcement is delayed, but the maximum

---

[2] If you have a sharp eye for experimental design, you may have realized that Grice did not, in fact, eliminate all possible sources of secondary reinforcement. If the color of the correct alley also gave rise to a persisting trace, then this color could have acted as a secondary reinforcer for the correct response. Indeed, this might be why Grice still obtained a small amount of learning with delays of up to 5 seconds.

FIGURE 5.8   Learning curves for Grice's six groups experiencing different delays of reinforcement. (Grice, 1948)

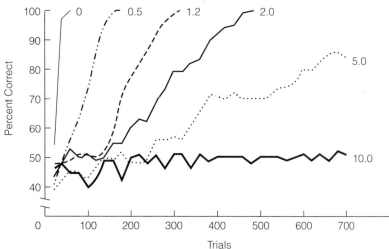

delay at which learning will occur seems to be somewhat longer. Lattal and Gleeson (1990) were able to train rats to press a bar with delays as long as 30 seconds between a response and the delivery of food, but learning under these conditions took many hours, and subjects pressed the bar at a very low rate.

The Role of Interference

Grice's results left little doubt about the importance of immediate reinforcement for learning. Less clear, however, was why immediate reinforcement was so critical. You might think that a 2-second gap between a correct response and reinforcement would not be all that harmful; yet, in Grice's experiment it clearly was. Why? One possible explanation was that the rat, with its very small brain (only about 0.003 the size of a human brain), has only a limited capacity for storing events, and unless food is delivered quickly, no trace of the preceding response will be left to be reinforced. In the years since Grice's experiment, however, it has become clear that rats can remember what response they have made for periods as long as 24 hours (for example, Capaldi, 1971). Why, then, did delaying reinforcement for just a few seconds have such devastating consequences in Grice's experiment?

The most likely explanation is now thought to be interference from other responses (Revusky, 1971; B. A. Williams, 1978). From the vantage point of the experimenter, it might seem obvious that food was contingent on entry into the white alley, but from the rat's perspective the situation was altogether more confusing. In the first place, there was no particular reason for the rat to believe that the food was contingent on its behavior at all. Perhaps the rat thought that the goal box contained food intermittently, in the same way that a tree produces nuts only in some seasons, with the availability of food in both cases being entirely independent of the rat's behavior. (See also Lawrence & Hommel, 1961.) Even if the rat suspected that food was response-contingent, any number of responses could have been responsible. Perhaps it was one of the responses that followed entry into the alley (R_c)—sniffing in a corner, rearing, walking down one side, and so forth—or perhaps it was one of the many responses made before entering the alley that was responsible for the food. From the rat's perspective, food was preceded by an almost infinite string of responses:

$$R_{-4} \quad R_{-3} \quad R_{-2} \quad R_{-1} \quad R_c \quad R_1 \quad R_2 \quad R_3 \rightarrow food$$

There was no obvious basis for identifying which of these responses actually produced the food. Moreover, at any given moment the rat was performing not one response but many responses—not just entering the white alley, for example, but breathing at a certain rate, holding its head at a particular angle, and so on.

From the rat's point of view, then, the situation was not the simple one illustrated in Figure 5.9a, but more nearly that shown in Figure 5.9b. Any reinforcer would be preceded by literally thousands of responses—in the case of reinforcement in humans, a rich profusion of thumb twitches, stomach contractions, leg flexions, and eyeblinks. From this vast array, the subject must somehow extract the one response that actually produced the reinforcer. Viewed in this light, the wonder is that Grice's rats ever solved the problem at all!

Implications for Human Learning

The evidence we have been reviewing suggests that even brief delays in reinforcement can severely impair learning. All the evidence, however, has come from rats, and you might be wondering whether brief delays would have nearly such serious effects in humans, given our larger brains and greater intelligence.

Delay reduces learning. The perhaps surprising answer seems to be yes—when human subjects are tested under conditions similar to those used with animals, the effects of delaying reinforcement also appear to be similar. In an experiment by Shanks, Pearson, and Dickinson (1989), for example, subjects were asked to press the space bar on a computer keyboard, and 75% of these responses were followed by illumination of a triangle on the computer's screen. Subjects were allowed to respond for 2 minutes, and were then asked to estimate the extent to which their responses had caused these illuminations on a scale from 0 to 100.

FIGURE 5.9   A rat's task in a maze when reinforcement is delayed. (a) The experimenter's view: A turn to the right (R_{turn}) produces food. (b) The rat's view: The correct response is preceded by many responses (R_1, R_2, and so on) and followed by many responses (for example, R_1). Moreover, at any moment in time the rat is engaged in multiple behaviors (R_a, R_b, and so on). Thus, the correct response is only one of a vast array of responses that preceded food, and identifying which response produced the food is not simple.

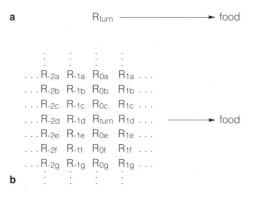

When illumination occurred immediately after a response, subjects estimated the response-outcome contingency at 80. (Their estimate was below 100 because not all responses produced illumination.) When the outcome was delayed for 4 seconds, however, estimates fell to around 30. Even this estimate, moreover, probably exaggerated the degree to which subjects perceived the relationship between their responses and the outcome, as the same estimate was produced by subjects exposed to illuminations presented at random, independently of their responses. When the outcome was delayed for 4 seconds, in other words, subjects were very poor at realizing that their behavior was producing the outcome—almost exactly the result observed by Grice in rats.

Delay reduces incentive. In real life, rewards sometimes maintain our behavior even when the rewards are delayed for periods much longer than 4 seconds—insofar as studying is reinforced by good grades, for example, the reinforcer occurs days or weeks after the response. In most of these cases, however, more immediate reinforcement was probably available when the behavior was first being established. Also, even in situations where reinforcement is not delivered immediately (for example, if a boy cleans his room when his parents are not present), the response and reinforcer can still be brought into temporal contiguity through the medium of language: "I see you cleaned your room this morning; you can stay up late tonight as a reward."

The use of language undoubtedly helps to mitigate the effects of long delays for humans, but it would be a mistake to conclude that delays in the presentation of reinforcers are therefore unimportant. One problem is that language does not always allow us to fully reinstate the response we wish to reinforce. If you are teaching someone to play tennis, for example, saying "That was a very good serve" after the game is over may be of little value, because the person will no longer be able to recall the serve in enough detail to be able to reproduce it.

A further problem is that a delayed reinforcer might be a less effective incentive for changing behavior. The term **incentive** refers to the attractiveness of a reinforcer, as measured by how hard we will work to obtain it. If you offer a neighbor's child $10 to mow your lawn, for example, the child will probably be much more interested if you offer to pay as soon as the job is completed than if you promise to pay a week later. In both cases the child might be confident that she or he will ultimately receive the reinforcer, but an immediate reinforcer might nevertheless be a stronger incentive.

Rachlin and Green (1972) conducted an experiment on choice behavior in pigeons using a situation that is analogous to that facing the lawn-mowing child. They trained their pigeons in a Skinner box containing two keys: If the birds pecked the key on the left, they received 2 seconds worth of grain immediately, whereas if they pecked the key on the right, they received 4 seconds' worth of food after a delay of 4 seconds:

$$R_1 \longrightarrow \textit{2 seconds of food}$$
$$R_2 \longrightarrow \textit{4 seconds of food}$$

Even though the second response produced twice as much food, the birds preferred the immediate reinforcer on 95% of the trials.

You might be tempted to dismiss this result as just another example of the irrationality of animals, but Kirby and Herrnstein (1995) have provided evidence that humans discount delayed reinforcers in much the same way. To assess the value of delayed rewards, they offered University students a choice between a small amount of money to be delivered soon and a larger amount to be delivered later. For example, subjects were asked if they would prefer $12 in 6 days or $16 in 12 days. The students were offered a number of these choices, and to ensure that they would take these choices seriously, they were told that one of their choices would be selected at random at the end of the session, and they would actually receive whichever option they had chosen on that trial.

Rationally, you might think that the students would have preferred receiving $16 to $12, even if it meant waiting a few more days. The result, however, was that most subjects preferred the smaller sum delivered sooner. Like pigeons, we seem to strongly prefer immediate rewards, and the longer we have to wait for a reward, the more it loses its attractiveness. (See also Kirby, 1997.)

Reinforcing homework. The practical implications of this principle are nicely illustrated in a study by Phillips (1968). To improve procedures for treating

FIGURE 5.10   Percentage of homework assignments completed by Tom under different reinforcement conditions. (Adapted from Phillips, 1968)

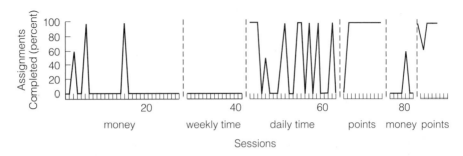

juvenile delinquents, Phillips established a residential home for boys called Achievement Place. One problem shared by most delinquents is failure in school, which in turn reflects an almost total failure to do any assigned homework. As one component of the treatment program, therefore, Phillips set out to encourage homework completion through the use of reinforcers. Whenever an assignment was completed to an acceptable standard, the boys were allowed to stay up for one hour past their normal bedtime on weekends. This reward was known as "weekly time." The effect of this reward on the behavior of one boy, Tom, is shown in Figure 5.10. Over a 14-day period, Tom did not complete a single assignment.

One possible explanation for this failure was that the reinforcer being used was not sufficiently attractive; maybe Tom just didn't value being allowed to stay up late. Another possible explanation was the delay between completing an assignment during the week and being allowed to stay up on the weekend. To find out, Phillips used exactly the same reinforcer in the next phase of the study—one hour of late time for each correct assignment—but now allowed Tom to stay up on the night that an assignment was completed rather than waiting until the weekend. These results are also shown in Figure 5.10, in the section labeled "daily time." We can see that the percentage of homework assignments completed rose immediately from 0 to an average of 50%. Even though the same reinforcer was used in both conditions, its effectiveness varied dramatically depending on the delay in its presentation. Thus, although reinforcers can be effective after a delay, as a general rule they should be delivered as soon after a response as possible if they are to achieve their full potential. Failure to adhere to this principle may be one of the most important reasons that reinforcers are sometimes ineffective.

At the beginning of the chapter, we referred to the puzzle of why students have difficulty studying despite the potent rewards—good grades, a job that pays well—contingent on this behavior. One important reason is almost certainly the delay involved in reinforcement. The reinforcers for studying arrive only after very long delays, whereas those for alternative activities, such as going to a movie or a football game, are essentially immediate.

$$R_{movie} \longrightarrow S^R$$
$$R_{studying} \longrightarrow S^R$$

The student who doesn't study might thus be behaving much like the pigeon in the Rachlin and Green study: Both may know that in the long term one response produces much more valuable consequences, but they are nevertheless unable to resist the temptation of immediate gratification. The moral to this section can thus be summarized very simply: *For a reinforcer to be maximally effective, it should be presented as soon as possible after a response.* (We will further consider the implications of this principle for behaviors such as studying and overeating in our discussion of self-control, in Section 6.5.)

5.5 SCHEDULES OF REINFORCEMENT

One of the most important factors determining the effect of reinforcement was discovered by accident. When Skinner was carrying out the research for his Ph.D., he ran his experiments on weekends as well as during the week, and one Saturday he discovered that his supply of pellets would not last until Monday. Instead of reinforcing every bar-press as he had always done in the past, therefore, he decided to reinforce only one per minute. This had two gratifying consequences:

1. His supply of pellets lasted almost indefinitely.

2. The rats continued to respond and, after some initial perturbations, did so at a steady rate.

Over time, Skinner tried several different rules, or **reinforcement schedules,** for deciding which responses to reinforce, and he found that the choice of schedule had important consequences for how his animals responded. We will begin by defining some of the schedules he used and then look at their effects on behavior.

Ratio and Interval Schedules

The schedules. The simplest schedule is to reinforce a response every time it occurs. This schedule is known, not unreasonably, as a **continuous reinforcement (CRF) schedule.** In the real world, though, behavior is rarely reinforced so consistently. Children, for example, are not praised every time they tell the truth, and factory workers are not paid every time they tighten a screw. Instead, most behavior is reinforced on intermittent, or partial, reinforcement schedules.

Two types of partial reinforcement schedules have been studied most commonly: **ratio schedules** and **interval schedules.** In a ratio schedule, reinforcement depends on the number of responses that have been emitted. In piecework, for example, a worker's wages depend solely on the number of units completed, regardless of how long the job takes. In an interval schedule, on the other hand, the passage of time since the last reinforcement, rather than the number of responses, determines whether the next response will be reinforced. Whether you find mail the next time you go to your mailbox, for example, will depend on how long it has been since the last time you found mail, not on how often you visited the mailbox in the interim. Note that obtaining mail in this example still requires a response: You do not obtain it unless you go to the mailbox. In an interval schedule, the length of the interval determines when reinforcement becomes *available*: a response is still necessary to actually obtain it.

Further complicating matters, ratio and interval schedules can be subdivided according to whether the requirement for reinforcement is fixed or variable. In a *fixed interval (FI)* schedule, the interval that must elapse before a response can be reinforced is always the same, whereas in a *variable interval (VI)* schedule this interval is varied. In an FI 60-second schedule, for example, 60 seconds must always elapse following a reinforcement before a response can be reinforced again, whereas in a VI 60-second schedule, the interval might be as short as 5 seconds or as long as 2 minutes. (The 60 seconds in the schedule's name refers to the average.) Ratio schedules are subdivided in a similar way. In a *fixed ratio (FR)* schedule, the number of responses required for reinforcement is always the same. In a *variable ratio (VR)* schedule, the number of responses required to obtain reinforcement varies across successive reinforcements. For example, FR 30 means that every 30th response will be reinforced; VR 30 means that an average of 30 responses (sometimes only 5 responses, sometimes 50, and so on) will be required for reinforcement. A slot machine in a casino is a classic example of a VR schedule: payoffs depend on how many times the machine is played, but the jackpot is made unpredictable to prevent players playing only when a machine has been in use by others for a long time. Figure 5.11 summarizes the four main types of intermittent, or partial, reinforcement schedules by the requirement for reinforcement (interval or ratio) and whether it is fixed or variable.

Patterns of responding. Learning the distinctions among the various schedules can be tedious, but each schedule has somewhat different effects on behavior, and these differences can be important. Figure 5.12 presents cumulative records illustrating the typical patterns of responding obtained under FI and FR schedules of reinforcement.

In an FI schedule (Figure 5.12a), reinforcement becomes available only after a fixed period of time has elapsed following the previous reinforcement;

FIGURE 5.11   Four main types of ratio and interval schedules. These are categorized according to whether the criterion for reinforcing a response is the passage of time or the number of previous responses, and whether this criterion is fixed or variable.

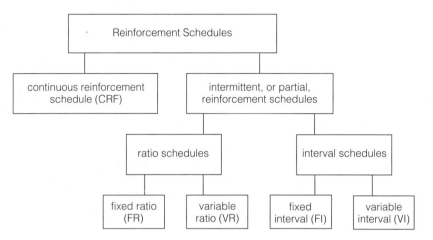

FIGURE 5.12   Typical cumulative response records generated by two types of schedules: (a) fixed interval (FI); (b) fixed ratio (FR). The short diagonal marks indicate presentations of a reinforcer.

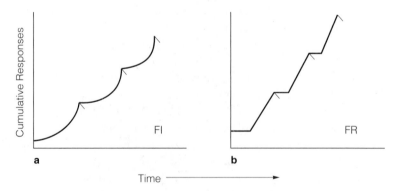

each short diagonal mark on the record indicates the occurrence of a reinforcer. We can see that immediately after reinforcement, subjects respond at a very low rate, but this rate steadily accelerates and reaches a peak just before the next reinforcement is due. Thus, subjects tend to respond in a cyclical pattern.

Because of its appearance when graphed, this positively accelerated response pattern is called an *FI scallop,* and it can have important implications for the practical use of FI schedules. For example, if you were a parent who wanted to encourage your daughter to study by praising this behavior, it would be a great mistake to visit her room only at regular, hourly intervals. If your

FIGURE 5.13   Typical responding under variable ratio (VR) and variable interval (VI) schedules with the same average rates of reinforcement. As in Figure 5.12, the short diagonal marks indicate presentations of a reinforcer.

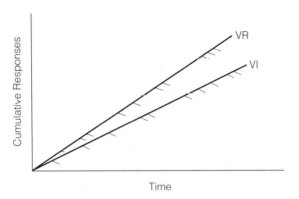

praise were the main reinforcer for studying, it is likely that your daughter would be studying at regular, hourly intervals. Ironically, psychology professors (including those teaching learning) seem to make exactly this mistake by scheduling exams at predictable, fixed intervals, with the result that students' studying often takes the form of a classic FI scallop: a zero or very low rate of studying immediately after an exam, gradually rising to a frantic peak the night before the next exam! Evidence that studying really does follow this pattern was reported by Mawhinney, Bostow, Laws, Blumenfeld, and Hopkins (1971), who monitored the use of course material in the library. When exams were scheduled daily, students maintained a constant rate of studying of around 60 minutes per day; when exams were scheduled at 3-week intervals, studying immediately after an exam fell to around 15 minutes, and then increased steadily to a peak of almost two hours just before the next exam.

Figure 5.12b shows the pattern of responding typically maintained by an FR schedule. Here, reinforcement is contingent on a fixed number of responses, and the result is generally "pause-and-run" behavior. The subject pauses for a while after reinforcement (the greater the response requirement, the longer the pause), and then switches to a steady rate of responding, which is maintained until the next reinforcement is earned. If the ratio requirement is too great, however, *ratio strain* may be observed: The subject will begin to respond, then pause, respond a bit more, pause again, and so on. If the schedule requirement is not reduced at this point, the subject soon ceases to respond altogether.

Finally, Figure 5.13 shows typical responding on VI and VR schedules. Because reinforcement can occur at any time on these schedules, subjects respond much more consistently over time; when the responses are plotted on a cumulative record, responding appears as a straight line.

The partial reinforcement effect. One puzzling consequence of presenting reinforcement on a partial reinforcement schedule is what happens when reinforcement is discontinued—that is, during extinction. Suppose, for example, that two groups of rats are allowed to run down a straight alley 100 times, with one group finding food in the goal box on every trial (CRF), and the other only on every second trial (FR 2). If both groups are now extinguished, which group of rats would you expect to stop running sooner?

On the surface, the answer might appear to be simple. Reinforcement, as we all know, strengthens responding, and nonreinforcement weakens it. If one group is reinforced 100 times and another only 50, responding should obviously be weaker in the latter group. And if responding were weaker in this group, we should certainly expect that it would be easier to eliminate responding in this group. However, we would be wrong. Not only would responding in the partially reinforced group not be easier to extinguish, it would be harder, and the less often responding were reinforced, the harder it would be.

Lewis and Duncan (1956) nicely demonstrated this effect in an experiment with college students. The students were given an opportunity to play a slot machine; they were told that they could play as long as they wanted, and that each time they won they would earn five cents. For their first eight plays, they were reinforced for between 0 and 100% of their responses; thereafter, no reinforcement was given. Figure 5.14 shows how long subjects continued to play the slot machine after reinforcement was discontinued: The lower the percentage of reinforcement during the initial phase, the longer subjects persisted in playing. The fact that partial reinforcement during training increases responding during extinction is known as the **partial reinforcement effect (PRE)**.[3]

One way of explaining this initially surprising result is in terms of how subjects know that conditions have changed and that it is no longer appropriate to continue responding. For subjects who have always been reinforced, the transition to extinction is obvious, and they are likely to quit responding quickly. For subjects who have become accustomed to nonreinforcement during training, on the other hand, the transition to extinction is less obvious, and they are more likely to persist in the hope that they will eventually be reinforced.

Tantrum behavior in children provides a real-life example of the partial reinforcement effect. When parents pay attention to a child having a tantrum, their attention can reinforce this behavior. Sometimes parents realize this is the case, so they try hard to ignore the tantrum. If, with great effort, they man-

---

[3] In the Lewis and Duncan experiment, the no-reinforcement condition (0%) resulted in the highest levels of responding during extinction, but this is not usually the case. The persistent responding in this group was probably due to the wording of the instructions, which implied that some reinforcement would be given if subjects responded. When this reinforcement was not forthcoming following the first eight plays, subjects kept trying.

FIGURE 5.14   The effect of partial reinforcement on responding during extinction. The lower the percentage of reinforcement college students received for playing a slot machine during training, the longer they persisted in playing during extinction. (Adapted from Lewis & Duncan, 1956)

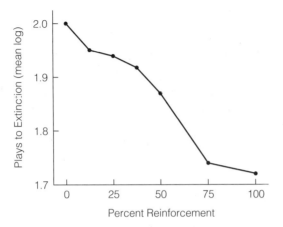

age to ignore the the their child's tantrums 90% of the time, they might then be baffled when the tantrums continue, but this persistence follows directly from the partial reinforcement effect: By reinforcing the behavior on a partial reinforcement schedule (in this case, a VR10), the parents are in fact increasing the persistence of the behavior, as the child learns that persistence will eventually pay off. If parents do want to eliminate tantrums by ignoring them, it is vital that they are consistent in not reinforcing them. We will discuss the partial reinforcement effect, and also its implications for tantrums, in greater depth in Chapter 7.

Choosing a schedule. Having described the properties of the five schedules most often studied—CRF, FI, FR, VI, and VR—can we now say which one is the best? The answer, you may not be surprised to hear, depends on how we define *best*. If your sole concern was that a response have a high probability of occurrence—that a child, for example, always tell the truth—then continuous reinforcement would have considerable attractions, because consistent reinforcement induces a very strong preference for the reinforced response over possible alternatives. This schedule, however, also has serious disadvantages. One problem is that continuous reinforcement is often costly: In monetary terms, it costs whatever the value of the reinforcer is, but it also requires considerable time and effort of the person delivering the reinforcer to ensure that he or she is always present when the desired response occurs. A further problem is that continuous reinforcement does not encourage persistent behavior. As we saw in our discussion of the partial reinforcement effect, subjects who have been reinforced every time they respond are less likely to persist in situations where reinforcement is infrequent.

Where persistence in the face of nonreinforcement is important—and this is probably the case in most practical applications involving reinforcement—the optimum strategy is to establish responding initially using continuous reinforcement, but then to gradually reduce the rate of reinforcement to the lowest level that will maintain a satisfactory response rate. Schedules with variable reinforcement requirements are generally preferable for this purpose to schedules with fixed requirements, because the unpredictability of reinforcement generates more consistent and rapid responding. Our search for the "best" schedule, therefore, has narrowed to two candidates: VR and VI. Which should you use?

The answer turns out to be a bit complicated. A VR schedule normally generates a higher rate of response than a VI schedule, because reinforcement on a VR schedule directly depends on the number of responses: If a subject doubles the number of responses he or she makes, that subject will also double his or her reinforcements. A similar increase in responding in a VI schedule is likely to have much less effect, because in a VI schedule only a single response is necessary once a reinforcer has become available. On the other hand, if the VR requirement is set too high, subjects will abruptly quit, whereas VI schedules can maintain a low but steady rate of responding even when reinforcement is infrequent. In sum, a VR or a VI schedule is generally the most effective in maintaining persistent responding; a VR schedule will tend to generate higher response rates, but if reinforcement is to be delivered only infrequently, then a VI schedule is more likely to sustain responding.

DRL and DRO Schedules

We have discussed only a few of the schedules of reinforcement that have been studied in the laboratory. Space considerations preclude coverage of all the others, but we will briefly mention two schedules that researchers encounter relatively frequently. (For a more thorough review, see Zeiler, 1977.) In a *differential reinforcement of low rate (DRL)* schedule, responses are reinforced only if they are separated by a minimum temporal interval. In a DRL 2-second schedule, for example, a response is reinforced only if it occurs at least two seconds after the preceding response. DRL schedules thus encourage low rates of responding—hence its name.

If the goal is to eliminate responding rather than reduce it, a very useful alternative is a *differential reinforcement of other behavior (DRO)* schedule. In this schedule, reinforcement is contingent on a specified period's having elapsed without a single instance of the response in question. In a study by Lowitz and Suib (1978), for example, a DRO one-minute schedule was used to eliminate persistent thumbsucking in an eight-year-old girl. She was given a penny whenever

60 seconds passed without any instances of thumbsucking, and within five sessions the behavior had been eliminated entirely.

Schedule Effects in Humans

Research on the effects of reinforcement schedules on humans has shown that they are broadly similar to those observed in animals, but there are exceptions. When animals are reinforced on an FI schedule, for example, we have seen that a graph of their cumulative responses resembles a scallop, with a low rate of responding at the beginning of each FI interval gradually increasing to a maximum just before reinforcement is due. When adults are reinforced on an FI schedule, however, this pattern is less common. Some subjects instead respond at a high and steady rate throughout the interval, while others do not respond at all until reinforcement is due. (See Lowe, 1983.)

The role of language. One way to understand this difference is through the two-level hypothesis discussed in Chapter 4. We suggested there that classical conditioning might involve two distinct learning systems, associative and cognitive, and these systems might also be involved in reinforcement. In an FI schedule, the FI scallop seen in animals might be the product of the associative learning system: As the time for reinforcement approaches, animals become increasingly excited (Zamble, 1967), and this can in turn lead to faster responding. This associative system might also be active in humans—think of drivers at a red light impatiently gunning their engines as the time for the light to change approaches—but in humans the more analytical or expectation-based cognitive system might play a greater role. If subjects on an FI schedule notice that their responses are reinforced only after a certain interval has elapsed, they might express this knowledge verbally in the form of a rule ("Respond only after one minute") and then use this rule to suppress responding early in the interval.

According to this analysis, humans have the same basic tendency to respond on an FI scallop as animals do, but this tendency is suppressed by verbal rules generated by the cognitive system. If so, humans who don't possess language—for example, infants who have not yet learned to speak—should respond similarly to animals, and this prediction has been confirmed. In an experiment by Lowe, Beasty, and Bentall (1983), for example, infants were reinforced on an FI schedule for touching an object, and their responding increased over the interval in exactly the same way as animals' did.

A criminally successful application. By now, your feelings about schedules might resemble those of the child whose review of a book about penguins began, "This book told me more about penguins than I wanted to know." Learning the technical distinctions among schedules is tedious and may appear pointless. As we suggested earlier, though, different schedules can have very different effects, and when used imaginatively, schedules can be a powerful tool for altering behavior.

In a striking demonstration of the importance of the schedule used, Kandel, Ayllon, and Roberts (1976) used reinforcement as part of a remedial high school education program in a Georgia state prison. The subjects were two inmates, one with a measured IQ of 65, the other with an IQ of 91. To reinforce studying, they were awarded points whenever they passed a test with a score of 80% or better, and these points could then be exchanged for a variety of reinforcers such as cigarettes, cookies, and extra visiting privileges. With 1000 points, for example, a convict could buy a radio as a present for his family.

The program produced significant progress, but not as much as the authors had hoped. One possible explanation was that the inmates simply were not bright enough to progress any faster. (With IQs of 65 and 91, it was perhaps remarkable that they had progressed as fast as they had.) Another possibility was that the reinforcement schedule did not provide sufficient incentive for the hard work required. To find out, the authors devised a new schedule in which the faster the inmates progressed, the more points they earned. If an inmate completed one grade level in a subject in 90 days, for example, he received 120 points; if he did it in only 4 days, he received 900 points; and if he did it in only 1 day he received 4700 points. The result was a quite staggering rate of progress. Under the old schedule, one of the convicts, Sanford, had completed ninth-grade English in three months—all things considered, not unimpressive. Under the new schedule, he completed tenth-, eleventh-, and part of twelfth-grade English in just one week. He often missed recreational periods and stayed up all night to work. As he remarked to one of the instructors, he wanted to "get when the gettin' was good." During the five months of the program—standard reinforcement schedule as well as enriched—he advanced 4.6 years in high school arithmetic, 4.9 years in reading, and 6.6 years in language. In other words, he completed almost five years of high school in five months—roughly 12 times the normal rate. And Sanford was the one with an IQ of 65!

These results have at least two important implications. First, and most relevant to our current concern, they illustrate how powerfully the choice of reinforcement schedule can determine the effectiveness of reinforcement. More generally, they hint at how often we underestimate people's ability to learn and change. Knowing Sanford's criminal record and apparent IQ, few would have believed that he was capable of such progress. But under appropriate learning conditions, all of us—learning disabled as well as gifted, criminal as well as noncriminal—might be capable of far more learning than is commonly assumed. Too often, we blame failure on the learner: "Oh, he's too stupid." "She's just not trying." A much more productive reaction to failure might be to assume that our teaching methods are at fault and to search for better methods. We have now seen two examples in which a critical reexamination of teaching procedures led to dramatic improvements in learning—Phillip's change to immediate reinforcement at Achievement Place, and the Kandel group's imaginative use of a new reinforcement schedule—and we shall encounter others as we proceed. The famous department store motto notwithstanding, the customer is not always right; sometimes the student really is at fault. However, greater faith in human potential can sometimes pay handsome dividends.

5.6 MOTIVATION

Whether you respond to obtain a reinforcer depends not only on your knowing that the response will produce the reinforcer (*learning*) but also on your desire to obtain it (**motivation**). Motivation, in turn, depends partly on deprivation and partly on the attractiveness of the reinforcer. How much you eat, for example, will depend not only on how hungry you are but also on how much you like the food. In this section we will examine how each of these factors influences the effectiveness of reinforcement, starting with deprivation.

Drive

The role of deprivation in reinforcement is nicely illustrated in an experiment by Clark (1958). In the first phase of Clark's study, rats were trained to press a bar to obtain food on a VI one-minute schedule. After all the rats had learned to bar-press, Clark arranged them into groups and deprived them of food for between 1 and 23 hours before running the next session. As shown in Figure 5.15, the longer the rats had been deprived, the faster they pressed the bar to obtain food. Studies have shown that hungry rats will also press the bar harder (Notterman & Mintz, 1965).

In addition to indicating the importance of deprivation in determining behavior, these results also suggest that we need to distinguish between *learning* and *performance*. The different response rates in the various groups could not have been caused by differences in learning because all the rats had had identical training. The likelihood of the rats' performing this learned response, however, depended on how long they had been deprived of food. Performance thus depends on motivation as well as on learning.

Psychologists have proposed several theories about the mechanism through which motivation controls behavior. One of the most influential learning theorists, Clark Hull, proposed that deprivation induces an internal aversive state, which he called a **drive,** and that such drives increase the vigor of all behavior (Hull, 1943). There is some evidence that drives do have a general energizing effect. (For example, hunger or anxiety can make you generally restless or fidgety.) It has since become clear, though, that the main effect of a drive is to selectively increase behaviors likely to reduce the drive. (For a review, see Bolles, 1975.) If you are hungry, for example, you will be particularly likely to engage

FIGURE 5.15   Average rate of bar-pressing as a function of hours of deprivation. (Adapted from Clark, 1958)

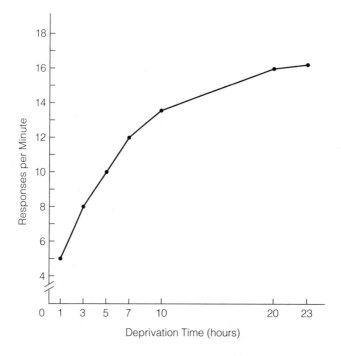

in behaviors that reduce hunger, such as going to the refrigerator or a nearby restaurant. As with the rats in the Clark study, the hungrier you are, the faster and more vigorously you are likely to carry out these responses.

In summary, performance depends on motivation as well as learning, and one determinant of motivation is deprivation level, or drive. Drives act to selectively increase responses that will reduce them, and they also increase the vigor with which these responses are performed.

Incentive

A second determinant of motivation is the attractiveness, or incentive value, of the reinforcer. As we noted earlier, some reinforcers are more attractive to us than others, and we will work harder to obtain them. In one study illustrating this point, Crespi (1942) trained rats to run down a straight-alley maze to a goal box containing either 1, 16, or 256 pellets of food. The larger the amount of food presented, the more attractive the reinforcer should be as an incentive for running, and thus the faster the rats should have run down the alley to obtain it. As shown in the left-hand section of Figure 5.16, this was what Crespi found.

FIGURE 5.16   Effect of amount of reinforcement on running speed. During the initial phase (left portion of the graph), groups received either 1, 16, or 256 pellets of food on each trial; all groups then received 16 pellets (shown on the right side of the graph). The group previously given 1 pellet ran faster than the group already accustomed to 16 pellets, resulting in an elation effect, or positive contrast. The group previously given 256 pellets ran slower than the group accustomed to 16 pellets, resulting in a depression effect, or negative contrast. (Adapted from Crespi, 1942)

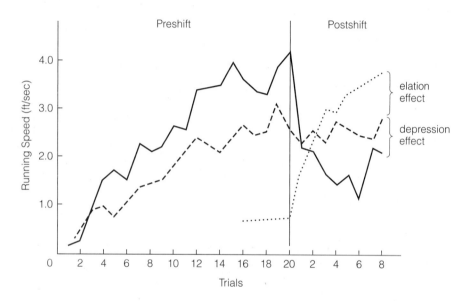

Learning or motivation? Crespi's results demonstrate the importance of the amount of a reinforcer as a determinant of performance, but they do not tell us whether it affects learning or motivation. According to Thorndike, the effect is on learning. The Law of Effect states that satisfaction stamps in an association between the response and the situation in which it occurs, with greater satisfaction producing a stronger association. In the maze, greater amounts of food produce a stronger association between the cues of the maze and the response of running, so the cues will elicit running more strongly.

An alternative possibility is that amount affects motivation. According to the cognitive analysis of learning proposed by Tolman (1932), reinforcement would lead to the formation of an expectation that food is available in the goal box. The rats then run to the goal box because they know that it contains food, and they are motivated to obtain it because they are hungry. According to

Tolman's analysis, rats that find greater amounts of food in the goal box don't learn *better,* they learn *differently;* that is, they learn to expect a greater amount rather than a smaller amount, and the expectation of a larger amount motivates faster running.

According to Thorndike, then, larger reinforcers produce better learning of the response, whereas according to Tolman, they increase motivation. To find out which account was right, Crespi ran a second phase in which he gave all three groups 16 pellets of food. The right-hand section of Figure 5.16 shows the results of this second phase: The rats that shifted from 256 pellets to 16 pellets decreased their speed of running, whereas those that shifted from 1 pellet to 16 increased theirs.

The fact that running speed decreased in the group that shifted from 256 to 16 pellets has devastating implications for a learning interpretation. Although the amount was reduced, the rats in this group were nevertheless still receiving food in the goal box; according to the Law of Effect, associative strength should have continued to increase. Running speed, therefore, should · either have increased or, if already at asymptote, remained stable. The fact that it fell suggests that the primary effect of reinforcer size was on motivation rather than on learning. This does not necessarily imply that the magnitude of a reinforcer has no effect on learning. Indeed, most learning theorists would now probably agree that amount does affect learning, but that the effect is on what is learned rather than on how well it is learned. In the acquisition phase of the Crespi study, the rats in the 16- and 256-pellet groups might have learned equally quickly that there was food in the goal box; but whereas the rats in one group learned to expect 256 pellets, the rats in the other group learned to expect 16 pellets. Similarly, when amount was changed in the test phase, this would have affected learning about what was in the goal box. In the words of Logan and Wagner:

> *If a rat's speed of running decreases over a series of trials after its reward has been reduced, it is unreasonable to conclude that the current trials have caused the animal to know less about the runway or about the appropriateness of running. Common sense says that the animal simply learned that he would receive a smaller reward as a consequence of the running.*
> (Logan & Wagner, 1965, p. 43)

In this study, then, the magnitude of the reinforcer had some effect on learning, in the sense that the amount presented is itself one of the things a subject learns, but its main effect was on motivation. In assessing motivation, therefore, we need to consider the attractiveness of the reinforcer (incentive) as well as the length of deprivation (drive). These two factors contribute independently to motivation, as shown by the fact that Crespi's rats were all deprived of food equally but nevertheless ran at different speeds depending on the amount of food available. To use a carrot-and-stick analogy, deprivation functions as a stick to drive us forward, and the reinforcer functions as a carrot to attract us; we need to consider both in predicting how hard someone will work to obtain a reinforcer.

Contrast effects. Crespi's results also have some important practical implications. Look again at Figure 5.16. You will see that the group that shifted from 1 to 16 pellets not only reached the level of those given 16 pellets throughout, but significantly exceeded it. Crespi called this overshoot an *elation effect,* implying that it was caused by the subject's euphoria at receiving more food than it had expected. Conversely, running speed in the 256/16 group not only fell to the level of the group trained throughout on 16 pellets but dropped significantly below it, a phenomenon Crespi labeled the *depression effect.*

The terms *elation* and *depression* imply emotional effects that should disappear as subjects become accustomed to the new levels of reinforcement. In some cases, however, the effects seem enduring. (For a review, see Flaherty, 1996.) Psychologists have thus come to prefer the more neutral terminology of **contrast effects** to describe these phenomena, emphasizing that the effect of any reinforcer depends on how it contrasts with reinforcers experienced previously. Crespi's elation effect is now called **positive contrast,** and the depression effect is called **negative contrast.**

Contrast effects suggest that the effects of reinforcement depend on subjects' expectations. If you expect 1 pellet (or 1 dollar, or a course grade of C), 16 pellets may seem marvelous; if you expect 256 pellets, then 16 pellets may be distinctly less impressive. The importance of expectations in reinforcement might remind you of classical conditioning, where we saw a very similar phenomenon in our discussion of the Rescorla-Wagner model. There too the effect of a US was assumed to depend on subjects' expectations, and the same US could produce either an increase or a decrease in associative strength, depending on what subjects were expecting. (Compare Figures 4.5 and 5.16.) When an important event such as food or shock occurs, we seem to evaluate it relative to our expectations, and this comparison or contrast then plays an important role in determining how we react. (For a more detailed analysis of the mechanisms underlying contrast effects, including a discussion of factors not considered here, see Williams, 1997.)

One practical implication is that in choosing a reinforcer we need to consider what reinforcers a person has experienced previously. If you own a car and a color television, the promise of a bicycle as a reward might not be very exciting, but if you grew up in poverty in Asia, it might seem priceless. A corollary of this principle is that, with extended exposure, large rewards can progressively lose their effectiveness. A heroin addict, for example, needs ever larger fixes to generate the same high. Similarly, a child accustomed to large rewards might need ever greater incentives to produce the same level of satisfaction. This might explain the age-old parental complaint, "Kids today just don't appreciate the value of money. Why, when I was a kid . . ." When standards of living improve, people become accustomed to the new levels; what was once a powerful reinforcer might now have little effect.

The Yerkes-Dodson Law

In discussing reinforcer magnitude, we suggested that its main effect was on motivation rather than on learning. The learned response in Crespi's study, however, was simply running down an alley; where more difficult tasks are involved, there is some evidence that motivation affects learning as well as performance. In an experiment by Broadhurst (1957), rats were trained on a visual discrimination in a Y-maze. The maze was flooded with water, but a platform located in one arm of the Y allowed the rats to escape. The position of the platform was shifted randomly over trials, but its current location was always signaled by the illumination of the arms; the brighter of the two arms always contained the platform. To determine the effects of motivation on learning, Broadhurst varied how long the rats were held underwater before being allowed to swim through the maze; the confinement period ranged from zero to eight seconds. In addition, he examined the role of problem difficulty by varying the relative brightness of the alleys in different groups. For the easiest problem, the correct alley was 300 times brighter than the incorrect one, whereas for the most difficult problem the illumination ratio was only 15 to 1.

The results for the different groups are shown in Figure 5.17, which plots in three-dimensional form the percentage of correct responses over the first 100 trials as a function of both drive level and problem difficulty. In all three problems, drive level did influence the speed of learning, but the optimal level of motivation varied with the difficulty of the problem. On the easy problem, drive seemed to enhance learning uniformly: The longer that subjects were deprived of air, the fewer errors they made while learning. On the difficult problem, on the other hand, the fastest learning occurred with deprivations of only two seconds; increases in deprivation beyond this value resulted in a substantial decrease in learning.

Broadhurst's results suggest that motivation does affect learning rate, but that the relationship is a complex one. With relatively simple problems, increasing motivation enhances learning, but on more difficult problems high motivation might actually be harmful. This inverse relationship between task difficulty and optimum motivation—the more difficult the problem, the lower the optimum level of motivation—has been observed in a number of other studies (for example, Bregman & McAllister, 1982; Hochauser & Fowler, 1975). The phenomenon is known as the **Yerkes-Dodson law,** named for the two psychologists who first discovered it.

FIGURE 5.17   Results of a visual discrimination experiment to determine the effects of motivation on learning. The percentage of correct responses on a discrimination learning task was affected by both motivation and problem difficulty. (Broadhurst, 1957)

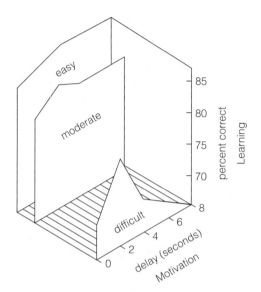

The reasons that high motivation interferes with the learning of difficult tasks are not fully understood, but one plausible explanation involves the effect of motivation on attention (Easterbrook, 1959). According to this hypothesis, attention becomes more highly focused when we are aroused; we concentrate more intensely on only a few stimuli while effectively ignoring all others. For simple problems, in which the relevant cues are obvious, focused attention is likely to facilitate learning. For problems in which the important cues are more subtle, however, a subject that focuses attention too narrowly might miss the critical cues and thus take much longer to solve the problem. (For experimental support, see Telegdy & Cohen, 1971; Geen, 1985; for an alternative explanation of the effects of motivation, see Humphreys & Revelle, 1984.)

Figure 5.18 provides a summary of our discussion of motivation. The performance of a response depends not only on whether subjects have learned that this response produces a reinforcer but also on their motivation to obtain the reinforcer. This motivation depends partly on the nature of the reinforcer, including its amount and how that amount contrasts with previous reinforcers, and partly on how long subjects have been deprived of the reinforcer. Finally, although the main effect of motivation is on performance, in some instances motivation can also influence learning, and the optimum level of motivation for learning becomes lower as the task becomes more difficult.

FIGURE 5.18   One possible view of the relationships between motivation, learning and performance. During reinforcement, subjects learn that the response produces the reinforcer ($R \rightarrow S^R$); motivation affects the value of the reinforcer (S^R).

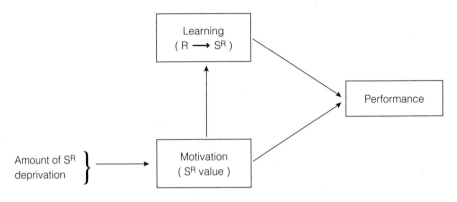

5.7 STIMULUS CONTROL

We have assumed that whenever someone presents a reinforcer it strengthens whatever response preceded it. If you were given $100 every time you spent one hour studying, for example, it seems a safe bet that this would increase your studying time. This view of reinforcement, however, can be misleading, as revealed in the following, classic experiment by Guttman and Kalish (1956).

The Concept of Stimulus Control

Guttman and Kalish used pigeons as subjects in their experiment, first training them to peck at a circular plastic disk, or key, mounted on one wall of a Skinner box. The key was illuminated with a yellowish-orange light of 580 nanometers (nm)[4]; pecks at the key were occasionally reinforced with access to a grain magazine located below the key. To find out what the birds had learned during the training phase, Guttman and Kalish ran a test session in which they varied the color on the key. Sometimes it was illuminated with a green light (550 nm), sometimes with a red light (640 nm), and so on. As shown in Figure 5.19, the birds responded vigorously whenever the key was illuminated with the training stimulus (580 nm), but responding fell off sharply when the test wavelengths diverged from this value. Contrary to our earlier analysis, reinforcement did not result in a general tendency to peck the key, but rather to peck the particular

---

[4] A nanometer is a measure of a light's wavelength, which determines its color.

FIGURE 5.19   Generalization of responding to colors of different wavelengths. The pigeons' pecking was reinforced during training only in the presence of the 580-nm stimulus (indicated by the arrow). (Adapted from Guttman & Kalish, 1956)

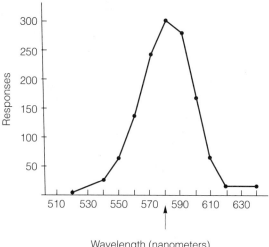

stimulus that had been present during reinforcement. Subsequent experiments have extended this finding, showing that even seemingly irrelevant features of the training situation (for example, the appearance of the walls; the texture of the floor) can acquire control over the reinforced response, so that subjects respond less when these stimuli are altered. (See Balsam & Tomie, 1985.)

In Guttman and Kalish's experiment, the response to the training stimulus spread to similar stimuli, a phenomenon known as **generalization.** As the training and test stimuli became less similar, responding declined, and this progressive decline in response is called a **generalization gradient.**

This gradient illustrates the phenomenon of **stimulus control,** in which the probability of a response varies depending on what stimuli are present. In this case, the color of the key acquired control over the birds' pecking, so that changes in color changed the rate of pecking. Similarly, human behavior often comes under the control of the cues that are present when we are reinforced, sometimes without our realizing it. A businessman, for example, may give generously to charity when in church while watching every penny at work, and most of us behave more deferentially when in the presence of a superior—a teacher, say, or an employer—than when we are with friends.

Thorndike was thus right: Reinforcement does not strengthen a response universally, but rather increases its likelihood to the stimuli present when it is reinforced. This principle, however, needs one further qualification: Although responding can come under the control of *some* of the stimuli present during reinforcement, it might not come under the control of them all.

In a study by Rincover and Koegel (1975), for example, the authors set out to teach autistic children to imitate—if the children could learn to imitate whenever they were told "Do this" and shown a behavior, then this technique could be used for teaching them new behaviors. One of their subjects, a boy named Joey, was given training trials in which the therapist said "Do this," and then touched his head. At first, the therapist would *prompt* the response by gently taking Joey's hand and moving it to his head; he would then reinforce the behavior by praising Joey and giving him a sweet. Joey required almost 300 trials to learn to imitate this action reliably. The experimenters then checked to see whether the response would generalize to a different context. Joey was taken outside the building where training had been given, and an adult Joey didn't know modeled the response and told Joey "Do this." Despite responding perfectly in the training environment, Joey did not imitate the response once during 20 test trials.

Why didn't the response generalize to the new setting? During training, the therapist had started each trial by holding Joey's hands in his lap, to ensure that he would attend to the subsequent instruction, and the experimenters wondered whether the stimulus of holding Joey's hands might have acquired control over his imitative behavior. To test this, they arranged further test trials in which the stranger began each trial by holding Joey's hands and then saying "Do this;" Joey now responded correctly on 60% of the trials. When the stranger returned to only saying "Do this," without holding Joey's hands, Joey again failed to imitate. Finally, the stranger simply held Joey's hands, without saying "Do this" or modeling the response; Joey immediately responded by moving his hands to his head. In other words, Joey's behavior was entirely controlled by the stimulus of someone holding his hands; he had learned nothing about the verbal instruction "Do this." The experimenter had inadvertently provided two cues at the beginning of every reinforced trial, and Joey had learned about only one of them.

These results make it clear that the stimuli present during reinforcement do not necessarily all acquire control over the response. We can thus reformulate the principle of reinforcement as follows: When a response is reinforced, some subset of the stimuli present is likely to acquire control over it, so that the response will become more likely when these stimuli, or others similar to them, are present.

Encouraging Discrimination

In situations where a stimulus has not acquired control over a response, we can increase the likelihood that it will do so by providing **discrimination training.** In this procedure, behavior is reinforced in the presence of the desired stimulus (S+)

but not in the presence of other stimuli (S–). The two kinds of trials are presented in a random sequence, and responding is reinforced only on the S+ trials:

$$S+: R \rightarrow S^R$$
$$S-: R \rightarrow \underline{\quad\quad}$$

If Joey's therapist had wanted to teach Joey to imitate only when the therapist said "Do this," for example, the therapist could have given Joey discrimination training in which the therapist said "Do this" on some trials and said "Don't do this" on others; the two kinds of trials would be presented in a random sequence, and Joey would be reinforced for imitating only on the S+ trials. Had Joey learned to respond differently to S+ and S–, this differential response to the two stimuli would be called a **discrimination.**

One interesting example of the use of discrimination training was reported by Azrin and Hayes (1984). Their goal in this study was to increase males' sensitivity to cues signaling females' level of interest in males. Subjects were shown 24 film clips of couples conversing, and after each film clip they were asked whether or not the female was interested in the male. They were then told whether or not they were correct. (The feedback was based on information provided by the females.) Subjects could rate the female's interest either positively or negatively, but to clarify the logic of the study we will focus on instances where subjects believed the female was interested. On clips where subjects were right—the female really was interested—they would receive positive feedback at the end of the trial, and this would reinforce their rating behavior. On the other hand, on clips where the females were not interested, the subjects' positive ratings would not be reinforced. In effect, subjects were receiving discrimination training in which positive ratings were reinforced on S+ trials (those in which the female was interested) and not reinforced on S– trials (those in which the female was not interested):

$$S_{interest}+ \; : \; R_{interest} \; \rightarrow S^R$$
$$S_{no\ interest}- : \; R_{interest} \; \rightarrow \underline{\quad\quad}$$

The result was that the accuracy of males' estimates of female interest increased by 50% over the trials, as the feedback taught them to discriminate more accurately the subtle social cues signaling interest.

Encouraging Generalization

In some situations we want to encourage discrimination, because it is important that a response occur only in appropriate contexts—a child, for example, needs to learn to discriminate between green and red lights at a street corner, and cross only when the light is green. In other situations, though, we want to ensure that behavior occurs in a wide range of settings, rather than being confined to the particular situation in which training occurred. Suppose, for example, that a little girl admitted stealing a friend's toy and that her mother praised her for being honest. The mother might have meant to encourage a general tendency to be honest, but the effect might be to increase honesty only when a toy is involved, or when the mother is present. How, then, can we reduce stimulus control to ensure that a reinforced response will generalize widely across situations? The answer, in brief, is to provide training in a variety of settings. To encourage honesty, for example, we would need to reinforce it in different situations—in different places, with different people, and so forth.

At first, this requirement might seem discouraging; people encounter an almost infinite variety of situations in real life, and we could hardly reinforce behavior in all of them. Fortunately, it is not necessary to do so: As long as reinforcement is provided in more than one setting, the reinforced behavior will often generalize quite widely.

In a study by Stokes, Baer, and Jackson (1974), for example, retarded children in a state institution were trained to greet people by waving. The experimenter first prompted the desired response by demonstrating it and, if necessary, physically guiding the children's arms through the movement. This response was then reinforced by the experimenter's smiling, saying hello, and serving candies to the children. After the children had learned to greet the experimenter reliably with a wave, generalization of this response was measured by observing the percentage of occasions on which other members of staff were greeted with a wave.

The training was effective—the children learned to wave whenever the experimenter greeted them in the training room—and the authors then observed the children's behavior in other areas of the hospital to see if this greeting behavior generalized. At first, it did—the percentage of occasions in which one of the subjects, Bruce, greeted other members of staff rose from approximately 0 to 40%—but the percentage rapidly fell back to zero. A second training phase was therefore instituted, but with a different staff member acting as the trainer. The result was that greeting behavior now generalized widely, with Bruce greeting more than 20 members of staff whenever he encountered them, regardless of where in the hospital (or even in the city) the encounter took place. This behavior was maintained for more than six months, even though the only reinforcement was the natural one provided by having people return the greeting and smile. Thus, by providing reinforcement in a variety of contexts (in this case, different trainers), it is possible to substantially increase the likelihood that a response will generalize widely. Also, although material reinforcers were used to establish the behavior initially, reinforcers in the natural environment (the friendly reactions of the people who were greeted) were then able to maintain it.

Let us summarize our discussion of stimulus control. Some subset of the stimuli present during reinforcement generally will acquire control over the response, so that the response will be particularly likely to occur when those stimuli are present. Such control can be enhanced by providing discrimination training, in which the response is reinforced only when a discriminative stimulus is present. Conversely, generalization of a response can be encouraged by reinforcing the response in a variety of contexts, with training in even two or three different settings sometimes being sufficient to ensure widespread generalization. (For more extensive discussion of the processes that underlie the development of stimulus control, see Chapter 9.)

The principle of stimulus control might sound a bit dry and technical, but, like the other reinforcement principles we have discussed, it can have important practical implications. In trying to eliminate undesirable habits, for example, it can be important to consider the stimuli that are associated with the habit. If someone is having trouble sleeping, for example—perhaps tossing and turning for hours before falling asleep—then the stimulus of the bed may become associated with this restless behavior, so that the very act of going to bed will tend to elicit restlessness. To break the link between the stimulus of the bed and worrying, Bootzin (1972) advised an insomniac client to ensure that being in bed was associated only with sleeping and not other activities. He encouraged the client to go to bed only when genuinely sleepy and not to engage in any other activities while in bed such as reading or watching TV. If he could not sleep, he was to get up and engage in other activities until he again felt tired. Within a few weeks, the patient was reliably falling asleep within minutes of getting into bed, and subsequent studies have reported similar successes (Lichstein & Riedel, 1994). We will discuss applications of stimulus control further in Section 6.5; in the meantime, you might want to imagine that you were a therapist and consider how you might use stimulus control to help clients with problems such as smoking and overeating, or to help yourself to study more.

5.8 SHAPING

To reinforce a response, the first requirement is that the response occur. In some situations, however, the desired behavior occurs so infrequently that it is difficult to train. One solution to this problem is a technique known as the *method of successive approximation*, or **shaping.** The first step in shaping is to reinforce whatever aspect of a subject's behavior is closest to the desired response. Once this behavior begins to occur more frequently, the experimenter withholds reinforcement until some closer approximation to the desired response occurs, and so on until the desired response has been established.

The Principle of Shaping

Suppose that an experimenter wanted to train a rat to press a bar. The first step would be to reinforce the rat for moving toward the section of the box containing

FIGURE 5.20   The role of response generalization in shaping. (a) Before reinforcement, the rat's average distance from the bar is 12 inches. If a response at a distance of 6 inches is reinforced (arrow), then (b) the probability of that response will increase, as will that of similar responses.

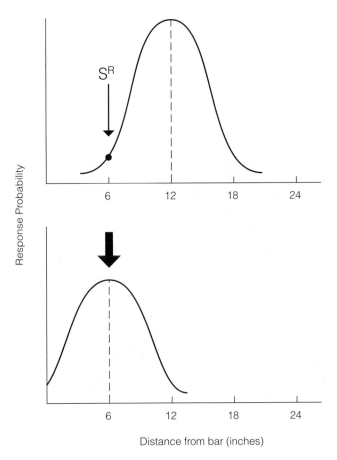

the bar. If the closest the rat approaches the bar is 8 inches, the experimenter might give it food for this movement. When this movement is reinforced, the rat would become more likely to repeat it, and this would also increase the rats' tendency to perform similar responses. The experimenter would now withhold reinforcement until the rat moved to within 6 inches, and so on, until eventually the rat learned to approach the bar, rear above it, and, finally, push down on it.

Shaping takes advantage of the fact that reinforcing a response strengthens not only that response but also similar responses. This is called *induction*, or **response generalization.** In our bar-pressing example, suppose that at the beginning of training the rat's average distance from the bar was 12 inches, with the rat sometimes standing closer and sometimes further (Figure 5.20a). If it was given food when it was 8 inches away, its tendency to approach this area would increase, which in turn would increase the likelihood of activity in adjacent areas (Figure 5.20b). As each movement closer to the target response was reinforced, response generalization would increase the likelihood of still closer approximations, until eventually the target response was emitted.

The Importance of Shaping

The principle of shaping has proven to be useful in a wide range of practical situations. One example comes from a case study reported by Wolf, Risley, and Mees (1964), which nicely illustrates several principles of reinforcement that we have discussed in this chapter. The subject was a boy named Dicky. Until he was nine months old, Dicky's behavior was normal, but then he developed cataracts in both eyes, which in turn led to a series of aberrant behaviors. He had difficulty falling asleep, for example, and would cry unless his parents remained by his bedside until he was asleep. Similarly, in other situations in which he didn't get what he wanted, he would have violent tantrums in which he would bang his head, slap his face, and pull his hair. After one of these tantrums, his mother commented that "he was a mess, all black and blue and bleeding" (Wolf, Risley, & Mees, 1964, p. 305).

Dicky underwent an eye operation for his cataracts, and his parents were told that he had to wear corrective glasses if his vision was to recover. Despite strenuous efforts, however, they could not get Dicky to wear the glasses. When Dicky was three years old, he was diagnosed as schizophrenic and was admitted to a mental hospital for children. The staff there again tried to get Dicky to wear his glasses, but again without success. After six months of failure, Dicky's ophthalmologist warned that unless he began to wear his glasses within the next six months, he would lose his vision permanently.

At this point, the hospital staff sought the assistance of Wolf, Risley, and Mees. They decided to teach Dicky to wear the glasses using the principles of reinforcement that had been identified in experiments with animals. First, recognizing the importance of immediate reinforcement, they repeatedly paired the noise of a clicker with presentations of candy, so that the noise would become a secondary reinforcer that could then be presented the instant Dicky responded appropriately. Then, since the desired response was one that, to put it mildly, occurred infrequently, they decided to use the technique of shaping, which had originally been developed to train rats to press bars. A shaping program was planned in which Dicky would be reinforced—immediately with the clicker, followed as soon as possible by food—first, simply for picking up the glasses, then for holding them for progressively longer periods, then for moving them toward his head, and so on.

When the authors instituted this program, the result was almost total failure. Although Dicky would hold the glasses, he would not wear them properly on his head. If you had been one of the psychologists involved, what would you have done at this point? One reasonable response would have been to give up, on the grounds that Dicky was simply too psychotic to be treated. The authors, however, believed that reinforcement can work with any individual, no matter how disabled or disturbed; if reinforcement did not work, they believed, then the fault must lie in the way it was being used, rather than in the subject. Specifically, they speculated that the reason Dicky wasn't working to obtain the reinforcer might have been that the incentive value of the reinforcer was not great enough.

To obtain a more effective reinforcer, therefore, the experimenters made bites of meals contingent on appropriate behavior. Dicky still responded poorly at breakfast, and again at lunch. But a third session was given at 2:00 P.M., when Dicky was hungrier, and the shaping program then worked beautifully! Dicky was trained to put his glasses on, then to wear them for longer and longer periods. His eyesight was saved, and over the years a similar training program was used to alter other aspects of his behavior. He learned to talk, to play with other children, and, eventually, to read and write. By the time he was 13, his measured IQ had increased from 50 to 110, and he was enrolled in a class for normal children (Nedelman & Sulzbacher, 1972).

The circumstances of Dicky's case are particularly dramatic, but shaping can be a powerful and useful tool in a wide range of more mundane situations. Consider, for example, the problem of teaching children to swim. You might have had the experience, at a swimming pool or beach, of watching a father trying to train his child to swim. At first, the father may cheerfully encourage the child: "Come on, there's no danger, Daddy will hold you." Then, as the child continues to resist, the father becomes increasingly impatient and the encouragements increasingly grim: "Don't be such a baby; come here right now!" The child ends up terrified, the parent in a rage.

A more fruitful approach in situations such as this, where a response is difficult to establish, is to shape it gradually. Professional programs for teaching swimming are modeled very closely on the principles we have been discussing. The key is to proceed gradually, asking children to advance at each stage only as much as they feel comfortable. At first, they may be asked to sit by the side of the pool, with only their legs in the water, then to practice kicking in the water while holding onto the side, then while holding onto a board, then with inflated water wings on their arms to support them. Finally, the air pressure in the wings may be reduced, until the child is swimming with no support. At each step, the advance is only a small one, and, with encouragement and social reinforcement, almost all children learn quickly.

The general principle underlying shaping is that when a task is difficult, begin with a simpler situation and move only gradually to the more complex one. This principle can be applied very widely. In the case of delayed reinforcement, for example, we have seen that delays of even a few seconds may prevent learning. If at first reinforcement is given immediately, however, and the delay then lengthened gradually, behavior can eventually be maintained despite delays of minutes or even hours. Similarly, in schedules of reinforcement, abruptly imposing a requirement of 500 responses for reinforcement can result in equally abrupt extinction of the response. If the requirement is introduced gradually, however—first requiring 1 response, then 2, 5, 10, and so on— behavior can be maintained even with quite substantial ratio requirements.

5.9 SUMMARY

Anecdotal evidence has suggested that animals are capable of great intelligence. When Thorndike studied animal learning under controlled conditions, however, he found that rewards produced only a gradual strengthening of the response that was rewarded, rather than the rapid improvement that would be expected if the animals had any insight into the nature of the problem. He summarized his observations in the Law of Effect, which stated that rewards stamp in an association between the rewarded response and the situation in which it was made.

This law was challenged on several grounds. Some psychologists argued that animals are capable of greater insight than Thorndike's results revealed, and the conflict between associative and cognitive accounts of learning has continued to this day. A second, less fraught, issue concerned Thorndike's use of the subjective term *satisfaction* in his statement of the Law. Some psychologists objected to the implication that rewards are always pleasurable, and this eventually led to the replacement of the term reward with the more neutral term *reinforcer*. Still a third issue concerned the relationship between Thorndike's research on reinforcement and Pavlov's on classical conditioning. The procedures are clearly different—food is presented following a response in reinforcement and following a stimulus in classical conditioning—but both involve the detection of a relationship between successive events, and the processes involved in detecting these relationships may be the same.

One of the most influential of the psychologists who emerged to carry on Thorndike's work was B. F. Skinner. He tested rats and pigeons in a box that resembled Thorndike's puzzle box, but he studied responses that could be easily repeated—for example, pressing a bar. He shaped his subjects to perform the response and then observed the effects of different reinforcement contingencies on the rate at which they responded.

Studies of learning in the Skinner box and in mazes revealed a number of factors that determine whether reinforcement is effective. One obvious one is the reinforcer used—some reinforcers are more effective than others. It is less easy to identify the characteristics shared by these effective reinforcers, but the Premack principle suggests that good reinforcers can be identified by observing what activities individuals engage in when offered a free choice: The higher the probability of an activity, the more likely that it will be an effective reinforcer. Because activities differ in their probability from moment to moment and from individual to individual, the Premack principle suggests a much more fluid and relativistic approach to identifying reinforcers than more traditional views.

In addition to primary reinforcers that require no training, learned or secondary reinforcers can also be very potent. Secondary reinforcers such as money acquire their reinforcing properties through pairing with primary reinforcers; in general, the principles involved are the same as those in classical conditioning.

One of the most important determinants of a reinforcer's effectiveness is the delay until it is presented. Studies with animals suggest that reinforcement of some kind—primary or secondary—must occur almost immediately if a response is to be strengthened, with delays of even a few seconds leading to a dramatic decrease in learning. In humans, the availability of language can help to bridge the gap symbolically between a response and a delayed reinforcer. Language, however, cannot always fully reproduce the important aspects of the response that is being reinforced, and in any case delayed reinforcers are generally perceived as much less attractive, and thus provide less incentive for repeating a response. Even in humans, therefore, delays in presenting a reinforcer can seriously undermine its effects, and this might be one main reason why reinforcement is sometimes ineffective in changing behavior.

Another important determinant of a reinforcer's effectiveness is the schedule on which it is presented. Skinner experimented with a number of partial reinforcement schedules and found that each had somewhat different effects on the rate and pattern of responding. To generate a high rate of responding, continuous reinforcement is less effective than partial reinforcement—especially variable ratio and interval schedules, in which the reinforced response cannot easily be predicted. Another advantage of partial reinforcement schedules is that they encourage more persistent responding during periods when reinforcement is not available: When subjects are accustomed to being reinforced only occasionally during training, they are more likely to persist in the face of non-reinforcement during extinction.

Whether we respond to obtain a reinforcer depends not only on learning but also on our motivation to obtain the reinforcer. This motivation depends on how long we have been deprived of the reinforcer (deprivation is assumed to generate an internal state called a drive), and the attractiveness or incentive value of the reinforcer. Incentive value in turn depends partly on the reinforcer's quantity and quality, but also on the recipient's previous experience with other reinforcers. If rats are used to receiving large amounts of food as reinforcers, for example, this will reduce the attractiveness or incentive value of smaller amounts (contrast effects).

The main effect of motivation is on whether a learned response is performed, but the level of motivation during training can also influence how a response is learned. The Yerkes-Dodson law says that the optimum level of motivation for learning depends on the difficulty of the task. For simple tasks, high motivation is helpful; on more difficult tasks, strong motivation can narrow attention in a way that interferes with learning. In general, then, using a powerful reinforcer is likely to enhance learning and performance. When a task is difficult, though, the use of large incentives can actually be counterproductive.

The effects of reinforcement also depend on the situation in which the reinforcer is given. Reinforcement does not result in a uniform increase in the probability of a response; rather, a subset of the stimuli present when a response is reinforced tends to acquire control over it, so that the response becomes more likely in the presence of these and similar stimuli. In situations in which it is desirable that a response occur widely, it is important that training occur in a variety of settings. Fortunately, the number of such settings need not be very great; in some cases, training in just two situations is sufficient to produce wide generalization. Conversely, when it is desirable that a response occur in only one situation, stimulus control can be enhanced by discrimination training in which the response is reinforced in that situation but not in others.

A final principle, and one that is too often ignored, involves introducing difficult tasks or contingencies gradually. When a response is difficult to learn, it is possible to shape it by first reinforcing a simpler response, and only gradually requiring closer approximations to the target behavior. Similarly, if it is difficult to maintain behavior with a particular delay or schedule, the problem can sometimes be circumvented by starting with more powerful reinforcement contingencies—reinforcing every response immediately—and then gradually moving toward the more difficult contingencies.

Once the principles of reinforcement are stated, they can seem almost trivially simple—just common sense. In practice, however, we tend not to appreciate how important some of these principles really are. For example, few parents or teachers would probably worry much if they reinforced a response a few seconds or minutes after it occurred, but we now know that such delays can have remarkably powerful effects. Similarly, when a response is difficult to train, we rarely consider the possibility of starting with a simpler situation and moving only gradually towards the more complex one.

When reinforcement is used in accordance with all of the principles discussed in this chapter, it can be far more powerful than our everyday experience might suggest. The examples we have discussed include a schizophrenic child who wouldn't wear glasses, an uneducated prison inmate with a measured IQ of 65, and teenage delinquents who would not do their homework. In all these cases, months or even years of effort produced no alteration in behavior, suggesting that these individuals were just too difficult to change. The appropriate use of reinforcement, however, produced dramatic changes in behavior almost immediately.

Glossary

Latency The time from when a response becomes possible until it actually occurs. In a puzzle box, for example, the latency of the escape response is the time from when the animal is placed in the cage until it escapes.

Law of Effect Thorndike's statement that the presentation of a reward would strengthen the connection between the response that preceded it and the stimuli present at the time.

Reinforcer An event that increases the probability of a response when presented after it. A **primary reinforcer** is a reinforcer that requires no special training to be effective; a primary reinforcer will thus be effective for all members of a species from birth. A **secondary** or **conditioned reinforcer** is a stimulus that acquires its reinforcing properties through experience. In most cases, secondary reinforcers are established by pairing a stimulus with a primary reinforcer.

Reinforcement The procedure of presenting a reinforcer following a response, or, alternatively, the typical outcome of this procedure, an increase in response probability as a result of presentation of a reinforcer following the response.

Operant A response that operates on the environment to produce a consequence, and whose probability of occurrence is then altered by this consequence. In a typical experiment with rats, bar pressing is an operant response that increases when it is followed by food.

Premack principle A basic law that states that the opportunity to perform a response can be used to reinforce any other response whose probability of occurrence is lower.

Response deprivation hypothesis This says that whether an activity will serve as a reinforcer depends on whether the current level of the activity is below its preferred level. Suppose, for example, that a subject is given free access to two responses, R_1 and R_2, and that the time spent in these activities during this baseline phase is measured. If the subject is then required to perform R_1 to gain access to R_2, then R_1 will increase only if the level of R_2 during this test phase would otherwise fall below its baseline level.

Incentive The attractiveness of a reinforcer, as measured by how hard we will work to obtain it. The incentive value of a reinforcer is in turn determined by both its quality (ice cream, for example, is widely regarded as more desirable than cod liver oil) and its quantity.

Reinforcement schedules Rules that determine when a response will be reinforced. In a **continuous reinforcement (CRF)** schedule, every response is reinforced. In a **ratio schedule,** reinforcement depends on the number of responses that have been emitted. In an **interval schedule,** whether a response is reinforced depends on how much time has elapsed since the last reinforcement.

Partial reinforcement effect (PRE) The higher the proportion of responses that are not reinforced during training, the more persistent responding is during extinction.

Motivation We can define motivation subjectively as the desire to obtain some goal. We can also define it more objectively (and, alas, more cumbersomely) in terms of the relationship between environmental conditions and behavior. We infer the existence of a motivational state if the probability of a response varies according to some antecedent condition that is reversible (for example, how likely we are to eat depends on how long we have been deprived of food). The motivation to obtain a reinforcer depends on the reinforcer's properties (incentive) as well as the antecedent conditions (**drive**).

Contrast effect A change in a reinforcer's effectiveness caused by prior experience with other reinforcers. An increase in a reinforcer's effectiveness caused by previous experience with less valued reinforcers is called **positive contrast;** a decrease in a reinforcer's effectiveness caused by previous experience with more valued reinforcers is called **negative contrast.**

Yerkes-Dodson law An inverse relationship between task difficulty and optimum motivation: the more difficult the problem, the lower the optimum motivation.

Stimulus control We say that a response is under stimulus control if the probability of its occurrence varies depending on what stimuli are present.

Discrimination Differential responding to two stimuli. In **discrimination training,** differential responding to two stimuli is encouraged by presenting both stimuli but reinforcing responding only in the presence of one. The stimulus that signals that responding will be reinforced is called a *discriminative stimulus* (S^D), or S+; the stimulus that signals nonreinforcement is called an S-delta (S^Δ), or S–.

Generalization Responding to one stimulus as a result of training involving some other stimulus. In most cases, the amount of generalization depends on the similarity of the training and test stimuli. If the probability of a response decreases as stimulus conditions diverge from those present during training, we refer to the decline as a **generalization gradient.**

Discrimination and generalization are two sides of the same coin, and both can be defined by the generalization gradient obtained after training with one stimulus. Insofar as subjects respond to a test stimulus, this defines generalization; insofar as the generalized response is weaker than that to the training stimulus, this defines discrimination. Terrace (1966) has argued for the replacement of both terms by that of **stimulus control.** The steeper the overall shape of the generalization gradient, the more the response is under stimulus control.

Shaping A technique for training responses that are initially unlikely to occur. The first step is to reinforce whatever aspect of an individual's behavior is closest to the desired response. As this behavior begins to occur more often, the trainer withholds reinforcement until some closer approximation to the desired response occurs, and so on.

Response generalization An increase in the strength of a response due to its similarity to a reinforced response.

Review Questions

1. Define the following terms: transituationality, T-maze, Skinner box, magazine training, operant level, free-operant and discrete-trial procedures, sensory reinforcers, social reinforcers, spatial and visual discriminations, proprioceptive stimuli, cumulative record, partial reinforcement, FI scallop, ratio strain, and drive.

2. Why didn't Thorndike trust anecdotal observations? How did he study learning instead?

3. What is the Law of Effect? What objections have been raised to it?

4. How do classical conditioning and reinforcement differ?

5. What evidence suggests that associative learning is a gradual, trial-and-error process? What evidence suggests that it is a sudden, insightful process?

6. How does the response deprivation hypothesis differ from the Premack principle?

7. How did Spence account for the discrepant results of early experiments on delayed reinforcement? How did Grice test Spence's explanation?

8. Why do even short delays of reinforcement have such devastating effects on learning in animals? Why are delays still sometimes harmful in humans, despite the availability of language to bridge the temporal gap between response and reinforcer?

9. Define the following schedules: CRF, FI, VI, FR, VR, DRL, DRO. What are the characteristic effects of these schedules on the rate and pattern of responding? If your goal were to produce persistent responding, which one of these schedules should you use?

10. Why does the Crespi experiment suggest that the amount of a reinforcer influences motivation rather than learning?

11. What does the Yerkes-Dodson law imply about the use of monetary incentives to encourage students to get good grades?

12. What can be done to increase or decrease stimulus control?

13. How can the principle of gradual change be applied to training a response, establishing a discrimination, and introducing delayed and intermittent reinforcement?

14. Every vertical mark on the "response" line in the record below represents a response. If response 1 has just been reinforced, what other responses will be reinforced if the schedule is

   a. FI 60 seconds?

   b. VI 60 seconds, with the first two intervals being 30 and 60 seconds?

   c. FR 3?[5]

15. What are the main principles that determine whether reinforcement will be effective? To what extent are these principles the same in animals and humans?

---

[5]*Answers to the schedule problems:*
   a. Responses 7 and 9. In an FI 60-second schedule, an interval of 60 seconds must elapse after every reinforcement before another response can be reinforced. Response 7 was the first response to occur at least 60 seconds after response 1 was reinforced, and response 9 was the first response to occur at least 60 seconds after response 7.
   b. Responses 4 and 8.
   c. Responses 4, 7, and 10.

CHAPTER SIX

APPLICATIONS OF REINFORCEMENT

In the introduction to Chapter 5, we considered the paradox that the principles of reinforcement appear so simple, yet in real life behavior is often remarkably difficult to change. One explanation, we suggested, was that the principles of reinforcement might not be as simple as they first appear; in the course of that chapter, we encountered evidence supporting that view. Even brief delays of reinforcement, for example, have far more severe effects on learning than is commonly realized, and our understanding of phenomena such as motivation and stimulus control is still limited. Therefore, we could readily account for our difficulty in using reinforcement effectively by our incomplete understanding of the principles governing its use.

There is, however, another possibility. Even in those cases in which we do understand the principles of reinforcement, it can appear ineffective because we fail to apply the principles in a coherent and systematic way. That is, we might already know enough to use reinforcement effectively, if only we would apply that knowledge systematically. This, at any rate, was the belief of a number of influential learning psychologists and has led to a major effort during the past two decades, under the rubric of **behavior modification,** to apply the principles of reinforcement developed in the animal laboratory to practical problems of human behavior. In this chapter we will review some of these programs, considering the extent to which they have been successful, and, insofar as they have failed, what these failures can tell us about the remaining gaps in our knowledge. We will begin by looking at some of the attempts that have been made to apply the principles of reinforcement to education.

6.1 Reinforcement in the Classroom

Reinforcement principles have been applied to a wide range of educational problems and institutional settings. We will focus our attention in this section on examples involving schoolchildren, teenage delinquents, and university students.

Classroom Behavior

One of the most difficult problems for any teacher is children who are severely disruptive in class. By talking, moving around, and so on, they not only fail to learn themselves but also seriously interfere with the work of those around them. To test a reinforcement-based program for dealing with this problem, Hall, Lund, and Jackson (1968) went to a school in a severely deprived urban area. They asked the teachers and principal to identify the children in the school whose behavior posed the most serious problems. One child, a third-grade boy named Robbie, had been in trouble ever since he entered the school. He had received repeated scoldings, been sent to the principal, and even been spanked—all to no avail. A classroom observer found that Robbie spent only 25% of his time on assigned tasks, the remainder of the time being devoted to activities such as talking, snapping rubber bands, drinking milk very slowly and then playing with the carton, and so on. His teacher often urged him to work; indeed, 55% of her contacts with Robbie occurred at times when he was not working.

If you were the teacher in charge of the class, what would you do? One natural reaction would be to punish him, but this had already been tried repeatedly without success. The experimenters' analysis was that the teacher was actually encouraging Robbie's misbehavior by giving him attention when he misbehaved. As we saw in our discussion of social reinforcement, attention from others, even when that attention comes in the form of scolding, can be reinforcing. The experimenters therefore recommended that the teacher use attention to reinforce appropriate behavior. They asked her to ignore Robbie whenever he misbehaved. When he behaved appropriately for one minute, however, she was to come over and praise him, making comments such as, "Very nice, Robbie, you've been working very well."

The results are shown in Figure 6.1. When reinforcement was introduced, there was an immediate increase in the proportion of time Robbie spent studying. When the teacher returned to the baseline condition—that is, scolding inappropriate behavior—studying fell; it improved again, however, when reinforcement was reinstated. This improvement, moreover, proved durable: Observations made 14 weeks after the training program had ended revealed that Robbie was still spending 79% of his time working, compared with only 25% during the baseline phase. Not surprisingly, this change in the amount of time spent working also led to a substantial improvement in the quality of Robbie's work. On spelling tests, for example, his performance improved from 57% to 97%.

This improvement was not achieved without effort. To ensure that Robbie would be reinforced immediately when he studied, his behavior had to be monitored constantly. To help the teacher, the classroom observer signaled surreptitiously whenever the criterion for reinforcement was met. In the early stages of

FIGURE 6.1   Effect of praise on the proportion of class time Robbie devoted to studying. (Hall, Lund, & Jackson, 1968)

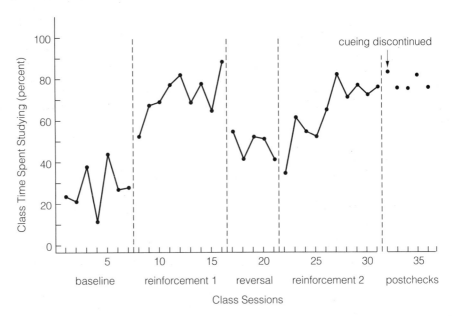

the program, therefore, considerable effort was needed to implement it, but in the long term, the improvement in Robbie's behavior meant that he required substantially less of the teacher's attention, and this improvement was maintained when cueing was discontinued. The experimenters obtained similar results with the other children studied. Thus, even a seemingly trivial reinforcer—just a little bit of praise and attention—produced remarkable changes in the behavior of the most severely disruptive children in the school, provided that this reinforcement was both immediate and consistent.

Teaching Sports

Allison and Ayllon (1980) reported an application of reinforcement to a different type of teaching problem. The subjects were university students in a physical education course. The normal teaching technique consisted of an explanation of the required behavior—for example, how to serve when playing tennis—after which the instructor modeled the behavior, then the students carried out the behavior themselves, and the instructor gave verbal feedback on the students' success. The training program was fairly standard, but a good one, with lots of explanation and demonstration. Progress, however, was very slow. Figure 6.2 plots the results for a student named Greg: On only a single

FIGURE 6.2   Greg's improvement in tennis serving under standard and behavioral coaching. (Adapted from Allison & Ayllon, 1980)

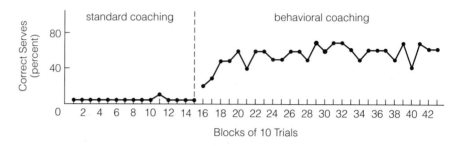

occasion did he manage to serve correctly, and there was no evidence of improvement even after 150 trials.

In an effort to improve learning, the experimenter made several changes in the teaching procedure; at the heart of these changes was the principle of immediate reinforcement. Students were again asked to execute the required stroke; if they did so correctly, the instructor immediately praised them. If they made an error, however, the instructor blew a whistle and told them to freeze. The instructor gave a verbal explanation of the students' mistakes while the students were stationary; then the instructor modeled the correct position and asked the students to assume it. The freezing served several purposes. First, it provided immediate feedback following an error, eliminating the delay of waiting until students finished their serve. Second, having students move from the wrong position to the correct position allowed them to compare directly the resulting sensations; in future, the sensory feedback from the correct position could act as a source of immediate secondary reinforcement. Finally, the requirement to freeze might also have served as an immediate punishment for the actions involved in serving incorrectly.

As shown in Figure 6.2, this seemingly small change in the immediacy of feedback resulted in dramatic improvement in the quality of Greg's tennis serve. Similar improvements were observed in other students in the class, and also in other sports such as football and gymnastics. One implication of these results is that if a student is not doing well, it might not help very much to leave the student alone to practice over and over again—each time practicing incorrectly. To improve at any task—whether learning a sport or a foreign language, or developing social relationships—we need feedback on the success of our efforts, and this feedback should be immediate and frequent if it is to be maximally effective. Providing such feedback can initially be very time-consuming for a teacher, but close monitoring of a student's behavior might require less teaching time in the long run because of the rapid improvement that results.

The Token Economy

The preceding studies support the view that failures of reinforcement might be the result of reinforcement's being used in a perfunctory, haphazard way. When reinforcement is used more systematically, and, in particular, when it is immediate and consistent, then even relatively small changes in reinforcement—a pat on the back, or providing exam results immediately instead of days or weeks later—can produce dramatic changes in behavior.

It would be misleading, however, to imply that applications of reinforcement principles are always this effective. Consider, for example, the "reinforce good behavior, ignore bad behavior" strategy used by Hall, Lund, and Jackson. In many of the studies that used this method, the results were similar to those reported by Hall's group; in others, though, students whose disruptive behavior was ignored have really gone haywire, finally forcing premature cancellation of the program (for example, O'Leary, Becker, Evans, & Saudargas, 1969).

In some of these failures, the problem was that the teachers did not implement the system properly. In the Hall, Lund, and Jackson study, for example, the technique was successful in six of the seven classes in which it was tried. In the one case where it failed, the experimenters found that the teacher had been unable to ignore bad behavior and had continued to become angry and to scold the student whenever he was disobedient.

In other cases, the problem could have been that the social reinforcers used were not effective reinforcers for the students concerned. As we noted in Chapter 5, social reinforcers gain or lose their effectiveness partly through experience; for some children, social reinforcers such as praise and attention are not effective (at any rate, not from their teachers). Where praise fails, a possible alternative is the **token economy,** in which points or tokens are established as secondary reinforcers through pairings with a variety of more potent reinforcers. If children behave appropriately in class, for example, they are immediately given points that can later be exchanged for backup reinforcers such as candy. The advantages of using tokens as reinforcers are these:

1. Because they are easily dispensed, they can be delivered immediately after the child makes a response.

2. Because they are exchangeable for a wide variety of backup reinforcers, they are always likely to be attractive. Even if a child does not want candy at a particular moment, the token might still be desirable because it can also be exchanged for other reinforcers such as toys.

One example of a token economy that we have already encountered is the study by Phillips (1968) in which juvenile delinquents were treated in a residential center called Achievement Place. The boys were given points for appropriate behavior, and these points could be exchanged for reinforcers such as snacks, money, permission to go into town, and so forth. When permission to stay up late was used to reinforce completion of homework assignments, the average percentage completed was 50%; when points were made contingent on completion, this percentage rose to 100%. (See Figure 5.10.)

Token economies have produced similar improvements in a wide range of settings. In one striking example, a token economy was used to reduce injuries in two mines. Workers were given trading stamps at the end of each month in which they suffered no injuries, and they received extra stamps if their work group was also injury-free. The stamps could then be exchanged for a wide variety of items at redemption stores. Over a 12-year period, the number of injuries fell by 68% in one of the mines and by 85% in the other. The program was highly cost-effective for the owners: The cost of injuries fell by more than $260,000 a year, whereas the stamps cost only around $12,000. And the program also proved highly attractive to the workers: A union representative at one of the mines even asked that the token program be written into the workers' contracts (Fox, Hopkins, & Anger, 1987).

As we shall see, token economies need to be used with some caution. Nevertheless, they provide a potentially useful alternative for situations in which reinforcers such as praise prove ineffective.

6.2 THE PROBLEM OF MAINTAINING BEHAVIOR

When psychologists first attempted to apply the principles of reinforcement to problem behaviors, there was considerable doubt that they would succeed. Could the behavior of delinquents, much less of children with severe learning disabilities or of psychotics, really be altered just by reinforcing them for appropriate behavior? Over the years, it has become clear that the answer is yes: Provided that reinforcement is used in a coherent and systematic way, it can be effective in settings as diverse as elementary schools and universities, prisons and psychiatric wards. It is now well established that behavior can be altered by reinforcement; the greater problem has proved to be maintaining these gains when the reinforcement program is terminated.

The Problem of Extinction

Consider, for example, the token economy used in Achievement Place. The initial results obtained with this program were highly positive. Boys who participated in this program were found to have substantially lower rates of court appearances during the two year period following their participation than did boys with similar backgrounds, and they also had higher grades in school (Fixsen, Phillips, Baron, Coughlin, Daly, & Daly, 1978). When their behavior was examined over a longer period, however, much of this improvement was eventually lost (Wolf, Braukmann, & Ramp, 1987). When you think about it, this is perhaps not surprising: If delinquents return to the environment that produced their delinquent behavior, it is understandable that they might return to the patterns of behavior that they had previously found to be effective in these environments.

We can see evidence of this effect on a smaller scale in the homework program we described earlier. If you look again at Figure 5.10, you will see that when points were made contingent on Tom's completion of homework, the percentage of assignments completed rose to 100%. When points were eventually discontinued, however, the percentage of completions fell back to zero. In other words, when Tom received a reward he valued for studying, he studied; when this reward was discontinued, he stopped studying. After all, why should anyone persist in a behavior if it no longer produces reinforcement?

The implicit assumption in the programs we have been reviewing is that there are sources of reinforcement in the natural environment that will maintain the desired behavior if only it can be established initially. A delinquent might need external incentives to learn to read, for example, but once the behavior is established, the inherent pleasure available from reading books, newspapers, and so on should maintain the behavior. In some cases, though, it can take time for these natural reinforcers to develop; if the reinforcement program is to be effective, then, it might be necessary to ensure that the reinforced behavior will continue long enough for the natural reinforcers to assume control.

Tactics for Encouraging Maintenance

Partial reinforcement. Several of the principles reviewed in the previous chapter can be used to encourage the persistence of behavior long enough for these natural reinforcers to assume control. One such technique is partial reinforcement. As we noted in Chapter 5, the greater the intermittency of reinforcement during training, the longer behavior will persist after reinforcement is terminated. In most reinforcement programs, therefore, continuous reinforcement is used to establish a behavior initially, but the frequency of reinforcement is progressively reduced as training continues.

Reinforcing in a variety of settings. Another technique for maximizing the persistence of behavior is to reinforce it in a variety of settings. According to the principle of stimulus control, reinforcement strengthens behavior most in the particular setting in which training is given. By reinforcing behavior in a variety of settings, however, we can increase the likelihood that it will generalize widely, and thus not extinguish the instant there is a change in conditions (for example, on leaving the classroom in which training was given).

Fading. A third potentially useful technique involves *fading* out the reinforcement program gradually, rather than terminating it abruptly. In our discussion of shaping, we saw that a reinforced response is more likely to persist if any changes in the reinforcement program—for example, in the number of responses required for reinforcement—are introduced gradually rather than abruptly, and this principle also applies to the termination of the program. In a study by Hall, Axelrod, Tyler, Grief, Jones, and Robertson (1972), for example, the experimenters were students in a university course on behavior modification. These students carried out projects in their own homes using the principles studied in the course. One such project involved a boy named Jerry, who had started wearing an orthodontic device when he was eight years old. Jerry was supposed to wear the device for 12 hours a day. In practice, though, he wore it for only a few hours a day because he hated it. After eight years, four dentists, and $3,300 in bills, Jerry's condition was essentially unchanged.

As a first step toward altering this behavior, Jerry's mother began to keep careful records of how often he wore the device, so she could accurately assess the effects of any treatment. During this baseline period, Jerry wore the device only 25% of the time. (See Figure 6.3.) To increase this percentage, his mother first tried social reinforcement. She did not reprimand her son when he failed to wear the device, but she praised him when he did. This social reinforcement produced a substantial increase in the desired behavior—he wore the device 36% of the time—but for practical purposes the increase was not sufficient. In the next phase, therefore, his mother tried a more powerful reinforcer: money. If Jerry was wearing the device when his mother checked, he received 25 cents; if he was not, he lost 25 cents. His mother paid him at the end of each month, and the amount of time Jerry spent wearing the device increased to 60%. To increase it still further, his mother changed to immediate reinforcement—Jerry received payment immediately after each inspection—and the amount of wearing time now rose to 95%! As we have seen again and again (and again . . .), a reinforcer presented after a delay is generally far less effective than the same reinforcer given immediately.

At this point, the reinforcement program was discontinued, and the amount of time Jerry spent wearing the device immediately declined to 64%. This still represented a substantial improvement over the original figure of 25%, but the change was still not sufficient to cure Jerry's dental problems. The immediate reinforcement condition was therefore reinstituted, and Jerry returned to wearing the device reliably (the percentage this time was 99%). Instead of terminating the program abruptly, his mother now faded it out gradually. The frequency with which Jerry's behavior was checked was gradually reduced from five times a day to only once every two weeks, and the behavior was now maintained. Eight months later, Jerry's dentist told him that he had made great progress and no longer needed to wear the device. By using reinforcement and then fading it out gradually, Jerry's mother was able to establish and maintain a behavior that years of scolding and nagging had proved powerless to influence.

FIGURE 6.3   Effects of three different reinforcement techniques: social reinforcement in the form of praise, money with a delayed payoff, and money with an immediate payoff. The reinforced behavior was the wearing of an orthodontic device. (Hall et al., 1972)

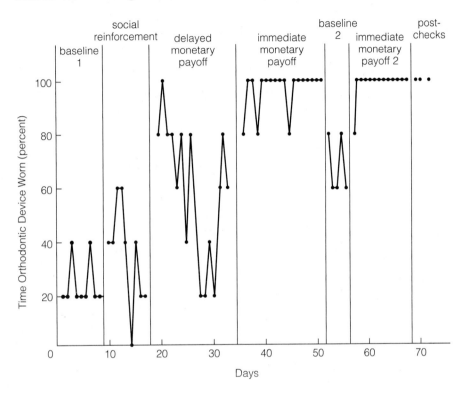

6.3 HARMFUL EFFECTS OF REINFORCEMENT

The material reviewed in the previous sections testifies to the beneficial effects that reinforcement can have when used properly. When encouraged to use reinforcement more frequently, however, parents and teachers sometimes react with suspicion, especially when the proposed reinforcer is a material one such as tokens or money. In this section, we will consider some of the reasons for this suspicion and the extent to which it might be justified.

Moral Objections

Bribery. One common objection to the use of reinforcement is that it seems to be a form of bribery. Why should a child be offered money or other rewards to mow the lawn or do other chores? Many people perceive these tasks as a duty; if so, a material inducement is nothing more than a bribe.

This view has some appeal: There is something disturbing about offering a reward to get someone to do something they should be doing anyway. However, we need to consider this issue in the context of available alternatives. There is no problem if children accept responsibility, but what alternatives are available if they do not? We could admonish them to do their duty, or threaten them with punishment if they disobey, and these strategies might be appropriate in some circumstances. In at least some situations, however, these disciplinary techniques are ineffective as well as unpleasant. Consider the examples we have already seen: Robbie's teachers tried punishment to eliminate his misbehavior without success, and eight years of reprimands had no effect on getting Jerry to wear his orthodontic device. In both cases, however, the introduction of reinforcement led to a rapid and substantial improvement in behavior, which was then maintained even after reinforcement was discontinued. These examples do not prove that reinforcement is always preferable to punishment, but they do suggest that reinforcement can be more effective than traditional forms of discipline in at least some circumstances, and might avoid harmful side effects that sometimes come with punishment. (See Chapter 7.) O'Leary, Poulos, and Devine (1972) discuss other issues concerning the relationship between reinforcement and bribery.

Greed. A second objection to the use of rewards—particularly material rewards—is that they promote greed. If children were offered $20 for cleaning their rooms, in this view, they would soon begin demanding money for doing other chores too, rather than accepting the chores as a necessary aspect of cooperative living. In fact, we have already encountered indirect evidence that material reinforcers can have this effect. In Chapter 5, we saw that extended exposure to a particular reinforcer devalues lesser reinforcers: A rat that had run down an alley to obtain 64 food pellets would not work nearly as hard to obtain 16 pellets as it would have before exposure to 64 pellets. In other words, it looked very much as if the rat had become greedy!

Similar effects have sometimes been observed in applications involving material reinforcers. In one study, delinquent female adolescents were reinforced with money when they behaved appropriately in class—for example, not talking while the teacher was explaining something. The program was run during classes held in the morning, and it produced a significant improvement in students' behavior. However, disruptive behavior *increased* during the afternoons, when the program was not in effect. As one student said to the experimenters, "If you don't pay us, we won't shape up" (Meichenbaum, Bowers, & Ross, 1968, p. 349).

To avoid these kinds of problems, most reinforcement programs begin by using relatively mild reinforcers such as social praise. Material reinforcers are used only if these milder forms of intervention prove ineffective.

Undermining Intrinsic Motivation

A further objection to the use of reinforcers is that they can devalue the activity on which they are contingent. One view is that a person should be directed toward a certain behavior by **intrinsic motivation**—motivation that comes from the activity itself rather than from any consequences that might follow it. In the words of A. S. Neil, a Scottish educator who founded an influential school known as Summerhill:

> The danger in rewarding a child is not as extreme as that of punishing him, but the undermining of the child's morale through the giving of rewards is more subtle. Rewards are superfluous and negative. To offer a prize for doing a deed is tantamount to declaring that the deed is not worth doing for its own sake. . . . A reward should, for the most part, be subjective: self-satisfaction for the work accomplished.
> (Neil, 1960, pp. 162–163)

In practice, it is sometimes difficult to distinguish precisely intrinsic and extrinsic reinforcers. Take, for example, the activity of eating. Should eating be considered intrinsically motivated because the pleasure derives from eating itself, or is the food an extrinsic reinforcer? In theory, however, the distinction seems reasonably clear: Intrinsically motivated behaviors are those that are relatively independent of external or arbitrary reinforcers.

Powerful support for Neil's view comes from a study by Lepper, Greene, and Nisbett (1973). The purpose of their experiment was to investigate the effects of reinforcement on children's behavior in drawing pictures. In the first phase, the spontaneous level of drawing was determined by providing a nursery class with free access to felt-tip markers and paper and observing how much time they spent in drawing during a three-hour period. One week later, the children were told that there was a visitor who would like to see what kinds of pictures children draw with markers. A reward group was told that they would receive a Good Player award—consisting of a card with a gold star, a red ribbon, and their names inscribed—if they drew a picture. A control group was also asked to draw a picture, but no reward was mentioned.

To test the effects of the reward, markers were again made available in the nursery one to two weeks later. Children in the control group spent almost exactly the same amount of time drawing as they had during the baseline phase, but the children who had been rewarded spent only half as much time as they had before.

Determinants of Undermining

If reinforcement reduces long-term interest in an activity, why was it so effective in the studies reviewed earlier in this chapter, in which changes in behavior were maintained even after reinforcement was discontinued? Clearly, reinforcement does not always reduce interest; the outcome must somehow depend on the particular circumstances in which it is used. In this section we will consider several possible factors suggested by recent research.

Level of initial interest. One obvious difference between the Lepper group study and earlier applications is that the activities reinforced in most of the earlier studies were not all that exciting to begin with. Robbie, for example, hardly derived pleasure from studying, nor did Jerry enjoy wearing his orthodontic device. In contrast, the Lepper study involved reinforcing a very attractive activity—drawing pictures. Perhaps reinforcement reduces interest only when intrinsic interest is high to begin with.

Support for this hypothesis comes from Lepper, Greene, and Nisbett's data. During the baseline phase, most of the children spent considerable time drawing; for these children, as we have seen, reinforcement significantly reduced interest. Some children, however, showed little interest in drawing initially, and these children became more interested in drawing following the reward. In practical terms, if a child hates lawn mowing, there is probably little danger that his or her interest will be reduced by the offer of a reinforcer; in fact, the pleasure derived from earning money and feeling grown-up might actually enhance interest. However, for those children who already enjoy mowing lawns—a rare and much prized species—the offer of a reward might be more likely to prove counterproductive.

Reinforcing obedience versus competence. Lepper (1981) and Deci and Ryan (1980) have suggested that when children are reinforced for engaging in an activity, they might feel that they are being controlled or manipulated. This sense of being controlled is aversive and could be responsible for their subsequent loss of interest in the task.

According to this analysis, whether reinforcement will have a damaging effect should depend on whether recipients perceive it as an attempt to control their behavior. To test this hypothesis, Ryan (1982) gave students a number of interesting puzzles to solve. In one group, the experimenter said "Good" whenever the students solved a puzzle; in a second group, the experimenter said "Good, you're doing as you should." As predicted by the control hypothesis, subsequent interest in the task was significantly lower in the second group. (See also Feehan & Enzle, 1991.) The more we feel controlled, the less we enjoy the task we are being forced to perform.

We might expect quite different results if reinforcers were delivered in a way that encouraged feelings of competence. If reinforcement was contingent on the quality of performance rather than simply on completing the task, it might be more likely to increase feelings of competence and thus lead to greater enjoyment and interest. In one study supporting this prediction, Enzle and Ross

(1978) offered university students $1.50 for working on difficult puzzles. In one group, the reward was promised simply for participating in the experiment; in a second group, it was contingent on achieving a level of competence well above average (this level was not specified, but all the subjects in this group were told that they had attained this high level). As in earlier studies in this area, subjects who were reinforced simply for participation showed significantly less interest in the task after the experiment was over, but subjects reinforced for their skill showed greater interest. When reinforcement implies a greater level of competence, the pleasure we experience is likely to enhance our enjoyment of the task rather than diminish it: "This is something I'm good at; what fun!"

Praise versus material reward. Still another factor determining whether reinforcement will undermine intrinsic interest is the nature of the reinforcer. In a review of the now-extensive literature in this area, Cameron and Pierce (1996) compared the results of studies that used material rewards with those that used social rewards such as praise. On average, they found that the studies using material reinforcers reported a small undermining effect on interest in the task, but those in which subjects were praised found a long-term increase in interest. This finding might be related to the evidence we just discussed on control: When we are praised, we might be more likely to perceive this as a genuine expression of appreciation for the quality of our work, rather than as an attempt to control our behavior. Conversely, when an attractive material reward is promised for performance, the frustration involved in waiting for it to be delivered can become associated with the task, making it aversive rather than pleasurable.

Evaluation

We can summarize these findings by saying that although reinforcement can reduce interest in certain circumstances, whether it has this effect depends critically on exactly how it is used. If the initial level of interest in a task is high, and a material reward is offered for performing it, there is a real danger that reward will reduce long-term interest, but even here reinforcement can increase interest if it is contingent on the quality of performance. If you wanted to encourage children to practice the piano, for example, it would probably be better to praise them for practicing rather than offering a material reward, because praise seems less likely to be perceived as a mechanism of control. Moreover, this praise is much more likely to be effective if it emphasizes their competence ("That sounds lovely; you've really improved") rather than their obedience ("That's wonderful; you've practiced for an hour just as I told you").

For further guidance on what has rapidly become a controversial area, you can consult papers by Lepper, Keavney, and Drake (1996) and Cameron and Pierce (1996). Although they fundamentally agree on the circumstances in which reinforcement can have undesirable side-effects, they offer different perspectives on how seriously the problem should be viewed.

The principle of minimal force. Despite the sometimes spectacular success of applied reinforcement programs such as token economies, parents and teachers are often resistant to the use of reinforcement, and it is now clear that at least some of their concerns are justified. Rewards can encourage greed and lead to a sense of being controlled, which will reduce long-term interest in the reinforced activity. Finally, there is one more problem, which we touched on in Chapter 5. Reinforcement can increase motivation, and when a task is difficult, this heightened motivation can paradoxically impair performance.

These difficulties do not mean that we should never use reinforcement. When a task is unattractive, reinforcement can be a far more pleasant—and effective—technique than are alternatives such as threats or admonitions to be good. To minimize the problem of harmful side effects, however, current evidence suggests that when reinforcement is used it is best to follow what might be called the *principle of minimal force*—that is, to use the least powerful reinforcer that is likely to be effective. (See Lepper, 1981.) In general, it is best to start with relatively mild reinforcers such as praise, turning to material reinforcers only if praise proves ineffective. Whatever the reinforcer chosen, wherever possible it should be administered in a way that encourages feelings of competence rather than mere obedience.

Behavioral contracts. No one likes to be manipulated or controlled, and the more reinforcement is perceived as part of a caring relationship, the more likely it is to be effective. One technique that might be helpful in this respect is a **behavioral contract,** in which the parties involved agree on what behaviors they want to be changed and the consequences that will follow. In a family setting, for example, parents and children could first discuss what behaviors they want from each other. The parents, for example, might want the children to clean their rooms; the children might want their parents to stop nagging them. They would also agree on what reinforcers or punishers would be used to encourage compliance. Such contracts might reduce feelings of being controlled, provided that both parties are reciprocally exerting control over each other, or that both have an active role in designing the contract (Dickerson & Creedon, 1981). When used in this way, there is evidence that behavioral contracts can be very useful in dealing with family problems. (See Kirschenbaum & Flanery, 1983; Miller & Kelley, 1994.)

Another way to state this idea is that the more individuals are involved in the design of a reinforcement program—choosing the goals, the reinforcers to be used, the contingencies—the more likely it is that they will cooperate in its implementation. An interesting example comes from a recent study by Ludwig and Geller (1997). Although the study did not involve reinforcement, it nicely

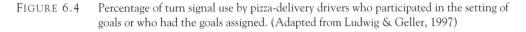

FIGURE 6.4   Percentage of turn signal use by pizza-delivery drivers who participated in the setting of goals or who had the goals assigned. (Adapted from Ludwig & Geller, 1997)

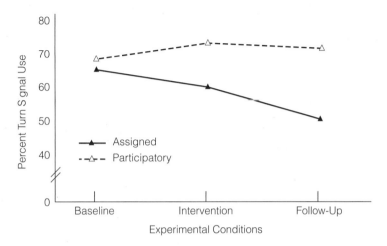

illustrates the importance of individuals participating in the design of programs affecting their behavior. The study focused on the desire of a pizza firm to reduce accidents involving their drivers. One group of pizza deliverers were assembled for a meeting to discuss the importance of coming to a full stop before joining the main road outside their store; they decided for themselves what targets to set for the percentage of occasions on which drivers should behave in this way, and they then received feedback for several weeks on the group's success. A group at another store was treated similarly, except that they were told what target to aim for.

The drivers' behavior was monitored without their knowledge, not only during the four weeks of the program but for 5½ months after it ended. Both groups showed similar behavior in terms of the explicit target of coming to a full stop, but drivers who had participated in the setting of a target were found to also improve in other safety behaviors, not mentioned in the program. Figure 6.4 shows the percentage of occasions on which drivers signaled before turning onto the main road. The subjects in the participatory group improved substantially on this behavior, and the improvement was maintained even after the program was terminated. The performance of subjects who had been assigned targets, however, if anything deteriorated, and was indistinguishable from that of control subjects who were never asked to change their safety behavior.

All attempts to change others' behavior can potentially be seen as coercive, and much depends on exactly how these programs are implemented. The more individuals feel that they are valued, and their needs and wishes are being considered, the more likely it is that they will cooperate in changing their behavior over the long term. (See also Grolnick & Ryan, 1989.)

6.4 ALTERNATIVES TO REINFORCEMENT: MODELING

The evidence we have discussed suggests that reinforcement can be counter-productive in some situations, particularly when the behavior to be encouraged already possesses some attractiveness. Is there any other way of encouraging such behaviors?

The Influence of Models

One potential alternative is **observational learning,** or **modeling.** Evidence from animal studies suggests that one of the most important ways in which animals learn what foods are edible, or what predators to avoid, is by observing the behavior of their parents or peers. For example, some species of birds respond to predators by "mobbing" them—flying toward them in groups while emitting distinctive calls. Curio, Ernst, and Vieth (1978) showed that black-birds who observed other blackbirds mobbing a target would then themselves mob the target, even though the target was initially neutral. Similarly, rhesus monkeys learn how to behave toward snakes by observing the behavior of other monkeys. Cook, Mineka, Wolkenstein, and Laitsch (1985) found that lab-reared monkeys, who have no fear of snakes, became intensely frightened of snakes if they observed other monkeys behaving fearfully toward snakes. Conversely, monkeys who saw another monkey behaving calmly with snakes were significantly less likely to later become afraid of snakes (Mineka & Cook, 1986).

Anecdotal evidence suggests that human behavior is also strongly influenced by the behavior of those around us—our parents' religion, our friends' drinking or smoking habits, the fashions worn by Hollywood stars, and so on. Laboratory experiments have confirmed this. In a classic series of studies, Albert Bandura and his colleagues at Stanford University showed that children have a strong tendency to imitate adult behavior, and other studies have shown similar effects in adults. Garlington and Dericco (1977), for example, studied the influence of peers on college students' drinking of alcohol. Subjects were told that they were participating in a study of normal drinking patterns and were asked to drink in pairs in a simulated tavern. One member of each pair was a confederate of the experimenter, and for the first few sessions the confederate matched his rate of drinking to that of the real subject. In subsequent phases, however, he sharply increased or decreased his own rate of drinking. The effects on one subject are shown in Figure 6.5. With remarkable precision, the subject matched his rate of drinking to that of the model.

Researchers have found that models also influence altruistic or helping behavior. People in a shopping center, for example, have been found to be far more likely to make a donation to the Salvation Army if they see someone else make a donation. Similarly, motorists are more likely to stop and help someone

FIGURE 6.5   The influence of a model on the rate of drinking alcoholic beverages. Initially, a confederate of the experimenter matched his own rate of drinking to that of the subject, but at two points he sharply increased and then decreased his own rate of drinking. (Adapted from Garlington & Dericco, 1977)

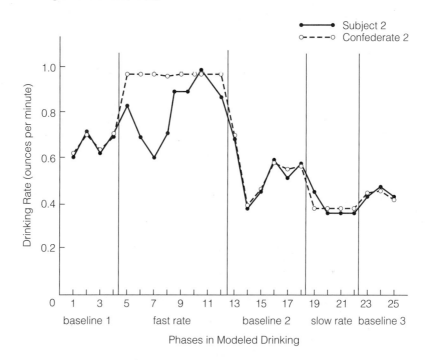

change a flat tire if they have just seen someone else receiving help a quarter of a mile earlier (Bryan & Test, 1967).

Determinants of Imitation

People, of course, do not imitate every behavior they see. We see scores of people every day engaging in hundreds of behaviors, and we could not begin to imitate all of these behaviors. What, then, determines whether we imitate a particular behavior?

We cannot discuss all the determinants of imitation here, but one factor is the *social status* of the model. In one amusing example, Lefkowitz, Blake, and Mouton (1955) observed what happened if a confederate of the experimenter crossed a street against a red light. If the model was dressed in a freshly pressed suit and tie, 14% of the pedestrians observing the model followed; if the same model was dressed in scuffed shoes, soiled trousers, and a blue denim shirt, only 0.007% followed. The social status of the model is clearly one important factor in determining imitation; this is one reason that companies hire famous athletes to promote products such as breakfast cereal and sneakers.

A second characteristic of a model that affects whether we will imitate them is the model's warmth or *friendliness*. In one study illustrating this point, Mischel and Grusec (1966) found that children were more likely to imitate the behavior of an adult if that adult had previously behaved in a friendly towards them. This study also demonstrated a third important characteristic of models, which is their *power*—the extent to which they control resources we value. The children in this study were more likely to imitate the adult if they believed she was going to be their future teacher rather than just a visitor. Interestingly, this imitation occurred even though it served no apparent purpose because the children believed themselves to be alone and unobserved at the time. Summarizing this evidence, it appears that the more we like or admire models and the greater their power, the more we tend to imitate them. (For a more comprehensive review, see Rosenthal & Bandura, 1978.)

Modeling in the Treatment of Phobias

One of the most vivid illustrations of the power of models—and of how that power can be harnessed constructively—comes from a study by Bandura, Blanchard, and Ritter (1969). The subjects were adults with an intense fear of snakes—so intense that they could not engage in normal outdoor activities such as gardening and hiking. After testing the subjects to measure their fear, the experimenters arranged the subjects in four groups. A control group received no treatment, a second group received systematic desensitization, and a third group was shown a film of children and adults handling snakes without any signs of fear. The final group was exposed to a combination of live modeling and participation. They were first taken to a room with a one-way mirror, through which they watched the model handling a live, four-foot king snake for 15 minutes. They were then invited into the room and encouraged to gradually move closer to the snake. Then, while the model held the snake securely by head and tail, the subjects were invited to touch the snake with their gloved hand. If they were unable to do this, they placed their hand on top of the model's, and then gradually slid their hand down the model's until they were directly touching the snake. With the model always demonstrating the required behavior first, they then moved through a series of progressively more difficult behaviors.

To assess the subjects' fear levels after treatment, the experimenters again administered the objective test, which involved a 29-step sequence of progressively more frightening actions. In the first stage, subjects were simply asked to approach the glass cage containing the snake; the final step involved holding the snake in their laps and allowing it to move around them while they kept their hands at their sides. The results are shown in Figure 6.6. Although the control subjects showed little change, the systematic desensitization and film model groups both

FIGURE 6.6   Phobics' fear of snakes before and after three forms of therapy. Fear was assessed by progress through a progressively more frightening set of interactions with a four-foot king snake; the higher the score, the less the subject's fear. (Bandura, Blanchard, & Ritter, 1969)

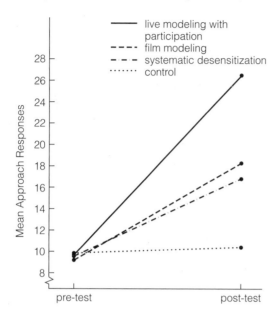

improved substantially, from a test score of about 10 to a test score of about 17. The group exposed to live modeling with participation, however, showed the most spectacular improvement of all, with an average score of 27.

The experimenters made a separate analysis of the percentage of subjects who reached point 29—that is, who allowed the snake to crawl over them and didn't move. None of the controls reached this level, compared with 25% of the systematic desensitization group, 33% of the modeling group, and an extraordinary 92% of the live modeling group. Seeing a live model holding a snake without fear thus produced an almost unbelievable reduction in fear; after only two hours of training, most subjects overcame what had previously been an intense, highly debilitating phobia. A follow-up study one month later revealed that this improvement was maintained in virtually all subjects, with many now engaging in outdoor recreational activities that previously had been barred to them. An additional study by Blanchard (1969) suggested that approximately 60% of the improvement was due to the use of a live model, with the remaining 40% accounted for by the subjects' active participation.

In addition to highlighting one of the most effective therapies ever reported, the Bandura, Blanchard, and Ritter study provides powerful evidence for the extent to which behavior can be influenced by seeing how others behave in similar situations. If you wanted to encourage some behavior, therefore, one alternative to reinforcing it would be to engage in the behavior yourself. If you wanted to encourage a child to practice the piano, for example, you could practice the piano yourself or, better still, practice it with the child. In this way, the child would receive not only a model of the importance you attach to piano playing but also the social reinforcement derived from doing it together. Once the behavior is sufficiently established to supply its own intrinsic reinforcement, modeling can be faded gradually.

Modeling and Reinforcement in the Treatment of Autism

We have so far discussed modeling as an alternative to reinforcement, but the two approaches can also be combined, with modeling used to encourage a behavior initially and reinforcement to maintain it. One of the most striking examples comes from the work of O. Ivar Lovaas and his colleagues on the treatment of autistic children. Autism is a psychiatric disorder in which children become totally isolated from their social environment, having neither verbal nor physical contact with other human beings. Typically, autistic children spend much of their day rocking back and forth and fondling themselves, sometimes engaging in bizarre and highly stereotyped gestures. Attempts to treat autism have largely been unsuccessful; in one long-term study of young children with this condition, more than 60% remained severely handicapped and had to be confined to hospitals (Rutter, 1970).

To treat this severely debilitating condition, Lovaas developed a program based almost entirely on the principles of reinforcement we have been discussing. He viewed autism as a set of maladaptive behaviors, and so set out to encourage more appropriate behaviors using reinforcement, shaping, discrimination learning, and so on. To train autistic children to talk, for example, Lovaas used a shaping procedure similar to that described in Section 5.8 to train Dicky to wear his glasses; children were immediately reinforced with food whenever they made the desired response, and training started with simple responses such as pronouncing a single word. Modeling was a fundamental component of this training: The experimenters would first pronounce the desired word or phrase, and then reinforce the children as soon as they repeated it. Once the children had learned to pronounce the desired words, they were given discrimination training to help them to learn how to use it properly—for example, they would be shown a toy and asked its name, with reinforcement given only if they gave the correct name.

Training was a demanding process, spread over many months, but the children did gradually make impressive progress (Lovaas, Koegel, Simmons, & Long, 1973). This preliminary success allowed Lovaas to obtain funds to extend his program. His initial program had been restricted to a small group of children in a psychiatric hospital, but Lovaas was now able to train therapists to work with children in their own homes; the children were all under 4 years of age, and they were assigned therapists who worked with them 40 hours per week for approximately 2 years. The children's parents were also given training in the appropriate use of learning principles, so that appropriate behavior could be reinforced whenever it occurred.

To assess the effectiveness of the treatment program, Lovaas (1987) compared the behavior of the 19 children who participated with that of a control group who were either not treated or else treated only 10 hours per week. The results were quite remarkable. The IQ of the treated group increased by an average of 30 points compared with that of the controls, and 47% of the treated children improved sufficiently to be enrolled in public schools, where their behavior was indistinguishable from that of normal children. In contrast, only 2% of children in the control conditions showed this level of improvement. Lovaas has prepared a film showing the behavior of the children before treatment and after, and the transformation in their behavior is so dramatic that it is sometimes hard to believe that you are seeing the same children.

The results reported by Lovaas and his colleagues are very, very impressive, but it must be added that the evidence for the treatment's effectiveness is not yet conclusive. One problem concerns the relatively small number of children in the study, and questions have also been raised about other aspects of the study such as the procedures used for measuring improvement. (See Gresham & MacMillan, 1997.) A further problem is that the treatment requires intensive tuition for an extended period, and is thus very expensive. On the other hand, as Lovaas (1987) has pointed out, the cost of one full-time teacher for 2 years is approximately $40,000, "in contrast to the nearly $2 million incurred (in direct costs alone) by each client requiring life-long institutionalization."

Given the potentially profound implications of Lovaas' treatment, with its apparent capacity to transform the lives of children suffering from autism, his results need to be replicated in other studies. Studies to this end are already underway (see Smith & Lovaas, 1997), but the expensive nature of the treatment, together with its extended time scale, mean that it will be many years before the current debate over Lovaas' findings is resolved. In the one attempt to systematically replicate his procedures reported to date, however, the results have been encouraging: Birnbrauer and Leach (1993) reported that 4 of the 9 children in their treatment group approached normal levels of functioning after 2 years of treatment, almost exactly the level of improvement reported by Lovaas.

6.5 ALTERNATIVES TO REINFORCEMENT: SELF-CONTROL

We have seen that the greatest weakness of reinforcement programs lies not in establishing behaviors initially but, rather, in maintaining them when the program is discontinued. If no reinforcement is provided, the response might simply extinguish. Also, in cases where the reinforcement program is seen as coercive or manipulative, interest in the task can actually be less than it was originally.

A potential solution to both of these problems is to encourage **self-control**—that is, training people to control their own behavior rather than relying on reinforcement from external sources. Before considering how we might help people to exercise greater self-control, though, we need to discuss what we mean by this term.

The Concept of Self-Control

To understand self-control, let us start with a concrete example. Suppose that a man named Tom wants to lose weight, but every time he tries to diet he fails. He has a particular weakness for chocolate bars and eats several every night before going to bed. Each time he diets he vows that he will give up these chocolates, but when he goes to bed he just can't resist eating them.

Willpower. How can we explain Tom's inability to diet? The conventional explanation for failures like this is poor willpower—Tom just doesn't have the self-control or willpower to make himself adhere to his diet. But what does it really mean to blame his failure on lack of willpower? The term willpower implies that we have a will that we can use to make ourselves do what we want, but is there really one part of our mind that forces other parts to obey its bidding? If so, and if some people have stronger wills than others, we should expect that individuals with strong wills would be uniformly good at making themselves perform difficult tasks, but this does not appear to be the case. For example, you might know people who are very good at making themselves study, but cannot resist cigarettes or overeating. (See also Mischel & Mischel, 1977.)

Another problem with the concept of willpower is that it seems to leave us helpless. If some people have greater willpower than others, what can people like Tom, who are deficient, do to suddenly endow themselves with more?

Difficulties like this have persuaded some psychologists that the concept of willpower is not really useful in explaining self-control—indeed, that it is simply an explanatory fiction that we invoke to explain behaviors that we don't understand. If Tom has difficulty dieting, we attribute his difficulty to poor willpower, but we have no independent evidence that willpower exists—we can't see it, and even Tom can't feel it. The explanation is circular: We attribute Tom's failure at dieting to poor willpower, but the only way we know that he lacks willpower is that he is having difficulty in dieting. It is a bit like the medieval belief that people who behaved strangely were possessed by demons—the strange behavior was attributed to demons, but the only evidence for the existence of demons was the strange behavior. Both explanations might make us feel better because they seem to provide an explanation for behavior that would otherwise be mysterious, but they are really only pushing the mystery a step further away. In the case of willpower, lack of willpower seems to explain Tom's difficulty in dieting, but we don't then consider what willpower really is, and why Tom has less of it than others.

The claim that willpower doesn't exist might strike you as obviously mistaken because we have all been exposed to this concept for so long that we simply take it for granted. Suppose for the moment, though, that the claim were correct and willpower really did not exist—how then could we explain why some people succeed at dieting or giving up smoking, while others fail?

Reinforcement contingencies. Behavioral psychologists such as B. F. Skinner (1953) and Howard Rachlin (1974) have proposed one possible explanation. They argue that difficulties in self-control arise not from a lack of willpower but, rather, from reinforcement contingencies that favor immediate gratification over our long-term interests. Consider again Tom's problems with eating chocolates. If he eats a chocolate bar before going to bed, he obtains immediate reinforcement from its taste. If he leaves it uneaten, he will lose some weight, but the amount he loses will be so small as to be undetectable. Only if he diets for an extended period will he lose enough so that he can begin to see the difference in a mirror, or to feel healthier. In other words, although there are strong reinforcers available for dieting, they are substantially delayed. Given a choice between eating a chocolate bar and not eating it, Tom may chose to eat it because he obtains a small but immediate form of reinforcement for doing so; dieting produces greater reinforcement, but only after a much longer delay:

$$S_{night} : \begin{array}{l} R_{eat} \longrightarrow S^R_{chocolate} \\ R_{diet} \xrightarrow{\hspace{5cm}} S^R_{weight\,loss} \end{array}$$

The situation is much like that faced by the pigeons in the Rachlin and Green experiment that were given a choice between a small amount of food immediately or a large amount after a delay, or students who have to choose between studying and going to a movie (Section 5.4). And unfortunately for Tom, the outcome is also the same—the small but immediate reinforcer exerts greater control.

In this view, choosing between eating chocolate or abstaining is no different from choosing whether to have a hamburger or a hot dog for lunch, or what clothing to wear to a party. They are all simply choice situations in which we choose between alternative responses, and the choice we make largely depends on the reinforcement available for each. As to why some people are better at refusing chocolate, one factor might be differences in the reinforcement contingencies affecting them. If Tom faces greater-than-average stress, for example, then the soothing properties of chocolate may make it a more powerful reinforcer for Tom than for others, thereby increasing the likelihood of his eating. Also, people who are good at dieting might have learned coping or self-control responses that help them in these situations.

A painful example. To illustrate the concept of self-control responses, we will use an experiment by Kanfer and Seidner (1973). To measure self-control, they asked one group of subjects to keep one hand in a bucket of ice water for as long as they could stand it. The water was very cold, and the average immersion time was only 57 seconds. A second group, however, was given access to a slide projector containing pictures of holiday scenes, and they were allowed to look at these images while their hands were in the water. The subjects in this group were able to keep their hands immersed for an average of 149 seconds, almost three times as long as those in the control group. Note that this result cannot be explained by willpower—because subjects were assigned to groups at random, the levels of willpower in the two groups would have been roughly equal. The reason that subjects in the slide group could keep their hands in the water was that they had a response they could perform—looking at pictures—that allowed them to distract themselves from their pain.

In this analysis, self-control is viewed simply as a set of responses that individuals can perform to alter their own behavior. This might at first seem contrary to the principle of determinism that we discussed in Chapter 1: If all behavior is determined, you might wonder, how can people be said to control their own behavior? B. F. Skinner (1953) suggested a solution to this apparent paradox. His argument was that behavior is indeed controlled by the environment, but that an individual's behavior can also alter that environment. An individual can thus perform a response now to alter his or her environment and thereby indirectly alter the probability of his or her future behavior. In the Kanfer and Seidner experiment, for example, when subjects turned on the slide projector they changed their visual environment, and this helped them to reduce the amount of attention they paid to their pain. The greater self-control of individuals in the slide group was thus not because of greater willpower but, rather, because they used a specific response that allowed them to modify the situation.

Psychologists have studied a variety of techniques that we can all use to modify our behavior. We will focus on three: stimulus control, distraction, and self-reinforcement.

Techniques of Self-Control

Stimulus control. In considering how you can change your behavior, one useful principle that we have already encountered is that of stimulus control. We saw in Section 5.7 that when a response is reinforced, this usually results not in a general increase in the probability of the response but rather in an increase in the specific situation in which it was reinforced. The idea is that the stimuli present when a response is reinforced become associated with the response, so that the response is more likely to occur when these stimuli are present.

This principle turns out to have several useful applications in programs for changing behavior. One example we have already encountered was Bootzin's work on insomnia. To help clients who had difficulty falling asleep at night, Bootzin (1972) advised them to get up from bed whenever they had difficulty in sleeping, so that the stimulus of being in bed would not become associated with their restless behavior and thereby come to elicit it. This treatment, as we have seen, proved very effective. (See also Turner, 1986.)

Another interesting application of stimulus control was reported by Stuart (1967), as part of a program he developed for treating obesity. As one part of his program, Stuart asked his patients not to eat while engaging in other activities such as reading or watching television. The purpose was to break the association between these stimuli and eating, so that there would be fewer situations that elicited this behavior. This program proved to be remarkably effective— his eight patients lost an average of 38 pounds in one year, making it one of the more successful dieting programs ever reported. Subsequent studies using his techniques have largely confirmed this success, but, as in most other diets, participants often find it hard to maintain their weight loss after the program has ended (Wadden, Foster, & Letizia, 1994). Because of the very powerful reinforcement that food provides, it is not easy to change eating behavior, but the principle of stimulus control does seem to be helpful and can contribute to impressive losses over periods of at least a year.

Distraction. Another useful self-control technique is distraction. The Kanfer and Seidner study illustrates the usefulness of distraction in coping with pain, but it can also be helpful in dealing with situations in which reinforcement is delayed. Walter Mischel and his colleagues have investigated the ability of children to tolerate delay of gratification by giving them a task in which they can have a less preferred reinforcer immediately (for example, a marshmallow) or a preferred reinforcer (for example, a pretzel) if they are willing to wait for a specified interval. In one experiment by Mischel, Ebbesen, and Zeiss (1972), children who were given no special instructions endured the delay for an average of less than 30 seconds before opting for the immediately available reinforcer. Children who were encouraged to spend the delay interval thinking of something that was fun to do, on the other hand, waited 12 minutes. (For a review of related research, see Mischel & Mischel, 1977.)

Self-reinforcement. We have suggested that one of the main reasons that reinforcement is sometimes ineffective is that the delay between response and reinforcer is too long. Consider the behavior of studying. There are a number of powerful reinforcers for studying—good grades, parental approval, improved career prospects, and so on—but these reinforcers are delayed for weeks, months, or even years. To take a wildly hypothetical example, imagine a college student who has to choose between reading a psychology text and going out on a date. The reinforcement for the date is relatively immediate; the reinforcement for studying is delayed days or weeks. From a reinforcement perspective, it is hardly surprising that many students have difficulty studying under these conditions.

When the environment does not provide immediate reinforcement for a behavior, one possible strategy is for individuals to reinforce themselves. This might at first sound implausible (how can we reinforce our own behavior?), but some evidence suggests that it is not only possible but effective. In one of the first studies on self-reinforcement, Bandura and Perloff (1967) invited children to turn a toy wheel. Children in the control group received no reinforcement for playing, but those in a self-reinforcement group were given a supply of tokens and told to take as many as they wanted whenever they turned the wheel a specified number of times. At the end of the experiment, they were told, the tokens would be exchanged for prizes, and the more tokens they had, the better the prizes they would receive. To encourage them to feel free to take as many tokens as they wished, the experimenter left the room while they played the game. An external reinforcement group was also included; these children received tokens automatically when they turned the wheel, with the number of tokens set at a level to match that of the children in the self-reinforcement group.

As you might expect, the children who were given tokens for turning the wheel did so significantly more than did those in the unreinforced control group. Perhaps more surprisingly, however, so too did the children in the self-reinforcement group. Indeed, these children turned the wheel as often as those reinforced by the experimenter. Self-reinforcement, in other words, was just as effective as reinforcement from an external agent, and in some subsequent studies self-reinforcement has actually been more effective (for example, Jackson, & Van Zoost, 1972).

The Development of Self-Control

Bandura and Perloff's results suggest that people can successfully reinforce their own behavior, but you might find yourself feeling skeptical. The tokens were freely available and the children could take as many as they wanted without the experimenter knowing, so why didn't they just take the tokens they wanted without increasing their rate of playing?

A reinforcement analysis. The concept of self-reinforcement might at first seem to resemble that of willpower, in that one part of a person appears to be reinforcing another part for good behavior. In Skinner's (1953) analysis of self-control, however, self-control is viewed simply as a set of responses, with the same properties as all other responses. We will learn to use self-control responses, therefore, if we find that these behaviors produce reinforcement. Children, for example, will learn to reinforce themselves—perhaps with candy or, more likely, with praise ("I've been such a good girl")—if such behavior is reinforced by others. When children praise themselves appropriately, they might in turn be praised by others. (Tommy: "I did a good job cleaning my room, didn't I, Mommy?" Mother: "Yes, Tommy, you did it beautifully.") If the children cheat, they might be reprimanded. Provided that we get enough appropriate feedback, we eventually learn to praise ourselves only when such praise is merited, and this self-praise can then help to maintain our behavior.

Training self-reinforcement. This analysis suggests that the children in the Bandura and Perloff study reinforced themselves appropriately—that is, only when they had genuinely reached the criterion—because they had learned in the past that accurate self-reinforcement is itself likely to be reinforced. There is little evidence to tell us whether self-reinforcement is actually learned in this way, but a study by Drabman, Spitalnik, and O'Leary (1973) suggests that it could be. The subjects were 10-year-old boys in a class for children with academic and emotional problems. Eight of the most disruptive boys in the class were selected for special training, and a token economy was established in which the boys were given points on a five-point scale for good behavior and for completing assignments; at the end of each lesson, the points could be exchanged for cakes, candies, or pennies.

The program was highly effective: The frequency of disruptive behavior fell by two-thirds, and the average number of assignments completed rose from 83 to 130. It was not possible, however, to maintain the token economy indefinitely. What, then, could be done to ensure that the gains would be sustained once the program was withdrawn?

Since a teacher could not always be available to provide reinforcement, Drabman and his colleagues decided to train the children to reinforce themselves. At the end of each lesson, the boys were to award themselves points on the basis of how they had behaved, with these points then being exchanged for other reinforcers in the usual way. To ensure that the boys would reinforce themselves appropriately, they instituted a training program in which the boys were initially reinforced by the teacher for accurate self-reinforcement. Once this behavior had been learned, the frequency of checking by the teacher was progressively reduced.

Specifically, the teacher monitored the boys' behavior during the self-reinforcement phase, and at the end of each lesson the boys' self-ratings were compared with the teacher's ratings. If the boys' ratings were within one point of the teacher's, they received the points they had given themselves; if the ratings matched accurately, the boys also received a bonus point; but if they had deviated from the teacher's ratings by more than a point, they received no points. To reduce the likelihood that the checking would be seen as a form of control, the experimenters explained that being selected for checking was a privilege, because only those boys who were checked would have the chance to earn bonus points.

Over days, the proportion of boys selected for checking was gradually reduced, until all the boys were receiving whatever points they had awarded

FIGURE 6.7   Mean number of disruptive behaviors in successive phases of a self-control program. (Adapted from Drabman, Spitalnik, & O'Leary, 1973)

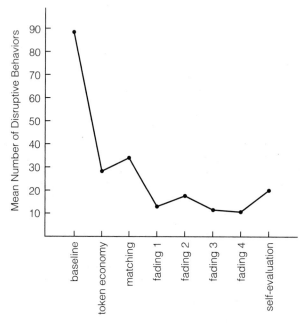

themselves without any formal checking. On days when their self-ratings exactly matched the teacher's, though, the teacher strongly praised them.

The results are shown in Figure 6.7. During the final phase, in which they received whatever points they had awarded themselves, their behavior was not only maintained at the levels achieved when the teacher controlled reinforcement, but, if anything, actually exceeded those levels. This final phase continued for only 12 days, so we cannot be certain how long this behavior would have been maintained. However, the results of a subsequent study by Wood and Flynn (1978) are encouraging. In this study, 13-year-old delinquents in a program based on Achievement Place were trained to clean their rooms to an extremely high standard. (For example, their shoes not only had to be put away in a closet but had to be placed neatly next to each other.) The room's cleanliness was judged on a 15-point scale. Before training was instituted, the boys averaged only 3.4 points; after training in self-reinforcement, this rose to 13 points. The use of points was then discontinued, so that the boys received no reinforcement for cleaning their rooms other than occasional praise, but the high standard of cleanliness established during the self-reinforcement program was nevertheless maintained without decrement over 60 days. These results support the view that self-reinforcement is a behavior that can itself be reinforced and that, once learned, can be effective in maintaining other behaviors.

Improving Your Studying

To summarize some of the self-control principles we have been discussing, we will conclude by briefly considering how you can use self-control principles to increase the amount of time you spend studying. According to several successful programs (for example, Goldiamond, 1965; Fox, 1966), your first step should be to find a quiet spot where you can work with minimal disturbance—for example, an isolated desk in a library. Begin by setting yourself a modest target for how long you will study, and then reinforce yourself (self-reinforcement) when you reach your target (the reinforcer could be coffee, a break with friends, or even just a notation on a special record card—an accurate record of progress can be a surprisingly powerful reinforcer). Then, over days, gradually increase your target (shaping).

For this strategy to work, it is important to choose an effective reinforcer. Some evidence suggests that a public declaration of both your goals and your progress—for example, posting a graph of your studying time where your friends can see it and thus encourage you—can also be important. (See Hayes, Rosenfarb, Wulfert, Munt, Korn, & Zettle, 1985.) Also, you need to set goals that are realistically attainable. If you are very poor at concentrating, you might need to set your initial goal at only 15 minutes, or even 5 minutes, and then increase your target gradually.

To maximize the probability that your desk will become a cue for studying and not for other behaviors, ensure that studying is the only activity you engage in while there. If you feel an uncontrollable urge to daydream or have a snack, leave immediately, and return only when you feel able to resume concentrating on your work (stimulus control). These are by no means the only useful techniques for improving studying habits. (For some other techniques, see Fox, 1966; Weinstein & Meyer, 1986.) However, if you do want to improve your studying, you might find this approach a helpful component of a broader program based on careful reading, underlining, reviewing what you have read as soon as you finish a section, and other basic study skills.

6.6 SUMMARY

In this chapter and the preceding one, we have reviewed a wide range of material on the practical applications of reinforcement—to disruptive and schizophrenic children, to convicts, even to university students—and there can be little doubt of its potential effectiveness. Even seemingly minor changes, such as praising youngsters when they are good instead of scolding them when they are bad, can sometimes produce dramatic changes in behavior, provided that this reinforcement is immediate and consistent.

These programs have been based on the assumption that once the desired behaviors are established, reinforcers in the natural environment will then serve to maintain them. In many cases, this assumption is justified. Once a child has learned to read, for example, the pleasure derived from this activity will maintain it without any need for support or encouragement from others. In other cases, however—such as a delinquent trying to study or an alcoholic trying to abstain from drinking—the naturally available reinforcers might not be sufficient.

One of the most difficult questions now facing researchers is how to encourage the long-term maintenance of behavior following termination of a reinforcement program. One strategy is to provide more time for the natural reinforcers to assume control, by ensuring that the learned behaviors do not immediately extinguish. To this end, partial reinforcement is used during training, behavior is reinforced in a variety of settings, and, finally, the entire reinforcement program is faded gradually rather than terminated abruptly. As we saw in the case of Jerry, who eventually learned to wear his orthodontic device without supervision, this fading strategy can be very effective.

In other situations, though, reinforcement might have harmful side effects that make its use undesirable. Opinions differ about whether some uses of reinforcement should be considered bribery, but there is little doubt that the use of material reinforcers can encourage greed and undermine intrinsic motivation in some situations. To minimize the likelihood of these outcomes, the principle of "minimal force" should always be applied: Use the mildest reinforcer that is likely to be effective (generally, this will be praise), and, whenever possible, use reinforcement in a way that encourages feelings of competence and skill rather than mere obedience. Parents or teachers who reinforce children for sitting quietly or for doing as they "should" might succeed initially, but at a long-term cost to the children's pride and intrinsic motivation.

One possible alternative to reinforcement of desired behavior is modeling. We are all influenced by the behavior of those around us, and the evidence reviewed in this chapter suggests that models who are liked or admired can play a powerful role in shaping behavior. If a child—or anyone else, for that matter—is not behaving as you wish, one useful question to consider is whether *you* are behaving as you wish!

A second alternative to reinforcement is self-control. The phenomenon of self-control is not well understood; we do not fully understand, for example, why some individuals find it easier to control their behavior than others do. In this chapter we have focused on B. F. Skinner's approach, which interprets self-control as a set of controlling responses that alter the environment in order to change the probability of subsequent responses. This is by no means the only possible interpretation of self-control, but it has the advantage of suggesting that self-control can be learned rather than being a form of willpower that you either have or do not have. Research on self-control techniques such as stimulus control, distraction, and self-reinforcement have supported this analysis by showing that individuals can learn to increase their self-control substantially. The reason that some individuals exhibit better self-control than others do might not be their superior willpower, but simply that they have learned more effective coping behaviors.

Here are two final thoughts. In Chapter 1, we discussed the assumption that animal and human behavior is similar in important respects, so that research in the animal laboratory might someday make important contributions to our understanding of human behavior. We have since encountered considerable support for this assumption. The importance of immediate reinforcement, the usefulness of gradual shaping, and the role of motivation in impairing as well as enhancing learning—all these principles were discovered initially in experiments on animals, and all have proved of real value in practical programs to use reinforcement more effectively.

It is also important, however, to recognize the limitations of animal research and how research with humans has revealed principles not suggested by work with animals. One example is the finding that reinforcement can reduce intrinsic motivation, as when children reinforced for drawing a picture become less likely to do so outside the experimental situation. Research in this area suggests that the effect of reinforcement can depend on the recipient's perception of the motivation of the giver: If reinforcement is seen as a means of control for the benefit of the controller, then it is less likely to be effective.

Similarly, we shall see in the next chapter that the effectiveness of punishment depends on whether it is accompanied by a clear and fair explanation. If we believe that the punishment we receive is fair, we are more likely to cooperate in future with the person who has punished us. A third example comes from research on modeling, which has shown that the extent to which we imitate the behavior of a model depends on whether we perceive the model as friendly. The common theme in all these examples is that the outcome of reinforcement does not depend simply on the reinforcer used: Reinforcement is often embedded within a complex social relationship between the person giving the reinforcer and the person receiving it, and a reinforcer's effectiveness can depend not just on its physical characteristics but also on the recipient's perception of the motive underlying its presentation. If a child feels that a reinforcer is being used as an expression of caring, the effect might be very different than if it is perceived as a means of exacting obedience ("If you sit quietly, you can have a candy").

In sum, reinforcement can be highly effective and is generally more fun for all concerned than alternatives such as reprimands or punishment. It is not a panacea for all problems, though, and, above all, it is not simple: You will not get very far by popping candy into people's mouths whenever they do what you want. Reinforcement is part of a complex social relationship, and we are only beginning to understand the nature of such relationships and how they determine the effects of reinforcement. Laboratory research has significantly increased our ability to use reinforcement effectively, but the application of these principles needs to proceed with some caution and even some humility.

Glossary

Behavior modification An approach that conceptualizes human problems in terms of behaviors rather than mental states and then uses learning principles to change these behaviors. In some cases, the term *behavior therapy* is used interchangeably with behavior modification.

Token economy A systematic procedure for reinforcing behavior in which tokens are made contingent on the performance of desired behaviors; the tokens can later be exchanged for backup reinforcers such as candy. In early applications in mental hospitals, access to the backup reinforcers was restricted so that they could be obtained only with tokens; this was the basis for the term economy.

Intrinsic motivation Motivation to perform an activity that derives from the activity itself, rather than from any consequences that might follow the activity.

Behavioral contract A written agreement (for example, between a parent and a child) specifying the behaviors to be reinforced and the consequences for their occurrence and nonoccurrence.

Observational learning The learning of new behaviors by observing the behavior of others. The individual exhibiting the behavior is called a model, and observational learning is sometimes referred to as *imitation* (which emphasizes the behavior of the observer) or **modeling** (which emphasizes the behavior of the model).

Self-control According to Skinner, the performing of one response to alter the probability of some subsequent response.

Review Questions

1. The principle of "minimal force" suggests starting with relatively mild reinforcers such as praise, whenever possible. Can social reinforcers such as praise really modify difficult behaviors? If they fail, what other reinforcers can be used?

2. What can be done to increase the likelihood that behaviors will persist long enough after a reinforcement program is terminated to allow natural reinforcers to acquire control?

3. What are the potentially harmful effects of reinforcement? In what situations are these most likely to occur?

4. What alternatives are there to reinforcement for encouraging behavior?

5. What determines whether we imitate the behavior of a model?

6. What are some of the techniques by which people control their own behavior? How can they be applied to studying?

7. Self-control is often attributed to willpower, which is seen as a unitary trait that people either have or don't. How does Skinner explain self-control? How does his account differ from that of willpower? What does each approach say about variability in self-control? In other words, should a person who shows strong self-control in one situation (for example, giving up smoking) also have above-average self-control in other situations (for example, studying)?

PUNISHMENT AND EXTINCTION

Of several responses made to the same situation . . . those which are accompanied or closely followed by discomfort to the animal will, other things being equal, have their connection with the situation weakened, so that, when it recurs, they will be less likely to occur.
(Edward L. Thorndike, *Animal Intelligence*, 1911, p. 244)

We are gradually discovering—at an untold cost in human suffering—that in the long run punishment doesn't reduce the probability that an act will occur.
(B. F. Skinner, *Walden Two*, 1948a)

7.1 PUNISHMENT

Punishment is one of society's oldest techniques for controlling behavior, and also one of its most controversial. Does it really work? If we spank a child for disobeying an order or send an adult to prison for stealing, will the treatment really be effective? Or are we only building up a reservoir of hostility and bitterness that will lead to even more antisocial behavior in the future?

Methodological Issues

Punishment refers to a reduction in the likelihood of a response caused by the presentation of an aversive stimulus or, in the case of **negative punishment,** caused by the removal of a reinforcing stimulus. Spanking a child is an example of punishment; taking away the child's allowance is an example of negative punishment. It is important not to confuse either form of punishment, both of which involve the suppression of behavior, with **negative reinforcement,** which is defined as an increase in the probability of a response caused by the removal of an aversive stimulus. (The behavior of taking aspirin, for example, is negatively reinforced by the termination of pain.) Both reinforcement and punishment involve a change in the probability of a response caused by a consequence that follows it; in reinforcement, the change is an increase in the response, in punishment, it is a decrease. In both cases, the term *positive* is used if the consequence involves presenting a stimulus (food, shock); the term *negative* is used if the response results in the removal of a stimulus.

Observation versus experiment.   There has been no lack of debate over the effectiveness of punishment, but rarely can either side produce unequivocal evidence to support its position. This is perhaps not surprising. How, after all, can we evaluate the long-term effects of punishment? Let's use spanking as an example: It might seem easy enough to compare the behavior of children who are spanked with those who are not, but in practice such data are often difficult to interpret. In a study by Eron, Walder, Toigo, and Lefkowitz (1963), for example, parents of 451 schoolchildren were interviewed to find out what kinds of punishment they used in different situations. If their children were rude, for example, they were asked whether they would say, "Young men (ladies) don't do that sort of thing," or "Get on that chair and don't move until you apologize," or would spank the child until he or she cried. The researchers found that the harsher the punishment chosen by the parents, the more likely the children were to be aggressive at school. Punishing aggression, in other words, seemed to increase the frequency of this behavior rather than reduce it.

As we shall see later, there is some support for this conclusion, but this study nevertheless poses serious problems of interpretation. First, even though the parents said they would have used a certain form of punishment, this does not necessarily mean that they would actually have done so. And even if they did, we cannot be sure that it was their use of this punishment that made their children aggressive. Might not some other aspects of the parents' behavior—a lack of love or concern, for example—have produced both the punitiveness and the aggression? Or perhaps the causal relationship is reversed: Perhaps the children's persistent aggression and disobedience, produced by other causes, progressively forced the parents to use punishments of ever-increasing severity. The fact that punishment and aggression are correlated, in other words, does not necessarily mean that punishment has caused the aggression. Thus, although studies based on questionnaires or on more direct forms of observation can be an important source of hypotheses about causal relationships, it is difficult to reach unequivocal conclusions by observing behavior in a complex social environment.

Animals versus humans.   The obvious alternative is experimentation under the controlled conditions of the laboratory. For punishment, though, this raises serious problems. For obvious reasons, psychologists are extremely reluctant to use severe punishment in studies that involve human subjects. If punishment is to be studied in the laboratory, therefore, we must either use very mild punishments, such as verbal rebukes, or else employ animals as our subjects.

Each of these alternatives has its drawbacks. It is certainly useful to know how a child will react to being told "No, that's wrong" by a stranger, but this might not be a reliable guide to the effects of being spanked by an enraged parent. So, what are the drawbacks to using animals as experimental subjects? As we have already seen, there are many similarities in the laws of learning across different species; by no stretch of the imagination, however, could a human being be described simply as a very large rat.

In trying to determine the effects of severe punishment, then, is it better to extrapolate from the effects of mild punishment in humans or severe punishment in animals? In practice, psychologists have resolved this dilemma by using both approaches; in the course of this chapter we will look at the results obtained with each, and at the extent to which they have contributed to a unified picture of the effects of punishment. We will begin by examining the effects of punishment on the punished response and consider whether punishment really produces long-term suppression of behavior. We will first look at the results of experiments using animals and then consider the extent to which the principles of punishment found in animals also apply to humans. Finally, we will consider the effects of punishment on other behavior; that is, even in situations in which punishment does suppress the punished response, might it have side effects that would make its use inadvisable?

Punishment in Animals

By studying punishment under controlled conditions, we have argued, it should be considerably easier to determine its effects. Even in the confines of the animal laboratory, however, these effects have proved controversial. The early evidence was largely negative, suggesting that punishment had little or no effect on behavior. Thus, although Thorndike had accorded punishment equal status with reinforcement in his first statement of the Law of Effect, his own research subsequently convinced him that punishment led to no permanent reduction in behavior. Similarly, B. F. Skinner (1938) was persuaded by the results of his research with rats that the effects of punishment were at best only temporary. In one of these experiments, a group of rats was first trained to press a bar to obtain food, then presentations of the food were discontinued. This is known as an *extinction* procedure; the typical result is a gradual decrease in responding, until subjects eventually stop responding altogether. To evaluate the effects of punishment, Skinner divided his subjects into two groups during the extinction phase, with subjects in one of the groups being punished every time they pressed the bar during the first 10 minutes of extinction. The punishment consisted of a slap on the rat's paw.

Figure 7.1 shows the cumulative number of responses made during extinction. Initially, the punishment contingency appeared highly effective; subjects

FIGURE 7.1   The effect of punishment on responding during extinction. Bar-presses during the first
10 minutes of extinction were punished in the extinction + punishment group but not
in the extinction group; the figure plots the cumulative number of responses during
extinction. (Skinner, 1938)

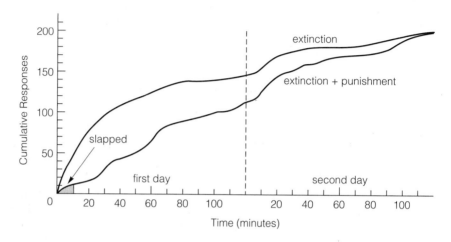

stopped responding for as long as it was in effect. After the punishment period
ended, however, they gradually began to respond again, until by the end of the
second session they had emitted the same total number of responses during extinction as the control subjects who had never been punished. Punishment, in
other words, seemed to suppress responding only temporarily, leading Skinner
and others to conclude that it was an ineffective and undesirable technique for
changing behavior.

This conclusion, however, was based on very little evidence. Because of
their reluctance to inflict pain, most experimenters either avoided punishment
altogether or chose relatively mild stimuli as their punishers. As we have mentioned, Skinner used a slap on the paw to punish his rats, and Thorndike's conclusions were based on experiments with humans using the word "wrong" as
the aversive event. Only in the past few decades have experiments using more
intense punishers been reported in any number, and the effect has been to reverse dramatically the earlier negative conclusions: At least insofar as the white
rat is concerned, there is now compelling evidence that punishment can produce powerful and enduring suppression of behavior. Boe and Church (1967),
for example, repeated Skinner's bar-pressing experiment but used electric shock
as the punishing event rather than a slap on the paw. To evaluate the importance of punishment severity, they varied the intensity of the shock for different groups from 0 to 220 volts.

With mild intensities of shock, their results resembled Skinner's, as Figure
7.2 shows. The brief period of shock at the end of training produced little

FIGURE 7.2   The effect of shock intensity on responses during extinction. Different groups received shocks ranging in intensity from 0 volts (the control group) to 220 volts during a 15-minute period at the beginning of extinction, marked P on the x-axis. The measure of responding was the cumulative number of responses during extinction, expressed as a percentage of responding during the last session of training. In the 220-volt group, for example, the total number of responses during extinction was less than 10% of responses during the final session of reinforcement. (Boe & Church, 1967)

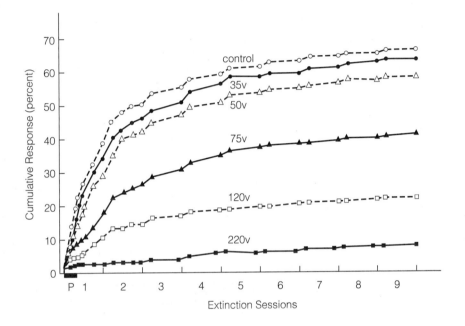

enduring reduction in the number of responses emitted during extinction. As the intensity of the shock was increased, however, the effect on subsequent responding became increasingly pronounced, until, in the 220-volt group, responding was not only suppressed during the punishment period but showed virtually no signs of recovery over nine subsequent sessions. If the punishment used is of sufficient severity, in other words, even a brief period of punishment can result in profound and enduring suppression of behavior.[1]

Intensity. One important determinant of a punishment's effectiveness, then, is the intensity of the punisher used. This might at first seem to imply that when

---

[1] Although the shock used in this study was undoubtedly aversive, it was not as intense as you might think. The aversiveness of a shock depends on the amount of current passing through the body rather than the shock voltage; under the conditions of this study, the shocks were intense but not physically harmful.

punishment is used, the intensity of the punishment should be as strong as possible, but there are obvious objections to this conclusion: Punishment, after all, is painful, and it is clearly undesirable to inflict more pain than absolutely necessary. (As we shall see in the following section, intense punishment is objectionable on practical as well as ethical grounds.) On the other hand, if the punishment used is too mild, it might be ineffective, and the problem might not be remedied easily by then switching to a stronger punishment. In a study by Azrin, Holz, and Hake (1963), for example, pigeons were punished with electric shock for pecking a key that also produced food. When the intensity of the shock was set at 80 volts, responding was totally suppressed. When the voltage was initially set at 60 volts, however, it had little effect, and when its intensity was then increased in gradual steps, subjects continued to respond even when the voltage reached 300 volts! In other words, if punishment intensity is set at low levels initially and then increased only gradually, it might prove ineffective, apparently because subjects adapt to the gradually increasing intensity.

These results pose a painful dilemma for those, such as parents, considering the use of punishment. On the one hand, it makes sense to inflict as little pain as possible, and therefore to use mild forms of punishment wherever possible. On the other hand, if the punisher is too mild, it is likely to fail, and it can undermine the effectiveness of more intense punishers. A parent might start with a mild punishment, find that it fails; graduate to a more intense punishment, find that it too fails, and so on. In the end, many more punishments might have to be used, and the intensity of punishment ultimately required might be much greater than if a stronger form of punishment had been used in the first place.

There is no simple solution to this dilemma. We shall see later that there are strong arguments for using the mildest form of punishment that is likely to be effective. The minimum level that will be effective, however, is likely to vary from individual to individual (perhaps because of their past histories of punishment), and it will also vary from response to response (when powerful reinforcers are maintaining a behavior, the level of punishment required to suppress it will inevitably be greater). It is thus not possible to provide universal guidelines: Choosing the optimum level of punishment comes down, in the end, to trial and error.

Delay. A second important factor determining the effectiveness of punishment is the delay between the response and the punisher. In an experiment by Solomon, Turner, and Lessac (1968), dogs were offered a choice between two foods, one highly preferred and the other less so. The foods were presented in two dishes, located on either side of the experimenter's chair. If the dogs approached the dish that contained the less preferred food, they were allowed to eat freely; but if they began to eat the preferred food, the experimenter would hit them on the snout with a rolled-up newspaper. The delay interval between the moment when the dogs started eating and the time they were punished was either 0, 5, or 15 seconds for different groups.

Regardless of which delay was used, all the subjects learned quickly, requiring an average of only three or four punishments before avoiding the preferred food entirely. To determine the extent to which these punishments had resulted in an enduring change in behavior, the dogs were deprived of food and exposed to a daily series of 10-minute temptation trials. During these tests, the hungry dogs were returned to the room in which they had previously been trained, but with the experimenter now absent; one food dish contained 500 grams of the preferred food, and another dish contained only 20 grams of the nonpreferred food. The question was, how long would the hungry dogs be able to resist the temptation of eating the preferred food under these circumstances?

For the group that was punished with a 15-second delay during training, the answer was about three minutes. The dogs that had been punished after a delay of 5 seconds, however, resisted eating for 8 days, whereas those that had been punished immediately went without eating for 2 weeks. A delay of only a few seconds in punishing a response, therefore, might have profound implications for the effectiveness of punishment—in this case, resisting eating for 3 minutes versus 2 weeks.

Schedule. The effects of punishment also depend critically on the schedule used. In the Azrin, Holz, and Hake (1963) experiment referred to earlier, for example, pigeons were first trained to peck a key to obtain food; then shock was also made contingent on pecking, while the reinforcement contingency remained in effect. The schedule on which the shock was presented varied from FR 1 (every response punished) to FR 1000 (only one response in 1000 punished). Punishment of every response resulted in total suppression of pecking, but as the probability of punishment was reduced, responding was much less affected. As common sense would suggest, for punishment to be effective it should be delivered as immediately and consistently as possible.

Stimulus control. Another important factor in determining the effectiveness of punishment is the similarity between the conditions during training and testing. If the dogs in Solomon's study had been tested in the training room with the experimenter still present, for example, it seems likely that they would have resisted eating even longer, whereas if they had been tested in a totally different room, without any experimenter and with different dishes, they would probably have given in to temptation much sooner.

Support for this prediction comes from an experiment by Honig and Slivka (1964), who looked at the effects of punishment on key-pecking in pigeons. During preliminary training, a plastic key was illuminated with one of seven alternating colors, varying in wavelength from 490 to 610 nanometers (nm), and

FIGURE 7.3   Generalization of a punished response. During the baseline condition, key-pecking was reinforced in the presence of each of seven different colors. The remaining curves show the changes in responding to each of these colors following the introduction of punishment in the presence of the 550-nm stimulus. (Honig & Slivka, 1964)

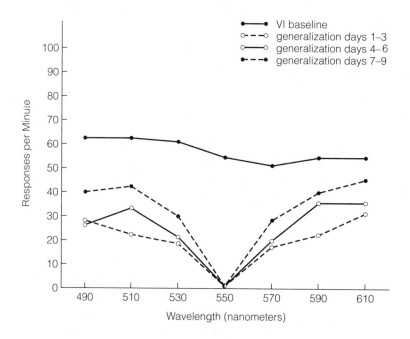

pecking was reinforced in the presence of each. When the rate of pecking to each color was roughly equal, Honig and Slivka began to selectively punish responding in the presence of the 550-nm stimulus by presenting an electric shock whenever this color was pecked.

The results of this selective punishment are illustrated in Figure 7.3, which shows the rate of responding to each stimulus recorded over nine days of punishment training. Punishment of responding to the 550-nm stimulus was highly effective from the outset, because the birds almost immediately stopped responding whenever this color appeared on the key. The extent to which responding was suppressed in the presence of the other colors, however, depended on their similarity to the punished stimulus. Responding to the 530- and 570-nm stimuli, for example, was also strongly suppressed, but as the test stimuli became increasingly dissimilar to the punished stimulus, the amount of suppression decreased. (Note that what is generalizing in this case is *inhibition* of responding, rather than responding: The weaker the inhibition, the more likely subjects are to respond. That is why response levels increase as the test stimulus becomes less similar to the training stimulus, rather than becoming lower, as in the generalization gradients we have encountered previously.)

As training continued, and the birds learned that punishment occurred only in the presence of the 550-nm wavelength, their rate of responding to the non-punished wavelengths progressively increased. In other words, if punishment is delivered in one situation, its effects might generalize at first, but if subjects repeatedly find that responding in other situations is safe, then responding might eventually be suppressed only in the setting in which it is actually punished.

One important implication of this finding is that if you want to eliminate a response entirely it might not be sufficient to punish it in only one situation. Suppose, for example, that you wanted to train young children not to play in the street. Ideally, an explanation of the dangers involved would be sufficient, but if this failed you might then find it necessary to punish the children every time you caught them playing in the street. If the children were punished only when you were nearby, however, they might very well learn a discrimination: If a parent is nearby, playing in the street is dangerous; if a parent is not nearby, then it's perfectly safe! To ensure that behavior is suppressed more generally, you would need to ensure that it was punished in different streets, by different adults, and, if possible, when no adult was present at all, so that the children would learn that playing in any street is dangerous, regardless of whether anyone appears to be watching.

The Honig and Slivka study, then, suggests some of the practical difficulties that can arise in trying to use punishment effectively in the natural environment. Like the Boe and Church experiment and the Solomon, Turner, and Lessac experiment, the Honig and Slivka study also illustrates the potential power of this procedure: Only a small number of shocks was necessary to eliminate responding in the presence of the 550-nm wavelength, and once responding to this stimulus was reduced, it remained at very low levels for at least the nine days during which responding was measured.

Insofar as animal behavior is concerned, then, there can now be little doubt that punishment, used appropriately, can produce profound and enduring suppression of behavior. There are some fascinating exceptions to this rule—situations in which, far from reducing responding, punishment may paradoxically strengthen it (for example, Fowler & Wischner, 1969; Morse & Kelleher, 1977). In general, though, punishment does seem to be effective in suppressing behavior in animals.

Punishment in Humans

Punishment of self-injurious behavior. Are the effects of intense punishment on humans the same as those observed on animals? For obvious reasons, the data on this point are limited, but the evidence we do have suggests a number of similarities. In a clinical study reported by Bucher and Lovaas (1968), for example, electric shock was used to treat self-destructive behavior in autistic children. (See Section 6.4 for a discussion of autism.) One of the most horrifying manifestations of this syndrome is self-destructive behavior, in which children repeatedly and viciously attack their own bodies. In the case of a seven-year-old boy named John, the resultant physical damage was so serious that he had to be hospitalized and kept in complete physical restraint 24 hours a day. "When removed from restraint he would immediately hit his head against the crib, beat his head with his fists, and scream. . . . He was so unmanageable that he had to be fed in full restraints; he would not take food otherwise. His head was covered with scar tissue, and his ears were swollen and bleeding" (Bucher & Lovaas, 1968, p. 86).

Because of the risk of permanent physical damage resulting from continued confinement, it was vital that some way be found to eliminate this behavior as quickly as possible. One technique that had previously been found to be effective consisted of ignoring the self-injurious behavior (thereby eliminating adult attention as a possible source of reinforcement) and simultaneously rewarding incompatible behaviors such as hand-clapping or singing songs. Because of the particular circumstances involved, however, this approach was not feasible, and Bucher and Lovaas decided instead to use punishment. This might at first seem to be a bizarre choice of treatment, since John's behavior suggested that, if anything, he enjoyed being hurt. Nevertheless, once a day John was taken to a special room where his restraints were removed, and he was given an immediate electric shock every time he hit himself. The results are shown in Figure 7.4, which plots the number of self-destructive responses observed during successive treatment sessions. During the first 15 baseline sessions, the experimenters did not administer punishment, and John hit himself an average of almost 250 times during each session. When punishment was introduced in session 16, however, this behavior disappeared almost immediately.

To determine the extent to which self-injurious behavior would be suppressed in other situations, different experimenters were present in the test room on different days. Only the first experimenter ever punished hitting, and whenever this experimenter was present, self-destructive behavior remained at very low levels. When the other experimenters were present, however, there was a perceptible increase in its frequency (though still far below baseline levels), and as testing continued it began to rise alarmingly. As with the pigeons in the Honig and Slivka experiment, John seemed to be learning that punishment occurred only in a particular situation, and, as a result, suppressed his self-destructive behavior only in that situation. During session 30, therefore, experimenter 3 was also instructed to use punishment whenever John hit himself, and thereafter there were no further recurrences of this behavior, regardless of which experimenter was present in the room. Using a total of only 12 shocks, Bucher and Lovaas were able to completely eliminate a response that had occurred previously at a rate of several thousand times a day for more than five years. Similar results were obtained with the other children treated.

FIGURE 7.4   The frequency of self-destructive behavior before and after punishment. The experimenter present during each session is indicated; experimenter 1 (E_1) or experimenter 3 (E_3) administered shocks during the sessions marked by an arrow. (Adapted from Bucher & Lovaas, 1968)

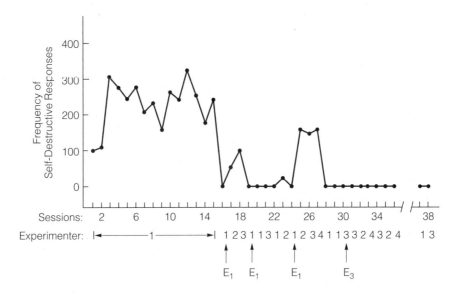

Similarities between animal and human reactions.   Bucher and Lovaas' results suggest that punishment can produce long-term suppression of human behavior in much the same way as in animals. The results further suggest that one of the principles discovered in animal research—that the environment in which punishment is administered can come to control the punished response (*stimulus control*)—also holds in humans, leading to almost identical patterns of behavior.

Studies of the other principles identified in animal research—intensity, schedule, and delay—suggest that these principles also have similar effects in humans. Williams, Kirkpatrick-Sanchez, and Iwata (1993), for example, studied the role of *punishment intensity* in suppressing severe self-injurious behavior. The subject was a profoundly retarded young woman who engaged in self-mutilating behaviors such as hitting and biting her body and gouging her eyes. (Her body was covered in open wounds when she was admitted to hospital, and she had to be kept in restraints almost continuously to prevent further damage.) Initial treatment with a relatively mild form of shock was ineffective, but when her therapists switched to more intense shock, her self-injurious behavior was very rapidly suppressed, and staff were later able to maintain this suppression solely by using reprimands that had previously been paired with the shock (secondary punishment).

298 PART III / OPERANT CONDITIONING

To explore the role of *schedule of punishment*, Larzelere, Schneider, Larson, and Pike (1996) asked mothers to keep diaries of when their children were misbehaved and whether they were punished. The researchers found that the higher the proportion of disobedient acts that mothers punished, the less likely their children were to disobey. Similarly, Brennan and Mednick (1994) found that criminal behavior is affected by the probability of punishment: The higher the proportion of an individual's arrests followed by some form of punishment, the less likely they were to re-offend.

Finally, Aronfreed (1968) studied the role of *delay of punishment* in humans using a procedure very similar to that developed by Solomon. Instead of offering dogs a choice of food dishes, Aronfreed asked schoolchildren to choose one of two toys, and then to describe the chosen toy to the experimenter. One of the toys was highly attractive, the other much less so. If they selected the unattractive toy, the children were allowed to describe it, but if they chose the attractive toy the experimenter would punish them by saying "No" and taking away a candy from a pile they had been given previously. For some of the children, this punishment took place as soon as they began to reach for the attractive toy, but for others it was delayed for either 2, 6, or 12 seconds. This procedure was then repeated for each of 10 different pairs of toys, with choices of the attractive member of each pair always being punished.

As in Solomon's study, the delay of punishment had little apparent effect on initial learning; virtually all the children learned to avoid the attractive toy after only two or three punishments. Again as in Solomon's study, however, the effect of the delay interval proved more dramatic when behavior was measured in the experimenter's absence. During this testing phase, just as the experimenter finished laying out a new pair of toys, he would explain that he had suddenly remembered something he needed to do elsewhere and would leave the child alone with the toys for 10 minutes. Of those children who had been punished immediately during training, only half made any attempt to play with the attractive toy, and the majority of these children waited at least five minutes before doing so. Of the children whose punishment had been delayed for even six seconds during training, however, almost all transgressed during the temptation period, and most did so within less than a minute of the experimenter's departure. Thus, delays of even a few seconds seemed to reduce substantially the effectiveness of punishment.

The importance of explanation. To this point, the results of punishment research in humans seem almost uncannily similar to those obtained with animals. As we argued earlier, however, the fact that the principles of animal and human learning are sometimes similar does not necessarily mean that they are identical. In particular, it would be very strange indeed if the cognitive and linguistic capacities of humans did not play some role in determining how we react to punishment.

This point is neatly illustrated in Aronfreed's experiment. In addition to the immediate and delayed punishment groups that we have described, Aronfreed included another delayed punishment group in which children were not only punished when they picked up an attractive toy, they were also given an explanation for why they should not do so. This toy was difficult to tell about, they were told, and was therefore only for older children. The children in this group were subsequently found to be significantly more likely to resist temptation than those not given an explanation.

Similar findings have been reported from field studies in which parents have been interviewed to determine what sorts of punishment they used. In a study by Sears, Maccoby, and Levin (1957), for example, mothers who made extensive use of reasoning reported punishment to be far more effective than those who reported using punishment alone. Similarly, in the Larzelere et al. study described earlier, the authors assessed the immediate effects of punishment in young children by calculating the average time interval separating successive instances of misbehavior such as fighting, and how this was affected by the mother's reaction to each incident. The data revealed that punishment on its own had no effect: Following a fight, the average time until another fight was the same whether or not the child was punished. When the punishment was accompanied by an explanation, however, the average time until the next fight increased by almost 40%.

Why should the addition of even a few words of explanation make punishment so much more effective? One possibility is that an explanation helps to clarify what behavior is being punished. If a child were punished in the evening for something he did that morning, for example, in the absence of some explanation he would clearly have considerable difficulty connecting these events. In addition, explanations can provide children with justification for why they are being punished. In Aronfreed's experiment, the children were not only being told which behavior to avoid (playing with the attractive toy), but why (because it was only appropriate for older children). If the explanation helped the children to perceive the punishment as fair, it might have reduced their resentment and thus increased their willingness to cooperate.

Cheyne (1969) has provided evidence that clarification and justification are both important. Using a procedure similar to Aronfreed's, Cheyne punished one group of children by saying "That's bad" when they chose a certain toy. With a second group of children, he told them explicitly which response was forbidden: "That's bad, you shouldn't play with that toy." As expected, the clarification group deviated significantly less in a later temptation situation, suggesting that the effectiveness of delayed punishment does depend on how clearly the punished response is identified. The least deviation of all, however, occurred in a third group of children, who were told not only which response was forbidden but why: "That toy belongs to someone else." If a punishment is perceived as fair or reasonable, in other words, it is more likely to be effective.

In addition to making punishment more effective, explanations can also play an important role in a child's moral development. Hoffman (1989) has suggested that when a child misbehaves in a way that involves harm to others, it is important to explain the consequences for the other person, rather than simply to say "Stop that." Children who receive such explanations seem to be more likely to develop empathy for others and accept responsibility for their own behavior.

The Role of Reason and Emotion

One question of interest to psychologists has been *why* punishment suppresses behavior. The important role of explanations could be taken as evidence that the process is essentially cognitive or rational: When we experience an aversive event, we try to figure out what caused it, and if we conclude that the cause was some aspect of our behavior, we might rationally decide not to repeat this response to avoid the unpleasant consequence. However, emotional factors can also play a key role. In Aronfreed's study, for example, we saw that delayed punishment was less effective than immediate punishment. In rational terms, this makes sense, because the delay would have made it harder for the children to figure out what aspect of their behavior was being punished. If the children in the delayed group were given an explanation, so that they understood what behavior was being punished ("you shouldn't play with that toy"), then the delayed punishment should be just as effective as the immediate one. This, however, is not what Aronfreed found: Even when explanations were provided, delayed punishment was still less effective than immediate.

This result makes more sense if we assume that the suppression of behavior depends not just on rational knowledge of a response's consequences—"If I touch this toy, I will be punished"—but also on how much fear the response produces. Suppose, for example, that a child's hand is slapped just as he or she reaches into a cookie jar. The proprioceptive cues produced by the reaching movement would be closely followed by a slap, with the result that fear would be classically conditioned to these cues. The next time the child approaches the jar, therefore, the reaching response would elicit fear, and this fear would in turn inhibit the response. (For a more detailed analysis, see the section on avoidance in Chapter 10.) If there is a delay between the response and punishment, however, less fear will be conditioned. Thus, even though the child might still know that he or she will be punished for responding, there will be less fear present to prevent the response.

As children grow older and their cognitive capacities increase, there might be a shift in the balance between cognitive and emotional factors, with cognition becoming progressively more important. In the Cheyne study cited earlier, children were told not to play with a certain toy because "That toy belongs to someone else." This added instruction increased obedience in third-grade children, but it had no effect on those in kindergarten. In other words, as children grow older, their behavior seems to come increasingly under the control of generalized moral codes or rules. Thus, although punishment might play a role in establishing these rules with younger children, it might be increasingly possible as the children grow older to rely on verbal appeals to these ethical codes, rather than on the direct elicitation of fear.

Summarizing the evidence to this point, it appears that punishment is most effective when it is immediate, firm, consistent, delivered in a variety of settings, and accompanied by a clear (and fair) explanation. Used under these conditions, punishment can be a powerful technique for suppressing behavior.

7.2 SIDE EFFECTS OF PUNISHMENT

Insofar as we confine our attention to the effects of punishment on the response being punished, it is clear that Thorndike was right—punishment can suppress behavior. But does this necessarily mean that we should use it? In addition to weakening the response that it follows, punishment might produce damaging effects on other aspects of behavior, so that we need to weigh the advantages of punishment against its disadvantages before deciding whether to use it. In this section, we will examine evidence about punishment's side-effects.

Fear

The problem is that aversive stimuli have a variety of effects. We have seen that one effect is to suppress preceding behavior, but aversive events can also elicit powerful emotions such as fear and anxiety, and these emotions could have a variety of undesirable consequences.

Reduced interest. Suppose, for example, that a teacher publicly criticized a schoolchild for poor performance. For some children, such criticism might act as a spur to greater effort, but for others the consequences might be less benign. If schoolwork were repeatedly associated with failure and punishment, studying might eventually become a source of fear rather than pleasure, so that the child would begin to avoid studying (and school) whenever possible. In one experimental analogue of this situation, J. A. Martin (1977) gave six-year-old boys a series of tasks to perform. On some tasks, the boys were praised when they worked; on others, they were reprimanded when they did not work; on a third set of tasks, they were ignored regardless of their behavior. On the surface, the reprimands seemed to be effective, in that the boys worked the hardest on tasks where they were reprimanded for not working. However, when they were given an opportunity to perform the tasks when the experimenter was not present, Martin found that the children never chose the tasks that had been associated with reprimands.

FIGURE 7.5   The effect of punishment intensity and explanations on a child's obedience to instructions. Intense punishment produced greater obedience than moderate punishment in children not given an explanation, but intense punishment was less effective for children who did receive an explanation. (Based on data from Cheyne, Goyeche, & Walters, 1969)

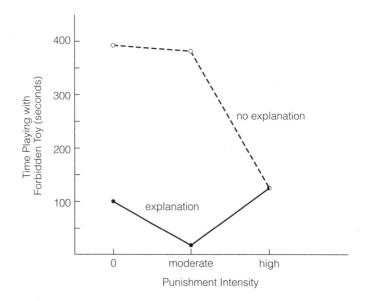

Impairment of attention. Even in situations where the fear of punishment makes us work harder, this anxiety can lead to poorer performance. In our discussion of the Yerkes-Dodson law, we noted that increases in motivation can result in a narrowing of attention, so that on complex tasks highly motivated subjects actually do worse (for example, Zaffy & Bruning, 1966). If children are punished for doing poorly on a difficult task, therefore, their anxiety could result in even poorer performance.

Indirect evidence that punishment can interfere with attention comes from a study by Cheyne, Goyeche, and Walters (1969). Using a situation similar to that developed by Aronfreed, the researchers asked children to select one of two toys. If the children selected the wrong toy, a buzzer was sounded; the intensity of the buzzer was 0, 88, or 104 decibels (db) for different groups of children. In addition, half the children were then given a verbal explanation of what they had done wrong. To measure the effectiveness of the punishment, the experimenters observed how much time the children spent playing with the forbidden toy during a subsequent temptation test. If no explanation was given, more intense punishment reduced playing time (Figure 7.5). For children who received an explanation, however, the 104-db buzzer produced *less* obedience than the weaker buzzer.

On the surface, this result is bizarre: Why should an intense punishment be less effective than a mild one? This result, however, is exactly what an attentional analysis would predict: The anxiety aroused by the more intense buzzer would interfere with children's attention to the explanation, leading to poorer performance. Supporting evidence for this interpretation comes from comparing the behavior of the children who received an explanation with the behavior of those who did not. Adding an explanation increased obedience for children in the 0- and 88-db groups but had no perceptible effect on children who received the 104-db buzzer. The children in this group, in other words, behaved exactly as if they had not heard what the experimenter was saying.

Learned helplessness. The potentially harmful effects of punishment on performance can be exacerbated if behavior is punished often. Returning to our school example, suppose that when a child is punished for doing poorly on an assignment, the anxiety this produces makes her perform even more poorly the next time. If the teacher then becomes even angrier ("You're not trying!"), the child might become even more anxious, hence becoming even more likely to fail, and so on, in a vicious circle. Eventually, if the child fails often enough, she might conclude that it is not worth even trying, even though she might actually have the ability to do well.

The first evidence that punishment can lead to individuals giving up came from a very influential series of experiments by Seligman, Maier, and Overmier. In the first of these experiments, Seligman and Maier (1967) trained dogs in a rectangular shuttle box with a shoulder-high barrier set in the center. A 10-second warning light was occasionally presented, followed by a 50-second shock delivered through the floor of the cage. If the dog jumped over the barrier while the shock was on, the shock was immediately terminated; if it jumped before the shock was presented, the light was terminated and the scheduled shock was canceled. The dogs could thus either escape the shock or avoid it altogether if they jumped across the barrier when the light came on.

Naïve dogs learned very quickly: after just one or two experiences of shock, the dogs began to jump over the barrier as soon as the shock was presented, and within a few more trials they learned to avoid almost all shocks. A second group, however, behaved very differently. These dogs were given pretraining in which they were confined in a harness and given 64 shocks that they could neither escape nor avoid. When these pretrained subjects were transferred to the avoidance task, their behavior was initially similar to the first group, as they ran about the cage when they received the shock. After about 30 seconds, however, they typically lay down on the floor and remained there, whining quietly, until the shock was terminated. In other words, it looked very much as if they had given up, and most of these subjects showed no signs of learning over successive trials.

There was, moreover, another puzzling feature of the behavior of these dogs. On most trials, as we have seen, they made little or no effort to escape, but occasionally one would jump over the barrier and thereby terminate the shock. In naïve dogs, a single success was usually enough to firmly establish the jumping response, so that the dogs would repeat it on all subsequent trials. But the dogs given inescapable shock during pretraining showed no sign of learning from a successful escape; on the trial following a successful escape, they immediately reverted to the pattern of passive acceptance shown earlier.

To explain these results, Overmier and Seligman (1967) suggested that during pretraining the dogs had learned that they were helpless—no matter how hard they struggled, they could not escape the shock. When they were transferred to the shuttle box, therefore, they made no effort to escape the shock because they had learned that such efforts were futile. And on those occasions when they did escape, they did not repeat the response, because such apparent successes during pretraining had always proved to be illusory. If on one pretraining trial a dog had lifted its paw just as the shock was terminated, for example, it would have found repeating this response on subsequent trials had no effect.

This **learned helplessness** hypothesis provoked considerable controversy—would dogs really think in such complex ways?—and subsequent research has suggested that other processes might also be involved. (See Maier & Jackson, 1979, and Maier, 1989, for reviews.) At present, however, it does look as if part of what animals learn when they are exposed to inescapable shock is that they are helpless, so that there is no point in even trying to escape.

Carol Dweck and her colleagues have suggested that learned helplessness can also occur in schools. Children who repeatedly fail at math, for example, might conclude that they are helpless and thus stop trying. In an experimental analogue of this phenomenon, Dweck and Repucci (1973) had two teachers give fifth-grade children a series of problems. One of the teachers always gave the children solvable problems, and the other presented only insoluble ones. When the second teacher finally gave the children some solvable problems, they failed to solve them, even though they had solved exactly the same problems earlier for the first teacher. (See also Dweck & Licht, 1980; Peterson, Maier, & Seligman, 1993.)

It is important to emphasize that effects of this kind are not inevitable. Children differ widely in their reactions to anxiety: For some, a particular punishment can be incapacitating; for others, the same punishment can be an incentive to greater effort. The available evidence, however, suggests that the use of punishment can pose special dangers in education, where it can lead to dislike of the subject and even a deterioration in learning.

Aggression

Pain-elicited aggression. Another possible consequence of presenting an aversive stimulus is that it can elicit aggression. This effect is known as *pain-elicited aggression*. In a study by Ulrich and Azrin (1962), pairs of rats from the same litter were placed in a test cage and given electric shocks through the floor of the cage. The authors reported that the rats responded to the shocks by rearing up on their hind legs and beginning to push each other. If the shocks were very intense, and continued long enough, the rats would begin to bite each other.

In subsequent experiments, Ulrich and his colleagues reported similar results with virtually every species tested, including species as diverse as cats, raccoons, monkeys, and alligators. In other words, it appears as if the tendency to attack when hurt is one of the most powerful and universal of all animal instincts. (Though see also Blanchard, Blanchard, & Takahashi, 1977.)

For obvious reasons, there has been little direct research on pain-elicited aggression in humans, but some research suggests that we too behave more aggressively when we are hurt. In one experiment by Berkowitz, Cochrane, and Embree (1979), university women were asked to act as teachers and either reinforce or punish a partner who was engaged in a learning task. Some of the "teachers" had one of their hands in a tank of cold water; others had one of their hands in a tank of warm water. Teachers whose hands were in cold water were significantly more likely to be punitive toward their partners than were teachers whose hands were in warm water. (See also Berkowitz, 1989.)

Modeling.   There is evidence that the use of punishment can also serve as a model for aggressive behavior. Children, after all, are highly imitative, particularly when the model is important or influential in their lives (Flanders, 1968). If a parent frequently uses physical force to control a child, therefore, the child might learn to imitate this behavior. In an early study on imitation by Bandura, Ross, and Ross (1963), nursery school children were exposed to an adult model who punched and kicked a large inflated doll. When the children were later left alone with the doll, they proved significantly more likely to attack the doll than were children in control groups who had not seen the model.

You might think that the measure of aggression used in this study was highly artificial: Does the fact that a child is more likely to attack a doll really tell us anything about the likelihood that the child will punch a friend? A field study by Leyens, Camino, Parke, and Berkowitz (1975) suggests that the answer might be yes. In their study, adolescents at a Belgian residential center for juvenile delinquents were exposed for two weeks to one of two sets of recreational films; one set emphasized physical violence, including films such as *Bonnie and Clyde* and *The Dirty Dozen*. To determine the effect of these films, the experimenters recorded the frequency of aggressive behavior during morning and evening play periods. (Aggression was defined as "physical contact of sufficient intensity to potentially inflict pain on the victim" and included hitting, slapping, choking, and kicking.) The result was that the adolescents exposed to the violent films became significantly more likely to attack one another, with the frequency of such attacks almost tripling from the first to the second week of the treatment period. Adolescents exposed to the nonviolent films, on the other hand, showed a significant decrease in aggression over the same period.

This effect is not confined to juvenile delinquents. In a more recent study by Josephson (1987), boys in a Canadian elementary school were shown either a 14-minute excerpt from a television program involving violence (a police SWAT team ambushing and shooting a gang of killers) or an equally exciting film without violence (a bike race with dramatic stunts). The boys were then given an opportunity to play floor hockey, and the experimenters observed levels of aggression during the game—for example, how often the participants pushed or elbowed their opponents. They found that the boys who had just seen the violent film engaged in almost 50% more acts of aggression. (See also Wood, Wong, & Chachere, 1991.)

Long-term effects. If exposure to a single violent film could have such a substantial effect, it seems at least possible that repeated exposure to violence from a model as influential as a parent might play a major role in determining a child's aggressiveness. In accordance with this prediction, research has shown that children who are severely punished by their parents are far more likely to be physically aggressive toward their peers (Eron et al., 1963), to later become juvenile delinquents (Glueck & Glueck, 1950), and, when adults, to develop emotional problems such as depression, alcoholism, and spousal abuse (Straus & Kantor, 1994). Moreover, more recent evidence suggests that these effects are not confined to severe punishment, as even milder forms such as spanking are correlated with increases in aggression. In a representative study by Strassberg, Dodge, Pettit, and Bates (1994), parents of 273 young children were interviewed to determine the methods of discipline they used. To separate the effects of spanking from more violent forms of punishment, the authors focused on a subgroup of parents who reported using spanking but not more severe forms such as hitting. They then observed the children of these parents in kindergarten and recorded how often these children behaved aggressively towards other children—for example, hitting or bullying them. They found that children who were spanked were roughly twice as likely to behave aggressively as those who were not.

We have cited only a few studies here, but there is now overwhelming evidence for a correlation between the use of physical punishment in childhood and the development of aggression. We need to be cautious, however, in interpreting this correlation. One problem, as discussed at the beginning of this chapter, is that a correlation between punishment and aggression does not necessarily mean that punishment causes aggression. The true relationship could actually be the reverse, with high levels of aggression leading to greater use of punishment. If a child is very aggressive or disobedient, this could gradually push a parent into using stronger punishment, as milder forms prove inadequate. The fact that punishment is correlated with aggression, therefore, doesn't necessarily mean that it causes it (Muller, 1996).

A further problem is that even if there is a causal relationship between punishment and aggression, this does not mean that punishment inevitably leads to aggression. There is evidence that whether punishment produces harmful side-effects depends on many factors, including the intensity of the punishment and the extent to which parents provide explanations for its use (Strassberg et al., 1994; Larzelere, 1986). Another important factor seems to be whether punishment is used in a reliable and consistent way, so that children know what will happen if they break rules. Punishment is much more likely to produce serious side effects when parents behave unpredictably, blowing up one minute over a relatively minor problem and then ignoring much more serious misbehaviors (Patterson, Reid, & Dishion, 1989).

The relationship between punishment and aggression is thus not simple, and it would be misleading to conclude that any use of punishment inevitably leads to aggression. On the other hand, the consistency with which researchers have observed a correlation between corporal punishment and aggression, and the experimental evidence that exposure to violence can lead to aggression—recall the effects of seeing a violent film on children's aggression during a game of hockey—suggest a powerful link between the two. Physical punishment might not always produce aggression, but it does seem to produce a strong impulse in this direction.

7.3 APPLICATION: CHILDREN'S MISBEHAVIOR

What should we conclude about the use of punishment? The evidence we have reviewed in the preceding sections seems to point to diametrically opposed conclusions. On the one hand, we have seen that punishment, if used properly, can be very effective in suppressing behavior. On the other, we have seen that intense forms of punishment can elicit fear and pain, potentially leading to such undesirable effects as a dislike of school and increased aggression. (See Figure 7.6.) In this section we will try to reconcile the conflicting evidence, focusing in particular on the use of punishment with children.

Reinforcement as an Alternative

The first point that needs to be emphasized is that the fact that punishment can cause harmful side-effects does not necessarily mean that it will always do so. When electric shock has been used to suppress self-destructive behavior in autistic children, for example, researchers have reported no signs of harm in some cases (Risley, 1968) and beneficial side-effects in others (Lovaas, Schaeffer, & Simmons, 1965). Whether side-effects will occur seems to depend on several factors, including the intensity of the punishment and its social context—as we have seen, parents who are loving and make extensive use of reasoning consistently report punishment to be more effective. Indeed, Baumrind (1991) has observed that the healthiest children—friendly, cooperative, and

FIGURE 7.6   The problems of punishment. (Drawing by Jack Ziegler from Cartoonbank.com ©1991. The New Yorker Collection. Reprinted by permission of the Cartoon Bank. All rights reserved.)

self-reliant—often come from families where parents use punishment, including spanking, to enforce rules consistently, but these parents also go to great lengths to explain the rules and (especially as the children grow older) to involve their children in setting them.

Baumrind's research suggests that when mild punishment is used in a consistent manner to enforce clear rules, and in the context of a loving and supportive family, it need not have damaging effects. On the other hand, the clear danger of side-effects suggests that it is worth minimizing the frequency and severity of punishment wherever possible. Indeed, in some situations it might be possible to avoid the use of punishment altogether. One alternative is to reinforce children when they are good instead of punishing them when they are bad. In one study of this approach, Madsen, Becker, Thomas, Koser, and Plager (1970) compared the use of reinforcement and punishment in getting first-grade children to stay in their seats during lessons. In the first phase, observers in the classroom recorded how often the children got out of their seats at times when they shouldn't during a six-day period. The teachers were then asked to punish the children for standing by ordering the children to sit down whenever they got up. As you might expect, the immediate effect of this command was that the children sat down, so that from the teacher's point of view the

FIGURE 7.7   The frequency of first-grade children leaving their seats as a function of the teacher's reaction. (Adapted from Madsen, Becker, Thomas, Koser, & Plager, 1970)

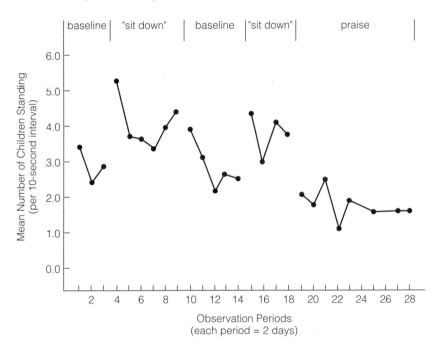

command might have appeared highly effective. When the frequency of inappropriate standing was measured over the course of the entire day, however, the introduction of punishment was found to produce an overall *increase* in standing (see Figure 7.7). The fact that the teacher paid attention to the children when they stood up, in other words, seemed to be reinforcing this behavior. After repeating the baseline and punishment phases to establish the reliability of this result, Madsen and colleagues asked the teacher to stop punishing standing and instead to reinforce incompatible behavior. Specifically, they asked the teacher to praise the children or smile at them whenever they were sitting down and working. As Figure 7.7 shows, this proved highly effective: For the first time, the frequency of standing fell significantly below its baseline level.

The punishment used in this study was a relatively mild reprimand, and a stronger form of punishment might well have been more effective. On the other hand, we have already encountered evidence that even stronger forms of punishment are sometimes not as effective as reinforcement. In Chapter 6 we discussed the Hall, Lund, and Jackson (1968) study involving children in an elementary school who had been identified as having the most serious disciplinary problems. Years of scolding and even corporal punishment had proven ineffective in reducing the disruptive behavior of children such as Robbie, but the introduction of praise for good work produced rapid and dramatic transformations.

Further evidence that reinforcement can be more effective than punishment in the classroom comes from a recent study by Tulley and Chiu (1995). They asked 135 student teachers to recall which disciplinary incidents in the previous month they felt they had handled the most successfully and which the least successfully. Three behaviors proved to be particular problems—disruption, defiance and inattention. Strong punishment, in the form of yelling or corporal punishment, proved to be the least effective strategy for dealing with these problems, as they were reported to be effective on only 4% of the occasions on which they were used. Milder forms of punishment such as detention and loss of privileges were somewhat more effective, working 53% of the time. Providing an explanation of the desired behavior was more effective still—this approach was effective 78% of the time. By far the most effective strategy, however, turned out to be reinforcement, as praising or rewarding more appropriate behavior was successful on 92% of the occasions where it was used.

The use of reinforcement in this way can require considerable effort and imagination. When children misbehave, and especially when they seem to be deliberately disobeying instructions, a parent or teacher's first reaction is often anger. It is far easier to yell at children in these situations than to stop and think, "I wonder how I could reinforce good behavior instead." The available evidence, however, suggests that the effort involved might be worthwhile: Reinforcement is not only more enjoyable than punishment, in some situations it is also more effective.

Using Minimal Force

As attractive as reinforcement might be as an alternative to punishment, there are some situations where reinforcement on its own does not seem to be sufficient. Gerald Patterson, for example, established a project to help parents of children with serious antisocial behavior, a project that eventually involved hundreds of families. At first, they relied on reinforcement, training parents to reinforce positive behaviors such as cooperation and compliance. In a summary of this work, Patterson, Reid, and Dishion (1989) wrote,

> This approach simply did not work. Even though the children became slightly more cooperative, they still hit others and had temper tantrums. (p. 2)

To produce lasting changes in this behavior, Patterson and his colleagues found that parents needed to use a combination of consistent reinforcement for appropriate behavior with nonviolent punishments such as time-out and response cost for misbehavior. (We will discuss these forms shortly.)

In some situations, then, punishment might be necessary. (See also Acker & O'Leary, 1987.) As we have seen, however, the use of punishment carries the risk of side-effects, and these effects are far more likely to occur when the punishment is intense or harsh. Where punishment is employed, therefore, it is desirable to use the mildest form of punishment that is likely to be effective. (Note that this is essentially the same principle of minimal force that we advocated in our discussion of reinforcement in Chapter 6.) In this section we will review four relatively mild alternatives to corporal punishment: ignoring, reprimands, time-out, and response cost.

Ignoring. In our discussion of the Hall, Lund, and Jackson study in Chapter 6, we noted that one reason why children such as Robbie might have continued to misbehave despite years of admonitions and scolding was that these might have provided him with attention that unintentionally reinforced his misbehavior. As counterintuitive as it sounds, therefore, many therapists recommend ignoring minor forms of misbehavior while praising appropriate behavior. Wierson and Forehand (1994), for example, describe a highly successful program developed by Forehand for training parents to cope with difficult behavior, and one component of the program is teaching parents to ignore minor forms of misbehavior such as whining.

This approach is only likely to work where the problematic behavior is being maintained by attention, and this is not always the case—stealing and aggression, for example, might have very different sources of reinforcement. Also, where children have been accustomed to receiving attention for their misbehavior, withdrawing this attention can at first result in even worse behavior, as the children try other tactics to regain attention. Wierson and Forehand have found that if parents ignore this behavior consistently, it will often disappear, and they recommend ignoring minor forms of misbehavior as one component of a broader package including reinforcement for good behavior and time-out to punish more serious misbehavior (see later). We will shortly return to this approach when we discuss extinction (Section 7.4).

Reprimands. A *reprimand* is a verbal statement conveying disapproval of a behavior. Although the use of reprimands carries a danger that the attention it provides can reinforce behavior, research by Susan O'Leary and her colleagues suggests that when used properly, reprimands can make a useful contribution to reducing misbehavior. Based on extensive research into disciplinary procedures used by mothers, the researchers identified three common mistakes in the use of reprimands: laxness, harshness, and verbosity. Laxness basically involves a failure to enforce rules consistently; harshness involves reacting in an angry or irritable way; and verbosity involves getting trapped into lengthy arguments with children about their misbehavior.[2] (The danger in verbosity is again that the attention the child gains may serve to reinforce their misbehavior.) To overcome these problems, O'Leary recommends that when parents do use reprimands, these should be *immediate, brief,* and *firm in tone* (for example, a firm "no"). When reprimands are used in this way, she and her colleagues have found that they can be effective (O'Leary, 1995).

Time-out. A second, relatively mild form of punishment is **time-out,** a procedure in which children are removed to a less reinforcing environment when they misbehave. A very mild form of time-out is being required to sit at the edge of a group and allowed to watch the others play but not participate (White & Bailey, 1990); more aversive forms include sitting in a chair facing a corner, or having to go to a bare room.

A study by Rortvedt and Miltenberger (1994) provides a nice example of how time-out can be used. The study focused on two four-year-old girls who frequently refused to comply with their parents' requests. During an initial observational phase carried out in the home, one of the girls, Morgan, failed to follow 87% of her mother's instructions, despite her mother's pleading and scolding. When the time-out phase was initiated, her mother was asked to praise her whenever she complied with a request; if she refused, she was taken to another room and told to sit quietly facing the wall for one minute. If she was sitting quietly at the end of the minute, she was allowed to leave the chair, but if not, the time-out period was extended until 10 seconds elapsed without noise. Figure 7.8 shows that this procedure resulted in an immediate improvement in Morgan's behavior, and after only seven sessions she was complying with every single instruction. This improvement was still present when her behavior was observed again six weeks later, and similar gains were shown by the other girl.

Time-out might seem to involve little more than the classic punishment of sending children to their rooms, and indeed this is a form of time-out. The classic version, however, suffers from at least two defects. First, a child's room is usually a fairly reinforcing environment because of the toys it contains, reducing its effectiveness as a form of punishment. Second, children who are sent to their rooms often have to stay there for extended periods, but research with time-out has shown that even quite brief periods in a chair, sometimes just 1–2 minutes, can be equally effective (Brantner & Doherty, 1983).

Time-out has proved to be effective with a very wide range of problems and children, but difficulties can sometimes arise. One is where a child refuses to

---

[2] The distinction between verbosity and explanation can be a source of potential confusion. As we have seen, punishment is much more effective when it is accompanied by a clear and fair explanation. This is not the same as engaging in a long debate with a child about whether a particular behavior is wrong, particularly if the purpose of the rule in question has been explained on previous occasions.

FIGURE 7.8   The percentage of her mother's instructions that Morgan followed. Compliance is shown for a period before training, during a time-out phase in which noncompliance resulted in having to sit in a chair in the corner, and during observations six weeks after the termination of training. (Adapted from Rortvedt & Miltenberger, 1994)

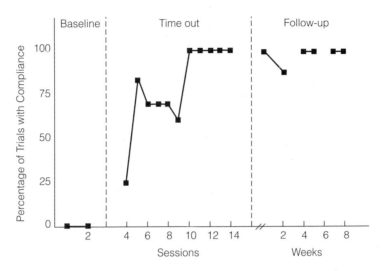

cooperate and attempts to leave the chair. A variety of approaches have been tried for dealing with this problem, ranging from gently holding the child in the chair to a quick spank, but it is not yet clear which of these approaches is most effective (McNeil, Clemens-Mowrer, Gurwitch, & Funderburk, 1994; Roberts & Powers, 1990; Reitman & Drabman, 1996). A further limitation is that time-out is inappropriate as a punishment for certain kinds of behavior. Suppose, for example, that a child repeatedly creates a disturbance in class to escape from work that she finds difficult. In this case, using time-out would only make matters worse, as it would allow her to succeed in her aim of escaping from work (Taylor and Miller, 1997). In most of the situations where time-out has been tried, however, it has proven highly effective.

Response cost. **Response cost** is a form of negative punishment in which a reinforcer is taken away whenever the target response occurs. The reinforcer that is removed is often points or money—a typical example would be a parking fine in which $50 is lost whenever a car is parked illegally.

Reynolds and Kelley (1997) have reported a treatment for aggression using response cost. The subjects were four preschool children who displayed high rates of aggression. Randy, for example, was a four-year-old boy whose parents were both psychology professors and who engaged in aggressive acts such as throwing toys or destroying structures built by classmates. During the baseline

FIGURE 7.9   The rate of aggressive behavior per hour exhibited by Randy. During baseline periods, aggression was not punished; during response-cost phases, aggression resulted in the loss of "smiley faces," which in turn canceled later access to reinforcers such as snacks. (Reynolds & Kelley, 1997)

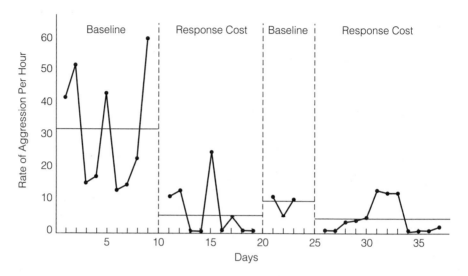

phase, he was observed to behave aggressively over 30 times per hour. To reduce this behavior, a blue chart with five yellow smiley faces attached with Velcro was posted in the classroom at the beginning of each day. Each time Randy behaved aggressively, his teacher briefly explained what he had done wrong and removed one of the smiley faces. If he still had at least one smiley face on his chart at the end of the period, then he was allowed to choose an attractive reward such as a special snack or being allowed to be the teacher's helper. (He had helped to select the rewards at the beginning of the study, when the teacher had also explained the procedure that would be followed.) In addition, if he earned a reward on at least 4 days during the week, then at the end of the week he was allowed to choose a small toy.

The effect on Randy's behavior can be seen in Figure 7.9. When the response cost procedure was initiated, his average rate of aggression fell from 31 incidents an hour to only 6. When the baseline condition was reinstated, his level of aggression rose somewhat, but quickly fell when response cost was reinstated. Similar results were obtained for the other participants, and when interviewed all said that they had enjoyed it. (Randy expressed disappointment when the treatment ended.) The teachers reported that they had found the treatment easy to use, and all four parents asked the experimenter to help them set up similar programs in their homes. A further positive feature, relative to time-out, was that the children did not have to be removed from the class, and so their education was not interrupted. Combining punishment with enhanced levels of reinforcement was clearly very effective.

Conclusions

We have seen that punishment can lead to a variety of undesirable side-effects, and for this reason we have suggested reinforcing good behavior, rather than punishing bad, wherever possible. In some situations, reinforcement is not only more enjoyable than punishment but also more effective, partly because punishment can inadvertently strengthen misbehavior by providing it with attention.

Although a strategy based on reinforcement can be surprisingly effective, it does not always work, and in these cases parents and teachers might need to use punishment. To minimize the risk of side-effects, we have suggested that the punishment used be the mildest form likely to be effective. Possible forms include ignoring minor forms of misbehavior, using brief reprimands, removing a child to a less reinforcing environment such as a chair, or removing a reinforcer. It can be difficult to predict in advance which of these alternatives will be most effective, and it will probably depend on the age of the child as well as the child's personality or discipline history. (See Forehand & Wierson, 1993; Roberts & Powers, 1990.)

Whatever form of punishment is selected, it is important that it be presented immediately, used reliably and consistently, and accompanied by a clear explanation. (This does not mean that every use of punishment has to be accompanied by a long justification for its use but, rather, that the child should always understand why he or she is being punished.) Also, the use of punishment for misbehavior should be combined, wherever possible, with encouragement for appropriate behavior.

Our understanding of punishment is still far from complete. Punishment, like reinforcement, is embedded within a complex social relationship between two individuals, and we are only beginning to understand how the different facets of this relationship combine to determine when punishment will work, why it is more effective for some children than others, and so on. There is still much to be learned, but our understanding of punishment has advanced a long way since Thorndike and Skinner first disagreed about whether punishment has any lasting effect.

7.4 EXTINCTION

One reason that children persist in certain forms of undesirable behavior is that they are strongly reinforced for doing so. Stealing, for example, might be reinforced not only by the obvious material benefits it brings but also by the respect and admiration it elicits from peers. In trying to eliminate such behavior, therefore, one possible alternative to punishment is simply to withhold the reinforcers that have been maintaining the behavior. In the case of stealing, this could be very difficult: How do you ensure that stealing will never be successful, or that a child's friends will never admire it? In situations in which the sources of reinforcement can be controlled, however, this technique can be surprisingly powerful.

A Practical Application

In one case reported by C. D. Williams (1959), the subject was a two-year-old boy who had been seriously ill for the first year and a half of his life. Even after he recovered physically, he continued to demand special attention and to throw tantrums whenever he did not get his way. On going to bed, for example, he insisted that both his parents stay with him until he was asleep, and if either of them left the room—or even tried to read—he would cry bitterly until they returned to the room and resumed giving him attention. Since falling asleep typically required from 30 minutes to 2 hours, his demands became a considerable strain on his parents, and they consulted Williams for advice.

One analysis of the boy's behavior might have been that he had suffered severe psychological trauma as a result of his earlier illness, and now needed all the love and attention he could get. Williams, however, felt that he had simply become used to receiving attention during his illness, and that his tantrum behavior was now being maintained by the attention it produced. To eliminate this behavior, therefore, Williams recommended that the parents simply ignore any crying that took place after they put the child to bed. On the first night, the child screamed and raged for 45 minutes before finally falling asleep (Figure 7.10, solid line). The parents did not go in, however, and on the following night he didn't cry at all. Crying reappeared briefly on a few subsequent nights, but within a week it had disappeared completely.

One week later, the boy's aunt baby-sat for him so his parents could have a night out. When she put him to sleep, he again began to cry, and she went in to him. As shown in Figure 7.10 (broken line), this single reinforcement was enough to trigger another massive burst of crying on the following night, but the parents again refused to go in, and within a week the crying had disappeared again, this time permanently. Simply by ignoring his tantrums, therefore, his parents were able to eliminate this behavior within a matter of days, and follow-up observations two years later suggested that he had become a friendly and outgoing child, with no sign of any harmful aftereffects.

Extinction as Punishment

Extinction, or the nonreinforcement of a previously reinforced response, obviously works, but it also poses something of a theoretical puzzle. Nonreinforcement

FIGURE 7.10   Extinction of a child's tantrum behavior. (C. D. Williams, 1959)

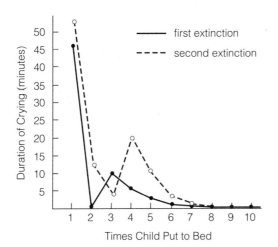

simply means that a response is followed by nothing: Why should nothing weaken a previously well-learned response? One possible explanation is that extinction is simply a form of rational decision making. When a response is repeatedly reinforced, we learn to expect that each response will be followed by a reinforcer. When we discover that the response is no longer producing the reinforcer, we logically conclude that there is no point in continuing to respond.

This explanation makes a lot of sense, but if we watch an angry monkey screeching when pressing a bar no longer produces food, or a man kicking a vending machine in which he has just lost a dollar, their behavior doesn't look as if it is guided by rational calculations of the optimal strategy. Instead, it appears as if the absence of an expected reinforcer causes an emotional response of frustration or anger. If this emotion is aversive, then extinction might actually be a form of punishment, with the frustration produced by the omission of the reinforcer punishing the response that produces it.

Rather than viewing extinction as a rational process, then, we can interpret it as a form of punishment in which our emotions act as the punishing event. Of course, these interpretation are not necessarily incompatible (reason and emotion could both play important roles), but the punishment interpretation leads to an interesting prediction: If extinction is really a form of punishment, then we should expect extinction to have exactly the same properties as other forms of punishment, albeit potentially in a milder form.

Extinction-induced aggression. Just as punishment elicits aggression, for example, we should expect extinction to do the same. Azrin, Hutchinson, and

Hake (1966) reported striking support for this prediction. They placed two pigeons in a cage, one free to move around and the other (the target bird) immobilized in a stocklike apparatus. A key was mounted on one wall, but during the baseline phase pecks had no effect. Then, during the experimental phase, pecks made by the free bird were alternately reinforced and extinguished. The reinforcement periods were signaled by a tone, and the pigeon soon learned to respond steadily whenever the tone was on. Whenever an extinction period began, however, the free pigeon would immediately turn away from the key and begin to attack the target bird. These attacks, moreover, were not mere feints; they "consisted of strong pecks at the throat and head of the target bird, especially around the eyes. The feathers of the target bird were often pulled out and the skin bruised" (Azrin, Hutchinson, & Hake, 1966, p. 204). The ferocity of these attacks gradually diminished over several minutes, but each new extinction period would bring a renewed burst of aggression. The absence of reinforcement during the baseline period, on the other hand, did not produce any such aggression. As predicted by our punishment analysis, nonreinforcement by itself appears to be quite neutral; it is only when it follows a history of reinforcement that it becomes aversive.

Nation and Cooney (1982) report evidence suggesting similar effects in humans. They gave college students a task in which they had to move a rod in a certain direction; successful responses automatically produced a reinforcer. Subjects were told that a loud noise would sometimes be played during the experiment, and that they could turn the noise off either by pressing a button or hitting a pad—the latter response required considerably more force. During the training phase, subjects preferred to turn the noise off by pushing the button, but when extinction began, and they found that they were no longer receiving reinforcement, subjects began to hit the pad instead. Moreover, the force with which they hit the pad increased dramatically during the early stages of extinction, then gradually fell back. It looked very much as if the omission of reinforcement initially produced intense frustration, and that this gradually subsided as subjects became accustomed to its omission.

The frustration effect. Further evidence for the frustrating nature of extinction comes from a study by Amsel and Roussel (1952). They hypothesized that frustration was an aversive drive, so that, like hunger and other drives, it should produce an increase in the vigor of behavior known as the **frustration effect.** To test this proposition, they trained rats in a double-alley apparatus in which there were two goal boxes, located in the middle and at the end of a long runway (Figure 7.11). During initial training, food was available in both goal boxes. During the test phase, however, food was absent from the first goal box on half the trials. On trials where food was not present in this goal box, Amsel and Roussel predicted that the food's absence would produce frustration, and this motivational state would act as a drive to energize subsequent

FIGURE 7.11   An overhead view of the double-alley apparatus used in the Amsel and Roussel (1952) frustration experiment.

behavior. The rats, in other words, should run down the second alley faster on trials in which food was omitted, and this is what happened. Furthermore, as in the case of aggression, it has been shown that it is not nonreinforcement per se that produces frustration, but nonreinforcement following a response that was previously reinforced (Wagner, 1959). This again supports the view that the omission of an expected reinforcer is aversive and, thus, that extinction is a form of punishment.

One practical implication is that the use of extinction to eliminate undesirable behaviors can generate anger and aggression. One dramatic example comes from a study by Herbert, Pinkston, Hayden, Sajwaj, Pinkston, Cordua, and Jackson, (1973), in which the mothers of six deviant children were instructed to ignore their children when they misbehaved, to prevent misbehavior being reinforced by attention. This technique has been very effective in many studies, but when the children in this group found that they were no longer receiving attention, they became furious: Four of the six children assaulted their mothers, and one kicked out a window of the room in which training was being given! Thus while extinction is normally a relatively mild form of punishment, it can produce powerful side effects in some circumstances. (This frustration effect could also explain why the boy in the Williams study cried so long the first night that his parents ignored his tantrums.) Also, extinguishing a response can require many trials; in situations where it is important to suppress a behavior immediately—for example, where a child is in danger of injuring himself—then punishment may be more appropriate.

The Partial Reinforcement Effect

In our discussion of the partial reinforcement effect (PRE) in Chapter 5, we saw that when responding is reinforced only occasionally during training, subjects persist in responding during extinction far longer than if every response had been reinforced. If rats are trained to run down a straight alley to obtain food, for example, a group that is reinforced on only 50% of the trials during training will run longer when food is no longer presented in the goal box than will a group that is reinforced on every trial. In situations like this, it looks as if nonreinforcement during training is actually strengthening the response, a very peculiar result indeed.

The discrimination hypothesis. The **discrimination hypothesis** provides a possible explanation for the partial reinforcement effect. According to this hypothesis, when subjects first encounter extinction, it might take them some time to realize that conditions have changed—that is, to discriminate the conditions in effect during extinction from those that prevailed during training. If you're accustomed to receiving reinforcement every time you respond, the omission of reinforcement will be obvious, and you will probably stop responding very quickly. If your responses are only occasionally reinforced, however, then the omission of reinforcement will be a familiar occurrence, and it will take you much longer to realize that conditions have changed.

Capaldi's sequential model. The discrimination hypothesis provides a plausible framework for understanding the partial reinforcement effect, but it does not provide a detailed account. More detailed theories have been proposed by several theorists (for example, Amsel, 1994; Daly & Daly, 1982), but we will focus here on just one, put forward by E. J. Capaldi (1971; 1994). To see how this model works, suppose that two groups of rats are trained to run down a straight alley to obtain food in the goal box. One group is reinforced on every trial, while the second is reinforced on only half the trials. Both groups are then given extinction trials in which food is never available in the goal box.

According to Capaldi's model, when the rats are put in the maze at the beginning of each trial, the cues of the maze will remind them of their experiences the last time they were in the maze. If the previous trial ended in food, for example, the rat will recall this, in the same way that if you revisited a restaurant, you might recall the dishes you had eaten on your previous visit.

Suppose that the rat now runs down the alley and obtains food. Capaldi, like Thorndike, assumes that the presentation of a reinforcer strengthens the connection between the preceding response and the stimuli present at the time. In this case, the delivery of food will strengthen the connection between the response of running down the alley and the cues that were present—for example, the color of the maze walls:

$$S^{maze} \text{---} R_{running} \rightarrow Food$$

However—and this is now the crucial assumption—Capaldi assumes that the memory of the previous trial will also act as a stimulus. Suppose, for example, that the previous trial ended in nonreinforcement. If we represent the memory of nonreinforcement by the symbol S^N, then this memory will form part of the stimulus complex that precedes running, and so this memory will also become associated with running down the alley:

$$S^N - R_{running} \rightarrow Food$$

When the extinction trials begin, neither group will be reinforced, and so each trial will begin with the rats remembering receiving no reinforcement on the previous trial. For subjects in the partial reinforcement group, this memory, S^N, will have been associated with running, and so it will elicit a tendency to run down the alley. For subjects reinforced on every trial, on the other hand, S^N will not have been associated with running, and they will be less likely to run.

New predictions. This might at first seem a rather cumbersome restatement of what the discrimination hypothesis says much more simply—that if we are accustomed to nonreinforcement during training, we will be more likely to continue to respond when we encounter nonreinforcement during extinction. However, Capaldi's model includes detailed assumptions about the rats' memory—for example, that at the beginning of a trial they will remember not only the outcome of the previous trial but the exact sequence of outcomes from a number of trials—and these assumptions allow the model to predict behavior over a wide range of situations. In some cases these predictions have been little more than common sense, but in others the model's predictions have not only gone beyond common sense but strongly contradicted it. To take just one example, suppose that two groups of rats were trained to run down a straight alley for food, with three trials a day arranged according to the following sequence of reinforcement (R) and nonreinforcement (N):

Group I: R N R

Group II: R R N

If we analyzed this situation using the discrimination hypothesis, we might argue that both groups should respond equally during extinction, because both received the same number of N and R trials, arranged in what seems a similarly haphazard sequence. According to Capaldi's analysis, however, the results in the two cases should be very different. In the first group, nonreinforcement on the second trial precedes reinforcement on the third, so that S^N will be associated with responding on this trial. In the second group, however, the nonreinforced trial is not followed by reinforcement. S^N, therefore, will not be present on a reinforced trial, and hence should not become associated with responding. To all intents and purposes, this final N trial might just as well not have taken place: Subjects in this group not only should respond less during extinction than subjects in the first group, but they should respond just as if they had been reinforced continuously throughout.

This prediction has now been tested in a number of experiments, and in every case the results have supported Capaldi's analysis. In one particularly striking experiment by Capaldi and Kassover (1970), one group received three times as many nonreinforcements during training as another, but when these trials were presented at the end of each daily sequence—so that they were never followed by reinforcement—they proved to have absolutely no effect on responding during extinction. It is not simply the experience of nonreinforcement during training that produces the PRE, then, but the particular sequence of nonreinforcement followed by reinforcement—hence Capaldi's naming of his theory the *sequential model*.

Capaldi's model has enjoyed substantial success (see also Capaldi, Alptekin, & Birmingham, 1996), and it illustrates how seemingly mysterious phenomena such as the PRE can sometimes be explained through a careful analysis of the stimuli present. More generally, it suggests again, as did the Rescorla-Wagner model earlier, the surprising power of even a few simple assumptions to predict behavior, provided that these assumptions are stated clearly. The principles of learning sometimes seem little more than common sense: It is hardly surprising, for example, that reinforcement strengthens behavior, or that responding is more likely in a situation in which training is given. When these principles are combined in a clear and explicit model, however, they can lead to predictions that go beyond—and sometimes even contradict—anything suggested by intuition or common sense.

7.5 SUMMARY

Punishment has long been a controversial method of suppressing behavior. Early research suggested that punishment had only a temporary effect, but more recent research has reversed this conclusion. When punishment is immediate, firm, accompanied by a clear (and fair) explanation, and when it occurs in a variety of settings, it can be a very powerful tool for eliminating undesirable behavior.

Evidence of the effectiveness of punishment, however, has not ended the controversy over its use, because the positive effects on the punished response must be weighed against the danger of harmful side effects. One problem is that the presentation of an aversive stimulus elicits fear, and this fear can be classically conditioned to the stimuli that precede punishment. If children are punished for poor schoolwork, for example, this can act as an incentive to try harder, but the resulting anxiety might narrow attention, so that in some cases a child who is punished for poor schoolwork might actually do worse. This may lead to a vicious circle in which failure increases anxiety, which then leads to still more failure, until the child eventually learns to stop trying altogether.

A second undesirable consequence of punishment is that it can increase aggression. Aversive stimuli directly elicit aggression; even if this aggression is not expressed immediately, there is a danger that it will later be directed at the individual administering the punishment or else displaced onto other, less powerful targets. Also, adults' use of punishment can provide a model for a child that the use of physical force is an appropriate way to get what you want. Observational studies have revealed a strong correlation between the use of severe punishment and the development of antisocial behaviors such as delinquency and violence. Even milder forms of corporal punishment such as spanking have been found to be associated with increases in aggression, though whether this occurs depends on factors such as parental use of reasoning.

Given the potential dangers posed by the use of punishment, it makes sense to consider alternative strategies where possible. One such strategy is to reinforce good behavior instead of punishing bad behavior, and this approach has proven surprisingly effective. Where punishment is necessary, the principle of minimal force suggests using the mildest form of punishment likely to be effective. Alternatives include ignoring minor misbehavior in cases where attention might be reinforcing that behavior; using brief reprimands; removing a child to a less reinforcing environment such as a time-out chair; and the response cost procedure in which misbehavior results in the loss of reinforcers such as points or money.

Another alternative to punishing a response is to extinguish it by withholding whatever reinforcer maintains it. Extinction, like punishment, seems to reduce behavior through a blend of reason and emotion. We might rationally decide not to repeat a response that has no payoff or a negative one, but both processes also seem to involve strong emotion. With extinction, the omission of an expected reinforcer can elicit frustration, and this aversive state may then act to punish the response that produced it. This punishment interpretation predicts that extinction should produce exactly the same side effects as punishment, and there is evidence that extinction can elicit aggression in humans as well as animals, as well as increasing the vigor of subsequent activity. Normally, though, extinction is a relatively mild form of punishment, and for this reason might be preferable in situations where it is possible to withhold the reinforcer that is maintaining a behavior.

Partial reinforcement during training produces more persistent responding during extinction than does continuous reinforcement. This partial reinforcement effect is puzzling in some respects: Surely more frequent reinforcement should produce a stronger response, and hence greater resistance to extinction? To explain this paradox, the discrimination hypothesis suggests that responding during extinction depends on the similarity of conditions during extinction to those prevalent during training: The greater the similarity, the more likely we are to continue to respond. In particular, animals or people who experience more frequent nonreinforcement during training will find it harder to discriminate the change of conditions during extinction, and thus will respond longer.

Capaldi's sequential model provides a detailed account of how the stimuli present during training influence subsequent responding during extinction. If a rat is occasionally reinforced for running down an alley, for example, Capaldi's model suggests that when the rat is returned to the alley to begin each trial, the cues of the alley will remind it of its experiences on previous trials. If it remembers not receiving reinforcement on the previous trial, this memory of nonreinforcement will be one of the stimuli present as it runs down the alley. If it is reinforced at the end of this trial, therefore, the memory of nonreinforcement will become associated with running, thus making it more likely that nonreinforcement during extinction will also elicit running. This model makes some surprising and counterintuitive predictions about the effects of different patterns of reinforcement, and these predictions have received substantial support.

Glossary

Punishment A decrease in the likelihood of a response caused by the presentation of an aversive stimulus or, in the case of **negative punishment,** the removal of a reinforcing stimulus. The term *punishment* is also sometimes used to refer to the procedure of presenting an aversive stimulus following a response, rather than to the outcome. Neither punishment nor negative punishment should be confused with **negative reinforcement,** which is defined as an increase in the probability of a response caused by the removal of an aversive stimulus. Reinforcement—including negative reinforcement—always involves the strengthening of a response, and punishment always involves its weakening. Reinforcement is called positive when the effect is caused by the presentation of a stimulus; it is called negative when a stimulus is removed.

Learned helplessness An impairment in learning to escape or avoid an aversive stimulus such as shock, caused by previous experiences in which the subject could not control the shock. The *learned helplessness hypothesis* attributes this impairment to subjects' learned belief that they are helpless to alter the aversive event's probability.

Time-out A form of punishment in which misbehavior results in removal to a less reinforcing environment for a specified period (time out from reinforcement). Commonly used forms of time-out for children include having to sit in a chair in a corner or having to stay in a bare room.

Response cost This is a form of negative punishment in which a reinforcer is taken away following a response. Typically, the reinforcer that is lost is points or tokens.

Extinction Nonreinforcement of a previously reinforced response. The typical result of the extinction procedure is a gradual decrease in responding.

Frustration effect An increase in the vigor of the behavior that immediately follows nonreinforcement of a previously reinforced response.

Discrimination hypothesis A theory that attempts to explain the partial reinforcement effect. It states that the level of responding in any situation is determined by the similarity of the stimuli present to those that prevailed during training.

Review Questions

1. Define *pain-elicited aggression* and S^N.

2. What are the advantages and disadvantages of using animal experiments to study punishment?

3. What determines whether punishment is effective?

4. To what extent are the principles of punishment the same in animals and humans?

5. Why do explanations enhance the effectiveness of punishment?

6. Extinction and punishment could both be explained as examples of rational decision making in which subjects decide how to respond on the basis of the consequences they expect to follow. What evidence points to an important role of emotion in both these procedures?

7. What are the possible harmful effects of punishment? What conditions make these harmful effects more likely? Less likely?

8. What is your own conclusion about whether punishment should be used, and, if so, when?

9. What are some possible alternatives to punishment for eliminating undesirable behavior?

10. What is the procedural difference between extinction, response cost, and time-out? What feature do they share that might explain why they all weaken the response that produces them?

11. What is the partial reinforcement effect? How does the discrimination hypothesis account for it?

12. How does Capaldi's sequential model account for the PRE?

13. In what ways are the Capaldi and Rescorla-Wagner models similar?

PART IV

THEORETICAL PROCESSES IN ASSOCIATIVE LEARNING

CHAPTER EIGHT

WHAT IS LEARNED?

A hungry cat is placed in a box with a dish of food located just outside the box. At first, the cat struggles frantically, biting and clawing at the walls of the box in a frenzied effort to reach the food. Eventually, in the course of its struggles, it strikes against a latch and the door to the box opens, allowing it to escape and eat the food. Over subsequent trials, the time period between placing the cat in the box and the cat's striking the latch gradually decreases, until eventually the cat begins to run directly to the latch and paw it immediately on being placed in the cage. Why? What has the cat learned to produce such a radical transformation in its behavior?

At first, the answer to this question might appear so simple that it is hardly worth discussing. In fact, however, the related issues of what the cat learns, and how it learns it, have proved to be among the most complex and difficult in all psychology, and it will require the whole of the rest of this book to set forth even the tentative outlines of a possible solution. In this chapter, we will focus on the first of these questions: What is learned when a response is reinforced?

8.1 EARLY VIEWS

One obvious answer to the question of what the cat learned is an expectation: "If I press the latch, the door will open." According to this interpretation, learning in animals is essentially a rational process, so when the cat is first put into the box it immediately tries to figure out how to reach the food. If it succeeds in escaping by pressing the latch, then the next time it is placed in the box it will recall this success, and, being hungry, will deliberately repeat the response in order to reach the food. Now this explanation is not quite as simple as it may sound; some fairly complex memory and reasoning processes are implicitly assumed. (For example, having opened the door once, the cat cannot simply repeat the exact same movements the next time, because the movements required to operate the latch will vary depending on the cat's position. The cat must thus learn something more than a specific sequence of muscular contractions—it must somehow abstract the general principle that it needs to make the latch move downward.) Nevertheless, this explanation does provide a plausible framework for understanding the cat's behavior.

The Development of S–R Theory

Thorndike's associative analysis. Thorndike, who first carried out the experiment we have been describing, considered an explanation along these lines, but closer analysis of his subjects' behavior led him to reject it. First of all, when a cat was initially placed in the puzzle box, there was no obvious indication of rational deliberation, of the cat's coolly looking the situation over in an effort to plan its escape. Instead, there was immediate frenzied activity. Thorndike observed, "It tries to squeeze through any opening; it claws and bites at the bars or wire; it thrusts its paw through any opening and claws at everything it reaches" (Thorndike, 1911, p. 35). Eventually, after 8 or 10 minutes of such scrambling about, the cat might accidentally contact the release mechanism and escape.

If the cat formed a rational appreciation of the situation, we might expect it to repeat this response immediately on subsequent trials:

> *If there were in these animals any power of inference, however rudimentary, however sporadic, however dim, there should have appeared among the multitude some cases when an animal, seeing through the situation, knows the proper act, does it, and from then on does it immediately upon being confronted with the situation. There ought, that is, to be a sudden vertical descent in the time-curve.*
> (Thorndike, 1911, p. 73)

In all the scores of animals Thorndike tested, however, not once did he observe sudden and enduring improvement of this kind. In most instances, improvement over trials was a slow, gradual affair. (See Figure 5.2 for some representative records.) Latencies did sometimes drop sharply after an early success, but after a series of such successes there would often be an equally sharp increase in latency. Indeed, two cats, after performing the escape response successfully a number of times—six times in one case, eight in the other—abruptly ceased to perform it at all, and even when left in the box as long as 20 minutes, never again managed to get out.

To Thorndike, this gradual improvement in performance, with its occasional reversals and failures, did not at all resemble the behavior of a rational animal fully aware of the relationship between the latch and the door:

> *The gradual slope of the time-curve . . . shows the absence of reasoning. They represent the wearing smooth of a path in the brain, not the decisions of a rational consciousness.*
> (Thorndike, 1911, p. 74)

As we saw in Chapter 5, Thorndike proposed that when the cat managed to escape and eat the food, the resultant pleasure stamped in an association between the impulse to make the response and the sense impressions that accompanied it. The more the response was rewarded, the stronger this association would become until, eventually, as soon as the cat was placed in the box, the sensations aroused would automatically elicit an impulse to perform the response. Rather than appealing to complex reasoning processes to explain the cat's behavior, in other words, Thorndike argued that it could be explained solely in terms of the stamping in of simple associations.

Watson's behaviorism. Although Thorndike's analysis differed markedly from earlier cognitive accounts, in one respect it was still not sufficiently radical for early behaviorists such as John B. Watson (1913). The problem, for Watson, was that Thorndike still assumed that associations were formed between sensations and impulses—mental events inside the animal's head. The stamping in of an association, moreover, was attributed to the feelings of pleasure that followed it. But how could anyone know what sensations or feelings were going on inside an animal's head? And what value is there in explaining an animal's behavior in terms of its mental states if there is no way of determining the truth of these explanations?

The essence of the scientific method—the quality that distinguishes it from other intellectual pursuits such as literary criticism or philosophy—is that scientific debates are settled by evidence. If a physicist makes what on the surface seems a totally absurd claim—for example, that no object can move faster than the speed of light, and that no matter how much energy is invested, this maximum speed cannot be exceeded by even one millimeter per second—then this claim is evaluated solely by how it fits with evidence, rather than whether it sounds plausible. This emphasis on evidence rather than on opinion allows science to progress rather than becoming bogged down in endless arguments. ("I'm right!" "No, I am!") In the case of mental explanations, however, Watson argued that it was not possible to obtain such evidence because we cannot know what an animal is thinking or feeling.

Watson's claim might sound strange, because we often interpret animals' behavior in terms of their feelings. If you stroked a cat and it began to purr, for example, you would almost certainly conclude that it was feeling the same sort of pleasure as you would in that situation. Our tendency to attribute human thoughts and feelings to animals is so strong that it has even been given its own name, *anthropomorphism*. In a number of situations, however, we have good reason to believe that anthropomorphic interpretations such as this are misleading.

One example comes from a study of grey-lag geese by Tinbergen (1951). When an egg rolls out of the nest, the goose will retrieve it by extending its beak beyond the egg and then moving its beak back towards its body, thereby moving the egg closer to the nest. Watching this behavior, the almost irresistible conclusion is that the goose is deliberately maneuvering the egg to guide it to the nest. However, Tinbergen found that if he removed the egg just as the movement was beginning, the goose would nevertheless persist in the movement exactly as if the egg was still present. In other words, the beak movement was essentially an instinct (technically, a *fixed-action pattern*), in which contact of the beak with the egg initiates an automatic and rigid series of muscular contractions designed to guide the egg back to the nest. The goose was not deliberately planning and controlling the movement of the egg in the way a person in this situation might have done, however much its actions might have given this impression.

The fact that an animal *appears* to be having a certain thought or feeling, then, does not necessarily mean that it is. If we can't be sure what an animal is thinking, however, then any explanation of its behavior based on its thoughts cannot be tested. Watson therefore argued that in trying to understand an animal's behavior, we must look for the behavior's causes in the environmental and hereditary influences operating on it, rather than in its thoughts or feelings. Explanations that attribute behavior to external influences might seem cold and mechanical when compared with mental accounts—when we attribute others' behavior to thoughts and feelings like our own, we can identify with them and feel that we understand them—but environmental explanations have the priceless advantage that they can be tested, allowing inadequate explanations to be discarded, and progress to be made.

Injunctions to avoid all references to the mind were hard enough to accept with animal behavior; but Watson went further and argued that the same prohibition should apply to explanations of human behavior. The problem is fundamentally the same: We can observe other people's behavior—we see them smiling, for example—but we cannot directly observe their emotions, and the inferences we make about these emotions might be very wrong. (As Shakespeare's Hamlet warned, "one may smile, and smile, and be a villain. . .") Any explanation that attributes people's behavior to their thoughts or feelings, therefore, is untestable, because we cannot be sure what these feelings are.

S–R theory.   Given the difficulty of observing mental processes, behaviorists argued that learning should be described solely in terms of changes in visible behavior, which could be observed objectively. Thus, although Watson and other behaviorists welcomed Thorndike's emphasis on the importance of simple associations, they rejected the assumption that these were formed between mental events. Where Thorndike spoke of a sense impression or sensation, behaviorists substituted the visible object in the environment that gave rise to it—the stimulus. And when he spoke of mental impulses to respond, they substituted the muscular movements that resulted—the response. Learning, in this view, consisted of the formation of associations between stimuli and responses—or, as they eventually came to be known, S–R associations.

S–R theory was thus the natural, perhaps inevitable, outgrowth of two fundamental beliefs: (1) *Associationism*—a belief that learning is the result of fundamentally simple associations, and (2) **behaviorism**—a belief that behavior must be explained by events that can be observed objectively.

A Cognitive View

Cognitive psychologists vigorously rejected both of these assumptions. Learning, they said, was far too complex and subtle to be explained by simple associations. As for the suggestion that psychologists should ignore what a person thinks or feels, a vivid rejoinder came from William McDougall, a social psychologist and contemporary of Watson's. In the course of an entertaining and sometimes caustic debate with Watson, staged in 1929, he asked his listeners to imagine the following scene:

> *I come into the hall and see a man on the platform scraping the guts of a cat with hairs from the tail of a horse; and, sitting silently in attitudes of rapt attention, are a thousand persons who presently break out into wild applause. How will the Behaviorist explain these strange incidents: How explain the fact that vibrations emitted by the cat-gut stimulate all the thousand into absolute silence and quiescence; and the further fact that the cessation of the stimulus seems to be a stimulus to the most frantic activity? Common sense and psychology agree in accepting the explanation that the audience heard the music with keen pleasure and vented their gratitude and admiration for the artist in shouts and hand clappings. But the Behaviorist knows nothing of pleasure and pain, of admiration and gratitude. He has relegated all such "metaphysical entities" to the dust heap, and must seek some other explanation. Let us leave him seeking it. The search will keep him harmlessly occupied for some centuries to come.*
> (Watson & McDougall, 1929, pp. 68–69)

Agreement between the two camps was clearly less than complete. It's important to note, however, that the dispute was not about the mind's existence—with the possible exception of Watson himself, most behaviorists fully accepted its reality—but about whether mental states should play any role in the scientific explanation of behavior. Because of the difficulties in testing mental explanations, Watson and other behaviorists argued that we should explain behavior solely through the hereditary and environmental variables that give rise to it. If someone becomes a murderer, for example, we should focus on the experiences that led to this behavior—for example, abandonment or harsh punishment during childhood. Only by identifying these environmental causes can we prevent the recurrence of such behavior in the future. Psychologists such as McDougall, on the other hand, argued that people's thoughts and feelings play a crucial role in determining their behavior, and that to ignore mental states simply because they are sometimes difficult to observe would be folly, not unlike an ostrich hiding its head in the sand to avoid having to face an awkward reality.

Test: Learning without Responding

Applying their analyses to learning, S–R theorists argued that learning should be explained by S–R associations, whereas cognitive psychologists argued that learning was the result of the formation of expectations. One way to evaluate the competing approaches was suggested by Thorndike. In an article published in 1946, entitled simply "Expectation," he compared the S–R and cognitive views of learning and suggested a simple way of distinguishing them. According to the S–R view, a reward stamps in whatever muscular response precedes it (or, more accurately, an association between that response and the stimuli present at the time). According to cognitive theorists, on the other hand, learning is fundamentally a perceptual process in which subjects perceive the relationships between events.

These two views have very different implications for what should be learned in a situation in which no response is made. If what is learned is a muscular response, then if no response is made, no S–R association will be formed. Learning, therefore, can occur only if a response is made. According to cognitive theorists, however, it is not the response itself that is crucial, but the opportunity to perceive appropriate relationships among events. Provided the experimental situation allows these relationships to be perceived, learning should be possible even in the absence of a response.

Stated in this abstract form, the differences between the two positions might not be clear, but we can illustrate them more concretely using an experiment by McNamara, Long, and Wike (1956). Two groups of rats were placed in a simple T-maze in which food was available in the goal box on the right. One group of rats was allowed to run through the maze by themselves, but in the second group, the rats were carried through in a wire basket pushed by the experimenter. The sequence of trips to the left and right goal boxes matched exactly the sequence for the first group: When a subject in the first group freely turned to the right and received food, its yoked partner was carried to the same goal box and fed; when the first subject went to the left and found nothing, so did the other. The subjects in the two groups thus received exactly the same sequence of turns and reinforcements; the only difference was that in one group the rats ran through the maze by themselves and in the other they were carried.

Following training, both groups were given nonreinforced test trials in which they were placed in the start box and allowed to run freely through the maze. (The experimenters withheld food to ensure that no further learning occurred during testing.) According to an S–R analysis, because subjects in the basket group never performed the correct response during training, this response would not have been associated with the cues of the maze. According to a cognitive analysis, however, these subjects would have had just as much opportunity to observe the appropriate relationship (that food is in the goal box on the right, not on the left) as those in the control group, and so should have learned equally.

This was exactly the result obtained: The preference for the correct side was virtually identical in the two groups (64% versus 66%). The fact that the turning response was not made clearly did not prevent its being learned. Learning, therefore, must involve something more than just the stamping in of particular movements.

Results like these suggest that animals can acquire new habits simply by observing the world around them. (See also Whiten, Custance, Gomez, Teixidor, & Bard, 1996.) If learning is to be characterized by the formation of associations, therefore, clearly these associations must sometimes involve covert events inside the organism that cannot be directly observed.

8.2 HULL'S S–R THEORY

Behaviorism arose out of a growing revulsion with the seemingly endless bickering of the introspectionists, with each observer studying his or her own private world and no two observers able to agree. The solution, as Watson saw it, was to eliminate all references to mental states from psychology. The evidence for learning without responding, however, showed that learning could not be described solely in terms of visible behavior. This created a painful dilemma for behaviorists: Could S–R theory be salvaged? Or did its failure in this instance require a repudiation of behaviorism and concomitant return to introspection, with all its faults?

In fact, few thought of repudiation, and the history of science would provide few precedents for an abrupt reversal of this kind. Any theory is built on a complex network of assumptions, and although an incorrect prediction might mean that one of these assumptions is wrong, it hardly invalidates the entire set. Put less charitably, none of us likes to admit to being totally wrong—a small oversight, perhaps, but surely not a total failure! The practical problem confronting S–R theorists, then, was not so much whether to abandon their theory as how to modify it to account for learning without responding while doing the least damage to the theory's basic structure.

Neobehaviorism

Intervening variables. Clark Hull provided the answer, and it was breathtaking in its simplicity: If we must assume covert behaviors, he said, let these behaviors have exactly the same properties as overt ones. Covert activities should be viewed as muscular responses, obeying exactly the same behavioral laws (laws of reinforcement, classical conditioning, generalization, and so forth) as their overt counterparts. Rather than abandoning an S–R analysis, in other words, Hull proposed that it be extended to cover covert responses as well as overt ones.

But how could a behaviorist assume invisible responses? The very essence of behaviorism lay in its insistence on studying only those behaviors that can be observed objectively, and by no stretch of the imagination could invisible muscle twitches be said to meet this criterion. Hull's response, in essence, was that a blanket refusal to countenance unobservable events was based on a misreading of the practice in other sciences. Although it was true that all sciences insisted that disputes could be settled only by objectively observable evidence, this did not mean that hypothetical or invisible states could not be allowed at a theoretical level. Newton's theory of gravity, for example, assumed a force that was totally invisible, but it specified the precise effects this force should have on objects such as falling apples and orbiting planets, and these predictions made the theory testable. As long as a hypothetical state meets this criterion of leading to testable predictions, there is no scientific reason for not allowing it. Applying this analysis to psychology, Hull argued that there could be no objection to assuming that some unobservable event (X) intervened between a stimulus and response,

$$S \rightarrow [X] \rightarrow R$$

provided that the relationships between S and X and between X and R were specified clearly enough to allow the unambiguous derivation of predictions.

The hypothetical event X in this equation is called an **intervening variable,** and for the theory to be testable, statements about intervening variables must satisfy two conditions:

1. The relationship between S and X must be clearly specified, so that it is possible to predict in advance what situations will produce X:

$$S \rightarrow X$$

2. The relationship between X and R must be clearly specified, so that when the unobservable event X occurs, we can predict what overt response will follow:

$$X \rightarrow R$$

If these requirements are satisfied, then the theory can predict what behavior will occur in any situation, and the predictions can then be tested.

To be able to predict when a covert response would occur, Hull assumed that covert responses would have exactly the same properties, and obey the same laws, as their overt counterparts. For example, if a rat receives food in a goal box, the laws of classical conditioning suggest that the responses elicited

FIGURE 8.1   Hull's view of classical conditioning in a maze. Food or other unconditioned stimuli presented in the goal box would elicit an unconditioned goal response, R_{Goal}, which would be conditioned to the cues of the goal box. Hull used the symbol r_g to represent the conditioned form of this response.

by food should be conditioned to the stimuli that are present. Based on this law, Hull simply *assumed* that such conditioning would occur whenever a reinforcer was presented, regardless of whether the conditioned response could be seen (Figure 8.1).

This approach came to be known as **neobehaviorism:** it retains behaviorism's emphasis on overt behavior as the only measure of a psychological explanation's accuracy. Neobehaviorism differs from behaviorism in allowing the postulation of unobservable events at a *theoretical* level, provided that the theory leads to testable predictions about overt behavior.

Conditioned responses as expectations. At this point you might fairly be wondering how assuming the existence of invisible conditioned responses can allow neobehaviorism to account for phenomena such as learning without responding. In a series of ingenious papers, Hull (1943, 1952) showed how his approach could do exactly that, accounting for a wide range of phenomena that, on the surface, provided seemingly irrefutable evidence against S–R theory. The heart of his new theory was the assumption we have just outlined, that any situation in which a reinforcer is presented will result in the conditioning of covert responses to the stimuli present.[1] He argued that these conditioned responses could bear much of the explanatory burden that cognitive theories assigned to expectations.

To see how this can be done, we will examine how Hull's theory can be used to explain the frustration effect, which we discussed in Section 7.4. In the

---

[1] Hull further assumed that these conditioned responses would produce proprioceptive feedback in the same way as any other response. If food is presented, for example, he argued that this could result in the conditioning of responses such as chewing, and that these covert chewing movements would produce proprioceptive stimuli. Hull called the conditioned response a *fractional, anticipatory goal response*, and he used the symbols r_g-s_g to represent the conditioned response and the proprioceptive stimulus that it produced. These proprioceptive stimuli can be associated with reinforced responses that follow, and these hypothetical associations allow Hull's theory to account for many phenomena that, when first discovered, seemed to strongly support the existence of expectations. (For examples, see Moltz, 1957; Amsel, 1994.)

initial demonstration of this phenomenon, Amsel and Roussel (1952) trained rats in a double alley in which the rats ran down one alley to a goal box and then into a second alley leading to a second goal box. During the training phase, both goal boxes contained food, but in the test phase food was sometimes omitted in the first goal box. The rats ran down the second alley much faster on trials when they did not receive food in the first goal box.

A simple cognitive explanation of this frustration effect is that during the training trials the rats learned to expect food in both goal boxes. When food was omitted in the first goal box, the absence of the expected reward produced frustration, and this emotional state led to more vigorous running down the second alley.

Amsel (1962) proposed an alternative explanation along Hullian lines, with conditioned responses taking the place of expectations. According to his analysis, when food was presented during training, any unconditioned response elicited by food would have been conditioned to the goal boxes. When the rats entered the goal boxes during the test phase, therefore, the goal box cues would have elicited this conditioned response. When this conditioned food response was not followed by food, Amsel proposed that this would induce a motivational state of frustration, which in turn would energize ongoing behavior. (One of the core assumptions of Hull's theory was that motives act to increase the vigor of all behavior—when an animal is hungry, for example, this will lead to an intensification of whatever behavior it engages in.)

The two explanations we have considered have very substantial similarities. Both assume that the training phase results in the learning of an internal response (either an expectation or a conditioned response), and both assume that when this internal response is not followed by food, the result is a state of frustration that then energizes ongoing behavior. The Hullian interpretation, however, avoids using the term expectation to describe this internal response, on the grounds that this term implies a conscious state of awareness about what events are about to occur, and that there is no way to know whether rats are really experiencing such conscious thoughts.

Some Masochistic Rats

The fact that S–R theory can account for phenomena such as the frustration effect does not necessarily mean that its explanation is correct: As we have just seen, a cognitive analysis can also explain this behavior. When two theories can account for existing evidence, we need to invoke a more demanding criterion to separate them: Which one is better at correctly predicting new phenomena? S–R researchers have tested a number of S–R theory predictions; we will examine a test of one of the most remarkable (and thoroughly counterintuitive) of these predictions.

Fowler and Miller (1963) reported a study in which rats were once again trained to run down a straight alley to a goal box containing food. As soon as the subjects reached the food, however, they were given a brief electric shock before being allowed to consume it. For some subjects, the shock was delivered to their hind paws; for others, it was delivered to their forepaws; control subjects received no shock at all. From a cognitive perspective, we would expect the rats in both of the shock conditions to run down the alley more slowly than the controls: If you know you're going to receive a painful shock as soon as you reach your goal, your enthusiasm for getting there is likely to be diminished.

Up to a point, an S–R analysis points to the same conclusion: Thorndike's Law of Effect says that punishment will weaken an S–R association, just as reinforcement will strengthen it. According to Hull's revision of S–R theory, however, in predicting the effects of shock we also need to take into account the conditioned responses it elicits, and these responses would be very different for shocks delivered to the forepaws and the hind paws. Specifically, whereas shocks to the hind paws elicit a tendency to jump forward, thus moving away from the source of the shock, shocks to the forepaws elicit a tendency to recoil. Rats in the forepaw group would thus move backward when shocked in the goal, and this unconditioned response would become conditioned to the goal box cues, and, because the entire apparatus is made of the same material and painted the same color, this conditioned response would then generalize to the rest of the alley. When returned to the apparatus for subsequent trials, therefore, the alley cues would elicit a tendency to move backward, which would interfere with the reinforced response of running. Rats in the hind paw group, on the other hand, would jump forward when shocked, so generalization of this response to the start box should result in an increase in the speed of running. Hull's version of S–R theory thus leads to the curious prediction that under some circumstances punishment should actually strengthen the punished response!

This prediction was supported: Rats in the hind paw group actually ran faster to reach the goal box than did subjects that had not been shocked at all (Figure 8.2). Furthermore, rats that received a 75-volt shock to their hind paws ran faster than those that received only a 60-volt shock, exactly as if they liked being shocked and couldn't wait to obtain it. From the standpoint of a cognitive analysis, this result is quite bizarre: If rats think ahead to what is going to happen in the goal box, surely those expecting a shock should run more slowly. But these results are exactly what an S–R analysis would lead us to expect. Or, to be more precise, this is *one* of the predictions made by S–R theory. As noted previously, shock in the goal box should have two effects in the hind paw group: punishing the preceding response of running, but also eliciting this behavior as an unconditioned response. It is difficult to predict in advance which of these effects will be stronger. What is noteworthy is that an S–R analysis can predict that shock will increase running, whereas a cognitive analysis cannot. Thus, although Hull's modification of S–R theory is in many ways counterintuitive—it denies that a rat running down an alley knows why it is doing so, and instead insists on describing its behavior in terms of habits elicited automatically by the

FIGURE 8.2   Mean speeds of rats running down an alley to a goal box containing food. When the rats reached the goal box, they received either a shock to the forepaws, a shock to the hind paws, or no shock, depending on the group to which they belonged. (Adapted from Fowler & Miller, 1963)

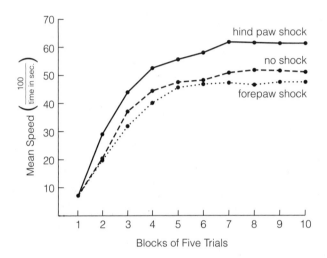

environment—in at least some situations animals appear to behave in just the simpleminded way that Hull's theory predicts.

8.3 TOLMAN'S EXPECTATIONS

Hull's neobehaviorist approach represented a major liberalization of S–R theory, as for the first time the existence (and importance) of covert processes inside the organism was formally acknowledged. The notion that these internal processes involved nothing more than simple associations, however, was still totally unacceptable to cognitive theorists such as Edward C. Tolman.

Tolman's Theory

Tolman, like Hull, was a behaviorist. He believed that introspection was an unreliable guide to mental processes, and thus that psychology needed to use visible behavior as the data for testing any theory. Also like Hull, however, he was prepared to speculate about processes that might occur between the reception of a stimulus and the performance of a response, provided that any theory about these internal processes led to testable predictions about behavior. Both men thus accepted the use of intervening variables to explain behavior:

$$S \rightarrow [X] \rightarrow R$$

Indeed, Tolman actually devised this approach.

The two theorists differed sharply, however, in their beliefs about the nature of these internal processes. Whereas Hull believed that these internal processes were basically associative in nature, Tolman felt that this approach failed to capture the purposive nature of behavior. When a trained rat ran down a maze, he suggested, it was not simply responding to stimuli blindly and automatically but, instead, was engaged in a purposeful effort to reach the goal box and obtain food. Comparing his views with those of Hull, he wrote,

> We agree with the other school that the rat in running a maze is exposed to stimuli and is finally led as a result of these stimuli to the responses which actually occur. We feel, however, that the intervening brain processes are more complicated [and] more autonomous than do the stimulus-response psychologists.
>
> (Tolman, 1948, p. 192)

To test the competing interpretations, Tolman and his students at the University of California at Berkeley carried out a number of experiments to test the two theories' predictions. We will focus here on two, involving what Tolman called docility and disruption.

Docility. **Docility** was Tolman's term for flexibility of behavior in trying to reach a goal. Suppose, for example, that a rat is reinforced for running down an alley. If all it has learned is an S–R association, then we might expect it to repeat mechanically whatever movement was reinforced on the first trial on all subsequent trials. If it has learned an expectation that food is in the goal box, however, then we might expect it to respond flexibly by selecting whatever movements will get it to the goal most efficiently.

One example of docility comes from an experiment by Macfarlane (1930). In the first phase, rats were trained to run through a partially flooded complex maze to reach a goal box containing food. Then, after the correct sequence of left and right turns had been well learned, the water level of the maze was increased so that running was no longer possible. If the rats had only learned a particular set of muscular movements during training, they should no longer have been able to find the correct path to the goal because with the maze flooded these particular movements were no longer possible. In fact, Macfarlane found that his rats simply swam down the correct paths instead of running, without any errors. To Tolman, these results indicated that during training the rats had learned not a particular set of movements, but rather a general expectation that food was available in the goal box, and they were flexibly choosing whatever movements would be most effective in getting them there.

Disruption. A second prediction of Tolman's expectancy theory was that behavior would be disturbed if an expectation was not met. Perhaps the most striking evidence of **disruption** comes from an experiment by Tinklepaugh (1928) in which monkeys were trained to reach under one of two cups to retrieve a reward that they had earlier seen the experimenter place there. On some trials, the reward was a banana; on others, it was a piece of lettuce—a food that monkeys consider less desirable but will normally eat readily. On special test trials, after baiting the cup with a banana, Tinklepaugh would reach under the cup while the monkey wasn't looking and replace the banana with lettuce. Tinklepaugh reports the monkey's typical reaction when he told it to "come get the food":

> She jumps down from the chair, rushes to the proper container and picks it up. She extends her hand to seize the food. But her hand drops to the floor without touching it. She looks at the lettuce but (unless very hungry) does not touch it. She looks around the cup and behind the board. She stands up and looks under and around her. She picks the cup up and examines it thoroughly inside and out. She has on occasion turned toward observers present in the room and shrieked at them in apparent anger. After several seconds spent searching, she gives a glance towards the other cup, which she has been taught not to look into, and then walks off to a nearby window. The lettuce is left untouched on the floor.
> (Tinklepaugh, 1928, p. 224)

Observations of this kind might not prove that the monkey expected a banana, but it is difficult to think of another explanation.

Reinforcer Devaluation

One possible reaction to the Tinklepaugh experiment by an S–R theorist might be to concede that monkeys form expectations but to argue that "lower" species such as rats learn only associations. Recent evidence, however, suggests that even this fallback position might not be tenable. Convincing evidence that rats, too, form expectations comes from experiments using a reinforcer-devaluation procedure very similar to that used in studies of classical conditioning (Chapter 4). The basic procedure is to train a rat to press a bar to obtain food and then to make the food aversive by pairing it with an aversive stimulus. If the rat had learned an S–R association during training, subsequent devaluation of the reinforcer should have no effect: The stimuli of the Skinner box, for example, should still automatically elicit bar-pressing. If the rat had learned to expect food, however, then when this food became unattractive, the rat should no longer respond to obtain it.

One of the first experiments to use this procedure was reported by Adams and Dickinson (1981), but we will focus on a more sophisticated variant developed by

FIGURE 8.3   Performance during extinction of a response that previously produced sucrose, following the conditioning of an aversion to either sucrose or food pellets. (Adapted from Colwill & Rescorla, 1985)

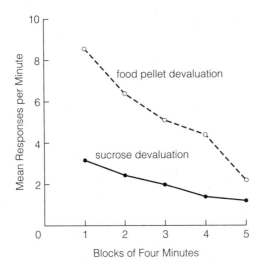

Colwill and Rescorla (1985). In the first phase, Colwill and Rescorla trained rats to make two responses (pressing a lever and pulling a chain) to obtain two different reinforcers (sucrose or food pellets). For example, one group learned to press a bar to obtain sucrose and to pull a chain to obtain food pellets:

$$R_{lever} \rightarrow Sucrose$$

$$R_{chain} \rightarrow Food\ pellets$$

One of these reinforcers was then paired with a mild dose of a toxin, lithium chloride (LiCl), until the rats would no longer consume it. There were thus two main groups: one in which sucrose was devalued, and a second in which food pellets were devalued:

Devaluation: $Sucrose \rightarrow LiCl$ **or** $Food\ pellets \rightarrow LiCl$

Finally, the rats were again allowed access to the lever and chain, and responding was measured during an extinction test in which neither was reinforced.

Figure 8.3 shows the extinction data for responses that had previously been reinforced with sucrose. Because no responses were reinforced during the extinction test, there was a significant decrease in responding as testing progressed. More important, performance depended on which reinforcer had been associated with illness. Rats for whom sucrose had been devalued responded significantly less to obtain sucrose than did rats for whom food pellets had been devalued. The almost inescapable implication is that the rats knew which reinforcer each response produced, so that when sucrose was devalued they ceased to make the response that produced it. (See also Colwill & Motzkin, 1994.)

8.4 HABITS AND EXPECTATIONS

In reviewing the conflict between S–R and cognitive theories, we have seen persuasive evidence for both views. S–R theorists, for example, could point to the gradual learning that occurred with Thorndike's cats, and to the behavior of the rats in Fowler and Miller's experiment, in which shock increased the rats' running to get to the goal box, a behavior that hardly seemed to reflect a keen awareness of consequences. On the other hand, the flexibility of behavior in Macfarlane's rat-swimming experiment and the striking reactions of Tinklepaugh's monkeys provided equally strong support for a cognitive account. We could continue to cite evidence supporting each side. (For persuasive evidence supporting an S–R analysis, see Powell & Perkins, 1957; Morgan, 1974. Equally impressive support for a cognitive interpretation is available in Hulse, Fowler, & Honig, 1978; Premack & Woodruff, 1978.) But the fundamental dilemma would remain the same: There is a considerable body of evidence on both sides, making it very difficult to decide which is correct. Why should this be so? Why, after decades of effort and many hundreds of experiments, is it still so difficult to say which theory is right?

Why Was the Issue So Difficult to Resolve?

Theoretical convergence.   One reason the debate was so difficult to resolve is that, over time, the assumptions of the two camps became increasingly similar, making it harder and harder to separate them experimentally. At first, the gulf between them was very wide: S–R theorists refused to allow any internal processes, and cognitive theorists concentrated on them to the exclusion of virtually everything else. As experimental evidence accumulated, however, there was a gradual convergence of the two positions, as theorists on both sides adjusted their views to accommodate the new evidence. The evidence for phenomena such as learning without responding led Hull to accept the importance of internal states, and the demonstrated inadequacies of introspection led Tolman to accept the behaviorist position that these internal states could not be observed directly. Both sides, therefore, agreed that statements about internal states must be regarded as theoretical hypotheses, and the validity of these hypotheses must be judged not by introspection but by the accuracy of their predictions.

The specific content of the proposed theories certainly sounded very different, but, in practice, Hull's conditioned responses served many of the anticipatory functions of an expectation, occurring in the same sort of situations and playing a similar function in directing behavior. In our analysis of the frustration effect, for example, we saw that both theories assumed that training would result in the learning of an internal response that would occur in the alley (an expectation or a conditioned response), and that if this learned response was not followed by food, the result would be frustration. The theories gave this response different names, but they end up making very similar predictions. These similarities do not mean that the two accounts were identical in all respects; they were not. But the similarities do help to explain why psychologists have had such difficulty devising experiments that would clearly separate them.

Theoretical ambiguity.   One problem in evaluating the claims of S–R and cognitive theory, then, is that the two theories are far more similar structurally than the differences in their terminology might suggest. A second, even more serious obstacle has been the vagueness with which each theory was formulated. As we have seen, a crucial requirement for testing any theory involving an intervening variable X is that this variable be clearly and unambiguously tied to antecedent stimuli (S) and consequent responses (R), so that the behavior to be expected in any situation can be clearly predicted:

$$S \rightarrow [X] \rightarrow R$$

Unfortunately, neither Hull nor Tolman ever really succeeded in meeting this criterion. Although Tolman certainly intended to provide clear definitions of what he meant by an expectation, in practice his definitions often turned out to be frustratingly vague. Consider again, for example, McNamara, Long, and Wike's experiment in which one group of rats was pushed through a maze in a basket while a second group was allowed to walk through normally. One possible prediction based on a cognitive analysis was that the subjects in the cart group would learn as well as the controls because both groups would have the same number of reinforced and nonreinforced trials, and thus an equal opportunity to learn which goal box contained food. On the other hand, cognitive theorists could have predicted with equal plausibility that these rats would learn nothing about which side was correct, but only that if they sat quietly in the basket they would sometimes be rewarded with food! An expectation analysis simply doesn't tell us which outcome to expect: The crucial link between S and X is not specified, so we don't know which of the possible expectations would actually be learned in a given situation.

A similar ambiguity prevails at the link between a subject's expectation and its overt behavior. Tolman tells us that if an expectancy is not met, we should expect some kind of disruption—but *what* disruption? If a monkey finds a lettuce leaf instead of an expected banana, will it shriek and throw the lettuce away, or merely gaze at the experimenter mournfully and eat the lettuce anyway? To simply say that subjects learn expectations does not go very far toward helping us to predict what effect a particular expectation will have on behavior. This problem was neatly captured in a famous gibe by Guthrie (1952), who accused Tolman of leaving his subjects "buried in thought" at the choice point.

In Tolman's theorizing, then, an expectation is not clearly tied either to the environmental conditions that produce it or to the behavior that follows, so that any predictions were much more the products of Tolman's intuitions—"Now what would I do if I were in that situation?"—than of any clearly stated set of rules. If cognitive theorizing was plagued by vagueness, however, S–R theory had its own share of ambiguity. As we have already seen, the main virtue in treating internal events as if they are covert muscle twitches is that their occurrence can then be predicted objectively using the same laws of behavior known to govern overt responses. But what if all these rules are not known? Or if those principles that are known sometimes predict opposite effects? Unless all the laws of overt behavior are known, we cannot hope to predict covert behavior unambiguously, and the sad truth is that these laws are not fully known even in outline form, much less in the quantitative detail required to predict what will happen when different principles conflict. In Fowler and Miller's punishment experiment, for example, we saw that an S–R analysis could equally predict faster or slower running in subjects shocked on their hind legs; equally ambiguous predictions can be derived in other cases. (See, for example, Gleitman, Nachmias, & Neisser, 1954.) On the surface, S–R theory might appear considerably more precise and objective than cognitive theory, but in practice its predictions often depend just as much on theorists' intuitions as do the predictions derived from cognitive theories. (For a more detailed—and devastating—critique of Hullian theory along these lines, see Koch, 1954.)

The Two-Level Hypothesis

Given the similarity of the two theories, and the ambiguity with which each was formulated, it is perhaps less surprising that psychologists have had so much difficulty determining which one is right. There is, however, still a third possible explanation that, if correct, would readily account for the difficulty in establishing which theory is correct: Perhaps they both are.

Throughout this chapter we have implicitly assumed that there could only be one kind of learning, but there is no logical reason why there could not be two. Perhaps, as we suggested in our analysis of classical conditioning, a relatively primitive associative system evolved first, but with the development of the neocortex a more sophisticated system evolved that allowed the anticipation of consequences. Each system could have important advantages, with the associative system allowing rapid and automatic responses in simple or dangerous situations, and the cognitive system allowing sophisticated planning in situations in which time permits consideration of alternative plans of actions and their consequences. Whatever their precise functions, the existence of the two systems would obviously explain why behavior appears so flexible and intentional in some situations, yet so rigid and mechanical in others.

Indeed, there is evidence that the two processes not only might coexist in the same organism but, in some cases, might even influence the same behavior simultaneously. In describing the results of the Colwill and Rescorla experiment, we noted that pairing of sucrose with illness resulted in a significant decrease in responding for sucrose. If you look back at Figure 8.3, however, you will see that although responding in the sucrose-devaluation group declined substantially, the rats in this group still did respond initially. Thus, despite the fact that the food had become highly aversive, to the point where the rats would not eat it, they nevertheless responded to obtain it; in some of the other experiments reported by Colwill and Rescorla (1986), this responding was quite substantial. One plausible explanation is that an S–R association was formed during training as well as an expectation, so that the experimental cues continued to automatically elicit responding, even though at another level the rats knew that they did not want the food for which they were responding. (See also Morgan, 1974.)

Whether or not associations and expectations can influence performance simultaneously, the hypothesis that animals can learn both has a number of attractions—not the least of which is that it would allow us to account for all the conflicting evidence on S–R versus cognitive learning.

Habits and Expectations in Human Behavior

One way of stating the hypothesis we have been considering is that knowledge can be stored in the brain in two distinct forms, forms that perhaps have developed independently in the course of evolution. The first is as an S–R habit, in which the occurrence of a stimulus automatically elicits a response without any anticipation of the consequences. In the other, knowledge is stored in the form of an expectation that can be recalled as needed to plan behavior. All the evidence we have considered so far for this distinction comes from animals, but research on human learning and memory has suggested similar distinctions.

Controlled versus automatic processing. One simple example suggesting the role of both habits and expectations in human behavior is the learning of motor skills such as driving a car. At first, learners have to pay close attention to what they are doing, frantically monitoring every wheel movement and trying to anticipate what will have to be done next. With practice, however, these movements become increasingly smooth and automatic, until eventually the learner can drive without thinking about it and can even carry on a conversation at the same time.

Similar automation occurs in perceptual learning. Suppose, for example, that you were presented with a sheet of paper containing a long list of randomly chosen letters, and your task was to identify each instance of the letter A. Research by Schneider and Shiffrin (1977) using a related (though more demanding) task suggests that you would respond relatively slowly at first, and that you would have to concentrate in a way that would leave you little time to carry out other tasks simultaneously. With practice, however, you would improve substantially, until eventually you could carry out the task automatically, without any interference with your performance on simultaneous tasks. (For a particularly dramatic demonstration along these lines, see Hirst, Spelke, Reaves, Caharack, & Neisser, 1980.)

To explain perceptual and motor learning of this kind, Shiffrin and Schneider (1977) have proposed that there are two fundamentally different kinds of cognitive processes in the brain. **Controlled processes** correspond roughly to what we normally mean by attention: largely conscious processes of limited capacity, so that only one task can be carried out at a time. In **automatic processes,** on the other hand, a stimulus elicits a response, or one set of neurons activates another set, automatically, meaning that the occurrence of the first almost invariably activates the second. Automatic processes presumably do not require attention, so a very large number of automatic processes can occur simultaneously without interfering with one another or with tasks that require controlled processing. In the letter-identification task, subjects initially must use controlled processes to identify the letter A; with sufficient practice, strong connections or associations are formed between the perceptual and response units involved (that is, between seeing the letter A and announcing it). When these connections become sufficiently strong, the process occurs automatically, at great speed and without conscious attention.

The Shiffrin and Schneider model emphasizes the processes involved, but the end result is that in some situations a stimulus will elicit a response automatically, whereas in others responding will be slower and will require conscious attention. This view clearly has strong similarities to the distinction in animal learning between automatic S–R habits and cognitive expectations.

Procedural versus declarative memories. Further evidence that knowledge might be stored within the brain in two different forms has come from studies of amnesia. Individuals who suffer certain forms of brain damage develop an *anterograde amnesia,* which means that they can remember experiences predating their injury but cannot form new memories. One example comes from the most intensively studied patient with this condition, identified in the literature as H. M. He had had an operation on his brain to treat severe epilepsy, but the removal of some of his brain tissue had the unfortunate result of impairing his ability to form new memories. If he was tested by a psychologist all morning, for example, when the psychologist returned for the afternoon session, H. M. would not recognize him and would not remember the morning session. In one poignant incident, he was told that his uncle had died and experienced intense grief, but he soon forgot this experience and thereafter often asked when his uncle would come to visit. Each time he was told that his uncle was dead his reaction was one of surprise, and his grief as intense as on the first occasion (Milner, 1966).

Similarly, when H. M. was given daily training on a mirror drawing task, in which he had to trace over a drawing that he could see only through a mirror, he was unable to remember each day ever having performed the task previously. The crucial point in the present context, however, is that, despite having no memory of ever performing the task before, H. M.'s performance improved significantly over days (Milner, 1962). As he worked on the drawing task, he seemed to be forming associations between the visual cues from the mirror and the correct tracing movement, and the strengthening of these associations over days allowed him to improve.

Evidence of this kind has suggested to many cognitive theorists that experience might be stored within the brain in two different forms, referred to by different theorists as *procedural* versus *declarative*, or *implicit* versus *explicit*. (For a review, see Squire, 1987.) The various theories are not identical, but their common theme is that some aspects of experience are coded in a procedural or habitual form, in which one event activates another automatically, without conscious awareness, whereas other events are stored in a more autobiographical form to which subjects can gain conscious access. Thus, H. M. retained the ability to form **procedural memories,** so that experience with the mirror drawing task strengthened the associations necessary for perceptual-motor coordination; as a result of his injury, though, he could no longer form (or perhaps retrieve) **declarative memories,** and thus could not recollect or "declare" the experiences that produced this improvement. Again, this distinction between unconscious habits and conscious recollections bears obvious similarities to the distinction between S–R habits, in which stimuli elicit responses automatically, and expectations that allow us to anticipate the consequences of our actions.

It is by no means certain that the various distinctions we have been discussing—S–R associations versus expectations, controlled versus automatic processing, procedural versus declarative memories—all refer to the same events. The fact that theorists from so many different areas of investigation have converged on similar distinctions, however, does encourage the belief that they might be tapping some fundamental property of the brain's operations, and to this extent supports the hypothesis that associative learning can take two forms: automatic habits and expectations.

Conclusions

The view that learning can take two fundamentally different forms has become increasingly popular in recent years (for example, Bolles, 1972; Mackintosh &

Dickinson, 1979; Rescorla, 1987). After decades of theoretical warfare, it is almost as if a truce has been declared, with both sides agreeing that the other had a good case after all, and everyone getting together for drinks and a barbecue.

This emerging consensus is highly gratifying. It suggests that years of theoretical battles have not been in vain, and it also clarifies why the war was so hard for each side to win. Not all of the differences, however, have disappeared. Although there is now impressive agreement about fundamental concepts, shadings of the earlier split still exist, and this is reflected in continuing differences in terminology. For example, Rescorla (1987), who describes himself as an "unreconstructed associationist," still prefers to use the language of associations in describing learning: Instead of talking of *expectations*, he uses the term *response–reinforcer* or *response–outcome* (R–O) association. In some respects, the distinction is purely linguistic, because what Rescorla means by a response–outcome association seems almost identical to what Tolman meant by an expectation—a link between a response and an outcome that allows subjects to anticipate what will occur. A case can be made, however, that the choice of terms to describe this unit, whether associative or cognitive, has potentially important implications.

The advantage of the term *association* is that its meaning is more clearly defined: Two events are associated when one elicits or activates the other. Thus, the term avoids some of the excess (and ambiguous) theoretical baggage that the term expectation brings with it from its use in everyday discourse. On the other hand, for precisely this reason the term *expectation* might be preferable, because its richer (albeit ambiguous) meanings allow it to explain behavior that a strictly associative account has considerable difficulty with. The searching behavior of Tinklepaugh's monkeys is much easier to understand if we assume that they had learned to expect a banana under the cup, rather than simply forming a response–banana association.

The real problem here is that both interpretations need to be spelled out more clearly. If we say that animals learn expectations, we need to define these clearly enough so that we can predict exactly what behaviors a frustrated monkey will exhibit. Similarly, if we say that a monkey has learned an R–O association, we need to specify how this association will be translated into behavior.

We will return to this issue in later chapters. For the moment, however, let us not disturb the prevailing mood of peace with calls to further battle; in most respects, associative and cognitive theorists have converged on remarkably similar accounts of learning.

8.5 COMPLEX LEARNING

The expectations we have considered so far in this chapter have been relatively simple: "Food is available in the goal box at the end of this alley"; "If I press this lever, I will obtain a food pellet." Tolman (1948), however, suggested that expectations could vary in their complexity, and in concluding this chapter we will look at some of the evidence for more complex forms of learning. We will look at evidence that when animals obtain food, they might store information on exactly where in their environment the food was obtained (space), the time of day (time), and even the number of food pellets involved (number).

Space

In a paper contrasting his own position on learning with that of Hull, Tolman (1948) introduced the idea of a cognitive map. He compared the brain to a central control room and suggested that when a rat traveled through a maze:

> . . . incoming impulses are usually worked over and elaborated in the central control room into a tentative, cognitive-like map of the environment. And it is this tentative map, indicating routes and paths and environmental relationships, which finally determines what responses, if any, the animal will finally release.
> (Tolman, 1948, p. 192)

The suggestion that rats could form **cognitive maps** of their environment, charting areas of importance to them and possible paths between them, was met with considerable skepticism, and the concept of a cognitive map gradually faded from view. It was revived in an influential book by O'Keefe and Nadel (1978), and since then there has been a substantial increase in research to determine whether animals are really capable of forming cognitive maps.

Cognitive maps. We will introduce this research with a study of Clark's nutcrackers, birds that appear to have quite remarkable memories for locations in their environment. They live in alpine regions where little or no food is available in the long winters, so they harvest conifer seeds in the autumn and store them in underground caches. Scientists have estimated that, since each cache contains an average of only four seeds, a bird needs to recover a minimum of 2500 caches each winter if it is to survive. One explanation for the birds' success is that they actually remember 2500 different locations—a phenomenal memory load. A simpler and perhaps more plausible alternative is that the birds search for distinguishing cues—for example, signs of disturbance in the soil—to identify where seeds have been hidden.

To test these hypotheses, Vander Wall (1982) allowed two Clark's nutcrackers to hide seeds in a fenced-in enclosure that contained a soil and gravel floor and a number of landmarks such as rocks, shrubs, and logs. Several days later, he released these birds into the enclosure, along with two other birds that had not hidden seeds, releasing them one at a time to search for the hidden caches. If the birds relied solely on local visual or olfactory cues to identify

FIGURE 8.4   Overhead view of the caching enclosure used by Vander Wall. The solid lines show the layout at the time the birds buried their food; the broken lines show the new positions of the objects and the right perimeter during the test trial. (Based on Vander Wall, 1982)

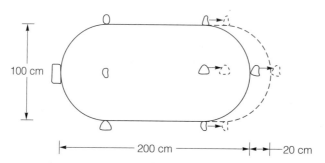

caches, all four birds should have been equally successful in discovering the caches, but this was not the case. When the noncaching birds were released into the enclosure, they hopped along the surface and occasionally probed it with their beaks, but only about 10% of these probes uncovered a cache. In contrast, the birds that had hidden the seeds flew directly to the cache sites and obtained food on 70% of their probes. Moreover, each of these birds recovered almost exclusively their own caches: 52 of the 55 recoveries made by one bird were of its own caches, as were all 44 of the other bird's recoveries. The birds clearly were not searching at random; they remembered where they had hidden their seeds and flew directly to those sites.

To explore what cues the birds were using to guide their performance, Vander Wall covered the floor with a plastic sheet, leaving only a 1 × 2 meter oval area exposed, and provided eight large objects as landmarks, four in the left quadrant and four in the right quadrant (Figure 8.4). After the birds had hidden their seeds, the experimenter moved the four objects in the right area 20 centimeters further to the right. If the birds were using these objects as landmarks to guide their search, their probes in the right quadrant should be displaced 20 centimeters to the right, and this was precisely the result obtained: Probes in the left side of the enclosure occurred within an average of 1.3 centimeters of the caches, whereas those in the right side were displaced an average of 20.5 centimeters to the right. For objects located midway between the stable and shifted landmarks, moreover, the average displacement was 11 centimeters to the right; this suggested that the birds were using at least two objects, one to the left and one to the right, to guide their search, so that when these objects provided conflicting information, the birds split the difference between them. These results indicate that Clark's nutcrackers do form some sort of cognitive map of their environment, and these maps might contain entries for up to 2500 items—perhaps many more if landmarks are included. (See also Bednekoff, Balda, Kamil, & Arla, 1997.)

FIGURE 8.5   Overhead view of the Tolman and Honzik rat maze. (Tolman & Honzik, 1930b)

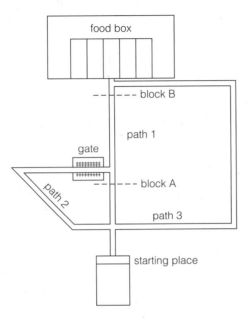

Spatial reasoning. A number of experiments suggest that animals not only form maps, but can use them to intelligently plan optimal routes to their destinations. In one of the first demonstrations of this kind of spatial reasoning, Tolman and Honzik (1930a) trained rats in the maze illustrated in Figure 8.5. There were three possible paths from the start box to the goal box containing food, with path 1 being the shortest and path 3 the longest. At first, the rats were allowed to enter any path. Once they had acquired a preference for path 1, Tolman and Honzik blocked path 1 at point A. When the rats found that they could not proceed along path 1, they chose the next shortest path, path 2, on 91% of the test trials.

This result was readily explicable in terms of S–R theory as well as Tolman's cognitive map hypothesis. According to S–R theory, the sooner reinforcement is delivered following a response, the more effective it is in strengthening behavior. Because path 2 was shorter than path 3, entry into path 2 was followed by reinforcement more quickly, so that this response would have been strengthened more. According to Tolman, on the other hand, the rats chose path 2 because they had formed a cognitive map of the maze's layout and realized that path 2 was the shortest available path to the goal.

To separate these two explanations, Tolman and Honzik simply moved the block on path 1 from point A to point B. According to S–R theory, when the rats found that they could not get through path 1 and returned to the choice point, they should have made the next strongest response; that is, they should choose path 2. If the rats had a cognitive map, on the other hand, they would realize that the block at B also blocked access to the goal via path 2, and thus should now choose path 3, even though it was the longest path during training. Rather remarkably, this is exactly what the rats did: 93% of the rats chose path 3 on the first test trial. (See also Menzel, 1978; Brown, Rish, Von Culin, & Edberg, 1993.)

These experiments, and others like them, suggest that animals can learn a great deal about the locations of objects in their environment. When a rat runs through a maze, it might not be simply memorizing a series of left and right turns, but forming a detailed picture of the maze's layout. The complexity of these maps, and the cognitive processes involved in forming them, are still being investigated, but recent research suggests an impressive degree of sophistication (Suzuki, Augerinos, & Black, 1980; Benhamou & Poucet, 1995; Brown, & Terrinoni, 1996; Greene & Cook, 1997).

Time

It is important for an animal to know where food is located in its environment, because some locations are usually much more likely to contain food than others. Predators like lions, for example, need to know where prey such as antelope are likely to be found, and seed-eating birds need to know where in their territories their favored seeds are situated. Similarly, for many species it is also important to know *when* food will be available. Bees, for example, collect pollen from flowers to produce nectar, and the time at which pollen is most likely to be available varies for different flowers. (See Gallistel, 1989.) It would thus be very helpful for a bee if it had some sort of internal clock to tell it the time of day, so that it could learn to visit each flower at the optimal time.

Circadian timing. There is now considerable evidence that many animals have just the kind of 24-hour clock that is required. It is easy, for example, to demonstrate bee's time sensitivity in the laboratory by making a food source such as honey available in a dish at, say, 2:00 P.M. each day; bees will quickly learn to visit the dish at almost exactly this time. This, however, does not necessarily prove that the bee is capable of measuring time—it could be relying on an external cue such as the position of the sun in the sky to know when to visit the feeding site. To determine which explanation was right, Renner (1960) designed a simple but clever experiment. He trained a colony of bees in Paris to obtain food from a feeder at a particular time. After they had mastered this task, and emerged from their hives only at the appointed hour, he flew the hive to New York. If their behavior was controlled by external cues such as light, then they should have emerged at the same local time as before—if trained to feed at 3:00 P.M. in Paris, they should have emerged from their hive at 3:00 P.M. in

FIGURE 8.6   Responding during Roberts' (1981) peak procedure. The figure shows the rate of responding at different times after the onset of a signal. The curve on the left shows responding to a signal previously associated with the delivery of food after 20 seconds; the curve on the right is for a signal previously associated with a delay interval of 40 seconds. The plotted data was obtained after 10 training sessions. (Adapted from Roberts, 1981)

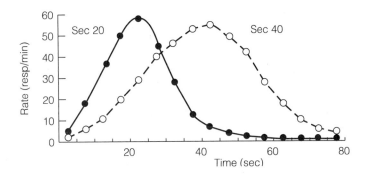

New York. Suppose, however, that the bees truly possessed an internal clock, and had learned to feed when their clock read 3:00 P.M. Because of the time difference between Paris and New York, it is 10:00 A.M. in New York when it is 3:00 P.M. in Paris, and so the bees should have emerged at 10:00 A.M., New York time. This is precisely what Renner found, suggesting that bees do have some sort of internal clock that allows them to measure the passage of time. This ability to time events on a 24-hour cycle, so that you can respond at the same time each day, is known as *circadian timing* (from the Latin *circa,* meaning about, and *diem,* meaning day).

Interval timing. In addition to having 24-hour clocks that indicate time of day, more recent evidence suggests that animals might possess something resembling a stopwatch, which allows them to time shorter intervals between events. In a particularly clear demonstration of this phenomenon, Roberts (1981) trained rats to press a bar to obtain food on a discrete-trials version of a fixed interval (FI) schedule. Some trials began with the illumination of a light, and on these trials he reinforced the first response to occur 20 seconds after the light's onset. On other trials he would present a noise, and on these noise trials food was made available after 40 seconds. To find out what the rats had learned about the two time intervals, Roberts occasionally presented probe trials during which food was not presented, and the light or tone remained on for a minimum of 80 seconds.

Figure 8.6 shows responding on these probe trials. When the light was presented, the rats gradually increased their rate of response following the light's onset, with responding reaching a peak at 22 seconds, almost exactly the time at which reinforcement had occurred during this stimulus. (With any FI schedule, reinforcement usually occurs somewhat after the scheduled time because subjects do not respond every second.) Similarly, when the noise was presented, peak responding occurred at 41 seconds. Roberts called this method of testing the *peak procedure*, and his results show that rats can time short intervals with great accuracy.

Pursuing our stopwatch analogy, most commercial stopwatches allow you to temporarily halt the stopwatch and then resume timing when you are ready. A second experiment by Roberts suggests that rats can pause in the middle of timing an event in exactly the same way. In this study, he trained rats to obtain food after 40 seconds in the presence of a light. On the probe trials, he presented the light for 80 seconds without food, but he also sometimes turned off the light for 10 or 15 seconds during the trial. Suppose, for example, that the light came on for 10 seconds, was then turned off for 10 seconds, and then turned on again for the remainder of the trial. When would you expect the rats' responding to reach its peak?

If a rat's stopwatch cannot be interrupted once it starts, peak responding should occur 40 seconds after the light's initial onset. Alternatively, if the rat restarts its stopwatch whenever the light comes on, peak responding should occur 40 seconds after the light's second illumination—that is, 60 seconds into the trial. Suppose, however, that the rat uses its stopwatch to time the total period of illumination, and that it halts the clock whenever the light goes off, and then restarts it when the light returns. In this case, we should expect peak responding at around 50 seconds (40 seconds of light plus 10 seconds of dark). The latter prediction was supported, as peak responding occurred very close to 50 seconds after the trial's onset (the actual value was 53 seconds). The rats seemed to be able to start and stop their stopwatches at will.

The internal clock. In addition to a 24-hour clock, then, it appears that animals have something like a stopwatch for measuring shorter intervals. Gibbon and Church (1984) have proposed one possible model of how this internal clock works, and part of their model is illustrated in Figure 8.7. The model starts by assuming a *pacemaker*—some part of the body that generates a steady stream of pulses at regular intervals. The pulses are fed through a *switch* to an *accumulator*, which effectively counts the pulses and stores the total. Suppose, for example, that the pacemaker generates one pulse every second. If a rat is trained on an FI 40 sec schedule, and if the switch is closed when the light comes on to begin a trial, then at the end of 40 seconds there will be 40 pulses registered in the accumulator, and the rat can then associate this value with the delivery of food. On probe trials, the rat will be more likely to respond when the accumulator contains a total similar to this value (38, say, or 42) then when the total is different. And if the light is turned off during a trial, the switch is opened so that pulses no longer reach the accumulator; when the light resumes, the switch is closed again and the count resumes.

The Gibbon and Church model is much more detailed than our brief summary would suggest, and it makes some very precise predictions about timing

FIGURE 8.7   A simplified version of Gibbon and Church's (1984) model of the internal clock.

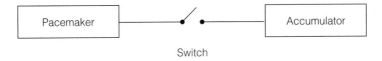

behavior. Experimental tests of these predictions have so far provided considerable support for the model in animals, and similar results have been found in tests with humans (for example, Raitkin, Gibbon, Penney, Malapani, Hinton, & Meck, 1998). Other models of timing have also been proposed (for example, Killeen, & Fetterman, 1993; Wearden & Doherty, 1995), and it is too soon to say which model is best. (See also Carr & Wilkie, 1997.) Whatever the precise mechanism of the clock eventually proves to be, clearly animals can time events with very considerable accuracy.

Number

We've seen that when animals obtain food, they might store information about where in their environment the food was located and when they obtained it. Recent evidence raises the provocative possibility that animals also remember the amount of food by counting the number of pellets or seeds, and so on.

Rosencrantz can count! Even the suggestion that animals might be able to count may seem surprising, but there is intriguing evidence that we need to take this possibility seriously. One procedure that has been used to study this issue involves presenting subjects with two sets that differ only in the number of objects or events they contain, and seeing if subjects can learn to respond differently when each is presented. Suppose, for example, that we place rats in a box containing two levers and occasionally present them with a sequence of brief tones, each lasting for one second. When the sequence contains two tones, responding on one lever is reinforced, whereas when it contains 3 tones, responding on the second lever is reinforced. Rats are able to learn such discriminations (for example, Meck, & Church, 1983; Breukelaar & Dalrymple-Alford, 1998), a result that is consistent with the notion that they can count the number of tones.

The fact that rats can discriminate two tones from three tones, however, does not necessarily mean that they count in the same way as people. For example, we cannot conclude from these results that the rats interpreted three tones as a larger quantity than two tones (Davis & Perusse, 1988). The rats might know that the two numbers differ, without assuming that one is larger than the other, just as humans know that a red apple is different from a green apple without regarding one as a larger quantity. Other evidence, however, suggests that in at least some situations animals do recognize one number of objects as being larger than another. In a recent—and quite remarkable—paper by Brannon and Terrace (1998), two rhesus monkeys, Rosencrantz and Macduff, were shown pictures containing different numbers of objects. During the training phase, four pictures were presented simultaneously, each containing either 1, 2, 3 or 4 objects. To obtain reinforcement, the monkeys had to touch the pictures in order of their numerosity—that is, they had to touch the picture containing one object first, then the picture containing two objects, and so on. After extensive training with this set of pictures, the monkeys were shown a second set of pictures, again containing 1–4 objects, and so on, through a total of 35 sets.

Both Rosencrantz and Macduff did very well during this training. On the final sets, for example, they touched the pictures in the correct sequence on more than half the trials, which was far above chance. (Had they responded to the pictures in a random sequence, they would been correct on only 5%.) The monkeys had clearly learned, but at this point it was not clear *what* they had learned. Suppose, for example, that one of the pictures contained a single circle, and another contained two triangles. The monkeys could have solved the problem on the basis of number—"Touch the picture with one object first, then the picture with two objects"—but they could also have solved the problem by using the pictures' perceptual characteristics—for example, "Touch the circle first, then the triangle." In other words, it wasn't clear if the monkeys were responding on the basis of number or some other, simpler characteristic.

To find out, Brannon and Terrace presented test trials involving new numbers of objects. They presented two new pictures on each test trial, and in order to obtain food the monkeys had to choose whichever picture contained more objects. On one test trial, for example, the monkeys might be shown one picture containing five objects and another picture containing six objects. Figure 8.8 shows two of the pairs used during testing. On half the trials, the smaller set of objects covered a larger surface area, but on the remaining trials the larger set covered a larger area. The subjects therefore could not use the size of the objects as a clue about which to select; the only clue to which picture was correct was the number of objects present.

If during training the monkeys had learned the abstract rule, "Touch the smallest number of objects first," then they should touch the picture with five objects first. (Note that to do so, they would have to be realize that the pictures contained five and six objects, and that five is smaller than six.) On the other hand, if all they had learned during training was to touch particular pictures ("Touch picture A first"), without attending to the number of objects present, then they would have no basis for deciding which of the two pictures to touch first because they had never seen them before.

FIGURE 8.8   Sample test stimuli used by Brannon and Terrace (1998). The correct stimulus, S+, contained 6 objects, and the incorrect stimulus, S–, contained 5 objects. On half the trials, (a) the total surface area of the objects in S+ was greater than in S–, while on the remaining trials (b) the surface area in S– was greater. (Adapted from Brannon & Terrace, 1998)

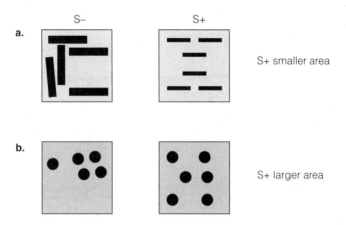

The quite remarkable result was that the monkeys responded correctly on approximately 90% of the test trials. This result suggests not only that they were capable of estimating the number of objects in a picture, and understood that some numbers are larger than others, but also that during training they had abstracted the general principle of selecting pictures in order of number. (They could have solved the problem simply by learning the specific sequence 1–2–3–4, rather than the more general principle of selecting whichever number is smallest.) Rosencrantz and Macduff's performance suggests an impressively sophisticated understanding of number.

Implications.   This evidence suggests that evolution might have endowed animals as well as humans with the capacity to estimate quantities. In nature, this would be a very useful skill, whether in coping with danger (think of a group of monkeys encountering a second group in a forest—if the intruding group is larger, a tactical retreat might be in order) or in obtaining food (where more than one area is available for exploration, searching normally should be concentrated in the area that has the highest number of visible food sources). In the course of evolution, therefore, many species might have developed an ability to estimate quantities. (See also Emmerton, Lohmann, & Niemann, 1997.)

We still need to be cautious, however, before concluding that animals form these estimates by counting. Counting, in the strictest sense, involves assigning a number to an object, then assigning a higher number to the next object, and so on. It is not yet clear whether animals estimate quantity in this way. Indeed, it is not even clear to what extent humans rely on counting in this formal sense. If you were briefly shown two photographs of herds of sheep, for example, and asked to say which herd contained more sheep, you might be able to respond almost instantly, in a time so brief as to almost certainly preclude counting in the normal sense. Thus, although it is clear that animals have some ability to estimate quantities, it is not yet clear whether they do so by counting in a formal sense. (See Roberts, 1998, for an excellent review of the evidence in this area, and Beran, Rumbaugh, & Savage-Rumbaugh, 1998, for tantalizing evidence of genuine counting in chimpanzees.) On the other hand, as Dr. Johnson, the author of the first dictionary, said two hundred years ago, in a somewhat different context:

> [It] is like a dog's walking on his hinder legs. It is not done well, but you are surprised to find it done at all.
> (Samuel Johnson, quoted in Boswell, 1791/1964, p. 463)

Summary

In summary, considerable evidence now indicates that rats engaged in a relatively simple task such as discovering which arm of a T-maze leads to food, might be doing far more than learning to turn left: They might also form a cognitive map of the maze's layout, and remember the amount of food that was present and the time at which it was obtained. Moreover, there is evidence that they might retain detailed memories of what happened on earlier visits to that location—when a rat is placed in a maze at the beginning of trial, for example, it might recall the exact sequence of rewards and nonrewards that it experienced on previous trials (for example, Capaldi, Miller, Alptekin, & Barry, 1990). A task such as discovering which arm of a T-maze might appear quite simple, but the processes that animals use in solving such problems might be remarkably complex. We will examine these processes further in subsequent chapters.

8.6 SUMMARY

When we observe a well-trained rat running down an alley to a goal box containing food, it is natural to assume that the rat is doing so because it knows that food is there and wants to obtain it. S–R theorists, however, rejected this account on two grounds:

1. We cannot know what a rat is thinking, so an explanation that refers to its expectations is untestable.

2. Behavior that seems to involve complex cognitive processes can often be explained in terms of simpler associations.

Together, these assumptions led to S–R theory—the assumption that reinforcement produces an association between environmental stimuli and the successful response. Thorndike's observations of learning in animals—its slow, erratic course and the rigidity with which a successful response was blindly repeated—provided strong initial support for this analysis.

Evidence for learning in situations in which subjects simply observed the environment, without making any active response, convinced neobehaviorists such as Clark Hull that learning could not be described solely in terms of visible behavior: We had to assume some kind of internal processes. Hull, however, continued to interpret learning in terms of simple associations; the only change was that these associations could involve unobservable covert responses as well as visible overt ones. Tolman, on the other hand, believed subjects learned expectations that allowed them to anticipate the consequences of their behavior. Both Hull and Tolman agreed, however, that the processes of learning could not be determined by introspection, because too much of the brain's functioning is simply inaccessible. The question of whether we learn associations or expectations, therefore, could only be settled by seeing what predictions each theory made about overt behavior, and then determining which of these predictions was correct:

$$S \rightarrow [X] \rightarrow R$$

A series of clever experiments designed to test the two theories provided support for both sides. In some situations, animals behaved as if they were executing S–R habits blindly, without any anticipation of the consequences that would follow. Fowler and Miller's (1963) study provides a good example, as rats ran faster to reach a goal box when they received a shock there as well as food. In other situations, however, animals behaved as if they had very clear expectations of the consequences of their actions—when Tinklepaugh's chimpanzees found a lettuce instead of a banana, this produced vigorous searching for the missing banana.

This conflicting evidence made it very difficult to determine which theory was right. One factor that contributed to this difficulty is that the two theories have more in common than the differences in their terminology might suggest. A second, even more important factor was the ambiguity of both theories. A crucial requirement for testing any theory is that it make clear and unambiguous predictions, but neither side was ever able to state its position with sufficient precision to allow this. Still a third reason that it has been so difficult to establish which theory is right, however, could be that both are right. The first learning system to have evolved may have been of the fundamentally simple kind described by S–R theory, in which stimuli automatically elicit a response without any anticipation of the goal. In vertebrates, however, this might have been supplemented by a more sophisticated cognitive system involving the acquisition of abstract knowledge, or expectations.

Both kinds of learning have advantages, and there is evidence in humans that we can alternate between the two systems. In learning to drive a car, for example, at first you have to pay constant attention to what you are doing, but, with practice, these movements become increasingly automatic, until eventually you can drive without thinking about it. This transfer of control over behavior to a simpler, automatic system leaves the more sophisticated system free to cope with new demands. (See also Schneider & Shiffrin, 1977.) If the automatic component of this system can be equated with the associative system described by S–R theorists, then human learning might indeed be a blend of associative habits and cognitive expectations.

In addition to habits and expectations, learning can take several other forms. One is a cognitive map, charting the location of objects in the environment. Clark's nutcrackers, for example, appear to be able to remember the locations of hundreds or even thousands of caches of seeds that they have hidden, and rats appear to use cognitive maps to plan new routes to goals when previously used paths are blocked. Another complex form of learning involves the ability to measure the passage of time: Many species seem to have internal clocks that allow them to monitor both the time of day and the interval between successive events. Gibbon and Church have suggested that this clock might consist of a pacemaker connected by a switch to an accumulator that stores the number of pulses. Finally, there is evidence that animals can accurately estimate numbers of objects, perhaps—though this is by no means yet certain—by counting.

The evidence for cognitive maps, timing and counting suggests that even in apparently simple situations, animal learning might be remarkably complex. In subsequent chapters, we will try to understand the processes that make this complex learning possible.

Glossary

S–R theory A theory that assumes that learning involves the formation of associations between environmental stimuli and the responses made in their presence.

Behaviorism A difficult term to define because behaviorists come grouped in a number of different schools, and their views diverge on many issues. A common theme is a distrust of introspection as a tool for scientific investigation, and a consequent emphasis on explaining behavior in terms of environmental causes rather than mental states.

Within this broad framework, behaviorists disagree about the precise role that should be accorded the mind within psychology. *Methodological behaviorists* believe that psychology should study only events that can be observed objectively—that is, about which independent observers can agree. Because the mind cannot be observed objectively, methodological behaviorists oppose any use of mental concepts within psychology.

Skinner, on the other hand, is a *radical behaviorist:* He has no objection to studying the mind, but does not believe that overt behavior should be attributed to mental states. The ultimate cause of behavior, he argues, lies in the environment (and genetics), and behavior must be explained in terms of these environmental determinants if psychology is to be of practical value. Also, Skinner was emphatically not an S–R theorist, as he did not believe that a stimulus elicited a reinforced response. Instead, he believed that reinforcement increased the probability that the response would be made in the presence of that stimulus; he regarded the stimulus as only "setting the occasion" for the response, rather than eliciting it.

Intervening variable A variable used in a theory to represent a hypothetical internal state. This state is elicited by a stimulus and helps to determine the eventual response; it thus intervenes between the independent variable (environment) and dependent variable (behavior).

Neobehaviorism is a variant of behaviorism whose adherents are willing to accept internal or mental states at a theoretical level as intervening variables, provided that the theory is stated clearly enough to allow the derivation of predictions about overt behavior. The validity of the theory is then determined solely by the accuracy of its predictions about overt behavior, not by how well it accords with introspective knowledge.

Cognitive behaviorists share with neobehaviorists a willingness to accept mental states at a theoretical level—indeed, Tolman first introduced the concept of an intervening variable (see Hull, 1943)—but differ in the kinds of intervening variables they employ. Whereas neobehaviorists view internal events as covert responses that obey the same laws as their overt counterparts, cognitive behaviorists postulate internal processes that correspond much more closely with those suggested by conscious experience: expectations, memory, attention, and so on.

Docility Flexibility in choosing a new response when a previously used behavior is not effective. If the path that a rat normally takes to a goal box is blocked by a barrier, for example, and the rat attempts to climb over the barrier, this would be an example of docility. Tolman regarded such flexibility as evidence for the presence of an expectation: The rat had not simply learned an S–R habit but, rather, had formed an expectation that there was food in the goal box, and it was flexibly choosing whatever response would get it there.

Disruption A term Tolman used to describe the disturbance of behavior that is observed when an expected outcome is not obtained.

Automatic processes and **controlled processes** Two categories of cognitive processes proposed by Shiffrin and Schneider. An automatic process is one that occurs rapidly, without any need for attention. Because conscious attention is not required, numerous automatic processes can be carried out simultaneously. A controlled process is a cognitive process that does require attention. Controlled processes are relatively slow, and only a limited number can be carried out at one time. With practice, however, controlled processes can become automatic.

Declarative memories and **procedural memories** Two forms in which experiences are stored in memory. Declarative memories are stored in a form to which subjects can gain conscious access—in other words, conscious recollections. Procedural memories are stored in a procedural, or habitual, form in which one event automatically activates another, without conscious involvement. Declarative memories include the recall of autobiographical experiences such as where you ate lunch yesterday (also called *episodic memory*) and the recall of factual information, such as the meaning of words (also called *semantic memory*); procedural memories, on the other hand, provide the basis for skills and habits such as riding a bicycle.

Cognitive map A mental representation of the spatial layout of an environment, indicating the location of different features of the environment and the paths linking them.

Review Questions

1. Define the following terms: anthropomorphism, reinforcer devaluation, anterograde amnesia, circadian timing, and the peak procedure.

2. How did Thorndike and Watson contribute to the development of S–R theory?

3. What was the central disagreement between early cognitive and behavioral learning theorists?

4. What is the evidence that learning can occur without an overt response being made? Why was this evidence regarded as a critical test of S–R and cognitive theories of learning?

5. What is neobehaviorism? How did Hull, as a behaviorist, justify talking about internal events?

6. How did Hull's modified S–R theory account for animals' apparent ability to anticipate the consequences of their action? What evidence supports Hull's theory?

7. Why did Tolman reject Hull's neobehaviorism? What evidence supports Tolman's claim that animals learn expectations?

8. Why was it so difficult to decide whether S–R or cognitive theories of learning are correct?

9. What is the two-level hypothesis presented in this chapter? How could the Colwill and Rescorla experiment be said to support it?

10. What evidence suggests that human learning also takes two different forms, roughly comparable to habits and expectations?

11. How has the associative account of learning evolved from Thorndike to Hull to Rescorla? In what ways has it changed, and in what ways has it remained the same?

12. What is a cognitive map? What evidence suggests that animals form such maps?

13. What evidence supports the existence of internal clocks? How does the Gibbon and Church model account for this evidence?

14. What evidence suggests that animals are capable of estimating quantities? Why do we need to be cautious in attributing their performance to counting?

CHAPTER NINE

THE ROLE OF MEMORY
AND ATTENTION

In Chapter 8 we saw that learning can take a number of forms. When a rat runs through a maze to a goal box containing food, it might learn a series of right and left turns; it might form an expectation that the goal box contains food; and it might form a detailed cognitive map of the spatial layout of the maze. Our ability to understand these forms of learning, however, was hampered by the vagueness of the theories proposed to account for them. In our maze example, will the rat learn a simple S–R habit, an expectation or both? And if it forms an expectation, what will the content of this expectation be? Will the rat simply expect something good in the goal box, will it expect food, or will it expect two oval-shaped pellets with a sweet taste?

Equivalent questions arise in the case of human behavior, and the answers can be of considerable practical importance. Consider a girl who is punished by her father for lying. Will she learn that it is dangerous to tell this particular lie, that it is dangerous to tell any lie to her father, or that all lying is wrong? We need to be able to predict what will be learned in situations like this if we are to use reinforcement and punishment effectively.

To be able to understand the determinants of learning, we can start by studying the processes involved in relatively simple situations. Even in the simplest learning situations, however, it can be difficult to predict what will be learned. Consider a salivary conditioning experiment in which a dog is presented with a bell followed, after several seconds, by food. Because we know the purpose of the experiment, the relationship between the bell and food may seem obvious, but try to imagine the situation from the dog's perspective. Thousands of stimuli impinge on it every second—a myriad of lights, sounds, and odors—and any of these stimuli potentially predict the availability of food. Moreover, we have seen that conditioning can occur to stimuli encountered long before the US—rats, for example, develop an aversion to food eaten up to 24 hours before they become ill. (See Chapter 3.) From our dog's point of view, therefore, food is preceded not only by a bell but also a vast array of sights, sounds, and odors, stretching back over many minutes or even hours (Figure 5.9). Which of these thousands of stimuli will it associate with food?

One important factor is likely to be how much attention the dog paid to the stimuli when it first encountered them: If a stimulus is not attended to, it is unlikely to be associated with any subsequent event. Similarly, conditioning is likely to depend on which of these stimuli the dog recalls when it receives the food. To predict what will be learned, in other words, we need to understand the processes of memory and attention, the focus of this chapter. To provide a foundation for our discussion, we will begin with an overview of the memory system. We will then look in more detail at the components of this system and try to understand how each of these components influences what is learned during classical and operant conditioning.

9.1 A MODEL OF HUMAN MEMORY

Before we begin our analysis of memory, a word of warning is in order: The literature on memory and attention is vast and would be difficult to summarize adequately in an entire book, much less in one section. The review that follows, therefore, is highly selective and will present only those principles that are most obviously and directly relevant to associative learning. Also, in most cases we will consider only one interpretation of how memory works, the interpretation that currently seems the most widely accepted. It is important to bear in mind that other views are possible; more detailed discussion of alternative approaches can be found in excellent texts by Baddeley (1997), Ashcraft (1994) and Parkin (1993).

An Information-Processing Perspective

Over the past few decades, a theoretical perspective known as information processing has guided most research on memory. This approach had its origins in the development of computer technology in the late 1940s, and to understand the rationale behind it, we first consider briefly the properties of computers.

Computers. In essence, a computer is a machine that can perform only a few very simple operations. To add the numbers 5 and 3, for example, a computer first stores the numbers in separate cells in its electronic memory, along with instructions, or a "program," that tells it how to add them. Using these instructions, the computer then retrieves from its memory these two numbers (5 and 3), and transfers them to a central processing unit (CPU) where they are added together. The computer then transfers the sum obtained to another memory cell and stores it there. Finally, it conveys the result to us by printing it on paper or displaying it on a screen.

This summary is something of an oversimplification. The steps outlined above would be broken down into tens or hundreds of separate operations. But it does accurately convey how computers solve problems by breaking them down into a series of small steps. Each of these steps considered by itself (for example, adding 3 and 5) is extremely simple, but by performing the steps at almost unimaginable speed, the computer can solve problems of staggering complexity. As this ability of computers to solve problems became clear in the 1940s and early 1950s, psychologists became increasingly fascinated by the mechanisms involved. If computers could solve complex problems by breaking them down into simpler steps, was it possible that human thinking might be based on the same strategy?

The information-processing approach in psychology is based on this assumption. It views problem solving as a sequence of simple operations, in each of which the information output of the preceding stage (for example, the sum 8 from our earlier example of 5 + 3) is subject to one further process or modification (for example, storage in a memory cell). The claim here is not that humans and computers solve problems in exactly the same way—they almost certainly do not. But although the exact sequence of operations may differ in humans and computers (just as they differ in different computer programs), the assumption is that both solve complex problems by breaking them down into a series of simpler operations. If this assumption is right, it follows that if we want to understand human thought, we need to understand the operations at each stage.

Coding, storage, and retrieval. In the case of memory, information-processing theorists have adopted as an organizing framework the three stages a computer goes through in remembering material: coding the input, storing it, and then retrieving it.

When information is presented to a computer, the first thing it does is transform, or code, that input into a form that it can process. This is known as **coding**. In the addition problem discussed earlier, for example, we might have typed in the numbers to be added, using the computer keyboard. For the computer to be able to use this information, it would first have to convert, or code, the information in the form of a series of electrical signals. These signals are then stored in electromagnetic cells located in the computer's memory. (The occurrence of a particular electrical impulse, for example, might be stored by magnetizing a particular memory cell.) This process is known as **storage**. Finally, when the stored information is needed for some purpose, such as addition, it is retrieved from its location in memory and copied into the computer's central processing unit, where any required arithmetic operations can be carried out. This is known as **retrieval**.

Similarly, memory in animals and humans can be understood as the sequential coding, storage and retrieval of information. In the remainder of this section, we will briefly review current theories about these three stages in human memory, based largely on studies of memory for words. With this material as a foundation, we will then turn to studies of coding and retrieval in contexts more directly relevant to classical and operant conditioning.

Coding

To provide a concrete focus for our discussion, imagine that a stranger came up to you in the street and, without saying a word, handed you a piece of paper containing the single word *dog*. What would determine whether you were later able to recall this word?

Sensory coding.   The first requirement for remembering any stimulus is to identify it correctly when it occurs. Perception is itself a complex process involving a number of stages, and we will only hint at this complexity here. In our *dog* example, when the light from the paper reached your eye, it would trigger chemical activity in millions of receptors located in the retina at the back of the eye; this chemical activity would in turn initiate electrical activity in millions of neurons; this activity would be transmitted to a second set of neurons located deeper in the brain and so on, until eventually a set of neurons in the brain's surface or cortex would become active. If this set of neurons is activated whenever the word *dog* is presented, and if it is not activated by other stimuli, then it is called a *node*. A node thus "represents" a stimulus, in the sense that it is active only when that stimulus is presented.

Short-term or working memory.   Suppose that the printed word *dog* has led to activation of the node in your brain that represents this word. How long will you now remember having seen this word? Early experiments on human memory showed that people could recall word lists hours or even days later, but the subjects in these studies were free to keep thinking about the words during the retention interval. The observed recall was, therefore, potentially the fruit of extended practice. To find out how long material could be remembered without such practice, Peterson and Peterson (1959) gave subjects a consonant trigram (for example, CHJ) and then, after a delay of between 3 and 18 seconds, asked them to recall it. To prevent subjects' practicing the trigram during the retention interval, they had to count backward by threes from a designated number.

On the surface, the task was almost ridiculously easy: The subjects were being asked to remember a simple trigram for only a few seconds. However, as Figure 9.1 shows, the task proved to be exceedingly difficult. After only 3 seconds, 20% of the subjects could no longer recall the trigram; within 15 seconds, nearly all the subjects had forgotten it. Simply recognizing a word is not enough to ensure that it will be remembered: Unless subjects are allowed to continue working on or processing the code they have formed, it will decay and become inaccessible within a matter of seconds.

FIGURE 9.1   The percentage of consonant trigrams correctly recalled after retention intervals of between 3 and 18 seconds. (Peterson & Peterson, 1959)

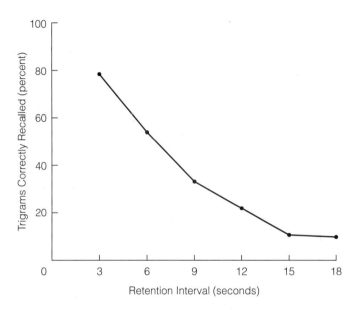

Early theories based on the Petersons' research used the term **short-term memory (STM)** or *short-term store* to describe the initial stage of memory in which a memory is held only briefly. Subsequent research, however, suggested that it might be more useful to think of short-term memory as a state of temporary activity, rather than simply as a way station on the path to more permanent storage. Consider the activity of reading a sentence. As you read the sentence, different nodes representing these words will be activated in succession, and you will need to use the relationships between these words to decipher the overall meaning of the sentence. (The word *hit*, for example, has very different meanings in "The boy hit the ball" and "The show was a hit"; we might need to consider the meaning of many words in a sentence before we can decipher the intended meaning of one of them.) Short-term memory, in other words, is not simply a passive storage area where we hold information on the way to long-term storage; it is a kind of mental workbench where we assemble information (activate nodes) and then work on this information for purposes such as interpreting sentences. To emphasize the active nature of this initial stage in memory, Baddeley (1992) and others have proposed calling it **working memory,** and this term has become increasingly common. Working memory can be thought of as the set of nodes that are active at a given moment, together with the processes that are brought to bear on them while they are in this state.

Long-term memory. Let us return to the word *dog*, which we have now assumed is being held in a state of temporary activation. If this activity lasts for only a matter of seconds, how do we manage to remember it for long periods? The answer, according to a memory model proposed by Shiffrin and Schneider (1977), is that **long-term memory (LTM)** depends on the formation of associations between nodes while they are active in short-term memory. In our *dog* example, for you to be able to recall later the word that had been written on the paper, it would not be sufficient for it to have activated the *dog* node in your brain; it would be just one more coding of a word that you would have heard thousands of times in your life, indistinguishable from all the others. To remember the particular occurrence, you would have to associate the word *dog* with the context in which it occurred: the presence of the stranger, the place, the time of day, and so on. Only with the coding of such word-context associations would you be able to distinguish this experience of the word from all its predecessors.

To remember the word *dog,* then, you would have to associate this word with the contextual cues that accompanied it—or, in neural terms, form associations between the nodes that were simultaneously active in short-term memory. Shiffrin and Schneider suggested that such associations can be formed only during the time the nodes are active. The Petersons' results suggest that nodal activity decays rapidly but that subjects can get around this limitation by repetition or **rehearsal** of the word they want to remember: Every time a subject repeats a word, activity in the node is reinitiated, extending the time available for forming new associations. (A common example is repeating a telephone number during the interval between looking it up and actually dialing: By continually repeating the number, we keep the node in an active state, thereby preventing its decay.) The formation of long-term memories thus depends on rehearsing material in short-term memory so that it remains active long enough to allow the formation of new associations. (The term *rehearsal* was originally confined to repetition of verbal material, but it is now used more generally to refer to the maintenance of a neural center in an active state.)

Attention. A central assumption of information-processing theories is that the brain's capacity to process information is limited. Our brains are massive—an adult brain contains on the order of 10 billion neurons—but so too is the amount of information reaching our senses. Our eyes alone contain over 200 million receptors, and there are many more millions of receptors in our ears, nose, skin, and so on. We simply don't have the capacity to process every aspect of this sensory input, and in many situations we can carry out only one or a few operations simultaneously. The term **attention** describes this kind of limitation in processing capacity.

Rehearsal is one of these limited processes: We can rehearse or attend to only a limited number of items in short-term memory at one time. To experience this limitation for yourself, repeat the following number after reading it only once:

683

You probably found it easy, but now try the following:

74095682153

The problem with repeating the longer number is that codes must be rehearsed periodically if they are to remain active, but we can rehearse only a small number of codes at a time. Indeed, according to Shiffrin and Schneider, we can rehearse only a single code at a time; to remember more items than that we must rehearse them sequentially. With the number 683, for example, you rehearse the 6 first, then the 8, then the 3. After finishing the 3, you can return to the 6, and repeat the entire sequence as often as necessary. If the list of digits to be remembered is too long, however, then the first digit will have faded from memory before you can return to rehearse it. It is rather like the plate-spinning act in a circus, where the juggler runs from one plate to the next, giving each a reviving spin (rehearsal) as he goes. Each new spin returns the plate to its original level of activity, but if the juggler tries to maintain too many plates at once, the first plate will already have fallen to the table by the time he reaches the last one. The number of items that can be kept active simultaneously in memory is known as the *memory span*; for most people, it seems to be about seven items.

If several items are presented together repeatedly, their nodes may be associated together to form a new, higher-level node. The letter sequence *aksolptzvbgw*, for example, is much harder to recall than the sequence *constitution*; the reason is that we have experienced the sequence *constitution* so often that we have associated its elements together to form a new, single code. The process of associating codes together to form a single code is known as *chunking*; the result is that a word such as *constitution* requires no more rehearsal to remember than a single letter such as *c*. Although chunking is of some help in overcoming the limited rehearsal capacity of short-term memory, we can still remember only a small fraction of the stimuli that are constantly inundating us. One of the most important determinants of memory, then, is how we allocate processing capacity or attention among the myriad of stimuli competing for it.

Storage

Given that a stimulus is successfully encoded and that we can remember it, say, one week later, you might think that we would then remember it forever, but this is clearly not the case. Why do we forget material after having successfully learned it? One obvious possibility is that memory traces decay with the passing of time. The ancient Greek philosopher Aristotle likened memory to a soft clay tablet: When an impression is first made, it is clear and vivid, but over time it becomes increasingly blurred, finally disappearing altogether. Similarly, the

FIGURE 9.2   The number of nonsense syllables recalled after intervals spent either awake or asleep.
(Jenkins & Dallenbach, 1924)

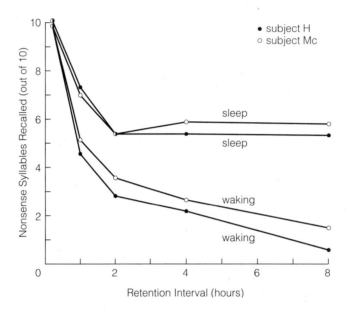

neural encoding of a stimulus might deteriorate over time, until it can no longer
be deciphered.

As plausible as this explanation might sound, experimental research has
provided only limited evidence for decay. In a classic study by Jenkins and
Dallenbach (1924), for example, the experimenters gave subjects a list of
nonsense syllables to memorize and then asked them to recall as many as they
could after delays of up to eight hours. In one condition, the subjects spent
the retention interval engaged in normal daily activities; in the other, they
stayed in the laboratory and went to sleep. If forgetting is caused solely by the
passing of time, then it should have been equal in both conditions, but, as
Figure 9.2 shows, this was far from being the case. Subjects who were awake
during the retention interval forgot much more than those who slept. That
subjects who slept did forget some of what they had learned could mean that
time also causes forgetting, or it could have been the result of the subject's
residual activity in the time before they fell asleep. Whatever the role of time
may be, it is clear that forgetting is not caused solely by the passing of time:
How subjects spend that time is critical.

Retroactive interference. In particular, the formation of new memories while
we are active seems to interfere with the recall of older memories. This interference of new memories with our ability to recall older ones is called **retroactive**

interference (RI). A lovely example (alas, apocryphal) concerns an aging professor of fish biology who reported that every time he learned the name of a new student, he forgot the name of a species of fish.

In this example, the addition of any new material to the professor's overloaded memory seemed to necessitate the ejection of material already there, but in reality retroactive interference seems to be greatest between memories that are similar. In a study by Tulving and Psotka (1971), for example, subjects learned a list of words and were then asked to recall it 20 minutes later. Subjects who spent the retention interval working on an arithmetic reasoning task showed virtually no forgetting. Subjects who memorized new lists during the period, however, did forget, and the more lists they memorized, the more of the original list they forgot. Activity itself, therefore, does not produce forgetting any more than time does: It is the encoding of new, similar material that seems to cause forgetting.

Proactive interference. Memory for a word list may also be impaired by material learned previously. This phenomenon, termed **proactive interference (PI),** was first identified in a classic paper by Underwood (1957), who analyzed published studies in which subjects had memorized a list until they could repeat it perfectly and were then tested for recall 24 hours later. The more lists subjects had memorized before the experiment, the more of the target list they forgot over the 24 hours. It does not seem to matter very much, therefore, whether interfering material is learned before or after a target: The more similar the material residing in memory, the harder it is to recall a particular item.

In this respect, memory seems to be like a rapidly expanding library that receives books faster than it can catalog them. As the library continues to expand and the piles of uncataloged books grow ever higher, the task of searching through the piles to find a particular volume becomes greater and greater. The main cause of forgetting seems to be difficulties in locating or retrieving material from storage.

Retrieval

What, then, determines our success in retrieving memories? One key factor is how well we organize material while we are learning it. If books are properly catalogued as they arrive at a warehouse, it will be much easier to find them later. Similarly, we are more likely to remember experiences if we think about them and try to relate them to material already in memory. In reading a text, for example, you are much more likely to recall it later if you actively think about the material you are reading—for example, how it relates to earlier topics, or to your own life—than if you try to memorize the words by rote.

In addition to organizing material during original learning (memory's equivalent of a cataloging system), two other factors seem to be particularly important in determining later retrieval: retrieval cues and cue overload.

Retrieval cues. One determinant of retrieval is the similarity of the contextual cues present during retrieval and coding. In discussing working memory, we saw that a word or other stimulus is not coded in isolation: In order to establish permanent memories, associations are formed between the word to be remembered and contextual cues present at the time. If one of these cues is again present during retrieval, activation will spread from its node to all the others linked to it (Collins & Loftus, 1975). The more such cues are present—that is, the greater the similarity of training and test conditions—the more excitation will spread to the target node from the associated contextual nodes, and the greater the likelihood of the word's being recalled.

Some of the contextual cues that form part of the coding of an experience are surprisingly subtle. In a study by Smith (1979), for example, subjects memorized a word list and were then asked to recall it 20 minutes later. Subjects tested in the room where they had originally studied the list recalled 33% more words than did subjects tested in a different room. Other seemingly unimportant cues, such as your mood and physical condition, can also form part of the stored memory trace, and the presence of these "irrelevant" cues at recall can substantially improve memory. (See also Bower, 1981; Eich, 1980.)[1]

Cue overload. A second factor that influences retrieval is the number of different memories associated with a retrieval cue. We have suggested that when a node is activated, activation spreads to all the other nodes connected to it. The greater the number of these connections, however, the less excitation will flow to any one of them and, thus, the less likely it will be that a particular memory will be retrieved (Figure 9.3). If you've eaten in a restaurant only once, for example, returning to it may evoke vivid memories of your earlier meal there. But the more often you eat there, the more memories will become associated with the contextual cues of the restaurant, and the more difficult it will be for you to remember any particular meal: They all blur together. This phenomenon has been termed **cue overload** and seems to be one of the most important factors causing proactive and retroactive interference (Watkins & Watkins, 1976; Anderson, 1995).

Summary

Let us summarize some of the points discussed so far. Whether we remember a stimulus such as the word *dog* depends on whether we succeed in coding, storing, and retrieving it. In coding, we analyze a stimulus into its constituent

---

[1] Before you decide to do all your exam studying in the room where you will be tested, we should add that contextual cues are relatively unimportant in the case of meaningful textual material. For such material, the main determinant of recall is how deeply you understand its meaning.

FIGURE 9.3   The cue-overload hypothesis. If a retrieval cue node is associated with only one other node, it will stimulate that node strongly (symbolized by the thick arrow); the more nodes with which it is associated (represented by N_1, N_2, and so on), the less it will stimulate any one of them.

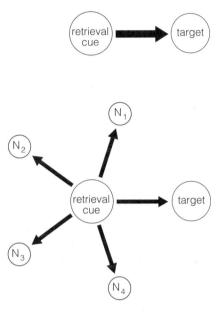

features and then use these features to infer what the original stimulus must have been. The final step in this sensory coding process seems to be activation of one or more cells in an integrated unit called a node. The nodes that are active simultaneously are collectively referred to as short-term memory; as implied by this term, activity in a node normally decays quite rapidly after the initiating stimulus is no longer present.

For the mind to form a permanent memory of a word, that word must be associated with the contextual cues that accompany it; in neural terms, associations must be formed between the nodes that are active in short-term memory. The formation of a memory takes time, however, and to ensure that nodes remain active long enough for an association to be formed, subjects can repeat or rehearse the material they are trying to remember.

Once a code for an item has been successfully stored in memory, current theories suggest that it will remain there with little if any decay. Forgetting, according to these theories, is attributable not to the disappearance of items from storage but rather to difficulties in retrieving ones that are there. Retrieval is greatly facilitated if contextual cues associated with the word during encoding are again present: The more of these cues that are present, the more activation will spread from their nodes to the target node, and the greater the likelihood of its reactivation. The effectiveness of a retrieval cue is diminished, however, if it is also associated with other memories. The more connections radiating out from a node, the less activation seems to flow through any one of them.

9.2 WORKING MEMORY

Having established a general framework for understanding memory, we will now consider how memory and attention can help us understand associative learning. We will start in this section with research on working memory in animals.

Delayed Matching to Sample

Learning psychologists have developed several techniques to study short-term or working memory in animals. One of the most popular is a procedure known as **delayed matching to sample (DMTS).** In this procedure, the subject is shown one stimulus, called the *sample,* and then, after a delay, is offered a choice between that stimulus and another stimulus. If the subject chooses the same stimulus as the sample (matching), it is rewarded. Performance on this task provides a simple index of how well the subject remembers the sample.

We can illustrate this procedure with an experiment by Grant (1976). He was interested in the effects of sample duration on memory—the longer a sample was visible, he speculated, the more time subjects would have to process it, and the better they would remember it. To find out, he ran a DMTS experiment using pigeons as subjects and colors as stimuli. On a typical trial, the center key of a three-key array was illuminated with a red light, and then, after a delay, the side keys were illuminated with red and green lights (Figure 9.4). If the bird matched the sample by pecking the red side key, it was reinforced; if it pecked the green key, the trial terminated without reward. Grant varied the duration of the sample and also the interval between presentation of the sample and comparison stimuli. As shown in Figure 9.5, the longer the delay interval, the poorer subjects' performance. The longer the sample had been presented, however, the better the subjects recalled it, suggesting that increased processing time leads to better memory.

Rehearsal

One possible interpretation of Grant's results is that they demonstrate the importance of rehearsal. When the sample was exposed for a longer period, subjects would have had more time to rehearse their cortical representation of the sample, leading to a stronger memory. But it is possible to explain Grant's results without appealing to rehearsal. In human research, rehearsal is normally thought of as a voluntary process that subjects can deliberately initiate or

FIGURE 9.4   Delayed matching-to-sample (DMTS) procedure. The sample is presented on the center key and then, after a delay during which the keys are dark, the same stimulus is presented on one of the side keys and an alternative on the other. Pecks to either side key terminate the trial; the pigeon is reinforced only if it has pecked the stimulus that matched the sample. In many DMTS experiments, the center key is initially white and the pigeon must peck it to produce the sample.

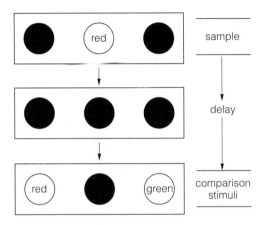

FIGURE 9.5   Percentage of correct matching responses as a function of the duration of the sample and the delay between the sample and comparison stimuli. (Grant, 1976)

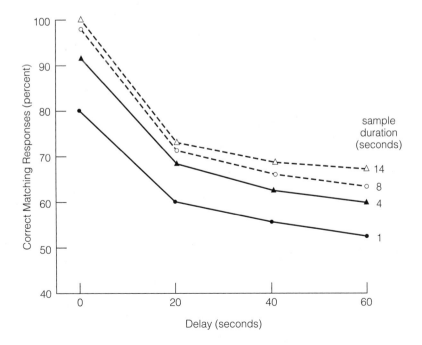

terminate—what in Chapter 8 we described as a *controlled process*. In Grant's experiment, however, there is no need to assume that the pigeons could control the allocation of their processing capacity—processing could have been directly driven by continuing sensory input from the sample on the key.

Surprise. Stronger evidence for what might be called "internally generated" rehearsal in animals (that is, processing not under the direct control of an external stimulus) comes from an experiment by Maki (1979). The intuition underlying this experiment was that the amount of attention paid to any stimulus would depend on how surprised subjects were by its occurrence: The more unexpected a stimulus is, the more attention it should attract, and the better it should be remembered. Maki tested this prediction using food as the stimulus to be remembered. Pigeons were first trained on a visual discrimination task in which they had to peck either a red key or a green key: If food was presented approximately 12 seconds before the trial began, then a peck to the red key was reinforced; otherwise, a peck to the green key was reinforced. In order to respond correctly, in other words, the birds had to remember whether the trial had been preceded by food.

To find out whether surprising events received greater processing, Maki then gave the birds separate training in which they were reinforced for pecking vertical lines (S+) but not horizontal ones (S–). Finally, the birds were returned to the red-green discrimination; now, though, presentations of food were preceded by either the former S+ or S–. Since S– had never before been followed by food, the presentation of food following S– should have occasioned far more surprise than the same presentation following S+. The subjects should thus have paid more attention to the food on these trials and hence remembered it better. Performance on the following red-green presentations confirmed these expectations: The birds were significantly more likely to respond correctly on trials in which food was preceded by S– (72%) than S+ (54%).

Note that this result cannot be explained by stimulus exposure time, because the food sample was available for the same period in both groups. It was not stimulus exposure that determined memory in this experiment but the surprise value of the stimulus, and this result is consistent with the idea that animals allocate greater processing time or rehearsal to unexpected events. (See also Grant, Brewster, & Stierhoff, 1983.)

Directed forgetting. Further evidence that animals can control rehearsal has come from a procedure known as **directed forgetting** (Maki & Hegvik, 1980). The idea here is that if animals deliberately rehearse a stimulus in order to remember it, they should do so only in situations in which they believe that remembering the stimulus will be of value. Suppose, for example, that on some DMTS trials a sample is presented but not followed by any comparison stimuli, so that remembering the sample on these trials will not lead to food. If subjects were given a cue signaling that memory would not be tested on these trials, they should be less likely to rehearse the sample.

To test this prediction, Grant (1981) trained pigeons on a standard DMTS procedure. On half of the trials, the sample was followed by a *forget cue* (illumination of the key with a horizontal line), and on these trials no comparison stimuli followed. On the remaining trials, the sample was followed by a *remember cue* (a vertical line), and the appropriate comparison stimuli followed. According to the logic sketched above, the pigeons should have learned that memory was not tested on *forget* trials, and thus should have spent less time rehearsing the sample on these trials. To see if this was so, Grant introduced unexpected probe trials in which the *forget* cue *was* followed by comparison stimuli. As predicted, he found that performance on these *forget* trials was poorer than on *remember* trials.

In a clever refinement of this procedure, Grant also varied when in the delay interval the *remember* and *forget* cues were presented. If subjects begin to rehearse a sample when it is presented and then stop when a forget cue appears, then delaying the forget cue should result in more rehearsal and thus better performance. Again this prediction was confirmed: The later the *forget* cue was presented during the delay interval, the better subjects remembered the sample. These results strongly suggest that pigeons can control whether or not they rehearse a stimulus while it is in memory. (See also Grant & Soldat, 1995.)

Retrospective versus Prospective Coding

So far, we have implicitly assumed that animals simply remember the stimulus that was presented. If a key is illuminated with a red light, for example, then pigeons will remember that red light. In our discussion of computers, however, we saw that the code computers assign to a stimulus may differ substantially from the original stimulus—the number 7, for example, may be stored in a digital code that more closely resembles a series of 0's and 1's. Similarly, the codes animals assign to stimuli differ from these stimuli, sometimes dramatically. We will be discussing coding in more detail in the next two sections, but we will introduce the topic here with an example.

Honig (1981) introduced a distinction between two kinds of memory, retrospective and prospective. In **retrospective memory,** we remember an experience we have had in the past, whereas in **prospective memory** we remember what we intend to do in the future. Consider a pigeon in a DMTS procedure that has been presented with a red sample. It might attempt to remember the red sample, which would be a form of retrospective memory, or it might try to remember what it needs to do in the future, which is to peck the red comparison stimulus. In this example, the difference between the retrospective and prospective memories is relatively small, but in other situations the difference can be much greater, and there is evidence that animals can form both kinds of memories.

FIGURE 9.6   Overhead view of the Olton radial maze. All eight arms of the maze are baited. The rat is placed on the center platform and allowed to enter the arms in whatever order it chooses. (Olton & Samuelson, 1976)

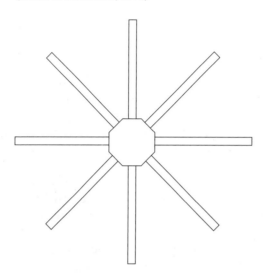

In one experiment illustrating this point, Kesner and DeSpain (1988) trained rats on a radial maze, an apparatus for studying memory developed by Olton and Samuelson (1976). In its original version, the maze consisted of eight arms radiating out from a central platform (Figure 9.6), but the version used by Kesner and DeSpain had 12 arms. At the start of each trial, food was placed at the end of each arm, and subjects were allowed to move freely between the arms to collect this food. After they had gotten food from a specified number of arms—this varied on different trials between 2 and 10 arms—the rats were removed from the maze for a period of 15 minutes. Then, to find out how well they remembered their earlier choices, the rats were returned to the maze and allowed to choose between two arms, one they had previously entered and one they had not. (Doors leading to the other arms were closed.) If the rats remembered their earlier choices, they should choose the arm that still contained food.

The key issue in this study was how performance on the test trial would vary as a function of the number of arms that had been visited. If rats form retrospective memories—in this case, remembering each of the arms they have visited— then the more arms they visited, the harder they should find it to remember all of their choices. Performance, in other words, should progressively deteriorate as the number of visits increased. Suppose, though, that rats form prospective memories, and attempt to remember what arms they still need to visit. In this case, the more arms already visited, the fewer arms remain to visit, and thus the smaller the burden on memory. If rats form prospective memories, therefore, performance should *improve* as the number of arms visited increases, because subjects will have fewer

FIGURE 9.7   Number of errors made by rats and humans during a test of spatial memory. Rats (left) and humans (right) were tested after exposure to a number of locations that varied on different trials; for rats, the maximum number of locations was 12, for humans it was 16. (Adapted from Kesner & DeSpain, 1988)

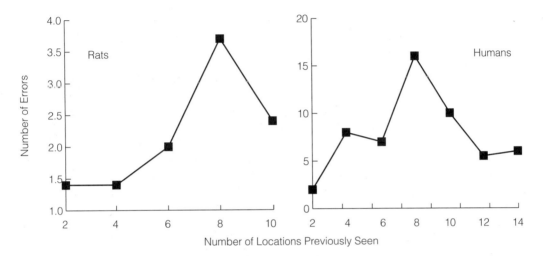

arms to remember. Finally, consider what might happen if rats can form both retrospective and prospective memories and can use whichever strategy requires less memory. In this case, early in a trial, when only a few arms have been visited, it is easier to remember the arms actually visited than the arms that still remain. As the number of entries increases past the halfway point, however, the situation reverses: The number of arms remaining is now smaller than the number of arms visited, so the rats should switch to remembering the arms that remain.

It might seem unbelievable that rats could follow such a complex strategy, switching from retrospective to prospective memory as the optimum strategy changes, but the results presented in Figure 9.7 (left panel) suggest that this is exactly what they did. As the number of visits increased, the number of errors initially also increased, suggesting that the burden on the rat's memory was increasing. (This, of course, is what we would expect if they were trying to remember an ever-increasing number of visits.) When the test was conducted after 10 choices, on the other hand, performance improved sharply, suggesting that the rats were trying to remember fewer items. The right hand panel in Figure 9.7 shows comparable data obtained from a group of human subjects who were trained on an equivalent task. (They had to remember which of 16 squares in a grid contained an X; one X was shown at a time.) The pattern of errors is clearly very similar in the two graphs, suggesting that both rats and humans switched coding strategies when a prospective code became easier to remember than a retrospective code. If, as this data suggests, subjects at the end of a trial were remembering the arms still to be visited rather than the choices they had just made, this illustrates how the code assigned to an experience in memory can differ radically from the actual experience.

9.3 THE ROLE OF ATTENTION IN CODING

One of the earliest theories of stimulus encoding was proposed by S–R theorist Kenneth Spence (1936). As we saw earlier, the central tenet of S–R theory was that reinforcement stamps in associations between the reinforced response and whatever stimuli are present at the time. Regarding the nature of these stimuli, Spence proposed that any object or event could be regarded as a set of discrete elements, and that each of these elements would be associated with the reinforced response. If a pigeon is reinforced for pecking a key with a picture of a large red triangle on it, for example, then Spence's theory predicts that every aspect of this triangle—its color (red), shape (triangle) and size (large)—will become associated with the response (Figure 9.8a).

Cognitive theorists rejected this analysis on the grounds that it grossly oversimplified the role of perception in learning. Rather than directly associating the elements of a stimulus with a response, they argued, subjects would first transform or elaborate the raw sensory data in order to identify the objects in the real world that gave rise to them. It was only this transformed, or coded, stimulus—what Lawrence (1963) called the *stimulus as coded* (SAC)—that would be associated with the response (Figure 9.8b).

One of the coding processes suggested by cognitive theorists was *attention*. The brain, they argued, does not have sufficient capacity to process all aspects of the stimuli bombarding our senses, so that only some subset—the elements to which the subject attend—will be associated with any response. The issue was thus a very simple one: Do all stimuli present during reinforcement become associated with responding, or only a subset of those stimuli?

Selective Attention

This simple issue proved remarkably difficult to answer. (For a review, see Mackintosh, 1965.) Many of the early skirmishes were won by S–R theory, but in the end it was the cognitive view that won the war. It is now clear that only some of the stimuli present during reinforcement become associated with the response, so that some sort of selective mechanism must be taken into account.

We will not try to unravel the intricate skein of argument that eventually led to this conclusion, but an experiment by Reynolds (1961) nicely illustrates the central point. Using two pigeons as subjects, Reynolds trained them on a successive discrimination in which two stimuli were presented alternately for three minutes at a time. When the key was illuminated with the outline of a white

FIGURE 9.8   Three theories of stimulus coding: (a) S–R theorists assumed that all elements of a stimulus would be associated independently with a reinforced response. (b) Cognitive theorists assumed that raw sensory input would be processed to produce a transformed or coded stimulus, and that it was this coded stimulus that would enter into any association. (c) One form of coding is attention. Dimensional models of attention assume that subjects can process only a limited number of stimulus dimensions at one time. If a pigeon attended only to the dimension of color, for example, then it would perceive a red triangle and a green circle simply as red and green. If it pecked the red and received food, the food would reinforce not only the overt response of pecking red but also the observing response (OR) of attending to color.

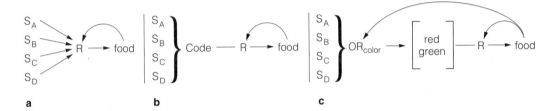

triangle against a red background (S+), pecking was occasionally reinforced, but not when the stimulus was the outline of a white circle against a green background (S–). (See Figure 9.9a.) According to S–R theory, both components of S+ (the triangular shape and the red color) should have acquired control over pecking. According to an attentional analysis, on the other hand, only a subset of the stimuli present can be fully processed, and although this does not necessarily mean only one stimulus will receive attention—processing capacity is not necessarily that limited—it does leave open the possibility that Reynolds's birds would learn only about the triangle or only about the color red.

To test what the birds had learned, Reynolds simply presented the elements of each compound separately, illuminating the key with either the circle, the triangle, red, or green. Figure 9.9b shows the results for bird number 1. According to S–R theory, the red and triangle components should have elicited roughly equal responding, but this was not the case: The bird responded vigorously when the key was red, but ignored the triangle. The second bird, on the other hand, responded at a high rate when the triangle was present, but virtually not at all when the key was red! (See Figure 9.9c.) Both birds, in other words, learned about only one of the two stimuli present. This result illustrates the empirical phenomenon of *selective attention*, in which only a subset of the stimuli present comes to control responding. (See also Langley & Riley, 1993.)

Theories of Attention

Given that selection does occur, what determines which stimuli will be selected? In Reynolds' experiment, for example, why did one bird attend to red while the other attended to triangle?

FIGURE 9.9   Selective attention. During training, responses to a white triangle on a red background
(S+) were reinforced; responses to a white circle on a green background (S–) were not. Test
trials presented each element—triangle, red, circle, green—separately. Bird 1 responded to
the color red, but not the triangle; bird 2 responded to the triangle, but not the color red.
(Adapted from Reynolds, 1961)

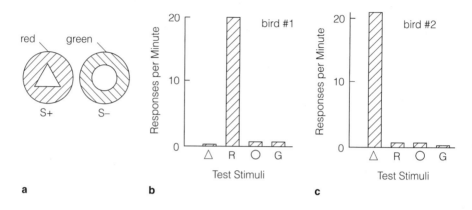

Dimensional models.   Several theorists have proposed that attention is organized in terms of stimulus dimensions (for example, Zeaman & House, 1963;
Sutherland & Mackintosh, 1971). According to this approach, we analyze different dimensions of a stimulus—for example, color and shape—separately. If
you were looking at a red ball, for example, one part of your perceptual system
would analyze its color while another part was simultaneously analyzing its
shape. Dimensional models of attention, however, assume that we do not have
the attentional capacity to analyze all the dimensions of a stimulus simultaneously; instead, we select only a subset for analysis. In Reynolds' experiment, for
example, suppose that his pigeons could analyze only one dimension at a time
(Figure 9.8c). If one of his birds attended to the dimension of color, it would
see only the color of the discriminative stimulus, red or green, and not its shape.

    As to which dimensions will be analyzed, dimensional models assume that a
preference for some dimensions is in part innate. Both monkeys and young children, for example, are more likely to attend to the color of objects than to their
shape (Warren, 1954; Zeaman & Hanley, 1983). In addition, these models assume that attention to a dimension can be strengthened by reinforcement, in
the same way as an overt response. In Reynolds' experiment, suppose that on
one of the trials the red triangle was presented and the bird attended to the dimension of color. If it pecked the red key, the delivery of food would strengthen
not only the overt response of pecking red but also the internal response of attending to the dimension of color. On subsequent trials, therefore, the bird would
be even more likely to attend to the color of whatever stimulus was present.

One way to test this prediction is to train subjects on one problem involving colors and then to give them a second problem involving different colors. If they have learned a general tendency to attend to color while solving the first problem, they will start the second problem already attending to the relevant dimension and hence should solve it faster. In order to control for alternative interpretations, this is usually done by comparing **intradimensional** or **ID shifts** (where the relevant cues change between problems but are still drawn from the same dimension) to **extradimensional** or **ED shifts** (where the relevant dimension in the second problem differs from that in the first problem). For example, suppose that one group is trained to solve a red-green problem before being transferred to a yellow-blue problem (an intradimensional shift, because the stimuli that are relevant in the second problem lie on the same dimension as the relevant stimuli in the first). A second group is trained on a triangle-circle discrimination before transferring to the same yellow-blue problem (an extradimensional shift, because the relevant dimension has changed between the problems). According to dimensional theories of attention, intradimensional shifts should be easier than extradimensional shifts, because the dimension that subjects have learned to attend to in the first problem is still relevant in the second problem. This prediction has been confirmed with both children and adults: When we are reinforced for attending to a dimension on one problem, we become more likely to attend to that dimension in subsequent problems (for example, Eimas, 1966; Kemler & Shepp, 1971). Several studies with animals have also found intradimensional shifts to be easier than extradimensional shifts (for example, Shepp & Schrier, 1969; Mackintosh & Little, 1969), but somewhat greater caution is necessary here as this result has not always been obtained (Hall, 1991).

Salience models. More recently, several theorists have proposed that we learn to attend to individual stimuli rather than to entire dimensions. In classical conditioning, for example, Mackintosh (1975) proposed that pairing a CS such as a red light with food will result in an increase in attention to the red light, rather than to the entire dimension of color. To account for the results of ED–ID shifts, he suggests that increased attention to one stimulus can generalize to other stimuli lying on the same dimension, but the primary effect is a change in the **salience** of the CS—that is, the extent to which it attracts attention. (For a fuller statement of the theory, see Mackintosh, 1975.)

Pearce and Hall (1980) have also proposed a theory that emphasizes changes in the salience of individual stimuli. But they suggest that learning usually involves a *decrease* in attention to a stimulus rather an increase. The central intuition of their model is that we need to concentrate our limited capacity for attention on events that we do not understand. If we hear an unfamiliar tone, for example, we need to attend to it carefully because we are not sure what other events might follow. If we have learned that the tone is always followed by food, on the other hand, then we no longer need to monitor it as carefully—we already understand its significance, and we can devote our limited capacity for attention to events whose significance is less certain. Pearce and Hall do not suggest that we ignore the tone totally—we still need to pay it sufficient attention to ensure the appropriate conditioned response—but they argue that we respond to it automatically rather than making it a focus of attention.

In essence, their model suggests a distinction between two kinds of attention, paralleling Shiffrin and Schneider's (1977) distinction between two levels of processing, *controlled* and *automatic*. (See Section 8.4.) When learning to drive a car, for example, we need to concentrate fully and use controlled processing. With practice, however, we learn to carry out the same processes automatically, freeing our attention for other tasks such as talking to passengers or planning our day. Similarly, Pearce and Hall suggest that early in conditioning we attend fully to a CS, but that as conditioning proceeds we respond automatically and reserve for more demanding tasks our limited capacity for controlled processing.

Thus, where Mackintosh suggests that conditioning results in an increase in attention to the CS, Pearce and Hall suggest that it leads to a decrease. In one test of the competing accounts, Hall and Pearce (1982) gave a group of rats conditioning trials in which a tone was paired with a mild shock. They then gave the rats a second set of conditioning trials in which the same tone was paired with a stronger shock:

Pretraining group: *Tone* → *mild shock*   *Tone* → *strong shock*

The question was how conditioning with the mild shock in the first phase would affect conditioning with the stronger shock in the second phase.

Common sense suggests that conditioning with the mild shock should greatly facilitate conditioning in the second phase, because fear would already be partly conditioned. Mackintosh's model makes a similar prediction: During the first phase, pairing of the tone with mild shock would increase attention to the tone, thereby facilitating learning in the second phase. The Pearce-Hall model, however, makes exactly the opposite prediction. During the first phase, subjects would learn that the tone is reliably followed by shock, and this would lead to a decrease in attention to the tone. When transferred to the second phase, they would start with a moderate level of fear (the tone would be eliciting fear automatically), but because they were not attending to the tone they would be less likely to learn that the tone was now being followed by a strong shock. In other words, although fear would start at a moderately high level in the second phase, it would increase only very slowly over trials.

To assess the effects of the pretraining, Pearce and Hall compared the performance of the pretraining group with that of a control group that also received pairings of the tone with the strong shock, but without preconditioning:

Control group: *Tone* → *strong shock*

FIGURE 9.10   Fear conditioning when a tone is paired with a strong shock. Rats in the pretraining group had previously received pairings of this tone with a mild shock; rats in the control group had no earlier experience with the tone. (Adapted from Hall & Pearce, 1982)

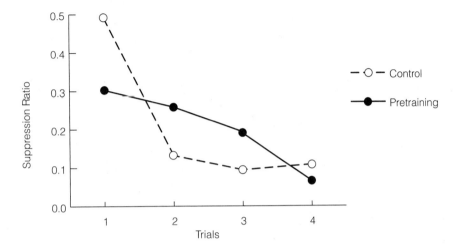

As shown in Figure 9.10, the predictions of the Pearce-Hall model were supported. Initially, fear was higher in the pretraining group. (Recall that low suppression ratios represent high fear.) Fear levels increased only very gradually in this group, however, and the control group reached asymptotic levels of fear significantly faster. As predicted by the Pearce-Hall model, pairing a tone with a mild shock seemed to reduce attention to the tone rather than to increase it.

In this case, the Pearce-Hall model predicted behavior more accurately than the Mackintosh model, but in some other situations the outcome has been reversed (for example, Mackintosh, 1973). And, complicating the situation still further, Wagner (1981) has proposed still a third model of attention based on changes in the salience of individual stimuli, and his model has also proved successful in some situations (for example, Lovibond, Preston, & Mackintosh, 1984). In situations such as this, where several theories each do well in some tests, the temptation is strong to suppose that each is capturing part of the truth about a complex process, and that ultimately we will need a theory that combines the best elements of each. In the case of attention, this might be a theory that allowed for increases as well as decreases in attention, and that incorporated a mechanism for altering attention to whole dimensions as well as to individual stimuli. Until such a theory appears, we can summarize current evidence by saying that we do not fully process all aspects of our environment simultaneously, and that how we allocate our limited capacity for attention depends in part on past experience. The precise details of how experience affects attention, however, remain to be determined.

9.4 CODING RELATIONSHIPS

In the introduction to the previous section, we discussed the conflict between Spence's S–R theory of discrimination learning and the perceptual account proposed by cognitive theorists. Spence suggested that when a response is reinforced, all elements of the stimuli that are present will be independently associated with the response (Figure 9.8a). Cognitive theorists, on the other hand, believed that a stimulus must be extensively processed or elaborated before a code can finally be assigned to it, and that it is only this coded version that can be associated with a response (Figure 9.8b). They identified attention as one of these processes, and subsequent evidence supported this view: Contrary to Spence, only some of the stimuli present when a response is reinforced become associated with it.

What, then, of the second assumption in Spence's model, that each element is processed independently, and thus each forms its own, separate association with the response? Cognitive theorists also challenged this assumption. (As you may have begun to sense, cognitive and S–R theorists were not in total agreement.) In order to make sense of the world, cognitive theorists argued, we need to look at the relationship between stimuli, rather than processing each in isolation. To identify an animal as a cat, for example, we cannot process its legs, tails and body in isolation: It is only by considering the spatial relationships between these elements that we can recognize the object as a cat. Thus where S–R theorists believed that each element of a stimulus is processed independently, cognitive theorists argued that we are constantly searching for the relationships between stimuli, and that we use these relationships to decide how they should be coded.

Transposition

These two views lead to very different predictions concerning discrimination learning. If subjects are trained to choose between two stimuli, S+ and S–, S–R theorists believed that subjects would code each stimulus separately, whereas cognitive theorists believed that they would code the stimuli in terms of their relationships.

Kohler's experiment. To determine which of these views was correct, the Austrian psychologist Wolfgang Kohler (1918/1939) trained chimpanzees to choose between two rectangular cards. One of the cards was 9 x 12 centimeters, the other was 12 x 16 centimeters, and food was always located behind the latter. This was a simple problem for the chimpanzees, and they solved it readily. But the question of interest was what precisely they had learned.

According to Spence's S–R analysis, each card should have been coded independently. Because the chimpanzee was looking at the 12 x 16 centimeters card just before obtaining food, it should have associated this card with the

FIGURE 9.11   Training and test cards used by Kohler (1918/1939). Food was located behind the 12 x 16 centimeter rectangle during training.

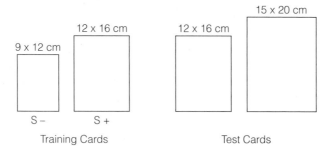

food. According to cognitive theorists, on the other hand, subjects would have compared the two cards before responding. In doing so, they would have noticed that one card was larger than the other, and they would have used this relationship in assigning codes to the two stimuli. Thus, whereas Spence would have predicted that subjects would learn to approach the 12 x 16 card, cognitive theorists predicted that they would learn to approach the *larger* card. To put this another way, S–R theorists believed that subjects would code the absolute properties of any stimulus, regardless of what other stimuli were present, whereas cognitive theorists believed that they would respond to the relational properties of the stimulus, as determined by its stimulus context.

To determine which of these predictions was correct, Kohler gave his subjects test trials in which the formerly positive 12 x 16 centimeter rectangle was paired with a new rectangle measuring 15 x 20 centimeters (Figure 9.11). If the chimpanzees had coded the positive stimulus during training as a 12 x 16 centimeter card, they should continue to choose this card during the test phase; if they had learned to approach the larger card, they should prefer the 15 x 20 centimeter rectangle. In some respects, this is an extraordinary prediction—that after repeated reinforcement for approaching a particular card, subjects should ignore it and go to one they had never previously encountered—but this is exactly what Kohler found. The chimpanzees preferred the larger card on more than 90% of the test trials. This result, moreover, could not be attributed to any special intellectual capacities of chimpanzees, because Kohler obtained the same results using baby chicks as subjects.

The most obvious explanation for the performance of Kohler's animals was that they had learned about the relationship between the cards during training, and that they based their responding during the test phase on this same relationship. Because they seemed to be transferring, or transposing, the relationship they had learned during training to the test problem, this phenomenon became known as **transposition**.

Spence's S–R model. Transposition seemed to provide conclusive evidence that stimuli are coded in terms of their relationships. In a brilliant paper published in 1937, however, Spence argued that transposition could be explained in terms of simple associative principles, without invoking complex perceptual processes. The first principle Spence appealed to was reinforcement: A response followed by a reinforcer will be associated with whatever stimuli are present at the time. Spence's second principle was extinction: If a response is not reinforced, an inhibitory connection will be established between the stimuli present and the response. The third principle was generalization: Both excitatory and inhibitory tendencies generalize to similar stimuli.

To see how these three simple principles could account for transposition, we will trace one of the hypothetical examples provided by Spence. Suppose, he said, that subjects were trained on a size discrimination involving cards of 256 and 160 square centimeters, with food available behind the larger card (hereafter referred to as 256+). As a result of reinforcement in the presence of this stimulus, an excitatory connection would be formed between it and the response. Similarly, nonreinforcement of responding to 160– would result in an inhibitory association between this stimulus and the response. Both of these tendencies would generalize to similar stimuli, and although very little information about the shape of generalization gradients was available at the time Spence wrote, he speculated that both excitatory and inhibitory generalization gradients would have the concave form illustrated in Figure 9.12. (If the shape of these generalization gradients looks somewhat strange, it is because we know from subsequent research that typical generalization gradients have a shape more like that of a bell—see, for example, Figure 9.13.)

The first point to notice about Figure 9.12 is that, because of generalization, most stimuli would have both excitatory and inhibitory associations with the response. There was no experimental evidence to suggest how these opposing tendencies would combine to determine responding, so Spence chose the simplest possible combination rule: that the net associative strength of any stimulus would be the sum of its positive and negative tendencies. If a stimulus had a generalized excitatory strength of +4.0 units, for example, and an inhibitory strength of –1.5 units, then its net associative strength would be:

$$4.0 + (-1.5) = +2.5$$

Assigning arbitrary values to the positive and negative stimuli used during training, Spence was then able to calculate how these tendencies would generalize to other stimuli and how these generalized values would combine to determine the response. This value for several representative stimuli is represented graphically in Figure 9.12 by the height of the line separating the excitatory and inhibitory gradients (that is, by the difference in their strengths) and is also given numerically. Looking at stimulus 256+, for example, we can see that its

FIGURE 9.12   Hypothetical generalization gradients proposed by Spence to account for transposition. Reinforcement of choices of a 256-square-centimeter card would produce a positive generalization gradient around 256; nonreinforcement of a 160-square-centimeter card would produce an inhibitory generalization gradient around 160. The net associative strength of any stimulus would be the difference between the positive and negative gradients; the numerical values for selected stimuli are indicated. (Adapted from Spence, 1937)

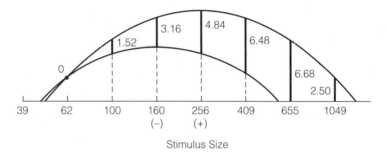

net strength after training would be 4.84 units, whereas that of stimulus 160– would be only 3.16. At the end of training, therefore, we should expect subjects to prefer 256+ to 160–, because its net associative strength would be greater. Notice, however, what would happen if subjects were presented with a choice between 256+ and the still larger stimulus of 409 square centimeters. Even though 409 had never been presented previously, its net associative strength would be greater than that of the 256+ stimulus, which had been reinforced. By taking generalization into account, in other words, Spence was able to explain transposition without invoking any of the internal processing mechanisms postulated by cognitive theorists.

Peak shift.   As well as accounting for Kohler's data on transposition, Spence's model allows predictions about learning in many other situations. For example, the model can be applied not only to transposition experiments in which the training stimuli are presented simultaneously, but also to successive discrimination studies in which only one stimulus is present at a time. In an experiment on pigeons by Hanson (1959), for example, a key was illuminated alternately with lights of 550 and 590 nm, with pecking reinforced only in the presence of the 550-nm wavelength. The birds then received a series of nonreinforced presentations of other wavelengths to measure generalization.

According to Spence's analysis, during training an excitatory gradient should have been established around 550+ and an inhibitory gradient around 590–. If these gradients combined in the manner predicted by Spence, then peak response during the test phase should have occurred not to 550+ but rather to some shorter wavelength, away from 590–. As shown in Figure 9.13, this **peak shift** is what Hanson found. In a control group trained only with 550+,

FIGURE 9.13   Generalization gradients following training with only a 550-nm stimulus (control) or discrimination training between 550+ and 590− (discrimination). (Adapted from Hanson, 1959)

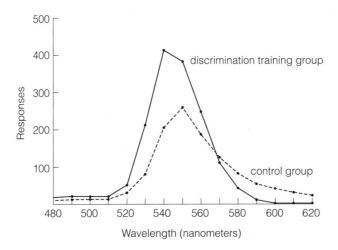

peak responding during the generalization test was to the 550-nm wavelength, but in the discrimination training group the peak was shifted to 540 nm. Spence's model thus correctly predicted the almost bizarre finding that peak responding occurred not to the stimulus reinforced during training but to one displaced away from the negative stimulus (S−).[2]

Relational learning. The occurrence of peak shift, even under conditions in which S+ and S− were never present at the same time during training, provides strong support for Spence's assumption of interacting generalization gradients. (See also Honig, Boneau, Burstein, & Pennypacker, 1963.) But other evidence suggests that although excitatory and inhibitory gradients do play an important

---

[2]One aspect of this study that was certainly not as Spence predicted was the height of the postdiscrimination gradient. Spence's generalization-of-inhibition analysis predicts that peak responding should shift from 550 nm to a shorter wavelength and that the level of responding to this wavelength should be less than in the control group. As shown in the graph, however, responding to 540 nm was substantially greater in the group given nonreinforced trials with 590−. The cause of this elevation is probably related to the phenomenon of contrast effects discussed in Chapter 5. Experience with a small amount of reinforcement, we saw then, enhances the effectiveness of larger amounts; in a similar fashion, it has been found that low rates of reinforcement may enhance the effectiveness of higher rates—a phenomenon known as *behavioral contrast*. In the group given discrimination training, nonreinforcement in the presence of 590 nm may have enhanced the effectiveness of reinforcement in the presence of 550 nm, thereby increasing responding. The final generalization gradient might thus be determined by an interaction among at least three processes: generalized excitation, generalized inhibition, and behavioral contrast.

FIGURE 9.14   Training and test stimuli used by Lawrence and DeRivera (1954). The cards varied in brightness between white (card 1) and black (card 7). The bottom card during training was always card 4. If the top card was 1, 2, or 3, a turn to the right was reinforced; if the top card was 5, 6, or 7, a turn to the left was reinforced.

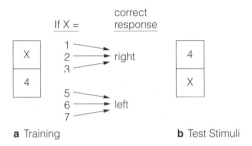

a Training   **b** Test Stimuli

role in discrimination learning, they cannot account for all of the evidence concerning transposition. A particularly neat illustration of this point comes from an experiment by Lawrence and DeRivera (1954), who trained rats on a brightness discrimination involving seven cards ranging in brightness from white (card 1) to black (card 7) in roughly equal steps. During training, the mid-gray card (card 4) was present on every trial, with one of the other cards mounted above it (Figure 9.14a). If the top card was light (card 1, 2, or 3), the rat was reinforced for going to the right; if it was dark (card 5, 6, or 7), the rat was reinforced for going to the left.

According to relational theory, the rats should have solved this problem on the basis of the relationship between the cards: If the top card was brighter, go right; if darker, go left. According to S–R theory, on the other hand, responding should be conditioned independently to each of the elements present on a reinforced trial. Turning to the right, therefore, should have become conditioned to cards 1, 2, and 3, since each would have been present on trials in which this response was reinforced. Similarly, cards 5, 6, and 7 should have become associated with a turn to the left. As for card 4, since it was present on trials in which turns to both right and left were reinforced, it should have become associated with both responses, and hence effectively neutral.

Since both theories predict successful learning, how can we decide which one is correct? Lawrence and DeRivera's solution was simple: They reversed the cards. Instead of presenting card 1 on top of card 4, for example, they presented 4 on top of 1 (Figure 9.14b). If subjects had solved the original problem on the basis of relationships, they should now reverse their responses, because the top card was now darker than the bottom one. If the response had been conditioned to each of the elements separately, on the other hand, subjects should continue to respond as they had during training, because card 4 would still be neutral and card 1 would still elicit a turn to the right. Unfortunately for S–R theory, more than 75% of the responses were reversed, indicating that the relationship between the cards was crucial in determining the response.

Together with other evidence (Hebert & Krantz, 1965; Dreyfus, Fetterman, Stubbs, & Montello, 1992; Kirkpatrick-Steger, Wasserman, & Biederman, 1998), these results make it clear that subjects do sometimes code stimuli in terms of their relationship to each other. The fact that subjects can code relationships, however, does not mean that they always respond on this basis: There is considerable evidence that subjects also respond to the absolute properties of stimuli, and the current consensus is that subjects normally code both aspects of stimuli. In the Kohler experiment, for example, it is likely that the chimpanzees coded the correct card in terms of its absolute properties ("It is a 12 x 16 centimeter rectangle") as well as its relation to surrounding stimuli ("It is the larger rectangle"). According to this view, which property of a stimulus governs response depends on the precise characteristics of the stimuli used during testing, with transposition being observed with some test stimuli but absolute responding with others (Lane & Rabinowitz, 1979; Thomas, Mood, Morrison, & Wiertelak, 1991).

Configural Learning

Further evidence that stimuli are not always coded independently comes from experiments on configural learning. In one of the first experiments of this kind, Woodbury (1943) gave dogs trials with either a high-pitched buzzer (H), a low-pitched buzzer (L), or both together (HL). If the buzzers were presented on their own, a response on a lever was reinforced, but not if the buzzers were presented together:

$$H : R \rightarrow food$$

$$L : R \rightarrow food$$

$$HL : R \rightarrow \underline{\quad}$$

The results for one of Woodbury's dogs, Chuck, are shown in Figure 9.15. When the buzzers were presented separately, Chuck responded on virtually every trial. When they were presented in compound, at first Chuck also responded; as training continued, though, this response gradually extinguished. Thus, even though both elements of the compound elicited vigorous responding, when presented together there was no response.

This result is utterly mystifying if a compound is coded solely in terms of its constituent elements. If H elicits a response, and L elicits a response, then H and L together should also elicit a response. The result begins to make sense, however, if we assume that stimuli presented together can form a unique

FIGURE 9.15   Configural learning. Presentations of high-pitched (H) and low-pitched (L) tones by themselves were reinforced, but the compound (HL) was not. (Adapted from Woodbury, 1943)

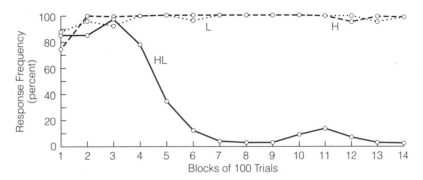

stimulus, or configuration, that is not like either of its components. If we relabel the HL compound as C to emphasize its unique qualities, then Woodbury's procedure can be represented as:

$$H : R \rightarrow food$$

$$L : R \rightarrow food$$

$$C : R \rightarrow \underline{\qquad}$$

Viewed in this light, it is hardly surprising that subjects eventually ceased to respond when the compound was presented.

The assumption that a compound is a totally unique stimulus, however, raises its own problems: If the HL compound bore no resemblance to its components (and this assumption is necessary to explain why the response to H and L did not generalize to HL), then why did the dogs continue to respond to the compound for hundreds of trials, even though responses on this trial were never reinforced? Rescorla suggested a possible solution. (There are those who believe that Rescorla is not a person, but a team of brilliant researchers working night and day who share the name.) According to Rescorla's "unique stimulus" hypothesis (Rescorla, 1973), an AB compound can be viewed as consisting of three stimuli: A, B, and a unique stimulus arising from their conjunction, which we will again label C. Thus, in Woodbury's experiment, H and L were paired with reinforcement, but the HLC compound was not. Applying the Rescorla-Wagner model to this situation, Rescorla (1973) was able to show that the compound would initially elicit a response because of the reinforcement given to H and L, but that with continued training C would become sufficiently inhibitory to block the response on the compound trials. This analysis can

FIGURE 9.16   Possible coding of a compound presented during configural learning. When an AB compound is presented, subjects may code A, B, or the AB configuration. Any or all of these codes may then be associated with a subsequent response.

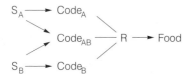

account for a wide range of experiments involving children (Zeaman & Hanley, 1983) as well as animals (Rescorla, 1973).

Pearce (1994) has proposed an alternative model of configural learning. To see how his analysis differs from that of Rescorla, consider a discrimination experiment in which an AB compound is followed by food, but A and B on their own are not:

$$AB \rightarrow Food$$

$$A \rightarrow \underline{\quad}$$

$$B \rightarrow \underline{\quad}$$

According to Rescorla, three associations would be formed on the AB compound trials: A, B, and the AB configuration would each form their own association with the US. According to Pearce, on the other hand, only a single association would be formed, between the AB configuration and food. When A and B are presented on their own, each would elicit some responding through generalization—A, for example, clearly resembles the AB compound, because it is present in both. Nevertheless, A would not itself have a direct association with food.

On the surface, the difference between Rescorla's and Pearce's accounts seems very small, but it turns out that they lead to some quite different predictions. Several attempts to test these predictions have produced some support for each (for example, Rescorla, 1997b; Pearce, Aydin, & Redhead, 1997). As with transposition, the most likely explanation seems to be that we are capable of coding stimuli in different ways. As illustrated in Figure 9.16, we can code compounds in terms of their individual elements, the configuration of these elements, or both. (See also Williams, 1996; Schmajuk, Lamoreux, & Holland, 1998.) If so, the task for future research will be to identify the conditions that promote each type of coding. (For a discussion of some of these conditions, see Shepp, 1983, and Rescorla, 1985b.)

9.5 RETRIEVAL

The coding of a stimulus is clearly a far more complex process than S–R theorists first supposed. Subjects selectively attend to stimuli in their environment, they search for relationships among these stimuli, and, after all that, they may remember an experience not in terms of the stimuli that were present but rather the response that they will need to make. The code that is eventually assigned to a stimulus in memory is clearly the product of extensive processing.

Suppose, now, that this coding process has been completed, and that a representation of the original stimulus has been stored in memory. If this stimulus is followed by an event such as food, will the two events be associated?[3]

According to the theory of memory sketched at the beginning of this chapter, the presentation of a stimulus results in the activation of a node in the cortex. Furthermore, an association can be formed between two nodes only while they are both active. For an association to be formed between a CS and a US, therefore, the nodes that represent them would have to be active at the same time.

The simplest way this could occur would be if the CS is still present at the time that US is delivered, and thus both nodes were active at the same time. Suppose, however, that activity in the CS node has already faded by the time the US appears, as in the case of taste-aversion conditioning, where hours may elapse between one's eating a food and becoming ill. How is it possible for an association to be formed under these circumstances?

Surprise!

Kamin (1969) suggested that the presentation of a US can trigger a search through memory for events that occurred previously. Specifically, he proposed that this search would occur whenever the occurrence of the US was unexpected. If rats received an unexpected electric shock, for example, they would need to search their memories to identify possible predictors, to help them to avoid that shock in the future. But a memory search requires effort. To save time and energy, therefore, subjects would search their memories for predictors only if the US surprised them—if they expected it, then by definition a cue predicting its occurrence must already have been available, so that no further search was necessary.

---

[3]Although we will largely concentrate on examples drawn from classical conditioning in this section, similar or identical processes occur during operant conditioning. That is, although classical conditioning involves stimulus–stimulus relationships, and operant conditioning involves response–stimulus relationships, the processes involved in the formation of associations between two events appear to be the same in both cases. That, at any rate, will be our guiding assumption in this section, and we will occasionally use evidence drawn from research on reinforcement as well as classical conditioning. We will return to the assumption that classical and operant conditioning are fundamentally similar in Chapter 10, where we will examine it more closely.

Kamin based this analysis on his studies of blocking. (See Section 3.4.) In the first phase of these experiments, he gave rats conditioning trials in which a noise was paired with shock, followed by a second set of trials in which a noise-light compound was paired with shock:

$$Noise \rightarrow Shock \qquad Noise\text{-}Light \rightarrow Shock$$

He found no conditioning to the light during the compound trials, and he argued that this was because subjects had learned during the first phase that the noise would be followed by shock. When the shock was presented following the compound, subjects were not surprised, and as a result they did not initiate a memory search to identify possible predictors.

However, blocking could also be explained quite differently, in terms of attention. We have seen that our brains have only a limited capacity to process stimuli in our environment; the more we attend to one stimulus, the less we can attend to others. When the noise was paired with shock during the first phase, subjects would have learned to attend to the noise. When presented with the noise-light compound, therefore, they might have attended to the noise and ignored the light, and this would explain why no fear was conditioned to the light.

Kamin considered this attentional explanation implausible on several counts. For one thing, the noise and light were presented together for three minutes during compound trials. Although a rat's processing capacity might be limited, it does strain credulity to suppose that it could attend to only a single stimulus in the course of three minutes! Moreover, Kamin was able to present empirical evidence that his rats *had* detected the light. Both the pretraining and the compound trials had taken place during sessions in which the rats were also pressing a bar to obtain food, so Kamin could measure whether the stimuli suppressed responding on every trial. On the final trial during pretraining, the noise produced a suppression ratio of 0.02 (that is, strong conditioning). When the light was introduced on the next trial, however, the suppression ratio rose to 0.15. In other words, the rats clearly had detected the light, since its introduction produced an immediate change in their behavior.

To provide a further test of whether blocking was because of a failure to attend to the light or a failure to retrieve it, Kamin ran an additional group. This group also received a pretraining phase in which a noise was paired with shock, followed by compound trials in which a noise-light compound was followed by shock. In the compound trials, though, the shock at the end of each 3-minute trial was followed by a second shock five seconds later:

$$Noise \rightarrow Shock \qquad Noise\text{-}Light \rightarrow Shock...Shock$$

According to an attentional analysis, adding the second shock should have no effect. During pretraining, the rats would have learned to attend to the noise, so that when the light was introduced they would not process it. Adding a second shock should not change this result: If the rats did not notice the light, they could not associate it with the second shock any more than with the first.

According to Kamin's surprise analysis, on the other hand, the introduction of this second shock should significantly alter the outcome. During pretraining, the rats would have learned that the noise was followed by a shock, so that on the compound trials they would again expect the shock to follow. The second shock, however, would come as a complete surprise, so the rats would search their memories for possible causes, notice the preceding light, and associate it with the shock. The presence of the second shock, in other words, should restore conditioning to the light. This was what Kamin found. When fear conditioning was assessed in a CER test, the light produced powerful suppression of responding. Conditioning thus seemed to depend on whether the US was surprising: In Kamin's first experiment, shock was expected on compound trials because of earlier pairings with the noise, and no conditioning occurred; when the outcome was made surprising in his second experiment by adding an extra shock, conditioning was restored.

Subsequent research has confirmed the importance of surprise for conditioning. Dickinson, Hall, and Mackintosh (1976), for example, manipulated surprise by removing a shock during compound trials instead of adding one. Their subjects received two shocks during the pretraining phase; half of the subjects continued to receive two shocks during the compound trials, while half were switched to one shock. No conditioning occurred to the light for subjects who continued to receive two shocks (no surprise), whereas strong conditioning was found in subjects switched to one shock. As in Kamin's research, conditioning occurred only when the US was unexpected.

Retrieval Cues

A second factor that could determine whether a CS is retrieved from memory is the availability of retrieval cues. According to the theory of memory that we have been using as our guide, an event is retrieved from storage when its node receives activation from other nodes that are already active. When a CS is presented in a conditioning experiment, for example, the CS node is assumed to become associated with the nodes of other stimuli that are present at the time. If these stimuli are again present at the time of retrieval, then activation will spread from their nodes to that of the CS. Whether we retrieve a CS from memory should thus depend on whether retrieval cues are present that were previously associated with that CS.

Reactivation. One way to test this analysis is to deliberately introduce retrieval cues prior to a memory test, to see if they will enhance recall. This strategy has been used in a number of experiments on classical and operant conditioning, and the results have strongly confirmed the importance of retrieval cues. In one of these experiments, DeWeer, Sara, and Hars (1980) trained rats to run through a complex maze in order to obtain food and then tested performance 25 days later. A control group was placed directly in the maze, but a reminder group was first placed in a mesh cage next to the maze and held there for 90 seconds before being transferred to the maze. The control group showed substantial forgetting compared to their performance at the end of training: They took almost five times as long to reach the goal box, and made many more errors while on route. The reminder group, on the other hand, showed virtually no deterioration. Placement next to the maze for 90 seconds apparently gave these reminder subjects more time to recall their earlier experiences in the maze, compared to control subjects who probably began to run almost as soon they were placed in the maze. (The situation is perhaps comparable to that facing students taking a multiple-choice exam; students who pause to think before answering are likely to have a better chance of remembering the correct answer.)

This procedure—exposing subjects to some aspect of the training situation prior to testing, to see if it will help them remember what they had learned in that situation—is called **reactivation.** Spear (1978) and Gordon (1981) pioneered this procedure, and they and their colleagues have reported extensive evidence for its effectiveness. It now appears that a very wide range of the cues present during training can act as retrieval cues, including the texture of the floor, the room where the apparatus was located, the time of day, and, in the case of classical conditioning, the CS and the US. (Presenting either of these stimuli on their own before a test can substantially increase conditioned responding during the test.)

There is even evidence that internal cues present at the time a response is reinforced can become associated with the response. In one study by Overton (1964), rats were trained to turn right in a maze when they had previously been given an injection of sodium pentobarbital; they had to turn left during sessions when they had not been drugged. When the rats were later tested in a drugged state, they turned right, whereas when tested without drugs they turned left. These results suggest that internal cues—in this case, generated by drugs—can act as retrieval cues in exactly the same way as external cues. (See Overton, 1985, for further examples involving internal stimuli such as hunger.)

The renewal effect. Further evidence for the importance of retrieval cues in associative learning comes from a phenomenon called the **renewal effect.** In one of the first demonstrations of this phenomenon, Bouton and King (1983) gave rats fear conditioning trials in which a tone was paired with shock. They then extinguished this conditioning by presenting the tone by itself. For one group, the extinction trials were conducted in the same apparatus (Context A) as the conditioning trials. For a second group, extinction took place in a different apparatus (Context B). The two chambers differed not only in visual

FIGURE 9.17   The renewal effect. The curves on the left show suppression ratios during extinction trials; the curves on the right show suppression during a subsequent test in which the CS was again presented on its own. For Group AAA, conditioning, extinction and test trials were all conducted in the same apparatus; for Group ABA, extinction trials were conducted in a different apparatus. When testing was conducted in the same apparatus as conditioning but not extinction (Group ABA), the previously extinguished response reappeared. (Adapted from Bouton & King, 1983)

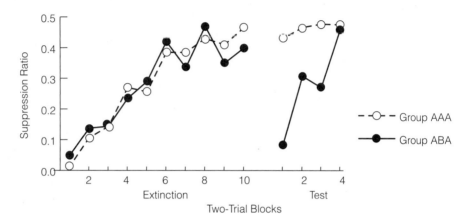

appearance (for example, the presence of stripes on the walls) but in aspects such as floor texture and odor (one was scented with vinegar, the other with Vick's Vaporub). When extinction was complete, both groups were returned to Context A for some additional extinction test trials:

	Conditioning	Extinction	Test
Group AAA:	A: CS → US	A: CS → ___	A: CS → ___
Group ABA:	A: CS → US	B: CS → ___	A: CS → ___

Fear was successfully conditioned in both groups, and their performance during extinction was virtually identical (Figure 9.17). The question of interest in this study, though, was how the two groups would respond during the final test.

Since fear had been completely extinguished in both groups by the end of extinction, it seems reasonable to suppose that the strength of the CS–US association was the same in both groups—that is, zero—and thus that the two groups would respond identically in the final test. Suppose, however, that during conditioning subjects formed associations not only between the CS and US but also between these stimuli and other cues that were present. In the case of group AAA, they would have associated the cues of context A first with conditioning and then with extinction. When returned to the apparatus for the test trials, therefore, the cues of context A would have reminded them of both experiences. Since the test trials followed shortly after many days of extinction, however, we would expect subjects to resolve any conflict by deciding that the extinction conditions were still likely to be in effect. (See also Brooks & Bouton, 1993.) In line with this analysis, the CS produced virtually no fear in this group.

Let us turn now to group ABA. When they were returned to context A for testing, the stimuli of this context would have reminded them more strongly of their previous experiences in this context (conditioning) than of their experiences in context B (extinction). In other words, these subjects should have remembered conditioning more strongly than extinction, and hence should once again have been frightened when the tone was presented. As shown in Figure 9.17, this is what happened.

Bouton and his colleagues have called this phenomenon the renewal effect because the fear extinguished in context B reappeared or was renewed when subjects were returned to context A. These results indicate again that conditioning does not occur in a vacuum: The contextual stimuli present during conditioning may become associated with the CS and US that are presented, and these contextual stimuli may then act as retrieval cues to remind subjects of these pairings. The renewal effect thus provides further evidence of the central role of retrieval cues in determining what we remember. More information on this topic can be found in extensive reviews by Bouton (1993) and Miller, Barnet, and Grahame (1995).

Interference

A third determinant of retrieval in human memory is the number of events that occurred in the same context. If people are asked to memorize a list of words, for example, they find it harder to later remember this list if they memorized other lists either beforehand (proactive interference) or afterwards (retroactive interference).The reason for this, we suggested at the beginning of the chapter, is cue overload: The effectiveness of any one link from a retrieval cue is reduced in proportion to the number of other links from that same cue (Figure 9.3).

Interference effects have also been reported in studies of classical and operant conditioning. In the case of classical conditioning, Revusky (1971) studied the role of interference in the formation of taste aversions. He gave rats a saccharin-flavored solution to drink and then, one hour later, an injection of lithium chloride to make them ill. As expected, the rats developed an aversion to the taste of the saccharin, as demonstrated by a substantial reduction in drinking of this solution in a later test. A second group was also exposed to saccharin and then poisoned one hour later, except that 15 minutes into the delay interval the second group was given a vinegar solution to drink. When this group was later tested, they drank significantly more of the saccharin solution than the control group, indicating that drinking vinegar during the delay interval had interfered with association of the saccharin with illness (retroactive interference). In a second experiment, Revusky found that tastes given before the CS also interfered with conditioning (proactive interference). The presence of other stimuli during conditioning, in other words, interferes with conditioning to the CS, and this is true whether the competing stimuli occur before or after the target.

Proactive and retroactive interference have also been demonstrated in experiments on reinforcement. Grant and Roberts (1973), for example, explored the role of proactive interference in delayed matching to sample in pigeons. They used colors as their samples, and on a typical trial they presented a red stimulus as a sample and then, after a delay, offered subjects a choice between red and green comparison stimuli; if the birds chose the red comparison stimulus on this trial, they received food. On some trials, however, they presented two samples in quick succession—the center key was illuminated with a green light, for example, immediately followed by illumination with a red light. The second cue was the true sample, so that subjects still needed to peck the red comparison stimulus to obtain reinforcement. Performance, however, was substantially poorer on these interference trials.

In the Grant and Roberts experiment, we cannot be sure whether the second cue interfered with subjects' ability to recall the sample, or whether the presence of two samples left subjects confused as to which sample was the real one. In some other studies of delayed matching to sample, however, illumination of the chamber during the delay interval has been used as an interfering stimulus. (Normally the chamber is dark during this period.) Illumination of the chamber is clearly not a sample, but this procedure also interferes with performance, apparently because illumination allows subjects to see other stimuli during the retention interval (Grant, 1988). Experiments on conditioning in animals thus point to the same conclusion as experiments on memory in humans: The more events occur in the same context, the harder it is to recall any one of them.

9.6 THE ASSOCIATIVE STAGE

Suppose, finally, that a CS has been coded, that it is followed by a US which initiates a memory search, and that this search successfully retrieves a memory of this CS. Can we now, at last, conclude that the CS and US will be associated? Or, rephrasing the question in the terms of the theoretical model we have been pursuing, if two nodes are simultaneously active in working memory, does this guarantee that they will be associated?

Is Contiguity Sufficient?

Some evidence suggests that the answer may be *yes*. In our discussion of retrieval cues, for example, we saw that a very wide range of the stimuli present during conditioning trials can be employed as retrieval cues, implying that most or all of these stimuli became associated with the CS and US when they occurred together. Further support for this possibility is available in an interesting study by Ward-Robinson and Hall (1996). In the first stage of their experiment, they exposed rats to pairings of neutral stimuli such as a click and a light. In the second phase, they paired the click with shock:

Preconditioning: *Click → Light*

Conditioning: *Click → Shock*

Finally, they used a CER test to see if the light elicited any fear.

On the surface, this might seem a rather strange result to expect: Since the light was never paired with shock, why should it produce fear? If associations are formed between any nodes that are active at the same time, however, this is exactly the result that would be expected. During the preconditioning phase, subjects would have associated the click and the light. When the click was presented during the conditioning phase, therefore, activation of the click node would have spread to the light node. And, since the light node would then have been active at the same time as the shock node, an association could have formed between them:

Click → [Light] → Shock

The results confirmed this prediction: When the light was presented in the CER test, it elicited significant levels of fear. This fear could simply have generalized from the click—we have seen many times that a response conditioned to one stimulus will generalize to similar stimuli—but the click and light used in this study were not obviously similar, and, more to the point, Ward-Robinson and Hall used control procedures that allowed them to eliminate this interpretation. The most plausible interpretation of their results seems to be that simultaneous activation of the light and shock nodes on conditioning trials was sufficient to establish an association between them, even though the light was not actually present. In effect, pairing an image of a stimulus with shock was sufficient to condition fear to that stimulus.

If this hypothesis seems familiar, it may be because it is the rationale for therapies such as systematic desensitization, where subjects are asked to imagine a feared object, such as a spider, while trying to relax. It is the *image* of the spider that is paired with relaxation, rather than an actual spider. In desensitization, subjects are deliberately trying to associate the image with relaxation, but the Ward-Robinson and Hall results imply that this process may happen automatically whenever two nodes are simultaneously active. (See also Dwyer, Mackintosh, & Boakes, 1998.)

There is evidence, however, that active nodes are not always associated. In our discussion of taste-aversion learning, for example, we described the Garcia and Koelling (1966) experiment in which rats received a taste-noise-light compound followed immediately by either shock or irradiation (causing illness). The irradiated rats developed an aversion to the taste, but the shocked rats did not.

Why didn't the rats associate the taste with the shock? The explanation cannot be that the rats did not attend to the taste, because when the taste was followed by illness, other subjects had no difficulty associating the two experiences. Nor can it be argued that the rats did not attend to the shock, because an aversion was conditioned to the noise on shock trials. Both the taste and the shock, therefore, must have activated their neural centers on these trials. That an association was not formed suggests that we do not associate all active centers, but only some subset. Associative learning, in other words, is apparently not nearly as promiscuous as contiguity models sometimes imply. Selection can occur during at least three phases: during the coding of a stimulus, when we selectively attend to some aspects of the situation; at retrieval, when we recall some memories but not others; and, finally, during the actual formation of associations, when we associate only some of the nodes in an active state.

The Role of Rehearsal

We have been developing a model of memory based on several simple assumptions. First, associations are formed between nodes in the brain only while these nodes are active. Second, the formation of an association takes time, and we use rehearsal to maintain the nodes in an active state long enough to allow the process to be completed. Third, our capacity for rehearsal is limited so that our ability to rehearse an association will be reduced if we allocate too much attention to other events occurring at the same time. Finally, we assume that how much attention we devote to any event depends in part on how much we are surprised by it: The more we are surprised by an event, the more attention we are likely to pay to it.

We introduced this model in the context of coding, where we suggested that our ability to remember a stimulus depends on associating it with contextual stimuli present at the time, but these assumptions apply to the formation of any association, including associations between a CS and a US, and a response and a reinforcer. Our ability to form any of these associations should depend on how much time we have to rehearse them in the absence of distraction from other events.

Wagner, Rudy, and Whitlow (1973) tested this prediction in an ingenious experiment. They gave rabbits eyeblink-conditioning trials in which one

FIGURE 9.18   The effect on conditioning of stimuli presented after a trial. Each conditioning trial was followed 10 seconds later by either a surprising post-trial episode—for example, a previously established CS– followed by a US—or an unsurprising episode. (Adapted from Wagner, Rudy, & Whitlow, 1973)

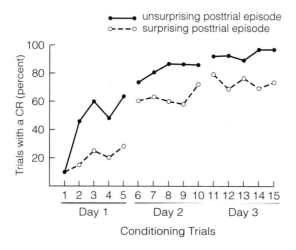

stimulus, S+, was followed by a mild shock to the region of the eye, and another stimulus, S–, was presented on its own:

$$S+ \rightarrow US$$

$$S- \rightarrow \_\_$$

After the rabbits had learned to blink only to S+, they were given additional conditioning trials in which a new stimulus, X, was paired with the shock:

$$X \rightarrow US$$

For some subjects, each conditioning trial was followed after a 10-second delay by a distracting event, to see if the distractor would interfere with formation of the X–US association. And, to test the assumption of our memory model that the amount of attention devoted to an event depends on how surprising it is, they varied the surprise value of the distracting event. Specifically, on some trials the distractor involved an unexpected event—either S+ presented without the shock, or S– presented with the shock. For the remaining subjects, the pairings were in accord with earlier training—S+ followed by shock or S– without shock. According to the preceding analysis, subjects exposed to surprising posttrial episodes should have paid more attention to them, and, as a result,

FIGURE 9.19   The impact of a surprising episode on conditioning as a function of the delay interval between the conditioning trial and the episode. (Adapted from Wagner, Rudy, & Whitlow, 1973)

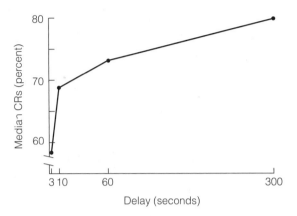

learning of the preceding CS–US association should be impaired. As shown in Figure 9.18, this was what Wagner's group found: Eyeblink conditioning was significantly slower when conditioning trials were followed by a surprising event.

In a second experiment, the experimenters varied the time interval between the CS–US pairing and the presentation of the unexpected posttrial episode. The more time that subjects are allowed to associate the CS and US, the less this association should be affected by a diversion of attention to other events; again, this was what Wagner's group found. As shown in Figure 9.19, the longer the delay between the conditioning trial and the posttrial unexpected event, the stronger conditioning was to the CS. These experiments support the view that conditioning depends on how long two events are simultaneously active in memory. The more time subjects have to rehearse events and to maintain them in working memory, the greater the likelihood that they will form permanent associations.

9.7 SUMMARY

We saw in Chapter 8 that classical and operant conditioning can produce a very wide range of outcomes; our goal in this chapter has been to better understand the processes that determine which S–R association, or which expectation, will actually be learned. We began by examining an information-processing model of memory developed from research on human memory. According to this model, the sensory processes involved in the perception of an event eventually lead to the activation of a group of neurons in the brain called a node. A node represents an event, and once a node has been activated, it normally remains active only briefly. The set of nodes active at any one time is called short-term or working memory.

To form a more enduring memory of an event, we need to associate it with the contextual stimuli that accompany it; in neural terms, we need to associate its node with other nodes that are currently active. The formation of such associations takes time, and we use rehearsal to maintain nodes in an active state long enough for associations to be completed. Our capacity for rehearsal is limited—in the case of words, we seem to be able to maintain only around seven words in working memory at a time.

Once contextual stimuli have been associated with an event, they can act as retrieval cues to allow us to recall the event. If these stimuli are present when we try to recall the event, then activation will spread from their nodes to that of the target event, thereby retrieving the event into working memory.

With this model as a framework, we turned to the role of memory in conditioning. Considerable research suggests that animals use rehearsal to maintain events in working memory in a manner similar to humans. Pigeons rehearse a stimulus longer if they are surprised by its occurrence; they stop rehearsing it if they are given a cue that memory will not be tested. In a further demonstration of the similarity of coding processes in animals and humans, Kesner and DeSpain found that rats and humans will use either retrospective codes (remembering a stimulus) or prospective codes (remembering the response that they will need to make), depending on which strategy is easiest.

The code assigned to a stimulus in memory also depends on what other stimuli are present at the time. We cannot attend fully to all of the stimuli impinging on our senses, and we seem to attend more to stimuli or stimulus dimensions that we have learned are good predictors of important events. Nevertheless, Pearce and Hall have found that in some situations we might also pay less attention to stimuli that are good predictors, precisely because we already understand their significance and, therefore, do not need to devote full attention to them.

We also code stimuli in terms of their relationship to the other stimuli that are present. If animals are presented with a problem in which the larger of two cards contains food, they will learn to choose the larger card, and if given a choice between the positive card and a still larger card, will choose the larger card. Spence was able to provide an ingenious explanation for transposition in terms of excitatory and inhibitory generalization from the positive and negative cards, but other evidence eventually confirmed that animals do sometimes code stimuli in terms of their relationships to each other. Configural learning also demonstrates the coding of stimuli in terms of relationships: Subjects might code a compound stimulus, not simply as a set of independent elements, but as a unique configuration.

Whether a coded stimulus is then associated with a subsequent event depends in part on whether that event is sufficiently surprising to trigger a memory search. If a search does occur, the outcome seems to depend on the retrieval cues that are present: If cues are present that were present when a response was reinforced, for example, subjects are more likely to recall that response (reactivation). Similarly, an extinguished response will reappear if stimuli associated with conditioning are presented (the renewal effect). On the other hand, retrieval is impaired if other events occurred in the same context; retrieval cues seem to be less effective in reactivating one event when they are also associated with other events.

If memory for a CS is successfully retrieved after a US is presented, it might seem that the hard work has been done, and that the formation of an association is assured. Indeed, in many situations it does look as if associations are formed whenever two nodes are active at the same time. In a particularly dramatic example, Ward-Robinson and Hall (1996) found that a CS can be associated with a US even if the CS is not actually present—it is sufficient that some other stimulus reminds the subject of the CS. In some situations, however, simultaneous activity is not sufficient for the formation of an association— taste-aversion learning is an example.

The strength of the associations formed between two nodes depends on how long the nodes are simultaneously active. Wagner, Rudy, and Whitlow (1973) have shown that the presentation of distracting events following a conditioning trial will reduce conditioning: The more attention is paid to the distraction, the less rehearsal capacity is available for associating the CS and US.

One final point concerns the convergence in recent years between theories of animal and human learning. To a remarkable extent, the concepts being used to explain associative learning in animals are the same as those used to account for learning and memory in humans. Examples discussed in this chapter include the distinction between short- and long-term memory, the assumption that the capacity for active memory is limited but that this capacity can be extended through rehearsal, and the importance of interfering events and retrieval cues. In part, this similarity reflects the historical roots of human memory research in animal learning. Some of the early theories of human learning were derived from learning concepts developed through research on animals, and these concepts have remained influential. (For a historical survey, see Postman, 1985.)

In recent years, however, the direction of influence has been much stronger from human to animal learning. The success of information-processing approaches in human research has helped to validate, and make acceptable, the use of cognitive concepts such as memory, attention, coding, and retrieval; animal-learning theorists using these concepts have been heavily influenced by the models developed by their human-learning colleagues. (See Wagner, 1981.) That current theories of animal and human learning are often strikingly similar, therefore, does not necessarily prove that the underlying processes are equally similar: It could simply be that the theorists in the two camps have been busily borrowing each other's theories. But if this convergence reflects a genuine similarity in underlying mechanisms, then animal learning may be far more cognitive—and human learning far more associative—than traditional views have suggested.

Glossary

Coding, storage, and **retrieval** Terms originally used to distinguish different phases of a computer's operations, and now used in information-processing theories of human learning to distinguish analogous phases of the brain's operations. In human memory, *coding* is the process by which an external stimulus is eventually assigned a neural representation or code within the brain; *storage* refers to the maintenance of these codes in long-term memory; and *retrieval* refers to recall of these memories.

Short-term memory (STM) and **long-term memory (LTM)** Events that are re-membered only for relatively brief periods (seconds or minutes) are said to be in short-term memory, whereas events remembered for longer periods are said to be in long-term memory. Current theories suggest that neurons are activated temporarily during the coding of a stimulus (short-term memory), and that associations are formed between the active neurons or nodes. If these associations are strong enough, then a permanent record of the experi-ence will be retained (long-term memory).

Working memory The set of active nodes in short-term memory is also sometimes referred to as working memory. The term *working memory* emphasizes the fact that nodes may be activated not only when an event is first presented but also when it is later retrieved in the course of thinking or problem solving.

Rehearsal A term originally confined to repetition of verbal material by saying it out loud or subvocally, but now used to refer to any maintenance of a neural center in an active state when the initiating stimulus is no longer present.

Attention Within associative learning, a term referring to the fact that only some of the stimuli present at a given moment influence our behavior. In this empirical usage, attention, or **selective attention,** is largely synonymous with our earlier definition of stimulus control.

   Confusion may arise because the term *selective attention* is also used to refer to each of the following: (1) a *theory* of selective attention—namely, that selection is due to limitations in our perceptual processing capacity; (2) a *process* that maintains activity in a neural center (also called rehearsal) or selectively facilitates some other aspect of processing; (3) a *conscious expe-rience*. When we say we are paying attention to what someone is saying, we mean in part that we are consciously aware of the person's words.

   These meanings—an empirical relationship, a theory, a process, and a conscious experience—are very different, and it is often unclear which meaning is intended. The underlying theme shared by all these meanings is that we cannot do everything at once.

Proactive interference (PI) and **retroactive interference (RI)** Two types of memory interference. Memory theorists now believe that forgetting is largely because of difficulties in retrieving material stored in memory, and that this difficulty is caused by interference from other stored memories. *Proactive interference* refers to interference from experiences that preceded the event to be remembered; *retroactive interference* refers to interference from experiences following the target event.

Cue overload A reduction in the effectiveness of a retrieval cue in activating an associated memory, due to the cue's association with other memories.

Delayed matching to sample (DMTS) A procedure used for studying short-term memory. In experiments with pigeons, subjects are presented with a sample stimulus on the center key and then, after a delay, the sample and a comparison stimulus are presented on keys on either side of the center key. Subjects are reinforced only if they peck the stimulus that matches the original sample; reinforcement thus depends on the pigeons' remembering what sample stimulus was presented before the delay.

Directed forgetting A procedure in which a cue is presented after a stimulus that normally needs to be remembered; the forget cue signals that the usual memory test will not take place at the end of the trial. (Although, in the perfidious way of psychologists, a test is occasionally presented after a forget cue in order to assess the cue's effect on memory.)

Retrospective and **prospective memory** In *retrospective coding*, we code an event in terms of its physical properties; in *prospective coding*, we code the event in terms of a response that we will later need to perform. If presented with a red light that signals we should later sneeze, for example, remembering the red light would be an example of retrospective coding; remembering to sneeze would be an example of prospective coding.

Extradimensional (ED) shift and **intradimensional (ID) shift** Test procedures for determining whether subjects who learn to discriminate between stimuli that differ along a dimension such as color acquire a general tendency to attend to that dimension. To answer this question, subjects are tested on a second discrimination involving new stimuli. In an intradimensional shift, the new stimuli differ along the same dimension that was relevant during training; in an extradimensional shift, the relevant stimuli shift to a new dimension. For example, suppose that subjects are trained to discriminate between a green object and a red object and are then required to solve a new discrimination involving either color or shape. If the subjects learn a general tendency to attend to color in the first problem, they should do better if the second problem also requires attention to color (an intradimensional shift) than if it requires attention to shape (an extradimensional shift).

Salience The degree to which a stimulus attracts attention. Salient stimuli are more likely to attract attention and to enter into associations.

Transposition In a transposition experiment, subjects are trained to choose one of two stimuli and then are given a choice between a second set of stimuli. If they base their choices between the test stimuli on a relationship that was also present between the first pair (for example, that one card is larger than the other), they are said to have transferred, or transposed, the relationship from training to testing.

Peak shift A shift in the peak of a generalization gradient away from S–. If subjects are given a generalization test following reinforced training with a single stimulus, the peak of the generalization gradient will be located at the training stimulus. However, if subjects are given discrimination training involving two stimuli, the greatest responding during the generalization test occurs not to S+ (the stimulus reinforced during training) but to a stimulus further away from S– (the nonreinforced stimulus during training).

Reactivation The presentation, before a memory test, of one of the stimuli present during training, to see whether this stimulus will act as a retrieval cue to reactivate a memory of the training episode. The stimulus that is presented is also referred to as a *reminder*.

Renewal effect The reappearance of an extinguished response due to a return to the training environment, instead of the environment used during extinction.

Review Questions

1. Define the following terms: node, memory span, retrieval cue, controlled and automatic processing, behavioral contrast, stimulus as coded (SAC), and blocking.

2. What is the information-processing approach? In what respects is it similar to earlier S–R and cognitive theories of learning?

3. What evidence suggests a need to distinguish between short- and long-term memory? What is the current view of how information is transferred from short- to long-term memory?

4. Once material has been coded and stored, why do we sometimes forget it?

5. How is short-term memory often studied in pigeons? What research suggests that short-term memory in pigeons depends on an active or controlled process of rehearsal?

6. What evidence suggests that rats can alternate between prospective and retrospective codes in a fashion similar to humans? Why do they do it?

7. What evidence is there for selective attention? How does the dimensional model account for this evidence? What evidence supports this model?

8. How do the salience models of attention proposed by Mackintosh and by Pearce and Hall differ from the dimensional model, and from each other? What evidence supports the Pearce-Hall model?

9. What evidence suggests that stimuli are coded in terms of their relationships to other stimuli?

10. S–R theorists opposed the postulation of internal processes; when such processes had to be invoked, they preferred the simplest possible mechanism that could account for the known facts. Cognitive theorists, by contrast, assumed that relatively complex internal processes would be required to explain learning. How does the history of transposition illustrate this conflict? How did Spence modify his original model to account for transposition? To what extent was his new model successful?

11. What seems to be the main determinant of whether stimuli, such as food and shock, initiate memory searches? What evidence supports this view?

12. Assuming that a memory search is initiated, what factors determine whether a particular memory will be retrieved?

13. What evidence suggests that retrieval cues play an important role in animal memory?

14. What evidence suggests that interference effects occur in classical and operant conditioning? How can retrieval cues account for these effects?

15. If two nodes are active at the same time, is this sufficient to produce an association between them?

16. The Wagner, Rudy, and Whitlow experiment provides a test of many of the assumptions about memory discussed in this chapter. Which ones?

17. In what respects do the properties of memory in animals and humans appear to be similar?

18. Do you believe that your brain has enough neurons to code all the material presented in this chapter?

CHAPTER TEN

THE ROLE OF THE REINFORCER

Of several responses made to the same situation, those which are . . . closely
followed by satisfaction to the animal will . . . be more firmly connected with the
situation
  (*The Law of Effect*, Thorndike, 1911, p. 24)

In Chapter 8 we discussed evidence that reinforcement can produce two quite different forms of learning: simple S–R associations, and more complex $R \to S^R$ expectations which allow subjects to anticipate the consequences of their actions.[1] Then, in Chapter 9, we examined the cognitive processes involved in producing these outcomes. We suggested that the code assigned to a stimulus depends on whether subjects attend to it, and also on the relationship between this stimulus and the other stimuli present. A reinforcer that follows might trigger a search that retrieves memories of preceding stimuli and responses, and associations can then be formed between the nodes in working memory that are active simultaneously.

In this chapter, we will continue our examination of the processes involved in reinforcement, focusing in particular on the processes that follow the reinforcer's presentation. Thorndike, in his Law of Effect, suggested that these processes were fundamentally simple, with the reinforcer stamping in a connection between the response that precedes it and the stimuli that are present:

<hr />

[1] Although we have sometimes referred to expectations involving $R \to S^R$ relationships, in the case of reinforcement expectations probably always involve $S–R \to S^R$ relationships—that is, we learn that a response in a particular situation produces the reinforcer. (See Seligman & Johnston, 1973). When we refer to $R \to S^R$ relationships, we are using this expression only as a form of shorthand.

We will find that he was right in some respects, but that the processes involved are often considerably more complex than his analysis implied.

10.1 IS REINFORCEMENT AUTOMATIC?

One of the most important characteristics of reinforcement, according to Thorndike, is that a reinforcer strengthens whatever response precedes it automatically, without any need for conscious deliberation:

> [A reward] does not pick out the "right" or "essential" or "useful" connection by any mystical or logical potency. It is, on the contrary, as natural in its action as a falling stone. . . It will strengthen connections which are wrong, irrelevant or useless, provided that they are close enough to the satisfier.
> (Thorndike, 1935, p. 39)

Superstition

Skinner's pigeons. Thorndike's claim that a reinforcer acts automatically suggests that a reinforcer should strengthen whatever response happens to precede it, even if this response played no role in producing it. Striking support for this view came from an experiment by B. F. Skinner (1948b). Using pigeons as subjects, Skinner placed them in a box and gave them grain to eat once every 15 seconds. The birds did not have to perform any response to obtain this food; the grain was presented every 15 seconds regardless of their behavior. Most of the birds nevertheless developed highly stereotyped behaviors, which they repeated over and over during the interval between reinforcements. One turned around in circles repeatedly, another brushed its head along the floor, a third tossed its head as if lifting an invisible bar, and so on.

The explanation for these strange behaviors, Skinner suggested, lay in the automatic nature of reinforcement. When the food was first presented, it would have strengthened whatever behavior the bird happened to be engaged in at the time. As a result, the bird would have been more likely to repeat this response, and if one of these repetitions happened to coincide with the next presentation of food, it would have been strengthened still further, and so on. This process, in which the accidental conjunction of a response and a reinforcer results in strengthening of the response, is called *adventitious reinforcement*. Not all of the repeated responses would have been followed by reinforcement, of course, and on some occasions food might have followed another response and strengthened it instead. In the end, however, Skinner found that six of his eight birds acquired highly stereotyped responses, even though these behaviors played no role in producing food. Skinner called these response patterns **superstitions** and suggested that a similar process might underlie the emergence of superstitious behavior in humans.

In a subsequent paper, however, Staddon and Simmelhag (1971) raised doubts about Skinner's interpretation of superstition. Using a procedure similar to Skinner's, they also found that subjects developed idiosyncratic patterns of behavior during the early stages of the interval between reinforcers. (They called these early responses *interim behaviors*.) As the time for reinforcement approached, however, all the birds began to behave in the same way, orienting toward the wall containing the grain magazine and pecking at it. The uniformity of this *terminal behavior* suggested that it could not have been due to adventitious reinforcement, since this would have produced different behaviors in each bird. Staddon and Simmelhag attributed this behavior instead to classical conditioning: Food elicited the bird's approach to the grain magazine and its pecking, and this behavior became conditioned to the time at which the food was delivered.

Staddon and Simmelhag's study provides compelling evidence that classical conditioning can play an important role in situations in which reinforcement is delivered at fixed intervals, and suggests that at least some of the behaviors that Skinner observed could have been the result of classical conditioning rather than reinforcement. However, Staddon and Simmelhag's conditioning interpretation predicts that all subjects will display the same terminal behavior as the time for reinforcement approaches, and this is not always the case: A number of studies have confirmed Skinner's observation that different subjects develop different responses (for example, Eldridge, Pear, Torgrud, & Evers, 1988; Justice & Looney, 1990). Thus, although Staddon and Simmelhag were undoubtedly correct that some of the responses observed in superstition experiments are due to classical conditioning, it appears that Skinner was also right that reinforcers can strengthen the behaviors that happen to precede them. (See also Neuringer, 1970.)

Particularly interesting evidence on this point has come from a study by Ono (1987) involving human subjects. Ono had his subjects sit at a table that contained three levers and a counter. He instructed the subjects to obtain as many points as they could and then exposed them to a fixed-time schedule in which a point was added to the counter every 30 seconds. Ono found, as had Skinner, that his subjects began to develop idiosyncratic behaviors, even though no response was necessary to obtain points. One subject, for example, developed a pattern of pulling a lever several times in succession and then holding it. He had just completed this sequence at the moment when he first received reinforcement, and as he repeated this pattern and continued to obtain reinforcement, the behavior became firmly established. (See also Wagner & Morris, 1987, Matute, 1995.)

Thomas's rats. Even more dramatic evidence for the power of reinforcers to strengthen whatever behavior precedes them comes from a line of research initiated by G. V. Thomas (1981). Whereas in Skinner's experiment responses had no effect on reinforcement, Thomas arranged matters so that responding actually reduced the probability of reinforcement.

Thomas placed rats in a Skinner box and gave them one pellet of food every 20 seconds. As in Skinner's study, the food was free; that is, the rats did not have to perform any response to obtain it. However, a bar was also present in the box, and if the rat pressed the bar during any 20-second interval, it would immediately receive the food pellet that had been scheduled for the end of that interval. However, this response also canceled the pellet scheduled to occur at the end of the following 20-second interval. Suppose, for example, that a rat pressed the lever 5 seconds into the session. It would immediately receive the pellet of food that had been scheduled to occur at 20 seconds, but it would lose the pellet scheduled for 40 seconds. If it responded again at, say, 42 seconds, it would immediately receive the pellet scheduled for 60 seconds but lose the pellet scheduled for 80 seconds. Thus, if a rat did not press the bar at all, it would receive food every 20 seconds, but if it responded regularly, food would be presented only once every 40 seconds.

In effect, Thomas was pitting the effects of contiguity against those of contingency. The response of pressing the lever was sometimes followed immediately by food (contiguity), but in the end this response reduced the probability of food. Thus, whereas in Skinner's experiment there was no contingency between responding and food, in Thomas's there was actually a negative contingency: The probability of food following a response was less than its probability in the absence of a response.

Despite this negative contingency, Thomas's rats learned to respond at a relatively high rate, and they continued to do so for many sessions. Figure 10.1 shows the results for a typical subject. The rat did not respond at all during the first two sessions, but once it began to do so, its response rate increased rapidly to approximately 2000 per hour. This high rate of responding halved its rate of reinforcement from about 180 to 90 reinforcements per hour; despite this, it continued to respond for 30 sessions.

Thomas's rats behaved as if they had inferred a causal relationship between bar-pressing and food because they sometimes occurred together. You might be tempted to think that this is yet more evidence for animals' stupidity and that humans would never behave so foolishly, but Wasserman and Neunaber (1986) have reported that people placed in similar situations behave almost identically. Their experimental design was essentially the same as Thomas's, except that they used college students as subjects. The students were told that they would earn points whenever a light came on, and that pressing or not pressing a telegraph key might increase the number of light flashes. For subjects in the control group, the light came on at fixed intervals, regardless of whether they responded. For subjects in the experimental group, however, the procedure was identical to that in Thomas's experiment: The first response in an interval moved forward the light flash that had been scheduled for the end of the interval, but canceled

FIGURE 10.1   Pitting contiguity against contingency. The solid line shows a rat's rate of bar-pressing. This response sometimes produced food immediately, but it reduced the overall rate of reinforcement. The dotted line shows the overall rate of reinforcement. (Thomas, 1981)

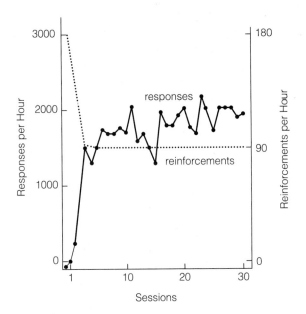

the light flash in the following interval. The results also mirrored those of Thomas: Subjects in the experimental group responded far more than those in the control group, even though this responding cost them points. When asked at the end of the experiment to describe the relationship between pressing the key and obtaining light flashes, they reported that responding increased the frequency of flashes, even though the actual effect was the opposite.

Contiguity versus contingency. These results make it clear that contiguity between a response and a reinforcer can lead both animals and humans into inferring a causal relationship where none exists. Langer (1975) refers to this overestimation of the extent to which we can control positive outcomes as the *illusion of control*; examples include gamblers who blow on a pair of dice to make them produce the desired outcome and lottery ticket purchasers who are convinced that they will win. The fact that contiguity is important, however, does not mean that it is the only factor that determines whether reinforcement strengthens a response. In our discussion of classical conditioning, we saw that conditioning depends not only on the contiguity of the CS and the US but also on their contingency. When Rescorla (1966) eliminated this contingency by presenting the US in the absence of the CS as well as in its presence, he found no conditioning. Similarly, there is evidence that animals are sensitive to the contingency between responses and reinforcers.

In one demonstration, Hammond (1980) trained rats to press a bar to obtain water. He divided the session into intervals of one second, and if a rat pressed the bar at least once during any of these intervals, then it would sometimes be reinforced at the end of the interval. (The actual probability of reinforcement was .05, meaning that, on average, 1 in 20 intervals containing a response terminated in water.) Once this response was well established, he introduced a new schedule in which bar presses continued to be reinforced as before, but water was also made available in intervals in which the rats did not press the bar. The probability that an interval would end in water was the same when subjects did not respond as when they did, so that there was no longer any contingency between responding and reinforcement. If contiguity between a response and a reinforcer was all that mattered, we should expect subjects to continue to respond during the second phase, because bar presses were still followed by water in the same way as in the first phase. If subjects are sensitive to the contingency between these two events, however, then responding should cease, and this is essentially what Hammond found, as the rate of responding gradually declined to almost zero.

As in classical conditioning, therefore, it appears that the effects of reinforcement depend on the contingency between a response and a reinforcer as well as on their contiguity. The relationship between these two variables is not yet clear, but one possibility is that contiguity is more fundamental. In our discussion of classical conditioning, we saw that the Rescorla-Wagner model was able to explain contingency effects in terms of contiguity. (The model assumed that shocks delivered in the absence of the CS caused conditioning of fear to the apparatus, and this ultimately interfered with conditioning to the CS.) It is possible—though by no means yet certain—that a similar mechanism operates in the case of reinforcement. In Hammond's experiment, the presentations of water in the absence of a response could have resulted in the formation of an expectation that water would be presented roughly every 20 seconds. When the rats responded and obtained water at the same rate, this too might have produced an expectation that responses would be followed by water after a delay of 20 seconds. If the rats realized that the average delay to water would be the same when they responded as when they didn't, then, clearly, they would have had little incentive to respond.

Note that in this analysis rats do not start by calculating the overall rate at which water is presented; rather, they learn about the delay between each response and the water presentation that follows. It is the cumulative effect of these individual response-reinforcer pairings that eventually generate an expectation about the average time to water. The crucial factor governing learning is assumed to be the contiguity between events, and this produces sensitivity to the probability of events in the presence and absence of a response. The powerful impact of contiguity also explains why the rats in Thomas's experiment behaved in what appeared as such an irrational manner. When a bar press produced food, this consequence followed immediately, whereas the cancellation of the following reinforcer did not occur until after a long delay. As we have seen many times, immediate consequences exert far more control over behavior than delayed ones, and Thomas's rats were misled by the immediate delivery of food into perceiving a positive relationship where none existed.

Reinforcement without Awareness

In general, reinforcement on superstition has strongly supported Thorndike's view that reinforcers act automatically and thus that a reinforcer can strengthen whatever behavior happens to precede it. A further implication of this view is that reinforcement should strengthen behavior even if subjects are not aware of the reinforcement contingency.

Thumb twitches. To test this prediction, Hefferline, Keenan, and Harford (1959) told subjects that they were participating in a study of the effects of stress on body tension. Electrodes were attached to their bodies to assess muscular tension, and the effect of stress was evaluated by randomly alternating periods of soothing music and a harsh noise. In reality, however, the duration of the noise was not random: The noise was terminated whenever the subjects contracted a very small muscle within their left thumb—a response so small that it could not be observed visually and could be detected only by an electrode mounted above the muscle. Over the course of the session, there was a dramatic increase in contractions of the muscle. When interviewed afterward, however, all the subjects "still believed that they had been passive victims with respect to the onset and duration of the noise, and all seemed astounded to learn that they themselves had been in control" (p. 1339). In a subsequent experiment, Hefferline and Keenan (1961) extended this result by showing that they could differentially reinforce subjects for contractions of particular magnitudes, so that subjects could learn to precisely control a muscle whose activity they could not detect.

A deceived experimenter. Further evidence that reinforcement can affect people's behavior without their awareness comes from an ingenious experiment by Rosenfeld and Baer (1969). Subjects were told that they were participating in a study of social attitudes and were asked questions about topics such as the Vietnam conflict. The interviewer—a graduate student recruited by the authors to carry out the study—was told to observe the subjects to see if they engaged in any distinctive mannerisms and then to reinforce one of these behaviors by nodding his head whenever the behavior occurred.

The first subject was observed to rub his chin occasionally as he talked, so the interviewer, in consultation with the authors, set out to reinforce this behavior. In fact, however, the "subject" was actually a confederate of the experimenter: He pretended to be naive, but he had been briefed in advance about what would happen and instructed to rub his chin whenever the interviewer said "yeah." In other words, while the interviewer was trying to reinforce the "subject" for rubbing his chin, the "subject" was actually using the desired outcome of chin rubbing to reinforce the interviewer for saying "yeah"!

The frequency with which the interviewer said "yeah" over the course of the experiment is shown in Figure 10.2. During the baseline phase, the "subject" rubbed his chin at random intervals, regardless of the interviewer's behavior. When chin rubbing was then made contingent on the interviewer's saying "yeah," the frequency of this verbal behavior increased substantially; when reinforcement was discontinued, it returned to low levels. In subsequent sessions, the frequency of "yeah" again increased when reinforced, but not when reinforcement was made contingent on a different verbal behavior ("mm-hmm"). Chin rubbing was thus clearly effective in reinforcing the response on which it was contingent, but the "experimenter" was totally unaware that his own behavior was being reinforced. When he was eventually told what had happened, his reaction was one of stunned incredulity. (The procedure, incidentally, is neatly summarized in the title of Rosenfeld and Baer's 1969 report: "Unnoticed Verbal Conditioning of an Aware Experimenter by a More Aware Subject: The Double-Agent Effect.")

Conclusions. The claim that reinforcement can strengthen people's behavior without their awareness has not gone unchallenged. Although subjects in these and many other experiments have said that they were not aware of the reinforcement contingency, critics have argued that we should not accept these reports at face value (Brewer, 1974; Shanks & St. John, 1994). Hefferline and his colleagues, for example, reported few details of the questions they used to assess awareness, and it is possible that their subjects were not given an adequate opportunity to reveal knowledge that they actually possessed. Also, even if they were not aware of the relationship between thumb contractions and noise termination, they could have possessed a correlated hypothesis—for example, that the noise stopped when they raised their arms, a movement which had the incidental effect of producing contractions of their thumb muscles. On the other hand, recent studies that have adopted stringent procedures for measuring awareness have also reported strong evidence for reinforcement without awareness (for example, Svartdal, 1995; Lieberman, Connell, & Moos, 1998). Because of the difficulties inherent in assessing mental states, this issue may never be resolved beyond doubt, but at present it does look as if people's behavior can be reinforced without their awareness.

It is important to recognize that even if this is so, in most cases we probably are aware of the reinforcement contingencies influencing our behavior—

FIGURE 10.2   The effect of a desired outcome (the interviewee's rubbing his chin) on the interviewer's saying "yeah." During different phases of the experiment, the interviewee rubbed his chin at random (baselines), after the interviewer said "yeah," or after he said "mm-hmm." (Rosenfeld & Baer, 1969)

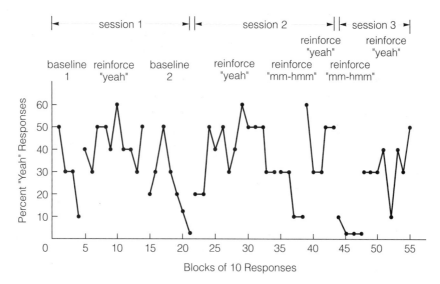

the subjects in the experiments we have described were not aware of these contingencies only because the experimenters went to extensive lengths to distract attention from them. Nevertheless, if reinforcement does sometimes affect us without our awareness, this could have important implications. Suppose, for example, that you were a Democrat and all your friends were Republicans; suppose, further, that they were obviously pleased whenever you referred positively to Republican politicians. Might social reinforcement of this kind lead you to shift your political beliefs, even if you were not consciously seeking to gain your friends' approval? An experiment by Scott (1959) suggests that it might. He staged a series of debates in which participants were told that winners would be selected on the basis of their style of presentation. (In fact, they were selected randomly.) Those who won the debate became significantly more likely to believe the positions they had advocated than those who had lost. Thus, even though approval was explicitly made contingent on style of presentation rather than content, those reinforced for stating a position became more likely to believe it.

To repeat, in most situations we probably are aware of the reinforcement contingencies that are influencing us, but there might be some situations in which our attitudes and behaviors are shaped without our realizing it.

10.2 Is Reinforcement Necessary for Learning?

Reinforcement theorists such as Thorndike and, later, Hull (1943), believed that some form of powerful event, a reinforcer or a punisher, must be present for learning to occur. The brain, in this view, is something like a coin-operated photocopier: Just as you have to put money in the machine to get it to produce a copy, so you have to supply a reinforcer to activate the brain's copying mechanism and get it to form an association.

A very different view of learning was proposed by cognitive theorists such as Tolman (1932, 1948). They argued that as we interact with the world around us, we are constantly noticing features of our environment and storing information about them. Reinforcement, in their view, does not cause learning; rather, the occurrence of a reinforcer is simply one of the many events in our environment that we learn about, and we then use this knowledge in deciding our behavior. If the brain is to be compared to any machine, in the cognitive view, then a more appropriate metaphor would be a powerful computer that carries out a complex sequence of operations on the information fed into it. The presentation of a reinforcer is simply one more bit of information, one more fact about the environment, to be used in calculating the optimal response.

Learning without Reinforcement

These two perspectives lead to very different predictions. According to the Law of Effect, learning should occur only if a reinforcer is presented, whereas the cognitive analysis suggests that learning can occur without reinforcement.

Latent learning. Tolman and Honzik (1930b) reported one early test of these opposing views. They trained two groups of rats to run through a complex maze with 14 choice points, but only one group was given food when they reached the goal box. If reinforcement is necessary for learning, then only the subjects in the reinforced group (R) should have learned the correct path to the goal box, and this was what Tolman and Honzik found: Whereas the number of errors made by the reinforced group steadily decreased, the performance of the nonreinforced group (N) improved only slightly. The failure of the nonreinforced subjects to *perform* the correct response, however, did not necessarily prove that they had not *learned* it. Perhaps they had learned the correct path to the goal box just as well as the reinforced subjects had, but did not choose this path because they had no incentive to do so.

To find out, Tolman and Honzik ran a third group (NR), which was not reinforced on the first 10 days but was reinforced thereafter. If these subjects had learned the correct path to the goal box during the nonreinforced trials, then they should begin to take it as soon as they realized that the goal box contained food. If reinforcement was necessary for learning, on the other hand,

FIGURE 10.3   Latent learning. Group R was given food in the goal box on every trial, group N was never given food, and group NR was given food starting on trial 11. (Adapted from Tolman & Honzik, 1930b)

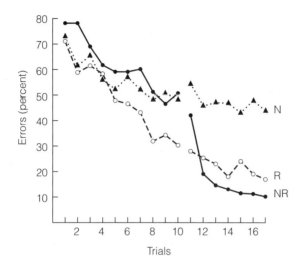

then learning should occur for the first time on trial 11, and their performance should then improve at the same gradual rate shown by the reinforced subjects at the beginning of the experiment. A cognitive analysis thus predicted immediate improvement after the introduction of food, whereas reinforcement theory predicted gradual learning.

As shown in Figure 10.3, it was the cognitive analysis that was supported: The performance of the switched subjects instantly matched that of the subjects who had already had 10 trials of reward. It thus appeared as if the rats had learned the correct path to the goal box during the nonreinforced trials, but that this learning had remained unused, or latent, until the introduction of a reinforcer provided an incentive for using it. This phenomenon is known as **latent learning.**

Perceptual learning. A second example of learning in the absence of reinforcement comes from experiments on **perceptual learning,** in which subjects' ability to discriminate between stimuli improves as a result of simple exposure. In an experiment by Gibson, Walk, Pick, and Tighe (1958), for example, rats reared with a metal triangle mounted on the walls of their cage were subsequently much better at solving a discrimination problem in which they had to discriminate this triangle from another shape. Similarly, human subjects in psychophysical experiments rapidly improved in their ability to hear a very weak tone or to discriminate between similar lights, even if given no feedback about the accuracy of their performance (Gibson, 1969).

You might have experienced similar improvements in your ability to recognize different musical instruments or different wines or beers. At first, all the stimuli sounded or tasted much the same, but with experience they became increasingly distinct, until eventually you might have found it difficult to understand how you could ever have confused them. This ability to distinguish stimuli can become quite remarkable with sufficient practice: Experts on wine, for example, can distinguish whether a sample of Madeira has come from the top half of a bottle or the bottom. (See Goldstone, 1998. Further discussion of perceptual learning, and the processes involved, can be found in Hall, 1991, and Mackintosh & Bennett, 1998.)

The common thread uniting these examples is that exposure to a stimulus can be sufficient to produce learning about its characteristics in the absence of any external reinforcement. In perceptual learning as in latent learning, reinforcement is not necessary for learning to occur.

Surprise!

The evidence for latent and perceptual learning suggests that we are constantly learning about the world around us, and research on classical conditioning points to a similar conclusion. In sensory preconditioning, for example, subjects exposed to pairings of neutral stimuli, such as a light and a tone, will form an association between them so that a response later conditioned to one of these stimuli will also occur to the other (Section 2.5). In all of these cases, we seem to be constantly learning about the relationships between events that we encounter. On the other hand, in our discussion of blocking we encountered evidence pointing to a quite different conclusion. There, we found that pairing a light with a shock was not sufficient to produce learning: Conditioning would occur only if the US was unexpected. Blocking thus seems to support the view of reinforcement theorists that contiguity between events is not sufficient for us to associate them; learning occurs only if a special event, an unexpected US, is present. How can we reconcile these apparently contradictory conclusions?

A surprising hypothesis. One possible resolution would be to accept the contention of reinforcement theorists that a special event of some kind is necessary for learning to occur, but to argue that this special event need not be a reinforcer as conventionally defined. Perhaps any surprising event—a new environment or an unexpected noise, as well as unpredicted food or a shock—will trigger a search through memory for possible causes.

A mechanism of this sort might have considerable survival value. A rat, for example, needs an accurate representation of its environment if it is to obtain food or escape from predators; similarly, it needs to attend to new stimuli to determine their possible significance. According to this analysis, curiosity, far from killing the cat, is probably what kept it alive. Once a situation becomes familiar, however, there is no need to continue to explore it; thus, familiar stimuli will elicit neither exploratory behavior nor memory searches for predictive cues.

Marking. According to this analysis, any salient and surprising stimulus should trigger a search for causes. Support for this prediction has come from a series of experiments by Lieberman and Thomas (for example, Lieberman, McIntosh, & Thomas, 1979; Lieberman & Thomas, 1986; Thomas, Robertson, & Lieberman, 1987). In the first of these experiments, Lieberman, McIntosh, and Thomas trained rats in a modified T-maze in which turns to the right were rewarded with food after a one-minute delay, and turns to the left were not. As we saw in Chapter 5, even quite small delays in reinforcement typically have devastating effects on learning, and the rats in this experiment were no exception: They consistently failed to learn to turn right—unless, that is, they were picked up by the experimenter immediately after they made their choice and then replaced in the maze and allowed to resume their journey! Subjects that were picked up in this way learned to enter the correct arm of the maze on an impressive 90% of trials, compared to only 50% for the unhandled controls.

As to why picking the rats up should have enhanced learning, the authors suggested that being hoisted into the air must have been a rather startling experience for the rats. According to the surprise analysis discussed previously, therefore, it should have triggered a search through memory for possible causes. Since the last response made before being picked up was the choice, the rats would have been particularly likely to identify this choice response as the cause of their misfortune. The experimenters suggested that the extra attention paid to this response would have effectively marked it in the rat's memory so the rat would remember the response better. When the rats received food at the end of the trial, this food would have triggered another memory search for possible causes, and the handled rats would have been more likely to recall the marked choice response and associate it with food. Lieberman, McIntosh, and Thomas called this phenomenon **marking.**

Lieberman and his colleagues speculated that any salient and unexpected stimulus will enhance memory for the behavior that preceded it. In line with this prediction, they were able to show that learning of the correct response was also enhanced if it was followed by a brief noise or light, rather than by handling. The evidence for marking is thus consistent with the view that any salient or novel stimulus triggers learning about preceding events.

Note that the surprise hypothesis does not say that surprise is the only factor that determines whether learning will occur; the innate or learned importance of the stimuli concerned is also important. Suppose, for example, that you were hit on the head by a feather or a baseball. The two events might be equally unexpected, but it would not be altogether surprising if the baseball attracted more of your attention and promoted a rather more vigorous search for the cause. Reinforcement theory, in other words, is not totally wrong: Some events are more

FIGURE 10.4   A typical shuttle box used for avoidance training. Electric shock is delivered through
the grid floor, but the shock can be avoided if the rat shuttles from one side of the box
to the other by jumping over the barrier.

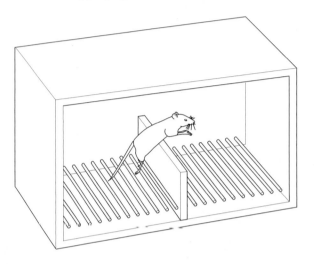

effective in producing learning than others. The class of events that will trigger
a memory search, however, is far broader than reinforcers as conventionally defined. Moreover, this class is probably even broader in the case of human behavior, where learning is in large measure a controlled or voluntary process. (See
the distinction between controlled and automatic processes in Section 8.4.) In
effect, we can switch on our learning mechanisms whenever we are appropriately motivated, whether to memorize baseball players' batting averages, multiplication tables, or textbooks. Thus while reinforcement theorists were right in
believing that reinforcers play an important role in initiating and guiding learning, a much wider set of events can also trigger learning.

10.3 THE AVOIDANCE PARADOX

One of the most difficult puzzles for reinforcement theorists concerns avoidance
learning. An **avoidance response** is one that postpones or prevents an unpleasant event. An **escape response** is one that terminates an unpleasant stimulus.

On the face of it, learning to avoid unpleasant events is quite straightforward. In a typical avoidance experiment, a rat is trained in a shuttle box with a
hurdle in the middle (Figure 10.4). A tone is presented for 10 seconds, followed
by an electric shock delivered through the floor of the cage. If the rat jumps
over the hurdle while the shock is on, the shock is immediately terminated. If

FIGURE 10.5   Diagram of a signaled avoidance procedure. Shock is typically presented following a 10-second warning stimulus. If the subject makes no response, the shock terminates after a fixed period; if the subject responds during the shock, both the warning stimulus and the shock are immediately terminated; if the subject responds before the shock, the warning stimulus is terminated and the forthcoming shock is canceled.

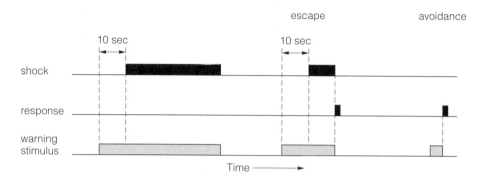

the rat jumps before the shock comes on, then the tone is turned off and the scheduled shock is canceled; this is even better, from the rat's point of view. Thus, depending on when the rat jumps over the barrier, it can either escape from the shock once it is on or avoid it altogether. The procedure is called **signaled avoidance,** because the experimenter provides a signal to indicate when the shock is imminent. Figure 10.5 diagrams the procedure.

Typical performance for one subject on this task (in this case, a dog) is shown in Figure 10.6. For the first seven trials, the dog's response latency was greater than 10 seconds, so it received a shock on every trial. It avoided shock on trial 8, however, and continued to do so on every trial thereafter.

In some respects, this result is hardly surprising: If an animal can avoid an unpleasant shock by jumping over a barrier, then of course it will do so. For reinforcement theorists, however, this learning posed a serious dilemma, because the consequence of a successful avoidance response was that absolutely nothing happened. How could *nothing* act to reinforce behavior?

Two-Factor Theory

An ingenious solution to this problem was proposed by O. Hobart Mowrer (1947), whose explanation has become known as **two-factor theory.** According to Mowrer, the pairing of tone and shock results in conditioning of fear to the tone. When the rat eventually jumps over the hurdle and terminates the tone, therefore, its level of fear is reduced. And, since fear is aversive, the termination of this aversive state reinforces jumping. Thus, the rat jumps over the barrier not because it wants to avoid shock, but in order to escape from the warning stimulus.

FIGURE 10.6   Avoidance learning of a typical dog. Shock was initiated 10 seconds after the onset of the warning stimulus, so responses that had a latency of less than 10 seconds avoided shock. (Adapted from Solomon & Wynne, 1953)

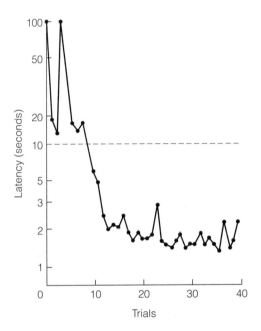

According to this theory, avoidance learning depends on two factors or processes: classical conditioning of fear to the tone, and reinforcement of the avoidance response by termination of the tone.

Fear as a motive. This analysis leads to a number of testable implications. The first derives from the assumption that fear provides the motive for avoidance behavior. In Chapter 5, we saw that motives such as hunger and thirst increase the vigor of responding. If fear provides the motive for avoidance behavior, therefore, then increasing subjects' fear should increase the speed of their avoidance responding.

In one test of this prediction, Rescorla and LoLordo (1965) trained dogs using a procedure known as **Sidman avoidance.** No warning stimulus is used in this procedure, and shock is programmed to occur at fixed time intervals (the shock–shock interval). If the subject makes an avoidance response, however, the next programmed shock is postponed for a fixed period (the response–shock interval). In Rescorla and LoLordo's experiment, shocks were programmed to occur every 10 seconds, but every time the dogs jumped over the hurdle in the shuttle box they ensured a shock-free period of 30 seconds. By jumping at least once every 30 seconds, therefore, the dogs could ensure that they would never receive a shock.[2]

Once the dogs learned the avoidance response, Rescorla and LoLordo confined them to one half of the shuttle box and gave them discriminative fear conditioning trials in which one tone (CS+) was followed by shock, but a second tone (CS−) was not. Sidman avoidance training was then resumed, and once the dogs were again responding reliably, CS+ and CS− were occasionally presented for five seconds at a time. When CS+ was presented the rate of jumping immediately doubled, despite the fact that the dogs were already responding at a rate that avoided shock. When CS− was presented, on the other hand, the rate of responding fell to almost zero. As predicted by two-factor theory, therefore, conditioned fear exerted powerful control over the rate of responding.

Escape from fear as a reinforcer. Mowrer's second assumption was that avoidance responses are reinforced by escape from the warning stimulus. To test whether termination of the warning stimulus on its own is really reinforcing, Brown and Jacobs (1949) gave rats conditioning trials in which a light-tone compound was paired with shock; the rats could not avoid the shock. A control group received the same light-tone compound but no shock. Then, in the test phase, the rats were placed in a test box and the light-tone compound was presented. If the rats jumped over the barrier, the compound was immediately terminated.

As shown in Figure 10.7, the latency of the jumping response declined substantially in the experimental subjects, as they scrambled across the hurdle to escape from the warning stimulus. Escape from a stimulus that has been paired with shock clearly is reinforcing. (See also McAllister & McAllister, 1991.)

There is thus considerable support for the two assumptions at the heart of two-factor theory: that conditioned fear motivates avoidance responding, and that termination of this fear reinforces it. Despite these successes, other evidence has been reported that poses some serious problems for two-factor theory. We will examine two of these problems in the following sections.

The Response Problem

One problem arose when psychologists tried to train rats to avoid shock by performing responses other than running in an alley. The most embarrassing of these

---

[2]Two-factor theory accounts for responding under Sidman avoidance by assuming that temporal cues play the role of the warning stimulus in signaled avoidance: As the time for shock approaches, fear increases, and the avoidance response reduces fear because this response is always followed by a shock-free period. One way of conceptualizing this analysis is in terms of two hypothetical stimuli, S_1 and S_2. The passing of a fixed amount of time, S_1, is followed by shock, whereas the feedback produced by the avoidance response, S_2, is not. Fear, therefore, is conditioned more strongly to S_1 than to S_2, and thus the occurrence of the response produces a transition to a lower level of fear.

FIGURE 10.7   The reinforcing properties of escape from a warning stimulus. Rats in a shuttle box were given a tone-light compound that they could terminate by jumping over a hurdle; the graph shows the change in the mean latency of the escape response over trials. For subjects in the experimental group, the compound had previously been paired with shock; for subjects in the control group, the compound had been presented without shock. (Adapted from Brown & Jacobs, 1949)

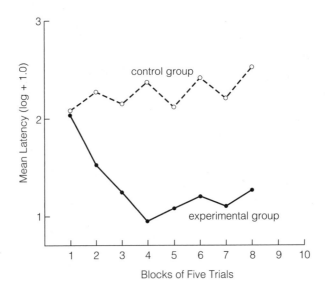

problems arose when experimenters tried to teach rats to press a bar to avoid shock. In previous chapters we have seen that rats are very good at pressing bars to obtain food, and we have now seen that they learn very rapidly to jump over a hurdle or run down an alley to avoid shock. So, bar-pressing is an easily learned response, and avoidance of shock is a very powerful reinforcer. You might think, therefore, that it would be very easy to train rats to press a bar in order to avoid shock. Certainly most learning psychologists thought so, but it gradually became clear that this optimism was misplaced. Whereas rats need an average of only six trials to learn to run down an alley to avoid shock, they need hundreds of trials to learn to press a bar to avoid shock, and many never do. (For a review, see Bolles, 1970.)

Since pressing the bar turns off the warning stimulus in exactly the same way as running down an alley, two-factor theory says that pressing the bar should produce a substantial reduction in the rat's fear, and hence should be easily learned. Why, then, do rats fare so badly on this simple task?

Bolles's SSDR model. Bolles (1970) offered a possible explanation. He began by arguing that two-factor theory was based on a fundamental misinterpretation of the role of avoidance learning in an animal's life, illustrating his point with a fable:

Once upon a time there was a little animal who ran around in the forest. One day while he was running around, our hero was suddenly attacked by a predator. He was hurt and, of course, frightened, but he was lucky and managed to escape. . . . Some time later our furry friend was again running around in the forest . . . when suddenly . . . he heard or saw or smelled some stimulus which on the earlier occasion had preceded the attack by the predator. Now on this occasion our friend became frightened, he immediately took flight as he had on the previous occasion, and quickly got safely back home. . . . I propose that this familiar fable . . . is utter nonsense. No owl hoots or whistles 5 seconds before pouncing on a mouse. . . . Nor will the owl give the mouse enough trials for the necessary learning to occur.
(Bolles, 1970, p. 32)

If an animal is to survive, Bolles argued, it needs innately programmed responses to allow it to react quickly to dangerous situations. Because each species has somewhat different behaviors for coping with danger, Bolles called these responses **species-specific defense reactions (SSDRs).** He suggested that rats have three main defensive reactions—broadly, freezing, flight, or fight—and that which of these responses will occur depends on the rat's environment at the time it is frightened. If the rat is in a confined space where escape is impossible, it is likely to freeze; if it is in an open field, it is more likely to run for cover.

The role of SSDRs in avoidance learning. Applying this analysis to laboratory research on avoidance learning, Bolles said that when shock is presented it elicits fear, and this fear is conditioned to the test chamber. The next time the rat is placed in the apparatus, it becomes frightened, and this fear elicits innate SSDRs. The reason the rat down an alley, therefore, is not that it was reinforced for doing so, but because running for shelter is its innate defensive reaction in an environment such as an alley. The result is that it is very easy to train a rat to run down an alley to avoid shock; indeed, Bolles (1989) suggests that training a rat to run in this situation is rather like teaching a child to sneeze if you stick a feather in his nose. A Skinner box, on the other hand, is a confined space, and here the rat's SSDR is to freeze; if a rat is freezing, it is clearly very hard for it to press a bar.

Bolles's hypothesis that rats have strong SSDRs, and that these SSDRs influence what other responses occur and are reinforced, makes a lot of sense. The details of the interaction between SSDRs and avoidance responses, however, are not yet well understood. For example, Bolles suggested that the reason why rats quickly learn to run down alleys to avoid shock is that running is the rat's SSDR in environments like alleys. Fanselow and Lester (1988), however, have reviewed extensive evidence that when rats are given unavoidable shocks in an alley, their conditioned response on future trials is not to run but to freeze. (They suggest that freezing is a more adaptive response to dangerous situations for a rat, in part because it minimizes the chances of a predator's detecting them.) If freezing is the rat's SSDR in alleys as well as in Skinner boxes, then it is not clear why this freezing does not interfere with learning to run in the same way as it interferes with learning to bar-press.

A two-factor analysis. Two-factor theorists have proposed an alternative explanation for this evidence. The key to their analysis lies in the fact that all of the avoidance responses that rats have difficulty learning—standing, turning, and bar-pressing—share the characteristic that they leave the rat in the situation where it became frightened. If a rat presses the bar in a Skinner box, for example, it still finds itself in exactly the same situation as before it responded, whereas in a straight alley running allows it to escape from the situation. This raises the possibility that the crucial factor is not the nature of the response to be learned—for example, pressing a bar versus running—but rather the extent to which the response produces a change in the animal's environment.

Why, though, should stimulus change be so important? The answer, according to two-factor theory, is that an avoidance response is reinforced to the extent that the stimuli that follow the response elicit less fear than the stimuli that precede it. If most of the stimuli present before a response are still present after it, then levels of fear will not change very much, and learning will be impaired. Thus, the reason rats have difficulty learning to press a bar to avoid shock could simply be that the stimuli present after a response are largely the same as those that were present before, so that responding produces little change in fear.

If this analysis is correct, rats should find it much easier to learn to press a bar to avoid shock if the response produced a greater change in its stimulus environment, and this prediction has been confirmed in a number of studies. In an experiment by D'Amato, Fazzaro, and Etkin (1968), for example, a noise was presented every time rats pressed a bar to avoid shock; as predicted by two-factor theory, they learned to press the bar much faster than control subjects who did not receive the noise. (See also Crawford & Masterson, 1978.)

In sum, we now have not one but two plausible-sounding explanations for why rats have difficulty in learning certain avoidance responses. According to Bolles, the problem lies in competition from innate defensive responses; according to two-factor theory, in the extent to which the response produces stimulus change. It is currently difficult to choose between these accounts because both are broad hypotheses rather than detailed theories, making it difficult to derive testable predictions. Bolles, for example, assumes that avoidance learning depends on the compatibility of the avoidance response with the animals' SSDRs, but this cannot be assessed unless we know what these SSDRs are in specific situations. Research is currently underway to identify these defensive behaviors (see Bouton & Fanselow, 1997), but it will be difficult to test the theory until more data becomes available.

Similarly, it will be difficult to evaluate the role of stimulus change until we have clear rules for measuring change. If a bar press produces a one-second noise, for example, to what extent is this change comparable to that produced by running down an alley? Until we can answer such questions, it will be hard to predict the speed of avoidance learning in advance.

At present, then, it is difficult to evaluate the relative merits of SSDR and stimulus-change explanations of why some avoidance responses are hard to learn. Both mechanisms seem plausible, and it will not be altogether surprising if both are eventually found to play a role.

The Fearlessness Problem

A further problem for two-factor theory came from evidence that fear and avoidance responding are not linked as firmly as the theory suggests. According to two-factor theory, fear provides the motive for avoidance responding, but once the response is well learned, subjects respond without apparent fear. For example, when dogs are first trained in a shuttle box, they urinate and defecate when the warning stimulus is presented; but as training continues, these signs of fear disappear, and eventually subjects jump over the barrier with apparent nonchalance (for example, Solomon & Wynne, 1953).

Avoidance without fear. Appearances, of course, can be deceptive, but more objective measures of fear point to the same conclusion. Kamin, Brimer, and Black (1963) trained four groups of rats on an avoidance task and tested fear levels at various stages of training by presenting the CS in a conditioned emotional responses (CER) test. The test was administered after subjects had avoided shock on either 1, 3, 9 or 27 consecutive trials. As training progressed, levels of fear at first increased: The suppression ratio after 9 trials was substantially lower than after 1 or 3 trials, indicating an increase in fear (Figure 10.8). By the 27th trial, however, presentation of the tone produced almost no suppression, confirming the anecdotal impression that fear disappears as the avoidance response becomes well established. (See also Cook, Mineka, & Trumble, 1987.)

This reduction in fear is not, in itself, damaging to two-factor theory; after all, once the avoidance response was learned, shock was no longer presented. According to the theory, however, the virtual disappearance of fear should be accompanied by a dramatic decline in avoidance responding, and this rarely happens. If you look back at Figure 10.6, for example, you will see that once the subject avoided shock on trial 8, it received no further shocks, but its response latencies nevertheless continued to improve, at first rapidly and then more slowly. Although all signs of fear had disappeared, there was no deterioration in avoidance responding.

This point is made even more dramatically in a study of avoidance learning by Solomon, Kamin, and Wynne (1953). In the first phase, dogs were trained to jump over a barrier to avoid shock, and they were then given extinction trials in which no shock was presented. Because the warning stimulus was no longer

FIGURE 10.8   The fear elicited by a CS at different stages of avoidance training. Fear was measured using a CER test, which was administered before avoidance training and then again after subjects had made either 1, 3, 9, or 27 consecutive avoidance responses. The pretest suppression score was subtracted from the final score to show how much the fear elicited by the tone had changed as a result of avoidance training, and it is this adjusted suppression score that is shown. The more fear increased during training, the more negative the score. (Adapted from Kamin, Brimer, & Black, 1963)

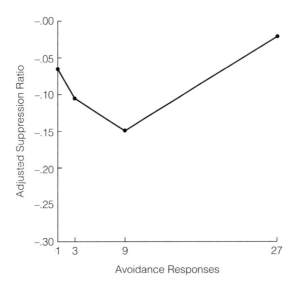

followed by shock, fear should have been extinguished, and thus (according to two-factor theory) avoidance responding should have stopped. The dogs, however, continued to respond for 200 trials without any sign of slackening, and one persisted for 650 trials—until the experimenters gave up. The dogs would probably have stopped responding had training continued long enough (Mackintosh, 1974; Levis, 1989), but according to two-factor theory there should have been at least some extinction of fear and thus some slowing down in the latency of the avoidance response to the warning signal. Quite the contrary, responding actually became faster during extinction and continued to show signs of improvement for 200 trials.

A cognitive analysis. To account for the persistence of avoidance responding in the apparent absence of fear, Seligman and Johnston (1973) proposed a cognitive theory of avoidance learning. Building on the work of earlier cognitive theorists such as Tolman, Seligman and Johnston proposed that avoidance responding is based not on fear, but on the subject's expectation that this response will avoid shock. During the initial training trials, when the warning stimulus is repeatedly followed by shock, it is assumed that subjects form an expectation that shock will occur whenever this stimulus is presented. When the animal finally jumps over the barrier and avoids the shock, it forms a new expectation—that shock does not occur if the response is made. The next time the warning stimulus is presented, the animal recalls both expectations—shock if it doesn't jump, no shock if it does—and since the outcome of no shock is clearly preferable, it performs the response that will produce this outcome.

Note that fear plays almost no role in this analysis. The subject jumps not because it is frightened, but because it prefers the outcome of no shock and, therefore, executes the response that will produce it. Seligman and Johnston do assume that fear is classically conditioned and that this fear plays an important role in directing the animal's initial reactions; they believe, however, that once the required avoidance response is performed successfully and the animal learns that this response will avoid shock, its behavior thereafter is based solely on this expectation.

Because of the small role allocated to fear in this theory, it can readily account for the evidence that was so embarrassing for two-factor theory. First, regarding the disappearance of fear during training, the theory assumes that once the avoidance response is learned, and thus the warning stimulus is no longer followed by shock, the fear conditioned to this stimulus will extinguish. The dog will continue to jump, however, because it still expects shock to occur if it doesn't, and it prefers to avoid this outcome. The situation is analogous to that of pedestrians at a traffic light: If they don't cross, it is not because they are frightened but because they know that if they were to cross they might be run over. It is this knowledge that restrains them, not any active sense of fear.

Regarding the difficulty of extinguishing avoidance behavior, this too follows directly from a cognitive analysis. The theory assumes that avoidance depends on two expectations: In the absence of a response, shock will occur; if a response is made, shock will not occur. On the first extinction trial, the dog holds both these expectations and, therefore, responds. When it does not receive a shock, its expectation that responding will not be followed by shock is confirmed, and it therefore continues to jump. With each new trial, this expectation receives further confirmation, so, if anything, the dog's tendency to jump is strengthened—exactly the result that Solomon's group found.

This analysis suggests that to extinguish an avoidance response, you must alter the expectations on which it is based. In normal extinction, the animal keeps jumping because it expects shock if it does not jump, and because it keeps responding it never gets to test this expectation. If it could somehow be prevented from jumping, however, it would discover that this expectation was no longer correct, and, hence, would stop responding. In one test of this prediction, Katzev and Berman (1974) trained rats to avoid shock in a shuttle box and then gave them 50 extinction trials during which shock was no longer presented. The CS was presented as always, and subjects in the normal extinction group were allowed to jump over the barrier to terminate it. Subjects in the response prevention, or **flooding,** group, however, had a barrier placed above the hurdle so they could no longer jump over it, although they still received the CS at the same time and for the same duration as subjects in the normal extinction group. Both groups thus received identical exposure to the CS; according to two-factor analysis, fear, and therefore avoidance, should have extinguished equally in both. When subsequently tested with the barrier removed, however, the two groups responded very differently: Subjects given normal extinction still responded on 59% of the test trials, whereas those prevented from responding responded on only 32% of test trials. As predicted by a cognitive analysis, response prevention, or flooding, does lead to rapid extinction of avoidance responding. (See also Mineka, 1979.)

A two-factor analysis. Seligman and Johnston's cognitive theory, then, not only can account for the evidence that proved so difficult for two-factor theory but can also generate accurate predictions of its own. Unfortunately, its strength is also its weakness: The fact that fear plays a minor role in the theory allows it to explain the independence of avoidance and fear; for the same reason, it has difficulty explaining evidence that fear *does* influence avoidance. The Rescorla and LoLordo experiment described earlier provides one example of this problem, but the theory's difficulties emerge in even sharper focus in an experiment by Grossen, Kostansek, and Bolles (1969).

These experimenters trained rats to jump over a barrier to avoid shock and then presented them with a tone that had previously been paired with food. What effect should the tone's presentation have on avoidance responding? According to two-factor theory, it should reduce responding. As we saw in Chapter 2, stimuli paired with food come to elicit a conditioned motivational state of hunger. Furthermore, it is known that motives such as hunger and fear are mutually inhibitory, so that increases in hunger produce decreases in fear (Dickinson & Dearing, 1979). According to two-factor theory, therefore, a tone that increases hunger should reduce fear, which in turn should reduce avoidance responding. According to Seligman and Johnston's cognitive analysis, on the other hand, the noise should have no effect. The tone might lead subjects to expect food, but the rats also know that they will receive a painful shock if they do not respond. Since no shock is preferable to shock, they should continue to respond. As predicted by two-factor theory, however, presentation of the tone produced a significant decrease in avoidance responding.

At present, then, neither two-factor theory nor cognitive theory seems able to encompass all of the evidence concerning the role of fear in avoidance responding. Perhaps, as we discussed in Chapter 8, the solution lies in recognizing that learning can take two different forms, S–R habits and cognitive expectations. In the case of avoidance, subjects may learn S–R habits that are motivated by fear, but they can also form expectations allowing them to anticipate that a response will prevent shock and, therefore, to keep responding even when shocks are no longer occurring. If so, avoidance responding is based on a mixture of fear and rational calculation, and we need to take both elements into account in trying to predict behavior. (See also Section 7.1 on punishment.)

Evaluation

Because this has been a long section, let us pause briefly to review the material we have covered. We've seen that avoidance learning seemed paradoxical to reinforcement theorists because a successful avoidance response did not seem to be followed by any consequence that could reinforce it. Mowrer's two-factor theory provided an ingenious solution by suggesting that avoidance learning was based on two factors, classical conditioning and reinforcement. He proposed that fear was classically conditioned to the warning stimulus, and that when the avoidance response terminated this stimulus, the resulting diminution in fear reinforced the response. Tests of the theory produced considerable support, but the theory's predictions proved to be erroneous in two important areas: Some avoidance responses were surprisingly hard to learn, and avoidance responding often continued even when subjects showed no signs of fear.

These problems led to the development of two alternative theories of avoidance, and both have had some success. Bolles showed that animals' innate defensive responses to danger strongly influence the development of avoidance responding. Seligman and Johnston argued that subjects respond because they expect this response to prevent a shock that would otherwise have occurred, and their theory correctly predicts that extinction will be facilitated if subjects are shown that shocks no longer occur when they don't respond. On the other hand, two-factor theorists have been able to provide ingenious explanations for some of the anomalous data, and they too can point to supporting evidence (Levis, 1989; McAllister & McAllister, 1991).

The result is that it has been difficult to unequivocally separate the various theories—each can account for some of the evidence but none can account for all of it. The obvious solution is to suppose that each theory is at least partly correct, and this may well be the case. The situation is perhaps analogous to the story of a group of blind men asked to identify an elephant by touching it. One (touching its trunk) reported that it was a snake; another (touching a leg) thought that it was a tree, and so on. Similarly in the case of avoidance, each theorist may have correctly described one aspect, and the task for the future will be to integrate these accounts into a coherent picture. This full account may well include processes such as fear conditioning, reinforcement by fear reduction, the formation of expectations, and innate defensive reactions. If this more optimistic assessment is right, then we may have already made significant progress towards understanding avoidance learning.

10.4 REINFORCEMENT AND CONDITIONING

At the heart of two-process theory is the assumption that learning involves two separate processes, conditioning and reinforcement. (When we use the term conditioning on its own in this section, we mean it as shorthand for classical conditioning.) Another possibility, however, is that conditioning and reinforcement are both the product of a single, underlying process. This issue—whether there is one basic learning process or two—is central to our understanding of associative learning, and it is this question that we will now consider.

One Process or Two?

The claim that reinforcement and conditioning are products of a single underlying process may seem strange at first, because the procedures used in studying these forms of learning are so different. In experiments on classical conditioning, subjects are exposed to pairings of two stimuli. In Pavlov's experiments, for example, dogs received pairings of a tone and food. In experiments on reinforcement, on the other hand, subjects must make a response in order to obtain food. The rules for presenting food in the two situations are thus completely different: In classical conditioning, food or some other stimulus (S*) is presented following a stimulus, while in reinforcement it is presented following a response:

$$classical\ conditioning: \quad S \rightarrow S*$$

$$reinforcement: \quad R \rightarrow S*$$

The fact that the *procedures* in these experiments differ, however, does not necessarily mean that the learning *processes* also differ. Consider a falling apple and the movement of the sun through the sky. On the surface, these appear to be very different phenomena, involving different objects and movements in different directions, but Newton was able to show that the underlying process, gravity, was the same in both cases. That conditioning and reinforcement involve different procedures, therefore, does not necessarily mean that they involve different processes.

How, then, can we decide whether conditioning and reinforcement involve two processes or just one? One approach is to consider the extent to which they share similar characteristics; if they are the products of the same underlying process, we should expect them to share common features. Suppose, for example, that you wondered whether two children that you saw sitting together on a bus came from the same family. To answer this question, you would probably examine their characteristics—the more they looked and acted alike, the greater the chances that they came from the same family. Similarly, if two instances of learning are the products of the same process, we should expect them to share a number of common features.

In fact, this does seem to be the case: To an impressive degree, the principles of conditioning and reinforcement are the same. For example, we have seen that one of the most important determinants of classical conditioning is the contiguity of the CS and US. Similarly in the case of reinforcement, learning depends critically on the delay between the response and the reinforcer. In both cases, learning depends on the temporal gap between the events to be associated, E_1 and E_2.

Similarly, conditioning depends on the intensity of the US, while in reinforcement the strength of the response depends on the intensity (amount) of the reinforcer that follows the response. And in both cases, omission of E_2 leads to extinction of the learned response; this extinction is slower if the two events were not always presented together during acquisition (the partial reinforcement effect); the response learned during acquisition generalizes to similar situations, and so on. Although there are some exceptions, in an impressive proportion of cases the principles of conditioning and reinforcement are similar if not identical. (See also Colwill & Rescorla, 1990; Williams, Preston, & de Kervor, 1990.)

One-Process Theories

If reinforcement and conditioning really are the products of a single process, what might this process be? We will consider three possibilities.

Reinforcement.   Some theorists have suggested that all learning is due to reinforcement. According to this view, the learning observed when a CS is paired with a US is actually due to reinforcement contingencies that are implicit in this procedure (for example, Hull, 1943). Consider a salivary conditioning experiment in which a tone is followed by food. From the experimenter's perspective, there is no reinforcement contingency: Food is presented in every trial, regardless of whether the dog salivates. Nevertheless, even though the experimenter does not arrange a reinforcement contingency deliberately, one could be present implicitly. Suppose, for example, that food tastes better when it is preceded by salivation—quite a reasonable supposition. If so, the amount of reinforcement will be greater for trials in which the dog salivates, and this implicit reinforcement contingency could be responsible for the increase in salivation over trials.

To evaluate this possibility, we need some way to pair a CS with a US without allowing the possibility of reinforcement. Sheffield (1965) reported an ingeniously simple procedure for achieving this. In his **omission procedure,** dogs were given standard salivary conditioning trials in which a tone was followed by food; if a dog salivated on any trial, however, the food scheduled for the end

FIGURE 10.9   Diagram of Sheffield's omission procedure. Food normally followed a tone but was omitted on any trials in which the dog salivated (response).

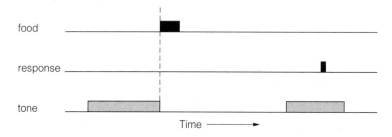

of that trial was canceled or omitted (Figure 10.9). Salivation was thus never followed by food, so that any increase in salivation could not be due to reinforcement. Because food continued to be presented on trials when the dog didn't salivate, however, the tone and food were still paired on some trials. A conditioning analysis thus predicted that the dogs might still learn to salivate, and this is what Sheffield found. One dog, Vicki, salivated on approximately half the trials and continued to do so for 800 trials, despite the fact that this salivation was costing her food. This increase in salivation could not have been due to reinforcement. (See also Williams & Williams, 1969.)

Classical conditioning. If one process is responsible for conditioning and reinforcement, that process is clearly not reinforcement. Could it, then, be classical conditioning? Just as reinforcement or R → S* contingencies are potentially present in experiments on classical conditioning, so S → S* contingencies are present in experiments on reinforcement, and these S → S* contingencies could be responsible for the learning observed.

    To see how this could be so, consider a reinforcement experiment in which a rat runs down an alley to receive food: How could running down the alley be the result of classical conditioning? One possible answer is *sign tracking*. In Section 2.4, we discussed evidence that animals approach or track stimuli that have been paired with food. One example is autoshaping: When a lit key is paired with food, pigeons will approach the key when it is illuminated and then peck at it. Though it might not be immediately obvious, this tendency to approach stimuli paired with food could also explain maze learning. When a rat receives food after running down an alley, the stimuli of the alley will be associated with the food and, therefore, elicit approach behavior. Moreover, the stimuli closer to the goal will be associated with food more strongly and will elicit approach behavior more strongly. When the rat is returned to the start box for the next trial, therefore, it will move towards the alley stimuli that were associated with food; as it approaches these stimuli, it will be attracted by stimuli that were still closer to food, and so on, until it reaches the goal box. The rat could be running down the alley for exactly the same reason that an autoshaped pigeon approaches the key—in order to move closer to stimuli that have been associated with food.

Evidence indicates that sign-tracking does influence behavior in many reinforcement experiments (for example, Peterson, Ackil, Frommer, & Hearst, 1972), but it cannot account for all the effects of reinforcement. In particular, classical conditioning can play a powerful role in experiments in which the reinforced response involves movement toward or away from a particular stimulus, but a conditioning explanation is much less plausible when the reinforced response is less clearly oriented toward a discrete stimulus. For example, it is easy to reinforce a dog for lifting its leg, and it is difficult to account for such learning in terms of the dog's trying to approach a stimulus that was previously correlated with food (Wahlsten & Cole, 1972; see also Bolles, Holtz, Dunn, & Hill, 1980; Davey, Oakley, & Cleland, 1981). Thus, just as we cannot account for classical conditioning solely in terms of reinforcement, we cannot explain reinforcement solely in terms of conditioning.

An Associative Analysis

We seem to be at something of an impasse. The remarkable similarity of the principles of conditioning and reinforcement points to a single process, but this process does not appear to be either conditioning or reinforcement. How, then, can we account for the similarities in their principles?

An E_1– E_2 associative system. One possibility is that conditioning and reinforcement both draw on a common system for detecting relationships between events (for example, Dickinson, 1980). It is perhaps easier to understand this idea if we begin by considering the evolutionary forces that are thought to have shaped learning. To survive in the world, animals must be able to predict where and when important events are going to occur: They must know which parts of their environment contain food, when a predator is nearby, which foods will make them ill, and so on. Some of this knowledge can be innately built in, but some of it needs to be learned, and to acquire this knowledge animals might have evolved a single learning system for detecting relationships between events. That is, if some event E_1 reliably precedes an important event E_2, animals possess a learning system to detect that these events tend to occur together:

$$E_1 \rightarrow E_2$$

In the case of reinforcement, the relationship is between a response and a stimulus (an R $\rightarrow$ S* association), whereas in classical conditioning the relationship is between two stimuli (an S $\rightarrow$ S* relationship), but the same learning system for detecting the co-occurrence of events could be involved in both cases. The reason that the principles of conditioning and reinforcement are so similar, therefore, could be that both rely on a common system for detecting relationships between events.

A new response problem. If reinforcement and conditioning are the products of a single associative process, we might also expect similarities in the responses that can be learned using the two procedures. Here, however, the evidence is less favorable to a single-process account. In the case of classical conditioning, it is easy to condition autonomic responses such as salivation and heart rate—indeed, there is evidence that most if not all autonomic responses can be conditioned. The number of skeletal responses that can be conditioned, on the other hand, is much smaller, because you need an unconditioned stimulus to elicit a response before you can condition it. Although some skeletal responses can be elicited by a US—blinking in response to a puff of air, for example, or jerking your knee when it is tapped—most skeletal responses are not reflexive and, therefore, cannot be conditioned. For better or worse, you cannot condition children to brush their teeth or condition adults to vote for a particular candidate.

The reverse is true in the case of reinforcement. It is relatively easy to reinforce most skeletal responses (we shall consider some interesting exceptions in Chapter 11), but much, much harder to reinforce autonomic responses (for example, Miller & Dworkin, 1974). The set of behaviors that can be strengthened by reinforcement and conditioning thus differ substantially: Whereas reinforcement is primarily effective with skeletal responses, classical conditioning is more effective with autonomic responses. If the same learning process is involved, why should this be?

The answer is not entirely clear. One possibility is that while the associative systems involved in conditioning and reinforcement share many characteristics, they also differ in certain respects. In particular, there might be differences in their propensity to form certain associations. In our discussion of the principle of preparedness in classical conditioning, we saw that some associations are easier to learn than others. In taste-aversion learning, for example, it is much easier to associate illness with an earlier taste than with a noise. We suggested that the reason might be that in nature the taste of a food is much more likely to be the cause of illness than, say, the call of a passing bird. As a result, the conditioning system might have evolved so as to favor some associations over others.

Preparedness of this kind might also explain why it is difficult to reinforce autonomic responses. If your pancreas happens to be particularly active at a moment when you discovered some food, it is highly unlikely that this pancreatic activity caused the food's appearance, and it would be positively dangerous to your well-being if this chance conjunction resulted in a long-term increase in pancreatic activity. As a result, the associative processes involved in reinforcement may have evolved in such a way as to prevent the formation of associations between autonomic responses and external events such as food and water. (See Mackintosh, 1983, for a discussion of other possibilities.)

This analysis seems plausible, but it is also speculative because we currently lack hard evidence on which to judge it. The question of why conditioning and reinforcement differ in the ease with which they affect skeletal and autonomic responses, therefore, cannot be definitively resolved at this time. Given the extensive similarities in the principles of the two forms of learning, however, there are strong grounds for believing that they do involve very similar processes.

10.5 CHOOSING A RESPONSE

We have been looking at how reinforcement influences learning; in this section we turn to the role of reinforcement in performance. On the surface, the relationship between reinforcement and performance can seem very simple—if you know that a certain response will lead to a reinforcer that you want, then you perform that response. In practice, the relationship is rarely this simple. For one thing, we rarely consider responses in isolation but instead choose from among a number of alternatives. Suppose, for example, that you knew that studying for two hours every day would guarantee that you would obtain an A for one of your psychology courses. Would you do it? In making this decision, you would probably take into account not only the possible consequences of studying but also the attractions of other activities such as meeting friends, listening to music, and so on. Unlike a hungry rat in a cage with a lever, you normally have many response alternatives available to you, and choosing among them can be far from simple.

Because making choices is so central to human behavior, researchers from a variety of disciplines have studied this process. We will focus on theories that have been developed by workers in three of these areas: learning, economics, and cognitive psychology. These fields are so large that we cannot examine each in detail, but we will try to provide a flavor of their different approaches by looking at a few examples from each.

The Matching Law

Learning psychologists have largely concentrated on how animals make choices in laboratory settings. This research has given rise to a number of theories about the effects of reinforcement and motivation on choice behavior, and we will focus on one that has been particularly influential in recent years.

Herrnstein's discovery. The primary determinant of choice behavior is the consequences that follow each response—in the broadest sense, the schedules of reinforcement. If one activity is more likely to produce reinforcement than another, we naturally prefer it, and similarly we prefer responses that produce larger amounts of reinforcement or involve shorter delays. In outline, then, the factors determining choice are well understood, but predicting their effects in detail has proved harder.

To study the processes involved, learning psychologists have often used a procedure called a **concurrent schedule.** In this procedure, subjects are given a choice between several possible responses; each response is reinforced on a different schedule, and subjects can alternate freely between the responses. Suppose, for example, that you had a choice between playing two adjacent slot machines that paid off, somewhat unusually, on VI schedules. (In a VI schedule, you may recall, reinforcement is made available at intervals that vary unpredictably, and the first response after this time produces the reinforcer.) Suppose that one outrageously generous machine produces reward on a VI 30-second schedule, while the other produces reward on an almost equally generous VI 60-second schedule. Since the VI 30 schedule produces a payoff more frequently, after a bit of experience you would probably begin to spend more of your time playing the VI 30 machine. However, because payoffs have been scheduled on VI schedules (remember, these are not typical machines), it would be a mistake to spend all of your time on just one—while you were working on the VI 30 machine, a payoff might have become available on the VI 60, so that just a single play on that machine would produce a bonanza. The optimum strategy is clearly to spend some time on both machines, but exactly how much time should you spend on each? Or, to consider a more complicated situation, suppose that one machine pays off on a VI 30 but that the other pays off on a VR 10 (an average of one response in 10 is reinforced). Again, how should you divide your time?

The optimum strategy in situations like these is not always obvious, but it turns out that animals faced with this problem divide their time according to a surprisingly simple rule. The rule was first identified in an experiment by Herrnstein (1961), in which he trained three pigeons to peck keys using concurrent VI VI schedules. Each bird was given a series of choices: In one condition, pecking on the two keys was reinforced on a concurrent VI 135 VI 270 schedule; once the bird's allocation of time between the two keys had stabilized, the schedule was changed to concurrent VI 180 VI 180, and so on. Figure 10.10 shows the terminal performance, after behavior had stabilized, for each bird. The graph shows that the percentage of pecks devoted to one of the keys matched almost exactly the percentage of the reinforcers obtained by responding on that key. When the birds were trained on a concurrent VI 135 VI 270 schedule, for example, reinforcement was available on the VI 135 schedule twice as often as on the VI 270 schedule, and this eventually led each bird to spend twice as much time responding on the VI 135 key.

Herrnstein termed this relationship the **matching law;** this states that if several responses are possible in a situation, the percentage of time you devote

FIGURE 10.10 The matching law. Pigeons were trained to peck two keys using concurrent VI VI schedules, and the percentage of their responses to one of these keys is shown as a function of the
percentage of the reinforcers they earned by pecking that key. Each data point represents
the results for one pigeon on one problem; the solid diagonal shows the predictions of the
matching law. (Adapted from Herrnstein, 1961)

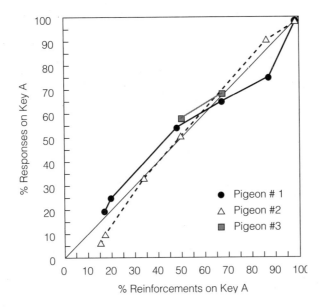

to one of them will match the percentage of the reinforcers you have obtained
by performing that response. In a situation where there are two possible responses, R_1 and R_2, and the number of reinforcements earned by each of these
reinforcements is S^R_1 and S^R_2, then the matching law says that the proportion of responses devoted to R_1 will come to match the proportion of reinforcements that have been earned by that response:

$$\frac{R_1}{R_1 + R_2} = \frac{S^R_1}{S^R_1 + S^R_2}$$

The matching law has been tested in a wide range of situations, involving
humans as well as rats and pigeons, and on the whole the results have supported
it (Davison & McCarthy, 1988). In one demonstration in humans, Conger and
Killeen (1974) asked groups of college students to participate in a 30-minute
discussion about drug abuse. The membership of the group was rigged so that
the real subjects had confederates of the experimenter sitting on their left and
right. As the conversation proceeded, the confederates occasionally reinforced
the subject by praising his or her comments (for example, saying "That's a good

point"). They found that the percentage of time subjects spent talking to each confederate came to match the percentage of the time that each had reinforced them. In one condition, the student on their left delivered 82% of the reinforcers, and by the end of the discussion, subjects were addressing 78% of their comments to this student!

Melioration.   In order to account for this behavior, Herrnstein and Vaughan (1980) proposed a new principle that they called **melioration.** The verb *meliorate* means to make things better, and the melioration hypothesis says that when one activity is more likely to produce reinforcement than another, we increase the proportion of time devoted to this activity. The goal is not to find the best alternative but simply to spend more time on whichever is better. Suppose, for example, that you were playing a game of tennis, and you had to choose between using a lob or a passing shot when your opponent came to the net. If you found that the lob was working better, you would begin to use this shot more often, and you would continue to increase the percentage of lobs for as long as it was more effective. As you used this shot more often, though, it would begin to lose its surprise value, until eventually you reached a point where lobs and passing shots were equally likely to win points. At this point, you would stop adjusting the proportion in which you used the two shots.

Herrnstein and Vaughan say that the same process is at work when pigeons are trained on a concurrent VI VI schedule. Suppose that a pigeon was reinforced for pecking one key on a VI 60 schedule and for pecking a second key on a VI 120 schedule. At first, it would probably peck the two keys equally often. As it discovered that the VI 60 key produced food more often, the melioration hypothesis says that it would increase the proportion of time that it devoted to pecking this key. On a VI schedule, however, changes in response rate have little effect on the number of reinforcements earned, so this increase in response rate would lead to a reduction in the percentage of responses reinforced. The more the bird responded on this key, the smaller the percentage of reinforced responses would become, until eventually the probability of a peck producing food would be the same on both keys. At this point, it would cease to redistribute its behavior.

A numerical example may help to clarify this point. Suppose that initially the bird responded 20 times a minute on the VI 60 key. In one minute, these 20 responses would produce, on average, one reinforcer, meaning that 5% of the bird's responses would be reinforced. If the bird doubled its rate of response, this would have little effect on the number of reinforcers it earned. (Remember that in a VI 60 second schedule, food becomes available on average once a minute, and the first response after this time produces the food. If a bird responds 20 times a minute, the average delay between responses would be only 3 seconds, so that it would obtain food within seconds of its becoming available; doubling its rate of response would have only a tiny effect on the average interval between successive food presentations.) Thus, even though the bird was now responding 40 times a minute, it would still earn only one reinforcer in that minute, so that the proportion of its reinforced responses would fall to 2.5%. If this payoff was still better than on the VI 120 key, the bird would increase the time it spent responding on this key still further, and this process would continue until the probability of a response being reinforced was the same on both keys. If you do the calculations for yourself, you will find that this point of equilibrium is reached when the percentage of responses on the key matches the percentage of reinforcements. The process of melioration, or increasing the effort devoted to the better alternative, thus eventually leads to matching.

Melioration can account for some of the data obtained in experiments using concurrent schedules, but it turns out that it cannot account for all of it (for example, Williams, 1993). Other theories have also been proposed, but they, too, have been only partially successful. (For a thorough review, see Williams, 1994b.) Thus, although psychologists have made considerable progress in understanding the outline of how reinforcement influences choice behavior, work still remains in filling in some of the details.

Behavioral Economics

At the same time as learning psychologists have been trying to understand the choice behavior of animals in the laboratory, economists have been trying to understand the choices made by consumers in the real world. Despite obvious differences in these situations, in both individuals have to decide how to use a limited resource to maximize their overall levels of reinforcement. In the laboratory, animals have to decide how to divide their limited time and energy between competing activities; in the economy consumers have to decide how to allocate a limited supply of money. In this section we will look at two of the principles that influence consumers' choices, and we will also consider whether these principles can help us understand the choices made by animals.

Price. When consumers are faced with a wide range of products, how do they decide which ones to buy? In economics, the amount of a product that is purchased is called the **demand** for that product, so in economics this question becomes what factors influence the demand for a product?

The most obvious influence is the product's price. The more an item costs, the less of it we tend to buy, and this relationship can be represented graphically in the form of a *demand curve,* which shows how demand (how much we buy) changes as prices increase. Figure 10.11 shows hypothetical demand curves for two products, salt and French chocolates. Looking first at the curve for chocolates, we can see that when the price is low, we tend to buy large quantities. As the price increases, however, demand begins to fall sharply. Demand in this situation is said to be **elastic**—it changes markedly as prices change. The

FIGURE 10.11 Hypothetical demand curves. Changes in the amount of salt and chocolate consumed (demand) as a function of their prices.

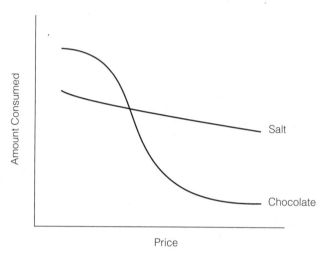

demand for salt, on the other hand, is less elastic; as price increases, demand remains relatively constant, because salt is a necessity that we are not prepared to do without. Demand in this case is said to be **inelastic.**

One other feature of this figure worth noting is the relationship between demand for the two products. At low prices, we consume larger amounts of chocolate than of salt, so it looks as if we prefer chocolate to salt. As prices increase, however, the demand for chocolate falls faster than does the demand for salt, because chocolate is a luxury we are willing to forego when it becomes too expensive. In judging whether consumers value one product more highly than another, therefore, we need to look at how demand compares over a range of prices, not just one price.

Would animals behave this way if faced with comparable situations? The answer turns out to be yes. In one experiment, Hursh and Natelson (1981) trained rats to press two levers on a concurrent schedule. Presses on one of the levers produced food pellets, while presses on the other produced a reinforcer that we have not previously encountered, electrical brain stimulation (EBS). In this procedure, a tiny electric current is delivered to the brain through implanted electrodes; if the current is delivered to certain areas of the brain ("pleasure centers"), it is intensely reinforcing, and rats will respond for hours to turn on this current. In one condition of the Hursh and Natelson experiment, the rats had to respond on each lever only twice to produce a reinforcer (FR 2), and in this condition they responded almost nine times as often on the EBS lever as on the food lever. This result was consistent with that of many earlier studies, demonstrating the powerful reinforcing properties of EBS. When the number of responses required for reinforcement on each lever was increased to eight, however, the rats responded more on the food lever! The rats seemed to regard EBS in the same way humans view chocolates—a wonderful luxury that they value highly when it is cheap, but for which they are no longer willing to work when it is expensive.

Income. Demand for a product depends not simply on the product's price but also on consumers' incomes. If you are living on an income of $10,000 a year, spending $40 on a box of chocolates might be unthinkable; if your income is $100,000, the same price might not cause you even to hesitate.

In animal experiments, the price of a reinforcer is the number of responses required to obtain it, while a subject's income is the number of responses it is capable of performing. Consider a pigeon reinforced for pecking a key on a VI 60-second schedule. In a VI schedule, only a single response is needed once reinforcement has become available, and a bird that pecks 20 times a minute will obtain virtually all of the reinforcers that are available during a session. The price of a reinforcer, therefore, is in the region of 20 responses a minute. The resource from which these responses are drawn, however, is considerably greater, as pigeons can peck keys in excess of 100 times a minute. In the case of a VI schedule, therefore, the price of a reinforcer is small relative to the bird's income.

This has often been the case in experiments on reinforcement. In effect, these experiments have looked at the effect of the price of chocolates on the behavior of a millionaire who could easily afford them. Would the effects of reinforcement look different if they were examined in a context where income was restricted?

Again, the answer turns out to be yes. In one experiment, Silberberg, Warren-Boulton, and Asano (1987) trained monkeys on a discrete-trials procedure in which two keys were occasionally illuminated with red and green lights. The first response to one of these keys produced a reinforcer and terminated the trial. If a monkey pressed the red key, it received a standard food pellet; if it pressed the green key, it received a pellet that was much larger but had a bitter taste. To assess the effect of income on preference, they varied the number of trials during a session: When there were many trials, subjects effectively had a high income that could be used to make many choices, whereas a small number of trials corresponded to a low income.

Silberberg and colleagues found that with a small number of trials (low income), the monkeys preferred the larger, more nutritious pellets. When they were allowed more choices, however—in effect, their disposable income was increased, so that they could afford to buy more pellets—they preferred the smaller but tastier pellets. A human analogy might be an assembly-line worker who buys hamburgers rather than steaks, but switches to steaks when promoted to a managerial position.

This experiment illustrates how principles derived from economics can shed light on choice behavior in other situations. Before psychologists became more aware of economic principles, the preference for the larger pellets in the first condition would have convinced most psychologists that these pellets were more reinforcing. The results for the second condition, however, made it clear that this conclusion would have been inappropriate: Which reinforcer was more effective depended crucially on subjects' incomes. Principles derived from economics thus can help to explain choice behavior in animals as well as humans.

Conversely, the fact that principles of economics also apply to animals points again to the similarities in animal and human behavior, and it raises the possibility that study of animal behavior under the controlled conditions of the laboratory could enhance our understanding of economics. Indeed, research with animals has already revealed areas in which economic principles need to be modified (for example, Myerson & Green, 1995). Developments like these have made psychologists and economists more aware of the potential benefits to cooperation between the disciplines, and this has given rise to a new field called *behavioral economics*, in which researchers have used behavioral techniques to explore economic principles. (See Bickel, Green, & Vuchinich, 1995.) Continued cross-fertilization between the two disciplines should ultimately help both in their efforts to understand behavior.

Behavioral Decision Theory

Cognitive psychologists have also looked at choice behavior in the laboratory, but they have studied the behavior of humans rather than of animals, and typically they have looked at relatively complex decisions, such as buying a car. In choosing a car model, you would probably consider factors such as its price, appearance, spaciousness, fuel economy, and so on. Cognitive psychologists have tried to understand how you combine information on all these features in reaching a decision.

Rational decision making? One obvious strategy for choosing a car is to evaluate each model on each feature. The value you assigned to each feature would inevitably be subjective—for one person, a red car might be highly desirable, whereas for someone else this color might be a serious drawback—and this subjective value is called the feature's **utility.** The first step in evaluating a car, therefore, is to assess the utility of each feature; you would then need to combine these utilities to arrive at an overall evaluation. The easiest way to combine utilities is simply to add them together, but some features are often more important to us than others—you may care more about a car's safety record than its value—so you would want to weigh some of these factors more heavily than others. To assess a car, therefore, you would need not only to assign utilities to each of its features but also to decide how heavily to weigh each of these features, and once you had calculated the overall utility of one model, you would need to go through the same process for every other model, in order to identify the car with highest overall utility.

You may have already realized that this is not how you make decisions, whether about buying a car, studying, or almost anything else. Introspectively, it doesn't *feel* as if we combine different factors in such a precise and logical way, and considerable evidence confirms that we don't. One way to see this is to examine the decision-making of experts—individuals with special expertise in a field who are regarded as particularly skilled at making judgments. Studies have revealed that even the decisions of experts are not as logical as the preceding model requires.

One example comes from studies of medical decision making. If doctors are interviewed about how they make their diagnoses, they often point to a wide range of factors that they consider, but research suggests that their decisions are actually based on a much smaller proportion of the evidence (for example, Elstein, Shulman, & Sprakfa, 1978). In one study bearing on this point, Einhorn (1972) studied the ability of doctors to assess the severity of Hodgkinson's disease in patients with terminal conditions. Three doctors, one of whom was one of the world's foremost experts, rated patients on nine characteristics, and on the basis of these scores each doctor rated the overall severity of the illness. However, Einhorn found that these ratings had no predictive value: Patients with the worst scores lived just as long as patients with the best scores. This could have been because the course of the disease was fundamentally unpredictable, but Einhorn went on to construct a simple mathematical formula for combining the doctors' ratings of the nine characteristics, and he found that this formula *was* successful in predicting longevity. The doctors had the necessary information; they just couldn't use it effectively. (See also Slovic & Lichtenstein, 1968.)

In making complex decisions, then, we don't normally perform the detailed calculations that would produce optimal decisions. Instead, faced with more information than we can handle, we simplify the decision process. Simon (1957) suggested that one way we do this is by abandoning the goal of a perfect solution and instead settling for one that is satisfactory. Instead of visiting every car dealer in your area, you might start with the ones that were nearest to you, and buy a car as soon as you found one that was acceptable. Simon called this strategy **satisficing,** meaning to look for a satisfactory solution rather than a perfect one. (Note the similarity to melioration, which also involves choosing the better outcome rather than the best.) A related strategy would be to concentrate on one of the features of each car and to eliminate the cars that were unacceptable on this feature. If price was your most important feature, you would start by eliminating cars that were too expensive, then narrow the field still further by considering another feature, and so on. (Tversky, 1972, called this strategy *elimination by aspects.*)

Uncertain outcomes. In the examples we have considered so far, we have known what the outcomes of different decisions would be—for example, a red

Ford or a silver Honda—and the only issue has been what value to assign to these outcomes. In many decisions, though, we are not sure whether the outcome we want will actually occur. If you decide to study two hours a day, for example, you cannot be sure that this effort will produce an A—it might, but it might not. In reaching decisions, therefore, we often need to take into account the probability of the possible outcomes as well as their utility.

The optimal strategy when outcomes are uncertain is to calculate the average or expected value of the various outcomes. Suppose, for example, that a generous friend offered to give you $5.00 every time you tossed a coin and it came up heads. The probability of this outcome would be .5, and if you tossed the coin repeatedly, the average amount of money that you would win on each toss would be:

$$expected\ value\ (heads) = (probability\ of\ outcome) \times (utility\ of\ outcome)$$
$$= .5 \times \$5.00 = \$2.50$$

In this case, we used the monetary value of a win as its utility, but the same approach can be taken with any decision by assigning a numerical value to utility. Suppose, for example, that you assigned a utility of 10 to the most desirable outcome that you could imagine and that you evaluated all other outcomes relative to this perfect score. On this scale, you might regard obtaining an A on an exam as having a utility of, let us say, 8. If you knew that the probability of obtaining an A if you studied was .5, then the expected utility of studying would be:

$$expected\ utility\ (studying) = (probability\ of\ \text{``A''}) \times (utility\ of\ \text{``A''})$$
$$= .5 \times 8 = 4$$

If the main alternative to studying was going to a party, you could also calculate the expected utility of that outcome. Suppose that the probability of having fun at the party was .6, and that the utility of this enjoyable outcome, if it materialized, was 5. Then the expected utility of the party would be

$$expected\ utility\ (party) = .6 \times 5 = 3$$

At least in this instance (rigged, to encourage you to study), the expected value of studying would be greater than that of going to a party.[3]

---

[3] To simplify our calculations, we have assumed that each decision had only one outcome. In the case of studying, for example, we considered only the possibility of an A, but of course other grades would also be possible. To take these into account, you would simply need to calculate the expected utility of each outcome. Suppose, for example, that studying was equally likely to lead to an A or a B, and that a grade of B had a utility for you of 3. The expected utility (E.U.) of studying would then be

E. U. (studying) = E. U. (“A”) + E. U. (“B”)
$$= (.5 \times 8) + (.5 \times 3) = 4 + 1.5 = 5.5$$

Heuristics. To be able to calculate expected utility, you need to know the probability of the different outcomes. In some situations, this is not difficult—both animals and humans are very good at estimating the probabilities of events in situations where they have extensive exposure to these events (for example, Estes, 1976). In many real-life decisions, though, we lack the necessary information. In these situations, cognitive psychologists have suggested that we again use simplifying strategies to help us in estimating probabilities. These shortcuts, called **heuristics,** are useful "rules of thumb"—they increase our chances of making a good decision, but they are not infallible. We will look at two of the heuristics that psychologists have identified, but before we do so, see if you can answer the following questions correctly:

1. Do more words begin with the letter k or have k as the third letter?

2. You meet someone at a party who is short, slim, and likes to read poetry. Is this person more likely to be:

    a. a professor of classics at an Ivy League university

    b. a truck driver

We will return to these questions shortly.

In a highly influential article, Tversky and Kahneman (1974) identified a number of heuristics that they believe people use in estimating probabilities. One, the **availability heuristic,** estimates the probability of an event by seeing how easy it is to find examples of this event in memory. If you have experienced an event frequently, then there should be many examples stored in your memory, and the ease with which you can remember examples—their availability—should give you a good idea of how often you have experienced the event. This seems reasonable, and in many situations the availability heuristic works well. If someone asked you whether more words begin with the letter a or the letter x, for example, you would undoubtedly select the letter a because you could think of words beginning with this letter more easily, and you would be right.

Unfortunately, the availability heuristic can also sometimes mislead us, because the ease of retrieving examples from memory is not always an accurate guide to event probability in the real world. Our earlier question about the letter k provides an example. It is much easier to think of words that begin with a letter than words than have that letter in a later position, so most people answer this question by saying that more words begin with the letter k. In fact, more than three times as many words have the letter k in the third position.

The issue of where letters occur most frequently in words is clearly trivial, but the availability heuristic can also lead us into error in more important situations. In one experiment, people were asked estimate the probability of dying from different causes. When asked whether more people died from tornadoes or asthma, for example, most people said tornadoes, but in fact people are more than twenty times more likely to die from asthma. The reason people make this error is almost certainly because newspapers devote far more coverage to deaths involving tornadoes, and as a result we find it easier to recall examples. This might also explain why people overestimate their chances of winning state lotteries—we often read about lottery winners, but in fact the chances of winning are about the same as those of being struck by lightening (Myers, 1995). The availability heuristic might even be one cause of marital discord. In a study by Ross and Sicoly (1979), married couples were asked to say which partner was more likely to perform each of 20 chores (for example, cooking and shopping). Husbands and wives *both* said that they were the ones more likely to do 16 of the 20 chores, probably because they found it easier to remember the occasions on which they had done these chores than their partners had. (The authors reported similar findings for lab partners in college courses.)

A second strategy identified by Tversky and Kahneman is the **representativeness heuristic.** In this strategy, we judge the likelihood that an event comes from a particular category by seeing whether the event seems to be typical or representative of the category. A robin, for example, is a typical bird, so if you were asked whether a robin is a bird, you would have no hesitation in saying that it was. In some cases, though, representativeness is not a good guide to category membership, and the truck driver question is an example. Most people asked this question say that the person is more likely to be a classics professor, because the characteristics (short, slim, poetry-loving) seem more typical of classics professors than of truck drivers. However, this conclusion ignores the fact that there are many, many more truck drivers than Ivy League classics professors. Suppose, as a rough approximation, that there are 50 Ivy League professors of classics, and 500,000 truck drivers. Even if half of the professors were short, slim and poetry-loving (unlikely), there would still only be 25 professors fitting this description, whereas if just 1% of truck drivers matched the description, there would be 5,000! Given these numbers, it is much more likely that the individual is a truck driver than a classics professor. (This example was drawn from Myers, 1995.)

In this example, we don't have the statistics to be sure that the representativeness heuristic has produced the wrong answer. When the appropriate statistics have been available, however, Tversky and Kahneman were able to show that use of this heuristic really does lead subjects to the kind of error illustrated here.

Framing. Economists have traditionally assumed that people are rational decision makers, meaning that they can evaluate evidence logically and reach the optimal conclusion. The research of cognitive psychologists, however, has made it clear that this assumption is fundamentally wrong because human reasoning is based not on pure logic but rather on simplifying strategies that sometimes lead us astray. We will conclude our brief introduction to decision theory by examining one further example, the phenomenon of **framing.**

Framing refers to how questions are phrased. In the context of decision making, Tversky and Kahneman (1987) have shown that even seemingly minor variations in how a question is framed can markedly alter which option subjects select. In one example, the subjects were employees of a company that developed high-technology engineering systems. They were given a description of a potential project and asked whether it should be funded. Two groups received the same description, except that the last sentence for one group said that the authors of the proposal had a 60% success rate in earlier projects, while the final sentence for the other group referred to a 40% failure rate. Even though the information in the two sentences is logically equivalent—a 60% success rate inevitably implies a 40% failure rate—subjects given the success description were significantly more likely to approve the project (Dunegan, 1993). Similarly, patients rated medical treatments more positively when they were told the percentage of patients that lived rather than the percentage of patients that died. More surprising, physicians given the same information made exactly the same mistake, rating treatments more positively when the outcomes were framed in terms of survival rather than mortality (McNeil, Pauker, Cox, & Tversky, 1982). Even experts can make fundamental errors in interpreting evidence, with potentially fatal consequences.

Conclusions

We have now looked at research on decision-making from three perspectives—learning, economics, and cognitive psychology—and each has revealed important facets of choice behavior. While research on learning has focused on the role of outcomes (reinforcers) in determining choice, economists have identified other important variables such as income, and cognitive psychologists have explored the processes involved in more complex decisions in which each outcome has many aspects, and the probability of these outcomes is difficult to estimate. These perspectives differ in some respects, but they also share some common themes. One, that we have now encountered many times, is that apparently complex and sophisticated forms of behavior are sometimes based on much simpler processes below the surface. We first saw this in classical conditioning, where the Rescorla-Wagner model showed how animals' exquisite sensitivity to different contingencies could be explained in terms of simple associations, and where performance was often based on simple rules ("If a predator is imminent, freeze"). Similarly in the case of reinforcement, complex decisions are often based on simplifying strategies, such as melioration, satisficing, and heuristics.

To return to the parable of the elephant and the blind men cited earlier, each of the three disciplines has focused on a different part of the elephant. In doing so, they have given us not only a clearer understanding of some of its parts, but also a sense of the enormity of the beast.

10.6 SUMMARY

Thorndike believed that a reinforcer would automatically strengthen whatever behavior preceded it. In accordance with this analysis, Skinner found that pigeons given free food every 15 seconds would begin to repeat whatever response happened to precede the food, even though there was no causal relationship between the two. There is evidence that under some circumstances reinforcement can also function automatically in humans and can strengthen subjects' behavior without their conscious awareness.

Thorndike also believed that some form of reinforcement is necessary for learning, but subsequent research has not treated this belief quite so kindly. Studies of latent learning showed that rats learn the correct path through a maze just as well when they were not reinforced as when they were. Similarly, studies of perceptual learning showed that we learn about the perceptual properties of stimuli simply through being exposed to them. On the other hand, learning does seem to be more likely when an event, such as food, occurs unexpectedly. The unexpected event need not be food: Research on marking suggests that any surprising event, even a light or a tone, can trigger a memory search for possible causes.

Another challenge to the Law of Effect has come from research on avoidance learning. In a typical avoidance experiment, rats are given a tone followed 10 seconds later by shock; if they jump over a barrier before the 10 seconds have elapsed, the warning signal is terminated and the shock delivery canceled. A rat will readily learn to jump over the barrier in this situation, but because a successful response is not followed by any stimulus, how could reinforcement account for this learning? Mowrer proposed an ingenious solution. According to his two-factor theory, pairings of the tone with shock condition fear to the tone; when the avoidance response turns off this tone, the subsequent reduction in fear reinforces the response.

The importance of fear is shown in studies in which a previously conditioned stimulus is presented while subjects are responding on an avoidance task: Stimuli that elicit fear increase responding, whereas stimuli that inhibit fear reduce responding. Similarly, the reinforcing properties of fear reduction are shown in studies in which rats learn to jump over a barrier in order to turn off a stimulus previously associated with shock.

One challenge to two-factor theory has come from evidence that some responses are much harder to learn than others. To account for this variability, Bolles proposed that animals have a set of innate, species-specific defense reactions (SSDRs) to fear, and that responses incompatible with these SSDRs are very difficult to learn. In contrast, two-factor theorists argue that responses such as bar pressing are hard to learn because they produce only minimal change in the animal's stimulus environment and thus provide less scope for fear reduction. There is evidence to support both factors, and it seems likely that both contribute to the difficulty in learning certain responses.

A second challenge to two-factor theory has come from evidence that avoidance responses are not as dependent on fear as the theory requires. Once subjects learn to avoid shock, conditioned fear should begin to extinguish because the warning stimulus is no longer followed by shock. Indeed, subjects do appear to become less frightened as training proceeds, but avoidance responding may nevertheless persist for hundreds of trials without weakening.

To account for the persistence of avoidance responding in the absence of fear, Seligman and Johnston (1973) have proposed a cognitive analysis in which responding is based not on fear but on the rational calculation that responding will reduce the likelihood of shock. According to their account, subjects in avoidance experiments learn that shock occurs following a warning stimulus, but does not occur if they respond; because they prefer not to receive a shock, they respond. The persistence of avoidance responding in extinction follows naturally from this analysis: Animals jump because they expect this response to be followed by no shock, and extinction trials simply confirm this expectation. For avoidance responding to extinguish, according to this analysis, subjects must have an opportunity to learn that shock no longer occurs if they do not respond, and experiments in which the response is prevented during extinction (flooding) have confirmed this prediction.

A cognitive analysis, then, can explain the persistence of avoidance responding after fear has extinguished, but it has difficulty accounting for experiments in which fear does influence avoidance responding. One obvious resolution is to assume that two-factor theory and cognitive accounts are both right, with avoidance responding being controlled by a mixture of fear (and the SSDRs this fear elicits) and the rational expectation that responding will avoid shock.

Two-factor theory assumes that classical conditioning and reinforcement involve different learning processes, but the principles of learning in the two cases are remarkably similar, and this has suggested to some theorists that the two might be different manifestations of a single underlying process. Possibly they both rely on a common system for detecting relationships between events. If event E_1 is followed by another event E_2, then whether E_1 is a stimulus (as in classical conditioning) or a response (as in reinforcement), the same processes may be involved in detecting the E_1–E_2 relationship. This interpretation faces problems in explaining why reinforcement and conditioning vary somewhat in the responses that they train—for example, it is much easier to condition autonomic responses than it is to reinforce them. The reason is not entirely clear, but in nature autonomic responses are unlikely to be the cause of external events such as obtaining food; as a result, our learning systems might have evolved so as not to form such associations.

In the final section, we looked at the role of reinforcement in choice behavior. We examined research on choice drawn from three very different perspectives: learning, economics and cognitive psychology.

Learning researchers have focused on the effects of reinforcement on choice behavior in animals, and to illustrate this approach we looked at research on the matching law. This states that we allocate our time between responses in proportion to the number of reinforcers earned by these responses. Herrnstein and Vaughan offered an explanation of matching in terms of melioration, which is a tendency to increase the amount of time spent on whichever response has had the highest probability of reinforcement. This redistribution of effort stops only when all responses are equally likely to produce a reinforcer, an equilibrium that is reached when the percentage of responses matches the percentage of reinforcement.

For animals, the cost of a reinforcer is the amount of time and energy needed to obtain it; for people, it is often the amount of money needed to purchase it. The higher the price of a product, the less likely consumers are to purchase it, but economists have found that the relationship between price and consumption (the demand curve) can vary widely for different products; demand for some products is more affected by price than others (elasticity). Demand also depends on income, and similar effects have been found in animals.

Cognitive psychologists have also studied human choice behavior, but in the laboratory rather than the real world, and they have found that decision-making is far less rational than economists have traditionally assumed. In making complex decisions, we are often overwhelmed by the amount of information that has to be considered, and we cope by using simplifying strategies such as satisficing. Making decisions is particularly difficult in situations where the outcomes are not certain, so that subjects have to take into account the probability of different outcomes as well as their subjective value or utility. Again, people often rely on simplifying strategies or heuristics to estimate probabilities. These heuristics can be very helpful, but under some circumstances they lead to serious errors, and this is one reason why human decision making, even that of experts, is often more deeply flawed than we realize.

Glossary

Superstition A response acquired as a result of its accidental contiguity with a reinforcer.

Latent learning Learning that occurs during nonreinforced trials but that remains unused until the introduction of a reinforcer provides an incentive for using it.

Perceptual learning An improvement in a subject's ability to discriminate between stimuli as a result of exposure to those stimuli.

Marking Enhanced memory for an experience because of the subsequent occurrence of a salient and unexpected event. The unexpected event is thought to trigger a search for causes that results in greater attention to preceding events.

Avoidance response A response that postpones or prevents an aversive event.

Escape response A response that terminates an aversive stimulus that is already present.

Signaled avoidance An avoidance-training procedure in which a warning stimulus is followed by an aversive event, such as shock; the shock is not presented if the subject responds before the shock is scheduled to occur.

Two-factor theory A theory proposed by O. Hobart Mowrer to explain avoidance learning. According to this theory, avoidance learning depends on classical conditioning of fear to a warning stimulus and reinforcement of the avoidance response by termination of this stimulus.

Sidman avoidance An avoidance procedure developed by Murray Sidman that does not employ a warning stimulus. An aversive event, such as shock, is scheduled to occur at fixed time intervals (the shock–shock interval); if the subject makes the required avoidance response at any time during this interval, the next programmed shock is postponed for a fixed period (the response–shock interval).

Species-specific defense reactions (SSDRs) Innate responses elicited by stimuli that signal danger. The reaction of a mouse to the approach of a cat, for example, is likely to be very different from the reaction of a pigeon in the same situation—hence the term species-specific.

Flooding A technique for overcoming conditioned fear by presenting the fear-evoking stimulus in a situation in which the subject cannot escape from the stimulus.

Omission procedure A technique developed by Sheffield for determining whether conditioned responses are really due to classical conditioning or to reinforcement contingencies implicit in the conditioning procedure. In an omission procedure, the US is omitted on any trial during which there is a response. Because responses are never followed by reinforcement, any increase in response cannot be the result of reinforcement.

Concurrent schedule A schedule in which two or more responses are available at the same time, and each is reinforced on a separate schedule.

Matching law In essence, the matching law states that when you have a choice among several activities, the percentage of your time that you devote to one of these activities will match the percentage of the available reinforcers that you have gained from this activity. A more formal statement would be that if the rate at which two responses are performed is represented by $Resp_A$ and $Resp_B$, and the rate of reinforcement obtained by these two activities is represented by $Reinf_A$ and $Reinf_B$, then:

$$\frac{Resp_A}{Resp_A + Resp_B} = \frac{Reinf_A}{Reinf_A + Reinf_B}$$

Melioration A theory of choice behavior assuming that if one response is producing a better outcome than another, then subjects will increase the amount of time they devote to this response.

Demand The amount of a product or reinforcer that is purchased or consumed at a given price. Demand is said to be **elastic** if it changes markedly with changes in price; if it remains relatively constant, it is said to be **inelastic.**

Utility The subjective value of an object or activity.

Satisficing A decision-making strategy based on finding a satisfactory solution rather than an ideal one.

Heuristic A method of solving a problem that often leads to the correct solution but not always. Availability and representativeness are heuristics for estimating the probability of events. The **availability heuristic** estimates the probability of an event in terms of how easy it is to retrieve examples of this event from memory. The **representativeness heuristic** estimates the likelihood that an event is drawn from a particular category by whether it has the typical properties of events from that category.

Framing How a question is phrased. Subtle differences in the framing of a question about a decision can lead to substantial differences in which option subjects select.

Review Questions

1. Define the following terms: adventitious reinforcement, interim behaviors, illusion of control, and demand curve.

2. What does the claim that reinforcement is "automatic" imply? How has this claim been tested, and have the results supported it?

3. What are the roles of contiguity and contingency in reinforcement? Is one more important than the other?

4. What evidence suggests that reinforcement can affect people's behavior without their realizing it? How common is this?

5. Thorndike believed that reinforcement was necessary for learning, whereas Tolman believed that reinforcement affected only performance, not learning. What evidence challenges Thorndike's view? What evidence challenges Tolman's view? How can the concept of surprise be used to synthesize the opposing evidence?

6. How does Mowrer's two-factor theory account for avoidance learning? What evidence supports this theory? What evidence opposes it?

7. Why do rats have difficulty in learning to press a bar to avoid shock?

8. How does Seligman and Johnston's cognitive analysis account for avoidance learning? What evidence supports it, and what evidence opposes it?

9. What is the difference between a learning procedure and a learning process? On what basis can we decide whether two instances of learning involve the same process?

10. What evidence suggests that reinforcement and conditioning involve one process?

11. If reinforcement and conditioning do involve a common process, what might that process be? Which of the proposed candidates seems the most plausible? Why?

12. When animals and humans are trained on concurrent schedules in which two responses are reinforced independently, how do they distribute their time between the two responses? Why?

13. What is behavioral economics? What experiments in this area have produced results that would not have been predicted by traditional learning principles?

14. According to rational decision-making models, how should people make decisions, such as whether to study for an exam? What evidence suggests that people don't behave in this way?

15. How do we use heuristics to estimate the probability of events?

16. What are some examples of erroneous decisions made by doctors? Why did they occur?

17. In the course of this chapter, we discussed several experiments that allowed comparisons of animal and human behavior in comparable situations. What were these experiments and what were their results?

CHAPTER ELEVEN

Learning in an Evolutionary Context

In preceding chapters we have treated classical conditioning and reinforcement as if they were entirely general processes whose effects were the same in all species. In discussing the principles of classical conditioning, for example, we based our conclusions on experiments involving, among other behaviors, salivation in dogs, nausea in rats, and key-pecking in pigeons. The implicit assumption was that the principles of classical conditioning were everywhere the same; regardless of the response or the species, the same basic process was at work.

This assumption is critical to attempts to apply the results of animal research to human behavior: Unless the principles of learning are fundamentally similar, there is little reason to think that studies of salivation in dogs or bar-pressing in rats will have much relevance to humans. But is this assumption correct? Are the fundamental principles of learning really the same in all animal species?

11.1 THE GENERAL PROCESS VIEW

Early research strongly supported the view that the principles of learning were identical in all species—or, more accurately, in all vertebrates, which were the species normally studied. In Pavlov's research on classical conditioning, for example, he found that it did not matter what stimulus he used as a US: Whether he presented dogs with food to elicit salivation or a mild electric shock to elicit leg flexion, the principles of conditioning were exactly the same. Similarly, it did not matter what stimulus he used as a CS: "Any natural phenomenon chosen at will may be converted into a conditioned stimulus . . . any visual stimulus, any desired sound, any odor, and the stimulation of any part of the skin" (Pavlov, 1928, p. 86). Regardless of the particular stimuli chosen as the CS and the US, the principles governing the formation of an association were identical.

467

Thorndike found exactly the same pattern in his experiments on reinforcement. As we noted in Chapter 5, Thorndike varied what response his cats had to make to escape from the puzzle box, but he found the same pattern of trial-and-error learning in every case. Similarly, he experimented with different species—chicks, dogs, monkeys, and so on—but again the pattern of behavior was the same. This uniformity led him to express his conclusions in the form of a universal Law of Effect.

Skinner, in his later experiments on reinforcement, observed the same uniformity. Skinner found that not all forms of behavior could be reinforced; he referred to those responses that could be modified by their consequences as operants. If a response had been shown to be an operant in one situation, however—that is, it could be strengthened by making a reinforcer contingent on it—he found that it could also be modified by other reinforcers and that the principles were the same in each case: "The general topography of operant behavior is not important, because most if not all specific operants are conditioned. I suggest that the dynamic properties of operant behavior may be studied with a single reflex" (Skinner, 1938, pp. 45–46).

As one example of this uniformity, Skinner and his colleagues found that reinforcement schedules had virtually identical effects regardless of the response or the species. In one of his papers, Skinner (1956) presented a figure showing the effects of a mixture of FI and FR schedules on rats, pigeons, and monkeys (see Figure 11.1), and challenged his readers to say which results came from which species:

> *Pigeon, rat, monkey, which is which? It doesn't matter. Of course, these three species have behavioral repertories which are as different as their anatomies. But once you have allowed for differences in the ways in which they make contact with the environment . . . what remains of their behavior shows astonishingly similar properties.*
> (Skinner, 1956, p. 230)

This similarity led Skinner to title his most important work *The Behavior of Organisms*, even though almost all of the reported research was on bar-pressing in white rats!

In both classical conditioning and reinforcement, then, it did not seem to matter what events were being associated: One association was formed as easily as another. Moreover, as we saw in the preceding chapter, the principles of classical conditioning and reinforcement are remarkably similar, suggesting that the same associative process might be responsible for both. If we combine all these observations, one obvious possibility is that only one learning system is responsible for the formation of associations, and that this same system is always involved, regardless of the events being associated or the species.

FIGURE 11.1   Cumulative response records of responding in a pigeon, a rat, and a monkey. All three
subjects were trained on a multiple FI FR, a schedule in which responding is reinforced on
an FI schedule in the presence of one stimulus and on an FR schedule in the presence of a
second stimulus. Despite the differences in the responses required, the reinforcers, and the
species, the patterns of responding in the three subjects were remarkably uniform. (Adapted
from Skinner, 1956)

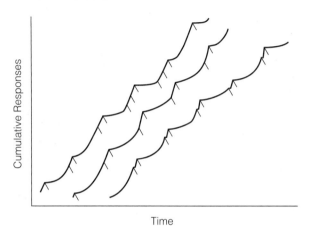

Seligman (1970) has called this the **general process view,** and it can be
stated somewhat more formally as follows:

1. *A general system.* Whenever an association is formed between two events,
   E_1 and E_2, the same learning process or system is responsible. In particular,
   it does not matter whether E_1 is a stimulus, as in the case of classical conditioning, or a response, as in the case of reinforcement: The same underlying associative mechanism is responsible for both.[1]

2. *Interchangeability of events.* One property of this associative mechanism is
   that it is indifferent to the events being associated. In the case of classical
   conditioning, any stimulus that is an adequate CS (that is, sufficiently
   salient to be capable of being associated with at least one US) can be associated with any US. Similarly, any reinforcer can strengthen any operant
   response (that is, any response capable of being modified by at least one reinforcer). Stated more generally, any member of the E_1 category can be associated with any member of the E_2 category. (Seligman called this the
   premise of *equipotentiality*.)

---

[1]This version of the general process view is broader than Seligman's, as he did not explicitly assume
that classical conditioning and reinforcement were a single process.

3. *Generality across species.* Associative learning in all vertebrate species is based on the same associative mechanism or system.[2]

As we have seen, early research provided considerable support for these assumptions, and as this evidence accumulated the general process view gradually became one of those fundamental beliefs that everyone takes for granted—an unchallengeable foundation stone of learning theory. If this assumption went largely unquestioned within learning theory, however, it was to come under increasing assault from workers outside this tradition. In the course of this chapter, we will be looking at some of these challenges and their possible implications.

In reading this material, you may find it helpful to bear in mind two extreme possibilities concerning the form learning takes in different species. At one extreme lies the general process view, with its assumption that seemingly different forms of learning are really manifestations of a fundamental mechanism that is always and everywhere the same. At the other extreme lies what might be called the multiprocess or "Let 1000 flowers bloom" view, which assumes that every species has evolved its own, unique forms of learning and that, because they have evolved independently, there is unlikely to be much relationship between them.

These extremes help to define a continuum of possibilities concerning the relationships between different forms of learning, from a single associative mechanism at one end to a myriad of unrelated forms at the other. In the remainder of this chapter, we will be considering where along this continuum reality lies.

11.2 AN EVOLUTIONARY PERSPECTIVE

One of the first challenges to the assumption that learning was uniform came from *ethologists*—behavioral biologists who study animal behavior under naturalistic conditions. Heavily influenced by Darwin's theory of evolution, ethologists take as their task not only observing animal behavior, but also trying to understand why it has evolved in the way it has. Why is it, for example, that male bluebirds of paradise—birds with brilliantly colored turquoise and purple feathers—court females by hanging upside down from a branch and flapping their wings? What in the history of the species could have led them to adopt such seemingly bizarre behavior?

This concern with how behavior evolved has made ethologists very sensitive to differences in the way species behave. To understand their views, we

---

[2] Vertebrates are animals that possess a hard backbone to support their bodies, in contrast to invertebrate species, such as jellyfish and insects, which either have no hard structures or else have a hard outer shell. The five main classes of vertebrates are fish, amphibians, reptiles, birds, and mammals.

will start by reviewing the main principles of evolution. We will then examine how this evolutionary perspective led them to a very different impression of learning than that of Pavlov, Thorndike, and Skinner.

Principles of Evolution

Charles Darwin did not invent the concept of evolution, but he was undoubtedly its most brilliant and influential advocate. In *The Origin of Species*, he proposed that species were not created simultaneously, but rather evolved gradually over many thousands of years from common ancestors.

Natural selection. To explain how this evolution occurred, he started from the observable fact that members of species vary, and suggested that some of these variants would make their possessors more likely to survive. Mice, for example, vary in their speed of running, and those that are faster are likely to be better at escaping from predators. Suppose, then, that at some point in mouse history, one mouse had the capacity to run faster than its peers. If so, it would have been likely to live longer and, crucially, to have more children. If we further suppose that whatever property made this mouse faster was heritable— that is, that its offspring would also generally be faster because of something they inherited from this parent—then these fast sons and daughters would also have been more likely to survive and reproduce, and so on; thus, the proportion of fast mice in the population would gradually have increased.

The way environmental conditions (in this case, the presence of predators) select out individuals who are fitter is known as **natural selection.** For natural selection to be effective, however, the adaptive characteristic must be transmitted to succeeding generations. The mechanism of transmission is now known to be a *gene*, a gigantic string of complex molecules. Many genes are linked together to form still longer units called *chromosomes,* and these chromosomes are present in the nucleus of every cell in our bodies. In organisms that reproduce sexually, half of each parent's set of genes is transmitted to the offspring (the male cells carrying the half-set are sperm, the female carriers are eggs). Once an egg is fertilized and, thus, the full number of chromosomes restored, the genes present in every cell act to control the chemical processes within that cell, and by this means ultimately control every aspect of the developing organism, from hair color to brain size.

Applying our knowledge of genes to evolution, we can rephrase our earlier explanation to say that if one mouse develops a gene resulting in stronger muscles and hence faster running, it will be likely to live longer and to have more offspring, so that over a number of generations this gene will come to be present in an ever larger proportion of the mouse population. Over time, then, mice will run faster, and as changes of this kind gradually accumulate, they may eventually result in a group of mice sufficiently different from their ancestors to constitute a new species.

Adaptive value. A crucial assumption in this analysis is that new traits will emerge only if they have some **adaptive value**—that is, if animals possessing the new trait are in some sense better adapted to their environment and, thus, more likely to reproduce and to pass on this trait. In deciding whether some trait has adaptive value, we need to consider not only the trait by itself, but also how well it fits the species to its particular environment. In our mouse example, we suggested that faster mice would be more likely to survive, but this is not necessarily so. Suppose, for example, that the genetic mutation we have been considering produced larger muscles, and these larger muscles enabled the mice to run faster. Being faster would undoubtedly help them evade predators, but their larger muscles would also mean that these mice weighed more and required more food to survive. If the environment provided sufficient food, the new gene would indeed have advantages, but in a harsher environment the costs might outweigh the benefits, and the gene would not be disseminated.

Niches. In assessing adaptive value, then, we need to consider carefully the environment of the species concerned. We tend to think of the world as a fairly uniform environment, perhaps subdivided into a few major regions such as earth, air, and water, but evolutionary theorists have found it more useful to conceptualize the world as composed of millions of local habitats known as *niches*.

Consider, for example, a tree in a forest. It might at first seem to provide a uniform environment for its inhabitants, so that we should expect to find the same species of birds living on all its branches, but this is not so. For one thing, lower branches receive less light than upper ones, and as a result they support different forms of lichen and insects; also, upper branches are accessible to predators such as eagles in a way that lower branches are not. The net result is that a number of different species of birds might inhabit different levels of a single tree, each specialized to take advantage of the properties of its unique niche. In evaluating the adaptive value of a behavior, then, we need to take into account the features of the species' niche.

Summarizing our account, the theory of evolution suggests that natural selection will lead to the reproductive success of individuals that are better adapted to their local environment, and that over time this will result in a gradual change in the properties of species. One result is that natural selection will tend to lead to the divergence of species, as each species becomes increasingly specialized to exploit the potential of its local environment, or niche.

Learning and Evolution

This evolutionary perspective has potentially important implications for the development of learning in different species. On the one hand, the descent of all vertebrates from a common ancestor suggests that there should be important similarities in their behavior. Consider, for example, the biological process of respiration. All mammalian species face the common problem of extracting oxygen from air, and this common problem has led to a common solution: The principles of respiration are fundamentally the same across mammalian species. Similarly, all vertebrates share a common environment in terms of causality: The cause of an event is always something that precedes it, and almost always something that precedes it closely. When an animal is injured, for example, the injury is likely to have been caused by something that happened just before the injury occurred. Thus, if at some point in evolutionary history a species developed a learning system that identified the stimuli that preceded injury—a system such as classical conditioning—it would not be surprising if this system were retained by all the species that descended from it. Thus, although we might expect some minor divergences in learning, as in respiration, the fundamental principles should remain the same. (See also Revusky, 1985.)

On the other hand, we must recognize that evolution involves not only the existence of common ancestors, but also descent from them, as species have been diverging from their ancestors over a period of many thousands of years. Thus, just as the physical structure of species changed as they became increasingly adapted to their local environments—birds developed wings, fish developed fins—so, too, we might expect divergences in learning mechanisms, as each species became increasingly adapted to the unique requirements of its niche. (See, for example, Gould, 1986.)

An evolutionary perspective, then, suggests that similar environments may lead to similar behaviors, but it also alerts us to the possibility that seemingly similar environments can nevertheless differ in important respects, and that these differences can lead to the evolution of different behaviors. It is difficult to predict in advance whether the similarities of two environments are more important than their differences and, thus, whether or not we should expect similar learning mechanisms. Because of ethologists' evolutionary perspective, however, they were more sensitive than psychologists to the possibility of differences, and in observing animals in their natural habitats, they discovered that learning did differ in significant respects. We will focus here on two examples involving birds: imprinting and song learning.

Imprinting. The first major challenge to the view that learning was the same in all vertebrates came from an Austrian ethologist, Konrad Lorenz. Earlier zoologists had noticed that precocial birds—species such as ducks and chickens that are able to walk as soon as they are born—will follow the first moving object they see after they hatch. Normally, this is their mother, with the happy result that families stay together when the mother goes off in search for food. If the first moving object a chick sees is a human being, however, it will instead become attached to that person, and will follow the person wherever he or she goes. If the chick is later reunited with its mother, it will show no interest, but instead hurry off after the person on whom it has imprinted, or even another human who happens to walk by.

These observations suggest that chicks have to learn to recognize their species, and that they do so by becoming attached to the first moving object they see. Lorenz called this development of a social attachment **imprinting,** and he suggested that imprinting differed from other forms of learning in several major respects.

First, whereas forms of learning such as classical conditioning can occur at any time in an animal's life, Lorenz said that imprinting would occur only during the first hours after hatching, which he called the **critical period.** If a duckling, for example, was not given an opportunity to imprint on its mother during its first few days, then it would never do so.

A second unique characteristic of imprinting, according to Lorenz, was that it was *irreversible*. "The process, once accomplished, is totally irreversible. . . . This absolute rigidity is something we never find in behavior acquired by associative learning, which can be unlearned or changed, at least to a certain extent" (Lorenz, 1937, p. 264). One consequence of this permanent attachment was that when the bird became an adult it would direct its sexual behavior either to the original imprinting stimulus or to one similar to it. In jackdaws, for example, adult males offer potential mates choice morsels of food as a way of courting them. Lorenz (1952) imprinted a male jackdaw on him when it was young, and found that when it reached sexual maturity it attempted to seduce him by offering him worms that it had thoughtfully predigested. When Lorenz refused this generous offer by keeping his mouth closed, the jackdaw instead deposited the worms in the nearest opening, his ear!

It appeared, then, that imprinting was unique in several respects: It occurred only in some species, it occurred only during a very brief critical period, and it was irreversible. Lorenz's evidence for these claims, however, came largely from naturalistic observations, and other ethologists and psychologists set out to test his claims under laboratory conditions, where alternative interpretations could be controlled for. In a typical experiment, a newly hatched duckling was placed in an apparatus like that shown in Figure 11.2: The stimulus on which it was to be imprinted was slowly rotated along the raised platform, and the duckling was allowed to follow behind it.

Laboratory research confirmed some of Lorenz's claims. For example, Lorenz believed that the crucial requirement for imprinting to take place was that the stimulus be moving, and experiments strongly confirmed this: Ducklings would imprint even to a milk bottle, provided that it was moving. Other experiments, however, revealed that imprinting was not as sharply differentiated from other forms of learning as he had supposed. The critical period, for example, is not as clearly defined as Lorenz's naturalistic observations had suggested, but can occur over a significantly longer period under some circumstances. (See, for example,

FIGURE 11.2   An apparatus for studying imprinting. (Adapted from Hess, 1959)

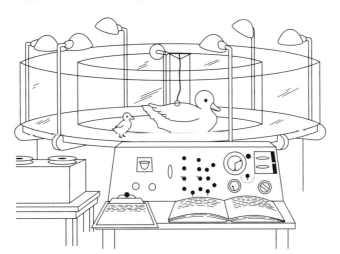

R. T. Brown, 1975.) As a result, the critical period is now usually referred to as the **sensitive period,** to emphasize that imprinting is more likely to occur during this period but is not necessarily limited to it.

Also, imprinting is not totally irreversible. In an experiment by Salzen and Meyer (1968), chicks were exposed to a colored ball for three days, at which point they showed typical attachment behavior—for example, preferring it to a second colored ball. Exposure to the second ball for a further three-day period, however, resulted in a reversal of this preference. Similarly, Guiton (1966) found that chicks exposed to a moving yellow glove when young later attempted to copulate with the glove in preference to a stuffed female chicken; if they were then allowed to live with other chickens rather than remaining in isolation, however, they developed a preference for the chicken model. Clearly, the preferences established during early life can be modified by later experience and, thus, are not as rigid as Lorenz had supposed.

If experimental studies led to qualifications of the conclusions Lorenz had drawn from his naturalistic observations, they nevertheless supported the view of ethologists that different species might evolve specialized forms of learning to cope with the requirements of their unique environments. Imprinting, for example, is found only in precocial species, whose young are mobile from the moment of their hatching. In these species, young birds that can quickly learn to identify their parents will obviously be better able to follow them and thus survive; in species that spend their early lives in nests, there is no advantage to the young in learning to identify their parents, and in these species imprinting does not occur.

Imprinting contradicts the general process view not only because it is present only in some species, but also because, when it is present, the process is much more selective than a simple associative account would suggest. The general process view assumes that the nature of the stimulus does not matter, but although imprinting *can* occur to a wide range of moving stimuli, it is far stronger if the moving stimulus resembles the parent: Ducklings, for example, imprint better if the model resembles the parent visually and if it emits a sound resembling the normal duck call. (For a review, see Bateson, 1991.)

Contrary to the general process view, then, imprinting occurs only in some species and, when it does, occurs more readily to some stimuli than others. Rather than possessing a totally indiscriminate learning system, capable of learning about all stimuli equally, birds seem biologically predisposed to imprint on certain stimuli—those that, not surprisingly, will maximize the chances that they will learn to follow their own mothers and not other adults or other species.

Song learning. A second respect in which learning in birds reflects strong biological predispositions concerns the acquisition of songs. In some species, the ability to produce the species-typical song is innate, but in others, parts of the song are learned by listening to adults sing. Only if a white-crowned sparrow is exposed to a recording of an adult's song while young, for example, will it reproduce that song when it reaches sexual maturity. (See Marler, 1991, for a review.)

Song learning has been found to possess many of the same properties as imprinting; indeed, song learning can be thought of as a form of imprinting in which young birds learn to identify the song of their species rather than its visual appearance. As with imprinting, learning seems to be most likely to occur during a sensitive period early in the bird's life. A white-crowned sparrow will reproduce a song if the song is played during the first 10 to 50 days of its life, but not if the song is played later.

Also, once a song is learned, this learning is hard to reverse. The white-crowned sparrow again provides an illustration: If it is exposed to one song during the sensitive period and a second song afterwards, the second song has no effect (Marler, 1967).

A third similarity between song learning and imprinting is that in both cases learning is guided by genetic predispositions. Although some species will learn virtually any song to which they are exposed, in most species there are strong predispositions to learn songs that closely resemble the characteristic song of the species. If young song sparrows and swamp sparrows are exposed to recordings of either their own song or that of the other species, learning occurs much more quickly if the song they hear is their own (Marler & Richards, 1989). The birds behave as if they possess a template or model of the ideal form, and the ease of learning is proportional to how closely the song fits this ideal. "It is as if the bird were a musician programmed to learn a single piece of Baroque music: Such an individual would be immune to the charms of Brahms or the Beatles, but would fixate instantly on anything by Bach or Vivaldi" (Staddon, 1983, p. 400).

Before leaving song learning, we will note some tantalizing parallels between song learning in birds and language learning in children. Just as birds are particularly likely to reproduce sounds that are characteristic of their species' song, human infants are more likely to attend to the sounds that are characteristic of human speech (Eimas, 1984). Also, once a bird has been exposed to a song, it will learn to imitate it by a trial-and-error process in which it produces a semi-random sequence of sounds, listens to itself, and then gradually modifies its song to make it resemble more closely the song to which it was exposed. Birds begin to produce these first approximations at a set age, even if they have been deafened just before this age and thus cannot modify the song they are producing. Similarly, human infants begin to produce a stream of sounds called *coos* at a particular age, and even naturally deaf children begin to coo at this age. Perhaps language learning in humans builds on some of the same instinctive patterns that are present in song learning. (See Gould, 1986.)

The adaptive value of learning. In both song learning and imprinting, species differ in whether they exhibit this learning, and, where it does occur, there are often strong predispositions to learn about particular stimuli. In both cases, moreover, the form of learning observed in a species seems to reflect the adaptive value of this learning. In the case of imprinting, we have seen that it occurs in precocial birds, for whom the ability to recognize one's parents is critical for survival, but not in tree-nesting birds, for whom recognition of the parent would have no value. Similarly, whether or not birds learn their songs seems to reflect the adaptive value of such learning. One example concerns *brood parasites*— birds that lay their eggs in the nests of other species, thereby tricking these other species into rearing their young (cuckoos are a notorious example). If young male cuckoos were to learn the song of the birds that reared them, when these cuckoos became adult they would be at a serious disadvantage in attracting the attention of female cuckoos, with potentially disastrous consequences for the propagation of their genes. As an adaptive value analysis would predict, no brood parasite species learns to sing; they rely instead on innate songs.

A common feature of both imprinting and song learning, then, is that both occur only in species for which such learning would have adaptive value. This also appears to be true of many other forms of learning in birds. For example, most birds do not learn to recognize their eggs, even though they see and handle them many times each day. Where there is an advantage to egg recognition— for example, in species whose nesting sites are closely packed together, so that there is a real danger of nests and eggs being confused—then the capacity for recognition is much more likely to be found. Similarly, birds that nest in trees have no need to recognize their young immediately after hatching and, in general, cannot do so. But these parents do begin to recognize their young when they fledge or develop the feathers necessary for leaving the nest—precisely the moment when such recognition would have some value. (See Gould, 1986.) In at least some circumstances, therefore, the capacity for learning does not seem to be a default option that is always present; rather, learning occurs only in those situations in which it is likely to be of value. Perhaps for birds the importance of being light enough to fly means that they cannot afford to develop or maintain the larger brain size that would be required to learn about the appearance of their eggs or of their progeny—unless, that is, this learning capacity has unequivocal adaptive value.

Summary. The evidence on imprinting and song learning suggests that the strong form of the general process view—that learning is always and everywhere the same—is simply not tenable. Learning does take different forms in different species, and these forms reflect the requirements of each species' unique niche. That learning in different species differs in some respects, however, does not imply that it differs in all respects; imprinting, for example, is not as sharply differentiated from other forms of learning as the early evidence for critical periods and irreversibility seemed to suggest. We will examine the similarities among different forms of learning more systematically in Section 11.4 and will consider the extent to which different varieties of learning may nevertheless share common mechanisms; for now, the critical point is that there are far more differences than early learning theorists realized.

11.3 ARE CLASSICAL CONDITIONING AND REINFORCEMENT UNIFORM PROCESSES?

The evidence for specialized forms of learning such as imprinting and song learning posed a serious challenge to the assumption of uniformity. At first, however, psychologists largely ignored this evidence. One reason was that the early evidence was largely observational, and, from Thorndike on, learning theorists have been deeply suspicious of purely observational evidence. In the case of imprinting, this suspicion proved to have some justification, as later experimental evidence did blur the sharp distinctions between imprinting and associative learning originally claimed by Lorenz.

A further reason why learning theorists paid little attention to the developing literature on imprinting was that it seemed to have little applicability to the central concern of these theorists, which was associative learning. Even if some species did develop specialized forms of learning, this did not necessarily mean that the mechanisms of associative learning in these species were different. Two species might differ in whether they were capable of imprinting, for example, but the effects of reinforcement in the two species might nevertheless be identical. And, as we have seen, decades of research on learning had consistently shown that the principles of classical conditioning and reinforcement were universal. Gradually, however, challenges to the general process view began to appear even within its associative heartland, and we now turn to this evidence.

Classical Conditioning

Taste-aversion learning. The most influential challenge arose from the work of John Garcia on taste-aversion learning. As we saw in Chapter 3, rats made ill after eating develop a strong aversion to the taste of the food they just ate, but not to its appearance. Garcia and Koelling (1966) showed that rats were differentially prepared to associate tastes with illness, and conversely, to associate auditory and visual cues with electric shock.

These results posed a fundamental challenge to the general process view. The strong form of this hypothesis states that there is a universal associative mechanism that will associate any two events that are paired. Garcia and Koelling's findings make it clear that this is not so: Animals are selectively prepared to associate some events more easily than others.

Gut defense versus skin defense. Garcia's challenge to the general process view, however, was even broader. He argued that classical conditioning involves at least two quite different subsystems: a gut-defense system, whose purpose is to protect animals from poisonous food, and a skin-defense system designed to protect them from predators (Garcia, Brett, & Rusiniak, 1989). These systems, he suggested, had evolved independently and, because of their different functions, had evolved quite different properties. Specifically, taste-aversion learning, which was a manifestation of the gut-defense system, differed from previously studied forms, such as fear and eyeblink conditioning (which are involved in skin defense), in at least three ways:

1. *The stimuli that can be conditioned.* As we have seen, Garcia and Koelling found strong conditioning to tastes, but not to noise or light, when they used illness as their US. When shock was the US, the results were reversed, with strong conditioning to audiovisual stimuli but none to tastes.

2. *The rapidity of conditioning.* Whereas most forms of conditioning are relatively slow—eyeblink conditioning, for example, can take hundreds of trials—taste-aversion conditioning is generally very rapid, with powerful conditioning observed after only one or two trials.

3. *The CS–US interval.* When conditioning involves external stimuli, we have seen that temporal contiguity between the CS and US is critical. In fear conditioning, for example, no conditioning is found with delays of more than a few minutes, and in eyeblink conditioning no learning occurs with delays of even a few seconds. In taste-aversion conditioning, on the other

hand, conditioning has been found even with a delay of several hours. (For a review, see Domjan, 1980.)

Such differences are bewildering if we assume a single associative mechanism, but they make far more sense if we assume that different subsystems evolved in response to particular needs. Consider first the case of fear conditioning. In nature, if you experience a sudden blow, it is almost certainly related to events that closely preceded it—for example, seeing an eagle circling in the sky, or hearing the sudden rush of its wings. There would be strong adaptive advantages, therefore, to developing a fear of the stimuli that immediately preceded attack. Becoming frightened of a robin seen two hours earlier, on the other hand, would not only be of little value but would probably be harmful because avoiding this irrelevant stimulus would interfere with crucial activities such as searching for food.

The situation is very different in the case of illness. Here, the interval between eating a poisonous food and becoming ill is often several hours, so that a system that produced an aversion to distant events would have considerable value, especially if, as Garcia and Koelling found, conditioning is focused on foods eaten earlier, rather than, say, sounds that were heard. The differences between fear and taste-aversion conditioning, in other words, become readily explicable if we assume learning systems that evolved separately to cope with different problems.

On the other hand, there are also substantial similarities between conditioning in the two cases. First, the same basic conditioning phenomena are found in both: extinction, generalization, blocking, and so on. Also, even in the three areas in which differences have been observed most clearly—preparedness, frequency of pairings, and contiguity—these differences appear to be more of degree than of kind. Thus, although tastes can be associated more easily with illness and visual stimuli with shock, it is nevertheless possible for the other associations to be made. Visual stimuli, for example, can be associated with illness; it just takes more pairings. (See, for example, Braveman, 1977.)

Similarly, taste-aversion conditioning is not always faster than other forms of classical conditioning: Fear conditioning can also occur very quickly, and taste-aversion learning can be slow in some circumstances.

Finally, although the longest interval at which conditioning will take place is clearly greater in taste-aversion conditioning, contiguity remains important even here: Just as in other forms of conditioning, there is a maximum interval at which conditioning is still possible, and within this range shorter intervals produce better conditioning than longer intervals. (See Figure 11.3.)

In summary, the work of Garcia and others has made it clear that taste-aversion learning differs in a number of respects from traditionally studied forms of learning, such as fear and eyeblink conditioning. (For evidence of further

FIGURE 11.3   Taste-aversion learning as a function of the delay between drinking saccharin and becoming ill. The measure of learning is the amount of saccharin consumed during a test following the conditioning phase. (Adapted from Andrews & Braveman, 1975)

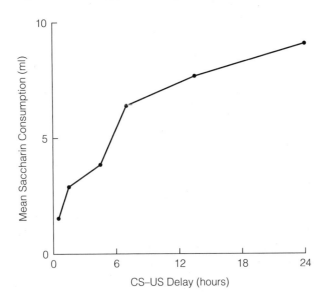

differences, see LoLordo & Droungas, 1989.) But there are also substantial similarities in the forms of learning observed, and where there are differences they often appear quantitative rather than qualitative. This pattern leads rather temptingly to the conclusion that the fundamental mechanism is similar, albeit modified in the course of evolution to cope with the requirements of different situations and different species. We will again postpone a systematic evaluation of the case for a common mechanism until the concluding section; for now, the crucial point is that the strong version of the general process view is not tenable for classical conditioning any more than it was for imprinting.

Reinforcement: The Misbehavior of Organisms

What, then, of reinforcement? Can the assumption of an invariant learning process be defended any better in this domain? As we have seen, early research suggested that the mechanism of reinforcement was universal. Thorndike, for example, tested his cats in a variety of puzzle boxes, requiring a variety of responses for escape, and he also tested a wide range of species. In every case, reinforcement was effective, and learning followed the same pattern—a gradual improvement over trials. Later research strongly supported the assumption of uniformity: Whether you reinforced bar-presses in rats, key-pecks in pigeons, or button-pushes in humans, the fundamental principles of reinforcement seemed to be the same.

Every once in a while, though, puzzling reports appeared of cases in which reinforcement did not work,[3] or at any rate was far less effective than usual. Indeed, the first hint of this problem came in Thorndike's own research.

Unlickable cats. In one of his experiments, Thorndike placed cats in a bare box; all they had to do to escape was to lick or scratch themselves. Given the frequency with which cats normally perform these responses, this should have been the simplest problem to solve, but, strangely, it proved the most difficult. Even after the cats had learned the required response, moreover, Thorndike observed

> *a noticeable tendency . . . to diminish the act until it becomes a mere vestige of a lick or scratch. . . . The licking degenerates into a mere quick turn of the head with one or two motions up and down with tongue extended. Instead of a hearty scratch, the cat waves its paw up and down rapidly for an instant. Moreover, if sometimes you do not let the cat out after this feeble reaction, it does not at once repeat the movement, as it would do if it depressed a thumbpiece, for instance, without success in getting the door open.*

(Thorndike, 1911, p. 64)

Defensive rats. Further evidence for the difficulty of reinforcing certain responses came from research on avoidance learning. As we saw in Chapter 10, it is surprisingly difficult to train rats to press a bar to avoid electric shock. The problem is clearly not that rats are incapable of learning to press bars—they are only too happy to do so when the reinforcer is food—nor is it that they are incapable of learning to avoid shock—when required to run down an alley to avoid shock, they typically learn in just a few trials. When required to press a bar to avoid shock, though, they often require hundreds of trials to learn this behavior.

Miserly raccoons. A third case in which reinforcement proved ineffective—and, in some ways, the strangest case of all—was reported by Keller Breland and Marion Breland in a delightful paper entitled "The Misbehavior of Organisms" (1961). After training as experimental psychologists at Harvard, the Brelands left academic psychology to start a company that trained animals to perform for commercial exhibitions. Everything went beautifully at first: They were able to use the principles of reinforcement developed in the laboratory to

---

[3] In our definition of reinforcement in Chapter 5, we noted that the term can refer to the *procedure* of presenting a reinforcer following a response or, alternatively, the typical *outcome* of this procedure, which is an increase in the probability of the response. In this case, the term is being used to refer to the procedure of presenting a reinforcer.

train species as diverse as cockatoos, pigs, reindeer, and whales. As time passed, however, they encountered more and more instances in which their subjects stubbornly refused to behave themselves.

In one project intended to illustrate the virtues of saving money, for example, they reinforced a raccoon with food first for picking up a coin and then for carrying the coin across its cage and depositing it in a piggy bank. At first everything went smoothly, but as training progressed, the raccoon became increasingly reluctant to release the coin. It would begin to put it into the bank, but then pull it back and rub it back and forth between its paws in a distressingly miserly fashion. This rubbing behavior was never reinforced—quite the contrary, the longer the raccoon rubbed the coin, the longer it had to wait to receive food—but the amount of time spent rubbing nevertheless continued to increase, until eventually the planned exhibit had to be abandoned. This failure, moreover, was not an isolated instance. The Brelands encountered cows that would not learn to kick, chickens that grabbed plastic capsules and pounded them up and down on the floor instead of pecking them, whales that swallowed beach balls they were supposed to be working with, and so on. In all these cases, the Law of Effect just didn't seem to be working.

Why Does Reinforcement Fail?

For many years, these failures and others like them were largely ignored: In most cases reinforcement was highly effective, so the occasional failure was easily dismissed as an aberration. With the publication of John Garcia's work on taste-aversion conditioning, however, the climate changed. Until then, most psychologists had enthusiastically accepted the assumption that the fundamental mechanisms of associative learning were universal. Garcia's research, however, demonstrated that taste-aversion conditioning was not the same as, say, eyeblink conditioning: Strong taste aversions could be conditioned in just a single trial, even with a delay between ingestion and illness of several hours. If the ease of conditioning could vary so greatly depending on the CS and US involved, then the notion that responses might also vary in their reinforceability suddenly didn't seem so unthinkable, and the failures that had been ignored for so long became a focus of considerable interest to experimenters.

The resulting research has not entirely resolved the question of why some responses are so much harder to reinforce than others, but it has identified several factors that might be important. We will concentrate here on two: inflexible reflexes and competition from conditioned responses. (For a review of other factors, see Domjan, 1983.)

Inflexible reflexes. Consider first Thorndike's difficulties in reinforcing licking and scratching. One possible explanation is suggested by the most obvious characteristic that these responses share: They are both reflexive behaviors, normally elicited by an unconditioned stimulus. One possibility, then, is that behaviors that are normally reflexive, or involuntary, might be more difficult to reinforce than other responses. In accordance with this analysis, research has shown that a number of other reflexive responses, such as face washing in golden hamsters and yawning in dogs, are also difficult to reinforce (Shettleworth, 1983; Konorski, 1967). Not all the evidence is favorable (for example, Konorski, 1967), but it does currently seem as if the reflexive nature of licking and scratching could be one reason that they are hard to reinforce. (For other reasons, see Pearce, Colwill, & Hall, 1978; Iversen, Ragnarsdottir, & Randrup, 1984.)

If reflexive responses do prove to be more difficult to reinforce, this could plausibly be viewed as another example of the role of preparedness in learning. In Chapter 10, we noted that autonomic responses are very difficult to reinforce, and we suggested that one reason could be that reinforcement of autonomic responses would be maladaptive. If every time we received a reinforcer it strengthened all the autonomic responses that happened to be in progress at the time, the result could be disastrous. The evidence on licking and scratching raises the possibility that all reflexive responses may be hard to reinforce, skeletal as well as autonomic, because these responses are unlikely to have a genuine causal connection to the reinforcer. If a lion or other cat obtains food, for example, its success might reflect the efficiency of its stalking behavior, but success probably would not be due to reflexive behaviors such as yawning or scratching. Natural selection, therefore, might have modified the reinforcement system to ensure that it does not strengthen reflexive behaviors because these are responses that have evolved to cope with very specific problems, such as a lack of oxygen, rather than as all-purpose behaviors capable of serving any of a variety of needs.

Competition from conditioned responses. What might be a more important factor in cases where reinforcement fails is our old friend classical conditioning. We saw in Chapter 4 that stimuli paired with food activate an animal's feeding system, which primes innately programmed behaviors for procuring and consuming food. Many of the failures of reinforcement we have discussed might be the result of competition between these conditioned responses and the response that the experimenter was trying to reinforce.

One example is the Brelands' study, in which a raccoon had difficulty learning to deposit a token in a piggy bank. Because the tokens were repeatedly paired with food in the early stages of training, and, critically, because the token's size and appearance resembled that of a raccoon's normal food, the raccoon might have learned to regard the token as food. Raccoons wash or rub prospective food before eating it, so the bizarre rubbing behavior might have been simply an attempt to prepare the coin for eating, and the racoon's refusal to deposit the coin in the bank an understandable reluctance to throw away its food.

Summary

Research on classical conditioning has shown that the ease of conditioning depends on the stimuli being associated. If a taste is paired with illness, for example, conditioning is faster, and occurs over a longer delay, than if a tone is paired with shock. Similarly in the case of reinforcement, some responses are much more difficult to reinforce than others, and this appears to depend in part on the response (reflexive responses appear harder to reinforce than voluntary responses) and in part on the combination of response and reinforcer used. It is easy to train rats to press a bar to obtain food, for example, but much more difficult to train them to press a bar to avoid shock. (See Chapter 10.) This difficulty, in turn, seems to be largely because of competition from classically conditioned responses. Whenever a reinforcer is presented, it is likely to condition responses to the stimuli that are present as well as to reinforce whatever behavior preceded it, and these two processes sometimes strengthen behaviors that are incompatible. If the classically conditioned response is stronger, it may prevent the emergence of the reinforced response in the first place, or, as in the case of the Brelands' raccoon, the CR may eventually take the place of the reinforced response.

Together, these results make it clear that associative learning is not general in the sense that any combination of events E_1 and E_2 will be associated as easily as any other combination. In classical conditioning and reinforcement, as in imprinting and song learning, animals seem prepared, or predisposed, to acquire some kinds of knowledge more readily than others, and this predisposition seems to reflect the greater value of this knowledge in the animals' natural environment.

11.4 VARIATIONS ON AN ASSOCIATIVE THEME

The general process view says that a single mechanism underlies all forms of associative learning. At this point, it might be worth reviewing the various assumptions that make up this hypothesis:

1. *A general system.* All associative learning is the product of a single system.

2. *Interchangeability of events.* Any member of the E_1 class can be associated with any member of the E_2 class.

3. *Generality across species.* This same mechanism underpins associative learning in all vertebrate species.

The evidence we have reviewed in this chapter makes it clear that at least some of these assumptions are wrong. The assumption of event interchangeability, for example, is clearly violated by the fact that a flashing light, which is a perfectly adequate CS in some contexts, is very difficult to associate with illness, and, conversely, that a taste is very difficult to associate with shock.

Similarly, the evidence on imprinting contradicts the assumption that learning is the same in all vertebrates: Although precocial birds develop an attachment to the first moving object they see, other birds do not. The mechanisms of learning in these species clearly cannot be identical.

On the other hand, when learning does occur, its characteristics are often very similar. In the case of taste-aversion learning and fear conditioning, for example, we have seen that the differences between these forms are more of degree than of kind: In both, conditioning depends on the contiguity of the CS and US, the number of pairings, the intensity of the US, and so on. Similarly, although imprinting differs from other forms of associative learning in that it occurs during a relatively brief period of life and is hard to reverse, these differences are again more of degree than of kind: For example, although imprinting is harder to reverse than most forms of conditioning, some strongly conditioned responses, such as intense fear, are also very hard to overcome.

An Adaptationist Perspective

One obvious way to integrate the evidence for both similarities and differences is to assume that the basic mechanisms of learning are similar across species, but that these basic mechanisms have been modified in the course of evolution to cope with the specialized requirements of different environments. For example, stimuli that predict damage to the skin, such as the appearance of a predator, usually occur immediately before the injury, whereas stimuli that predict gastrointestinal upsets, such as eating rotten food, are experienced many minutes or hours earlier. The result, as we have seen, is that taste aversions can be conditioned over far longer periods than fear. The fact that the two forms of conditioning share so many other properties, however, suggests that the two systems are still largely the same in other respects.

The idea that learning is basically a general process, but one that has often been modified in the course of evolution to cope with the demands of particular situations, has been called the **adaptationist approach** (for example, Beecher, 1988). According to this view, there are two powerful reasons why the mechanisms of learning are likely to be similar across species. First, the biological mechanisms underlying learning are not newly created in every species: Every species inherits genetic material from its ancestors, and this will inevitably lead to similarities in the mechanisms used by species descended from a relatively recent ancestor. Of course, if these species face different environments, the mechanisms they have inherited may be gradually modified and, therefore, diverge. Second, as far as learning is concerned, the broad outlines of the problems faced by different species are remarkably similar. For all species, causes precede effects, and in most instances there is close temporal contiguity between the two. It is thus hard to imagine a species in which the ability to identify the stimuli that immediately preceded an important event would not be advantageous. Similarly, it is hard to imagine a species for which it would not be advantageous to repeat responses that have consistently led to positive outcomes, such as food, and to suppress responses that have consistently led to negative outcomes, such as injury. So, it would not be surprising if once species evolved learning mechanisms for classical and operant conditioning, these mechanisms were retained by their descendants largely unaltered.

On the other hand, as we have seen repeatedly, there are differences as well as similarities in the environmental problems faced by different species. The adaptationist approach thus assumes that although the broad outline of any learning system will be largely constant, within this framework there may be significant modifications to the details so as to make the system more sensitive to the particular information needed for each species' survival. If so, the issue is not whether we should expect similarities or differences in learning in different species—there will inevitably be both—but rather to what extent the properties of the core system have been preserved as the system has been modified to cope with special problems.

Theme and Variations

In one sense, the answer to this question does not matter much: The extent to which a common system has been preserved is simply a matter for empirical inquiry and one that need no longer be a focus of great theoretical debate. Learning theorists, however, have long been attracted to the idea that learning could be explained in terms of a small number of basic principles, for much the same reason that physicists have searched for a small number of unifying principles such as gravity and electromagnetism. For all scientists, there is something elegant and attractive about being able to explain superficially unrelated phenomena in terms of a single, simple process. (Indeed, if scientists did not prefer a simple, orderly view of the universe to a complex and chaotic one, they probably would not have become scientists in the first place!) This preference for simpler explanations is expressed in the scientific principle of **parsimony,** which states that if alternative explanations can account for a phenomenon equally well, the simpler explanation—the one making the fewest assumptions—should be preferred. In particular, if two phenomena can be explained equally well with an assumption that they involve a single process or two separate processes, the single-process explanation is always to be preferred.

The principle of parsimony encourages us to explain learning in terms of as few processes as possible—ideally, just one. In this chapter, we have discussed four forms of learning: imprinting, song learning, classical conditioning and reinforcement. Could these diverse forms of learning all be based on just a single process?

Before considering the evidence relevant to this claim, it is important to emphasize that the issue is not whether these forms of learning are identical: The evidence we have reviewed makes it clear that they differ in a number of respects, and thus that the underlying processes almost certainly differ as well. The question that we will be considering is not whether the processes involved are identical, but how far we can push the claim that they are similar.

Conditioning and reinforcement. In the case of classical conditioning and reinforcement, we addressed this question in Chapter 10. We saw then that the principles of conditioning and reinforcement are almost identical (for example, the roles of contiguity, frequency and intensity), that both are affected by processes such as extinction and generalization, and so on. This similarity encouraged the view that conditioning and reinforcement rely on a common system for detecting E_1–E_2 relationships. In classical conditioning E_1 is a stimulus, whereas in reinforcement E_1 is a response, but in both animals learn that E_1 is followed by E_2. Once an E_1–E_2 relationship is detected, how this information is used seems to differ between the two forms—information that a response is followed by food normally leads to repetition of that response, whereas information that a stimulus is followed by food primes an innately programmed set of responses for obtaining and consuming this food. Conditioning and reinforcement thus embody different rules for translating knowledge into performance, but the systems for acquiring this information appear to be similar if not identical.

Imprinting and song learning. What, then, of imprinting and song learning? Could these forms of learning be due to the same associative processes as conditioning and reinforcement?

The perhaps surprising answer is yes. The argument is somewhat complicated, but we can begin by noting that both imprinting and song learning involve an initial stage in which animals are exposed to a complex stimulus—a song or a moving adult—and learn to recognize and remember this stimulus. This process bears strong similarities to the phenomenon of perceptual learning discussed in the previous chapter, in which exposure to stimuli increases our ability to discriminate these stimuli from other, potentially similar stimuli. A wine-taster, for example, becomes increasingly skilled at discriminating different classes of wine simply as a result of exposure to these wines. As to how this perceptual learning occurs, McLaren, Kaye, and Mackintosh (1989) have suggested that it is based on the same associative processes involved in conditioning.

We will not discuss their full model here, but one key assumption is that any stimulus—a wine, say, or a moving duck—consists of many elements, and that when we experience these elements together, we form associations between them. With extended exposure to a song, for example, a bird will associate each of the song's notes with those that follow, so that eventually hearing only the first few notes will allow the bird to recall all those that follow. (Notice the similarity of this account to the British Associationist account, in Chapter 2, of how we memorize passages such as the Lord's Prayer.)

One reason that exposure to a stimulus helps us to recognize it later, then, is that repeated exposure allows us to link its elements into a coherent unit, thereby producing a more accurate image or representation of the stimulus in our brains. As a result, exposure to even a small proportion of the elements—for example, hearing only a snatch of a song, or catching only a brief glimpse of a retreating duck—will summon up the entire representation, and this fuller representation will make it easier for us to discriminate the stimulus from otherwise similar stimuli. (See also the discussion of neural networks in Chapter 12.) When a duckling first glimpses its mother, then, perceptual learning allows it to form an accurate representation of its mother's features, and this perceptual learning could be based on the formation of associations. (See also Honey, Horn, & Bateson, 1993.)

Assume for the moment that this hypothesis is correct, and that a duckling remembers its mother and a sparrow remembers a song by forming associations between the elements of these stimuli. Why does the duckling then follow the mother, and why does the sparrow later reproduce the song? The answer in both cases may be classical conditioning. In our discussion of conditioning in Chapter 4, we saw that pairing of a CS with a US results in the formation of an S–S association, and this, in turn, leads to priming of responses appropriate to the US. If a chick is exposed to water for the first time, for example, its first reaction is to try to eat the water. After only a few experiences, however, it switches to drinking movements. To explain this behavior, we suggested that the sensation of water in the chick's beak activates the water center or representation in the chick's brain. (You can think of this as a flashing sign in the chick's brain saying "This is water.") When the visual cues of the water are paired with this sensation, they come to be identified as signs of water, so that thereafter these cues will elicit appropriate behaviors such as drinking.

The same conditioning process could be at work in imprinting and song learning. In the case of imprinting, some feature of the imprinting model might lead to its being identified as the parent—for example, the fact that it is moving, or emitting a duck's call. The visual properties of the model would then be associated with this critical property, so that henceforth these stimuli would also elicit the behaviors appropriate to a parent, such as following it wherever it goes (Hoffman, 1978). Thus, just as a chick learns to identify the stimuli that accompany drinking as water, the duckling learns to identify the stimuli that accompany a moving object as its parent, and both stimuli then trigger the appropriate innate responses.

This conditioning account of imprinting is not perfect. Whereas it is easy to extinguish most conditioned responses by presenting the CS by itself, we have seen that the attachment formed through imprinting is very difficult to alter, and it certainly does not seem to disappear simply through repeated exposure to the CS—the duckling will happily follow the model for many weeks. At present, therefore, it is not clear if classical conditioning provides a complete account of imprinting, but it does look as if the two phenomena involve similar processes. (See also van Kampen, 1996; Honey & Bolhuis, 1997.)

Implications

Clearly, at least some of the assumptions of the general process view are wrong: The events that can be associated are not interchangeable, and learning in different species differs in significant respects. Nevertheless, the substantial similarities in most cases support the view that a common process or processes may be at work.

In Chapter 9, we saw that classical conditioning and reinforcement are themselves based on a number of subprocesses. In conditioning, for example, the subject must attend to the CS when it is presented; it must then recall the CS when the US is presented; and, finally, it must form an association between their cortical representations. Classical conditioning, in other words, is not a unitary process, but is itself based on a number of subprocesses, or building blocks. In this context, the conclusion suggested by the material we have been reviewing is not that all forms of learning are identical, but rather that they all involve a number of component processes, such as memory and attention, and that the properties of these building blocks are similar. (For a similar analysis, see Hollis, ten Cate, & Bateson, 1991.)

It may be helpful to think of the relationships between different forms of learning as analogous to the relationship between different houses in a suburban housing development. The houses fall into a few basic types—for example, colonial versus ranch—and the houses within each type also differ in some respects. All ranch houses, for example, share a common design, but they might nevertheless differ in details, such as their color and size. Similarly, there seem to be a small number of types of learning, such as classical conditioning and reinforcement, and instances within these categories also differ in some respects. Taste-aversion learning and fear conditioning, for example, are both examples of classical conditioning and share common features—in both, for example, the strength of conditioning depends on contiguity—but they also differ in details, such as the maximum delay at which conditioning will occur.

The general process view claimed that all suburban houses (types of learning) were identical; the adaptationist approach acknowledges that they differ and attributes these differences to the need to adapt each house to the features of the local environment (for example, the steepness of the hill on which the house is built). The particular version of this approach that we are now proposing is that, despite the differences in appearance of these houses, evolution may have used a relatively small set of building blocks in constructing them, and that the properties of these blocks (core processes such as memory, attention, and association) have remained substantially unchanged.

In recent years, many ethologists as well as psychologists have been moving toward some form of the adaptive learning hypothesis, which, while acknowledging significant differences in learning in different species, views these differences as variations on a common theme. (See, for example, Gould, 1986; Bateson, 1991; Shettleworth, 1993.) Not all psychologists or ethologists agree (for example, Johnston, 1981), but especially in light of the yawning gap that once existed between the psychological and ethological traditions, this convergence is encouraging. Psychologists have learned much from ethologists' studies of animals in their natural habitats, and ethologists have also shown increasing appreciation of the value of experiments under controlled conditions in illuminating behaviors first observed in the wild (for example, Krebs, 1991; Marler, 1991).

11.5 SUMMARY

Early research on learning by Pavlov, Thorndike, Skinner, and others suggested that the principles of learning were identical in different situations and different species. This, in turn, suggested that all of these forms of learning might be based on the same basic process—a view we have called the general process view. According to this hypothesis, whenever an association is formed between two events, E_1 and E_2, the same associative mechanism is involved (a general system). Furthermore, this system is assumed to be largely indifferent to the particular events being associated, so that any member of the E_1 category can be associated with any member of the E_2 category (interchangeability of events). Finally, associative learning in different species is assumed to be based on the same associative mechanisms (generality across species).

The first major challenge to this view came from ethologists—biologists who studied animal behavior largely through observations under natural conditions, rather than through experiments in the laboratory. Their approach to animal behavior was strongly influenced by Darwin's theory of evolution, which suggested that all existing species have evolved from common ancestors. The main principle of evolution was natural selection, in which animals that were better suited to their environments were more likely to survive and reproduce and, thus, pass on their genes to succeeding generations. Over time, natural selection would lead to a gradual change in the characteristics of each species, with a trend toward divergence as each species became more specialized to exploit the potential of its particular environment or niche.

Insofar as species are closely related, and also face similar environments, an evolutionary perspective suggests that we should expect substantial similarities in learning. But this perspective also alerts us to the possibility that environments that seem similar can differ in subtle but important ways and, thus, that we should expect differences in learning as well as similarities. Observations of birds by ethologists, such as Konrad Lorenz, pointed to precisely such differences. He observed that in some species of birds, newly hatched birds would develop a strong attachment to the first moving object they saw and would then follow this object wherever it went. a phenomenon he called imprinting. Imprinting differs from other forms of associative learning in that it occurs largely during an early period of the bird's life, called the sensitive period, and once the attachment has developed, it is difficult to reverse.

Another form of learning observed by ethologists was song learning, in which the young of some species of birds learn to imitate the songs of adults. Song learning is similar to imprinting in that it occurs during a sensitive period, is hard to reverse, and is strongly guided by genetic predispositions to certain stimuli (for example, birds are much more likely to imitate songs that resemble the natural songs of their species). In both imprinting and song learning, whether learning occurs in a species seems to reflect the adaptive value of the learning for that species: Learning is found in species where it would be useful, but not in species where it would not. The implication is that evolution has not produced learning systems that are entirely general, capable of associating any events that occur contiguously but, rather, has encouraged more focused systems that are geared to detecting particular information that would help the species to survive. It is interesting to reflect on whether the human ability to learn might be constrained in similar ways.

The evidence on imprinting and song learning made it clear that learning is not entirely uniform; subsequent research on classical conditioning and reinforcement showed that here, too, learning is not as uniform as it once appeared. John Garcia showed that rats can associate tastes with illness and visual cues with shock, but they have great difficulty in associating either CS with the other US. The assumption of interchangeability was clearly wrong. Moreover, taste-aversion learning differed from conditioning involving other responses, such as fear, in aspects such as speed of conditioning and maximum delay interval at which conditioning could be obtained—differences suggesting that the associative mechanisms underlying these different forms must differ.

Research on reinforcement suggested a similar conclusion: A reinforcer that was effective for one response might be entirely ineffective for another response. The Brelands, for example, found that they could train a raccoon to deposit a coin in a piggy bank, but that it developed a disconcerting tendency to hold onto the coin and to rub it instead of depositing it. Other cases in which reinforcement appeared ineffective included cats not learning to lick themselves, and rats not learning to press a bar when the reinforcer was avoidance of shock. It currently appears as if two main factors are responsible for these failures: involuntary or reflexive responses might be hard to reinforce, and classically conditioned responses might interfere with performance of the response that has been reinforced.

This evidence makes it clear that learning does differ in different situations (for example, not all CSs can be associated with all USs) and in different species (imprinting occurs in some species but not others). However, learning in these situations is also similar in many respects. Thus, although taste-aversion learning and fear conditioning differ in their quantitative properties, such as the maximum CS–US interval that will sustain conditioning, they nevertheless obey the same general principles. One way to integrate the evidence for similarities as well as for differences is to assume that the basic mechanisms of learning are quite general across species, but that the details are modified in the course of evolution to allow species to adapt to the unique problems that each faces. This adaptationist approach suggests that there will be differences in learning in different situations and species, but that these differences can be understood as variations on a common theme.

We could, logically, have concluded our discussion at this point, but the scientific principle of parsimony drives psychologists to explain learning in terms of as few basic processes as possible. We went on, therefore, to consider the possibility that all forms of animal learning are based on a single associative mechanism. In the case of classical conditioning and reinforcement, the powerful similarities in their principles and properties support the idea that they rely on a common system for detecting relationships between events. On the surface, imprinting and song learning seem to have few similarities with conditioning, but there is growing evidence that they, too, might be based on associative processes. Both involve a learning phase in which animals learn to recognize a stimulus, and this perceptual learning might be based on the formation of associations between the elements of the stimulus, allowing a fuller and more accurate representation. Furthermore, the behavior that is then directed towards this stimulus may be the result of classical conditioning. In the case of imprinting, some elements of the imprinting model might trigger an identification of the stimulus as the duckling's parent, and other characteristics of the stimulus are then associated with the parental US. As a result, these characteristics elicit behaviors appropriate to the parent, such as following it. In sum, imprinting, song learning, classical conditioning, and reinforcement might all rely on a common core of associative processes.

This evidence suggests that a synthesis of the views of learning psychologists, such as Pavlov and Thorndike, and ethologists, such as Lorenz might be emerging. The ethologists have clearly been supported in their belief that learning differs in different species, but there are also substantial similarities, and recent evidence suggests that similar associative mechanisms might be involved. If different forms of learning, such as reinforcement and imprinting, are metaphorically pictured as houses, evolution might have constructed an impressive variety of houses by combining the same basic building blocks (associative mechanisms) in different ways.

Glossary

General process view In its strongest form, this view says that a single, universal mechanism is responsible for learning in all situations and all species. The mechanism is normally assumed to be an associative one: An association is formed between any two events that occur together, regardless of the nature of the events.

Natural selection A description of the environmental contingencies ensuring that individuals who are fitter are more likely to survive and reproduce.

Adaptive value The degree to which a trait helps individuals adapt to their environment, making them more likely to survive and reproduce.

Imprinting The development by an animal of a strong social attachment, normally to its mother, during the early period of its life. By a broader definition, imprinting is the process by which some species learn to recognize other members of their species during this early period.

Critical period A short, sharply defined period during the first few days of a bird's life during which Lorenz believed that imprinting could occur. Later evidence has suggested that this period is both longer and less clearly defined than Lorenz supposed; as a result, the period during which imprinting is most likely to occur is now called the **sensitive period.**

Adaptationist approach The idea that learning has evolved to help animals adapt to the unique requirements of their niches. In current usage, adaptationist positions seem to assume that the principles of learning are generally similar in different situations and species, but that variations on these common principles occur because of the different niches species occupy.

Parsimony The scientific principle that when different explanations of a phenomenon are equally consistent with the available evidence, we should prefer the simplest of the available explanations. The simplest explanation is the one that makes the fewest assumptions, or postulates the fewest processes, in order to explain a set of observations.

Review Questions

1. What is the general process view? What evidence supports it?

2. How does the theory of evolution account for the development of species?

3. According to an evolutionary perspective, under what circumstances should we expect learning in two species to be similar? Under what circumstances should it be different?

4. In what respects are imprinting and song learning similar?

5. In what respects did Lorenz believe imprinting to be unique? Was he right?

6. How would an evolutionary analysis explain why some forms of learning are found in some species but not in others?

7. Why does the evidence on taste-aversion learning pose a challenge to the general process view?

8. What evidence challenges the view that a reinforcer can strengthen any response that precedes it? How can this evidence be explained?

9. What is the adaptationist view? How can the evidence that the effects of reinforcement and classical conditioning vary across situations be reconciled with the claim that there is basically a single learning system?

10. How could a single, universal associative system account for the existence of imprinting?

11. In what respects have psychologists and ethologists converged on a common view of how learning varies across situations and species?

CHAPTER TWELVE

CONCEPT LEARNING: ASSOCIATIVE AND COGNITIVE PROCESSES

To explain classical conditioning, Pavlov proposed a very simple theory: If stimuli such as a tone and food are presented together, each will activate a cortical center, and a connection will be formed between these centers. Similarly, Thorndike suggested that the presentation of a reinforcer stamps in an association between the preceding response and the stimuli present at the time. Thus, both believed that learning could be explained in terms of the formation of associations between contiguous events.

Subsequent research supported the important role of associations in conditioning—recall, for example, the success of the Rescorla-Wagner model in integrating most of the known facts about classical conditioning (Chapter 4), and evidence that reinforcers will stamp in whatever behaviors happen to precede them, even if these behaviors actually reduce the overall rate of reinforcement (Chapter 10). Other evidence, however, pointed to more complex processes in conditioning. In classical conditioning, there is evidence that animals form expectations about what US will follow a CS, and we encountered similar evidence in the case of reinforcement—a particularly striking example was the monkey in Tinklepaugh's experiment that shrieked in anger when it found a lettuce leaf under a cup, instead of the banana that it had seen placed there earlier. In Chapter 8, we also encountered evidence for more sophisticated cognitive processes, including the formation of remarkably detailed cognitive maps of the environment.

To integrate this evidence, we proposed a two-level hypothesis according to which learning involves two separate systems: an associative system that forms associations between contiguous events, and a cognitive system that forms expectations about future events and uses them to plan effective action. In this chapter, we will be looking more deeply at the relationship between associative processes on the one hand, and more complex, cognitive processes on the other. In particular, we will focus on learning concepts. Our goal will be to understand the role of associative and cognitive processes in concept learning, and what this can tell us about the relationship between these two forms of learning.

12.1 CONCEPT LEARNING IN HUMANS

A **concept** is a remarkably difficult term to define, but one simple starting point is to think of a concept as a set of objects or events sharing common features. The concept *triangle*, for example, consists of all shapes that have three sides; *squares* are four lines of equal length joined at right angles, and so on. In this definition, a person is said to understand a concept if he or she can identify its members. Thus a child is assumed to understand the concept triangle if she can distinguish shapes that are triangles from those that are not.

Concepts provide the building blocks for logical thought, because by combining concepts we are able to think and reason. ("This new pet is an animal; animals all need food to live; this pet must need food.") The ability to form concepts, however, is not critical simply to intelligent thought; it is critical to our ability to function at all. One way to see this is to try to imagine a child born without the ability to group events into conceptual categories, so that he reacts to every new stimulus as if it is completely unique. If he encountered a dog, for example, he would not recognize it as similar to other dogs he had encountered in the past, and thus would have no basis for anticipating how it might behave. Indeed, he would not even be able to recognize this dog as one he had seen just moments earlier, because its perceptual properties would be different every time he encountered it—its limbs would be in a different position, it would be at a different distance and angle, and so on. If every stimulus is unique, this child would have no basis for bringing past experience to bear on present problems; the stimulus would be lost in a sea of unique events. The ability to group similar events together in concepts allows us to impose coherence on the turbulent stream of our perceptions.

Hypothesis Theory

Given the centrality of concepts to human thought and behavior, psychologists have long been concerned to understand what concepts are and how they are formed. We will not try to review their efforts in detail here, but one study that proved particularly influential was reported in 1956 by Bruner, Goodnow, and Austin. In one of their experiments, they showed their subjects an array of cards spread out over a table. The cards showed sets of objects that varied in a number of dimensions: One card might contain three large green squares, another two small red triangles, and so on. The subjects were told that some of the cards belonged to a single category and that their task was to identify the conceptual rule that defined this category. On each trial they could select one card that they thought might belong to the category, and the experimenter would then tell them whether their choice had been correct. If the concept was a simple one such as red, for example, then subjects were told that they were correct any time they selected a card containing this color.

By studying the sequence in which subjects selected cards, Bruner and colleagues were able to identify a number of strategies that subjects used to solve the problems. Although the details of these strategies differed, all involved formulating a hypothesis and then testing it. On the first trial, for example, a subject might guess that the concept was triangle, and select one of the cards containing a triangle. If the experimenter told her that she was wrong, she would conclude that this hypothesis must have been incorrect and she would select a new hypothesis for testing on the next trial.

Marvin Levine proposed one formal theory of how subjects test hypotheses in situations like this. (Similar models were proposed by other theorists such as Trabasso & Bower, 1968.) Levine's (1971) theory was based on three simple assumptions:

1. Subjects start any problem with a set of hypotheses about the solution.

2. On each trial, subjects select one hypothesis for testing and base their response on this hypothesis.

3. If the hypothesis is correct, they retain it for testing on the following trial; if it is incorrect, they abandon it and select another hypothesis from those remaining in the set.

As simple as this theory is, it leads to a number of interesting predictions about subjects' behavior while solving problems, and we will look at two of these predictions.

All-or-none learning.   The first concerns how quickly learning should occur. To illustrate this prediction, consider the following concept-learning experiment by Trabasso (1963). On every trial, subjects were shown a picture of a different flower, and the flowers differed in dimensions such as type (tulip, daisy, and so on), color, and leaf shape. The subject's task was to decide which of two categories each picture belonged to. The correct classification was based on just one of the flower's dimensions—for example, whether it was red or yellow— and subjects were told after each trial whether their response was correct.

How should we expect the probability of a correct response to change over trials? According to associative models of learning, reinforcement gradually strengthens an association between a response and the stimuli present. Therefore, as the response of saying "category A" is repeatedly reinforced on red trials, there should be a gradual increase in the probability that red will produce this response. According to hypothesis theory, on the other hand, subjects test only a single hypothesis on each trial. As long as the subject's hypothesis is wrong—for example, that flowers with smooth leaves belong in category A— then responding will remain at chance (50%), because values of the irrelevant dimensions were assigned randomly. Once subjects select the correct hypothesis, however, they should respond correctly on all subsequent trials, because the model assumes that they will retain this hypothesis as long as it leads to

FIGURE 12.1   Presolution performance during concept learning. The percentage of correct responses is shown for all trials prior to a subject's last error. (Adapted from Trabasso, 1963)

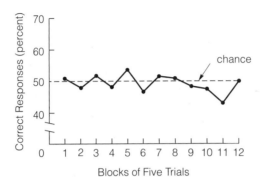

reinforcement. In other words, subjects should start at 50% and stay there until they finally select the correct hypothesis, whereupon they should immediately respond at 100%. Thus, whereas associative learning models predict a gradual improvement over trials, hypothesis-testing models predict **all-or-none learning,** or **one-trial learning.**

To test this prediction, Trabasso examined each subject's data to determine the last trial on which an error occurred. Then, for each trial, he calculated the average performance of subjects who had not yet begun performing perfectly. According to hypothesis theory, subjects must have been using incorrect hypotheses on all trials preceding the last error. (Had they adopted the correct hypothesis, they would not have made any further errors.) Performance across these trials, therefore, should remain at chance. According to an incremental learning analysis, however, reinforcement for saying "A" on red trials should lead to a gradual strengthening of this response. The results are shown in Figure 12.1. Note that performance did not improve over trials, suggesting that reinforcement of the correct response had no effect as long as subjects were testing hypotheses about irrelevant dimensions.

Nonlearning. A related prediction of the model concerns what happens when a subject's initial set of hypotheses does not contain the correct hypothesis. If the set is small—say, 5 to 10 hypotheses—subjects should soon realize that none of the hypotheses in this set is correct, and they should then generate a new set of hypotheses for testing. If the set is very large, however, they should continue to sample hypotheses from this incorrect set. If we now add the assumption that subjects learn only about the hypotheses they are testing, the theory predicts that subjects who start a problem with a very large set of hypotheses not including the solution should fail to solve it, no matter how simple the problem may be.

To test this prediction, Levine (1971) asked college students to select the letter A or B on every trial. If they said A, the experimenter told them that they were correct; if they said B, the experimenter told them that they were wrong. The problem was thus unbelievably simple: All subjects had to do was to learn to say A. Not surprisingly, subjects in a control group required an average of only three trials to solve it. To see what would happen if subjects did not include the correct solution in their hypothesis set, Levine gave a second group pretraining in which the correct letter on each trial was determined by a complex alternation sequence. The basis of solution for a typical problem was the sequence AABAAABABB, a sequence that was repeated over and over. If the subject did not solve the problem within 115 trials, the experimenter verbally explained the solution and then presented a new problem, again involving a complex alternation sequence. In all, subjects received six such problems during pretraining.

When transferred to the test problem, how should these subjects perform? Despite the utter simplicity of the problem, Levine predicted that subjects would find it unsolvable. On the first pretraining problem, subjects might begin by testing relatively simple hypotheses such as "A is always correct," but as simple hypotheses of this kind repeatedly proved inadequate, they would turn to more complex hypotheses. By the end of pretraining, Levine suggested, their hypothesis set would consist exclusively of such complex hypotheses. When transferred to the test problem, then, they would be unable to solve it, because their hypothesis set would not contain the simple hypothesis "A is correct."

The result was that 81% of the subjects failed to solve the problem, even when given 115 trials to do so. Indeed, there was no sign of any improvement in the performance of these subjects. On trials 91–100, for example, only 53% of their responses were correct, a figure statistically indistinguishable from chance. Thus, even though the response of saying A was reinforced every time it occurred, there was no increase in its probability. The implication is that reinforcement was not strengthening the overt response of saying A but, rather, whatever covert hypothesis gave rise to it.

Limitations of the theory. Hypothesis theory provides a simple and often impressive account of concept learning. (For more detailed reviews, see Levine, 1975, and Gholson, 1980.) Notwithstanding its success, hypothesis theory also has several limitations. One is that the theory provides us with little or no guidance concerning the origin of subjects' hypotheses. If a subject starts a problem with five hypotheses about its solution, for example, where do these hypotheses come from? In some cases we undoubtedly use our past experience with similar problems to decide what hypotheses are likely to be correct, but it is unlikely that we are born with a complete set of hypotheses about all the possible problems we might face in the course of our lives. At some point, we must begin to generate new hypotheses based on experience, and hypothesis theory has little to say about how this occurs. This does not mean that hypothesis theory is wrong—many of its predictions have been handsomely supported—but rather that the theory needs to be supplemented by assumptions about how hypotheses are generated before it can provide a comprehensive account of concept learning.

We also need to recognize that although we may solve some problems by consciously testing hypotheses, it is unlikely that we solve all problems in this way. For example, although learning sometimes follows the all-or-none pattern predicted by Levine's model, we have also encountered many situations in which learning is gradual: cats struggling to escape from a puzzle box, humans learning to drive a car or to contract an invisibly small muscle in their thumb. It seems unlikely that learning in the latter situations is based on the systematic testing of hypotheses. A more plausible interpretation is that while learning involves the testing of hypotheses in some situations, in others simpler, associative mechanisms are involved. (See also Kendler, 1979.) Or, restating this idea within the framework of the two-level hypothesis, complex cognitive processes at a conscious level might coexist with associative processes at a more primitive level.

Fuzzy Concepts

Hypothesis theory was developed to account for performance in problems where the concepts to be learned were defined by clear rules—the concept *triangle* is an example. Many of the concepts that we learn in real life, however, are not so easily defined. Consider the concept *dog*. This might at first seem a simple concept to define—for example, "A dog is a four-legged animal with a tail, fur, etc." As you think more about such definitions, however, they quickly begin to break down. Most dogs have four legs, but some may be born deformed, with only three; although some dogs have tails, others do not; and so on. Another way to see this difficulty is to form mental images of different breeds such as dachshunds, Saint Bernards, poodles, and bulldogs. What is it that unites these very different animals, yet distinguishes them from similar species such as a cat or a fox? There does not seem to be any clear rule that defines category membership.

Prototype theory. If the concept *dog* cannot be given a precise definition, how do we decide whether an animal that we encounter is a dog? One approach to this question was pioneered by a philosopher, Ludwig Wittgenstein (1953), and later elaborated by a psychologist, Eleanor Rosch (1975, 1978). They noted that although examples of a concept do not all share the same features (four legs, a tail, and so on), there is nevertheless a clear *family resemblance* between them. That is, just as members of a family may resemble each other even though there are no features that they all share, so too instances of a concept such as *dog* share broadly similar features. In this view, membership of a category is not determined by a precise rule but rather by the degree to which a candidate possesses the features characteristic of existing members; the more of these features a candidate possesses, the more likely it is to be a member. Concepts, in this view, are "fuzzy," in the sense that they are not demarcated by clear boundaries. For example, would you consider a rug an example of furniture? A pumpkin a fruit? When a group of 30 subjects were asked the latter question, 16 said that it was a fruit and 14 that it was not. And, even more remarkably, when interviewed a month later, 8 of the 30 subjects had changed their minds (McCloskey & Glucksberg, 1978). Although the concept *fruit* at first seems quite clear, when we examine it more closely its boundaries prove surprisingly fuzzy.

If concepts are only collections of similar objects and have no clear boundaries, this brings us back to the question of how we decide whether a new instance is a member. One suggestion is that as we encounter members of a concept, or *exemplars*, we begin to build a picture of what an average or typical member looks like. This average representation of the concept is called its **prototype.** If you hear the word "bird," for example, you may think of a typical example such as a robin; if you hear the word "chair," you may think of a typical chair, and so on. According to *prototype theory*, we combine the features of exemplars of a concept in order to form an average representation, and we then decide whether a new instance is a member by judging its similarity to this prototype. (See Posner & Keele, 1968; Rosch, 1975.) In our dog example, you would decide whether an animal is a dog by judging its similarity to your image of a typical dog. The process of forming a prototype, by identifying the common features shared by exemplars, is called **abstraction**.

If membership of a concept is determined by judging similarity to a prototype, one implication is that people should find it easier to judge category membership if the test stimulus closely resembles the prototype. To test this prediction, Rosch (1973) began by asking subjects to rate the extent to which various exemplars were typical of their categories. (Exemplars judged highly typical are likely to be very close to the prototype.) In the case of the concept *bird*, for example, she found that robins and sparrows were judged to be highly typical birds, whereas chickens and ostriches were rated as much less typical. Rosch then asked a different set of subjects to decide whether each of these exemplars was a member of the category. Subjects were shown sentences such as "A robin is a bird," and "A chicken is a bird," and asked to push a button marked "true" or "false" as quickly as they could. (They also read false sentences such as "A robin is a vegetable.") She found that subjects responded significantly faster when the exemplar was typical of the category then when it was not.

This finding—that subjects find it easier to judge category membership when an exemplar is typical of the category—is called the *typicality effect*. It supports the view that subjects classify stimuli by comparing them to prototypes—when a stimulus is close to the center of a category, and thus close to the prototype, subjects find it easier to decide whether they are members of the category. (See also Rosch, Simpson, & Miller, 1976.)

Exemplar theory. The existence of typicality effects at first seemed to provide compelling evidence that subjects create and use prototypes, but it later became clear that this evidence could be explained without appealing to prototypes. Suppose that all subjects do during the training phase is to associate each exemplar with its category label. Then, when they are shown new exemplars during the test phase, they compare these test stimuli to those they saw during training. If the test stimulus resembles exemplars from category A more then exemplars from category B, then they assume that this stimulus must also come from category A.

Exemplar theory, as this approach is called, assumes that classification of new stimuli is based on a comparison of these stimuli with previously learned exemplars. Thus, whereas prototype theory assumes that we decide whether an animal is a dog by comparing it to a prototypical dog, exemplar theory assumes that we compare it to particular dogs that we already know. (See Komatsu, 1992, for a review.) The basis for the typicality effect, according to this theory, is that typical exemplars, almost by definition, are very similar to other instances of the concept. If you see a typical bird, for example, it is likely to remind you of many other birds you have seen, and this will provide strong evidence that it too is a bird. If you see an atypical bird, on the other hand, it will remind you of fewer birds, and so you will be more hesitant to conclude that it is a bird.

It is possible to account for the typicality effect, then, purely in terms of associations, without assuming that subjects average together exemplars to form prototypes. Exemplar theory is essentially a version of the associative theories of learning that we encountered in earlier chapters. It assumes that when a stimulus is presented, it is associated with a response (in this case, the category label). Test stimuli are then classified by comparing them to existing exemplars, or, in the language of associative theories, by generalization, as the response associated with a training stimulus (an exemplar) generalizes to similar stimuli. Exemplar theory thus emphasizes relatively simple processes of association and generalization, whereas prototype theory is more in the spirit of cognitive approaches that assume much more complex processes, such as memory, attention, and, here, abstraction.

Evaluation

We have encountered three theories of concept learning—that subjects learn the rules that define the concept, that they form prototypes by averaging together exemplars, and that they simply associate exemplars with category labels. Can we now say which theory is correct?

As always, testing competing theories requires identifying situations in which they yield different predictions. To see how this can be done, we will begin by examining the predictions of these theories in a very simple situation. Suppose that subjects are shown a series of rectangles that differ in the lengths

FIGURE 12.2   Two sets of rectangles, A and B, arranged on the basis of their base and height dimensions.

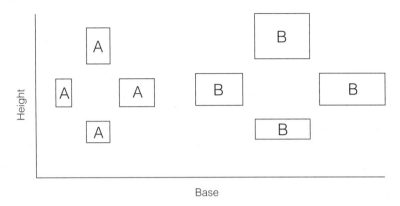

of their bases and heights, and they must learn to classify these stimuli into one of two categories, A and B. Figure 12.2 shows the rectangles used in this hypothetical experiment. They are arranged within the figure on the basis of their dimensions, and the category to which each rectangle belongs is indicated by the letter A or B.

According to hypothesis theory, subjects would solve this problem by testing hypotheses about the defining rule until they found one that worked. In this case, they might eventually realize that the category A rectangles all have bases shorter than 4 inches, whereas category B rectangles have bases longer than this value. In other words, they might learn the rule "category A if base less than 4 inches, category B if longer." This solution is shown in Figure 12.3a, where each rectangle is now represented by a small square, rather by a picture of the rectangle. The rule defining the boundary between the two categories is shown by a line separating the two sets of dots. If a test stimulus was presented for classification (the dot marked "T"), it would be judged in relation to the rule; since the test stimulus has a base smaller than 4 inches, it would be assigned to category A.

According to prototype theory, subjects would average together the rectangles in each category to form prototypes (P_A and P_B in Figure 12.3b). When a test stimulus was presented, it would be judged in terms of which prototype it resembled most closely.

Finally, Figure 12.3c represents the analysis of exemplar theory. According to this analysis, subjects simply learn to associate each rectangle with the appropriate label. If a test stimulus was presented, subjects would judge it on the basis of its similarity to one or more of these exemplars. In the example shown in the figure, the test stimulus is closer to exemplars in category A than to those in category B, so it, too, would be assigned to category A. (For simplicity's sake, we will hereafter assume that subjects compare a test stimulus only to the

FIGURE 12.3   Three theories of how subjects decide whether an object is a member of a concept. Each
small square represents a rectangle, and the letter T represents a test rectangle that must
be allocated to one of the two categories. (a) Hypothesis theory assumes that subjects
use a rule, represented by the vertical line, to distinguish the two categories. Membership is then judged relative to that line. (b) Prototype theory assumes that subjects
average together the exemplars of a concept to form a prototype (P_1 and P_2). Category
membership is then judged by similarity to the two prototypes. (c) Exemplar theory
assumes that category membership is judged by the similarity of the test stimulus to one
or more of the exemplars.

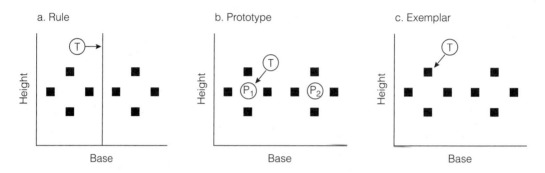

exemplar that it resembles most closely, but some versions of the theory assume
that subjects compare it to all the exemplars that they have encountered and
calculate the average resemblance.)

For the example we have shown, all three theories make the same prediction: The test stimulus would be assigned to category A. If changes are made to
the location of the test stimulus, however, and also to the exemplars presented
during training, then it is possible to produce situations in which the theories
lead to different predictions. Figure 12.4 illustrates one of the ways in which
this can be done. In this example, we are assuming that four exemplars are presented during the training phase, potentially leading to the creation of a prototype, P_1. Then, in the test phase, subjects receive two test stimuli, T_1 and T_2;
these stimuli are equally similar to the prototype but vary in their similarity to
one of the exemplars. According to prototype theory, the two test stimuli should
be equally easy to classify because they are equally similar to the prototype. If
subjects assess category membership by comparing a stimulus to the exemplar it
resembles most closely, however, then T_1 should be easier to classify than T_2
because it is more similar to this exemplar.

Using designs like this, we can tease apart the predictions of the three theories. Several tests of these predictions have now been reported, and the results
have increasingly converged on a common conclusion: The answer to which
theory is correct is that they all are. (See, for example, DeLosh, Busemeyer, &

FIGURE 12.4   A procedure for testing prototype and exemplar theories. The small squares represent four exemplars of a category, and T_1 and T_2 represent two test stimuli. According to prototype theory, category membership should be judged in terms of the similarity of the test stimuli to the prototype; according to exemplar theory, membership should be judged in terms of their similarity to exemplar E_1.

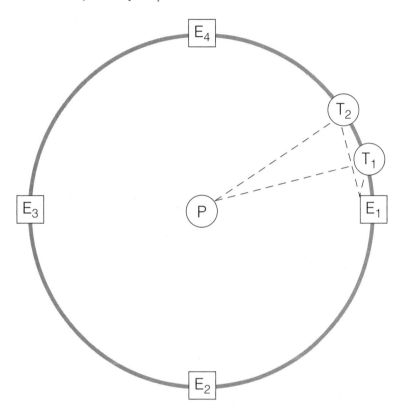

McDaniel, 1997; Smith, Murray, & Minda, 1997; Erickson & Kruschke, 1998.) That is, people have the ability to solve problems in different ways, and which solution we adopt depends in part on the characteristics of the problem. When confronted with a problem that reminds us of similar problems from the past, we might well test hypotheses derived from these earlier experiences. When the stimuli are more confusing—for example, a seemingly random collection of dots—we might combine stimuli to form prototypes. And, in both situations, we can also use our knowledge of old exemplars to aid us in classifying new ones. Doctors, for example, are taught rules for deciding whether a patient is suffering from a particular disease, but they also base their decisions on experiences with individual patients. In trying to decide if a patient is suffering from disease X, for example, they are significantly more likely to reach this conclusion if they have recently treated a patient with this disease who had a similar constellation of symptoms (Brooks, Norman, & Allen, 1991).

As our medical example illustrates, the three processes need not be mutually exclusive. While subjects are consciously testing hypotheses about the solution to a problem, they might be forming associations and prototypes at an unconscious level. Indeed, an unconscious process of abstracting common features could be the source of many of the hypotheses that are eventually tested consciously. If subjects are trying to solve a concept-learning task involving complex geometric shapes, for example, they might detect similarities between the positive exemplars at an unconscious level; these similarities could then form the basis for a conscious hypothesis. ("Hey, I wonder if . . .")

The concepts we have discussed so far have all been relatively simple. In discussing the concept *dog,* for example, we largely concentrated on its visual appearance, whereas an adult's concept of a dog also includes information about its eating habits, its behavior towards strangers, and so on. An adult's concept of a dog is thus much richer than the version presented here, and this richer version raises questions about how all the different components of the concept are interrelated. This issue is beyond the scope of our discussion, but if you would like to pursue this question further, you can find discussions of other theories of concept learning in papers by Medin (1989) and Keil (1994).

12.2 CONCEPT LEARNING IN ANIMALS

The ability to form concepts is so central to human thought and language that it was long taken for granted that this ability was exclusively human. Even if it had occurred to anyone to wonder whether animals might also have this ability, there was no obvious way to find out. Suppose, for example, that you wanted to know whether a pigeon could form a complex concept such as *human being.* To find out if a child understands a concept such as *dog* is relatively simple: We can present pictures of different animals and ask whether each is a dog. If the child consistently answers correctly, we assume that it has mastered the concept. A pigeon, however, cannot say "human being." How, then, can we determine whether it understands this concept?

A Pigeon's Concept of "Human Being"

In 1964, Herrnstein and Loveland provided an ingenious solution to this problem by taking advantage of one response that pigeons can make with ease and conviction: pecking. Using standard reinforcement techniques, they trained their birds to peck a key whenever a human being was present. The experimenters projected a series of slides onto a screen, some containing a human being but others not. If the picture contained one or more people, pecks at the screen were occasionally reinforced with food; if a human being was not present, pecks were not reinforced:

$$S_{people} : R_{peck} \rightarrow food$$

$$S_{no\ people} : R_{peck} \rightarrow \underline{\quad\quad}$$

If pigeons are capable of forming the concept of human being, we should expect the birds to learn to peck only when a human being was present.

To ensure that the birds were using a complex concept and not just relying on a simpler feature such as the presence of human flesh colors, Herrnstein and Loveland assembled a set of pictures that were matched in every possible respect except for the presence of a human:

> For any one session, approximately half the photographs contained at least one human being; the remainder contained no human beings—in the experimenter's best judgment. In no other systematic way did the two sets of slides appear to differ. Many slides contained human beings partly obscured by intervening objects: trees, automobiles, window frames, and so on. The people were distributed throughout the pictures: in the center or to one side or the other, near the top or the bottom, close up or distant. Some slides contained a single person; others contained groups of various sizes. The people themselves were clothed, semi-nude, or nude; adults or children; men or women; sitting, standing, or lying; black, white, or yellow. Lighting and coloration varied: some slides were dark, others light; some had either reddish or bluish tints, and so on.
>
> (Herrnstein & Loveland, 1964, p. 239)

The results were straightforward: The birds quickly learned to peck more to positive stimuli than to negative ones. On its own, this result does not prove that the birds had formed a concept; they could have learned to peck each reinforced picture individually, without realizing that they shared a common property. To determine whether the birds had truly formed a concept, therefore, Herrnstein and Loveland presented the birds with pictures they had never seen before. If they had learned only to peck the pictures they had seen, they should have pecked all the novel pictures at the same rate, whereas if they had learned that positive pictures all shared the presence of a human being, they should have pecked new positive pictures faster than new negative pictures. The latter prediction was confirmed, as the average rate of pecking to the novel stimuli was 10 to 100 times faster when a human being was present. Just as children learn to say "dog" whenever they see a new dog, so pigeons can learn to peck whenever they see a picture of a new human being.

In subsequent experiments, Herrnstein and his colleagues showed that pigeons are equally proficient at learning other concepts such as *tree*, *oak leaf*, and even *fish*. These concepts are learned, moreover, with quite astonishing speed.

In one experiment (Herrnstein, 1979), the correct concept was tree. The positive and negative slides did not obviously differ in any respect other than the presence of a tree. Pigeons typically require from two to nine sessions to master relatively simple discriminations such as color (learning, for example, to peck a green key but not a red one). The birds in this experiment, however, learned to respond differentially to pictures containing trees after only a single session.

Is It Really Learning?

The remarkable speed of this learning raised questions about whether the pigeons' performance was really based on learning. Were they really forming complex concepts so rapidly, or were they simply tapping existing concepts that had become genetically ingrained through the course of evolution? In the case of the concept tree, there are obvious advantages for a pigeon in being able to recognize trees and discriminate them from other objects such as bushes—this ability could be vital in activities such as finding food and locating appropriate locations for nests. Pigeons that possessed an innate ability to recognize trees would be more likely to survive and reproduce, thereby passing on this ability to their offspring.

An evolutionary analysis thus seems plausible in the case of trees, but it is difficult to imagine what evolutionary pressures could have encouraged pigeons to develop an innate concept of fish. Definitive evidence that pigeons can learn concepts, however, was provided in an experiment by Herrnstein, Loveland, and Cable (1976). The positive stimuli in this study were pictures of one person, and the negative stimuli were pictures of other people. Even though the pictures were closely matched in almost all respects (the negative pictures were taken in the same settings as the positive ones, and in some cases even involved people wearing the same clothing as the subject), the birds nevertheless had little difficulty learning to peck only when a particular person was present. It seems safe to infer that the birds in this experiment were genuinely learning something new, rather than tapping a preexisting concept.

Is It Really a Concept?

A rather more difficult issue is whether this learning involved the formation of a concept. The issue here is fundamentally one of definition—what do we really mean by a concept, and thus what evidence do we need to conclude that an animal has formed one? At the beginning of this chapter, we provisionally defined a concept as a set of objects or events sharing common features. Under this definition, it is clear that pigeons can form concepts, as they are able to sort stimuli into categories on the basis of their common features. But does this definition fully capture what we mean by a concept? When we say that a child understands the concept dog, for example, we don't simply mean that it can say the word "dog" whenever it sees one, because the child could learn to utter the appropriate noises by rote, without any understanding of what they meant. When we say that a child understands the concept *dog*, we are tacitly assuming that he or she has formed some sort of internal representation of a dog—for example, a prototype—so that when asked whether a new animal is a dog, it compares this animal to its internal representation. Did the pigeons in the Herrnstein and Loveland experiment form such a prototype?

One possibility is that they did. As they were repeatedly exposed to pictures containing human beings, they might have formed a visual prototype of what a human being looks like. However, it is also possible to explain the pigeons' behavior in purely associative terms. When the pigeons were reinforced for pecking pictures containing human beings, they could have associated each of these pictures with the response of pecking. When a new picture was presented which contained a human being who resembled one they had seen earlier, the response of pecking could have generalized to this picture. In other words, an exemplar model can account for learning in this situation in the same way that it can for some aspects of concept learning in humans. If Herrnstein and Loveland's pigeons relied solely on the formation of S–R associations to solve the problem, though, we might be reluctant to conclude that they form concepts in the same way as people.

We have seen that experimental techniques exist to separate associative and prototype analyses of concept learning, but these have not yet been applied in the case of animals' learning concepts. At present, therefore, there is no clear basis for deciding whether Herrnstein and Loveland's pigeons relied on purely associative methods, or whether they formed something resembling a prototype. Thus, although it is clear that pigeons satisfy our first definition of concept learning—they can sort stimuli into categories on the basis of their similarity, and they can do so with impressive skill—it is not yet clear whether they satisfy our second definition, which would require the formation of internal representations of the categories. (For reviews of the evidence in this area, and the criteria to be used in assessing concepts, see Herrnstein, 1990; Gallistel, 1990; Wasserman & Astley, 1994; Roberts, 1996.)

12.3 ABSTRACT CONCEPTS IN ANIMALS

The animal experiments we have examined to this point have involved perceptual concepts—stimuli that are united by common physical properties. This evidence makes it clear that pigeons can rapidly learn to respond appropriately to fuzzy categories, such as "pictures containing a human being," but leaves unresolved the question of whether this learning involves simple associations or the formation of concepts at a deeper level.

Another way to try to tackle this issue is to focus on more abstract concepts. In abstract concepts, the concept is defined by the relationship between stimuli, rather than by the properties of a single stimulus on its own. (See Herrnstein, 1990.) A simple example would be the concept *larger*: We judge whether one object is larger than another in terms of the relationship between them, rather than by any property intrinsic to just one. Precisely because abstract concepts are defined in terms of relationships, it is not possible to judge new instances in terms of their similarity to established members. In deciding whether one shoe is larger than another, for example, we cannot base our decision on the size of that shoe on its own, nor on its resemblance to any other shoe that we once categorized as "larger." If animals could sort stimuli on the basis of abstract relationships, therefore, this behavior could not be explained in terms of generalization from existing members of the category, and in this respect would come closer to what we intend by the term "concept."

We have already encountered evidence that animals can form complex concepts in earlier chapters—see, for example, the discussion of number in Chapter 8 and the discussion of transposition in Chapter 9. We will consider two further, perhaps more compelling, examples here.

The Concept "Same"

One example of an abstract relationship is sameness—are two stimuli the same or different? In a typical experiment to study this concept in animals, pigeons are trained on a *matching-to-sample* procedure in which they are shown a sample stimulus and asked to choose which of two comparison stimuli is the same as the sample. In the hypothetical example illustrated in Figure 12.5, a trial begins with the illumination of one of three keys with a sample—in this case, a triangle. When the pigeon pecks the sample on the center key, the two side keys are illuminated with comparison stimuli, a square and a triangle. (The position of the comparison stimuli would randomly alternate between trials, so that the triangle was sometimes on the left and sometimes on the right.) If the subject pecked the comparison stimulus that matched the sample, it would receive food.

Note that choice of the correct stimulus in this procedure does not necessarily mean that the subject has based its response on whether the comparison is the same as the sample. Rather than relying on this abstract relationship, it could solve the problem by associating the entire stimulus complex with the response that is reinforced. When confronted by the stimulus complex shown in Figure 12.5, for example, the pigeon is reinforced for pecking the key on the left, and it could simply associate this stimulus configuration with the response of pecking the left key.[1] To determine whether a subject is basing its response

---

[1] If this hypothesis is not clear, think of the stimuli present on the illustrated trial (square, triangle, triangle) as a single stimulus, S_1, and the stimuli present on another trial (triangle, triangle, square) as a second stimulus, S_2. When S_1 is present, the pigeon is reinforced for pecking the right key, and when S_2 is present the pigeon is reinforced for pecking the left key. In other words, matching to sample can be viewed as a discrimination learning procedure in which the stimulus is a configuration or pattern of illumination spread across three keys, rather than, as in the more common arrangement, concentrated on just one key.

FIGURE 12.5   A typical matching-to-sample trial. The trial begins with illumination of a sample on the center key; a peck illuminates comparison stimuli on the side keys, and a peck to the stimulus that matches the sample produces food.

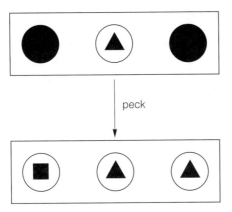

on the relationship of sameness, we need to present new samples and comparison stimuli. Suppose, for example, that we arranged a transfer test in which subjects were exposed to a green sample for the first time and had to choose between red and green comparisons. If they chose the correct stimulus, this would suggest that they had indeed learned to respond to the comparison that was the same as the sample, regardless of the particular stimuli involved.

In one experiment based on this procedure, Wright (1997) trained pigeons with three samples: cartoon drawings of a duck, an apple, and a bunch of grapes. Once the birds had learned to respond correctly to all three samples, Wright introduced transfer trials involving novel stimuli. He found that subjects responded correctly on 80% of these test trials, suggesting that they had indeed learned the general principle of matching the sample. (See also Cook, Cavoto, & Cavoto, 1995; Young, Wasserman, & Dalrymple, 1997.)

One noteworthy feature of Wright's experiment was that the outcome depended on how often subjects had to peck the sample in order to illuminate the comparison stimuli. The results we have cited were obtained from a group that had to peck the sample 20 times in order to produce the comparison stimuli. Another group, however, was required to peck the key only once, and the performance of this second group barely exceeded chance on test trials. In other words, this group solved the problem by associating each stimulus configuration with whatever response was reinforced on that trial, apparently without noticing that the correct comparison was always the same as the sample. Overall, these results support the two-level hypothesis, in that pigeons appear capable of solving matching problems by relying on either associative mechanisms or abstract concepts; which strategy they adopt seems to depend on the precise nature of their training. (For a plausible analysis of why the number of pecks to the sample should matter, see Wright, 1997.)

Language

The suggestion that animals can form concepts is surprising, perhaps even shocking, in light of the long-standing assumption that animals are fundamentally inferior to humans in intelligence. On the other hand, the ability to form concepts is only the foundation stone of the edifice of human thought; people are not only capable of learning concepts such as *tree* and *dog,* they can use words to symbolically represent these concepts, and they can combine these words in sentences to communicate ideas to others. Could animals use language in this way?

Sign language.   Chimpanzees are our closest relatives, so that if any animal could master the rudiments of language, many psychologists believed that it would be chimpanzees. Early attempts to teach chimpanzees to speak, however, met with little success. Hayes and Hayes (1951), for example, reared a chimpanzee named Vicki in their home, but after four years of effort Vicki had learned a grand total of only four words: mama, papa, cup, and up. However, subsequent research on the anatomy of the chimpanzee vocal tract revealed that they were not physically capable of producing the full range of sounds required for speech. Vicki's failure could have been because of this physical limitation rather than any deficiency in her intellectual capacity.

To test this hypothesis, Allen and Beatrice Gardner decided to teach a chimpanzee to use a language that did not require speech—American Sign Language for the deaf. The subject for their study was a baby chimpanzee named Washoe, and the results were dramatic. By the time she was five, Washoe had learned more than 130 signs and was able to use them reliably in a variety of situations. The sign for *dog,* for example, was elicited by a wide variety of dogs, both living and in pictures, and even by the barking of a dog that could not be seen. Washoe also demonstrated some ability to combine signs; when she wanted a refrigerator opened, for example, she signed "open food drink" (Gardner, Gardner, & Van Cantfort, 1989).

Terrace (1979) attempted to replicate these results with a chimpanzee named Nim (short for Nim Chimpsky, a pun on the name of a famous linguist, Noam Chomsky). Nim also succeeded in learning a large number of signs, but Terrace found little evidence that Nim could combine these signs in meaningful ways. When Nim did make several signs in combination, the ordering of the signs appeared random or an imitation of signs just made by one of his trainers. Terrace, Pettito, Sanders, and Bever (1979) argued that Washoe's achievements could also be explained in these ways, and a fierce controversy ensued over whether chimpanzees were capable of combining words meaningfully (for example, Terrace, 1985; Gardner & Gardner, 1985). One result was that the grant supporting the Gardners' research was not renewed.

Lexigrams. Fortunately, other research on teaching language to chimpanzees continued. One research program had been started by Duane Rumbaugh of Georgia State University and was later continued in collaboration with his wife, Sue Savage-Rumbaugh. They, too, believed that it was a mistake to try to teach chimpanzees to speak, but instead of using sign language, they developed a new language using geometrical shapes that they called *lexigrams* as words. The lexigrams were displayed on a keyboard linked to a computer, and subjects could choose words by pressing the appropriate symbol on the board.

The chimpanzees trained in this program soon showed performances very similar to those of Washoe. One of the participants, a female named Lana, developed an intriguing ability to create novel word combinations. Some of the foods that she ate were not assigned lexigrams by the experimenters, and Lana therefore invented her own names to request them. When she wanted a cucumber, for example, she asked for "banana which-is green," and she requested an orange by using the lexigrams for "apple which-is orange (color)" (Rumbaugh & Savage-Rumbaugh, 1994).

One of the most difficult issues in studying language in animals is knowing whether they understand the meaning of the words they are using, or whether they are using them only because they have been reinforced for doing so in the past. If a chimpanzee chooses the lexigram for "banana" in order to obtain a banana, for example, this might involve no greater intelligence than a rat's pressing a lever to obtain food pellets. Lana's creation of novel word combinations suggests more intentional and meaningful behavior, but it could be argued, as Terrace and his colleagues did in the case of Washoe, that such behavior was random, or cued by the experimenters. Before concluding that chimpanzees understand the meaning of the words they are using, a characteristic known as **semanticity,** we need evidence that words are evoking some sort of mental representations of the objects that they symbolize. If a chimpanzee sees the lexigram for banana, for example, does this evoke a representation of a banana in the chimpanzee's brain?

Unfortunately, it is not possible to observe animals' mental states, and so there will probably always be some level of doubt about the linguistic capacity of chimpanzees. Indirect evidence, however, supports the view that chimpanzees genuinely understand the meaning of words. One poignant example concerns Washoe. When she was 15, she had a baby. He was ill at birth, and Washoe had to be anesthetized so that the infant could be removed for treatment. He recovered and was returned to her, but several weeks later he again became ill, so that a pediatrician again needed to anesthetize her. When she saw the needle, she began to scream and sign "My baby, my baby."

Sadly, the infant died. When Washoe saw her trainer the next day, her first sign was "Baby?" The trainer replied by signing "Baby gone, baby finished." Washoe's response was dramatic:

> *Washoe dropped her arms that had been cradled in the baby sign position . . . broke eye contact and slowly moved away to a corner of the cage . . . She continued for the next several days to isolate herself from any interactions with the humans and her signing dropped off to almost nothing. Her eyes appeared to be vacant or distant.*
> (Fouts, Hirsch, & Fouts, 1982, p. 170)

It is difficult to read this account without feeling that Washoe had some understanding of the meaning of the signs that were used.

More formal (and less painful) evidence on this point comes from a study by Savage-Rumbaugh, Rumbaugh, Smith, and Lawson (1980). The subjects in this study were two male chimpanzees, Sherman and Austin. During the first phase, they were taught lexigrams for more than 20 different foods and tools. They were then taught to associate three of the foods with a new lexigram representing "food," and similarly to associate three of the tools with a new lexigram representing "tool." Finally, they were shown the lexigrams for the other foods and tools and asked to label each lexigram as either a food or a tool. Sherman labeled 15 of the 16 lexigrams correctly, and Austin correctly labeled 17 out of 17. If Sherman and Austin had seen the lexigrams simply as arbitrary geometrical patterns, it is difficult to see how they could have decided whether the lexigrams represented foods or tools; their success suggests that they knew what object each lexigram represented.

Kanzi's comprehension of English.   As impressive as Sherman and Austin's achievements were, they were eventually to be eclipsed by those of a bonobo chimpanzee named Kanzi. (Bonobos are one of two chimpanzee species.) Kanzi's mother was one of the early participants in the Georgia State training program, but the mother proved to be a very slow learner and made little progress. Though Kanzi was present during his mother's training sessions, the experimenters made no effort to train him. Nevertheless, when Kanzi was 2½ years old, the experimenters were astonished to discover that he understood the meaning of the lexigrams that the experimenters had tried and failed to teach his mother. Simply by watching this training, he seemed to have worked out for himself what the symbols meant. The experimenters then initiated an active training program for Kanzi, and by the time he was 5½, his lexigram vocabulary had increased to 149 words.

At this point, Kanzi astonished the experimenters for a second time when they discovered that he had also learned to understand human speech. Again, simply by listening to the conversations of his trainers as they taught him to use the lexigrams, Kanzi had learned the meaning of a number of English words and phrases. In one test of his abilities, he was placed in a room containing 12 objects and given verbal instructions about what to do with these objects. (The experimenter was located in an adjacent room behind a one-way mirror, in order to avoid inadvertently providing Kanzi with cues through gestures—see the discussion of Clever Hans in Chapter 1.) When Kanzi was given novel instructions such as "Hide the gorilla" and "Take the potato outdoors and get the apple," he responded correctly to 74%, even though he had never heard them before. To provide a baseline for comparison, the same instructions were given to Alia, the 2½-year-old daughter of one of Kanzi's caretakers, who had been given exactly the same training in the use of lexigrams; she responded correctly to 66% (Savage-Rumbaugh, Murphy, Sevcik, Brakke, Williams, & Rumbaugh, 1993).

One of the important characteristics of most human languages is that different meanings can be expressed by changing the order of the words in a sentence—the sentence "Tom bit the dog," for example, has a very different meaning from "The dog bit Tom." This characteristic is important because it helps to make possible the richness of human language—by changing word order, we can use a small number of words to express an enormous range of ideas. Savage-Rumbaugh and colleagues also tested Kanzi's sensitivity to word order by giving him instructions in which the same words were presented in different orders—for example, "Put the raisins in the shoe" versus "Put the shoe in the raisins." Again, Kanzi's performance was far above chance, as he responded correctly to 81% of these sentences; Alia was correct on only 64%.

Incredible though it may seem, Kanzi appears to have learned English simply by listening to the conversations of those around him, and his vocabulary and comprehension appear roughly on a par with those of a 2½-year-old child. More than 100 years ago, Charles Darwin wrote that "The difference in mind between man and the higher animals, great as it is, certainly is one of degree and not of kind." (Darwin, 1871/1920, p. 128) It is beginning to look as if he might have been right.

12.4 THE NEURAL NETWORK SOLUTION (TO ASSOCIATION, ABSTRACTION, AND EVERYTHING . . .)

It appears that animals are capable of forming concepts, and that the methods they rely on for doing so are often similar to those used by humans. In both, associative processes play an important role, as subjects associate exemplars with a response (for example, a name; pecking) and then generalize this response to similar stimuli. In at least some situations, however, animals as well as humans combine information from exemplars to form a more abstract representation of the concept, whether in the form of a rule or a prototype.

Given this evidence, we ideally would like a theory of learning that can encompass associative as well as abstractive processes, and learning in animals as well as in humans. In short, a theory of everything.

This might at first seem an outrageous requirement—or, at any rate, one exceedingly unlikely to be fulfilled—but a theory has recently emerged that supporters claim has the potential to meet it. It offers an explanation for virtually every aspect of learning, from classical conditioning in animals to concept and language learning in humans. And it achieves all this using what is essentially a single, simple principle.

A variety of terms have been suggested to describe this new approach: *connectionist*, *parallel-and-distributed processing*, and *neural network*. We will use the term neural network, because it conveys a clearer sense of the model's fundamental assumptions.

Brains and Computers

At the heart of this new approach is a belief that psychological theories should be modeled as closely as possible on the known properties of the brain. To understand this view, it may be helpful to begin by contrasting it with the computer or information-processing metaphor that has dominated cognitive psychology for the past few decades. As we saw in Chapter 9, the basic structure of a digital computer consists of a central processing unit (CPU) and a memory store: The CPU retrieves items from memory, carries out a sequence of operations, such as addition and subtraction, and then transfers the result back to memory. The computer is capable of carrying out only very simple operations, but by performing them in an appropriate sequence and at extraordinarily high speeds—more than a million operations in a single second—it can solve highly complex problems.

The brain, however, is organized very differently. For one thing, there is no obvious distinction in the brain between the processing of information and its storage; there is only one unit, the neuron, that must somehow carry out both functions. As we saw in Chapter 2, when a neuron is stimulated, it produces an electrical impulse that is transmitted along the long part of the cell called the axon. When this impulse arrives at the axon terminal, it causes the release of neurotransmitter chemicals that move across the synaptic gap to the next neuron in the chain; the arrival of these neurotransmitters causes the second neuron to produce an electrical impulse, and so on. The brain consists of an almost unimaginably large number of such neurons—more than 10,000,000,000—organized in densely interconnected networks called **neural networks.** A single neuron may receive inputs from up to 50,000 other neurons. Figure 12.6 shows a small section of the brain, with some of the connections between the neurons. The complexity of the interconnections is apparent.

In contrast to most computers, then, which carry out only a single operation at a time, the brain contains a vast array of neurons of which many millions

FIGURE 12.6   Drawing of cortical neurons, illustrating the dense network of interconnections. (Conel, 1963)

or even billions are active at a given moment. In the terminology of electrical circuitry, the brain is a massive parallel system in which an enormous number of circuits operate simultaneously. Unlike most computers, then, the brain is characterized by **parallel processing.**

This difference in architecture has important implications for function: The structure of the brain allows it to easily solve problems that computers find difficult, if not impossible. For example, most people find it easy to read other people's handwriting, but this trivial skill is beyond the power of most current computers. Neural network theorists believe that the computer has thus been a partially misleading model for the functioning of the brain, and that psychological models should be based instead on the architecture of the brain—that is, they should incorporate neuronlike units that can assume only a limited range of firing states, and that are interconnected in dense networks.

A Neural Network Model

In outline, neural network models are surprisingly simple and rest on three basic assumptions:

1. *Neural network.* There is a network of neurons, with every neuron in the network connected to every other neuron.

2. *Transmission.* When one neuron in a network becomes active, this activity is transmitted to the other neurons in the network; the amount of excitation transmitted between any two neurons depends on the strength of the neural connection between them.

3. *Learning.* If two neurons within the network are active at the same time, the connection between them will be strengthened, so that future activity in one of these neurons will be more likely to produce activity in the other neuron.

In essence, these assumptions are virtually identical to those made by Pavlov almost 100 years ago: When two cortical centers are active simultaneously, the connection between them will be strengthened. Neural network models, however, incorporate two changes in Pavlov's ideas, which have far-reaching implications for these models' ability to predict behavior. First, they assume that the networks involved are quite massive, so that associations will be formed simultaneously among very large numbers of active neurons. Second, they provide a mathematical formula that allows us to calculate exactly how much each of these connections will be strengthened. Together, these assumptions allow us to make predictions about the brain's functioning in a way that goes far beyond anything Pavlov ever attempted or could have attempted—because of the large number of connections, the model's predictions can be calculated only with the aid of computers.

The predictions of neural network models depend critically on the formula used for calculating how connections are strengthened. A number of formulas or rules have been suggested, but one of the most influential has been the *delta rule*.

Learning in a neural network. To understand this rule, it may be helpful to begin by considering some of the physiological mechanisms involved in learning. Suppose, for example, that a dog participated in a classical conditioning experiment in which a tone was repeatedly followed by food. How might these pairings result in the strengthening of a connection within the dog's brain?

Much of the research on neural mechanism in learning has been carried out with a sea slug called *aplysia*, because this slug has a very simple nervous system in which it is relatively easy to observe neural changes during learning. Our understanding of this system is still incomplete, but learning seems to depend on changes at the synapses where neurons connect to each other. In particular, Byrne (1985) has proposed that learning is mediated by changes in the capacity of neurons to produce and release neurotransmitters at their synapses. We will use his proposed system for *aplysia* to suggest how classical conditioning might occur in a dog, though the synaptic mechanisms in dogs will almost certainly prove more complex.

Figure 12.7a illustrates a simplified version of a synaptic connection between two neurons in the dog's brain, which we will call a CS neuron and a US neuron. When the CS neuron is activated, an electrical impulse is transmitted along its axon, and the arrival of this impulse at the neuron's terminals causes the release of chemical neurotransmitters. (See Section 2.1.) These neurotransmitters then move across the synaptic gap to the US neuron. Prior to conditioning, the amount of neurotransmitters released by the CS neuron is likely to be low, with the result that it is unlikely to trigger an electrical impulse in the US neuron. (Stimulation must exceed a certain threshold before an electrical impulse is produced in a neuron's axon.)

To help explain what happens during conditioning, Figure 12.7b provides a somewhat fuller illustration of the neurons involved. As shown in the figure, the CS and US neurons each receive input from sensory neurons. When a tone is presented, activity in the receptors in the dog's ear is transmitted through a Tone neuron to the CS neuron. (Remember, we are simplifying; many more neurons are almost certainly involved.) The CS neuron then produces its own

FIGURE 12.7   Neural connections. (a) A simplified, two-neuron representation of classical conditioning. Neurotransmitters released by the CS neuron stimulate the US neuron. (b) An expanded representation, showing sensory inputs to the CS and US neurons. (c) A section of a neural network, showing connections between neurons within the network, together with sensory input from outside the network.

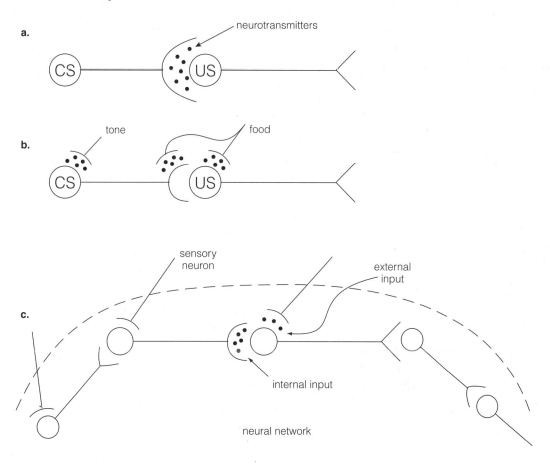

electrical impulse, which leads to the release of neurotransmitters from its terminals. Similarly, when food is presented, activity in receptors in the dog's mouth is transmitted through a Food neuron to the US neuron. However, as shown in the figure, Byrne proposed that the Food neuron is also connected to the terminals of the CS neuron. When food is presented, therefore, neurotransmitters are released at the Food–CS synapse as well as at the Food–US synapse.

According to Byrne, if neurotransmitters arrive at a CS terminal at a time when the terminal is already engaged in releasing neurotransmitters, a complex chemical sequence is initiated that results in a permanent increase in the terminal's capacity to produce neurotransmitters. (See Byrne, 1985, for details.) The next time the CS is presented, therefore, the terminals of the CS neuron will release a larger quantity of neurotransmitters, thereby increasing the likelihood of activating the US neuron. In other words, the connection between the CS and US neurons has been strengthened, so that activity in the CS neuron is more likely to trigger activity in the US neuron. Other models of how the connections between neurons are strengthened have also been proposed (for example, Hawkins & Kandel, 1984), but for our purposes the precise physiological mechanism is not important. The key point is simply that simultaneous activity in two neurons is likely to result in strengthening of the connection between them.

The delta rule. We can now return to the delta rule. So far, we have focused on two cortical neurons, a CS neuron and a US neuron; we will now assume that these are just two neurons within a much larger neural network. In the same way that the CS and US neurons received input from sensory neurons, we will assume that each of the other neurons in the network also receive input from sensory neurons lying outside the network. Figure 12.7c illustrates several neurons from this larger network, together with their sensory inputs. We will call the excitation that any of the neurons receives from a neuron within the network the *internal input*—that is, the input from within the network. We will call the excitation that each neuron receives from outside the network the *external input*.

According to the logic we have already sketched, if two neurons are active at the same time, then connection between them will be strengthened. How much, though, will this connection be strengthened? The delta rule states that the increase in the strength of any connection depends on the relationship between the internal and external inputs to the neuron. Ignoring some of the complexities of the actual formula, the delta rule in essence states that the change in the internal connection between two neurons (ΔI) is proportional to the difference between the internal and external inputs:

$$\Delta I = c \ (external \ input - internal \ input)$$

where c is some constant.

This formula has the effect of increasing the internal input to a neuron until it matches the external input. To illustrate this in concrete terms, suppose that in our classical conditioning example the presentation of food results in strong activation of the US neuron. Prior to conditioning, though, the connection between the CS and US neurons is weak, so that presentation of the tone does not induce any activity in the US neuron. If we assume, for purposes of illustration, that the external input to the US neuron has a value of 10 units, that the internal input has a value of 0 units, and that the constant c has a value of .5, then if the tone and food were presented together, the change in the strength of the CS–US connection would be:

$$\Delta I = c \ (external \ input - internal \ input)$$

$$= .5 \ (10\text{--}0) = .5 \ (10) = 5$$

In other words, the connection between the CS and US neurons would be substantially strengthened.

If the tone and food were now presented together for a second trial, the strength of the connection would again be increased, but not by quite as much. Specifically, on the second trial the strength of the internal input would initially be 5, and the change in the strength of the connection produced on this trial would be:

$$\Delta I = c \ (external \ input - internal \ input)$$

$$= .5 \ (10\text{--}5) = .5 \ (5) = 2.5$$

Over a series of conditioning trials, the strength of the CS–US connection would continue to be adjusted toward that of the Food–US connection, but at a progressively slower rate. Eventually, when the internal and external inputs matched, additional pairings would have no further effect. In this way, the delta rule adjusts the strength of the internal input from the network until it matches that of an external source; in the case of salivary conditioning, this means that the CS would eventually produce just as much salivation as the US.

The Rescorla-Wagner model. Does any of this seem familiar? As you perhaps have realized already, the delta rule achieves at the neural level exactly what the Rescorla-Wagner model achieves at the associative or behavioral level. The delta rule adjusts a neural connection so that it will match a value determined by input from outside the network; similarly, the Rescorla-Wagner model adjusts the strength of the CS–US association so that it will match an external value determined by the US used.

Indeed, not only is the logic of the two approaches the same, but it turns out the formulas used are mathematically identical (see Sutton & Barto, 1981), even though they were developed entirely independently. (The delta rule was developed by Widrow & Hoff, 1960, for use in designing optimal electrical circuits.) That workers in different areas have independently converged on the same rule might just be coincidence. But it could also be an indication that this rule is an optimal solution to the problem of how to modify electrical circuits to make them more adaptive—a solution that not only has been discovered by engineers for the design of electrical circuits, but also has emerged in the course of evolution as the basis for the operation of the brain's neural circuits.

Explaining Concept Learning

In one sense, then, neural network models are little more than the Rescorla-Wagner model applied not just to two neurons but to many thousands of neurons in a vast network. But how does all of this help us to understand the problem of concept learning with which we began?

McClelland and Rumelhart. Consider again a child learning the concept *dog*. No two dogs are identical—dachshunds, poodles, and bulldogs all differ greatly—but somehow the child abstracts the common features. McClelland and Rumelhart (1985) have shown how a neural network presented with many instances of *dog* could similarly abstract a prototype and then use this prototype to classify new examples. In a real network in the brain, many tens of thousands of neurons would be involved, but to simplify their calculations McClelland and Rumelhart assumed a much smaller network containing 24 units. We will simplify their analysis still further and assume a system with only 8 units.

Suppose, then, that a child's visual system contains only eight receptors, and that each responds to the presence of a single feature. We will assume that four of these receptors respond to features that are characteristic of dogs. Receptor D_{Legs} detects the presence of four legs; receptor D_{Tail} the presence of a tail; D_{Fur} the presence of fur; and D_{Ears} the presence of floppy ears. The other four receptors, which we will label N_1, N_2, and so on, are sensitive to features that are less typical of dogs, though some dogs might have them, nevertheless. (Receptor N_1, for example, might detect the presence of scars.) Each of these receptors is connected to one of the units in an 8-unit network within the brain (Figure 12.8). Thus, if the child sees an animal with a tail, unit D_{Tail} in the network will be activated; if the animal has four legs, unit D_{Legs} will be activated; and so on.

Suppose that our imaginary child was exposed to a dog. The visual cues from the dog would stimulate the receptors in the child's eyes, and these in turn would stimulate the corresponding units in the brain. According to the model, the connections between these active units would then be strengthened. To see what the consequences might be, McClelland and Rumelhart created a series of imaginary dogs and "presented" each dog individually to the child. That is, when one of these dogs was present, they assumed that the corresponding units in the network would be activated, and they then used the delta rule to calculate how much the strength of the connections between these active units would be modified.

The first requirement was a set of imaginary dogs to present to the network. To create these dogs, McClelland and Rumelhart began by creating a prototypical dog that would have all the typical features of a dog—in this simplified model, the features D_{Legs}, D_{Tail}, D_{Fur} and D_{Ears}. Real dogs, of course, do not have all the features of the prototype: Some have only three legs, some have no tails,

FIGURE 12.8   A simplified representation of the McClelland and Rumelhart (1985) model. (a) An 8-unit neural network, showing all possible interconnections. Each circle represents a single neuron in the network. (b) The same network after exposure to many exemplars of the concept *dog*. Strong connections involving the prototypical features are shown in heavy lines so that it is clear that these features have become strongly interconnected.

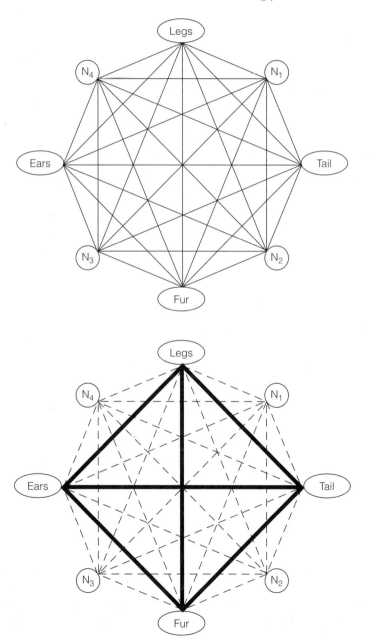

and so on. McClelland and Rumelhart therefore created individual dogs by assigning each dog somewhat different features. For example, one dog might be assigned the features $D_{Legs}D_{Fur}D_{Ears}N_1$—it would thus have had three features typical of dogs but also one atypical feature, in the same way that a dachshund has many typical dog features but also unusually short legs. A second dog might have the features $D_{Legs}D_{Tail}D_{Fur}N_3$, and so on. McClelland and Rumelhart created a total of 50 individual dogs in this way, and then calculated the effects of exposure to these dogs on connections within the neural network.

Suppose, for example, that the first dog to be presented possessed the features $D_{Legs}D_{Tail}D_{Fur}N_2$. Because the D_{Legs} and D_{Tail} units in the network would be activated simultaneously, the connection between them would be strengthened. Similarly, the connection from D_{Legs} to D_{Fur} would be strengthened, the connection between D_{Tail} and D_{Fur}, and so on. Using the delta rule, McClelland and Rumelhart calculated the changes in the strength of each of these connections. They then calculated the changes that would occur as a result of exposure to the second dog, and so on, until all 50 dogs had been presented.

The result is shown in Figure 12.8b, in which heavy lines have been drawn only between those units in the network that have become strongly connected. (Because nonprototype features often occurred together, some of these features also became associated with one another, but these connections were not as strong.) The crucial result stands out clearly: The features that are typical of dogs have all become strongly interconnected, with the result that activation of any subset of these features would be likely to activate the remainder.

Implications. This outcome might sound trivial, but it has some surprisingly powerful implications. One is that the network can *recognize new dogs*. For example, suppose that the network is presented with a new dog that it has never seen before. Because this new dog will have many typical dog features, it will activate the entire set of dog features in the network. As a result, the network will respond to this new dog in the same way as it responded to old ones. To see this, it may be helpful to imagine that all the dog features in the network are connected to a single output unit—for example, a unit that controls the child's vocal cords and produces the word "dog." Whenever a new dog was presented, its features would activate all the typical dog features, and these would in turn activate the word "dog." The network would thus respond to a new dog in exactly the same way as to an old one, because both would activate the complete set of dog units.

A second feature of this result is that the network would respond in this way *only* to dogs. That is, the network would not respond indiscriminately to any input by saying "dog"—it would respond in this way only to genuine exemplars of the category *dog*. To demonstrate this point, McClelland and Rumelhart ran a second simulation in which they presented the network with stimuli derived from three prototypes: one of a dog, another of a cat, and a third of a bagel. To help assess the network's ability to categorize these stimuli, another eight features were added to the network to represent the category names—*cat*, *dog*, or *bagel*. (The network now contained a total of 24 features, 16 of which could be used to represent the visual properties of each object and 8 to represent its category name.) The experimenters then exposed the network to 50 exemplars drawn from each of the three categories, and each of these exemplars was accompanied by its category name. On each of these simulated exposures, therefore, the network would strengthen the connections between all the perceptual features, and also between the perceptual features and the features representing the category name.

To find out what the network had learned, McClelland and Rumelhart then ran test trials in which they presented the network with new exemplars from the three categories. In each case, they found that the exemplars activated the correct category name. Furthermore, when they presented the network with just the name, they found that the network activated the appropriate set of visual features. In effect, when presented with the word *dog*, the network responded with an image of this animal; when presented with a picture of a dog, the network recalled its name. The response to cats and bagels was similarly accurate.

Summarizing the evidence to this point, when the network was exposed to exemplars from a category, it formed strong associations between the features that tended to occur together. This has the important effect that a subset of prototypical features will activate the full set. As a result, the network can respond appropriately to an incomplete or distorted version of a familiar stimulus. If part of a dog is obscured by a tree, for example, the presence of the remaining features might still be sufficient to activate the prototype and thus produce recognition. Similarly, the network can categorize stimuli it has never seen before: As long as enough features of the prototype are present, the entire prototype will be activated.

McClelland and Rumelhart went on to show that the network can preserve information about individual dogs as well as the prototype. In our discussion of concept learning, we saw that individuals can categorize new stimuli by comparing them to individual exemplars as well as to a prototype. Clearly, the brain can store information about individual exemplars as well as prototypes, and it turns out that neural networks also have this property. In one of the experiments demonstrating this, McClelland and Rumelhart used a computer to simulate the effects of exposing their network to two particular dogs—one named *Rover*, the other named *Fido*—as well as other dogs that were simply called *dog*. When they tested the network by activating the features representing the name dog, they found that this activity spread through the network's connections to activate the typical visual features of a dog—in effect, the network produced an image of a typical dog. Similarly, when they activated the features corresponding to the names *Rover* or *Fido*, the network responded by activating the neurons representing the visual characteristics of that dog. Their network thus satisfies all the criteria for a model of concept learning outlined in the previous sections: It stores information about individual exemplars of a category as well as the properties that they share, and it can use this information to accurately categorize stimuli it has never previously encountered.

And Everything . . .

In the brief time that neural network models have been in existence, they have proved able to account for a wide range of phenomena in classical and operant conditioning, including occasion setting, latent inhibition, shaping, and the formation of cognitive maps (for example, Brown & Sharp, 1995; Donahoe & Dorsel, 1997; Schmajuk, Lamoureux, & Holland, 1998). In addition, they also have accounted for a wide range of phenomena in the very different domain of concept learning (e.g., McClelland & Rumelhart, 1986; Gluck & Bower, 1988; Erickson & Kruschke, 1998). If this were all these models could do, it would be remarkable enough, but evidence suggests that they might be able to do much more. One example is their ability to account for many aspects of language and thought. An important problem in psycholinguistics, for example, concerns how children learn the rules governing the past tense of verbs. The most common method of forming the past tense of a verb in English is to add the letters *ed* to the end of the present tense form (jump—jumped, open—opened, and so on). However, many verbs follow different patterns (run—ran, send—sent, and so on). At first, children learn the correct form for all the verbs they know, but then, as their vocabulary grows, they begin to use the *ed* form for all verbs, even ones for which it is inappropriate (*runned, sended,* and so on), and for which they previously used the correct form. Finally, they return to using the correct form for all verbs. As complex as this developmental sequence is, Rumelhart and McClelland (1986) have shown that a neural network analysis predicts not only the sequence but also some of its finer details, including which forms are most likely to be confused.

There is also evidence that networks can learn the complex rules that govern English pronunciation. We tend to take our ability to read and pronounce English words for granted, but children and adults who learn English as a foreign language can testify to the baffling complexity of the rules governing its pronunciation. In a striking demonstration of the power of neural networks, however, Sejnowski and Rosenberg (1987) constructed a demonstration network that, when given examples of English words together with information about their pronunciation, can learn to read—in the sense that, when given the letters of an English word it has never previously encountered, it can pronounce that word correctly using a voice synthesizer. In one of their tests, they presented the network with a set of words that it had never seen before, and it pronounced 95% of these new words correctly. Given the extraordinary variability of English spelling rules—George Bernard Shaw once pointed out that, on the basis of how its components were sometimes pronounced, the made-up word *ghoti* could be pronounced "fish"—this is a quite remarkable feat.

A Preliminary Evaluation

The evidence we have reviewed suggests that neural network models might be able to account for some of the most sophisticated aspects of human thought, including our ability to learn concepts and languages, and to do so on the basis of a learning mechanism almost identical to that observed in slugs, a primitive creature with a brain of only a few hundred neurons. (See Gelperin, 1986.)

If the fundamental mechanism of the brain is the same in humans as in slugs, you might wonder, why are humans so much more intelligent? One difference lies in the sheer size of the networks involved: A network with millions of neurons can carry out computations and store data to a degree far beyond that of much smaller networks.

In addition, there are almost certainly critical differences in the organization of the networks. We have emphasized the role of parallel processing—many neurons operating at once—but we must also consider **sequential processing,** in which information processed in one subsystem is passed on to a second subsystem, and so on. Thus, although McClelland and Rumelhart assumed that a feature would be represented by a single neuron in the network, in reality the identification of features is in itself a massive undertaking, requiring many thousands or millions of neurons spread over a number of processing stages. In other words, before reaching our "prototype" network, visual input will already have undergone extensive processing; similarly, extensive processing will almost certainly follow this stage—for example, in combining concepts into sentences, plans of action, and so forth.

Neural networks, then, are not quite as simple as our initial discussion implied, and neural network models must eventually be made far more complex to account for sequential as well as parallel processing. (For contrasting views of the accomplishments of existing models, see Pinker & Prince, 1988, and Seidenberg, 1993.) Such complexity should not surprise us; it would be astonishing if a model of a system containing billions of neurons were not complex. What is far more remarkable is that the fundamental mechanism upon which the entire system is based appears to be genuinely simple, and that even small networks of randomly interconnected neurons can be very powerful.

A possible objection to the approach we have been outlining is that it is too mechanistic: Instead of dealing with thoughts, images, and emotions, we seem to be lost in a sea of neurons. The difference in the two accounts is perhaps akin to the anecdote about a swan swimming in a lake: seen from above, all cool grace and elegance, but underneath the surface, paddling away furiously. The two views are not contradictory; they simply describe different levels of analysis. A neural account does not deny the reality of thoughts or emotions any more than an analysis of atomic structure denies the reality of thunderstorms or planets. An understanding of what is going on beneath the surface, however, can enhance our ability to understand and influence events at the higher level.

12.5 ASSOCIATIVE LEARNING AND COGNITION

In a sense, this whole text has been about the tension between two views of learning. Pavlov believed that education and training "are really nothing more than the results of an establishment of new nervous connections" (Pavlov, 1927, p. 26), and that an understanding of how associations are formed during conditioning would inevitably lead to an understanding of all learned behavior. Cognitive theorists such as Tolman, on the other hand, argued that learning was far too complex, too goal oriented, to be explained in terms of simple associations: Something more complicated, more like an expectation or a cognitive map, was required.

The history of learning theory can be seen as a series of swings between these two views, with cognitive theorists providing seemingly decisive evidence against associative accounts, only to have associative theorists show how, with a relatively minor adjustment, their theories could account for the new evidence after all. Thus, when the evidence for learning without responding seemed to show that animals could anticipate the consequences of their actions, Hull showed how this behavior could be explained if S–R theory was broadened to include associations between covert events as well as overt ones. Similarly, Rescorla's demonstration that contiguity is not sufficient for conditioning—the CS and US must also be contingent—seemed at first to require that animals be capable of calculating complex probabilities of events over time. Eventually, however, Rescorla and Wagner showed how this behavior too could be understood in terms of associations, provided that the associative strength of all the stimuli present during conditioning was taken into account. And now, almost before learning theorists have had time to assimilate the evidence that animal learning is far more complex than had been supposed, with animals having the capacity to learn concepts and strategies and cognitive maps, an explanation of these behaviors in fundamentally associative terms has already been proposed by neural network theorists and others (for example, Astley & Wasserman, 1992; Couvillon & Bitterman, 1992).

In Chapter 8, we considered one possible reconciliation of the two viewpoints—that both might be right, with learning involving relatively simple associations in some situations but more complex expectations in others. Then, in Chapter 9, we considered some of the cognitive processes that contribute to

FIGURE 12.9   A three-level analysis of associative learning.

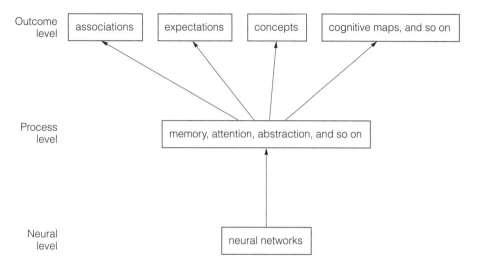

shaping the two outcomes, including how events are coded and retrieved. The material reviewed in this chapter can be interpreted as providing a number of amendments to this emerging model of learning, summarized in Figure 12.9.

First, at the level of outcomes, it might be useful to categorize learning not only in terms of relatively simple forms such as associations and expectations, but also in terms of more complex structures, such as cognitive maps, concepts and rules. It is still not clear whether these are truly distinct forms of learning or variants of a single basic process, but in our present state of ignorance it is perhaps worth listing them separately, if only to emphasize the breadth and variety of learning.

A second amendment to our model is the inclusion of abstraction among the cognitive processes that shape learning. The crucial role of abstraction in the learning of complex concepts and rules is probably clear by now, but abstraction might be equally important in even the simplest forms of learning. Consider, for example, a rat learning to press a bar to obtain food. We tend to think of this as a relatively trivial accomplishment, but from the perspective of the rat it certainly is not. On one occasion it presses the bar with 10 grams of force with its right paw while holding its head at an angle of 45 degrees and breathing rapidly; on another occasion, it presses with 12 grams of force with its left paw while holding its head at 60 degrees and raising its tail; and so on. We know that the requirement for reinforcement is simply how far the bar travels, but the rat does not: It must abstract the critical feature from experiences that have varied widely over many dimensions. Even seemingly simple learning thus requires the same cognitive processes of memory, attention, and abstraction required by more obviously demanding tasks such as problem solving and language learning. This does not mean that all forms of learning are equivalent in complexity—learning to press a bar is undoubtedly easier than coming to terms with Einstein's theory of relativity or the Rescorla-Wagner model—but the difference in the skills required may be less dramatic than the terms *associative* and *cognitive* tend to imply. Associative learning may be simpler, but this does not mean that it is simple.

Still a third change to our conception of learning, and the one that in the end might prove the most important, is the introduction of a third level of analysis based on interactions at the neural level. The fundamental unit of analysis at this third level consists of associations between neurons, and neural network models are thus closely related to earlier associative accounts, such as Pavlov's and Hull's. Indeed, if these models are able to explain concept learning and language acquisition as they claim to (that is, if the claims can be supported), they would provide striking confirmation for Pavlov's claim that an understanding of conditioning would ultimately lead to an understanding of all learned behavior. (Recall that the central principle of these network models, the delta rule, is essentially a restatement of the Rescorla-Wagner model of classical conditioning.)

In other respects, however, these models are much closer in spirit to cognitive analyses of learning than to S–R theory. S–R theorists argued that behavior should be analyzed in terms of simple, observable events, such as stimuli and responses. Neural network models, however, accept the crucial role of internal processes in determining how we respond to a stimulus. Rather than denying cognitive processes, such as memory, attention, or abstraction, network theorists make them a central focus of their investigations but then try to account for these cognitive processes by more primitive interactions at a neural level. In terms of our earlier swan analogy, network theorists do not deny that swans swim gracefully; instead, they try to explain how they do it.

Neural network models, then, represent a new and richer version of our earlier attempt to reconcile associative and cognitive approaches to learning. As in that earlier synthesis, network models accept the reality of both associations and expectations at a behavioral level, and they also accept the importance of cognitive processes, such as memory and attention, in shaping those outcomes. They suggest, however, that these processes can themselves be understood at a more primitive level, with the fundamental principle being the association. It is too soon to say whether these models will succeed, but their solid grounding in the known structure of the brain gives them an inherent plausibility. If they do succeed, the emergence of these models might someday be seen as the single most important step in the evolution of psychology.

12.6 SUMMARY

To benefit from past experience, it is vital that we be able to sort events into categories: If we reacted to every new stimulus as if it were unique, unlike any we had ever encountered, we could never bring our past experience to bear. One way people form concepts is by consciously testing hypotheses. If we are told that a group of stimuli come from the same category, for example, then we might systematically test hypotheses about the critical features that define this category. But we can also detect common features in a less formal manner. When exposed to a set of stimuli, we might abstract the features that they share and store this information in the form of a prototype. If shown a series of dogs, for example, we might form an image of a typical dog and then evaluate potential new members of the concept by comparing them to this prototype. Finally, we might categorize stimuli even more simply by comparing test stimuli to known exemplars of the category: If a test stimulus closely resembles a dog that we have already encountered, we may conclude that it, too, must be a dog.

It was long assumed that only humans had the ability to form concepts, but Herrnstein and Loveland (1964) showed that pigeons could learn to peck a key when pictures containing a human being were present but not when a human was not present. This suggested that pigeons could abstract the common properties of the positive stimuli—the presence of a human—and in this sense form a concept of human being. Subsequent research, however, suggested that their behavior could also be explained in terms of generalization—the pigeon would peck a new picture if it resembled one that it had seen previously. If the latter explanation were correct, we might be reluctant to conclude that pigeons form concepts in the same sense as humans.

More compelling evidence that animals can form concepts has come from research involving abstract concepts. Pigeons, for example, can learn the abstract concept *same*, responding only when two test stimuli are the same. The most impressive evidence for conceptual behavior, however, has come from studies of language in chimpanzees. This research suggests that chimpanzees not only can learn to name objects but also can combine these names and other words into meaningful sentences. We do not yet fully understand the processes involved, but it currently looks as if animals can form prototypes and abstract rules in much the same way people can.

To explain concept learning, theorists have recently developed an entirely new class of theories called neural network models. These models are based on the known properties of the brain; they assume that neurons are organized in interconnected networks and that activity in one neuron spreads to the other neurons in the network. The transmission of impulses between neurons depends on the strength of the connection between them, and most neural network models assume that this connection is strengthened whenever the neurons are simultaneously active.

A mathematical formula is used to calculate how much a connection is strengthened when two neurons are active at the same time. The most commonly used formula is called the delta rule, and it turns out to be mathematically identical to the formula used in the Rescorla-Wagner model. Neural networks are thus in essence another variant of the Rescorla-Wagner model, except that instead of predicting changes in just one neural connection at a time, these models take into account changes in hundreds or thousands of neurons simultaneously.

Computer simulations of these models have shown that strong connections are formed between elements of a network that are often activated together. If a network is exposed to many exemplars of a concept, for example, then features that are characteristic of the concept, and thus often occur together, will become strongly associated. If a new exemplar is presented that possesses a number of these characteristic features, they will activate the remaining features; as a result, the new exemplar will elicit the same responses as the familiar exemplars. In effect, the network has learned to recognize the concept, and it will respond to all exemplars of the concept in the same way. Neural network models can thus account for many of the features of concept learning, and preliminary evidence suggests that they might also be able to account for phenomena ranging from classical conditioning in slugs to the acquisition of language in humans.

Glossary

Concept A remarkably difficult term to define. One definition is a set of objects or events sharing common features. Another approach views concepts as the mental representations of these events; the idea of a mental representation captures an important element of what we intend by the term, but it is difficult to pin down the meaning of a mental representation in a definition.

All-or-none learning or **one-trial learning** A change in a single trial from responding at chance levels on a problem to responding correctly on all trials. Hypothesis theory attributes one-trial learning to the use of hypotheses: As long as subjects base their responses on incorrect hypotheses, they will respond at chance; but once they adopt the correct hypothesis, they will be correct on every trial. One-trial learning is also found in situations where hypothesis testing is unlikely; taste-aversion conditioning is an example.

Prototype A typical or average instance of a concept; a robin, for example, is considered a prototypical bird.

Abstraction The process of detecting the common features shared by a set of objects or events. Prototype theory proposes that we form a prototype of a concept by abstracting the common features shared by exemplars of the concept.

One way of doing this is to average together the features of the exemplars. If most dogs possess long tails, for example, then the tail of the prototype—formed by averaging the tails of the exemplars—will also be long.

Semanticity One of the characteristics of human language is that words have meaning. That is, words represent objects or events in the real world, and presentations of words are assumed to evoke these representations.

Neural networks Densely interconnected sets of neurons in the brain. Activity in one neuron is transmitted to other neurons within the net.

Parallel processing In the brain, any processes that occur simultaneously. Many of the brain's processes operate in parallel, and neural network theorists believe that this is an important factor in the brain's ability to solve problems, such as reading handwriting, that even the most powerful of modern computers cannot solve. Computers usually rely on **sequential processing,** in which only one operation is carried out at a time.

Review Questions

1. Define the following terms: family resemblance, fuzzy concept, exemplar, typicality effect, lexigram, and delta rule.

2. What is a concept? How does hypothesis theory account for the learning of concepts? What evidence supports this theory? What are its limitations?

3. What is the typicality effect? How do prototype and exemplar theories account for it? Which theory is correct?

4. What evidence suggests that pigeons can learn visual concepts? Why have some psychologists argued that this evidence is not conclusive?

5. Why does evidence for the learning of abstract concepts provide stronger evidence that animals can form concepts? What are examples of such abstract concepts?

6. What evidence suggest that animals can learn the abstract relationship "same"?

7. Two important characteristics of human language are semanticity—words have meanings—and syntax—the meaning of a string of words depends on the order in which they are expressed. What evidence suggests that chimpanzees are capable of using language in a way that satisfies these requirements?

8. How are brains thought to differ from computers in the way they process information?

9. If two neurons are active simultaneously, how could this result in a strengthening of the connection between them?

10. What are the fundamental assumptions of neural network models? How do these assumptions differ from those of Pavlov?

11. What is the delta rule?

12. How could a neural network, which is basically just a set of interconnected electrical units, learn a concept?

13. Aside from possible differences in personality, how do slugs and humans differ?

14. What is the essential difference between associative and cognitive approaches to learning? How many instances can you think of in which associative theorists have provided explanations for evidence that initially seemed irrefutable support for a cognitive analysis? What are the implications of neural network models for this conflict?

References

Acker, M. M., & O'Leary, S. G. (1987). Effects of reprimands and praise on appropriate behavior in the classroom. *Journal of Abnormal Child Psychology, 15,* 549–557.

Adams, C. D., & Dickinson, A. (1981). Instrumental responding following reinforcer devaluation. *Quarterly Journal of Experimental Psychology, 34B,* 109–121.

Ader, R., & Cohen, N. (1985). CNS-immune system interactions: Conditioning phenomena. *Behavior and Brain Sciences, 8,* 379–394.

Allan, L. G. (1993). Human contingency judgments: Rule based or associative? *Psychological Bulletin, 114,* 435–448.

Allen, K. E., Hart, B., Buell, J. S., Harris, F. R., & Wolf, M. M. (1964). Effects of social reinforcement on isolate behavior of a nursery school child. *Child Development, 35,* 511–518.

Allison, J. (1989). The nature of reinforcement. In S. B. Klein & R. R. Mowrer (eds.), *Contemporary learning theories: Instrumental conditioning theory and the impact of biological constraints on learning.* Hillsdale, NJ: Erlbaum.

Allison, M. G., & Ayllon, T. (1980). Behavioral coaching in the development of skills in football, gymnastics, and tennis. *Journal of Applied Behavior Analysis, 13,* 297–314.

Amsel, A. (1962). Frustrative nonreward in partial reinforcement and discrimination learning. *Psychological Review, 69,* 306–328.

Amsel, A. (1994). Précis of *Frustration theory: An analysis of dispositional learning and memory. Psychonomic Bulletin & Review, 1,* 280–296.

Amsel, A., & Roussel, J. (1952). Motivational properties of frustration: I. Effect on a running response of the addition of frustration to the motivational complex. *Journal of Experimental Psychology, 43,* 363–368.

Anderson, J. R. (1995). *Cognitive Psychology and its implications* (4th ed.). New York: W. H. Freeman.

Andrews, E. A., & Braveman, N. S. (1975). The combined effects of dosage level and interstimulus interval on the formation of one-trial poison-based aversions in rats. *Animal Learning and Behavior, 3,* 287–289.

Annau, Z., & Kamin, L. J. (1961). The conditioned emotional response as a function of intensity of the US. *Journal of Comparative and Physiological Psychology, 54,* 428–432.

Anrep, G. V. (1920). Pitch discrimination in the dog. *Journal of Physiology, 53,* 367–385.

Aronfreed, J. (1968). Aversive control of socialization. In D. Levine (ed.), *Nebraska symposium on motivation.* Lincoln: University of Nebraska Press.

Ashcraft, M. H. (1994). *Human memory and cognition* (2nd ed.). New York: Harper-Collins.

Astley, S. L., & Wasserman, E. A. (1992). Categorical discrimination and generalization in pigeons: All negative stimuli are not created equal. *Journal of Experimental Psychology: Animal Behavior Processes, 18*, 193–207.

Azrin, N. H., Holz, W. C., & Hake, D. F. (1963). Fixed-ratio punishment. *Journal of the Experimental Analysis of Behavior, 6*, 141–148.

Azrin, N. H., Hutchinson, R. R., & Hake, D. F. (1966). Extinction-induced aggression. *Journal of the Experimental Analysis of Behavior, 9*, 191–204.

Azrin, R. D., & Hayes, S. C. (1984). The discrimination of interest within a heterosexual interaction: Training, generalization, and effects on social skills. *Behavior Therapy, 15*, 173–184.

Baddeley, A. (1992). Working memory. *Science, 255*, 556–559.

Baddeley, A. (1997). *Human Memory: Theory and practice* (rev. ed.). Hove, UK: Psychology Press.

Baker, B. L. (1969). Symptom treatment and symptom substitution in enuresis. *Journal of Abnormal Psychology, 74*, 42–49.

Balsam, P., & Tomie, A. (eds.). (1985). *Context and learning*. Hillsdale, NJ: Erlbaum.

Bandura, A., & Perloff, B. (1967). Relative efficacy of self-monitored and externally imposed reinforcement systems. *Journal of Personality and Social Psychology, 7*, 111–116.

Bandura, A., Blanchard, E. B., & Ritter, B. (1969). Relative efficacy of desensitization and modeling approaches for inducing behavioral, affective, and attitudinal changes. *Journal of Personality and Social Psychology, 13*, 173–199.

Bandura, A., Ross, D., & Ross, D. A. (1963). Imitation of film-mediated aggressive models. *Journal of Abnormal and Social Psychology, 66*, 3–11.

Barber, T. X. (1976). *Hypnosis: A scientific approach*. New York: Psychological Dimensions.

Bateson, P. (1991). Is imprinting such a special case? In J. R. Krebs & G. Horn (eds.), *Behavioural and neural aspects of learning and memory*. Oxford: Oxford University Press.

Baumrind, D. (1964). Some thoughts on ethics of research: After reading Milgram's "Behavioral Study of Obedience." *American Psychologist, 19*, 421–423.

Baumrind, D. (1991). Parenting styles and adolescent development. In J. Brooks-Gunn, R. Lerner, & A. C. Petersen (eds.), *The encyclopedia of adolescence*. New York: Garland.

Bechara, A., Tranel, D., Damasio, H., Adolphs, R., Rockland, G., & Damasio, A. R. (1995). Double dissociation of conditioning and declarative knowledge relative to the amygdala and hippocampus in humans. *Science, 269*, 1115–1118.

Bednekoff, P. A., Balda, R. P., Kamil, A. C., & Arla, G. (1997). Long-term spatial memory in four seed-caching corvid species. *Animal Behaviour, 53*, 335–341.

Beecher, M. D. (1988). Some comments on the adaptationist approach to learning. In R. C. Bolles & M. D. Beecher (eds.), *Evolution and learning*. Hillsdale, NJ: Erlbaum.

Bellingham, W. P., Gillette-Bellingham, K., & Kehoe, E. J. (1985). Summation and configuration in patterning schedules with the rat and rabbit. *Animal Learning & Behavior, 13*, 152–164.

Belsky, J. (1993). Etiology of child maltreatment: A developmental-ecological analysis. *Psychological Bulletin, 114*, 413–434.

Benhamou, S., & Poucet, B. (1995). A comparative analysis of spatial memory processes. *Behavioural Processes, 35*, 113–126.

Beran, M. J., Rumbaugh, D. M., Savage-Rumbaugh, E. S. (1998). Chimpanzee (*Pan troglodytes*) counting in a computerized testing paradigm. *Psychological Record, 48*, 3–19.

Berkowitz, L. (1989). Frustration-aggression hypothesis: Examination and reformulation. *Psychological Bulletin, 106*, 59–73.

Berkowitz, L., Cochrane, S., & Embree, M. (1979). Influence of aversive experience and the consequences of one's aggression on aggressive behavior. Reported in L. Berkowitz, *A survey of social psychology* (2nd ed.). New York: Holt, Rinehart & Winston.

Bernstein, I. L. (1978). Learned taste aversions in children receiving chemotherapy. *Science, 200,* 1302–1303.

Best, P. J., Best, M. R., & Henggeler, S. (1977). The contribution of environmental non-ingestive cues in conditioning aversive internal consequences. In L. M. Barker, M. R. Best, & M. Domjan (eds.), *Learning mechanisms in food selection.* Waco, TX: Baylor University Press.

Bickel, W. K., Green, L., & Vuchinich, R. E. (1995). Behavioral economics (Editorial). *Journal of the Experimental Analysis of Behavior, 64,* 257–262.

Birnbrauer, J. S., & Leach, D. J. (1993). The Murdoch Early Intervention Program after 2 years. *Behaviour Change, 10,* 63–74.

Blanchard, E. B. (1969). *The relative contributions of modeling, informational influences, and physical contact in the extinction of phobic behavior.* Unpublished doctoral dissertation, Stanford University, Stanford, CA.

Blanchard, R. J., Blanchard, D. C., & Takahashi, L. K. (1977). Reflexive fighting in the rat: Aggressive or defensive behavior? *Aggressive Behavior, 3,* 145–155.

Blough, D. S. (1975). Steady state data and a quantitative model of operant generalization and discrimination. *Journal of Experimental Psychology: Animal Behavior Processes, 1,* 3–21.

Boe, E. E., & Church, R. M. (1967). Permanent effects of punishment during extinction. *Journal of Comparative and Physiological Psychology, 63,* 486–492.

Boland, F. J., Mellor, C. S., & Revusky, S. (1978). Chemical aversion treatment of alcoholism: Lithium as the aversive agent. *Behavior Research and Therapy, 16,* 401–409.

Bolles, R. C. (1970). Species-specific defense reactions and avoidance learning. *Psychological Review, 71,* 32–48.

Bolles, R. C. (1972). Reinforcement, expectancy, and learning. *Psychological Review, 79,* 394–409.

Bolles, R. C. (1975). *Theory of motivation* (2nd ed.). New York: Harper & Row.

Bolles, R. C. (1989). Acquired behaviors, aversive learning. In R. J. Blanchard, P. F. Brain, D. C. Blanchard, & S. Parmigiani (eds.), *Ethoexperimental approaches to the study of behavior.* Boston: Kluwer.

Bolles, R. C., Holtz, R., Dunn, T., & Hill, W. (1980). Comparisons of stimulus learning and response learning in a punishment situation. *Learning and Motivation, 11,* 78 96.

Bootzin, R. R. (1972). Stimulus control treatment for insomnia. *Proceedings of the 80th Annual Convention of the American Psychological Association, 7,* 395–396.

Borden, J. W. (1992). Behavioral treatment of simple phobia. In S. M. Turner, K. S. Calhoun, & H. E. Adams (eds.), *Handbook of clinical behavior therapy* (2nd ed.). New York: Wiley.

Boring, E. G. (1950). *A history of experimental psychology* (2nd ed.). New York: Appleton-Century-Crofts.

Boswell, J. (1791/1964). *The Life of Samuel Johnson.* Oxford: Clarendon.

Bouton, M. E. (1993). Context, time, and memory retrieval in the interference paradigms of Pavlovian learning. *Psychological Bulletin, 114,* 80–99.

Bouton, M. E. (1994). Context, ambiguity, and classical conditioning. *Current Directions in Psychological Science, 3,* 49–53.

Bouton, M. E., & Bolles, R. C. (1979). Contextual control of the extinction of conditioned fear. *Learning and Motivation, 10,* 445–466.

Bouton, M. E., & Fanselow, M. S. (1997). *Learning, motivation and cognition: The functional behaviorism of Robert C. Bolles.* Washington, D.C.: American Psychological Association.

Bouton, M. E., & King, D. A. (1983). Contextual control of the extinction of conditioned fear: Tests for the associative value of the context. *Journal of Experimental Psychology: Animal Behavior Processes, 9,* 248–265.

Bower, G. H. (1981). Mood and memory. *American Psychologist, 36,* 129–148.

Brannon, E. M., & Terrace, H. S. (1998). Ordering of the numerosities 1 to 9 by monkeys. *Science, 282,* 746–749.

Brantner, J. P., & Doherty, M. A. (1983). A review of timeout: A conceptual and methodological analysis. In S. Axelrod & J. Apsche (eds.), *The effects of punishment on human behavior.* New York: Academic.

Braveman, N. S. (1977). Visually guided avoidance of poisonous foods in mammals. In L. M. Barker, M. R. Best, & M. Domjan (eds.), *Learning mechanisms in food selection.* Waco, TX: Baylor University Press.

Bregman, N. J., & McAllister, H. A. (1982). Motivation and skin temperature biofeedback: Yerkes-Dodson revisited. *Psychophysiology, 19,* 282–285.

Breland, K., & Breland, M. (1961). The misbehavior of organisms. *American Psychologist, 16,* 681–684.

Brennan, P. A., & Mednick, S. A. (1994). Learning theory approach to the deterrence of criminal recidivism. *Journal of Abnormal Psychology, 103,* 430–440.

Breukelaar, J. W. C., & Dalrymple-Alford, J. C. (1998). Timing ability and numerical competence in rats. *Journal of Experimental Psychology: Animal Behavior Processes, 24,* 84–97.

Brewer, W. F. (1974). There is no convincing evidence for operant or classical conditioning in adult humans. In W. B. Weimer & D. S. Palermo (eds.), *Cognition and the symbolic processes.* Hillsdale, NJ: Erlbaum.

Broadhurst, P. L. (1957). Emotionality and the Yerkes-Dodson law. *Journal of Experimental Psychology, 54,* 345–352.

Brogden, W. J. (1939). Sensory pre-conditioning. *Journal of Experimental Psychology, 25,* 323–332.

Brooks, D. C., & Bouton, M. E. (1993). A retrieval cue for extinction attenuates spontaneous recovery. *Journal of Experimental Psychology: Animal Behavior Processes, 19,* 77–89.

Brooks, L. Norman, G., & Allen, S. (1991). Role of specific similarity in a medical diagnostic task. *Journal of Experimental Psychology: General, 120,* 278–287.

Brown, J. S., & Jacobs, A. (1949). The role of fear in the motivation and acquisition of responses. *Journal of Experimental Psychology, 39,* 747–759.

Brown, M. A., & Sharp, P. E. (1995). Simulation of spatial learning in the Morris water maze by a neural network model of the hippocampal formation and nucleus accumbens. *Hippocampus, 5,* 171–188.

Brown, M. F., Rish, P. A., Von Culin, J. E., & Edberg, J. A. (1993). Spatial guidance of choice behavior in the radial-arm maze. *Journal of Experimental Psychology: Animal Behavior Processes, 19,* 195–214.

Brown, M. F., & Terrinoni, M. (1996). Control of choice by the spatial configuration of goals. *Journal of Experimental Psychology: Animal Behavior Processes, 22,* 438–446.

Brown, P. L., & Jenkins, H. M. (1968). Autoshaping of the pigeon's key-peck. *Journal of the Experimental Analysis of Behavior, 11,* 1–8.

Brown, R. T. (1975). Following and visual imprinting in ducklings across a wide age range. *Developmental Psychobiology, 8,* 27–33.

Bruner, J. S., Goodnow, J. J., & Austin, G. A. (1956). *A study of thinking.* New York: Wiley.

Bryan, J. H., & Test, M. A. (1967). Models and helping: Naturalistic studies in aiding behavior. *Journal of Personality and Social Psychology, 6,* 400–407.

Bucher, B., & Lovaas, O. I. (1968). The use of aversive stimulation in behavior modification. In M. R. Jones (ed.), *Miami symposium on the prediction of behavior: aversive stimulation.* Coral Gables, FL: University of Miami Press.

Butler, R. A. (1954). Incentive conditions which influence visual exploration. *Journal of Experimental Psychology, 48,* 19–23.

Bykov, K. M. (1957). *The cerebral cortex and the internal organs.* New York: Chemical.

Byrne, J. H. (1985). Neural and molecular mechanisms underlying information storage in *Aplysia:* Implications for learning and memory. *Trends in Neurosciences, 8,* 478–482.

Cacioppo, J. T., Marshall-Goodell, B. S., Tassinary, L. G., & Petty, R. E. (1992). Rudimentary determinants of attitudes: Classical conditioning is more effective when prior knowledge about the attitude stimulus is low than high. *Journal of Experimental Social Psychology, 28,* 207–233.

Cameron, J., & Pierce, W. D. (1996). The debate about rewards and intrinsic motivation: Protests and accusations do not alter the results. *Review of Educational Research, 66,* 39–51.

Capaldi, E. D. (1996). *Why we eat what we eat.* Washington, DC: American Psychological Association.

Capaldi, E. D., Campbell, D. H., Sheffer, J. D., & Bradford, J. P. (1987). Conditioned flavor preferences based on delayed caloric consequences. *Journal of Experimental Psychology: Animal Behavior Processes, 13,* 150–155.

Capaldi, E. D., Hovancik, J. R., & Friedman, F. (1976). Effects of expectancies of different reward magnitudes in transfer from noncontingent pairings to instrumental performance. *Learning and Motivation, 7,* 197–210.

Capaldi, E. J. (1971). Memory and learning: A sequential viewpoint. In W. K. Honig & P. H. R. James (eds.), *Animal memory.* New York: Academic.

Capaldi, E. J. (1994). The sequential view: From rapidly fading stimulus traces to the organization of memory and the abstract concept of number. *Psychonomic Bulletin & Review, 1,* 156–181.

Capaldi, E. J., Alptekin, S., & Birmingham, K. M. (1996). Instrumental performance and time between reinforcements: Intimate relation to learning or memory retrieval? *Animal Learning and Behavior, 24,* 211–220.

Capaldi, E. J., & Kassover, K. (1970). Sequence, number of nonrewards, anticipation, and intertrial interval in extinction. *Journal of Experimental Psychology, 84,* 470–476.

Capaldi, E. J., Miller, D. J., Alptekin, S., & Barry, K. (1990). Organized responding in instrumental learning: Chunks and superchunks. *Learning and Motivation, 21,* 415–433.

Caramazza, A., & Hillis, A. E. (1991). Lexical organization of nouns and verbs in the brain. *Nature, 349,* 788–790.

Carr, J. A. R., & Wilkie, D. M. (1997). Rats use an ordinal timer in a daily time-place learning task. *Journal of Experimental Psychology: Animal Behavior Processes, 23,* 232–247.

Carr, W. J., Loeb, L. S., & Dissinger, M. L. (1965). Responses of rats to sex odors. *Journal of Comparative and Physiological Psychology, 59,* 370–377.

Champion, R. A., & Jones, J. E. (1961). Forward, backward, and pseudoconditioning of the GSR. *Journal of Experimental Psychology, 62,* 58–61.

Cheney, D. L., Seyfarth, R. M., & Silk, J. B. (1995). The role of grunts in reconciling opponents and facilitating interactions among adult female baboons. *Animal Behaviour, 50,* 249-257.

Cheng, P. W. (1997). From covariation to causation: A causal power theory. *Psychological Review, 104,* 367–405.

Cheyne, J. A. (1969). *Punishment and reasoning in the development of self-control.* Paper presented at the R. H. Walters Memorial Symposium at the Biennial Meeting of the Society for Research in Child Development, Santa Monica, CA.

Cheyne, J. A., Goyeche, J. R. M., & Walters, R. H. (1969). Attention, anxiety, and rules in resistance-to-deviation in children. *Journal of Experimental Child Psychology, 8,* 127–139.

Christianson, S. A., & Nilsson, L. G. (1989). Hysterical amnesia: A case of adversively motivated isolation of memory. In T. Archer & L.-G. Nilsson (eds.), *Aversion, avoidance, and anxiety: Perspectives on aversively motivated behavior* (pp. 289–310). Hillsdale, NJ: Erlbaum.

Cialdini, R. B. (1993). *Influence: Science and practice* (3rd ed.). New York: HarperCollins.

Clark, F. C. (1958). The effect of deprivation and frequency of reinforcement on variable-interval responding. *Journal of the Experimental Analysis of Behavior, 1*, 221–227.

Cole, R. P., Barnet, R. C., & Miller, R. R. (1997). An evaluation of conditioned inhibition as defined by Rescorla's two-test strategy. *Learning and Motivation, 28*, 323–341.

Collins, A. M., & Loftus, E. F. (1975). A spreading-activation theory of semantic processing. *Psychological Review, 82*, 407–428.

Colwill, R. M., & Motzkin, D. K. (1994). Encoding of the unconditioned stimulus in Pavlovian conditioning. *Animal Learning and Behavior, 22*, 384–394.

Colwill, R. M., & Rescorla, R. A. (1985). Postconditioning devaluation of a reinforcer affects instrumental responding. *Journal of Experimental Psychology: Animal Behavior Processes, 11*, 120–132.

Colwill, R. M., & Rescorla, R. A. (1986). Associative structures in instrumental learning. In G. H. Bower (ed.), *The psychology of learning and motivation* (Vol. 20). New York: Academic.

Colwill, R. M., & Rescorla, R. A. (1990). Evidence for the hierarchical structure of instrumental learning. *Animal Learning and Behavior, 18*, 71–82.

Comroe, J. H., Jr., & Dripps, R. D. (1977). *The top ten clinical advances in cardiovascular-pulmonary medicine and surgery, 1945–1975*. Final report. January 31, 1977. Bethesda, MD: National Heart, Lung, and Blood Institute.

Conel, J. L. (1963). *Postnatal development of the human cerebral cortex*. Cambridge, MA: Harvard University Press.

Conger, R., & Killeen, P. (1974). Use of concurrent operants in small group research. *Pacific Sociological Review, 17*, 399–416.

Cook, M., Mineka, S., & Trumble, D. (1987). The role of response-produced and exteroceptive feedback in the attenuation of fear over the course of avoidance learning. *Journal of Experimental Psychology: Animal Behavior Processes, 13*, 239–249.

Cook, M., Mineka, S., Wolkenstein, B., & Laitsch, K. (1985). Observational conditioning of snake fear in unrelated rhesus monkeys. *Journal of Abnormal Psychology, 94*, 591–610.

Cook, R. G., Cavoto, K. K., & Cavoto, B. R. (1995). Same-different texture discrimination and concept learning by pigeons. *Journal of Experimental Psychology: Animal Behavior Processes, 21*, 253–260.

Cooper, L. D. (1991). Temporal factors in classical conditioning. *Learning and Motivation, 22*, 129–152.

Couvillon, P. A., & Bitterman, M. E. (1992). A conventional conditioning analysis of "transitive inference" in pigeons. *Journal of Experimental Psychology: Animal Behavior Processes, 18*, 308–310.

Craighead, W. E. (1990). There's a place for us: All of us. *Behavior Therapy, 21*, 3–23.

Crawford, M., & Masterson, F. (1978). Components of the flight response can reinforce bar-press avoidance. *Journal of Experimental Psychology: Animal Behavior Processes, 4*, 144–151.

Crespi, L. P. (1942). Quantitative variation in incentive and performance in the white rat. *American Journal of Psychology, 55*, 467–517.

Culler, E. A. (1938). Recent advances in some concepts of conditioning. *Psychological Review, 45*, 134–153.

Curio, E. K., Ernst, K., & Vieth, W. (1978). The adaptive significance of avia mobbing II. Cultural transmission of enemy recognition in blackbirds: Effectiveness and some constraints. *Zeitschrift für Tierspsychologie, 48*, 184–202.

Daly, H. B., & Daly, J. T. (1982). A mathematical model of reward and aversive nonreward: Its application over 30 appetitive learning situations. *Journal of Experimental Psychology: General, 6,* 441–480.

Damasio, A. R. (1990). Category-related recognition defects as a clue to the neural substrates of knowledge. *Trends in Neurosciences, 13,* 95–98.

D'Amato, M. R., Fazzaro, J., & Etkin, M. (1968). Anticipatory responding and avoidance discrimination as factors in avoidance conditioning. *Journal of Experimental Psychology, 77,* 41–47.

Darwin, C. R. (1859). *On the origin of species by means of natural selection.* London: Murray.

Darwin, C. (1920). *The descent of man, and selection in relation to sex* (2nd ed.). New York: Appleton. (Original work published 1871)

Davey, G. (1989). *Ecological learning theory.* London: Routledge.

Davey, G. C. (1992). Classical conditioning and the acquisition of human fears and phobias: A review and synthesis of the literature. *Advances in Behaviour Research and Therapy, 14,* 29–66.

Davey, G., Oakley, D., & Cleland, G. G. (1981). Autoshaping in the rat: Effects of omission on the form of the response. *Journal for the Experimental Analysis of Behavior, 36,* 75–91.

Davis, H., & Perusse, R. (1988). Numerical competence in animals: Definitional issues, current evidence, and a new research agenda. *Brain and Behavioral Sciences, 11,* 561–579.

Davis, M. (1974). Sensitization of the rat startle response by noise. *Journal of Comparative and Physiological Psychology, 87,* 571–581.

Davison, G. C. (1968). Systematic desensitization as a counterconditioning process. *Journal of Abnormal Psychology, 73,* 91–99.

Davison, M., & McCarthy, D. (1988). *The matching law.* Hillsdale, NJ: Erlbaum.

De Houwer, J., Baeyens, F., & Eelen, P. (1994). Verbal evaluative conditioning with undetected US presentations. *Behaviour Research and Therapy, 32,* 629–633.

Deci, E. L., & Ryan, R. M. (1980). The empirical exploration of intrinsic motivational processes. In L. Berkowitz (ed.), *Advances in experimental social psychology* (Vol. 13). New York: Academic.

Delamater, A. R. (1996). Effects of several extinction treatments upon the integrity of Pavlovian stimulus-outcome associations. *Animal Learning and Behavior, 24,* 437–449.

DeLosh, E. L., Busemeyer, J. R., & McDaniel, M. A. (1997). Extrapolation: The sine qua non for abstraction in function learning. *Journal of Experimental Psychology: Learning, Memory, and Cognition, 23,* 968–986.

Descartes, R. (1650). The passions of the soul. In G. T. B. Ross (trans.), *The philosophical works of Descartes* (Vol. 1). Cambridge: Cambridge University Press.

DeWeer, B., Sara, S. J., & Hars, B. (1980). Contextual cues and memory retrieval in rats: Alleviation of forgetting by a pretest exposure to background cues. *Animal Learning and Behavior, 8,* 265–272.

Dickerson, E. A., & Creedon, C. F. (1981). Self-selection of standards by children: The relative effectiveness of pupil-selected and teacher-selected standards of performance. *Journal of Applied Behavior Analysis, 14,* 425–433.

Dickinson, A. (1980). *Contemporary animal learning theory.* Cambridge: Cambridge University Press.

Dickinson, A. (1989). Expectancy theory in animal conditioning. In S. B. Klein & R. R. Mowrer (eds.), *Contemporary learning theories: Pavlovian conditioning and the status of traditional learning theory* (pp 279–308). Hillsdale, NJ: Erlbaum.

Dickinson, A., & Dearing, M. F. (1979). Appetitive-aversive interactions and inhibitory processes. In A. Dickinson & R. A. Boakes (eds.), *Mechanisms of learning and motivation.* Hillsdale, NJ: Erlbaum.

Dickinson, A., Hall, G., & Mackintosh, N. J. (1976). Surprise and the attenuation of blocking. *Journal of Experimental Psychology: Animal Behavior Processes, 2,* 313–322.

Dickinson, A., Shanks, D. R., & Evenden, J. L. (1984). Judgement of act–outcome contingency: The role of selective attribution. *Quarterly Journal of Experimental Psychology, 36A,* 29–50.

Doleys, D. M. (1977). Behavioral treatments for nocturnal enuresis in children: A review of the recent literature. *Psychological Bulletin, 84,* 30–54.

Domjan, M. (1980). Ingestional aversion learning: Unique and general processes. In J. S. Rosenblatt, R. A. Hinde, C. Beer, & M. Busnel (eds.), *Advances in the study of behavior* (Vol. 11). New York: Academic.

Domjan, M. (1983). Biological constraints on instrumental and classical conditioning: Implications for general process theory. In G. H. Bower (ed.), *The psychology of learning and motivation* (Vol. 17). New York: Academic.

Domjan, M. (1992). Adult learning and mate choice: Possibilities and experimental evidence. *American Zoologist, 32,* 48–61.

Domjan, M., & Burkhard, B. (1986). *The principles of learning and behavior* (2nd ed.). Pacific Grove, CA: Brooks/Cole.

Donahoe, J. W., & Dorsel, V. P. (eds.). (1997). *Neural-network models of cognition: Biobehavioral foundations.* Amsterdam: Elsevier.

Drabman, R. S., Spitalnik, R., & O'Leary, K. D. (1973). Teaching self-control to disruptive children. *Journal of Abnormal Psychology, 82,* 10–16.

Dreyfus, L. R., Fetterman, J. G., Stubbs, D. A., & Montello, S. (1992). On discriminating temporal relations: Is it relational? *Animal Learning and Behavior, 25,* 234–244.

Dunegan, K. J. (1993). Framing, cognitive modes, and image theory: Toward an understanding of a glass half full. *Journal of Applied Psychology, 28,* 491–503.

Dutton, D. G., & Aron, A. P. (1974). Some evidence for heightened sexual attraction under conditions of high anxiety. *Journal of Personality and Social Psychology, 30,* 510–517.

Dweck, C. S., & Licht, B. G. (1980). Learned helplessness and intellectual achievement. In J. Garber & M. E. P. Seligman (eds.), *Human helplessness: Theory and applications.* New York: Academic.

Dweck, C. S., & Repucci, N. D. (1973). Learned helplessness and reinforcement responsibility in children. *Journal of Personality and Social Psychology, 25,* 109–116.

Dwyer, D. M., Mackintosh, N. J., & Boakes, R. A. (1998). Simultaneous activation of the representations of absent cues results in the formation of an excitatory association between them. *Journal of Experimental Psychology: Animal Behavior Processes, 24,* 163–171.

Easterbrook, J. A. (1959). The effect of emotion on cue utilization and the organization of behavior. *Psychological Review, 66,* 183–201.

Eich, J. E. (1980). The cue-dependent nature of state-dependent retrieval. *Memory and Cognition, 8,* 157–173.

Eikelboom, R., & Stewart, J. (1982). Conditioning of drug-induced physiological responses. *Psychological Review, 89,* 507–528.

Eimas, P. D. (1966). Effects of overtraining and age on intradimensional and extradimensional shifts in children. *Journal of Experimental Child Psychology, 3,* 348–355.

Eimas, P. D. (1984). Infant competence and the acquisition of language. In D. Caplan, A. R. Lecours, & A. Smith (eds.), *Biological perspectives on language.* Cambridge, MA: MIT Press.

Einhorn, H. J. (1972). Expert measurement and mechanical combination. *Organizational Behavior and Human Performance, 7,* 86–106.

Eisenberger, R., Karpman, M., & Trattner, J. (1967). What is the necessary and sufficient condition for reinforcement in the contingency situation? *Journal of Experimental Psychology, 74,* 342–350.

Eldridge, G. D., Pear, J. J., Torgrud, L. J., & Evers, B. H. (1988). Effects of prior response-contingent reinforcement on superstitious behavior. *Animal Learning and Behavior, 16,* 277–284.

Elkins, R. L. (1991). An appraisal of chemical aversion (emetic therapy) approaches to alcoholism treatment. *Behaviour Research and Therapy, 29,* 387–413.

Elstein, A. S., Shulman, L. S., & Sprafka, S. A. (1978). *Medical problem solving.* Cambridge, MA: Harvard University Press.

Emmerton, J., Lohmann, A., & Niemann, J. (1997). Pigeons' serial ordering of numerosity with visual arrays. *Animal Learning and Behavior, 25,* 234–244.

Enzle, M. E., & Ross, J. M. (1978). Increasing and decreasing intrinsic interest with contingent rewards: A test of cognitive evaluation theory. *Journal of Experimental and Social Psychology, 14,* 588–597.

Epstein, S. (1994). Integration of the cognitive and the psychodynamic unconscious. *American Psychologist, 49,* 709–724.

Erickson, M. A., & Kruschke, J. K. (1998). Rules and exemplars in category learning. *Journal of Experimental Psychology: General, 127,* 107–140.

Eron, L. D., Walder, L. O., Toigo, R., & Lefkowitz, M. M. (1963). Social class, parental punishment for aggression, and child aggression. *Child Development, 34,* 849–867.

Estes, W. K. (1959). The statistical approach to learning theory. In S. Koch (ed.), *Psychology: A study of a science* (Vol. 2). New York: McGraw-Hill.

Estes, W. K. (1976). The cognitive side of probability learning. *Psychological Review, 83,* 37–64.

Estes, W. K., & Skinner, B. F. (1941). Some quantitative properties of anxiety. *Journal of Experimental Psychology, 29,* 390–400.

Etscorn, F., & Stephens, R. (1973). Establishment of conditioned taste aversions with a 24-hour CS–US interval. *Physiological Psychology, 1,* 251–259.

Fanselow, M. S. (1989). The adaptive function of conditioned defensive behavior: An ecological approach to Pavlovian stimulus-substitution theory. In R. J. Blanchard, P. F. Brain, D. C. Blanchard, & S. Parmigiani (eds.), *Ethoexperimental approaches to the study of behavior.* Boston: Kluwer.

Fanselow, M. S., & Lester, L. S. (1988). A functional behavioristic approach to aversively motivated behavior: Predatory imminence as a determinant of the topography of defensive behavior. In R. C. Bolles & M. D. Beecher (eds.), *Evolution and learning.* Hillsdale, NJ: Erlbaum.

Fantino, E. (1977). Conditioned reinforcement. In W. K. Honig & J. E. R. Staddon (eds.), *Handbook of operant behavior.* Englewood Cliffs, NJ: Prentice-Hall.

Farris, H. E. (1967). Classical conditioning of courting behavior in the Japanese quail, *Coturnix coturnix japonica. Journal of the Experimental Analysis of Behavior, 10,* 213–217.

Feehan, G. G., & Enzle, M. E. (1991). Subjective control over rewards: Effects of perceived choice of reward schedule on intrinsic motivation and behavior maintenance. *Perceptual and Motor Skills, 72,* 995–1006.

Fixsen, D. L., Phillips, E. L., Baron, R. L., Coughlin, D. D., Daly, D. L., & Daly, P. B. (1978). The Boys' Town revolution. *Human Nature,* pp. 54–61.

Flaherty, C. F. (1996). *Incentive relativity.* New York: Cambridge University Press.

Flanders, J. P. (1968). A review of research on imitative behavior. *Psychological Bulletin, 69,* 316–337.

Forehand, R., & Wierson, M. (1993). The role of developmental factors in planning behavioral interventions for children: Disruptive behavior as an example. *Behavior Therapy, 24,* 117–141.

Fouts, R. S., Hirsch, A. D., & Fouts, D. H. (1982). Cultural transmission of a human language in a chimpanzee mother-infant relationship. In H. E. Fitzgerald, J. A. Mullins, & P. Gage (eds.), *Child Nurturance: Vol. 3. Studies of development in nonhuman primates* (pp. 159–193). New York: Plenum.

Fowler, H., & Miller, N. E. (1963). Facilitation and inhibition of runway performance by hind- and forepaw shock of various intensities. *Journal of Comparative Physiological Psychology, 56,* 801–805.

Fowler, H., & Wischner, G. J. (1969). The varied function of punishment in discrimination learning. In B. A. Campbell & R. M. Church (eds.), *Punishment and aversive behavior.* New York: Appleton-Century-Crofts.

Fox, D. K., Hopkins, B. L., & Anger, W. K. (1987). The long-term effects of a token economy on safety performance in open-pit mining. *Journal of Applied Behavior Analysis, 20,* 215–224.

Fox, L. (1966). Effecting the use of efficient study habits. In R. Ulrich, T. Stachnik, & J. Mabry (eds.), *Control of human behavior* (Vol. 1). Glenview, IL: Scott, Foresman.

Gallistel, C. R. (1989). Animal cognition: The representation of space, time and number. *Annual Review of Psychology, 40,* 155–189.

Gallistel, C. R. (1990). Representation in animal cognition: An introduction. *Cognition, 37,* 1–22.

Garcia, J. (1981). Tilting at the paper mills of Academe. *American Psychologist, 36,* 149–158.

Garcia, J., Brett, L. P., & Rusiniak, K. W. (1989). Limits of Darwinian conditioning. In S. B. Klein & R. R. Mowrer (eds.), *Contemporary learning theories: Instrumental conditioning theory and the impact of biological constraints on learning.* Hillsdale, NJ: Erlbaum.

Garcia, J., & Koelling, R. A. (1966). Relation of cue to consequence in avoidance learning. *Psychonomic Science, 4,* 123–124.

Gardner, R. A., & Gardner, B. T. (1969). Teaching sign language to a chimpanzee. *Science, 165,* 664–672.

Gardner, R. A., & Gardner, B. T. (1985). Signs of intelligence in cross-fostered chimpanzees. In L. Weiskrantz (ed.), *Animal intelligence.* Oxford: Clarendon.

Gardner, R, A., Gardner, B. T., & Van Cantfort, T. E. (1989). *Teaching sign language to chimpanzees.* New York: State University of New York Press.

Garlington, W. K., & Dericco, D. A. (1977). The effect of modeling on drinking rate. *Journal of Applied Behavior Analysis, 10,* 207–211.

Gauci, M., Husband, A. J., & King, M. G. (1992) Conditioned allergic rhinitis: A model for central nervous system and immune system interaction in IgE-mediated allergic reactions. In A. J. Husband (ed.), *Behavior and immunity.* London: CRC.

Geen, R. G. (1985). Test anxiety and visual vigilance. *Journal of Personality and Social Psychology, 49,* 963–970.

Gelperin, A. (1986). Complex associative learning in small neural networks. *Trends in Neurosciences, 9,* 323–328.

Gholson, B. G. (1980). *The cognitive-developmental basis of human learning: Studies in hypothesis testing.* New York: Academic.

Gibbon, J., & Church, R. M. (1984). Sources of variance in an information processing theory of timing. In H. L. Roitblat, T. G. Bever, & H. S. Terrace (eds.). *Animal cognition.* Hillsdale, NJ: Erlbaum.

Gibson, E. J. (1969). *Principles of perceptual learning and development.* New York: Appleton-Century-Crofts.

Gibson, E. J., Walk, R. D., Pick, H. L., Jr., & Tighe, T. J. (1958). The effect of prolonged exposure to visual patterns on learning to discriminate similar and different patterns. *Journal of Comparative and Physiological Psychology, 51,* 584–587.

Gleitman, H., Nachmias, J., & Neisser, U. (1954). The S–R reinforcement theory of extinction. *Psychological Review, 61,* 23–33.

Gluck, M. A., & Bower, G. H. (1988). From conditioning to category learning: An adaptive network model. *Journal of Experimental Psychology: General, 117*, 227–247.

Glueck, S., & Glueck, E. (1950). *Unraveling juvenile delinquency.* Cambridge, MA: Harvard University Press.

Goldiamond, I. (1965). Self-control procedures in personal behavior problems. *Psychological Reports, 17*, 851–868.

Goldstone, R. C. (1998). Perceptual learning. *Annual Review of Psychology, 49*, 595–612.

Goodall-van Lawick, J. (1968). *My friends the wild chimpanzees.* Washington, DC: National Geographic Society.

Gordon, W. C. (1981). Mechanisms for cue-induced retention enhancement. In N. E. Spear & R. R. Miller (eds.), *Information processing in animals: Memory mechanisms.* Hillsdale, NJ: Erlbaum.

Gorn, G. J. (1982). The effects of music in advertising on choice behavior: A classical conditioning approach. *Journal of Marketing, 46*, 94–101.

Gould, J. L. (1986). The biology of learning. *Annual Review of Psychology, 37*, 163–192.

Graham, J. M., & Desjardins, C. (1980). Classical conditioning: Induction of luteinizing hormone and testosterone secretion in anticipation of sexual activity. *Science, 210*, 1039–1041.

Grant, D. S. (1976). Effect of sample presentation time on long-delay matching in the pigeon. *Learning and Motivation, 7*, 580–590.

Grant, D. S. (1981). Stimulus control of information processing in pigeon short-term memory. *Learning and Motivation, 12*, 19–39.

Grant, D. S. (1988). Sources of visual interference in delayed matching-to-sample with pigeons. *Journal of Experimental Psychology: Animal Behavior Processes, 14*, 368–375.

Grant, D. S., Brewster, R. G., & Stierhoff, K. A. (1983). "Surprisingness" and short-term retention in pigeons. *Journal of Experimental Psychology: Animal Behavior Processes, 9*, 63–79.

Grant, D. S., & Roberts, W. A. (1973). Trace interaction in pigeon short-term memory. *Journal of Experimental Psychology, 101*, 21–29.

Grant, D. S., & Soldat, A. S. (1995). A postsample cue to forget does initiate an active forgetting process in pigeons. *Journal of Experimental Psychology: Animal Behavior Processes, 21*, 218–228.

Greene, C. M., & Cook, R. G. (1997). Landmark geometry and identity controls spatial navigation in rats. *Animal Learning and Behavior, 25*, 312–323.

Gresham, F. M., & MacMillan, D. L. (1997). Denial and defensiveness in the place of fact and reason: Rejoinder to Smith and Lovaas. *Behavioural Disorders, 22*, 219–230.

Grice, G. R. (1948). The relation of secondary reinforcement to delayed reward in visual discrimination learning. *Journal of Experimental Psychology, 38*, 1–16.

Grice, G. R. (1968). Stimulus intensity and response evocation. *Psychological Review, 75*, 359–373.

Grolnick, W. S., & Ryan, R. M. (1989). Parent styles associated with children's self-regulation and competence in school. *Journal of Educational Psychology, 81*, 143–154.

Grossen, N. E., Kostansek, D. J., & Bolles, R. C. (1969). Effects of appetitive discriminative stimuli on avoidance behavior. *Journal of Experimental Psychology, 81*, 340–343.

Groves, P. M., & Thompson, R. F. (1970). Habituation: A dual-process theory. *Psychological Review, 77*, 419–450.

Guiton, P. (1966). Early experience and sexual object-choice in the brown leghorn. *Animal Behaviour, 14*, 534–538.

Gustavson, C. R., Garcia, J., Hankins, W. G., & Rusiniak, K. W. (1974). Coyote predation control by aversive conditioning. *Science, 184*, 581–583.

Guthrie, E. R. (1952). *The psychology of learning* (rev. ed.). New York: Harper & Row.

Guttman, N., & Kalish, H. I. (1956). Discriminability and stimulus generalization. *Journal of Experimental Psychology, 51,* 79–88.

Hall, G. (1991). *Perceptual and associative learning.* Oxford: Clarendon.

Hall, G., & Pearce, J. M. (1982). Restoring the associability of a preexposed CS by a surprising event. *Quarterly Journal of Experimental Psychology, 34B,* 127–140.

Hall, R. V., Axelrod, S., Tyler, L., Grief, E., Jones, F. C., & Robertson, R. (1972). Modification of behavior problems in the home with a parent as observer and experimenter. *Journal of Applied Behavior Analysis, 5,* 53–64.

Hall, R. V., Lund, D., & Jackson, D. (1968). Effects of teacher attention on study behavior. *Journal of Applied Behavior Analysis, 1,* 1–12.

Hall, S. M., Rugg, D., Tunstall, C., & Jones, R. T. (1984). Preventing relapse to cigarette smoking by behavioral skill training. *Journal of Consulting and Clinical Psychology, 52,* 372–382.

Hammond, L. J. (1980). The effect of contingency upon the appetitive conditioning of free operant behavior. *Journal of the Experimental Analysis of Behavior, 34,* 297–304.

Hanson, H. M. (1959). Effects of discrimination training on stimulus generalization. *Journal of Experimental Psychology, 58,* 321–333.

Harlow, H. F., & Harlow, M. K. (1965). The affectional systems. In A. M. Schrier, H. F. Harlow, & F. Stollnitz (eds.), *Behavior of nonhuman primates* (Vol. 2). New York: Academic.

Hawkins, R. D., & Kandel, E. R. (1984). Is there a cell-biological alphabet for simple forms of learning? *Psychological Review, 91,* 375–391.

Hayes, K., & Hayes, C. (1951). The intellectual development of a home-raised chimpanzee. *Proceedings of the American Philosophical Society, 95,* 105–109.

Hayes, S. C., Rosenfarb, I., Wulfert, E., Munt, E. D., Korn, Z., & Zettle, R. D. (1985). Self-reinforcement effects: An artifact of social standard setting? *Journal of Applied Behavior Analysis, 18,* 201–214.

Hearst, E., & Jenkins, H. M. (1974). *Sign-tracking: The stimulus-reinforcer relation and directed action.* Austin, TX: Psychonomic Society.

Heath, R. G. (1963). Electrical self-stimulation of the brain in man. *American Journal of Psychiatry, 120,* 571–577.

Hebert, J. A., & Krantz, D. L. (1965). Transposition: A re-evaluation. *Psychological Bulletin, 63,* 244–257.

Hefferline, R. F., & Keenan, B. (1961). Amplitude-induction gradient of a small operant in an escape-avoidance situation. *Journal of the Experimental Analysis of Behavior, 4,* 41–43.

Hefferline, R. F., Keenan, B., & Harford, R. A. (1959). Escape and avoidance conditioning in human subjects without their observation of the response. *Science, 130,* 1338–1339.

Herbert, E. W., Pinkston, E. M., Hayden, M. L., Sajwaj, T. E., Pinkston, S., Cordua, G., & Jackson, C. (1973). Adverse effects of differential parental attention. *Journal of Applied Behavior Analysis, 6,* 15–30.

Herrnstein, R. J. (1961). Relative and absolute strength of response as a function of frequency of reinforcement. *Journal for the Experimental Analysis of Behavior, 4,* 267–272.

Herrnstein, R. J. (1979). Acquisition, generalization, and discrimination reversal of a natural concept. *Journal of Experimental Psychology: Animal Behavior Processes, 5,* 116–129.

Herrnstein, R. J. (1990). Levels of stimulus control: A functional approach. *Cognition, 37,* 133–166.

Herrnstein, R. J., & Loveland, D. H. (1964). Complex visual concept in the pigeon. *Science, 146,* 549–551.

Herrnstein, R. J., Loveland, D. H., & Cable, C. (1976). Natural concepts in pigeons. *Journal of Experimental Psychology: Animal Behavior Processes, 2,* 285–311.

Herrnstein, R. J., & Vaughan, W. (1980). Melioration and behavioral allocation. In J. E. R. Staddon (ed.), *Limits to action.* New York: Academic.

Hess, E. H. (1959). Imprinting. *Science, 130,* 133–141.

Hilgard, E. R., & Bower, G. H. (1981). *Theories of learning* (5th ed.). Englewood Cliffs, NJ: Prentice-Hall.

Hirst, W., Spelke, E. S., Reaves, C. C., Caharack, G., & Neisser, U. (1980). Dividing attention without alternation or automaticity. *Journal of Experimental Psychology: General, 109*, 98–117.

Hochauser, M., & Fowler, H. (1975). Cue effects of drive and reward as a function of discrimination difficulty: Evidence against the Yerkes-Dodson law. *Journal of Experimental Psychology: Animal Behavior Processes, 1*, 261–269.

Hoffman, H. S. (1978). Experimental analysis of imprinting and its behavioral effects. In G. H. Bower (ed.), *The psychology of learning and motivation.* (vol. 12, pp. 1–37) New York: Academic.

Hoffman, M. L. (1989). Empathy, social cognition, and moral action. In W. Kurtines & J. Gewirtz (eds.), *Moral behavior and development: Advances in theory, research and application* (Vol 1). Hillsdale, NJ: Erlbaum.

Holland, P. C. (1977). Conditioned stimulus as a determinant of the form of the Pavlovian conditioned response. *Journal of Experimental Psychology: Animal Behavior Processes, 3*, 77–104.

Holland, P. C. (1985). The nature of conditioned inhibition in serial and simultaneous feature negative discriminations. In R. R. Miller & N. E. Spear (eds.), *Information processing in animals: Conditioned inhibition.* Hillsdale, NJ: Erlbaum.

Holland, P. C., & Straub, J. J. (1979). Differential effect of two ways of devaluing the unconditioned stimulus after Pavlovian appetitive conditioning. *Journal of Experimental Psychology: Animal Behavior Processes, 5*, 67–78.

Hollis, K. L. (1982). Pavlovian conditioning of signal-centered action patterns and autonomic behavior: A biological analysis of function. *Advances in the Study of Behavior, 12*, 1–64.

Hollis, K. L. (1984). The biological function of Pavlovian conditioning: The best defense is a good offense. *Journal of Experimental Psychology: Animal Behavior Processes, 10*, 413–425.

Hollis, K. L., Pharr, V. L., Dumas, M. J., Britton, G. B., & Field, J. (1997). Classical conditioning provides paternity advantage for territorial male blue gouramis (*Trichogaster trichopterus*). *Journal of Comparative Psychology, 111*, 219–225.

Hollis, K. L., ten Cate, C., & Bateson, P. (1991). Stimulus representation: A subprocess of imprinting and conditioning. *Journal of Comparative Psychology, 105*, 307–317.

Homme, L. W., deBaca, P. C., Devine, J. V., Steinhorst, R., & Rickert, E. J. (1963). Use of the Premack principle in controlling the behavior of nursery school children. *Journal of the Experimental Analysis of Behavior, 6*, 544.

Honey, R. C., & Bolhuis, J. J. (1997). Imprinting, conditioning, and within-event learning. *Quarterly Journal of Experimental Psychology, 50B*, 79–110.

Honey, R. C., Horn, G., & Bateson, P. (1993). Perceptual learning during filial imprinting: Evidence from transfer of training studies. *Quarterly Journal of Experimental Psychology, 46B*, 253–269.

Honig, W. K. (1981). Working memory and the temporal map. In N. E. Spear and R. R. Miller (eds.), *Information processing in animals: Memory mechanisms.* Hillsdale, NJ: Erlbaum.

Honig, W. K., Boneau, C. A., Burstein, K. R., & Pennypacker, H. S. (1963). Positive and negative generalization gradients obtained after equivalent training conditions. *Journal of Comparative and Physiological Psychology, 56*, 111–116.

Honig, W. K., & Slivka, R. M. (1964). Stimulus generalization of the effects of punishment. *Journal of the Experimental Analysis of Behavior, 7*, 21–25.

Houts, A. C., Berman, J. S., & Abramson, H. (1994). Effectiveness of psychological and pharmacological treatments for nocturnal enuresis. *Journal of Consulting and Clinical Psychology, 62,* 737–745.

Hull, C. L. (1943). *Principles of behavior.* New York: Appleton-Century-Crofts.

Hull, C. L. (1952). *A behavior system.* New Haven, CT: Yale University Press.

Hulse, S. H., Fowler, H., & Honig, W. K. (eds.). (1978). *Cognitive processes in animal behavior.* Hillsdale, NJ: Erlbaum.

Humphreys, M. S., & Revelle, W. (1984). Personality, motivation, and performance: A theory of the relationship between individual differences and information processing. *Psychological Review, 91,* 153–184.

Hunt, G. L., Jr., & Smith, W. J. (1967). Pecking and initial drinking responses in young domestic fowl. *Journal of Comparative and Physiological Psychology, 64,* 230–236.

Hursh, S. R., & Natelson, B. J. (1981). Electrical brain stimulation and food reinforcement dissociated by demand elasticity. *Physiology and Behavior, 18,* 141–150.

Ince, L. P., Brucker, B. S., & Alba, A. (1978). Reflex conditioning in a spinal man. *Journal of Comparative and Physiological Psychology, 92,* 796–802.

Iversen, I. H., Ragnarsdottir, G. A., & Randrup, K. I. (1984). Operant conditioning of auto-grooming in vervet monkeys (*Cercopithecus aethiops*). *Journal of the Experimental Analysis of Behavior, 42,* 171–189.

Jackson, B., & Van Zoost, B. (1972). Changing study behaviors through reinforcement contingencies. *Journal of Counseling Psychology, 19,* 192–195.

Jacobsen, P. B., Bovbjerg, D. H., Schwartz, M. D., Andrykowski, M. A., Futterman, A. D., Gilewski, T., Norton, L., & Redd, W. H. (1993). Formation of food aversions in cancer patients receiving repeated infusions of chemotherapy. *Behaviour Research and Therapy, 31,* 739–748.

Janis, I. L., Kaye, D., & Kirschner, P. (1965). Facilitating effects of "eating-while-reading" on responsiveness to persuasive communications. *Journal of Personality and Social Psychology, 1,* 181–186.

Janssen, M., Farley, J., & Hearst, E. (1995). Temporal location of unsignaled food deliveries: Effects on conditioned withdrawal (inhibition) in pigeon signtracking. *Journal of Experimental Psychology: Animal Behavior Processes, 21,* 116–128.

Jenkins, H. M., & Moore, B. R. (1973). The form of the autoshaped response with food or water reinforcers. *Journal of the Experimental Analysis of Behavior, 20,* 163–181.

Jenkins, H. M., Barrera, F. J., Ireland, C., & Woodside, B. (1978). Signal-centered action patterns of dogs in appetitive classical conditioning. *Learning and Motivation, 9,* 272–296.

Jenkins, J. G., & Dallenbach, K. M. (1924). Oblivescence during sleeping and waking. *American Journal of Psychology, 35,* 605–612.

Johnston, T. D. (1981). Contrasting approaches to the theory of learning. *Behavioral and Brain Sciences, 4,* 125–139.

Jones, A., Wilkinson, H. J., & Braden, I. (1961). Information deprivation as a motivational variable. *Journal of Experimental Psychology, 62,* 126–137.

Jones, M. C. (1924). The elimination of children's fears. *Journal of Experimental Psychology, 7,* 382–390.

Josephson, W. L. (1987). Television violence and children' aggression: Testing the priming, social script, and disinhibition predictions. *Journal of Personality and Social Psychology, 53,* 882–890.

Justesen, D. R., Braun, E. W., Garrison, R. G., & Pendleton, R. B. (1970). Pharmacological differentiation of allergic and classically conditioned asthma in the guinea pig. *Science, 170,* 864–866.

Justice, T. C., & Looney, T. A. (1990). Another look at "superstitions" in pigeons. *Bulletin of the Psychonomic Society, 28,* 64–66.

Kamin, L. J. (1969). Predictability, surprise, attention, and conditioning. In B. A. Campbell & R. M. Church (eds.), *Punishment and aversive behavior*. New York: Appleton-Century-Crofts.

Kamin, L. J., Brimer, C. J., & Black, A. H. (1963). Conditioned suppression as a monitor of fear of the CS in the course of avoidance training. *Journal of Comparative and Physiological Psychology, 56*, 497–501.

Kandel, E. R. (1991). Cellular mechanisms of learning and the biological basis of individuality. In E. R. Kandel, J. H. Schwartz, & T. M. Jessell (eds.), *Principles of neural science*. New York: Elsevier.

Kandel, H. J., Ayllon, T., & Roberts, M. D. (1976). Rapid educational rehabilitation for prison inmates. *Behavior Research and Therapy, 14*, 323–331.

Kanfer, F. H., & Seidner, M. L. (1973). Self-control: Factors enhancing tolerance of noxious stimulation. *Journal of Personality and Social Psychology, 25*, 381–389.

Kasper, C. J., & Alford, J. M. (1988). Redecision and men who sexually abuse children. *Transactional Analysis Journal, 18*, 309–315.

Katzev, R. D., & Berman, J. S. (1974). Effect of exposure to conditioned stimulus and control of its termination in the extinction of avoidance behavior. *Journal of Comparative and Physiological Psychology, 87*, 347–353.

Kaufman, J., & Zigler, E. (1987). Do abused children become abusive parents? *American Journal of Orthopsychiatry, 57*, 186–192.

Kaye, H., & Pearce, J. M. (1987). Hippocampal lesions attenuate latent inhibition and the decline of the orienting response in rats. *Quarterly Journal of Experimental Psychology, 39*, 107–125.

Keil, F. C. (1994). The birth and nurturance of concepts by domains: The origins of concepts of living things. In L. A. Hirschfeld & S. A. Gelman (eds.), *Mapping the mind: Domain specificity in cognition and culture*. New York: Cambridge University Press.

Keller, R. J., Ayres, J. J. B., & Mahoney, W. J. (1977). Brief versus extended exposure to truly random control procedures. *Journal of Experimental Psychology: Animal Behavior Processes, 3*, 53–66.

Kemler, D. G., & Shepp, B. E. (1971). Learning and transfer of dimensional relevance and irrelevance in children. *Journal of Experimental Psychology, 90*, 120–127.

Kendall-Tackett, K. A., Williams, L. M., & Finkelhor, D. (1993). Impact of sexual abuse on children: A review and synthesis of recent empirical studies. *Psychological Bulletin, 113*, 164–180.

Kendler, T. (1979). Toward a theory of mediational development. In H. W. Reese & L. P. Lipsitt (eds.), *Advances in child development and behavior* (Vol. 13). New York: Academic.

Kesner, R. P., & DeSpain, M. J. (1988). Correspondence between rats and humans in the utilization of retrospective and prospective codes. *Animal Learning and Behavior, 16*, 299–302.

Killeen, P. R., & Fetterman, J. G. (1993). The behavioral theory of timing: Transition analyses. *Journal of the Experimental Analysis of Behavior Processes, 59*, 411–422.

Kimble, G. A., Mann, L. I., & Dufort, R. H. (1955). Classical and instrumental eyelid conditioning. *Journal of Experimental Psychology, 49*, 407–417.

Kirby, K. N. (1997). Bidding on the future: Evidence against normative discounting of delayed rewards. *Journal of Experimental Psychology: General, 126*, 54–70.

Kirby, K. N., & Herrnstein, R. J. (1995). Preference reversals due to myopic discounting of delayed reward. *Psychological Science, 6*, 83–89.

Kirkpatrick-Steger, K., Wasserman, E. A., & Biederman, I. (1998). Effects of geon deletion, scrambling, and movement on picture recognition in pigeons. *Journal of Experimental Psychology: Animal Behavior Processes, 24*, 34–46.

Kirschenbaum, D. S., & Flanery, R. C. (1983). Behaviorial contracting: Outcomes and elements. In M. Hersen, R. M. Eisler, & P. M. Miller (eds.), *Progress in behavior modification*. New York: Academic.

Kish, G. B. (1966). Studies of sensory reinforcement. In W. K. Honig (ed.), *Operant behavior: Areas of research and application*. New York: Appleton-Century-Crofts.

Kleinknecht, R. A. (1994). Acquisition of blood, injury, and needle fears and phobias. *Behaviour Research and Therapy, 32*, 817–823.

Knowlton, B. J., Mangels, J. A., & Squire, L. R. (1996). A neostriatal habit learning system in humans. *Science, 273*, 1399–1402.

Koch, S. (1954). Clark L. Hull. In W. K. Estes, S. Koch, K. MacCorquodale, P. E. Meehl, C. G. Mueller, Jr., W. N. Schoenfeld, & W. S. Verplanck, *Modern learning theory*. New York: Appleton-Century-Crofts.

Kohler, W. (1927). *The mentality of apes* (rev. ed.). London: Routledge & Kegan Paul.

Kohler, W. (1939). Simple structural functions in the chimpanzee and in the chicken. In W. D. Ellis (ed. and trans.), *A source book of gestalt psychology*. New York: Harcourt, Brace. (Original work published 1918)

Komatsu, L. (1992). Recent views of conceptual structure. *Psychological Bulletin, 112*, 500–526.

Konorski, J. (1948). *Conditioned reflexes and neuron organization*. Cambridge: Cambridge University Press.

Konorski, J. (1967). *Integrative activity of the brain*. Chicago: University of Chicago Press.

Krebs, J. R. (1991). Food-storing in birds: Adaptive specialization in brain and behaviour? In J. R. Krebs & G. Horn (eds.), *Behavioural and neural aspects of learning and memory*. Oxford: Oxford University Press.

Kremer, E. F. (1971). Truly random and traditional control procedures in CER conditioning in the rat. *Journal of Comparative and Physiological Psychology, 76*, 441–448.

Kuch, K., Cox, B. J., Evans, R., & Shulman, I. (1994). Phobias, panic, and pain in 55 survivors of road vehicle accidents. *Journal of Anxiety Disorders, 8*, 181–187.

Kuhn, T. S. (1970). *The structure of scientific revolutions*. Chicago: University of Chicago Press.

Lamon, S., Wilson, G. T., & Leaf, R. C. (1977). Human classical aversion conditioning: Nausea versus electric shock in the reduction of target beverage consumption. *Behavior Research and Therapy, 15*, 313–320.

Lane, D. M., & Rabinowitz, F. M. (1979). A rule-based theory of intermediate-size transposition. *Child Development, 48*, 412–426.

Langer, E. J. (1975). The illusion of control. *Journal of Personality and Social Psychology, 32*, 311–328.

Langley, C. M, & Riley, D. A. (1993). Limited capacity information processing and pigeon matching-to-sample: Testing alternative hypotheses. *Animal Learning and Behavior, 21*, 226–232.

Larkin, K. T., & Edens, J. L. (1994). Behavior therapy. In V. B. Van Hesselt & M. Hersen (eds.), *Advanced abnormal psychology*. New York: Plenum.

Larzelere, R. E. (1986). Moderate spanking: Model or deterrent of children's aggression in the family? *Journal of Family Violence, 1*, 27–36.

Larzelere, R. E., Schneider, W. N., Larson, D. B., & Pike, P. L. (1996). The effects of discipline responses in delaying toddler misbehavior recurrences. *Child & Family Behavior Therapy, 18*, 35–57.

Lattal, A. K., & Gleeson, S. (1990). Response acquisition with delayed reinforcement. *Journal of Experimental Psychology: Animal Behavior Processes, 16*, 27–39.

Lawrence, D. H. (1963). The nature of a stimulus: Some relationships between learning and perception. In S. Koch (ed.), *Psychology: A study of a science* (Vol. 5). New York: McGraw-Hill.

Lawrence, D. H., & DeRivera, J. (1954). Evidence for relational transposition. *Journal of Comparative and Physiological Psychology, 47,* 465–471.

Lawrence, D. H., & Hommel, L. (1961). The influence of differential goal boxes on discrimination learning involving delay of reinforcement. *Journal of Comparative and Physiological Psychology, 54,* 552–555.

Lazarus, A. A. (1971). *Behavior therapy and beyond.* New York: McGraw-Hill.

LeDoux, J. E. (1994). Emotion, memory and the brain. *Scientific American, 270,* 50–57.

Lefkowitz, M. M., Blake, R. R., & Mouton, J. S. (1955). Status factors in pedestrian violation of traffic signals. *Journal of Abnormal and Social Psychology, 51,* 704–706.

Lepper, M. R. (1981). Intrinsic and extrinsic motivation in children: Detrimental effects of superfluous social controls. In W. A. Collins (ed.), *Minnesota symposium on child psychology* (Vol. 14). Hillsdale, NJ: Erlbaum.

Lepper, M. R., Greene, D., & Nisbett, R. E. (1973). Undermining children's intrinsic interest with extrinsic rewards: A test of the overjustification hypothesis. *Journal of Personality and Social Psychology, 28,* 129–137.

Lepper, M. R., Keavney, M., & Drake, M. (1996). Intrinsic motivation and extrinsic rewards: A commentary on Cameron and Pierce's meta-analysis. *Review of Educational Research, 66,* 5–32.

Levine, M. (1971). Hypothesis theory and nonlearning despite ideal S–R reinforcement contingencies. *Psychological Review, 78,* 130–140.

Levine, M. (1975). *A cognitive theory of learning: Research based on hypothesis testing.* Hillsdale, NJ: Erlbaum.

Levis, D. J. (1989). The case for a return to a two-factor theory of avoidance: The failure of non-fear interpretations. In S. B. Klein & R. R. Mowrer (eds.), *Contemporary learning theories: Pavlovian conditioning and the status of traditional learning theory.* Hillsdale, NJ: Erlbaum.

Lewis, D. J., & Duncan, C. P. (1956). Effect of different percentages of money reward on extinction of a lever pulling response. *Journal of Experimental Psychology, 52,* 23–27.

Leyens, J. P., Camino, L., Parke, R. D., & Berkowitz, L. (1975). Effects of movie violence on aggression in a field setting as a function of group dominance and cohesion. *Journal of Personality and Social Psychology, 32,* 346–360.

Lichstein, K. L., & Riedel, B. W. (1994). Behavioral assessment and treatment of insomnia: A review with an emphasis on clinical application. *Behavior Therapy, 25,* 659–688.

Lieberman, D. A. (1979). Behaviorism and the mind: A (limited) call for a return to introspection. *American Psychologist, 34,* 319–333.

Lieberman, D. A., Connell, G. L., & Moos, H. F. T. (1998). Reinforcement without awareness: II. Word class. *Quarterly Journal of Experimental Psychology, 51B,* 317–315.

Lieberman, D. A., McIntosh, D. C., & Thomas, G. V. (1979). Learning when reward is delayed: A marking hypothesis. *Journal of Experimental Psychology: Animal Behavior Processes, 5,* 224–242.

Lieberman, D. A., & Thomas, G. V. (1986). Marking, memory, and superstition in the pigeon. *Quarterly Journal of Experimental Psychology, 38B,* 449–459.

Locke, J. (1961). *An essay concerning human understanding* (J. W. Yolton, Ed.). London: Dent. (Original work published 1690)

Logan, F. A., & Wagner, A. R. (1965). *Reward and punishment.* Boston: Allyn & Bacon.

Logue, A. W., Ophir, I., & Strauss, K. E. (1981). The acquisition of taste aversions in humans. *Behaviour Research and Therapy, 19,* 319–333.

LoLordo, V. M., & Droungas, A. (1989). Selective associations and adaptive specializations: Taste aversions and phobias. In S. B. Klein & R. R. Mowrer (eds.), *Contemporary learning theories: Instrumental conditioning theory and the impact of biological constraints on learning.* Hillsdale, NJ: Erlbaum.

Lorenz, K. (1937). The companion in the bird's world. *Auk, 54*, 245–273.

Lorenz, K. (1952). *King Solomon's ring.* New York: Crowell.

Lovaas, O. I. (1987). Behavioral treatment and normal educational and intellectual functioning in young autistic children. *Journal of Consulting and Clinical Psychology, 55,* 3–9.

Lovaas, O. I., Koegel, R. L., Simmons, J. Q., & Long, J. (1973). Some generalization and follow-up measures on autistic children in behavior therapy. *Journal of Applied Behavior Analysis, 6,* 131–166.

Lovaas, O. I., Schaeffer, B., & Simmons, J. Q. (1965). Experimental studies in childhood schizophrenia: Building social behavior in autistic children by the use of electric shock. *Journal of Experimental Research in Personality, 1,* 99–109.

Lovibond, P. F., Preston, G. C., & Mackintosh, N. J. (1984). Context specificity of conditioning, extinction and latent inhibition. *Journal of Experimental Psychology: Animal Behavior Processes, 10,* 360–375.

Lowe, C. F. (1983). Radical behaviourism and human psychology. In G. C. L. Davey (ed.), *Animal models and human behaviour.* Chichester, England: Wiley.

Lowe, C. F., Beasty, A., & Bentall, R. P. (1983). The role of verbal behavior in human learning: Infant performance on fixed-interval schedules. *Journal of the Experimental Analysis of Behavior, 39,* 157–164.

Lowitz, G. H., & Suib, M. R. (1978). Generalized control of persistent thumbsucking by differential reinforcement of other behaviors. *Journal of Behavior Therapy and Experimental Psychiatry, 9,* 343–346.

Lubow, R. E., & Moore, A. U. (1959). Latent inhibition: The effect of nonreinforced preexposure to the conditioned stimulus. *Journal of Comparative and Physiological Psychology, 52,* 415–419.

Lucas, G. A., & Timberlake, W. (1992). Negative anticipatory contrast and preference conditioning: Flavor cues support preference conditioning, and environmental cues support contrast. *Journal of Experimental Psychology: Animal Behavior Processes, 18,* 34–40.

Ludwig, T. D., & Geller, E. S. (1997). Assigned versus participative goalsetting and response generalization: Managing injury control among professional pizza deliverers. *Journal of Applied Psychology, 82,* 253–261.

Macfarlane, D. A. (1930). The role of kinesthesis in maze learning. *University of California Publications in Psychology, 4,* 277–305.

Mackintosh, N. J. (1965). Selective attention in animal discrimination learning. *Psychological Bulletin, 64,* 124 150.

Mackintosh, N. J. (1973). Stimulus selection: Learning to ignore stimuli that predict no change in reinforcement. In R. A. Hinde & J. Stevenson-Hinde (eds.), *Constraints on learning.* New York: Academic.

Mackintosh, N. J. (1974). *The psychology of animal learning.* New York: Academic.

Mackintosh, N. J. (1975). A theory of attention: Variations in the associability of stimuli with reinforcement. *Psychological Review, 82,* 276–298.

Mackintosh, N. J. (1983). *Conditioning and associative learning.* Oxford: Oxford University Press.

Mackintosh, N. J., & Bennett, C. H. (1998). Perceptual learning in animals and humans. In M. Sabourin, F. Craik, & M. Robert (eds.), *Advances in Psychological Science, vol. 2: Biological and cognitive aspects.* Hove, England: Psychology Press.

Mackintosh, N. J., & Dickinson, A. (1979). Instrumental (Type II) conditioning. In A. Dickinson & R. A. Boakes (eds.), *Mechanisms of learning and motivation.* Hillsdale, NJ: Erlbaum.

Mackintosh, N. J., & Little, L. (1969). Intradimensional and extradimensional shift learning by pigeons. *Psychonomic Science, 14,* 5–6.

Madsen, C. H., Becker, W. C., Thomas, D. R., Koser, L., & Plager, E. (1970). An analysis of the reinforcing function of "sit down" commands. In R. K. Parker (ed.), *Readings in educational psychology*. Boston: Allyn & Bacon.

Maier, S. F. (1989). Learned helplessness: Event covariation and cognitive changes. In S. B. Klein & R. R. Mowrer (eds.), *Contemporary learning theories: Instrumental conditioning theory and the impact of biological constraints on learning*. Hillsdale, NJ: Erlbaum.

Maier, S. F., & Jackson, R. L. (1979). Learned helplessness: All of us were right (and wrong): Inescapable shock has multiple effects. In G. H. Bower (ed.), *The psychology of learning and motivation* (Vol. 13). New York: Academic.

Maki, W. S. (1979). Pigeon's short-term memories for surprising vs. expected reinforcement and nonreinforcement. *Animal Learning and Behavior, 7*, 31–37.

Maki, W. S., & Hegvik, D. K. (1980). Directed forgetting in pigeons. *Animal Learning and Behavior, 8*, 567–574.

Marler, P. (1967). Comparative study of song development in sparrows. *Proceedings of the International Ornithological Congress, 14*, 231–244.

Marler, P. (1991). Song learning: The interface between behaviour and neuroethology. In J. R. Krebs & G. Horn (eds.), *Behavioural and neural aspects of learning and memory*. Oxford: Oxford University Press.

Marler, P., & Richards, S. (1989). Species differences in auditory responsiveness in early vocal learning. In R. Dooling & S. Hulse (eds.), *The comparative psychology of audition: Perceiving complex sounds*. Hillsdale, NJ: Erlbaum.

Martin, J. A. (1977). Effects of positive and negative adult-child interactions on children's task performance and task preferences. *Journal of Experimental Child Psychology, 23*, 493–502.

Matute, H. (1995). Human reactions to uncontrollable outcomes: Further evidence for superstitions rather than helplessness. *Quarterly Journal of Experimental Psychology, 48B*, 142–157.

Matzel, L. D., Held, F. P., & Miller, R. R. (1988). Information and expression of simultaneous and backward associations: Implications for contiguity theory. *Learning and Motivation, 19*, 317–344.

Mawhinney, V. T., Bostow, D. E., Laws, D. R., Blumenfeld, G. J., & Hopkins, B. L. (1971). A comparison of students' studying-behavior produced by daily, weekly, and three-week testing schedules. *Journal of Applied Behavior Analysis, 4*, 257–264.

McAllister, D. E., & McAllister, W. R. (1991). Fear theory and aversively motivated behavior: Some controversial issues. In M. R. Denny (ed.), *Fear, avoidance, and phobias: A fundamental analysis* (pp. 135–163). Hillsdale, NJ: Erlbaum.

McAllister, W. R. (1953). Eyelid conditioning as a function of the CS–UCS interval. *Journal of Experimental Psychology, 45*, 417–422.

McClelland, J. L., & Rumelhart, D. E. (1985). Distributed memory and the representation of general and specific information. *Journal of Experimental Psychology: General, 114*, 159–188.

McClelland, J. L., & Rumelhart, D. E. (1986). A distributed model of human learning and memory. In J. L. McClelland, D. E. Rumelhart, & the PDP Research Group, *Parallel distributed processing: Explorations in the microstructure of cognition: Vol. 1. Psychological and biological models*. Cambridge, MA: MIT Press.

McCloskey, M. E., & Glucksberg, S. (1978). Natural categories: Well-defined or fuzzy sets? *Memory & Cognition, 6*, 462–472.

McGuire, R. J., Carlisle, J. M., & Young, B. G. (1965). Sexual deviations as conditioned behaviour: A hypothesis. *Behaviour Research and Therapy, 2*, 185–190.

McLaren, I. P. L., Kaye, H., & Mackintosh, N. J. (1989). An associative theory of the representations of stimuli: Applications to perceptual learning and latent inhibition. In R. G. M. Morris (ed.), *Parallel distributed processing*. Oxford: Oxford University Press.

McNamara, H. J., Long, J. B., & Wike, E. L. (1956). Learning without response under two conditions of external cues. *Journal of Comparative and Physiological Psychology, 49*, 477–480.

McNeil, B. J., Pauker, S. G., Cox, H. C., Jr., & Tversky, A. (1982). On the elicitation of preferences for alternative therapies. *New England Journal of Medicine, 306*, 1259–1262.

McNeil, C. B., Clemens-Mowrer, L., Gurwitch, R. H., & Funderburk, B. W. (1994). Assessment of a new procedure to prevent timeout escape in preschoolers. *Child and Family Behavior Therapy, 16*, 27–35.

Meck, W. H., & Church, R. M. (1983). A mode control model of counting and timing processes. *Journal of Experimental Psychology: Animal Behavior Processes, 9*, 320–334.

Medin, D. L. (1989). Concepts and conceptual structure. *American Psychologist, 44*, 1469–1481.

Meehl, P. E. (1950). On the circularity of the law of effect. *Psychological Bulletin, 47*, 52–75.

Meichenbaum, D. H., Bowers, K. S., & Ross, R. R. (1968). Modification of classroom behavior of institutionalized female adolescent offenders. *Behaviour Research and Therapy, 6*, 343–357.

Menzel, E. W. (1978). Cognitive mapping in chimpanzees. In S. H. Hulse, H. Fowler, & W. K. Honig (eds.), *Cognitive processes in animal behavior*. Hillsdale, NJ: Erlbaum.

Miles, D. R., & Carey, G. (1997). Genetic and environmental architecture of human aggression. *Journal of Personality and Social Psychology, 72*, 207–217.

Milgram, S. (1963). Behavioral study of obedience. *Journal of Abnormal and Social Psychology, 67*, 371–378.

Milgram, S. (1974). *Obedience to authority*. New York: Harper & Row.

Mill, J. (1878). *Analysis of the phenomena of the human mind* (J. S. Mill, ed.). London: Longmans, Green, Reader & Dyer. (Original work published 1829)

Miller, D. L., & Kelley, M. L. (1994). The use of goal setting and contingency contracting for improving children's homework. *Journal of Applied Behavior Analysis, 27*, 73–84.

Miller, N. E., & Dworkin, B. R. (1974). Visceral learning: Recent difficulties with curarized rats and significant problems for human research. In P. A. Obrist, A. H. Black, J. Brener, & L. V. DiCara (eds.), *Cardiovascular psychophysiology: Current issues in response mechanisms, biofeedback, and methodology*. Chicago: Aldine.

Miller, R. R., & Barnet, R. C. (1993). The role of time in elementary associations. *Current Directions in Psychological Science, 2*, 106–111.

Miller, R. R., Barnet, R. C., & Grahame, N. J. (1995). Assessment of the Rescorla-Wagner model. *Psychological Bulletin, 117*, 363–86.

Miller, R. R., & Matzel, L. D. (1989). The comparator hypothesis: A response rule for the expression of associations. In G. H. Bower (ed.), *The psychology of learning and motivation* (vol. 22, pp. 51–92). Orlando, FL: Academic.

Millikan, G. C., & Bowman, R. I. (1967). Observations on Galapagos tool-using finches in captivity. *Living Bird, 6*, 23–41.

Milner, B. (1962). Les troubles de la memoire accompagnant des lesions hippocampiques bilaterales. In *Physiologie de l'hippocampe*. Paris: Centre National de la Recherche Scientifique.

Milner, B. (1966). Amnesia following operation on the temporal lobes. In C. W. M. Whitty & O. L. Zangwill (eds.), *Amnesia*. London: Butterworth.

Mineka, S. (1979). The role of fear in theories of avoidance learning, flooding, and extinction. *Psychological Bulletin, 86*, 985–1010.

Mineka, S., & Cook, M. (1986). Immunization against the observational conditioning of snake fear in rhesus monkeys. *Journal of Abnormal Psychology, 95,* 307–318.

Mischel, W., & Grusec, J. (1966). Determinants of the rehearsal and transmission of neutral and aversive behaviors. *Journal of Personality and Social Psychology, 3,* 197–205.

Mischel, W., & Mischel, H. N. (1977). Self-control and the self. In T. Mischel (ed.), *The self: Psychological and philosophical issues.* Oxford: Blackwell.

Mischel, W., Ebbesen, E. B., & Zeiss, A. R. (1972). Cognitive and attentional mechanisms in delay of gratification. *Journal of Personality and Social Psychology, 21,* 204–218.

Mitchell, G., & Brandt, E. M. (1972). Paternal behavior in primates. In F. E. Poirier (ed.), *Primate socialization.* New York: Random House.

Miyadi, D. (1964). Social life of Japanese monkeys. *Science, 143,* 783–786.

Moeller, G. (1954). The CS–UCS interval in GSR conditioning. *Journal of Experimental Psychology, 48,* 162–166.

Moltz, H. (1957). Latent extinction and the fractional anticipatory response mechanism. *Psychological Review, 64,* 229–241.

Montgomery, K. C. (1954). The role of the exploratory drive in learning. *Journal of Comparative and Physiological Psychology, 47,* 60–64.

Morgan, M. J. (1974). Resistance to satiation. *Animal Behavior, 22,* 449–466.

Morrow, G. R. (1986). Effect of the cognitive hierarchy in the systematic desensitization treatment of anticipatory nausea in cancer patients: A component comparison with relaxation only, counseling, and no treatment. *Cognitive Therapy and Research, 10,* 421–446.

Morse, W., & Kelleher, R. (1977). Determinants of reinforcement and punishment. In W. K. Honig & J. E. R. Staddon (eds.), *Handbook of operant behavior.* Englewood Cliffs, NJ: Prentice-Hall.

Mowrer, O. H. (1947). On the dual nature of learning: A reinterpretation of "conditioning" and "problem-solving." *Harvard Educational Review, 17,* 102–150.

Mowrer, O. H., & Mowrer, W. M. (1938). Enuresis: A method for its study and treatment. *American Journal of Orthopsychiatry, 8,* 436–459.

Muller, R. T. (1996). Family aggressiveness factors in the prediction of corporal punishment: Reciprocal effects and the impact of observer perspective. *Journal of Family Psychology, 10,* 474–489.

Munn, N. L. (1961). *Psychology* (4th ed.). Boston: Houghton Mifflin.

Myers, D. G. (1995). *Psychology* (4th ed.). New York: Worth.

Myerson, J., & Green, L. (1995). Discounting of delayed rewards: Models of individual choice. *Journal of the Experimental Analysis of Behavior, 64,* 263–276.

Nation, J. R., & Cooney, J. B. (1982). The time course of extinction-induced aggressive behavior in humans: Evidence for a stage model of extinction. *Learning and Motivation, 13,* 95–112.

Nedelman, D., & Sulzbacher, S. I. (1972). Dicky at 13 years of age: A long-term success following early application of operant conditioning procedures. In G. Semb (ed.), *Behavior analysis and education,* 1972. Lawrence: University of Kansas.

Neil, A. S. (1960). *Summerhill: A radical approach to child rearing.* New York: Hart.

Neuringer, A. J. (1970). Superstitious key pecking after three peck-produced reinforcements. *Journal of the Experimental Analysis of Behavior, 13,* 127–134.

Notterman, J. M., & Mintz, D. E. (1965). *Dynamics of response.* New York: Wiley.

Odling-Smee, F. J. (1975). Background stimuli and the interstimulus interval during Pavlovian conditioning. *Quarterly Journal of Experimental Psychology, 27,* 387–392.

O'Farrell, T. J., Choquette, K. A., Cutter, H. S. G., Brown, E., Bayog, R., McCourt, W., Lowe, J., Chan, A., & Deneault, P. (1996). Cost-benefit and cost-effectiveness analyses of behavioral marital therapy with and without relapse prevention sessions for alcoholics and their spouses. *Behavior Therapy, 27*, 7–24.

Öhman, A. (1988). Nonconscious control of autonomic responses: A role for Pavlovian conditioning? *Biological Psychology, 27*, 113–135.

Öhman, A., & Soares, J. J. F. (1998). Emotional conditioning to masked stimuli: Expectancies for aversive outcomes following nonrecognized fear-relevant stimuli. *Journal of Experimental Psychology: General, 127*, 69–82.

O'Keefe, J., & Nadel, L. (1978). *The hippocampus as a cognitive map*. Oxford: Clarendon.

Olds, J., & Milner, P. (1954). Positive reinforcement produced by electrical stimulation of septal area and other regions of rat brain. *Journal of Comparative and Physiological Psychology, 47*, 419–427.

O'Leary, K. D., Becker, W. C., Evans, M. B., & Saudargas, R. A. (1969). A token reinforcement program in a public school: A replication and systematic analysis. *Journal of Applied Behavior Analysis, 2*, 3–13.

O'Leary, K. D., Poulos, R. W., & Devine, V. T. (1972). Tangible reinforcers: Bonuses or bribes? *Journal of Consulting and Clinical Psychology, 38*, 1–8.

O'Leary, S. G. (1995). Parental discipline mistakes. *Current Directions in Psychological Science, 4*, 11–13.

Olton, D. S., & Samuelson, R. J. (1976). Remembrance of places passed: Spatial memory in rats. *Journal of Experimental Psychology: Animal Behavior Processes, 2*, 97–116.

Ono, K. (1987). Superstitious behavior in humans. *Journal of the Experimental Analysis of Behavior, 47*, 261–271.

Ost, L. G., Stridh, B. M., & Wolf, M. (1998). A clinical study of spider phobia: prediction of outcome after self-help and therapist-directed treatments. *Behaviour Research and Therapy, 36*, 17–36.

Overmier, J. B., & Seligman, M. E. P. (1967). Effects of inescapable shock upon subsequent escape and avoidance learning. *Journal of Comparative and Physiological Psychology, 63*, 23–33.

Overton, D. A. (1964). State-dependent or "dissociated" learning produced with pentobarbital. *Journal of Comparative and Physiological Psychology, 57*, 3–12.

Overton, D. A. (1985). Contextual stimulus effects of drugs and internal states. In P. D. Balsam & A. Tomie (eds.), *Context and learning*. Hillsdale, NJ: Erlbaum.

Parkin, A. J. (1993). *Memory: Phenomena, experiment and theory*. Oxford: Blackwell.

Patterson, G. R., Reid, J. B., & Dishion, T. J. (1989). *A social interactional approach: IV. Antisocial boys*. Eugene, OR: Castalia.

Paul, G. L. (1969). Outcome of systematic desensitization II: Controlled investigations of individual treatment, technique variations, and current status. In C. M. Franks (ed.), *Behavior therapy: Appraisal and status*. New York: McGraw-Hill.

Pavlov, I. P. (1927). *Conditioned reflexes* (G. V. Anrep, trans.). Oxford: Oxford University Press.

Pavlov, I. P. (1928). *Lectures on conditioned reflexes* (W. H. Gantt, trans.). New York: International Publishers.

Pavlov, I. P. (1941). *Conditioned reflexes and psychiatry*. New York: International Publishers.

Pearce, J. M. (1994). Similarity and discrimination: A selective review and a connectionist model. *Psychological Review, 101*, 587–607.

Pearce, J. M., Aydin, A., & Redhead, E. S. (1997). Configural analysis of summation in autoshaping. *Journal of Experimental Psychology: Animal Behavior Processes, 23*, 84–94.

Pearce, J. M., Colwill, R. M., & Hall, G. (1978). Instrumental conditioning of scratching in the laboratory rat. *Learning and Motivation, 9*, 255–271.

Pearce, J. M., & Hall, G. (1980). A model for Pavlovian learning: Variations in the effectiveness of conditioned but not of unconditioned stimuli. *Psychological Review, 87,* 532–552.

Penfield, W. (1958). *The excitable cortex in conscious man.* Liverpool: University of Liverpool Press.

Pepperberg, I. M. (1993). Cognition and communication in an African Grey parrot (*Psittacus erithacus*): Studies on a nonhuman, nonprimate, nonmammalian subject. In H. L. Roitblat, L. M. Herman, & P. E. Nachtigall (eds.), *Language and communication: Comparative perspectives* (pp. 221–248). Hillsdale, NJ: Erlbaum.

Perkins, C. C., Jr. (1947). The relation of secondary reward to gradients of reinforcement. *Journal of Experimental Psychology, 37,* 377–392.

Peterson, C., Maier, S. F., & Seligman, M. E. P. (1993). *Learned helplessness: A theory for the age of personal control.* New York: Oxford University Press.

Peterson, G. B., Ackil, J. E., Frommer, G. P., & Hearst, E. S. (1972). Conditioned approach and contact behavior toward signals for food and brain-stimulation reinforcement. *Science, 177,* 1009–1011.

Peterson, L. R., & Peterson, M. J. (1959). Short-term retention of individual verbal items. *Journal of Experimental Psychology, 58,* 193–198.

Petty, R. E., & Cacioppo, J. T. (1986). *Communication and persuasion: Central and peripheral routes to attitude change.* New York: Springer-Verlag.

Pfungst, O. (1965). *Clever Hans: The horse of Mr. von Osten.* New York: Holt, Rinehart and Winston.

Phillips, E. L. (1968). Achievement Place: Token reinforcement procedures in a home-style rehabilitation setting for "pre-delinquent" boys. *Journal of Applied Behavior Analysis, 1,* 213–233.

Pinker, S., & Prince, A. (1988). On language and connectionism: Analysis of a parallel distributed processing model of language acquisition. *Cognition, 28,* 73–193.

Posner, M. I., & Keele, S. W. (1968). On the genesis of abstract ideas. *Journal of Experimental Psychology, 77,* 353–363.

Postman, L. (1985). Human learning and memory. In G. A. Kimble & K. Schlesinger (Eds.), *Topics in the history of psychology* (Vol. 1). Hillsdale, NJ: Erlbaum.

Poulson, C. L. (1983). Differential reinforcement of other-than-vocalization as a control procedure in the conditioning of infant vocalization rate. *Journal of Experimental Child Psychology, 36,* 471–489.

Powell, D. R., Jr., & Perkins, C. C., Jr. (1957). Strength of secondary reinforcement as a determiner of the effects of duration of goal response on learning. *Journal of Experimental Psychology, 53,* 106–112.

Premack, D. (1965). Reinforcement theory. In D. Levine (ed.), *Nebraska symposium on motivation* (Vol. 13). Lincoln: University of Nebraska Press.

Premack, D. (1971). Catching up with common sense, or two sides of a generalization: Reinforcement and punishment. In R. Glaser (ed.), *The nature of reinforcement.* New York: Academic.

Premack, D., & Woodruff, G. (1978). Chimpanzee problem solving: A test for comprehension. *Science, 202,* 532–535.

Rachlin, H. (1974). Self-control. *Behaviorism, 2,* 94–107.

Rachlin, H., & Green, L. (1972). Commitment, choice, and self-control. *Journal of the Experimental Analysis of Behavior, 17,* 15–22.

Rachman, S., & Hodgson, R. J. (1968). Experimentally induced "sexual fetishism": Replication and development. *Psychological Record, 18,* 25–27.

Raitkin, B. C., Gibbon, J., Penney, T. B., Malapani, C., Hinton, S. C., & Meck, W. H. (1998). Scalar expectancy theory and peak-interval timing in humans. *Journal of Experimental Psychology: Animal Behavior Processes, 24,* 15–33.

Ramsay, D. S., & Woods, S. C. (1997). Biological consequences of drug administration: Implications for acute and chronic tolerance. *Psychological Review, 104,* 170–193.

Raymond, M. J. (1964). The treatment of addiction by aversion conditioning with apomorphine. *Behaviour Research and Therapy, 1,* 287–291.

Razran, G. (1971). *Mind in evolution.* New York: Houghton Mifflin.

Reiss, S., & Wagner, A. R. (1972). CS habituation produces a "latent inhibition effect" but no active "conditioned inhibition." *Learning and Motivation, 3,* 237–245.

Reitman, D., & Drabman, R. S. (1996). Read my fingertips: A procedure for enhancing the effectiveness of time-out with argumentative children. *Child and Family Behavior Therapy, 18,* 35–40.

Renner, M. (1960). Contribution of the honey bee to the study of time sense and astronomical orientation. *Cold Spring Harbor Symposium on Quantitative Biology, 25,* 361–367.

Rescorla, R. A. (1966). Predictability and number of pairings in Pavlovian fear conditioning. *Psychonomic Science, 4,* 383–384.

Rescorla, R. A. (1967). Pavlovian conditioning and its proper control procedures. *Psychological Review, 74,* 71–80.

Rescorla, R. A. (1968). Probability of shock in the presence and absence of CS in fear conditioning. *Journal of Comparative and Physiological Psychology, 66,* 1–5.

Rescorla, R. A. (1969). Pavlovian conditioned inhibition. *Psychological Bulletin, 72,* 77–94.

Rescorla, R. A. (1970). Reduction in the effectiveness of reinforcement after prior excitatory conditioning. *Learning and Motivation, 1,* 372–381.

Rescorla, R. A. (1973). Evidence for "unique stimulus" account of configural conditioning. *Journal of Comparative and Physiological Psychology, 85,* 331–338.

Rescorla, R. A. (1980a). *Pavlovian second-order conditioning.* Hillsdale, NJ: Erlbaum.

Rescorla, R. A. (1980b). Simultaneous and successive associations in sensory preconditioning. *Journal of Experimental Psychology: Animal Behavior Processes, 6,* 207–216.

Rescorla, R. A. (1981). Simultaneous associations. In P. Harzem & M. D. Zeiler (eds.), *Predictability, correlation, and contiguity.* New York: Wiley.

Rescorla, R. A. (1982). Simultaneous second-order conditioning produces S–S learning in conditioned suppression. *Journal of Experimental Psychology: Animal Behavior Processes, 8,* 23–32.

Rescorla, R. A. (1985a). Conditioned inhibition and facilitation. In R. R. Miller & N. E. Spear (eds.), *Information processing in animals: Conditioned inhibition.* Hillsdale, NJ: Erlbaum.

Rescorla, R. A. (1985b). Pavlovian conditioning analogues to Gestalt perceptual principles. In F. R. Brush & J. B. Overmier (eds.), *Affect, conditioning, and cognition: Essays on the determinants of behavior.* Hillsdale, NJ: Erlbaum.

Rescorla, R. A. (1987). A Pavlovian analysis of goal-directed behavior. *American Psychologist, 42,* 119–129.

Rescorla, R. A. (1988). Pavlovian conditioning: It's not what you think it is. *American Psychologist, 43,* 151–160.

Rescorla, R. A. (1997a). Spontaneous recovery after Pavlovian conditioning with multiple outcomes. *Animal Learning and Behavior, 25,* 99–107.

Rescorla, R. A. (1997b). Summation: Assessment of a configural theory. *Animal Learning and Behavior, 25,* 200–209.

Rescorla, R. A., Grau, J. W., Durlach, P. J. (1985). Analysis of the unique cue in configural discriminations. *Journal of Experimental Psychology: Animal Behavior Processes, 11,* 356–366.

Rescorla, R. A., & LoLordo, V. M. (1965). Inhibition of avoidance behavior. *Journal of Comparative and Physiological Psychology, 59*, 406–412.

Rescorla, R. A., & Wagner, A. R. (1972). A theory of Pavlovian conditioning: Variations in the effectiveness of reinforcement and nonreinforcement. In A. H. Black & W. F. Prokasy (eds.), *Classical conditioning II: Current research and theory*. New York: Appleton-Century-Crofts.

Revusky, S. (1971). The role of interference in association over a delay. In W. K. Honig & P. H. R. James (eds.), *Animal memory*. New York: Academic.

Revusky, S. (1985). The general process approach to animal learning. In T. D. Johnston & A. T. Petrewicz (eds.), *Issues in the ecological study of learning*. Hillsdale, NJ: Erlbaum.

Reynolds, G. S. (1961). Attention in the pigeon. *Journal of the Experimental Analysis of Behavior, 4*, 203–208.

Reynolds, L. K., & Kelley, M. L. (1997). The efficacy of a response cost-based treatment package for managing aggressive behavior in preschoolers. *Behavior Modification, 21*, 216–230.

Rincover, A., & Koegel, R. L. (1975). Setting generality and stimulus control in autistic children. *Journal of Applied Behavior Analysis, 8*, 235–246.

Risley, T. R. (1968). The effects and side effects of punishing the autistic behaviors of a deviant child. *Journal of Applied Behavior Analysis, 1*, 21–34.

Roberts, M. W., & Powers, S. W. (1990). Adjusting chair timeout enforcement procedures for oppositional children. *Behavior Therapy, 21*, 257–271.

Roberts, S. (1981). Isolation of an internal clock. *Journal of Experimental Psychology: Animal Behavior Processes, 7*, 242–268.

Roberts, W. A. (1996). Stimulus generalization and hierarchical structure in categorization by animals. In T. R. Zentall & P. M. Smeets (eds.), *Stimulus class formation in humans and animals* (pp. 35–54). Amsterdam: North Holland.

Roberts, W. A. (1998). *Principles of animal cognition*. Boston: McGraw-Hill.

Romanes, G. J. (1882). *Animal intelligence*. London: Kegan Paul.

Rortvedt, A. K., & Miltenberger, R. G. (1994). Analysis of a high-probability instructional sequence and time-out in the treatment of child noncompliance. Special Issue: Functional analysis approaches to behavioral assessment and treatment. *Journal of Applied Behavior Analysis, 27*, 327–330.

Rosch, E. (1973). On the internal structure of perceptual and semantic categories. In T. E. Moore (ed.), *Cognitive development and the acquisition of language*. New York: Academic.

Rosch, E. (1975). Cognitive representations of semantic categories. *Journal of Experimental Psychology: General, 104*, 192–233.

Rosch, E. (1978). Principles of categorization. In E. Rosch & B. B. Lloyd (eds.), *Cognition and categorization* (pp. 27–48). Hillsdale, NJ: Erlbaum.

Rosch, E., Simpson, C., & Miller, R. S. (1976). Structural bases of typicality effects. *Journal of Experimental Psychology: Human Perception and Performance, 2*, 491–502.

Rosenfeld, H. M., & Baer, D. M. (1969). Unnoticed verbal conditioning of an aware experimenter by a more aware subject: The double-agent effect. *Psychological Review, 76*, 425–432.

Rosenthal, R. (1966). *Experimenter effects in behavioral research*. New York: Appleton-Century-Crofts.

Rosenthal, T., & Bandura, A. (1978). Psychological modeling: Theory and practice. In S. L. Garfield & A. E. Bergin (eds.), *Handbook of psychotherapy and behavior change: An empirical analysis* (2nd ed.). New York: Wiley.

Rosenzweig, M. R. (1984). Experience, memory, and the brain. *American Psychologist, 39*, 365–376.

Ross, M., & Sicoly, F. (1979). Egocentric biases in availability and attribution. *Journal of Personality and Social Psychology, 37*, 322–336.

Roueche, B. (1954). *Eleven blue men*. Boston: Little, Brown.

Rozin, P., & Zellner, D. (1985). The role of Pavlovian conditioning in the acquisition of food likes and dislikes. *Annals of the New York Academy of Sciences, 443*, 189–202.

Rumbaugh, D. M., & Savage-Rumbaugh, E. S. (1994). Language in comparative perspective. In N. J. Mackintosh (ed.), *Animal learning and cognition* (pp. 307–333). San Diego: Academic.

Rumelhart, D. E., & McClelland, J. L. (1986). On learning the past tenses of English verbs. In J. L. McClelland, D. E. Rumelhart, & the PDP Research Group, *Parallel distributed processing: Explorations in the microstructure of cognition: Vol. 2. Psychological and biological models*. Cambridge, MA: MIT Press.

Rutter, M. (1970). Autistic children: Infancy to adulthood. *Seminars in Psychiatry, 2*, 435–450.

Ryan, R. M. (1982). Control and information in the intrapersonal sphere: An extension of cognitive evaluation theory. *Journal of Personality and Social Psychology, 43*, 450–461.

Salzen, E. A., & Meyer, C. C. (1968). Reversibility of imprinting. *Journal of Comparative and Physiological Psychology, 66*, 269–275.

Savage-Rumbaugh, E. S., & Lewin, R. (1994). *Kanzi: At the brink of the human mind*. New York: Wiley.

Savage-Rumbaugh, E. S., Murphy, J., Sevcik, R. A., Brakke, K. E., Williams, S., & Rumbaugh, D. M. (1993). Language comprehension in ape and child. *Monographs of the Society for Research in Child Development, 58*, 1–221.

Savage-Rumbaugh, E. S., Rumbaugh, D. M., Smith, S. T., & Lawson, J. (1980). Reference: The linguistic essential. *Science, 210*, 922–925.

Schacter, S., & Singer, J. E. (1962). Cognitive, social and physiological determinants of emotional state. *Psychological Review, 69*, 379–399.

Schmajuk, N. A., Lam, Y. W., & Gray, J. A. (1996). Latent inhibition: A neural network approach. *Journal of Experimental Psychology: Animal Behavior Processes, 22*, 321–349.

Schmajuk, N. A., Lamoureux, J. A., & Holland, P. C. (1998). Occasion setting: A neural network approach. *Psychological Review, 105*, 3–32.

Schneider, B. A., & Shiffrin, R. M. (1977). Controlled and automatic human information processing: I. Detection, search, and attention. *Psychological Review, 84*, 1–66.

Scott, W. A. (1959). Attitude change by response reinforcement: Replication and extension. *Sociometry, 22*, 328–335.

Sears, R. R., Maccoby, E. E., & Levin, H. (1957). *Patterns of child rearing*. Evanston, IL: Row, Peterson.

Seidenberg, M. S. (1993). Connectionist models and cognitive theory. *Psychological Science, 4*, 228–235.

Sejnowski, T. J., & Rosenberg, C. R. (1987). Parallel networks that learn to pronounce English text. *Complex Systems, 1*, 145–168.

Seligman, M. E. P. (1969). Control group and conditioning: A comment on operationalism. *Psychological Review, 76*, 484–491.

Seligman, M. E. P. (1970). On the generality of the laws of learning. *Psychological Review, 77*, 406–418.

Seligman, M. E. P., & Johnston, J. C. (1973). A cognitive theory of avoidance learning. In F. J. McGuigan & D. B. Lumsden (eds.), *Contemporary approaches to conditioning and learning*. Washington, DC: Winston-Wiley.

Seligman, M. E. P., & Maier, S. F. (1967). Failure to escape traumatic shock. *Journal of Experimental Psychology, 74*, 1–9.

Shanks, D. R., Pearson, S. M., & Dickinson, A. (1989). Temporal contiguity and the judgment of causality. *Quarterly Journal of Experimental Psychology, 41B*, 139–159.

Shanks, D. R., & St. John, M. F. (1994). Characteristics of dissociable human learning systems. *Behavioral and Brain Sciences, 17*, 367–447.

Sheffield, F. D. (1965). Relation between classical conditioning and instrumental learning. In W. F. Prokasy (ed.), *Classical conditioning*. New York: Appleton-Century-Crofts.

Sheffield, F. D., Wulff, J. J., & Backer, R. (1951). Reward value of copulation without sex drive reduction. *Journal of Comparative and Physiological Psychology, 44*, 3–8.

Shepp, B. E. (1983). The analyzability of multidimensional objects: Some constraints on perceived structure, the development of perceived structure, and attention. In T. J. Tighe & B. E. Shepp (eds.), *Perception, cognition and development: Interactional analyses.* Hillsdale, NJ: Erlbaum.

Shepp, B. E., & Schrier, A. M. (1969). Consecutive intradimensional and extradimensional shifts in monkeys. *Journal of Comparative and Physiological Psychology, 67*, 199–203.

Shettleworth, S. J. (1983). Function and mechanism in learning. In M. D. Zeiler & P. Harzem (eds.), *Advances in analysis of behaviour* (Vol. 3). Chichester, England: Wiley.

Shettleworth, S. J. (1993). Varieties of learning and memory in animals. *Journal of Experimental Psychology: Animal Behavior Processes, 19*, 5–14.

Shiffrin, R. M., & Schneider, W. (1977). Controlled and automatic human information processing: II. Perceptual learning, automatic attending, and a general theory. *Psychological Review, 84*, 127–190.

Siegel, S. (1972). Conditioning of insulin-induced glycemia. *Journal of Comparative and Physiological Psychology, 78*, 233–241.

Siegel, S. (1975). Evidence from rats that morphine tolerance is a learned response. *Journal of Comparative and Physiological Psychology, 89*, 498–506.

Siegel, S. (1978). A Pavlovian conditioning analysis of morphine tolerance. In N. A. Krasnegor (ed.), *Behavioral tolerance: Research and treatment implications* (NIDA Research Monograph No. 18). Washington, DC: U.S. Government Printing Office.

Siegel, S. (1984). Pavlovian conditioning and heroin overdose: Reports by overdose victims. *Bulletin of the Psychonomic Society, 22*, 428–430.

Siegel, S., & Allan, L. G. (1996). The widespread influence of the Rescorla-Wagner model. *Psychonomic Bulletin & Review, 3*, 314–321.

Siegel, S., Hinson, R. E., Krank, M. D., & McCully, J. (1982). Heroin "overdose" death: Contribution of drug-associated environmental cues. *Science, 216*, 436–437.

Siegel, S., & Castellan, N. J., Jr. (1988). *Nonparametric stastistics for the behavioral sciences.* New York: McGraw-Hill.

Silberberg, A., Warren-Boulton, F. R., & Asano, T. (1987). Inferior-good and Giffen-good effects in monkey choice behavior. *Journal of Experimental Psychology: Animal Behavior Processes, 13*, 292–301.

Silva, K. M., & Timberlake, W. (1997). A behavior systems view of conditioned states during long and short CS–US intervals. *Learning and Motivation, 28*, 467–490.

Simon, H. A. (1957). *Models of man.* New York: Wiley.

Singh, D. (1993). Adaptive significance of female physical attractiveness: Role of waist-to-hip ratio. *Journal of Personality and Social Psychology, 65*, 293–307.

Singh, D. (1995). Female judgment of male attractiveness and desirability for relationships: Role of waist-to-hip ratio and financial status. *Journal of Personality and Social Psychology, 69*, 1089–1101.

Siqueland, E. R., & DeLucia, C. A. (1969). Visual reinforcement of non-nutritive sucking in human infants. *Science, 165*, 1144–1146.

Skinner, B. F. (1938). *The behavior of organisms.* New York: Appleton-Century-Crofts.

Skinner, B. F. (1948a). *Walden two.* New York: Macmillan.

Skinner, B. F. (1948b). "Superstition" in the pigeon. *Journal of Experimental Psychology, 38*, 168–172.

Skinner, B. F. (1953). *Science and human behavior.* New York: Macmillan.

Skinner, B. F. (1955). Freedom and the control of men. *American Scholar, 25*, 47–65.

Skinner, B. F. (1956). A case history in scientific method. *American Psychologist, 32,* 221–233.

Slovic, P., & Lichtenstein, S. (1968). The relative importance of probabilities and payoffs in risk taking. *Journal of Experimental Psychology Monograph Supplement, 78* (3 Pt. 2).

Small, W. S. (1901). An experimental study of the mental processes of the rat. *American Journal of Psychology, 12,* 206–239.

Smith, G. H., & Engel, R. (1968). Influence of a female model on perceived characteristics of an automobile. *Proceedings of the 76th Annual Convention of the American Psychological Association, 3,* 681–682.

Smith, J. D., Murray, M. J., Jr., & Minda, J. P. (1997). Straight talk about linear separability. *Journal of Experimental Psychology: Learning, Memory, and Cognition, 23,* 659–680.

Smith, S. M. (1979). Remembering in and out of context. *Journal of Experimental Psychology: Human Learning and Memory, 5,* 460–471.

Smith, T., & Lovaas, O. I. (1997). The UCLA Young Autism Project: A reply to Gresham and MacMillan. *Behavioral Disorders, 22,* 202–218.

Solomon, R. L., Kamin, L. J., & Wynne, L. C. (1953). Traumatic avoidance learning: The outcomes of several extinction procedures with dogs. *Journal of Abnormal and Social Psychology, 48,* 291–302.

Solomon, R. L., Turner, L. H., & Lessac, M. S. (1968). Some effects of delay of punishment on resistance to temptation in dogs. *Journal of Personality and Social Psychology, 8,* 233–238.

Solomon, R. L., & Wynne, L. (1953). Traumatic avoidance learning: Acquisition in normal dogs. *Psychological Monographs, 67* (4, Whole No. 354).

Spear, N. E. (1978). *The processing of memories: Forgetting and retention.* Hillsdale, NJ: Erlbaum.

Spence, K. W. (1936). The nature of discrimination learning in animals. *Psychological Review, 43,* 427–449.

Spence, K. W. (1937). The differential response in animals to stimuli varying within a single dimension. *Psychological Review, 44,* 430–444.

Spence, K. W. (1947). The role of secondary reinforcement in delayed-reward learning. *Psychological Review, 54,* 1–8.

Spence, K. W. (1966). Cognitive and drive factors in the extinction of the conditioned eye blink in human subjects. *Psychological Review, 73,* 445–458.

Spence, K. W., Homzie, M. J., & Rutledge, E. F. (1964). Extinction of the human eyelid CR as a function of the discriminability of the change from acquisition to extinction. *Journal of Experimental Psychology, 67,* 545–552.

Squire, L. R. (1987). *Memory and brain.* New York: Oxford University Press.

Squire, L. R. (1992). Memory and the hippocampus: A synthesis from findings with rats, monkeys, and humans. *Psychological Review, 99,* 195–231.

Staddon, J. E. R. (1983). *Adaptive behavior and learning.* Cambridge: Cambridge University Press.

Staddon, J. E. R., & Simmelhag, V. L. (1971). The "superstition" experiment: A reexamination of its implications for the principles of adaptive behavior. *Psychological Review, 78,* 3–43.

Stokes, T. F., Baer, D. M., & Jackson, R. L. (1974). Programming the generalization of a greeting response in four retarded children. *Journal of Applied Behavior Analysis, 7,* 599–610.

Strassberg, Z., Dodge, K. A., Pettit, G. S., & Bates, J. E. (1994). Spanking in the home and children's subsequent aggression toward kindergarten peers. *Development and Psychopathology, 6,* 445–461.

Straus, M. A., & Kantor, G. K. (1994). Corporal punishment of adolescents by parents: A risk factor in the epidemiology of depression, suicide, alcohol abuse, child abuse, and wife beating. *Adolescence, 29,* 543–561.

Stuart, R. B. (1967). Behavioral control of overeating. *Behaviour Research and Therapy, 5,* 357–365.

Sutherland, N. S., & Mackintosh, N. J. (1971). *Mechanisms of animal discrimination learning.* New York: Academic.

Sutton, R. S., & Barto, A. G. (1981). Toward a modern theory of adaptive networks: Expectation and prediction. *Psychological Review, 88,* 135–170.

Suzuki, S., Augerinos, G., & Black, A. H. (1980). Stimulus control of spatial behavior on the eight-arm maze in rats. *Learning and Motivation, 11,* 1–18.

Svartdal, F. (1995). When feedback contingencies and rules compete: Testing a boundary condition for verbal control of instrumental performance. *Learning and Motivation, 26,* 221–238.

Swartzentruber, D. (1995). Modulatory mechanisms in Pavlovian conditioning. *Animal Learning and Behavior, 23,* 123–143.

Taylor, J., & Miller, M. (1997). When timeout works some of the time: The importance of treatment integrity and functional assessment. *School Psychology Quarterly, 12,* 4–22.

Telegdy, G. A., & Cohen, J. S. (1971). Cue utilization and drive level in albino rats. *Journal of Comparative and Physiological Psychology, 75,* 248–253.

Terrace, H. S. (1966). Stimulus control. In W. K. Honig (ed.), *Operant behavior: Areas of research and application.* New York: Appleton-Century-Crofts.

Terrace, H. S. (1979). *Nim.* New York: Knopf.

Terrace, H. S. (1985). Animal cognition: Thinking without language. In L. Weiskrantz (ed.), *Animal intelligence.* Oxford: Clarendon.

Terrace, H. S., Petitto, L. A., Sanders, R. J., & Bever, T. G. (1979). Can an ape create a sentence? *Science, 206,* 891–902.

Testa, T. J. (1975). Effects of similarity of location and temporal intensity pattern of conditioned and unconditioned stimuli on the acquisition of conditioned suppression in rats. *Journal of Experimental Psychology: Animal Behavior Processes, 1,* 114–121.

Thomas, D. R., Mood, K., Morrison, S., & Wiertelak, E. (1991). Peak shift revisited: A test of alternative interpretations. *Journal of Experimental Psychology: Animal Behavior Processes, 17,* 130–141.

Thomas, G. V. (1981). Contiguity, reinforcement rate, and the law of effect. *Quarterly Journal of Experimental Psychology, 33B,* 33–43.

Thomas, G. V., Robertson, D., & Lieberman, D. A. (1987). Marking effects in Pavlovian trace conditioning. *Journal of Experimental Psychology: Animal Behavior Processes, 13,* 126–135.

Thorndike, E. L. (1898). Animal intelligence: An experimental study of the associative processes in animals. *Psychological Review Monograph Supplement, 2*(8).

Thorndike, E. L. (1911). *Animal intelligence.* New York: Macmillan.

Thorndike, E. L. (1935). *The psychology of wants, interests, and attitudes.* New York: Appleton-Century-Crofts.

Thyer, B. A., & Birsinger, P. (1994). Treatment of clients with anxiety disorders. In D. K. Granvold (ed.), *Cognitive and behavioral treatment: Methods and applications.* Pacific Grove, CA: Brooks/Cole.

Tiffany, S. T., Martin, E. M., & Baker, T. B. (1986). Treatments for cigarette smoking: An evaluation of the contributions of aversion and counseling procedures. *Behaviour Research and Therapy, 24,* 437–452.

Tiffany, S. T., Maude-Griffin, P. M., & Drobes, D. J. (1991). Effect of interdose interval on the development of associative tolerance to morphine in the rat: A dose-response analysis. *Behavioral Neuroscience, 105,* 49–61.

Timberlake, W. (1984). The functional organization of appetitive behavior: Behavior systems and learning. In M. D. Zeiler & P. Harzem (eds.), *Advances in the analysis of behavior* (Vol. 3). New York: Wiley.

Timberlake, W. (1994). Behavior systems, associationism, and Pavlovian conditioning. *Psychonomic Bulletin & Review, 1,* 405–420.

Timberlake, W., & Allison, J. (1974). Response deprivation: An empirical approach to instrumental performance. *Psychological Review, 81,* 146–164.

Timberlake, W., & Grant, D. S. (1975). Autoshaping in rats to the presentation of another rat predicting food. *Science, 190,* 690–692.

Timberlake, W., & Lucas, G. A. (1989). Behavior systems and learning: From misbehavior to general principles. In S. B. Klein & R. R. Mowrer (eds.), *Contemporary learning theories: Instrumental conditioning theory and the impact of biological constraints on learning.* Hillsdale, NJ: Erlbaum.

Timberlake, W., Wahl, G., & King, D. (1982). Stimulus and response contingencies in the misbehavior of rats. *Journal of Experimental Psychology: Animal Behavior Processes, 8,* 62–85.

Tinbergen, N. (1951). *The study of instinct.* Oxford: Clarendon.

Tinklepaugh, O. L. (1928). An experimental study of representative factors in monkeys. *Journal of Comparative and Physiological Psychology, 8,* 197–236.

Titchener, E. B. (1915). *A textbook of psychology.* New York: Macmillan.

Tolman, E. C. (1932). *Purposive behavior in animals and men.* New York: Century.

Tolman, E. C. (1948). Cognitive maps in rats and men. *Psychological Review, 55,* 189–208.

Tolman, E. C., & Honzik, C. H. (1930a). "Insight" in rats. *University of California Publications in Psychology, 4,* 215–232.

Tolman, E. C., & Honzik, C. H. (1930b). Introduction and removal of reward, and maze performance in rats. *University of California Publications in Psychology, 4,* 257–275.

Trabasso, T. (1963). Stimulus emphasis and all-or-none learning of concept identification. *Journal of Experimental Psychology, 65,* 395–406.

Trabasso, T., & Bower, G. H. (1968). *Attention in learning: Theory and research.* New York: Wiley.

Tulley, M., & Chiu, L. H. (1995). Student teachers and classroom discipline. *Journal of Educational Research, 88,* 164–171.

Tulving, E., & Psotka, J. (1971). Retroactive inhibition in free recall: Inaccessibility of information available in the memory store. *Journal of Experimental Psychology, 87,* 1–8.

Turner, A. M., & Greenough, W. T. (1985). Differential rearing effects on rat visual cortex synapses: I. Synaptic and neuronal density and synapses per neuron. *Brain Research, 329,* 195–203.

Turner, R. M. (1986). Behavioral self-control procedures for disorders of initiating and maintaining sleep. *Clinical Psychology Review, 6,* 27–38.

Tversky, A. (1972). Elimination by aspects: A theory of choice. *Psychological Review, 79,* 281–299.

Tversky, A., & Kahneman, A. (1974). Judgment under uncertainty: Heuristics and biases. *Science, 185,* 1124–1131.

Tversky, A., & Kahneman, A. (1987). Rational choice and the framing of decisions. In R. Hogarth & M. Reder (eds.), *Rational choice: The contrast between economics and psychology.* Chicago: University of Chicago Press.

Ulrich, R. E., & Azrin, N. H. (1962). Reflexive fighting in response to aversive stimulation. *Journal of the Experimental Analysis of Behavior, 5,* 511–520.

Underwood, B. J. (1957). Interference and forgetting. *Psychological Review, 64,* 49–60.

Van Hamme, L. J., & Wasserman, E. A. (1994). Cue competition in causality judgments: The role of nonpresentation of compound stimulus elements. *Learning and Motivation, 25,* 127–151.

van Kampen, H. S. (1996). A framework for the study of filial imprinting and the development of attachment. *Psychonomic Bulletin and Review, 3,* 3–20.

Vander Wall, S. B. (1982). An experimental analysis of cache recovery in Clark's nutcracker. *Animal Behavior, 30,* 84–94.

Wadden, T. A., Foster, G. D., & Letizia, K. A. (1994). One-year behavioral treatment of obesity: Comparison of moderate and severe caloric restriction and the effects of weight maintenance therapy. *Journal of Consulting and Clinical Psychology, 62*, 165–171.

Wagner, A. R. (1959). The role of reinforcement and nonreinforcement in an "apparent frustration effect." *Journal of Experimental Psychology, 57*, 130–136.

Wagner, A. R. (1969). Incidental stimuli and discrimination learning. In R. M. Gilbert & N. S. Sutherland (eds.), *Animal discrimination learning*. London: Academic.

Wagner, A. R. (1981). SOP: A model of automatic memory processing in animal behavior. In N. E. Spear & R. R. Miller (eds.), *Information processing in animals: Memory mechanisms*. Hillsdale, NJ: Erlbaum.

Wagner, A. R., Rudy, J. W., & Whitlow, J. W. (1973). Rehearsal in animal conditioning. *Journal of Experimental Psychology Monograph, 97*, 407–426.

Wagner, G. A., & Morris, E. K. (1987). "Superstitious" behavior in children. *Psychological Record, 37*, 471–488.

Wahlsten, D. L., & Cole, M. (1972). Classical and avoidance training of leg flexion in the dog. In A. H. Black & W. F. Prokasy (eds.), *Classical conditioning II: Current research and theory*. New York: Appleton-Century-Crofts.

Ward-Robinson, J., & Hall, G. (1996). Backward sensory preconditioning. *Journal of Experimental Psychology: Animal Behavior Processes, 22*, 295–404.

Warren, J. M. (1954). Perceptual dominance in discrimination learning by monkeys. *Journal of Comparative and Physiological Psychology, 47*, 290–292.

Warren, V. L., & Cairns, R. B. (1972). Social reinforcement satiation: An outcome of frequency or ambiguity? *Journal of Experimental Child Psychology, 13*, 249–260.

Wasserman, E. A. (1973). Pavlovian conditioning with heat reinforcement produces stimulus-directed pecking in chicks. *Science, 181*, 875–877.

Wasserman, E. A. (1990). Attribution of causality to common and distinctive elements of compound stimuli. *Psychological Science, 1*, 298–302.

Wasserman, E. A., & Astley, S. L. (1994). A behavioral analysis of concepts: Its application to pigeons and children. In D. L. Medin (ed.), *The psychology of learning and motivation* (Vol. 31, pp. 73–132). San Diego: Academic.

Wasserman, E. A., & Neunaber, D. J. (1986). College students' responding to and rating of contingency relations: The role of temporal contiguity. *Journal of the Experimental Analysis of Behavior, 46*, 15–35.

Watkins, M. J., & Watkins, O. C. (1976). Cue-overload theory and the method of interpolated attributes. *Bulletin of the Psychonomic Society, 7*, 289–291.

Watson, J. B. (1913). Psychology as the behaviorist views it. *Psychological Review, 20*, 158–177.

Watson, J. B., & McDougall, W. (1929). *The battle of behaviorism*. New York: Norton.

Watson, J. B., & Raynor, R. (1920). Conditioned emotional reactions. *Journal of Experimental Psychology, 3*, 1–14.

Wearden, J. H., & Doherty, M.F. (1995). Exploring and developing a connectionist model of animal timing: Peak procedure and fixed-interval simulations. *Journal of Experimental Psychology: Animal Behavior Processes, 21*, 99–115.

Weingarten, H. P. (1983). Conditioned cues elicit feeding in sated rats: A role for learning in meal initiation. *Science, 20*, 431–433.

Weinstein, C. E., & Meyer, R. E. (1986). The teaching of learning strategies. In M. Wittrock (ed.), *The handbook of research on teaching* (3rd ed.). New York: Macmillan.

Westen, D. (1998). The scientific legacy of Sigmund Freud: Toward a psychodynamically informed psychological science. *Psychological Bulletin, 124*, 333–371.

White, A. G., & Bailey, J. S. (1990). Reducing disruptive behaviors of elementary physical education students with Sit and Watch. *Journal of Applied Behavior Analysis, 23,* 353–359.

Whiten, A., Custance, D. M., Gomez, J. G., Teixidor, P., & Bard, K. A. (1996). Imitative learning of artificial fruit processing in children (*Homo sapiens*) and chimpanzees (*Pan troglodytes*). *Journal of Comparative Psychology, 110,* 3–14.

Whitlow, J. W., Jr., & Wagner, A. R. (1984). Memory and habituation. In H. V. S. Peeke & L. Petrinovich (eds.), *Habituation, sensitization, and behavior.* New York: Academic.

Wickens, D. D., & Wickens, C. D. (1942). Some factors related to pseudoconditioning. *Journal of Experimental Psychology, 31,* 518–526.

Widrow, G., & Hoff, M. E. (1960). Adaptive switching circuits. *Institute of Radio Engineers, Western Electronic Show and Convention, Convention Record, 4,* 96–194.

Wierson, M., & Forehand, R. (1994). Parent behavioral training for child noncompliance: Rationale, concepts, and effectiveness. *Current Directions in Psychological Science, 3,* 146–150.

Wilcoxon, H. C., Dragoin, W. B., & Kral, P. A. (1971). Illness-induced aversions in rat and quail: Relative salience of visual and gustatory cues. *Science, 171,* 826–828.

Williams, B. A. (1978). Information effects on the response-reinforcer association. *Animal Learning and Behavior, 6,* 371–379.

Williams, B. A. (1993). Molar versus local reinforcement probability as determinants of stimulus value. *Journal of the Experimental Analysis of Behavior, 59,* 163–172.

Williams, B. A. (1994a). Conditioned reinforcement: Neglected or outmoded explanatory construct? *Psychonomic Bulletin and Review, 1,* 457–475.

Williams, B. A. (1994b). Reinforcement and choice. In N. J. Mackintosh (ed.), *Animal learning and cognition* (pp. 81–109). San Diego: Academic.

Williams, B. A. (1997). Varieties of contrast: A review of "Incentive Relativity" by Charles F. Flaherty. *Journal of the Experimental Analysis of Behavior, 68,* 133–141.

Williams, B. A., Preston, R. A., & de Kervor, D. E. (1990). Blocking of the response-reinforcer association: Additional evidence. *Learning and Motivation, 21,* 379–398.

Williams, C. D. (1959). The elimination of tantrum behaviors by extinction procedures. *Journal of Abnormal and Social Psychology, 59,* 269.

Williams, D. A. (1996). Comparative analysis of negative contingency learning in humans and nonhumans. In D. R. Shanks, K. J. Holyoak, & D. L. Medin (eds.), *The psychology of learning and motivation* (Vol. 34, pp. 89–131). San Diego, CA: Academic.

Williams, D. A., Overmier, J. B., & LoLordo, V. M. (1992). A reevaluation of Rescorla's early dictums about Pavlovian conditioned inhibition. *Psychological Bulletin, 111,* 275–290.

Williams, D. E., Kirkpatrick-Sanchez, S., & Iwata, B. A. (1993). A comparison of shock intensity in the treatment of longstanding and severe self-injurious behavior. *Research in Developmental Disabilities, 14,* 207–219.

Williams, D. R., & Williams, H. (1969). Automaintenance in the pigeon: Sustained pecking despite contingent non-reinforcement. *Journal of the Experimental Analysis of Behavior, 12,* 511–520.

Wittgenstein, L. (1953). *Philosophical investigations* (G. E. M. Anscombe, trans.). Oxford: Blackwell.

Wolf, M. M., Braukmann, C. J., & Ramp, K. A. (1987). Serious delinquent behavior as part of a significantly handicapping condition: Cures and supportive environments. *Journal of Applied Behavior Analysis, 20,* 347–359.

Wolf, M. M., Risley, T. R., & Mees, H. L. (1964). Application of operant conditioning procedures to the behavior problems of an autistic child. *Behavior Research and Therapy, 1,* 305–312.

Wolfe, J. B. (1934). The effect of delayed reward upon learning in the white rat. *Journal of Comparative Psychology, 17,* 1–21.

Wolfe, J. B. (1936). Effectiveness of token-rewards for chimpanzees. *Comparative Psychology Monographs, 12*(5, Serial No. 60).

Wolpe, J. (1958). *Psychotherapy by reciprocal inhibition.* Stanford: Stanford University Press.

Wolpe, J., & Lazarus, A. A. (1966). *Behavior therapy techniques.* London: Pergamon.

Wood, R., & Flynn, J. M. (1978). A self-evaluation token system versus an external evaluation token system with predelinquent youth. *Journal of Applied Behavior Analysis, 11,* 503–512.

Wood, W., Wong, F. Y., & Chachere, G. (1991). Effects of media violence on viewers' aggression in unconstrained social interaction. *Psychological Bulletin, 109,* 371–383.

Woodbury, C. B. (1943). Learning of stimulus patterns by dogs. *Journal of Comparative Psychology, 35,* 29–40.

Wrangham, R. W., McGrew, W. C., DeWall, F. B. M., & Heltne, P. G. (eds.). (1994). *Chimpanzee culture.* Cambridge, MA: Harvard University Press.

Wright, A. A. (1997). Concept learning and learning strategies. *Psychological Science, 8,* 119–123.

Yerkes, R. M., & Morgulis, S. (1909). The method of Pavlov in animal psychology. *Psychological Bulletin, 6,* 257–273.

Young, M. E. (1995). On the origin of personal causal theories. *Psychonomic Bulletin & Review, 2,* 83–104.

Young, M. E., Wasserman, E. A., & Dalrymple, R. M. (1997). Memory-based *same-different* conceptualization by pigeons. *Psychonomic Bulletin & Review, 4,* 552–558.

Zaffy, D. J., & Bruning, J. L. (1966). Drive and the range of cue utilization. *Journal of Experimental Psychology, 71,* 382–384.

Zahorik, D. (1977). Associative and non-associative factors in learned food preferences. In L. M. Barker, M. R. Best, & M. Domjan (eds.), *Learning mechanisms in food selection.* Waco, TX: Baylor University Press.

Zamble, E. (1967). Classical conditioning of excitement anticipatory to food reward. *Journal of Comparative and Physiological Psychology, 63,* 526–529.

Zamble, E., Hadad, G. M., Mitchell, J. B., & Cutmore, T. R. H. (1985). Pavlovian conditioning of sexual arousal: First- and second-order effects. *Journal of Experimental Psychology: Animal Behavior Processes, 11,* 598–610.

Zeaman, D., & Hanley, P. (1983). Stimulus preferences as structural features. In T. J. Tighe & B. E. Shepp (eds.), *Perception, cognition, and development: Interactional analyses.* Hillsdale, NJ: Erlbaum.

Zeaman, D., & House, B. J. (1963). The role of attention in retardate discrimination learning. In N. R. Ellis (ed.), *Handbook of mental deficiency: Psychological theory and research.* New York: McGraw-Hill.

Zeiler, M. (1977). Schedules of reinforcement: The controlling variables. In W. K. Honig & J. E. R. Staddon (eds.), *Handbook of operant behavior.* Englewood Cliffs, NJ: Prentice-Hall.

Zener, K. (1937). The significance of behavior accompanying conditioned salivary secretion for theories of the conditioned response. *American Journal of Psychology, 50,* 384–403.

ACKNOWLEDGMENTS

Fig. 1.4 from Premack, D., and Woodruff, G. (1978), "Chimpanzee Problem Solving: A Test for Comprehension," *Science, 202, 532–535.* Copyright 1978 American Association for the Advancement of Science and the author.

Fig. 1.5 from Davis, M. (1974), "Sensation of the Rat Startle Response by Noise," *Journal of Comparative and Physiological Psychology,* 87, 571–581. © 1974 by the American Psychological Association. Reprinted by permission of the publisher.

Fig. 2.13 from Kimble, G. A., Mann, L. I., and Dufort, R. H. (1955). Classical and instrumental eyelid conditioning. *Journal of Experimental Psychology, 49,* 407–417. Reprinted by permission of Gregory Kimble.

Fig. 4.8 from Bellingham, W. P., Gillette-Bellingham, K., and Kehoe, E. J. (1985). Summation and configuration in patterning schedules with the rat and rabbit. *Annual Learning and Behavior, 13,* 152–164. Reprinted by permission.

Fig. 4.11 from Jenkins, H. M., and Moore, B. R. (1973), "The Form of the Auto-Shaped Response with Food or Water Reinforcers," *Journal of the Experimental Analysis of Behavior, 20,* 163–181. Reprinted by permission of the publisher and the author.

Fig. 4.12 from Domjan, M., and Burkhard, B. (1986), *The Principles of Learning and Behavior.* © 1986 Brooks/Cole Publishing Company, Pacific Grove, CA 93950. Reprinted by permission of Wadsworth, Inc.

Fig. 4.15 from Spence, K. W., Homzie, M. J., and Rutledge, F. F. (1964), "Extinction of the Human Eyelid CR as a Function of the Discriminability of the Change from Acquisition to Extinction," *Journal of Experimental Psychology, 67,* 545–552. Reprinted by permission of the publisher and the author.

Fig. 4.16 from Wasserman, E. A. (1990). Attribution of causality to common and distinctive elements of compound stimuli. *Psychological Science, 1,* 298–302. Reprinted by permission of Blackwell Publishers.

571

Fig. 5.10 from Phillips, E. L. (1968), "Achievement Place: Token Reinforcement Procedures in a Home-Style Rehabilitation Setting for 'Pre-Delinquent' Boys," *Journal of Applied Behavior Analysis, 1,* 213–223. Copyright 1968 by the Society for the Experimental Analysis of Behavior. Reprinted by permission of the publisher.

Fig. 5.15 from Clark, F. C. (1958), "The Effect of Deprivation and Frequency of Reinforcement on Variable-Interval Responding," *Journal of the Experimental Analysis of Behavior, 1,* 221–228. Reprinted by permission of the publisher.

Fig. 5.16 Adapted from Crespi, L. P. (1942), "Quantitative Variation in Incentive and Performance in the White Rat," *American Journal of Psychology, 55,* 467–517. Copyright 1942 by the Board of Trustees of the University of Illinois. Used with the permission of the University of Illinois Press.

Fig. 6.1 from Hall, R. V., Lund, D., and Jackson, D. (1968), "Effects of Teacher Attention on Study Behavior," *Journal of Applied Behavior Analysis, 1,* 1–12. © 1968 by the Society for the Experimental Analysis of Behavior. Reprinted by permission of the author and the publisher.

Fig. 6.2 from Allyson, M. G., and Ayllon, T. (1980), "Behavioral Coaching in the Development of Skills in Football, Gymnastics, and Tennis," *Journal of Applied Behavior Analysis, 13,* 297–314. © 1980 by the Society for the Experimental Analysis of Behavior. Reprinted by permission of the author and the publisher.

Fig. 6.3 from Hall, R. V., Axelrod, S., Tyler, L., Grief, F., Jones, F. C., and Robertson, R. (1972), "Modification of Behavior Problems in the Home with a Parent as Observer and Experimenter," *Journal of Applied Behavior Analysis, 5,* 53–64. © 1972 by the Society for the Experimental Analysis of Behavior. Reprinted by permission of the author and the publisher.

Fig. 6.4 from Ludwig, T. D., and Geller, E. S. (1997). Assigned versus participative goalsetting and response generalization: Managing injury control among professional pizza deliverers. *Journal of Applied Psychology, 82,* 253–261. Reprinted by permission.

Fig. 6.5 from Garlington, W. K., and Dericco, D. A. (1977), "The Effect of Modeling on Drinking Rate," *Journal of Applied Behavior Analysis, 10,* 207–211. © 1977 by the Society for the Experimental Analysis of Behavior. Reprinted by permission of the author and the publisher.

Fig. 6.6 from Bandura, A., Blanchard, F. B., and Ritter, B. (1969), "Relative Efficacy of Desensitization and Modeling Approaches for Inducing Behavioral, Affective, and Attitudinal Changes," *Journal of Personality and Social Psychology 13,* 173–199. © 1969 by the American Psychological Association. Reprinted by permission of the author and the publisher.

Fig. 6.7 from Drabman, R. S., Spitalnik, R., and O'Leary, K. D. (1973), "Teaching Self-Control to Disruptive Children," *Journal of Abnormal Psychology, 82,* 10–16. © 1973 by the American Psychological Association. Reprinted by permission of the author and the publisher.

Fig. 7.8 from Rortvedt, A. K., and Miltenberger, R. G. (1994). Analysis of a high-probability instructional sequence and time-out in the treatment of child noncompliance. Special Issue: Functional analysis approaches to behavioral assessment and treatment. *Journal of Applied Behavior Analysis, 27,* 327–330. Reprinted by permission.

Fig. 7.9 from Reynolds, L. K., & Kelley, M. L. (1997). The efficacy of a response cost-based treatment package for managing aggressive behavior in preschoolers. *Behavior Modification, 21,* 216–230. Copyright © 1997 by Sage Publications. Reprinted by permission of Sage Publications.

Fig. 7.10 from Williams, C. D. (1959). The elimination of tantrum behaviors by extinction procedures. *Journal of Abnormal and Social Psychology, 59,* 269. Reprinted by permission.

Fig. 8.2 from Fowler, H., and Miller, N. E. (1963), "Facilitation and Inhibition of Runway Performance by Hind- and Forepaw Shock of Various Intensities," *Journal of Comparative Physiological Psychology, 56,* 801–805. © 1963 by the American Psychological Association. Reprinted by permission of the author and the publisher.

Fig. 8.3 from Colwill, R. M., and Rescorla, R. A. (1985), "Postconditioning Devaluation of Reinforcer Affects Instrumental Responding," *Journal of Experimental Psychology: Animal Behavior Processes, 11,* 120–132. © 1985 by the American Psychological Association. Reprinted by permission of the author and the publisher.

Fig. 8.4 from Vander Wall, S. B. (1982), "An Experimental Analysis of Cache Recovery in Clark's Nutcracker," *Animal Behavior, 30,* 84–94. Reprinted by permission of the author.

Fig. 8.5 reprinted by permission of The University of California Press.

Fig. 8.6 from Roberts, S. (1981). Isolation of an internal clock. *Journal of Experimental Psychology: Animal Behavior Processes, 7,* 242–268. Reprinted by permission.

Fig. 8.8 from Brannon, E. M., and Terrace, H. S. (1998). Ordering of the numerosities 1 to 9 by monkeys. *Science, 282,* 746–749. Copyright 1998. American Association for the Advancement of Science.

Fig. 9.7 from Kesner, R. P., & DeSpain, M. J. (1988). Correspondence between rats and humans in the utilization of retrospective and prospective codes. *Animal Learning and Behavior, 16*, 299–302. Reprinted by permission.

Fig. 9.9 from Reynolds, G. 5. (1961), "Attention in the Pigeon," *Journal of the Experimental Analysis of Behavior, 4*, 203–208. Reprinted by permission.

Fig. 9.10 from Hall, G., & Pearce, J. M. (1982). Restoring the associability of a preexposed CS by a surprising event. Quarterly Journal of Experimental Psychology, 34B, 127–140. Reprinted by permission.

Fig. 9.17 from Bouton, M. E., & King, D. A. (1983). Contextual control of the extinction of conditioned fear: Tests for the associative value of the context. *Journal of Experimental Psychology: Animal Behavior Processes*, 9, 248–265. Reprinted by permission.

Figures 9.18 and 9.19 from Wagner, A. R., Rudy, J. W., and Whitlow, J. W. (1973), "Rehearsal in Animal Conditioning," *Journal of Experimental Psychology Monograph*, 97, 407–426. © 1973 by the American Psychological Association. Reprinted by permission of the author and the publisher.

Fig. 10.1 from Thomas, G. (1981), "Contiguity, Reinforcement Rate and the Law of Effect," *Quarterly Journal of Experimental Psychology, 33B*, 33–43. Reprinted by permission of the University of Edinburgh.

Fig. 10.2 from Rosenfeld, H. M., and Baer, D. M. (1969), "Unnoticed Verbal Conditioning of an Aware Experimenter by a More Aware Subject: The Double-Agent Effect," *Psychological Review, 76*, 425–432. © 1969 by the American Psychological Association. Reprinted by permission of the author and the publisher.

Fig. 10.3 reprinted by permission of The University of California Press.

Fig. 10.8 from Kamin, L. J., Brimer, C. J., and Black, A. H. (1963), "Conditioned Suppression as a Monitor of Fear of the CS in the Course of Avoidance Training," *Journal of Comparative and Physiological Psychology*, 56, 497–501. © 1963 by the American Psychological Association. Reprinted by permission of the author and the publisher.

Fig. 10.10 from Herrnstein, R. J. (1961). Relative and absolute strength of response as a function of frequency of reinforcement. *Journal for the Experimental Analysis of Behavior, 4*, 267–272. Copyright 1961 by the Society for theExperimental Analysis of Behavior, Inc.

Fig. 11.2 from Hess, E. H. (1959), "Imprinting," *Science, 130*, 133*ff*, July 17, 1959. Copyright 1959 by the AAAS. Reprinted by permission of the American Association for the Advancement of Science.

Fig. 11.3 from Andrews, E. A., and Braverman, N. 5. (1975), *Animal Learning and Behavior, 3*, 187–189. Reprinted by permission of Psychonomic Society, Inc., and the author.

Fig. 12.1 from Trabasso, T. (1963), "Stimulus Emphasis and All-or-None Learning of Concept Identification," *Journal of Experimental Psychology,* 65,395–406. © 1963 by the American Psychological Association. Reprinted by permission of the author and the publisher.

Author Index

SUBJECT INDEX

Pages on which terms are defined are indicated by **bold** type.

A FINAL WORD

I hope you've enjoyed reading this text and found it stimulating. I would like to hear from you about your reactions–whether you enjoyed it, or whether there any aspects you'd like to see changed. You can reach me by mailing the form on the following pages or through e-mail at d.a.lieberman@stirling.ac.uk, or by mail at

Dr. David Lieberman
Department of Psychology
University of Stirling
Stirling FK9 4LA
Scotland
U. K.

It would be help if you included answers to the questions on the following pages, but this isn't necessary. Authors get a lot less feedback than you might think, and I'd be pleased to hear from you in any form.

David A. Lieberman

TO THE OWNER OF THIS BOOK:

I hope that you have found *Learning, Behavior and Cognition*, Third Edition useful. So that this book can be improved in a future edition, would you take the time to complete this sheet and return it? Thank you.

School and address: _____

_____

Department: _____

Instructor's name: _____

Course name: _____

1. How would you rank this text on a scale from –3 to +3, where –3 represents terrible and +3 represents

   excellent? _____

2. What did you like most about this text? _____

_____

_____

3. What did you like least? _____

_____

_____

4. Were all of the chapters of the book assigned for you to read? _____

   If not, which ones weren't? _____

5. In the space below, or on a separate sheet of paper, please write specific suggestions for improving this book and anything else you'd care to share about your experience in using this book.

_____

_____

_____

_____

OPTIONAL:

Your name: _____ Date: _____

May we quote you, either in promotion for *Learning, Behavior and Cognition*, Third Edition, or in future publishing ventures?

Yes: No:

Sincerely yours,

David A. Lieberman

FOLD HERE

FOLD HERE